GLOBAL CRIMINOLOGY AND CRIMINAL JUSTICE

GLOBAL CRIMINOLOGY AND CRIMINAL JUSTICE

CURRENT ISSUES AND PERSPECTIVES

Edited by Nick Larsen and Russell Smandych

broadview press

Library and Archives Canada Cataloguing in Publication

 Global criminology and criminal justice : current issues and perspectives / edited by Nick Larsen and Russell Smandych.

ISBN 978-1-55111-682-2

 1. Criminology—Cross-cultural studies. 2. Criminal justice, Administration of—Cross-cultural studies. 3. Transnational crime. I. Larsen, Nick, 1948-
II. Smandych, Russell Charles

HV6025.G64 2007   364   C2007-905614-8

Broadview Press is an independent, international publishing house, incorporated in 1985. Broadview believes in shared ownership, both with its employees and with the general public; since the year 2000 Broadview shares have traded publicly on the Toronto Venture Exchange under the symbol BDP.

We welcome comments and suggestions regarding any aspect of our publications—please feel free to contact us at the addresses below or at broadview@broadviewpress.com.

North America
PO Box 1243, Peterborough, Ontario, Canada K9J 7H5
2215 Kenmore Ave., Buffalo, New York, USA 14207
Tel: (705) 743-8990; Fax: (705) 743-8353
email: customerservice@broadviewpress.com

UK, Ireland, and continental Europe
NBN International, Estover Road, Plymouth, UK PL6 7PY
Tel: 44 (0) 1752 202300; Fax: 44 (0) 1752 202330
email: enquiries@nbninternational.com

Australia and New Zealand
UNIREPS, University of New South Wales
Sydney, NSW, Australia 2052
Tel: 61 2 9664 0999; Fax: 61 2 9664 5420
email: info.press@unsw.edu.au

www.broadviewpress.com

Typesetting by Aldo Fierro.

PRINTED IN CANADA

CONTENTS

FOREWORD

During the past two or so decades in which I have taught comparative criminology at the upper-level undergraduate and postgraduate levels, I have never once held my students hostage, so to speak, to the limited and seemingly arbitrary confines of a course textbook. To my way of thinking, the handful of comparative texts currently in print are mostly too conservative and too old-fashioned in their approach to crime and too instinctively pro-Western in their general attitude and content. Had I required my students to read one such text, I would have felt obliged to do battle with it, thereby consuming class time and diverting students' attention from what I really wanted to achieve in the course, namely, cultivation of a loosely supervised process of self-discovery about different societies. Rather than require students to purchase and read a single course textbook, therefore, I have over the years pointed each of them, depending on their individual interests and ambitions, to an essay here, an article there, a United Nations data set on this, an Amnesty International or Human Rights Watch report on that.

So, when I was asked if I would care to write a Foreword to this text of pedagogy, my immediate and—as it quickly turned out—very shortsighted reaction was "What's the point? I've never even used a course textbook myself!" Moreover, who on earth would ever bother to read a Foreword? Isn't a Foreword simply a thinly veiled advertising blurb disguised as scholarly pontification, a dust-jacket-like pat on the back designed more for the promotion of authors and editors than for the needs of students?

So, what's the point? Well, read on. Émile Durkheim once famously declared that comparative sociology is not a particular branch of sociology—*it is sociology itself*. Little did Durkheim realize that, by later scholars, who were otherwise sympathetic to the sociological tradition, his understanding of the term "comparative" would be challenged and then eventually relegated to secondary importance. Yet, this is precisely what is done in the collection *Global Criminology and Criminal Justice: Current Issues and Perspectives*. Because our world in the new millennium differs so profoundly from the twentieth-century one inhabited by Durkheim, recognition of this overwhelming difference is one of several organizing principles employed by editors Nick Larsen and Russell Smandych. As they rightly stress, a comparative approach to the understanding of crime and justice cannot properly capture the full complexity of globalization at the dawn of the twenty-first century. We need a global criminology now!

Two other organizing principles are at work in *Global Criminology and Criminal Justice*. One of these, according to the editors' own stated criterion, is that the book is meant to provide undergraduate students with an accessible and up-to-date collection of readings in the emerging field of global criminology and criminal justice. In this regard, the collection succeeds admirably. Important and influential work is represented between these covers.

The editors have also tried to give the book added coherence by including only readings that are critical in their intellectual and political orientation. I must admit that I have never been satisfied with the employment of the word "critical" in the term "critical criminology." It is difficult to imagine any useful sort of criminology—or, for that matter, any other "ology" or "ism"—that is not self-avowedly critical. By convention, "critical criminology" is wielded not only as a hostile epithet to distinguish its bearers from those with whom they have political and epistemological disagreement; it is also a convenient umbrella that shelters a healthy variety of leftist perspectives. These latter include, though are certainly not limited to, abolitionism, feminism, postmodernism, socialism, constitutive criminology, convict criminology, cultural criminology, green criminology, and peacemaking criminology. Many of these perspectives are represented in this collection. In that all the readings seem basically agreed that criminology should be a discourse whose mission is, on the one hand, to expose power and inequality and their ill effects and, on the other, to dissolve the legalistic category "crime" into harms—and also, occasionally, into pain, suffering, exclusion, and exploitation—then their collective effect is an empowering one.

The diverse processes of globalization ebb and flow like tidal currents across the borders and boundaries of all societies. Globalization's economic, political, social, and cultural movements seep and whirl into every nationality and religion, every labour market, every culture and subculture, and every social group and kinship network. Globalization exacerbates inequalities, increases mobilities, worsens relative deprivation, and fuels religious fundamentalism of every stripe and colour. At the same time, national states and international agencies are unable to properly address the basic needs of 1.5 billion undernourished people worldwide and 2.0 billion who have no adequate access to clean water. If the main locomotive of globalization is the transnational movement of capital, then the growth of transnational crime is surely one of its greatest and most inevitable accompaniments. Though transnational crime sometimes occurs in face-to-face situations, it is much more often committed by transnational corporations and criminal syndicates.

The forms of transnational crime are legion. They seem capable of infiltrating every nook and cranny on tiny planet Earth, not only on land but also underground, in oceans and seas, in the air, in space, and in cyberspace. Among the most well-known and most costly transnational harms are those involving trafficking in humans (e.g., slaves, women, and children traded for purposes of sexual slavery, domestic servitude, and other types of enforced labour), in human identities, in animals, and in human and animal organs; terrorism, which is committed and financed sometimes by individuals acting alone, sometimes by, or else sponsored by, more-or-less organized political and religious groups, and at still other times by states against the populations and ethnic groups of other societies; the waging of unjust wars; crimes committed by the military in war and against civilian populations and against environments; violations of the rights of prisoners, detainees, migrants, and guest workers; harms to environments and to animals other than humans; financial harms, such as fraud, price gouging, money-laundering, Internet scams, and violations of consumers' rights; drug trafficking; and the illegal buying and selling of art, antiques, archaeological artefacts, and precious stones.

Sometimes it is hard to determine where any given transnational crime originates, who profits from it and how, which people and what institutions it has affected, and in whose jurisdiction it has taken place. As *Global Criminology and Criminal Justice* demonstrates, criminal justice agencies, whether local, national or international, public or private, are often under funded, unprepared, and unable or unwilling to uncover and prosecute the perpetrators of transnational crime. Sometimes the very authorities who patrol and police national boundaries themselves engage in transnational crime.

I anticipate that there is at least one major question about which this book will encourage further debate. This can be found in the editors' implicitly supportive claim, voiced at the beginning of their Introduction, that, over the past three decades, an historical shift has occurred from comparative and international to global criminology. I do not for one moment doubt that this shift marks real and significant changes in the world(s) of crime. What concerns me, however, is what this shift might mean for the understanding of transnational crime and, specifically, what it implies about the usefulness of comparative criminology as an explanatory tool.

It is true that the various processes of globalization, including the rapid growth of transnational crime, have muddied the basic unit of comparative criminology, namely, the comparison of crime or other harms in two or more distinct societies. Globalization and transnational crime do indeed tend to blur the relatively distinct boundaries and mobilities that exist between nations and between sovereign territories. It is thus increasingly moot whether it makes sense to talk of crime in "Russia" or in "India" or in "Northern Ireland" or in the "United States," for example. It is also true that the comparison of crime and crime rates between one society and another is nowadays not as straightforward as it once was (if, indeed, largely because of relativist problems to do with method and epistemology, it ever was that straightforward).

But I believe that, in the understanding of crime, comparative criminology still has a vital role to play, both in its own terms and also adjacent to global criminology and as one of its key constituents. As I have argued on another occasion, the question of how globalization and transnational crime affect different societies—similarly, differently, both similarly and differently at the same time, or somewhere in between—is first and foremost a *comparative* one. As comparativists we might further ask, for instance, whether societies regarded as failed or collapsed states are more vulnerable to transnational crime than more stable societies. If so, why? If not, why not? Is transnational crime more likely to penetrate societies with weak or corrupt militaries, with corrupt politicians or ineffective polities, with weak informal social controls and with lengthy geographical borders? As such, I suggest, comparative criminology will remain a crucial avenue of inquiry for global criminology.

Be this anticipation as it may, Larsen and Smandych are genuinely to be congratulated for assembling and introducing this fine collection of twenty-two essays. As a sociologist and as someone who regularly asks students to examine crime and other harms in global and comparative contexts, I will undoubtedly recommend that students in my course on comparative criminology read and lean on *Global Criminology and Criminal Justice*. Put plainly, it will make the process of learning and teaching criminology that much more productive and enjoyable. Let's hope that, unlike globalization itself, global criminology and criminal justice are not stamped "Made in the USA."

Piers Beirne
University of Southern Maine

PREFACE

This text arose out of a recognition that the cross-cultural study of crime and justice has evolved from a "comparative" or "international" approach to what is now increasingly referred to as a "transnational" or "global" approach to crime and justice. Each co-editor of this book has taught comparative criminology and criminal justice at his respective university at both the undergraduate and graduate level for many years (Nick Larsen at Chapman University, USA and Russell Smandych at the University of Manitoba, Canada), and both editors have published research in the field. In this capacity, during the past fifteen or so years, we had witnessed the development of a new and challenging body of research literature that can be subsumed under the label of "global criminology and criminal justice." Despite this burgeoning literature, however, we are unaware of any serious attempt to outline the broad historical development of the field or to define its current contours and parameters. We hope that the current book will begin to fill this noticeable void.

We set out to achieve two main goals in designing this book. One of these goals was to provide undergraduate college and university students with an accessible, well-organized, and up-to-date collection of readings in the emerging field of global criminology and criminal justice. The chapters included in the book contain analyses of important issues by recognized experts in global criminology and criminal justice, and every attempt has been made to include authors from many different countries and regions of the world. The second goal was to outline the broad themes included in this emerging field and to defend our central argument that the effects of rapid globalization have changed social, political, and legal realities in such a way that comparative and international approaches to crime and justice are inadequate to capture the full complexity of these issues on a global scale. As will be detailed in the following general introduction, the broad themes emerging from recent research and analysis in global criminology and criminal justice include globalization and recent developments in global crime; global trends in policing and security; convergence and divergence in criminal justice and penal policy; and international criminal justice, war crimes, and the global protection of human rights.

A particular bias of this book that we must confess at the outset is that the selection process we used in deciding on chapters to be included favoured the literature on key topics and issues in global criminology and criminal justice written from a "critical" perspective. While we are aware of the rather conservative nature of the "criminological enterprise" generally, and particularly in North America (see also, Haen Marshall, Chapter 2 in this volume), it is our belief, based on an exhaustive review of recent literature in the field, that many of the most significant new insights and ideas on global crime and criminal justice are to be found in the work of authors who have approached the topics from a critical perspective that challenges the currently more dominant liberal and conservative theoretical and ideological orientations. In the end, of course, it will be up to you, as students and instructors who take up the challenge of moving into the field of global criminology and criminal justice, to decide on whether you agree with us in this regard.

While attempting to encourage readers to approach the study of global criminology and criminal justice from a more critical orientation, we have at the same time organized the following book in a way that should make it relatively easy for instructors teaching traditional courses on comparative criminology or comparative criminal justice to adopt the book for their courses. We already have some, at least anecdotal, evidence of this in the success we have had integrating earlier published versions of the chapters in our own teaching. From our experience of having "tested" with our own students many of the chapters and related study questions included in the book, we are cautiously optimistic that it can be used effectively as either a primary text in college and university courses on global criminology and criminal justice or as a supplementary text in other courses in which a global perspective on crime and criminal justice is needed. We would in particular like to thank many of our students who provided useful feedback on readings that were ultimately selected for inclusion in the book, and we hope that both instructors who decide to use the book in their courses and their future students also find them to be a valuable resource for learning more about current issues and perspectives in the emerging field of global criminology and criminal justice.

ACKNOWLEDGEMENTS

We would like to thank the many people who have contributed to the successful completion of this book. We have been fortunate to work with the dedicated editorial and marketing staff at Broadview Press, whose patience and flexibility made the completion of this book possible. We would like to acknowledge the excellent research assistance of Tim Smandych, Reagan Gordon, Kristen Tateishi, and Vanessa Gordon. We would also like to thank the University of Manitoba and Chapman University for the provision of research assistance and other editorial support. We would also like to acknowledge the many students we have had over the years in our comparative criminology and criminal justice courses, and especially to thank those who read and provided comments on several of the chapters included in our book. In addition, we would like to acknowledge the personal and collegial support of Joe Lelay, Brian Burtch, Rick Linden, Rod Kueneman, Ron Steiner, and Andrew Woolford. Russell Smandych would especially like to thank Kathyrn Smandych, for her encouragement and support. And finally, we would like to thank Piers Beirne for taking the time to write an insightful and detailed foreword to this book.

INTRODUCTION: FOUNDATIONS FOR A GLOBAL CRIMINOLOGY AND CRIMINAL JUSTICE

RUSSELL SMANDYCH AND NICK LARSEN

Recent years have witnessed a shift in the perspective criminologists have taken to the cross-cultural study of crime and justice, a shift from "comparative" or "international" criminology to what is now increasingly referred to as "transnational" or "global" criminology. Despite this striking paradigmatic shift, to date there has been no attempt that the current editors are aware of to compile examples of important literature in the new burgeoning field of global criminology and criminal justice. The current book brings together a selection of some of the most important recent literature in the field, and it situates the theoretical perspectives and research findings contained in the included chapters within a broader discussion of the historical shift over the past three decades from comparative and international to global criminology. We also contextualize the included chapters thematically, noting in particular how they each contribute to advancing knowledge on one or more of the themes: criminology, globalization, and recent developments and issues in global crime; global trends in policing and security; comparative systems of criminal prosecution, the courts, and social control; convergence and divergence in criminal justice and penal policy; and, challenges for global criminology, specifically human rights crimes and international criminal justice. Part of our effort at contextualizing the chapters included in the book is carried out in the following general introduction, in which we offer a brief overview of trajectories in the development of comparative and international criminology from the 1960s to the 1980s and of more recent calls for the development of a global criminology and criminal justice in the 1990s and 2000s. We also add to this general explanation of the relevance and importance of the included chapters by providing a more detailed overview of the specific content of each chapter in the introduction found at the beginning of the particular part of the book in which the chapter is included. Additional resources to assist readers to better appreciate the context and significance of the selected chapters include a set of study questions at the end of each chapter and a list of related current web links that provide additional information on the major topics and issues covered in specific chapters.

Over the years cross-culturally minded teaching criminologists have adopted different approaches to the way they typically teach undergraduate courses. The most basic dividing line in this regard is usually between those criminologists who decide to concentrate on the topic of "comparative criminology" (or the cross-cultural study of crime) and those who place more emphasis on "comparative criminal justice" (or the cross-cultural study of criminal justice and dispute settlement systems and practices). A good example of the first approach can be seen in the significant collection of original essays on *Transnational and Comparative Criminology* edited by James Sheptycki and Ali Wardak (2005), while recent examples of the second approach can be found in Francis Pakes's *Comparative Criminal Justice* (2004) and Philip Reichel's *Comparative Criminal Justice Systems* (2005a). Other recent popular textbooks and readers also tend to lean toward the second approach (Ebbe 2000; Fairchild and Dammer 2001; Fields and Moore 2005; Rounds 2000), with the exception of Philip Reichel's (2005b) assorted collection of readings included in his edited *Handbook of Transnational Crime and Justice*. Unlike most of these noted books, in *Global Criminology and Criminal Justice: Current Issues and Perspectives*, we adopt a more balanced approach by including selected studies that cover the topics of both global crime and global criminal justice. Specifically, of the 22 substantive chapters included in the book, nine deal primarily with issues and perspectives on global crime (in Part 1, 2, and 6), while thirteen give more emphasis to recent trends and issues affecting global criminal justice (in Part 3, 4, 5, and 6). By adopting this more balanced approach, we are, in substance, acknowledging our general agreement with Philip Reichel (2005a: 35), who argues that "because the phenomenon of transnational crime propels much of today's multinational cooperation, it behoves comparative criminal justice [researchers and students] to understand transnational crime and criminals." While having the advantage of being more balanced in the degree of attention it gives to issues of transnational or global crime and criminal justice, the organization of the current book is nonetheless also reasonably consistent with the way in which most popular textbooks and readers in the sub-field of comparative criminal justice are organized. Namely, it adopts a structural and procedural approach—taking the reader from policing, through courts, to corrections (see, for example Pakes 2004; Reichel 2005a)—rather than a "country-by-country" pedagogical approach (see, for example Barak 2000; Terrill 2003). Specifically in this regard, it gives particular attention to issues and perspectives on global trends in policing and security (Part 3); comparative systems of criminal prosecution, the courts, and social control (Part 4); and, convergence and divergence in criminal justice and penal policy, including prison privatization, prison populations, and US and European drug laws and drug control policies (Part 5). The purpose of the remaining portions of this general introduction is to provide a critical overview of the development of the field of global criminology and criminal justice and to highlight other key features of the structure and content of the current book.

FROM "COMPARATIVE" AND "INTERNATIONAL" TO "GLOBAL" CRIMINOLOGY AND CRIMINAL JUSTICE: A BRIEF HISTORY OF THE DEVELOPMENT OF THE FIELD

It is important to have an appreciation of the historical roots of the field of global criminology and criminal justice in traditional comparative and international criminology. One of the historical "facts" we will learn is that the call for a more "global" approach to the study of crime and criminal justice is not entirely a new development of the late twentieth century but actually began as far back as the 1970s. It is especially interesting to note early examples of the use various criminologists made of the terms "world" and "global" criminology (Hippchen 1987; Janeksela 1977).

The False Start of Global Criminology in the 1970s

Writing in the late 1970s, Leonard Hippchen (1977, 1981a, 1981b, 1987: 159) argued that "world criminology" was becoming "a new, developing field of serious scholarly study." According to Hippchen, budding recognition of the need for a world perspective on crime and justice was beginning to occur at this time for a number of reasons, including "the increasing magnitude of such global social disorders as violent crimes, terrorist activities, revolutions, and wars of liberation," along with "increasing global problems of over-population, energy shortages, ecological hazards and social injustices" that "threatened to produce social disorder of a magnitude which the world hitherto has not seen." Hippchen argued that the more energetic development of the field of world criminology could "aid us greatly in understanding the causative factors operating behind these problems," and thus, he challenged criminologists to "discover and develop new approaches which might be used by the statesmen of the world to avert or at least to lessen the impact of the predicted catastrophes" he linked to looming global geo-political, environmental, and social-justice related crises and issues of the day. Many readers of this book living in the early twenty-first century will probably already see that Hippchen's diagnosis of the global ills of the 1970s is quite similar to that offered by critics of globalization, war and terrorism, and global social injustices today, and, as we will see shortly, many of the same types of arguments are being made by those who have begun to call again for a more global approach to crime and criminal justice.

The Rise of Comparative Criminology and Criminal Justice

Although it would be presumptuous in this short introduction to attempt to explain definitively why Hippchen's dream of world criminology did not materialize in the 1970s, at least part of the reason probably resides in the fact that he did not clearly distinguish it from the co-emerging subfields of "comparative criminology" and "comparative criminal justice"; labels which many more criminologists at the time were beginning to use. For example, Hippchen himself (1987: 171) believed that "the subject of world criminology" included three major interests: "comparative criminology and criminal justice systems; special problems; and the development of world models." According to Hippchen (1987: 172), while "comparative criminology" was concerned with investigating "the similarities and differences of patterns of social disorder of the various cultures of the world," the study of "comparative criminal justice systems" investigated "the philosophical bases of law, police, courts, and corrections" across a range of cultures and countries. And the study of "special problem areas" included the investigation of "emerging problems which are significantly related to world order," such as "terrorism, skyjacking, riots, revolutions, trafficking in alcohol and narcotics, international white collar crime, genocide, organized crime, interpersonal violence, arms control and disarmament, law of the seas, airwaves, and outer space" and "planning for crime control, socio-economic planning for crime prevention, and control of environmental hazards." Moreover, Hippchen's (1987: 164, 169) recipe for the development of world criminology was rather conservatively value laden and naïve, based, as it was, on a set of rather contentious assumptions and principles including the idea that "Man [sic] is a species separate from and greatly superior to the other species" on earth and that the "achievement of world religious unity would enable a crucial spiritual contribution to be made to the achievement of [global] social justice" (see also, Janeksela's 1977 similarly naïve and contentious views).

Although, as we have seen, the terms "world" and "global" criminology have been used occasionally in the past to describe the field, with the exception of a few authors like Hippchen (1987), until recently, most cross-culturally minded criminologists have defined their work as falling into one of the subfields of "comparative" or "international" criminology and "comparative criminal justice." Although presaged by the often-cited earlier work of Glueck (1964) and Mannheim (1965), the growth of comparative criminology and criminal justice clearly took off in the 1970s and early 1980s, when an increasing number of primarily North American—and mainly mainstream and liberal—criminologists began publishing comparative research monographs (e.g., Archer and Gartner 1984; Clinard 1978; Clinard and Abbott 1973; Newman 1976; Shelley 1981a) and writing journal articles and book chapters advocating the pressing need for more research and teaching on "comparative" and "international" aspects of crime and criminal justice (Johnson 1979, 1983; Johnson and Barak-Glantz 1983; Haen Marshall and Marshall 1983; Newman and Ferracuti 1980; Newman 1977; Shelley 1981b; Szabo 1975; Terrill 1982). In the course of this advocacy and defence of the emerging field, a number of these authors offered their own—often overlapping—definitions of "comparative criminology." For example, Johnson and Barak-Glantz (1983: 7) stated that

> Comparative criminology is not merely the cross-cultural comparison of crime rates. Rather, it is a scientific approach and an exercise in macro-analysis whereby the qualities of a given phenomenon or the purposes and meaning of a given activity are seen to be derived from the broad setting in which they are located. Thus it (that is, comparative criminology) seeks to locate commonalities and differences in patterns of criminality and crime among divergent economic, political, social, or cultural systems.

Johnson and Barak-Glantz's definition embodied the idea that comparative criminology is concerned mainly with the cross-cultural study of crime so as to explain commonalities (or similarities) and differences in the patterns of crime that exist in different legal jurisdictions. This definition also implies that criminologists who undertake studies in the field recognize that the meaning of crime or the kinds of behaviours that are defined and dealt with as criminal vary from one cultural setting to another. Johnson and Barak-Glantz's (1983) definition overlapped considerably with Marshall B. Clinard and Daniel Abbott's definition offered in their earlier influential book *Crime in Developing Countries: A Comparative Perspective* (1973). Clinard and Abbott reported the findings of research they undertook when they were visiting professors at universities in Uganda in the late 1960s. The aim of this research was to gather information on, and attempt to explain, increases in the crime rates of a number of different developing African countries. In their introduction, Clinard and Abbott argued,

> A truly comparative criminology must approach existing data and conduct new research by using theoretical frameworks, propositions, or models that

can be tested across various societies. For an adequate comparative criminology it is essential to ascertain whether similar social processes account
for crime in technologically developed and less developed societies.

According to the definition advanced by Clinard and Abbott (1973), comparative criminology should be concerned with applying the positivist scientific method to the cross-cultural
study of crime. Clinard and Abbott's book moreover reflected the belief that, in addition to it
being ideally *positivist* (or concerned with systematic data collection and theory testing), comparative criminology should also be *applied* (or concerned with making use of knowledge of
crime to inform criminal-control policy). Consequently, Clinard and Abbott's pioneering work
had the effect of inspiring many other mainstream (or conventional-liberal) American-trained
criminologists to turn to the study of *applied comparative criminology.*

With the general political conservativism of comparative criminology came the development of cross-cultural theories of crime that fit the same ideological mould. In particular,
the 1970s and 1980s witnessed the growing popularity of various modernization and ecological-opportunity perspectives (Howard, Newman, and Pridemore 2000; Neuman and Berger
1988). The most popular variant of modernization theory as applied to the cross-cultural study
of crime was the Durkheimian-Modernization (DM) theory popularized by Louise Shelley
(1981a) in her influential book *Crime and Modernization: The Impact of Industrialization and
Urbanization on Crime.* Shelley built her theory around Durkheim's essential idea that, as society goes through periods of rapid economic and social change, traditional mechanisms of social
control become weaker and individuals within society are more likely to begin to experience
a state of normlessness or "anomie." Drawing on Durkheim, Shelley attempted to develop a
better understanding of the relationship between modernization and criminality (or changing
levels of industrialization and urbanization and changing levels and patterns of criminality).
Specifically, her theory predicted, first, that overall levels of crime will increase with modernization and, second, that patterns of crime will change with modernization, with violent crime
declining in relative proportion to the amount of property crime. Shelley argued that her theory
was supported by empirical evidence and that it represented a major advance over existing
sociological theories of crime, which collectively tended to be both ethnocentric (or limited to
explaining crime in only one social environment) and temporally limited (or unable to explain
changes in the type and distribution of crime over time).

The ecological-opportunity (EO) perspective that became popular in the 1980s attempted
to integrate an ecological approach to social change with an opportunity theory of criminal
behaviour (Neuman and Berger 1988). This "ecological" part of the theory originated from
the early work of Park and Burgess and Shaw and Mackay (members of the Chicago school of
criminology in the US in the 1920s and 1930s) who emphasized the importance of studying
interrelations between environmental conditions and population units. The "opportunity"
component of the theory was derived from the work of opportunity theorists such as Cloward
and Ohlin (1961), who popularized the idea that crime occurs in spatially and temporally
organized social contexts that provide favourable environmental conditions for the execution
of criminal acts. Applied to the cross-cultural study of crime, the EO perspective attempts to

explain "cross-national variation in crime by identifying societies where there is a mix of growing material resources and environments which provide increased opportunities for unsanctioned criminal behaviour" (Neuman and Berger 1988: 288). In essence, researchers guided by this perspective looked for cross-national evidence to test the validity of the proposition that having more opportunities to commit crimes would result in increasing crime rates. Since the 1980s, positivist theorizing and theory testing in comparative criminology has given rise to the development of a much broader variety of positivist, theory-driven cross-cultural research on crime and crime control than it is possible to discuss within the confines of this brief introductory chapter (see, for example Beirne and Nelken 1997; Evans, LaGrange, and Willis 1996; Heiland and Shelley 1992; Howard, Newman, and Pridemore 2000; LaFree and Tseloni 2006; Newman 1999; Newman and Howard 2001; Schneider 2001). Suffice it to say here, and as we illustrate in more detail shortly, that this general theoretical and ideological orientation has continued to dominate cross-cultural theorizing and theory testing in criminology to the present time.

However, comparative criminology did not develop entirely as, or remain, a North American (mainly US) and predominately "positivist" criminological enterprise (Haen Marshall, Chapter 2 in this volume). On the contrary, the 1980s also witnessed the beginning of the development of a self-consciously *critical comparative criminology and criminal justice* (Beirne 1983a, 1983b; Cohen 1982 [reprinted 1988]; De Haan 1992; Groves and Newman 1986, 1989; Horton and Platt 1986; Igbinovia 1986; Johnson 1985; Sumner 1982; West 1989), and this critical line of thinking has also continued to the present (see Agozino 2003, 2004, 2005a; Ganapathy 2005; Nelken 1994, 2002; Oriola 2006; Singh 2005; van Swaaningen 1999; see also the chapters in Part 2 in this volume).

The most famous early proponent of this type of explicitly critical approach was Peirs Beirne (1983a), who, in his provocative chapter on "Generalization and Its Discontents: The Comparative Study of Crime," offered a candid discussion of views on what comparative criminology should and should not be concerned with. First, Beirne (1983a: 21–22) argued that the comparative study of crime and criminal justice should not involve the imposition of criminological knowledge developed in one country onto another culture. In addition, he critiqued a range of positivist theorists, including Clinard and Abbott (1973) and Shelley (1981a), who were, in his view, naïvely committed to developing universally applicable cross-cultural theories of crime. In particular, Beirne rallied against what he saw as the too common practice of American criminologists going abroad and selling their crime-control "expertise" to the governments of Third World developing countries, many of which were led by undemocratic military or, at least, US Central Intelligence Agency compliant political regimes. Specifically, he criticized the type of "comparative" research done by most mainstream American criminologists, pointing out that

> ... any intellectual adventure abroad can be construed as comparative. This could include (as it now does) the export of American models of crime control to any country whose government has resources, human or financial, to waste, but comparative criminology must be firmly distinguished from the simple extension of the tenets of any national criminology to other cultures. (1983a: 22)

Beirne was only one of a number of criminologists who in the 1980s began arguing the need for a more critical comparative criminology that exposed the complicit manner in which mainstream American criminologists went about attempting to "sell" (or at least benevolently offer) their research findings and policy recommendations to the governments of Third World countries. For example, in an equally influential article on "Western Crime Control Models in the Third World: Benign or Malignant?" Stanley Cohen (1982 [reprinted 1988]) offered a similar critical view of the kinds of research that had in the past been considered to make up the field of comparative criminology. Like Beirne, Cohen was especially critical of the fact that much of what passed as comparative criminology really amounted to little more than criminologists from developed countries attempting to apply their theories and sell their crime control policy recommendations to other less developed countries. Indeed, Cohen (1988: 173) found it ironic that, most often, "the type of crime control models (and the criminological theories that sometimes inform them) being exported by criminologists, crime-control officials, international agencies, and various other 'experts,' are the very ones that are now being discredited in the West." The impact of Cohen's fundamental critique of mainstream comparative criminology and criminal justice cannot be overestimated. Since first published, his thought-provoking critical analysis has come to inform the thinking of many cross-culturally minded criminologists who have chosen to adopt a critical perspective in their research and teaching. This is most notable in the influence Cohen's (1988) writing has had on the leading proponents of the emerging critical paradigm of "counter-colonial" or "post-colonial" criminology, many of whom themselves currently live in or are part of the modern diaspora of criminologists and graduate students from developing countries, and particularly from African countries (e.g., Agozino 2004; Kalunta-Crumpton and Agozino 2004; Oriola 2006; Singh 2005).

One example of this is the recent provocative and penetrating analysis of the complicity of mainstream criminology in the process of Western colonialism offered by Biko Agozino (2004). Agozino (2004: 344) builds on "the theoretical footprints left on the sand by Stan Cohen" to argue that "Third World" criminologists must take control of the production and dissemination of their own indigenously produced criminological knowledge, instead of continuing to rely on the importation of Western theories and models of crime and crime control while also being complicit in doing nothing to promote a critical awareness of the "imperialist logic" underlying mainstream comparative criminology and criminal justice. As part of his proposal for the "decolonization of criminology," Agozino (2004: 355) argues critically that "human rights crimes are also criminological problems that should no longer be left out of fat volumes that pretend to be comprehensive handbooks of criminology" and that what is needed is "the establishment of Third World schools of theoretical criminology that could teach the West one or two things about crime." Echoing Cohen's earlier (1988) critique, he also prods Western criminologists to wake up to the reality that "[i]t is no longer credible for the imperialist countries who have the greatest crime problems and who perpetrate the greatest crimes to continue to posture as the standard-bearers of criminology from which the Third World should learn." At the heart of Agozino's call for a "counter" or "post"-colonial criminology is his contention that

All known administrative, empiricist and descriptive accounts of the invisibility of criminology in post-colonial locations serve to justify a more rigorous attempt to theorize the genealogy of criminology from the family tree of colonialism. We therefore need to develop critical scholarship in criminology to avoid the stultifying influence of the imperialist logic that sees criminology only in terms of police training, security agency and prison administrations, especially in post-colonial universities. The silence on the genealogical links of criminology with colonialism has produced two adverse effects: a) criminological theory has been constrained by the shackles of imperialist reason and, b) post-colonial countries have generally shunned criminology as an irrelevant colonialist pastime even while continuing to import the nuts and bolts of "made-for-export" imperialist technology. Both these consequences of the failure of the criminological imagination when it comes to colonialism need to be addressed in order to begin and further the decolonization of criminology for the good of all. (Agozino 2004: 355)

As we shall see in the next part of this introductory chapter, Agozino's call for the development of a criminology that is informed more by the work of researchers from non-North American and European countries is also consistent with the recent calls of both critical and mainstream criminologists for a more global criminology and criminal justice.

Calls for a Global Criminology and Criminal Justice in the 1990s and 2000s

Calls for the development of a global criminology and criminal justice have become increasingly widespread since the 1990s. This is reflected, in part, in the evident increasing concern among criminologists for producing and disseminating research on crime and justice issues undertaken from a global perspective. One sign of this concern is the burgeoning of new academic journals and other publication outlets. For example, since the early 1990s a number of either new or revamped peer-reviewed journals have been introduced, including *Global Crime* [formerly *Transnational Organized Crime*], the *European Journal of Crime, Criminal Law and Criminal Justice* [1993], the *European Journal on Criminal Policy and Research* [1993], the *Journal of Scandinavian Studies in Criminology and Crime Prevention* [2000], the *International Journal of Comparative Criminology* [2000], the *Journal of International Criminal Justice* [2002], the *European Journal of Criminology* [2004], and the *African Journal of Criminology and Justice Studies* [2005], while a number of established critical criminology journals, such as *Social Justice* and *Crime, Law and Social Change*, have begun to routinely feature relevant peer-reviewed articles, some leading examples of which have been edited and included in the current volume. It is also clear that at least some of these noted newer journals have been initiated, at least in part, as a counterbalance to the traditional dominance of American criminologists over the field of comparative criminology and criminal justice (Agozino 2005b; Smith 2004; see also the chapter by Haen Marshall in this volume). Comparably, in this vein, in his 2004 Academy of Criminal Justice Sciences published Presidential Address, Richard Bennett (2004: 21) lists thirteen comparative criminology and criminal justice journals, seven of which started being published after 1993, while in their recent textbook chapter on "International and Comparative Criminology," Adler, Mueller, and Laufer (2007: 389) list thirty-two English-language periodicals known for publishing comparative criminological research.

The call for a global criminology and criminal justice is also reflected more directly in the sustained thoughtful arguments and commentaries on the need for a shift in this direction written by criminologists from a variety of countries (Barak 2001; Beare 2003; Bennett 2004; Chan 2000; Duffy 2006; Findlay 2000; Gillespie 2006; Hardie-Bick, Sheptycki, and Wardak 2005; Marenin 2005; McDonald 1997; Muncie 2004, 2005; Muncie and Goldson 2006; Nelken 2002; Newburn and Sparks 2004; Stern 2006; see also, the chapters in Part 1 and 2 of this volume). For example, in her thought-provoking article on the topic, Janet Chan (2000: 19) explores "the challenges facing criminology in the new millennium" with a particular focus "on the processes of globalization and reflexive modernization which have consequences for criminology, criminal justice studies and law-and-order politics." Chan (2000: 20–21) adopts Anthony Giddens's (1990: 64) definition of "globalization" as a two-way process that involves "the intensification of worldwide social relations which link distant localities in such a way that local happenings are shaped by events occurring many miles away and vice versa," and, in her article, she provides a nuanced analysis of "the extent to which criminology and criminal justice policies have been affected by globalization." In the course of this analysis, Chan (2000: 122) addresses the question of whether the "global dominance of Anglo-American criminology" will necessarily lead "to the homogenization of criminology and criminal justice policy?" With regard to this she concludes:

> Globalization has brought about economic and cultural interdependence and a sense of commonality of risk faced by people in different locations. It has made the distribution of access to knowledge (information capital) more equitable, and increased the capacity of researchers to communicate and form support networks (social capital), but the flow of knowledge is still predominantly uni-directional, from the center (mainly the US and to a less extent the UK) to the periphery. Globalization has led to significant convergences in criminal justice policy, but the globalization of criminological knowledge is a double-edged sword: on the one hand, it may lead to the importation of inappropriate policies; on the other, it facilitates the communication of information that can be used to contest such importation. Hence the impact of globalization on the field of criminology may in fact be to reinforce its diversity through the formation of deterritorialized networks and communities. (2000: 130)

In their indicatively titled introductory chapter on "Transnational and Comparative Criminology in a Global Perspective," Hardie-Bick, Sheptycki, and Wardak (2005) agree with Chan's (2000) view of the globalization of the field of criminology. Specifically, they argue that "[c]riminology—that is the putative science for defining, measuring and governing 'the crime problem'—is, we believe, now thoroughly implicated in the project of globalization" while "[a]cademic criminology is only slowly beginning to develop the theoretical sophistication to be able to participate fully in this global discourse" (Hardie-Bick *et al.* 2005: 14). These authors also express their essential agreement with the stance taken by the editors of the current book, noting that their increasing cognizance of and concern with the process of globalization has prompted some criminologists "to move away from comparative concerns *per se*" and to "concentrate more attention on specific forms of transnational crime." More to the point, they note the following:

> Until relatively recently, practically the only criminological topic that was explicitly transnational in focus was drug trafficking. This is no longer the case. A variety of social practices have become defined as matters of trans-national or global crime concern and thriving new areas of criminology have been established. These raise new theoretical and practical issues with which traditionally nationally-focused criminologists are ill-equipped to deal. (Hardie-Bick *et al.* 2005: 3)

In recent years, criminologists representing the gamut of theoretical and ideological per-spectives that characterize their discipline have come to recognize the pressing need to ad-dress issues surrounding transnational or global crime. On the more conservative side of the ideological spectrum, in 2004, Richard Bennett (2004: 18) predicted to delegates of the annual conference of the Academy of Criminal Justice Sciences that "the continued globalization of business, economics, politics, and cultures will create a demand for global criminology and criminal justice research" and that "[a]s the demand grows, comparative research will also grow in popularity and prestige in all categories." Additionally, in their recent chapter on the topic, Adler, Mueller, and Laufer (2007: 385) note that today the circumstances of criminology "have changed drastically" and that "[c]omparative criminologists have become a necessity, simply because the world has become a 'global village.'" While the editors of the current book prefer, for the sake of accuracy, to use the terms "global crime" and "global criminologists," we, at the same time, agree with the points Adler, Mueller, and Laufer make concerning why criminologists need to be more globally minded. In addition to pointing to the globalization of world economies, communications, and transportation as motivating reasons, the authors note of particular importance that

> Europe is feeling the effects of globalization even more intensely than the rest of the world. The collapse of Communist dictatorships in Central and Eastern Europe and the virtual abolition of frontiers within Europe have brought crime problems until now unheard of in Europe. Consequently, na-tional criminology had to become international criminology. Criminology has in fact been globalized. (Adler *et al.* 2007: 385-386; footnotes omitted)

Interestingly, in recent years, more critical comparative (and now increasingly "global") criminologists have expressed similar views, but have, at the same time, approached the study of global crime and crime control from different theoretical perspectives. For example, in a recent critical criminological analysis of the development of modern "global capitalism" and its primary offspring, the modern "transnational corporation," Wayne Gillespie (2006) draws theoretically on "neo-Marxian world-system theory" and Gidden's (1990) "theory of globalization" to argue that, since the appearance of global capitalism, transnational corporations have come to dominate the world economy, with the consequences being that wealth is now more "heavily concentrated in the hands of an elite capitalist class" and that "[t]he resultant income inequality, coupled with increased state surveillance and formal control, increases structural violence throughout the periphery," or the less economically advanced countries of the world. Similarly, Rosaleen Duffy (2006: 29) draws on and critiques recent theories of "global governance" in an effort to better understand "the ways that global and illicit networks" have contributed to the problem of environmental damage, especially in periphery, or "Third World," developing countries. Duffy (2006: 27) argues that "global governance can be broadly regarded as denoting a global system where states are no longer the main sources of power (if they ever were), and about extending liberal political and economic values and practices justified and legitimated by reference to notions of reason, knowledge and expertise." According to Duffy's (2006: 26) analysis of the linkage between global governance and environmental crime, "[g]lobalization has accelerated the development of transnational networks that have changed states so that they might be better regarded as arenas where complex and illicit transactions are negotiated between locally based elites and representatives of the global economy." An unfortunate frequent impact of such transactions, she argues, is both local and more widespread global environmental degradation. John Muncie and Barry Goldson (Muncie 2004, 2005; Muncie and Goldson 2006) have also taken a theoretically informed critical approach to exploring issues related to the "globalization of crime control," using transnational developments in youth justice policy as a primary example. This approach is articulated in most depth by Muncie (2005), who, in a similar manner to other critical global criminologists, points to the link between the increasing global spread of neo-liberal economic and political theories and practices—dictated through international organizations like the World Bank and the World Trade Organization—and transnational changes in the nature of criminal victimization and crime control (see also, for example, chapters in this volume by Gros, Friedrichs and Friedrichs, Gilbert and Russell, and Mameli). Specifically in relation to criminal and youth justice policy, Muncie (2005: 37) observes "that since the 1960s penal welfarism has been undermined by the development of forms of neo-liberal or 'advanced' governance" and that "[t]his fundamental change in criminal and juvenile justice has been broadly characterized as placing less emphasis on the social contexts of crime and measures of state protection and more on prescriptions of individual/family/community responsibility and accountability." According to Muncie and Goldson (2006), the effects of neo-liberal economic and political globalization can be seen in the realm of transnational developments in youth justice policy; in signs of the increasing convergence, or growing similarity, of youth justice policies and legislative regimes across many different Western countries; and, in particular, in the movement now more common in Western countries toward introducing bifurcated youth justice systems that, at the same time, "crack down" harder on more serious repeat and violent young offenders while offering more preventative and restorative forms of treatment and punishment for criminally "at risk" youth and less serious young offenders. In this respect, Muncie and Goldson's (2006: 2) call for more critical research that can lead to "a deeper understanding of international convergence [and/or] diversity" in the realm of youth justice systems is in keeping with Janet Chan's (2000) call for research on international convergences and divergences in both criminology as a discipline and the global transfer of criminal justice polices. In recent years, this call has also encouragingly been taken up by other globally minded criminologists, including the authors of several chapters in the current volume (see, in particular, chapters by Haen Marshall, Aden, Jones and Newburn, and all of the chapters in Part 5, "Convergences and Divergences in Criminal Justice and Penal Policy").

Other coalescing concerns shared by international and global criminologists of various ideological persuasions and from many different countries are those of human rights, war crimes and genocide, crime and criminal justice reform in transitional democracies, and international criminal justice courts and tribunals. Indeed, within the last decade, criminological literature on these topics has grown at an incredibly rapid pace (Cohen 2001; Day and Vandiver 2000; Findlay and Henham 2005; Garapon 2004; Hafner-Burton and Tsutsui 2005; Hagan 2003; Hagan and Greer 2002; Hagan and Kutnjak Ivkovi 2006; Hagan and Levi 2004; Harrington, Milde, and Vernon 2006; Henham 2004; Jamieson 1998; Jamieson 1999; Jamieson and McEvoy 2005; Kalunta-Crumpton and Agozino 2004; McKay 2006; Mullins, Kauzlarich, and Rothe 2004; O'Connor 2005; Roche 2005; Stanley 2005; Sung 2006; Wilson 2006; Woolford 2006; in addition to numerous other related articles in journals such as the *International Criminal Law Review*, the *Journal of International Criminal Justice*, and *Criminal Law Forum*). This outpouring of literature has been sparked at least in part by events such as the ending of apartheid in South Africa; the Balkan wars and genocides in Rwanda, East Timor, and many other parts of the world in the 1990s; the terrorist attacks on the US on September 11, 2001 and subsequent wars in Afghanistan and Iraq; and the pivotal event of the creation of an International Criminal Court (ICC) in 2002. Whatever the motive forces that have led criminologists to begin pursing research on these topics, in the opinion of the editors of the current book, a move in this direction is long overdue. The three chapters contained in Part 6, under the covering theme of "Challenges for Global Criminology: Human Rights Crimes and International Criminal Justice," provide an introduction to the variety of research topics, approaches, and challenges that are now being taken up by global criminologists in this field.

Embarking on the Study of Global Criminology and Criminal Justice

We hope that you the reader, like us, find *Global Criminology and Criminal Justice* to offer a range of valuable current perspectives on key topics and issues in the emerging field of global criminology and criminal justice. In addition to trying to include carefully selected examples of the latest research in the field, the editors have designed the book to make it as "user friendly" as possible for students and course instructors. As noted earlier, specific features that have been incorporated in order to achieve this include more detailed overviews of each chapter provided in the introductions found at the beginning of each part of the book and study questions and a list of relevant current web links at the end of each chapter. In addition, each of the chapters has been edited, where necessary, to make its content more readily accessible to a wide range of undergraduate university and college students, for example, by removing excessive academic jargon and overly complicated data analysis and statistics. For students and instructors who are new to the field, welcome to the world of global criminology and criminal justice! We hope that you find the current volume to be a useful starting point for your study. For all of the book's readers, whether new to or on the cutting-edge of current developments in the field, we hope the present volume provides an accurate and fair-minded overview of current issues and perspectives of concern to globally minded criminologists.

REFERENCES

Adler, F., G. Mueller, and W. Laufer. 2007. *Criminology and the Criminal Justice System*. 6th ed. New York: McGraw-Hill.

Agozino, B. 2003. *Counter-Colonial Criminology: A Critique of Imperialist Reason*. London: Pluto.

Agozino, B. 2004. "Imperialism, Crime and Criminology: Towards a Decolonization of Criminology." *Crime, Law and Social Change* 41: 343–58.

Agozino, B. 2005a. "Crime, Criminology and Post-Colonial Theory: Criminological Reflections on West Africa." Pp. 117–34 in *Transnational and Comparative Criminology*, edited by J. Sheptycki and A. Wardak. London: Glasshouse Press.

Agozino, B. 2005b. "Editorial." *African Journal of Criminology and Justice Studies* 1: 1–3.

Archer, D. and R. Gartner. 1984. *Violence and Crime in a Cross-National Perspective*. New Haven: Yale University Press.

Barak, G. (Ed.). 2000. *Comparative Criminology: A Global View*. London: Greenwood Press.

Barak, G. 2001. "Crime and Crime Control in an Age of Globalization: A Theoretical Dissection." *Critical Criminology* 10: 57–72.

Beare, M. (Ed.). 2003. *Critical Reflections of Transnational Organized Crime, Money Laundering, and Corruption*. Toronto: University of Toronto Press.

Beirne, P. 1983a. "Generalization and Its Discontents: The Comparative Study of Crime." Pp. 19–37 in *Comparative Criminology*, edited by I. Barak-Glantz and E. Johnson. Beverly Hills: Sage.

Beirne, P. 1983b. "Cultural Relativism and Comparative Criminology." *Contemporary Crises* 7: 371-91.

Beirne, P. and D. Nelken (Eds.). 1997. *Issues in Comparative Criminology*. Aldershot: Ashgate.

Bennett, R. 2004. "Comparative Criminology and Criminal Justice Research: The State of Our Knowledge." *Justice Quarterly* 21: 1–21.

Chan, J. 2000. "Globalization, Reflexivity and the Practice of Criminology." *Australian and New Zealand Journal of Criminology* 33: 118–35.

Clinard, M.B. 1978. *Cities with Little Crime: The Case of Switzerland*. Cambridge: Cambridge University Press.

Clinard, M.B. and D. Abbott. 1973. *Crime in Developing Countries: A Comparative Perspective.* New York: John Wiley and Sons.

Cloward, R. and L. Ohlin. 1961. *Delinquency and Opportunity: A Theory of Gang Delinquency.* New York: Free Press.

Cohen, S. 1982 [reprinted 1988]. "Western Crime Control Models in the Third World: Benign or Malignant?" Pp. 85–119 in *Research in Law, Deviance and Social Control*, vol. 4, edited by S. Spitzer and R. Simon. Greenwich: JAI Press [reprinted in S. Cohen, *Against Criminology* (New Brunswick: Transaction Books, 1988), pp. 172–202].

Cohen, S. 2001. *States of Denial: Knowing About Atrocities and Suffering.* Cambridge: Polity Press.

Day, L.E. and M. Vandiver. 2000. "Criminology and Genocide Studies: Notes on What Might Have Been and What Still Could Be." *Crime, Law and Social Change* 34: 43–59.

De Haan, W. 1992. "Universalism and Relativism in Critical Criminology." *The Critical Criminologist* 14: 1–2, 7–8.

Duffy, R. 2006. "Global Governance, Criminalization and Environmental Change." *Global Crime* 7: 25–42.

Ebbe, O.N.I. (Ed.). 2000. *Comparative and International Criminal Justice Systems: Policing, Judiciary, and Corrections.* 2nd ed. Boston: Butterworth-Heinemann.

Evans, T. D., R. LaGrange, and C. Willis. 1996. "Theoretical Development in Comparative Criminology: Rekindling an Interest." *International Journal of Comparative and Applied Criminal Justice* 20: 15–29.

Fairchild, E. and H. Dammer. 2001. *Comparative Criminal Justice Systems.* 2nd ed. Belmont, CA: Wadsworth.

Fields, C. and R. Moore (Eds.). 2005. *Comparative and International Criminal Justice: Traditional and Nontraditional Systems of Law and Control.* 2nd ed. Long Grove, IL: Waveland.

Findlay, M. 2000. *The Globalization of Crime: Understanding Transitional Relationships in Context.* Cambridge: Cambridge University Press.

Findlay, M. and R. Henham. 2005. *Transforming International Criminal Justice: Retributive and Restorative Justice in the Trial Process.* Cullompton: Willan.

Ganapathy, N. 2005. "Critical Realist Reflections on Crime and Social Control in Singapore." Pp. 157–78 in *Transnational and Comparative Criminology*, edited by J. Sheptycki and A. Wardak. London: Glasshouse Press.

Garapon, A. 2004. "Three Challenges for International Criminal Justice." *Journal of International Criminal Justice* 2: 716–26.

Giddens, A. 1990. *The Consequences of Modernity.* Cambridge: Polity Press.

Gillespie, W. 2006. "Capitalist World-Economy, Globalization, and Violence: Implications for Criminology and Social Justice." *International Criminal Justice Review* 16: 24–44.

Glueck, S. 1964. "Wanted: A Comparative Criminology." Pp. 306–22 in *Ventures in Criminology*, edited by E. Glueck. Cambridge: Harvard University Press.

Groves, W.B. and G. Newman. 1989. "Against General Theory in Comparative Criminology." *International Journal of Comparative and Applied Criminal Justice* 13: 23–29.

Groves, W.B. and G. Newman. 1986. "Criminal Justice and Development: Some Critical Observations." *International Journal of Comparative and Applied Criminal Justice* 10: 1–16.

Haen Marshall, I. and Chris E. Marshall. 1983. "Toward a Refinement of Purpose in Comparative Criminological Research: Research Site Selection in Focus." *International Journal of Comparative and Applied Criminal Justice* 7: 89–97.

Hafner-Burton, E. and K. Tsutsui. 2005. "Human Rights in a Globalizing World: The Paradox of Empty Promises." *American Journal of Sociology* 110: 1373–1411.

Hagan, J. 2003. *Justice in the Balkans: Prosecuting War Crimes in the Hague Tribunal*. Chicago: University of Chicago Press.

Hagan, J. and S. Greer. 2002. "Making War Criminal." *Criminology* 40: 231–64.

Hagan, J., and S. Kutnjak Ivković. 2006. "War Crimes, Democracy, and the Rule of Law in Belgrade, the Former Yugoslavia, and Beyond." *Annals of the American Academy of Political and Social Sciences* 605: 130–51.

Hagan, J. and R. Levi. 2004. "Social Skill, the Milosevic Indictment, and the Rebirth of International Criminal Justice." *European Journal of Criminology* 1: 445–75.

Hardie-Bick, J. Sheptycki, and A. Wardak. 2005. "Introduction: Transnational and Comparative Criminology in a Global Perspective." Pp. 1–18 in *Transnational and Comparative Criminology*, edited by J. Sheptycki and A. Wardak. London: Glasshouse Press.

Harrington, J.M. Milde, and R. Vernon (Eds.). 2006. *Bringing Power to Justice? The Prospects of the International Criminal Court*. Kingston/Montreal: McGill-Queen's University Press.

Heiland, H.-G. and L. Shelley. 1992. "Civilization, Modernization and the Development of Crime and Crime Control." Pp. 1–19 in *Crime and Control in Comparative Perspectives*, edited by H.-G. Heiland, L. Shelley, and H. Katoh. Berlin: Walter de Gruyter.

Henham, R. 2004. "Theorizing the Penality of Sentencing in International Criminal Trials." *Theoretical Criminology* 8: 429–63.

Hippchen, L. 1977. "The Teaching of Comparative and World Criminology in Graduate Schools of Sociology and Criminal Justice." *International Journal of Comparative and Applied Criminal Justice* 1: 57–71.

Hippchen, L. 1981a. "A Social Justice Model for a World Criminology." *International Journal of Comparative and Applied Criminal Justice* 5: 107–18.

Hippchen, L. 1981b. "Importance of Teaching the International Aspects of Criminal Justice." *International Journal of Comparative and Applied Criminal Justice* 5: 221–27.

Hippchen, L. 1987. "World Criminology: A Developing Concept." *International Journal of Comparative and Applied Criminal Justice* 11: 159–75.

Horton, J. and T. Platt. 1986. "Crime and Criminal Justice under Capitalism and Socialism: Towards a Marxist Perspective." *Crime and Social Justice* 25: 115–34.

Howard, G., G. Newman, and W. Pridemore. 2000. "Theory, Method, and Data in Comparative Criminology." Pp. 139–210 in *Criminal Justice 2000*, edited by David Duffee. Washington, D.C.: National Institute of Justice.

Igbinovia, P. 1986. "Africanism, Consciencism, Paternalism, and Western Criminology." *International Journal of Comparative and Applied Criminal Justice* 10: 223–30.

Jamieson, R. 1998. "Towards a Criminology of War in Europe." Pp. 480–506 in *The New European Criminology: Crime and Social Order in Europe*, edited by V. Ruggiero, N. South, and I. Taylor. London: Routledge.

Jamieson, R. 1999. "Genocide and the Social Production of Immorality." *Theoretical Criminology* 3: 131–46.

Jamieson, R. and K. McEvoy. 2005. "State Crime by Proxy and Juridical Othering." *British Journal of Criminology* 45: 504–27.

Janeksela, G. 1977. "Typologies in Comparative Criminal Justice Research." *International Journal of Comparative and Applied Criminal Justice* 1: 103–10.

Johnson, E. 1979. "Institutionalization of Criminology: A Prerequisite to Comparative Criminology." *International Journal of Comparative and Applied Criminal Justice* 3: 27–33.

Johnson, E. 1983. "Criminology: Its Variety and Patterns Throughout the World." Pp. 5–30 in *International Handbook of Contemporary Developments in Criminology: Current Issues and the Americas,* edited by E. Johnson. Westport, CT: Greenwood Press.

Johnson, E. 1985. "Influence of American Criminology Abroad: A Critique." *International Journal of Comparative and Applied Criminal Justice* 9: 99–111.

Johnson, E. and I. Barak-Glantz. 1983. "Introduction." Pp. 7–18 in *Comparative Criminology,* edited by I. Barak-Glantz and E. Johnson. Beverly Hills: Sage.

Kalunta-Crumpton, A. and B. Agozino (Eds.). 2004. *Pan-African Issues in Crime and Justice.* Aldershot: Ashgate.

LaFree, G. and A. Tseloni. 2006. "Democracy and Crime: A Multilevel Analysis of Homicide Trends in Forty-Four Countries, 1950–2000." *Annals of the American Academy of Political and Social Sciences* 605: 26–49.

Mannheim, H. 1965. *Comparative Criminology.* 2 Vols. London: Routledge and Kegan Paul.

Marenin, O. 2005. "Building a Global Police Studies Community." *Police Quarterly* 8: 99–136.

McDonald, W. 1997. "Crime and Justice in the Global Village: Towards Global Criminology." Pp. 321 in *Crime and Law Enforcement in the Global Village,* edited by W. McDonald. Cincinnati, OH: Anderson.

McKay, L. 2006. "Characterizing the System of the International Criminal Court: An Exploration of the Role of the Court Through the Elements of Crimes and the Crime of Genocide." *International Criminal Law Review* 6: 257–74.

Mullins, C., D. Kauzlarich, and D. Rothe. 2004. "The International Criminal Court and the Control of State Crime: Prospects and Problems." *Critical Criminology* 12: 285–308.

Muncie, J. 2004. "Youth Justice: Globalisation and Multi-Modal Governance." Pp. 152–83 in *Criminal Justice and Political Cultures,* edited by T. Newburn and R. Sparks. Cullompton: Willan.

Muncie, J. 2005. "The Globalization of Crime Control: The Case of Youth and Juvenile Justice: Neo-Liberalism, Policy Convergence and International Conventions." *Theoretical Criminology* 9: 35–64.

Muncie, J. and B. Goldson. 2006. "States of Transition: Convergence and Diversity in International Youth Justice." Pp. 196–218 in *Comparative Youth Justice: Critical Issues,* edited by J. Muncie and B. Goldson. London: Sage.

Nelken, D. 1994. "Whom Can You Trust? The Future of Comparative Criminology." Pp. 220–43 in *The Futures of Criminology,* edited by David Nelken. London: Sage.

Nelken, D. 2002. "Comparing Criminal Justice." Pp. 175–201 in *Oxford Handbook of Criminology.* 3rd ed., edited by M. Maguire, R. Morgan, and R. Reiner. Oxford: Oxford University Press.

Neuman, W. and R. Berger. 1988. "Competing Perspectives on Cross National Crime: An Evaluation of Theory and Evidence." *Sociological Quarterly* 29: 281–313.

Newburn, T. and R. Sparks. 2004. "Criminal Justice and Political Cultures." Pp. 1–15 in *Criminal Justice and Political Cultures*, edited by T. Newburn and R. Sparks. Cullompton: Willan.

Newman, G. 1976. *Comparative Deviance: Perception and Law in Six Cultures*. New York: Elsevier.

Newman, G. 1977. "Problems of Method in Comparative Criminology." *International Journal of Comparative and Applied Criminal Justice* 1: 17–31.

Newman, G. (Ed.). 1999. *Global Report on Crime and Justice*. New York: Oxford University Press.

Newman, G. and F. Ferracuti. 1980. "Introduction: The Limits and Possibilities of Comparative Criminology." Pp. 7–16 in *Crime and Deviance: A Comparative Perspective*, edited by G. Newman. Beverly Hills: Sage.

Newman, G. and G.J. Howard. 2001. "Introduction: Varieties of Comparative Criminology." *International Journal of Comparative Sociology* 42: 1–8.

O'Connor, V. 2005. "Traversing the Rocky Road of Law Reform in Conflict and Post Conflict States: Model Codes for Post Conflict Criminal Justice as a Tool of Assistance." *Criminal Law Forum* 16: 231–55.

Oriola, T. 2006. "Biko Agozino and the Rise of Post-Colonial Criminology." *African Journal of Criminology and Justice Studies* 2: 104–31.

Pakes, F. 2004. *Comparative Criminal Justice*. Cullompton: Willan.

Reichel, P. 2005a. *Comparative Criminal Justice Systems*. 4th ed. Upper Saddle River, NJ: Prentice-Hall.

Reichel, P. (Ed.). 2005b. *Handbook of Transnational Crime and Justice*. Thousand Oaks, CA: Sage.

Roche, D. 2005. "Truth Commission Amnesties and the International Criminal Court." *British Journal of Criminology* 45: 565–81.

Rounds, D. (Ed.). 2000. *International Criminal Justice: Issues in a Global Perspective*. Boston: Allyn and Bacon.

Schneider, H.J. 2001. "Comparative Criminology: Purposes, Methods and Research Findings." Pp. 359–76 in *Contemporary Issues in Crime and Criminal Justice: Essays in Honor of Gilbert Geis*, edited by H. Pontell and D. Shichor. Upper Saddle River, NJ: Prentice Hall.

Shelley, L. 1981a. *Crime and Modernization: The Impact of Industrialization and Urbanization on Crime*. Carbondale: Southern Illinois University Press.

Shelley, L. (Ed.). 1981b. *Readings in Comparative Criminology*. Carbondale: Southern Illinois University Press.

Sheptycki, J. and A. Wardak (Eds.). 2005. *Transnational and Comparative Criminology*. London: Glass House Press.

Singh, A.-M. 2005. "Some Critical Reflections on the Governance of Crime in Post-Apartheid South Africa." Pp. 135–56 in *Transnational and Comparative Criminology*, edited by J. Sheptycki and A. Wardak. London: Glasshouse Press.

Smith, D. 2004. "Criminology in the Wider Europe." *European Journal of Criminology* 1: 5–15.

Stanley, E. 2005. "Truth Commissions and the Recognition of State Crime." *British Journal of Criminology* 45: 582–97.

Stern, V. 2006. *Creating Criminals: Prisons and People in a Market Society*. Halifax/London: Fernwood/Zed Books.

Sumner, C. 1982. "Crime, Justice and Underdevelopment: Beyond Modernization Theory." Pp. 1–39 in *Crime, Justice and Underdevelopment*, edited by C. Sumner. London: Heinemann.

Sung, H. 2006. "Democracy and Criminal Justice in Cross-National Perspective: From Crime Control to Due Process." *Annals of the American Academy of Political and Social Sciences* 605: 311–37.

Szabo, D. 1975. "Comparative Criminology." *Journal of Criminal Law and Criminology* 66: 366–79.

Terrill, R. 1982. "Approaches to Teaching Comparative Criminal Justice to Undergraduates." *Criminal Justice Review* 7: 23–27.

Terrill, R. 2003. *World Criminal Justice Systems: A Survey*. 3rd ed. Cincinnati, OH: Anderson.

van Swaaningen, R. 1999. "Reclaiming Critical Criminology: Social Justice and the European Tradition." *Theoretical Criminology* 3: 5–28.

West, G. 1989. "Towards a Global Critical Justice Problematic." *Journal of Human Justice* 1: 99–112.

Wilson, J. 2006. "Law and Order in an Emerging Democracy: Lessons from the Reconstruction of Kosovo's Police and Justice Systems." *Annals of the American Academy of Political and Social Sciences* 605: 152–77.

Woolford, A. 2006. "Making Genocide Unthinkable: Three Guidelines for a Critical Criminology of Genocide." *Critical Criminology* 14: 87–106.

PART 1

PERSPECTIVES ON THE GLOBAL STUDY OF CRIME AND CRIMINAL JUSTICE

The chapters included in this section deal with fundamental theoretical and practical problems that are now being addressed by criminologists at the cutting edge of the emerging field of global criminology and criminal justice. As noted previously in the general introduction of this book, globalization is one of the key recent developments that have prompted criminologists to move increasingly toward adopting a global perspective on crime and justice. Another development that has had an influence on this trend is the growing recognition of the problems associated with approaching the cross-cultural study of crime and justice issues from a parochial, regional, or single-nation-based theoretical or ideological perspective. Each of the three chapters in Part 1 offers examples of the manner in which current leading global criminologists have attempted to influence other criminologists toward recognizing the need for an explicitly global perspective on crime and justice issues, one that takes into account both the process of globalization and the need to move beyond limited parochial perspectives.

In Chapter 1, Susan Karstedt challenges criminologists to give more sustained attention to culture as an essential concept in the cross-cultural study of crime. Karstedt argues that, as the twenty-first century unfolds, globalization will intensify contacts, and perhaps conflicts, between different cultures more than ever in the history of humankind. Signs of this can already be clearly seen in developments that provide us with new experiences of difference and diversity as well as commonality, developments such as the increased flow of migrants around the world along with rising global business and global consumption. Coinciding with these developments, the concept of culture has recently begun to receive more sustained attention from cross-culturally minded criminologists. For example, in recent decades criminologists from Western countries have looked in awe at Asia, endeavouring to solve the enigma of how modern, affluent societies can maintain low crime rates especially of violent crimes, while Asian criminologists have looked to the West warning of the impact that Western culture might have in causing rising crime rates. Karstedt develops the argument that undertaking research aimed at comparing cultures and comparing crime can offer new insights, fresh theories, and

19

the chance of discovering new innovative perspectives. Karstedt contends that criminologists should give more attention to the following questions. What will be the fate of "general theories of crime" in different cultures? And will practices of criminal justice work when transported to another social and cultural environment? According to Karstedt, criminologists should develop a more nuanced sense of the problems that are related to comparing cultures and crime since cultures are not monolithic, and, in the past, cultural comparisons have often suffered from exaggerations of differences and produced exaggerated predictions and expectations. In this context, Karstedt contends that criminologists need to develop new research approaches to avoid former errors and to help solve the problems that lie ahead. As a step in this direction, she outlines a number of specific methodological strategies that she feels will help to more adequately meet the challenge of comparing cultures and crime in an increasingly globalized twenty-first century.

In her chapter on "The Criminological Enterprise in Europe and the United States," Ineke Haen Marshall addresses the problems that arise from approaching the cross-cultural study of crime and justice issues from a parochial, regional, or single-nation-based ideological perspective. Specifically, Haen Marshall points to the traditional international dominance of "American criminology" and the manner in which this has often undermined the development of criminology as a research and teaching-based social science discipline in other countries. Part of the reason for this is the extreme parochialism of American criminologists. As Haen Marshall states, for many American scholars, "criminology is *American* criminology. That is what they do, that is what they teach, the publications they read, and the congresses they attend." Using Europe as a specific counter example, Haen Marshall points to differences between the US and Europe with regard to the "criminological enterprise" (such as history, scale, degree of institutionalization, accessibility, diversity in theory and method, critical and self-reflexive stance, and focal research questions), along with differences in "doing science," "doing justice," and "doing crime." More generally, Haen Marshall claims that while European criminology has tended to be more international and eclectic in terms of theoretical and methodological orientations, traditionally American criminology has been pragmatic and policy-oriented, methodologically driven by the positivist scientific method, and consequently lacking in "theoretical lustre, diversity," and "critical edge." At the same time, however, Haen Marshall contends that American criminology has had a powerful influence in Europe and that the fear of the "Americanization" (or "cultural homogenization") of European criminology is well placed. In essence, what Haen Marshall does in her chapter is provide a good example of how the discipline of criminology itself is very much a "cultural product," which is to say that the dominant culture within which criminologists do their work in many ways shapes the way they individually and collectively approach the study of crime and crime control. She also, in effect, highlights how crucial it is to recognize indigenous national criminologies and place more value on the work completed by criminologists from outside of the United States. Specifically, Haen Marshall maintains it is inevitable that in the future "the criminological enterprise will centre more and more around questions that transcend national boundaries" and that "such a worldwide criminology can only prosper through the joint efforts of criminologists from all the continents and regions of the world."

Haen Marshall's argument on the pressing need for a more transnational or global criminology is provided added support in the chapter by Jean-Germain Gros on "Trouble in Paradise: Crime and Collapsed States in the Age of Globalization." Specifically, Gros argues the indispensability of approaching the study of transnational crime from a global perspective that takes into account both the heightened vulnerability of "failed states" to criminality and the contributing role of globalization. Gros's main contention is that the so-called failed or collapsed state is the principal actor in the criminalization of the world economy, while globalization itself is an unwitting but pre-eminent member of the supporting cast. According to his definition, failed or collapsed states "are those whose power grids have experienced sustained and massive breakdown, or political brownout, wherein state authorities are no longer able to project power either at the centre or at the periphery," while current examples of failed states include Afghanistan, Nigeria, Columbia, and Haiti, among many other countries. He, in turn, defines globalization as "the deregulation of national economies and financial markets, on the one hand, and their international integration under the aegis of free-market ideology on the other." Gros enumerates several interconnected reasons why "the failed state and globalization are fertile ground for criminality," and, in light of these, he proposes a number of potential means of reducing the many forms of transnational economic and political criminality with which the two are often linked. Among Gros's proposed remedies is a call for a greater role for international institutions, such as the United Nations and Interpol, in the fight against global criminality and a reconsideration of the notion of national sovereignty. In addition to adding support to Karstedt and Haen Marshall's earlier arguments for a more critical global criminology and criminal justice, Gros's analysis of the causes of and solutions to crimes linked to failed states and globalization also provides a good conceptual foundation for approaching the study of the different types of global criminality discussed by the contributing authors in Part 2 on "Global Crime: Developments and Issues."

Chapter 1

COMPARING CULTURES, COMPARING CRIME: CHALLENGES, PROSPECTS, AND PROBLEMS FOR A GLOBAL CRIMINOLOGY

SUSANNE KARSTEDT

THE PROBLEM OF CULTURE IN COMPARATIVE CRIMINOLOGY

There is an old myth about the dawn of human history: In the beginning, human beings were incapable of living together, and their cities were torn with violence and strife. Thus, the highest god feared that humankind was in danger of utter destruction. He sent his messenger, who was, remarkably, the god of merchants and thieves, down to earth with two gifts that should enable humankind to successfully establish communities and live together in safety and amity. These two gifts were shame and law.

When making a guess about the origin of this myth, many might assume that it is of Asian origin, but it is not. It was written in the dawn of what is called Western civilization, in Athens by the Greek philosopher Plato in one of his Socratic dialogues nearly 2400 years ago (Platon 1987; Stone 1988). This myth and its origin direct our attention to a central question of any approach in criminology that takes up the task of cross-cultural comparison. Is shame a *universal* common to all cultures and epochs? Or is it a *specific cultural characteristic* that is present in some cultures only, and absent in others? Was shame preserved in Asian cultures, while the West abandoned it on its long road toward modernization, and in particular with the adoption of individualistic values (Duerr 1988)?

It cannot be denied that there are universal phenomena of crime and control. In all cultures, girls and women commit ... [fewer] crimes than boys and men, in particular violent crimes; everywhere crime rates of adolescents and young adults are decisively higher than those of adults; a very high proportion of crimes is committed by a small group of persistent offenders (Braithwaite 1989). On the other hand, huge differences in rates of specific crimes, e.g., violent crimes, organized crime, or white collar crime and corruption, are found. There are differences in the proportion of property crimes compared to violent crimes between developing and developed nations (Heiland and Shelley 1992; Arthur and Marenin 1995; Shelley 1990). But if and to what extent these differences can be attributed to differences in cultural patterns is a highly contested problem in the field of criminology.

In contrast, criminologists consent that cultural patterns are decisive in shaping the systems of penal justice and of formal social control, thus producing a subsystem of the legal culture.[1] Which actions are criminalized, what kind of sanctions are provided by the punitive system, how offenders are dealt with on all levels of the system of justice is determined by cultural values and practices. Crime and social control are social and cultural phenomena: This is the main universal principle in criminology, which simultaneously accounts for the profound differences between societies and cultures.

In the social sciences, the concept of culture has moved from the periphery to the very centre of scientific investigation, and culture figures as a primary rather than dependent variable in global change (Featherstone 1995; Janos 1986). Criminology has made no exception to this development after lingering for decades between the Scylla of culture-blindness and the Charybdis of extreme cultural relativism. In a recent interview, Nils Christie argued that criminal justice policy is "cultural policy," and as such much less determined by crime rates than by the cultural identity that a nation wants to achieve. He gives as an example the case of Finland, where after World War II, the rate of prisoners was very close to that of the USSR. In the course of adopting a national identity as a Scandinavian country, Finland systematically changed its criminal justice policy until complete similarity with the other Scandinavian states was achieved (Kriminalität 1998).

The discourse on "Asian exceptionalisms" and "Western culture" is the most recent and prominent example of how culture is brought back into criminology. A "deepening cultural crisis" of the West and a growing "failure of Western culture" to control crime was contrasted with "Asian family values" and "Confucian traditions" that were named as decisive factors responsible for the low level of crime in these nations (Eckersley 1993; Stephens 1993; Westermann and Burfeind 1991). Asian criminologists found these cultural patterns endangered by the impact of Western culture. The "advanced nation disease" is the socio-cultural syndrome of individualistic and hedonistic value patterns, the neglect of collectivistic orientations, and the erosion of the social embeddedness of individuals, that they identify at the roots of rising crime rates and violence in Western market and consumer societies, and that is equally made responsible for rising crime rates mostly among juveniles throughout Asian nations (von Kopp 1998; Ariffin 1995). This perspective owes much, and in particular its flaws to the debate on "Asian exceptionalism" in the economy. Asian values and Confucian traditions served as ad-hoc cultural explanations for economic success and failure likewise.[2]

This perspective on Asian exceptionalism and the use it makes of culture as a concept seems to be burdened with prejudice and to be shaped by "cultural rhetoric" (Miyazawa 1994) more than by systematic analysis that takes culture seriously.[3] It is based on an extremely monolithic concept of culture. But East Asian cultures differ considerably: "Confucian traditions" did not influence the cultures of large parts of the region,[4] and a number of Asian nations include many different cultures (Anderson 1983). Neither do "Western values" represent a monolithic culture. Scandinavian societies differ from the South of Europe, and European cultures differ from US-American culture to a considerable degree. In particular, Asian societies vary considerably with regard to collectivism and interdependence, as do Western countries with regard to individualism and independence (Fiske, Kitayama, Markus, and Nisbett 1998).

In addition, this perspective ignores the rapid modernization of South East Asian societies and Japan during the downward changes of their crime rates. Therefore, it is not reasonable to assume that traditional cultural values are mostly responsible for the downward changes. Asian family values and the traditional cultural patterns of families were considerably affected by economic and social change in Japan, Korea, and China.[5] The process of economic improvement and concomitant changes of cultural patterns seem to have affected different types of crime in specific ways. Harada argues that social and cultural change contributed to a reduction of crime in the streets "while creating new sources of crimes in the schools" (Harada 1995: 58). Between 1950 and 1985 crime rates in Japan were not constantly below those of European countries and the US, and Japan is much less an exception and an outlier among Asian countries when ranked according to collectivistic value orientations and homicide rates (Vaughn and Tomita 1990; Fujimoto and Park 1994; Karstedt 2001). On the other hand, despite profound and rapid social change, basic cultural patterns seem to have a higher degree of inertia than is often assumed; as Inglehart has shown in his study of modernization and value patterns in 43 countries, the relative position of cultural patterns remains stable throughout decades.[6]

Which are the tasks of cross-cultural criminology that avoid "cultural rhetoric," and make use of the concept of culture in a more systematic way? Looking for guidance, criminology might turn to cross-cultural psychology that is most advanced in the field of the systematic integration of the concept of culture.[7] In following the most recent frameworks, the major goals of cross-cultural criminology can be defined as:

- *transport* of criminological theories to other cultures and *test* of their limits and potential of generalization;
- *exploration and discovery* of variations of crime and forms of social control;
- *integration* and *widening* of the data base for the development of an *universal* criminology (Lonner and Adamopoulos 1997).

In a first step I will outline a concept of culture and present a classification of cross-cultural research strategies in criminology. Next, I will analyze the transport and test of theories, and I will propose an additional strategy of *indigenizing criminological theories and concepts*. A third part will explore some seminal topics and research strategies for cross-cultural criminology. Finally, I will show how the global cultural sources can be tapped for models of crime control and criminal justice, and analyze strategies of transfer and modeling. I will mostly center on theories and research on the impact of culture on crime and criminal behavior than on cross-cultural differences of formal regimes of control and the penal law.

THE CONCEPT AND ROLE OF CULTURE IN CROSS-CULTURAL CRIMINOLOGY

There are two hundred or more definitions of culture in the literature of the social sciences (Lonner 1994). These definitions center around three problems and their respective solutions: First, is there an autonomous realm of culture that is at least partially independent and not congruent with structural and institutional arrangements of society? Second, is homogeneity, integration and high consensus a necessary requirement of a concept of culture? Third, how is culture related to the concept of values? A minimal though common core can be identified in the recent conceptualizations of culture. Culture is defined as a set of meanings, values and interpretations that forms a specific social force independently of and partially autonomous of social structure and institutional contexts (Alexander and Smith 1993). This allows for a more precise conceptualization of the relation between culture, structure and actors: cultural patterns originate from and result in typical environmental constraints and patterns of social structure. They produce and reproduce their economic and institutional context. They are embedded in the social system as much as in the minds of people (Hofstede 1994). Like structural conditions and institutional arrangements they are distinct sets of "shared restraints" of behavior (Poortinga 1990; Poortinga 1997).

Culture is a concept that stresses difference. It is a set of "ordered differences" that people adhere to, a normal recurrence of familiar differences (Geertz 1996: 75). Difference of cultures implies a certain amount of homogeneity and internal integration. Culture is a "necessary shared medium ... the minimal shared atmosphere within which (its) members can breathe and survive and produce" (Gellner 1984: 37). Comparative research has shown that different cultures form distinctive patterns with typically interrelated elements (Inglehart 1997). This concept of culture has two main components: shared activity, i.e., *cultural practices*, and shared meanings, i.e., *cultural interpretation and values* (Greenfield 1997). It does not imply a monolithic concept of culture but gives room to internal differences, and subsets of shared meanings, though it insists on a minimum of consensus on basic practices and meanings within the same cultural pattern.

Values are central to this concept of culture. An idealizing tendency in cultural analysis has exclusively identified values with images of the desirable and the good, and a monolithic concept of culture implied that this should be the common good. But their importance in cultural analysis is derived as much or even more from the fact that they set off "the good from the bad, the desirable from the detested, the sainted from the demonic,"[8] and that they define a set of proper reactions toward transgressions of these limits. Shared meanings include both, the good as well as the bad, and repression, exclusion and reconciliation lie at the inner core of cultural patterns. They define different concepts of the good, or at least establish consensus that more than one concept exists. Values, ideas and ideologies have an important and highly autonomous impact on the systems of crime control, as their history in the West shows. Crime and social control thus become expressions and illuminations of the wider culture, they indicate and produce evidence about the structure of its inner core (Nelken 1994; Melossi 2000). Since the undesirable and negative in culture is its natural topic, cross-cultural criminology has a chance to take a leading role in the analysis of culture in the social sciences.

Cross-cultural criminological inquiry that is based on this concept has to follow two general strategies: one that is based on a (multi-)dimensional concept of culture and uses extensive research strategies, and one that is based on singular cultural traits or "culture complexes," (Fiske et al. 1998) and uses intensive research strategies (see Table 1). The *dimensional-extensive* strategy starts from the assumption that cultures can be compared with regard to specific dimensions that are common to all. Typical dimensional concepts are individualism/collectivism, egalitarianism/authoritarianism, or solidarity.[9] The culture dimensions function as factors or variables in the explanatory equations. As such, their impact can be direct, and culture is conceptualized either as an independent or mediating variable. If an indirect impact is assumed, culture is either a contextual or a moderating variable; here culture defines the context in which other causes of crime and control operate, and it affects the way they do. The research strategy is extensive, i.e., mostly quantitative and based on considerably large samples of different nations. The dimensional-extensive strategy implies that different cultures are mainly studied with parallel research designs that use the same variables, operationalizations, and sampling techniques.

Table 1. The role of culture in criminological theory and research

Concept of Culture	Types/concepts	Role in theoretical framework	Strategies and methods
(Multi)-dimensional	-individualism/ collectivism -egalitarianism	*direct impact* -independent variable -mediating variable *indirect impact* -contextual variable -moderating variable	*strategy: extensive* -quantitative -large samples -*parallel* methods
Singular cultural traits Culture complexes	-religion(s) -US-southern "culture of honour" -machismo (Latin American) -"shame"-culture	*direct impact* -"culture as context" -culture as "overarching frame" *crime illuminating/ explaining culture* -culture as pattern	*strategy: intensive* -qualitative -ethnographic -small samples -case studies -contrasting cultures -*equivalent* methods

The *singular-trait-intensive* strategy starts from the assumption that differences between cultures are shaped by a specific characteristic or singular cultural trait, that pervades the total cultural pattern; it is present in one type of culture, but absent in others. Typical concepts are religion (e.g. Islamic religion [Groves, Newman, and Corrado 1987]), the so-called Southern-US culture of "honour and violence" (Nisbett and Cohen 1996), Latin-American "Machismo" (Neapolitan 1984) or "shame-cultures" (Braithwaite 1989). Culture complexes are "important components or organizing ethos of cultures," that "... involve patterns of actions, values, ... myths and all the complementary patterns of the psyche" (Fiske et al. 1998: 946). One or more of such culture complexes may be salient for the crime-culture relationship. Here, culture is conceived of as context or an overarching frame, with direct contextual impact or an indirect, 'framing' impact on crime and social control. Research strategies are intensive: Studies are qualitative, and often use ethnographic methods like Freund's (1982) study on miners in Nigeria or Birkbeck's (1982) study of a slum in Cali, Columbia. They rely on very small samples, case studies, or just contrast two cultures as do Melossi, and Westermann and Burfeind.[10] They often assign very different traits or complexes to each of the cultures studied, as well as different causal mechanisms that link them to crime. Equivalent instead of parallel research designs will be mainly used in cross-cultural singular-trait studies. In criminology, much more attention has been given to cultures of punishment than to cultures of crime: Skogan (1993) contrasted Catholic and Protestant countries, Melossi (2000) "soft" authoritarianism in Italy with democratic Protestant "exclusion" in the US, Westerman and Burfeind (1991) cohesion and solidarity in Japan versus individualism and social exclusion in the US.

These strategies do by no ways mutually exclude or are incompatible with each other. Both strategies are needed in cross-cultural research, at different stages and for different purposes. Comparative criminology in general mostly relied on extensive strategies while cross-cultural criminology focused its efforts mostly on specific examples in two or three countries. The adoption of a research strategy will depend on the differences between cultures that are included in the comparative strategy. The use of parallel procedures and variables works best when cultures are not too different, whereas equivalent procedures and variables will be required in the case of very dissimilar cultures, even if extensive strategies are applied (Greenfield 1997).

THE ROLE OF THEORY IN CROSS-CULTURAL RESEARCH

Transport and test of theories in different cultures

The transport and test of general theories of crime serves two purposes: It consolidates the foundations of knowledge in criminology, and—as far as the theories have implications for crime prevention and the handling of offenders—it will outline conditions of successful programs of crime prevention and control. The transport and test of theories in criminology cannot be directed at the universal confirmation of a specific model and specific strength of causal mechanisms, nor at the universal confirmation of outcomes. It is based on the assumption that universal causes and causal mechanisms exist. But universal causes will produce very different outcomes, depending on the extent and the ways ... [that] cultural patterns affect the variables and the causal mechanisms of the theoretical model. Even if the universal causal mechanism is confirmed, the transport and test of theories allows for a more exact specification of the impact of culture within a general model of crime. On the other hand, transport and test might show a failure of the theory in a specific cultural context; this result draws attention to culture-blindness of the original model and helps to situate it in its own historical and cultural context.

Theories differ with regard to the way culture is integrated into the model: they explicitly incorporate cultural and value patterns into the causal mechanism, they allow for a high cultural variability of the basic variables in the model, or they come with a claim to be universal and culture-free. I will present anomie theory as an example for the first case, the routine-activity approach for the second, and the theory of differential association and control theory as an illustration of the third case.

Anomie theory in its original version by Durkheim centers on the impact of cultural and structural change on the level of criminal behavior. Therefore, it will contribute to our understanding of the profound changes that globalization causes in Western industrialized countries, that are experienced in post-communist states of Eastern Europe, or that take place in the newly industrialized countries in South East Asia. Anomie theory allows for a global perspective that will remove the preoccupation with comparing so-called "developed" and "developing" nations. Messner and Rosenfeld (1994, 1997) have proposed an "institutional-anomie" theory that seems to be particularly apt for cross-cultural transport and test. It centers on the balance between market mechanisms and forces, and those cultural institutions that restrict and restrain these forces. Cultural values and practices—like solidarity and trust, or a tradition of welfare practices embedded in solidarity—counteract the impact of market forces on individuals, and contribute to mitigating economic distress. Imbalance between market forces and restraining social and cultural institutions causes crime. Messner and Rosenfeld base their theory on the Parsonian perspective of institutions as universal functional prerequisites. Consequently, they assume a universal causal mechanism, but allow for integrating different cultural contexts that each shape an institutional system of its own. Specific cultural contexts determine the way economic distress is experienced and defined by the population. Wagatsuma and De Vos (1984) studied a poor neighborhood in Tokyo where they found a high level of economic distress, but little crime. They attributed this to a set of attitudes that they called the "heritage of endurance." People accepted their distressful situation because they were convinced that their passive compliance would be rewarded in the future.

Institutional-anomie theory is based on the notion that the forces of the market and economic actors need institutional restraints. But culture-bound concepts of markets and economic transactions differ, as has been shown for markets in national and international Chinese communities. In particular, family and kinship ties emerge as a restraining force (Jones 1994; Appelbaum 1998). Consequently, an imbalance of the institutional settings of markets will have a decisively different shape and will emerge under different conditions depending on cultural concepts of markets, economic transactions and economic actors. Patterns of adaptation on the societal as well as on the individual level will vary accordingly. This will produce culture-specific types of adaptation, levels of deviant behavior and relations between different types of deviant behavior and crimes. Cross-cultural analysis might well change anomie theory as we know it, and produce culture-specific versions of the theory.

The routine-activity approach proposes a universal mechanism that explains why a crime happens in terms of the availability of crime targets. It relates suitable targets, the absence/presence of guardians and motivated offenders. This model holds constant the motivation of offenders, which seems to be, in particular, unreasonable in cross-cultural research. In fact, all three components of the universal causal mechanism are determined by cultural values and practices. Motivational patterns, practices of informal and formal control, and practices and habits of the routines of everyday-life are deeply embedded in the cultural fabric of societies. Therefore, the routine activity approach allows for a high cultural variability. In particular, transport and test will reveal the cultural sources of motivation and constraints which act in situations of "temptation."[11]

Within the framework of the routine activity approach, the cultural concepts of work and leisure, the rhythms of both, and the cultural practices of leisure are decisive in explaining levels of crime. Cultural concepts of "acting out" and drug consumption—in particular of alcohol, which is the most common drug in all cultures—will determine culture-specific relations between leisure activities, alcohol consumption and crime.[12] Integrating such cultural concepts into the routine activity approach will contribute to adapting the paradigm of routine activities to different cultures.

The theory of differential association has been applied in different cultures, but cross-cultural research and explicit and strong "transport-and-tests" in a comparative design have been rare.[13] Involvement with delinquent peers varies considerably, due to bonds with families and conform groups as in Japan (Vaughn and Huang 1992). In Africa, tribal networks and kinship have a decisive role in shaping criminal activities (Clinard and Abbot 1973). Cultural practices of juvenile leisure and entertainment activities differ with regard to involving the family as, e.g., in India. By comparing models of US and Indian juvenile delinquency, Hartjen and Kethineni (1996) show that the impact of delinquent peers as well as relationships with other variables in the model differ considerably between India and the US. The model is quite efficient in explaining juvenile delinquency in the US, but not in India. These examples of cross-cultural transport and test clearly demonstrate the limits of general models that have been developed within one culture. Transport and test therefore will specify and determine the impact of culture on the role of families, peers and educational institutions in the life of juveniles, and the way these patterns are combined into a specific cultural context that is more or less conducive to delinquent behavior. Cross-cultural comparisons of general involvement in delinquency, as well as of specifically situated involvement like after-school-crime will profit from transport and test of this theory.

A theory that claims to be a "general theory of crime" offers itself to transport and test. The control theory by Gottfredson and Hirschi (1990) comes with such a universal claim to building a culture-free theory of crime. They base their claim on the argument that cultural variability only affects the opportunity for crime, but not the nature of crime itself that they conceptualize as a lack of self-control. In particular, their propositions about a universal age-crime relationship have been transported and tested. For Japan, Harada rejects this universal claim (Harda 1995). In India, family attachment and control by the family are far from being as important factors for involvement in delinquency as in the US because of a generally higher and more equal level of family control (Hartjen and Kethineni 1996). But as Nelken (1994) pointed out, the core concept of crime and self-control in this theory is culturally determined: It cannot deny a strong foundation in Protestant ethics. The universal claim comes with a heavy burden of culture-blindness.

Cultures widely differ with regard to conceptions of the self, its relation to others, and the ways individuals learn and practice self-control. Practices of child rearing and socialization differ accordingly. Mothers in Japan react with much more empathy toward aggression than in Germany (Kornadt and Trommsdorf 1998). These practices are manifestations of cultural conceptions about the control of aggression by the self and others (Vaughn and Tomita 1990; Vaughn and Huang 1992; Kumagai 1981). We cannot exclude that in each culture equivalents of mechanisms of self control and their relationship to crime and criminal behavior may be found. Given the differences of the core concepts between cultures it is doubtful if there is a universal link between crime and self-control. Even if such culture-specific equivalents still support the claim of universality, they obviously undermine the claim of the theory to be culture-free.

The transport and test of theories of crime and criminal behavior might produce more cultural variability than universal "iron laws." This will give more importance to the task "to develop specific theories which are both consistent with and relevant to particular socio-cultural systems" (De Fleur 1969). Cultural variability will be the starting point and not the outcome of such a strategy in cross-cultural criminology. In the next section I will examine the potential of indigenizing theories and concepts in cross-cultural criminology.

Indigenizing criminological theories and concepts

In fact, the general conceptual frameworks and theories of crime and criminal behavior are in a way indigenous. They have been mostly developed within the US-American and Western culture, and refer to the specific problems of crime in these countries. Criminology therefore is simultaneously culture-bound and culture-blind, a characteristic that it shares with other social sciences. The overall process of internationalization and globalization gave momentum to the development of indigenous theories and concepts in the social sciences (Arrow and King 1990). Indigenization means the extent, to which concepts, problems, hypotheses and methods emanate from, represent and reflect back on the cultural context in which crime and social control are observed (Sinha 1997).

In cross-cultural psychology as well as in sociology, indigenization first evolved from traditional concepts of mental health and therapeutic practices (Sinha 1999). Western psychologists had to confront the notion that neither their definitions of mental health nor the Western therapeutic measures fitted the existing ones or were a priori superior to indigenous practices of handling mental problems; instead they were confronted with the iatrogenic effects of their measures. In his fervent attack on the transport of Western crime control models to the Third World, Stanley Cohen (1997) took to the most discouraging examples of the impact of Western health systems in the Third World, and compared their failures to those of Western crime control models. He strongly criticized that at a time when community control and the dispersal of social control into the community was favored in Western countries, traditional community control in Third World countries was increasingly destroyed by bringing in more police, courts and prisons. Local traditions needed a positive defence and strong reinforcement.[14]

Today, criminology is taking the first steps on the path toward indigenization. The social movement of restorative justice has started from and taken up traditional approaches toward handling crimes and offenders from different cultures all over the world. These traditions are rooted in Western cultures as well as in many others. Eliminated ago a long time in the West, they are now re-imported from Asia, Australia or Africa; in Canada or the USA, Indian communities reanimate their traditional justice systems (Braithwaite 1997). This process has been accompanied by building new theories and integrating new concepts into criminology, in particular Braithwaite's theory of reintegrative shaming.

Braithwaite's theory is a showcase of how the process of indigenization might work, and even result in some unintended consequences for theory and crime control. He started from the concept of shame as indigenous to Asian cultures. But he developed it into a universal concept and integrated it into the existing body of criminological theories. As a result, what started as indigenization became a universal theoretical approach, and shame was rediscovered as a factor in crime control in Western nations. In addition, he combined his theory with indigenous practices of restorative and reintegrative justice in New Zealand and Australia that afterwards were transported to Western and Asian justice systems (Braithwaite 1997). Braithwaite's theory clearly demonstrates that the process of indigenization does not necessarily result in the rejection of universal concepts, and that it is no one-way street, but allows for an exchange between universal and indigenous concepts. They are neither incompatible nor mutually exclusive, and what starts as an indigenous concept might become a universal one and vice versa. Indigenization furthers new perspectives on universal concepts, and thus contributes to integrating new general concepts into the ensemble of criminological theories.

Consequently, it is no paradox that general theories of crime and universal concepts might provide a foundation for the process of indigenization. The broadness of their core concepts and categorical frames can stimulate the search for indigenous concepts, and allow for their absorption into and subsequent substantive changes of the theories. Concepts of the "self" and "others," of the relation between self and community have been the seedbed of the process of indigenization in cross-cultural psychology. In an analogous way, criminology will center the process of indigenization on the relationship between formal and informal controls, and inclusionary and exclusionary concepts of crime and control. Religious traditions and culture-specific patterns of morality and moral emotions provide an important set of indigenous concepts, since they define dominant moral concerns that shape the practices of regulating and sanctioning deviant behavior (Fiske et al. 1998). Cultural concepts of self-esteem and respect, of trust and forgiveness will shape patterns of crime as well as of control.

STRATEGIES AND TOPICS FOR CROSS-CULTURAL CRIMINOLOGY

In this section, I want to explore selected strategies and topics for cross-cultural research in criminology that seem to be seminal for the development of theory and research: stability and change of cultural patterns, the relationship between cross-cultural and historical research and the culture of inequality. I have selected these topics because they have to do as much with understanding one's own culture as with understanding a foreign one, and they direct attention away from an altogether too stable, integrated and homogeneous concept of culture that mainly nourishes cultural rhetoric.

Stability and change of cultural patterns

Much of the debate on Asian versus Western values and their impact on crime and control implicitly centers on the problem of the stability and homogeneity of cultural patterns; it has been overrated by outsiders, and perhaps underrated by insiders. Global migration confronts societies with increasing and new crime problems. Migration and the establishment of ethnic and cultural diasporas offer a first-rate opportunity for criminology to study the stability of the culture-crime relationship. It allows for a perspective from within, and in addition for research strategies that circumvent many of the data problems that make comparative research in criminology such a difficult task. Migrants bring their own culture to the foreign country. At the beginning of this century immigrant Italians in the USA had rates of violent crime (homicides) that did not differ from those in their native country, and were higher than those of other immigrant groups, as were Italian homicide rates compared to other European countries (Gurr 1981, 1989). De Haan (1993) obtained analogous results for the immigrant Surinamese in the Netherlands, who—like the Italians in the USA—had high rates compared to other immigrant groups. These data hint to processes of cultural transfer and the stability of cultural patterns in immigrant communities that are related to crime.

But these patterns will change considerably during the process of integration and acculturation. Individual behavior is bolstered and enhanced by the specific cultural environment, and consequently "modal cultural traits" will change and adapt to a new cultural environment (Fiske et al. 1998). Nonetheless, in the situation of immigration, specific cultural patterns might be strengthened even if they are in contrast to the surrounding culture. Turkish immigrants in Germany seem to have a stronger collectivistic orientation than those who live in Turkey (Öztoprak 1998). The process of acculturation and cultural change will be most visible in the succession of generations. Stability and change of cultural patterns can be studied in first and second generation immigrant families, as well as in the respective ethnic communities. Cultural practices of socialization, patterns of control in families and communities will contribute to different levels of crime within ethnic groups, and in contrast to others. These patterns will in particular manifest themselves in the transfer, stability and change of gender roles, and resulting differences of involvement in deviant behavior between both genders.

Stability, adaption and transfer of cultural patterns equally influence levels of white collar crime on the national as well as on the global level. Cultural traditions in the political system and economy of Japan have been made responsible for the spread of white collar crime and corruption.[15] Organized crime is deeply rooted in cultural traditions, and embedded in ethnic and cultural minorities that preserve parts of their respective traditions. The very characteristic of cultural patterns—internal integration and homogeneity, and external difference—can be named as a precondition for the emergence of organized crime. "Trading diasporas" of ethnic communities establish global networks of ethnic and kin relationships that have a competitive advantage in legal and illegal economies (Kotkin 1993). Nonetheless, these cultural patterns are easily linked to modern markets and management strategies. Arlacchi (1986) shows how the Italian Mafia adapted its cultural pattern to social and economic change on a national and global scale, and how this gave it a competitive advantage in white collar crime and organized crime.

The role of cultural history

"The past is a foreign country:" The cultural values and practices of our own ancestors seem to us as strange and unfamiliar as those of a contemporary foreign culture (Lowenthal 1985). The diachronic perspective on our own culture thus becomes cross-cultural. But cross-cultural criminology should clearly avoid the erroneous path that modernization theory took by simply equating the diachronic with the cross-national perspective. The process of modernization in Western countries was taken as the universal model of the road to modernization for all countries, and consequently the development of crime and social control should follow the same pattern. Globalization has given evidence that this basic assumption of a universal model of modernization has to be rejected in favour of culture-specific trajectories of modernization. More recently, modernization theory relies more and more on the particular historical realities from which the process of modernization started and that accompanied it; cultural history has a major role in these new perspectives on the diversity of trajectories of change (Park and Chang 1999).

The "enigma of Japan" (Miyazawa) and the South East Asian states showed that the relationship between modernization and crime clearly deviated from what was assumed according to the Western model of modernization. The process of "cultural modernization"— from interdependent and collectivistic cultural patterns toward independent and individualistic patterns—cannot claim to be a universal model a priori. Instead, careful diachronic analyses of the relationship between cultural patterns and criminalization or decriminalization, the culture of punishment or crime waves will reveal unique paths of historical and cultural transformation of crime and social control. The historical reconstruction of the relationship between culture and crime will help to overcome the often ahistorical, typifying and monolithic conceptualizations of culture as in the juxtaposition of "Western" and "Confucian" cultural values.

Norbert Elias' (1994) "theory of civilization" though definitely restricted to Western cultures might serve as an example of cultural historical research. Elias argues that the long wave of Western modernization was accompanied by a change of the moral order and cultural practices of control. This process shifted the weight away from external to internal controls, to self-control and "inner shaming" in Western cultures (Braithwaite 1993). Elias' theory provides explanations for the change of penal cultures in Europe—in particular the ban of corporal punishment and sanctions that are overtly aggressive actions—and the trend toward the decrease of violent crime that started as early as the 17th century and continued until the 1960s (Gurr 1989). Until now it has not proved its usefulness as a conceptual framework and methodology for the study of different cultural traditions and culture complexes. But it directs attention to the potential of culture-specific theories of cultural change and might stimulate analogous studies and theories in other countries.

Cultures of inequality

When del Olmo (1975) criticized Latin American criminologists for not confronting the "Latin American reality" of violence, she in particular defined it as dominated by institutional, not individual violence. She gives a vivid account of the structural and cultural patterns of inequality, domination and dependency that are directly linked to the high levels of violence in these societies, in particular violence by the state and the institutions of social control. She directs attention to the fact that criminological theories are especially ill equipped to deal with such a cultural pattern of violence and inequality.

Violent crime is one of the most urgent problems in Western industrialized countries, new industrialized countries or post-communist states. Social inequality and social exclusion emerge as kind of universal factors across time and space in explanatory models of rates and types of violent crime (Messner 1982; Karstedt 2001; Land, McCall and Cohen 1990; Messner and Rosenfeld 1997). Nonetheless, non-egalitarian structures are likely to have different meanings in modern societies compared to "simple societies" (Rosenfeld and Messner 1991). The context of individualistic and independent cultures establishes the relationship between violence and inequality that might be missing in other contexts, and consequently, the relationship should be conceived of as context-dependent. In individualistic cultures, social inequality will produce types of social exclusion of minorities that are related to violence, while in collectivistic, more hierarchical and authoritarian cultures, inequality will contribute to violence between groups as well as to high levels of in group-violence e.g. in families, that often remains secret within their domain (Karstedt 2001). The study of immigrant groups is a first-rate opportunity for elaborating the context-dependency of the relationship between crime and cultures of inequality. Immigrants normally experience social inequality and discrimination on high levels. Which cultural patterns mitigate the impact of such a situation on crime rates, which cultural patterns further the commitment of crimes and violent actions?

This relationship between structural inequality and cultural context is but one facet of the culture of inequality. An examination of studies on the culture of violence like the "culture of machismo" or the "culture of honour" shows a common denominator: These are cultures that stress inequality—between genders as well as between groups of different "honour." Violence seems to be related not only to structural inequality but to ... different cultures of inequality.

Cultures of inequality are a seedbed of crimes by the state, corruption, and economic and corporate crimes that involve social elites. In a cross-cultural study on corruption in forty countries, the extent of authoritarian and non-egalitarian cultural orientations emerged as a most powerful predictor of the level of corruption (Karstedt 2004). Authoritarian political and corporate cultures make elites more invulnerable to threats of detection and punishment by shielding them from public blame and official prosecution. Pressure on middle and lower ranks to participate in such crimes is higher, as is the dependency of these groups. Simultaneously, such cultural patterns make potential victims much more vulnerable by assigning to them an inferior position and allowing for degrading mechanisms.

TAPPING CULTURAL RESOURCES, TRANSFER, AND MODELING: CRIMINAL JUSTICE IN CROSS-CULTURAL PERSPECTIVE

Tapping the different cultures of the world as sources of cultural knowledge is one of the foremost advantages that cross-cultural criminology offers to the field of criminal justice and its professionals. Exploration, transfer and modeling of crime prevention strategies are important modes of cross-cultural exchange in criminal justice. New strategies of crime prevention, procedures of dealing with offenses, offenders and victims, or models of institutions and therapeutic intervention for juvenile and adult offenders rapidly spread around the globe. More than a decade ago this seemed to be a one-way and dead-end road from western industrialized countries mainly to those in the Third World. This has changed meanwhile, and the model of restorative justice has in a way reversed the direction. There is more space and attention for indigenous developments of prevention and sanction systems. The idea of institutional and organizational isomorphism—that the same types of institutions spread in the course of modernization and globalization processes because of their success (DiMaggio and Powell 1983)—finds less support among criminal justice experts. On the other hand, Western countries might still provide models for prosecuting national and international corporate crime in particular after having become alert to profound cultural differences within their own group (Cohen 1997; Nelken 1994). Programs of restorative justice, community policing and prevention, and situational crime prevention were established in many countries and different cultures. They are confronted with problems that result from integration in and adaptation to the different cultures of control, including practices in families and communities as well as in the legal culture of penal justice. These are deeply embedded in cultural-historical realities and unique trajectories of development, as studies on the culture of punishment in Europe or respective comparisons easily show. Those criminal justice models that are based on universal causes have to be checked for specific conditions, qualifying mechanisms and different outcomes when being transferred or modeled in other cultural settings than their origin. Those that are based on a specific cultural tradition like restorative justice models have to be checked for differences and common ground with the cultural practices of control into which they will be integrated.

Not simple transfers, but modeling seems to be the best strategy for cross-cultural exchange of both types of crime prevention. Restorative justice—including reintegrative shaming, conferencing, victim-offender reconciliation and victim compensation programs—has emerged as a strategy of tapping the sources of cultural practices of control and penal justice mainly of non-western, indigenous cultures and often pre-colonial practices of social control. These models are embedded in informal practices of control, and modeling therefore touches the crucial point of the relationship between formal and informal cultural practices of control. Shame seems to be a specific characteristic of interdependent cultures, and therefore might work in a different way and needs a different environment in independent cultures.[16]

Lacey and Zedner (2000) compared the development of locally based criminal justice initiatives in Britain and Germany, two countries that share at least some dominant characteristics of Western culture. They found that the distinctive institutional and political cultures decisively shaped community based strategies of crime control in both countries, and accounted for remarkable differences between them. In Germany, its typical corporatist political culture and the ideology of professionalism significantly restricted volunteer involvement in contrast to Britain. Rhetorics of community were much more subdued than in Britain; instead the discourse on "community and crime" centered on foreigners—migrants and asylum-seekers. Cultural contexts and its specific dimensions thus shape implementation of programs, and might consequently often account for unintended consequences or failure of programs of locally based crime prevention (Zedner 1997).

Situational crime prevention comes with a high claim to a universal approach to crime prevention. Being ultimately based on rational choice theory, situational crime prevention programs start from the assumption of universal causes. Consequently, the principle of universal causes and (potentially) different outcomes in particular applies to cross-cultural transfers of situational crime prevention models. Such models should provide a framework for integrating culture-specific, contextual variables into situational crime prevention strategies. Exploration and discovery of traditional, culture-specific forms of situational crime prevention will contribute to widening the data base for refining the universal model, and might promote as well the indigenization of situational crime prevention.

PAROCHIALISM OR UNIVERSAL CRIMINOLOGY?

Taking the concept of culture serious in criminology implies stressing differences. This might generate a kind of radical cultural relativism, "relativizing particularism" (Fiske et al. 1998: 945) and parochialism in the study of crime and control, that finally does not encourage comparison, exchange, and understanding between cultures. Cultural relativism and particularism are not a necessary consequence of moving culture from the periphery more to the center of criminological research. In principle, understanding another culture is neither more nor less difficult than understanding our own culture or its past (Beirne 1997). The dichotomy 'unity versus diversity' or 'difference' does not further the tasks of cross-cultural criminology. Instead, we should shift our perspective systematically from differences toward universals and vice versa. Indigenization does not imply that universals or a universal theory are useless, but to the contrary: It directs attention to the culture-bound quality of those theories that we rate as universal theories, or directs the search toward hitherto neglected and potential universals. Any such tendencies toward such dichotomies are inimical to the development of the discipline.[17]

The different strategies of cross-cultural research each make specific contributions to a universal criminology. Dimensional cross-cultural research with large samples will contribute to understanding the relation between general types of cultural contexts, and crime and control. Singular-trait cross-cultural research will provide in-depth studies of the cultural contexts of crime and control, and enhance our knowledge about the relationship between crime and social control. They in particular will contribute to making crime and social control an independent variable that "explains" culture. Until now, mostly Western criminologists studied foreign cultures; a research strategy that makes the West not only a source for theoretical insights or models of crime control, but also an object of empirical scrutiny from the perspective of other cultures will make especially valuable contributions to a global criminology.[18]

Parochialism might emerge as a problem in crime prevention strategies and institutional practices of criminal justice that are based on cultural and indigenous practices. It easily implies a sort of romanticism and exoticism that neglects the changes of cultural traditions of social control and of its structural and economic environment. These practices might be especially ill equipped to deal with those crime problems that are caused by extreme inequality, authoritarianism and dependency. Controlling and regulating the powerful without strong centrally enforced legislation might deprive those who are in a situation of dependency and of lower social status from formal legal recognition of their rights (Cohen 1997: 151). This in particular applies to the illegal global economy and the enforcement of human rights. It would be a dangerous development to underrate the unifying power of common legal principles and the general principles of the rule of law in penal justice.[19]

Myths are culture-specific discourses on universals. Therefore we might return to the myth from Plato's "Protagoras" for an answer. It continues like this: The highest god gave orders to his messenger to distribute shame and law *equally* among human beings. Since then, humankind shares a moral sense and basic principles of justice and fairness.

NOTES

[1] See for the concept of legal culture Feest and Blankenburg (1997).

[2] This is not the first time in history that Western scholars promote Confucianism as a model. Particularly in the Age of Enlightenment, the European philosophers Voltaire, Leibniz and Wolff found Confucian China to be an ideal realization of the "enlightened state." See Lee (1997: 29). For the discussion of Asian values and economic development see Huntington (1996) and Fukuyama (1992, 1998: 3).

[3] Particularly when used from a Western perspective, it may be termed as "orientalism" following Said's influential concept (Said 1978).

[4] But see Reishauer (1988: 204) who contends that Japan is a society whose secularism is rooted in its essentially Confucian philosophical background: "... Confucian ethical values continue to permeate their thinking."

[5] For Japan see Fukaya (1998) and Kumagai (1979, 1981); for Korea, Lee (1997); and China, Gransow and Hanlin (1995).

[6] Inglehart (1997); when compared to the value dimensions of Hofstede's study, the relative stability of cultural patterns can be shown across 30 years (Hofstede 1984).

[7] See the various volumes of the *Handbook of Cross-Cultural Psychology*, in particular Berry, Poortinga, and Pandley (1997) and Berman (1989).

[8] Alexander and Smith (1993: 157); the authors argue "for studying the importance of the undesirable and negative in culture.... The conflict between good and bad functions inside of culture as an internal dynamic.... It is for this reason that transgression and purification are key rituals in social life" (158).

[9] For individualism see Messner (1982) and Karstedt (2001); for solidarity see Pampel and Gartner (1995); for individualism/collectivism in cross-cultural psychology see Triandis (1995).

[10] For small samples see Haferkamp and Ellis (1992) and Kersten (1997); for case studies see Arthur and Marenin (1995); for the contrast of two cultures, Melossi (2000) or Westermann and Burfeind (1991).

[11] See Miyazawa (1994: 92). Even when differences in opportunity structures are taken into account nations differ considerably with regard to the moral condemnation of deviant behaviour that is mostly regarded as being caused by opportunity structures, like claiming benefits, cheating on taxes, or avoiding transport fares (Inglehart, Basanez, and Moreno, 1998: V296–V319).

[12] See Hartjen and Kethineni (1996: 145), for differences in alcohol consumption among Indian and US adolescents.

[13] Hartjen and Kethineni (1996) included association with peers into their model. Clinard and Abbot (1973) used the theory of differential association as a framework; their research supports the main propositions of differential association theory but points to specific conditions, e.g., of migration to urban centers and the role of kinship and tribal networks.

[14] Nonetheless, Cohen makes a strong argument for the import of Western strategies for controlling crimes of the powerful.

[15] See, e.g., traditions of gift-offering and taking in Japan and China, where the line between legal and illegal gifts is drawn in a way different from other countries; for Japan see Abe (1992) and Kerbo and Inoue (1992); for China see Ong and Nonini (1997) and Yang (1994).

[16] Fiske et al. (1998: 943); see Levi (2000) for the impact of shame in different cultures and in the global economy.

[17] Archer (1991: 133) states for sociology that this "false dichotomy has done inestimable damage" to the discipline.

[18] See for Korea, Park and Chang (1999).

[19] According to Geertz (1996: 86–89), the principles of liberalism—freedom, rule of law, and universal human rights—provide a general and indispensable foundation for a world of cultural differences.

REFERENCES

Abe, K. 1992. "Wesen und Wandel der Reziprozität in Europa und Japan." Pp. 239–48 in *Zwischen den Kulturen. Die Sozialwissenschaften vor dem Problem des Kulturvergleichs*, Soziale Welt, Sonderband 8, edited by J. Matthes. Göttingen: Schwartz.

Akiwowo, A. 1999. "Indigenous Sociologies: Extending the Scope." *International Sociology* 14: 115–38.

Albrow, M. and E. King (Eds.). 1990. *Globalization, Knowledge and Society*. London: Sage.

Alexander, J.C. and Ph. Smith. 1993. "The Discourse of American Civil Society: A New Proposal for Cultural Studies." *Theory and Society* 22: 151–207.

Anderson, B. 1983. *Imagined Communities: Reflections on the Origin and Spread of Nationalism*. London: Verso.

Appelbaum, R.P. 1998. "The Future of Law in a Global Economy." *Social and Legal Studies* 7: 171–92.

Archer, M. 1991. "Sociology for One World: Unity and Diversity." *International Sociology* 6: 133.

Ariffin, J. 1995. "At the Crossroad of Rapid Development: Malaysian Society and Anomie." *International Journal of Sociology and Social Policy* 15: 8–18.

Arlacchi, P. 1986. *Mafia Business: The Mafia Ethic and the Spirit of Capitalism*. London: Verso.

Arthur, J.A. and O. Marenin. 1995. "Explaining Crime in Developing Countries: The Need for a Case Study Approach." *Crime, Law & Social Change* 23: 191–214.

Beirne, P. "Cultural Relativism and Comparative Criminology." Pp. 3–24 in *Issues in Comparative Criminology*, edited by P. Beirne and D. Nelken. Aldershot: Dartmouth.

Berman, J.J. (Ed.). 1989. *Cross-Cultural Perspectives*. Vol. 37, *Nebraska Symposium on Motivation*. Lincoln: University of Nebraska Press.

Berry, J.W., Y.H. Poortinga, and J. Pandey (Eds.). 1997. *Handbook of Cross-Cultural Psychology*, Vol. 1, *Theory and Method*. Boston: Allyn and Bacon.

Birkbeck, Ch.H. 1982. "Property Crime and the Poor: Some Evidence from Cali, Columbia." Pp. 161–91 in *Crime, Justice, and Underdevelopment*, edited by C. Sumner. London: Heinemann.

Braithwaite, J. 1997. *Restorative Justice: Assessing an Immodest Theory and a Pessimistic Theory*. Canberra: Australian National University.

Braithwaite, J. 1993. "Shame and Modernity." *British Journal of Criminology* 33: 1–18.

Braithwaite, J. 1989. *Crime, Shame and Reintegration*. New York: Cambridge University Press.

Christie, Nils. 1998. "Kriminalität ist eine unerschöpfliche Ressource—Interview mit Nils Christie." *Neue Kriminalpolitik* 10: 6.

Clinard, M.B. and D.J. Abbot. 1973. *Crime in Developing Countries: A Comparative Perspective*. New York: Wiley.

Cohen, S. 1997. "Western Crime Control Models in the Third World: Benign or Malignant?" Pp. 123–60 in *Issues in Comparative Criminology*, edited by P. Beirne and D. Nelken. Aldershot: Dartmouth.

De Fleur, L. 1969. "Alternative Strategies for the Development of Delinquency Theories Applicable to Other Cultures." *Social Problems* 17: 38–39.

de Haan, W. 1993. *Street Robbery in 1991 in Amsterdam*. Research Report for the Home Office, The Hague. Utrecht, NL: Dept. of Criminal Law and Criminology, University of Utrecht.

del Olmo, R. 1975. "Limitations for the Prevention of Violence: The Latin American Reality and its Criminological Theory." *Crime and Social Justice* 3: 21–29.

DiMaggio, P. and W.R. Powell. 1983. "The Iron Cage Revisited: Institutional Isomorphism and Collective Rationality in Organizational Fields." *American Sociological Review* 48: 147–60.

Duerr, H.-P. 1988. *"Der Mythos vom Zivilisationsprozeß."* Vol. 1, *Nacktheit und Scham*. Frankfurt: Suhrkamp.

Eckersley, R. 1993. "The West's Deepening Cultural Crisis." *The Futurist* (November/December): 8–12.

Elias, N. 1994. *The Civilizing Process*. Oxford: Blackwell.

Featherstone, M. 1995. *Undoing Culture: Globalization, Postmodernism and Identity*. London: Sage.

Feest, J. and E. Blankenburg (Eds.). 1997. *Changing Legal Cultures*. Oñati: International Institute for the Sociology of Law.

Fiske, A.P., S. Kitayama, H.R. Markus, and R.E. Nisbett. 1998. "The Cultural Matrix of Social Psychology." Pp. 915–81 in *The Handbook of Social Psychology*. 4th ed. Vol. 2. edited by D.T. Gilbert, S.T. Fiske, and G. Lindzey. Boston: McGraw-Hill.

Freund, W. 1982. "Theft and Social Protest among the Tin Miners of Northern Nigeria." *Radical History Review* 26: 68–86.

Fujimoto, T. and W.K. Park. 1994. "Is Japan Exceptional? Reconsidering Japanese Crime Rates." *Social Justice* 21: 110–35.

Fukaya, M. 1998. "Japanische Jugendliche im internationalen Vergleich—grundlegende Muster und aktuelle Tendenzen." Pp. 139–150 in *Gewalt unter Jugendlichen in Deutschland und Japan*, edited by G. Foljanty-Jost and D. Rössner. Baden-Baden: Nomos.

Fukuyama, F. 1992. *Trust. The Social Virtues and the Creation of Prosperity*. New York: Free Press.

Fukuyama, F. 1998. "Asiens Werte, Asiens Krise." *Die Zeit* (May 20/22): 3.

Geertz, C. 1996. *Welt in Stücken. Kultur und Politik am Ende des 20. Jahrhunderts.* Wien: Passagen-Verlag.

Gellner, E. 1984. *Nations and Nationalism.* Oxford: Basil Blackwell.

Gottfredson, M.R. and T. Hirschi. 1990. A *General Theory of Crime.* Stanford, CA: Stanford University Press.

Gransow, B. and L. Hanlin. 1995. *Chinas neue Werte. Einstellungen zu Modernisierung und Reformpolitik.* Berliner China-Studien 26. München: Minerva.

Greenfield, P.M. 1997. "Culture as Process: Empirical Methods for Cultural Psychology." Pp. 301–46 in *Handbook of Cross-Cultural Psychology,* Vol. 1, *Theory and Method,* edited by Berry, J.W., Y.H. Poortinga, and J. Pandey. Boston: Allyn and Bacon.

Groves, B., G. Newman, and Ch. Corrado. 1987. "Islam, Modernization and Crime: A Test of the Religious Ecology Thesis." *Journal of Criminal Justice* 15: 495–503.

Gurr, T.R., "Historical Trends in Violent Crime: A Critical Review of the Evidence." Pp. 24–59 in *Violence in America,* edited by T.R. Gurr. Newbury Park: Sage.

Haferkamp, H. and H. Ellis. 1992. "Power, Individualism and the Sanctity of Human Life: Development of Criminality and Punishment in Four Cultures." Pp. 261–80 in *Crime and Control in Comparative Perspectives,* edited by H.-G. Heiland, L. Shelley, and H. Katoh. Berlin: de Gruyter.

Harada, Y. 1995. "Adjustment to School, Life Course Transitions, and Changes in Delinquent Behavior in Japan." *Current Perspectives on Aging and the Life Cycle* 4: 58.

Hartjen, C.A. and S. Kethineni. 1996. *Comparative Delinquency: India and the United States.* New York: Garland.

Heiland, H.-G. and L. Shelley. 1992. "Civilization, Modernization and the Development of Crime and Control." Pp. 1–20 in *Crime and Control in Comparative Perspectives,* edited by H.-G. Heiland, L. Shelley, and H. Katoh. Berlin: de Gruyter.

Hofstede, G. 1984. *Culture's Consequences: International Differences in Work-Related Values.* 1st ed. 1980 and 2nd abridged ed. Beverly Hills: Sage.

Huntington, S.P. 1996. *The Clash of Civilizations.* New York: Simon Schuster.

Inglehart, R. 1997. *Modernization and Postmodernization: Cultural, Economic and Political Change in 43 Societies.* Princeton: Princeton University Press.

Inglehart, R., M. Basanez, and A. Moreno. 1998. *Human Values and Beliefs: A Cross-cultural Sourcebook. Political, Religious, Sexual and Economic Norms in 43 Societies: Findings from the 1990–1993 World Values Survey.* Ann Arbor: The University of Michigan Press.

Janos, A.C. 1986. *Politics and Paradigms: Changing Theories of Change in Social Science.* Stanford: Stanford University Press.

Jones, C.A.G. 1994. "Capitalism, Globalization and Rule of Law: An Alternative Trajectory of Legal Change in China." *Social and Legal Studies* 3: 195–221.

Karstedt, S. 2001. "Die moralische Stärke schwacher Bindungen: Individualismus und Gewalt im Kulturvergleich." *Monatsschrift fuer Kriminologie und Strafrechtsreform* 84: 226–43.

Karstedt, S. 2004. "Macht, Ungleichheit und Korruption: Strukturelle und kulturelle Determinanten im internationalen Vergleich." Pp. 384–412 in *Soziologie der Kriminalität*, edited by D. Oberwittler and S. Karstedt. Special issue, *Kölner Zeitschrift für Soziologie und Sozialspychologie* 43. Wiesbaden: VS Verlag Sozialwissenschaften.

Kerbo, H.R. and M. Inoue. 1992. "Japanese Social Structure and White Collar Crime: Recruit Cosmos and Beyond." *Deviant Behavior* 11: 139–54.

Kersten, J. 1997. *Gut und (Ge)schlecht. Männlichkeit, Kultur und Kriminalität.* Berlin: de Gruyter.

Kornadt, H.-J. and G. Trommsdorf. 1998. "Sozialisationsbedingungen von Aggressivität in Japan und Deutschland." Pp. 27–52 in *Gewalt unter Jugendlichen in Deutschland und Japan*, edited by G. Foljanty-Jost and D. Rössner. Baden-Baden: Nomos.

Kotkin, J. 1993. *Tribes: How Race, Religion and Identity Determine Success in the New Global Economy.* New York: Random House.

Kumagai, F. 1979. "Family Egalitarianism in Cultural Contexts: High-Variation Japanese Egalitarianism vs. Low-Variation American Egalitarianism." *Journal of Comparative Family Studies* 10: 315–29.

Kumagai, F. 1981. "Field Theory and Conjugal Violence in Japan." *Journal of Comparative Family Studies* 12: 413–28.

Lacey, N. and L. Zedner. 2000. "Community and Governance: A Cultural Comparison." Pp. 157–70 in *Social Dynamics of Crime and Control: New Theories for a World in Transition*, edited by S. Karstedt and K.-D. Bussmann. Oxford: Hart.

Land, K.C., P.L. McCall, and L.E. Cohen. 1997. "Structural Covariates of Homicide Rates: Are There Any Invariances across Time and Social Space?" *American Journal of Sociology* 95: 922–63.

Lee, E.J. 1997. *Konfuzianismus und Kapitalismus. Markt und Herrschaft in Ostasien.* Münster: Westfälisches Dampfboot.

Levi, M. 2000. "Shaming and the Regulation of Fraud and Business 'Misconduct': Some Preliminary Explorations" Pp. 143–56 in *Social Dynamics of Crime and Control. New Theories for a World in Transition*, edited by S. Karstedt and K.-D. Bussmann. Oxford: Hart.

Lonner, W.J. and J. Adamopoulos. 1997. "Culture as Antecedent to Behavior." Pp. 53–74 in *Handbook of Cross-Cultural Psychology*, Vol. 1, *Theory and Method*, edited by J. Berry, Y.H. Poortinga, and J. Pandey. Boston: Allyn and Bacon.

Lonner, W.J. 1994. "Culture and Human Diversity." Pp. 220–43 in *Human Diversity: Perspectives on People in Context*, edited by E.J. Trickett, R.J. Watts, and D. Birman. San Francisco: Jossey-Bass.

Lowenthal, D. 1985. *The Past is a Foreign Country.* Cambridge: Cambridge University Press.

Melossi, D. 2000. "Translating Social Control: Reflections on the Comparison of Italian and North-American Cultures Concerning Social Control, with a Few Consequences for a Critical Criminology." Pp. 143–56 in *Social Dynamics of Crime and Control. New Theories for a World in Transition*, edited by S. Karstedt and K.-D. Bussmann. Oxford: Hart.

Messner, S. F. 1982. "Societal Development, Social Equality and Homicide: A Cross-National Test of a Durkheimian Model." *Social Forces* 61: 225–40.

Messner, S.F. and R. Rosenfeld. 1994. *Crime and the American Dream.* Belmont, CA: Wadsworth.

Messner, S.F. and R. Rosenfeld. 1997. "Political Restraint of the Market and Levels of Criminal Homicide. A Cross-National Application of Institutional-Anomie Theory." *Social Forces* 75: 1393–1416.

Miyazawa, S. 1994. "The Enigma of Japan as a Testing Ground for Cross-Cultural Criminological Studies." *International Annals of Criminology.* 32: 81–103.

Neapolitan, J.L. 1984. "Cross-National Variation in Homicides: The Case of Latin America." *International Criminal Justice Review* 4: 4–22.

Nelken, D. 1994. "Whom Can You Trust? The Future of Comparative Criminology." Pp. 220–43 in *The Futures of Criminology*, edited by D. Nelken. London: Sage.

Nisbett, R.E. and D. Cohen. 1996. *Culture of Honor.* Boulder, CO: Westview.

Ong, A. and D.M. Nonini (Eds.). 1997. *Ungrounded Empires: The Cultural Politics of Modern Chinese Transnationalism.* New York: Routledge.

Öztoprak, Ü. 1998. "Individualistische und kollektivistische Wertorientierungen bei türkischen Jugendlichen." *Forschungsnetzwerk für ethnisch-kulturelle Konflikte, Rechtsextremismus und Gewalt, Newsletter* 10: 66–85.

Pampel, F.C. and R. Gartner. 1995. "Age-Structure, Socio-Political Institutions and National Homicide Rates." *European Sociological Review* 11: 243–60.

Park, M.-K. and K.-S. Chang. 1999. "Sociology Between Western Theory and Korean Reality: Accommodation, Tension and Search for Alternatives." *International Sociology* 14: 139–56.

Plato. 1987. *Protagoras.* Translated and commented on by H.-W. Krautz. Stuttgart: Philipp Reclam.

Poortinga, Y.H. 1990. "Towards a Conceptualization of Culture for Psychology." *Cultural Psychological Bulletin* 24: 2–10.

Poortinga, Y.H. 1997. "Towards Convergence?" Pp. 347–87 in *Handbook of Cross-Cultural Psychology*, Vol. 1, *Theory and Method*, edited by J. Berry, Y.H. Poortinga, and J. Pandey. Boston: Allyn and Bacon.

Reischauer, E.O. 1988. *The Japanese Today.* Cambridge, MA: Harvard University Press.

Rosenfeld, R. and S.F. Messner. 1991. "The Social Sources of Homicide in Different Types of Societies." *Sociological Forum* 6: 51–70.

Said, E. 1978. *Orientalism.* New York: Pantheon.

Skogan, W.G. 1993. "Reactions to Crime in Cross-National Perspectives." Pp. 257–70 in *Understanding Crime. Experiences of Crime and Crime Control*, edited by A. Alvazzi del Frate, U. Zvekic, and J.J.M. van Dijk, UNICRI Publ. No. 49. Rome: United Nations Interregional Crime and Justice Research.

Shelley, L. 1990. "The Internationalization of Crime: The Changing Relationship between Crime and Development." Pp. 110–45 in *Essays on Crime and Development*, edited by U. Zvekic, UNICRI Publ. No. 36. Rome: United Nations Interregional Crime and Justice Research.

Sinha, D. 1997. "Indigenizing Psychology." Pp. 129–169 in *Handbook of Cross-Cultural Psychology*, Vol. 1, *Theory and Method*, edited by J. Berry, Y.H. Poortinga, and J. Pandey. Boston: Allyn and Bacon.

Stephens, G. 1993. "The Global Crime Wave and What We Can Do About It." *The Futurist.* (July/August): 22–28.

Stone, I.F. 1987. *The Trial of Socrates.* Boston: Little, Brown.

Tonry, M. and N. Morris (Eds.). 1981. *Crime and Justice: An Annual Review of Research.* Vol. 3. Chicago: Chicago University Press.

Triandis, H.C. 1995. *Individualism and Collectivism.* Boulder, CO: Westview.

Vaughn, M.S. and N. Tomita. 1990. "A Longitudinal Analysis of Japanese Crime from 1926 to 1987. The Pre-War, War and Post-War Eras." *International Journal of Comparative and Applied Criminal Justice* 14: 145–70.

Vaughn, M.S. and F.F.Y. Huang. 1992. "Delinquency in the Land of the Rising Sun: An Analysis of Juvenile Property Crimes in Japan during the Showa Era." *International Journal of Comparative and Applied Criminal Justice* 16: 273–99.

von Kopp, B. 1998. "Schüler, Schule und Gewalt in Japan. Erscheinungsformen und Maßnahmen zur Gegensteuerung." Pp. 115–38 in *Gewalt unter Jugendlichen in Deutschland und Japan,* edited by G. Foljanty-Jost and D. Rössner. Baden-Baden: Nomos.

Wagatsuma, H. and G.A. De Vos. 1984. *Heritage of Endurance.* Berkeley: University of California Press.

Westermann, T.D. and J.W. Burfeind. 1991. *Crime and Justice in Two Societies: Japan and the United States.* Pacific Grove, CA: Brooks and Cole.

Yang, M.M. 1994. *Gifts, Favors and Banquets: The Art of Social Relationships in China.* Ithaca, NY: Cornell University Press.

Zedner, L. 1997. "German Criminal Justice Culture." In *Changing Legal Cultures,* ed. J. Feest and E. Blankenburg. Oñati: International Institute for the Sociology of Law.

CHAPTER STUDY QUESTIONS

- According to Karstedt, cross-cultural criminology has a chance to take a leading role in the analysis of culture in the social sciences. What are the arguments she uses to substantiate this point of view? Do you agree with her analysis? Explain.

- Traditionally, criminology has been "simultaneously culture-bound and culture blind." Why is this a problem? How are global criminologists attempting to overcome this problem?

- What are the different strategies that can be used to undertake cross-cultural criminological research? Are these strategies mutually exclusive? Explain.

- What are some of the different ways in which the cross-cultural study of crime can help to overcome the traditional parochialism of criminology?

- How is cross-cultural and global criminology relevant to the development of new strategies of crime prevention and criminal justice procedure? Discuss this question using the example of restorative justice.

RELATED WEB LINKS

What Is Culture?
http://www.wsu.edu/gened/learn-modules/top_culture/
> This site provides a starting point for the study of culture by anthropologists. It includes a range of important definitions and discussions of culture and links to other culture-related websites.

Human Development Report 2004
http://hdr.undp.org/reports/global/2004/?CFID=2456910&CFTOKEN=31217891
> This site provides access to the 2004 independent Human Development Report on "Cultural Liberty in Today's Diverse World" commissioned by the United Nations Development Programme (UNDP). This substantial (nearly 300 page) report contains a wealth of information on current developments and issues surrounding world cultures and cultural liberty, and it makes a case for respecting diversity and building more inclusive societies by adopting policies that explicitly recognize cultural differences.

The Centre for Restorative Justice (Simon Fraser University)
http://www.sfu.ca/crj/
> This site provides access to an extensive on-line library of publications, conference papers, and web links on restorative justice, in addition to providing current information on the activities of the Centre for Restorative Justice at Simon Fraser University, which is dedicated to promoting the principles and practices of restorative justice through education, research, and training.

Comparative Criminal Justice Resources
http://arapaho.nsuok.edu/~dreveskr/ccjr.html-ssi
> This site provides access to an extensive collection of on-line comparative criminal justice resources.

Chapter 2

THE CRIMINOLOGICAL ENTERPRISE IN EUROPE AND THE UNITED STATES: A CONTEXTUAL EXPLORATION

INEKE HAEN MARSHALL

> "Each of us is in some ways like *everybody* else, in some ways like *somebody else*, and in some ways like *nobody* else. What is true of individuals is also true of countries and nations." (Bell 1991)

INTRODUCTION

"A rose is a rose by any other name ... " so reads one of Shakespeare's most famous lines. A rose has a delicious fragrance, prickly thorns and velvety leaves regardless of whether you hold it in Amsterdam, Rome, Shanghai or New York. The same is not true of the thing called—by lack of a better name—the "criminological enterprise"[1] as it exists in the different regions of the world. There are as many criminologies as there are nations in the world. National social factors permeate the practice of science deeply. The sociology and philosophy of science and the history of ideas are replete with examples which demonstrate the social and contingent nature of knowledge (Smith 1975; Glick 1987; Goetzman 1992; Goonatilake 1998). Science and technology practices vary, "depending upon such factors as the country's history, funding sources, research and developmental allocations, and coordinatory mechanism ... " (Goonatilake 1998: 17). Criminology is no exception to this observation. There are many criminologies, but among the most significant are those in Europe and the US.

The purpose of this chapter is to (1) highlight how the criminological enterprise in North America (in particular the US)[2] differs from Europe; (2) to interpret some of these differences in the light of unique American socio-cultural national characteristics; and (3) to speculate about the degree to which these national differences will colour the criminological enterprise of the future.

Why Europe versus the United States?

Does it make sense to attempt sweeping comparisons between one particularly large nation-state (the US) and an aggregate of individual nation-states (Europe)? Comparing Europe *versus* the US is in many ways like comparing apples and oranges, yet we do it all the time. Such comparison builds on a long and well-established tradition, emphasising American "exceptionalism" (the phrase is De Tocqueville's). Almost since its very foundation, it has been believed that America is unique, and that it in crucial ways is different and distinct from other Western countries (Lipset 1991: 1). The US was created differently, and thus has to be understood differently—essentially on its own terms and within its own context, or so the belief goes (Shafter 1991). The assumption is that there are peculiarly American approaches to major social sectors—to government, to the economy, to culture, to religion, to education, and to public policy and to their interaction in the larger society around them (Shafter 1991: viii). A large literature on the subject dating back to the eighteenth century tries to specify the special character of the US in political and social terms (Lipset 1991: 4). Thousands upon thousands of books and articles have been written by foreign (mostly European) observers emphasising the differences in behaviours and institutions between Europe and the US. The American uniqueness is typically contrasted with "Europe" conceived as a cultural entity, where the whole (that is, Europe) is more than the sum-total of the individual nation-states. For many purposes, it is obviously appropriate to treat European culture as a distinct entity.

However, in many instances it would be misleading to overlook the fact that Europe (unlike the US) is made up of a number of separate individual nations, each with a distinct history, socio-political culture, and language. These deep-seated national differences within Europe remain of crucial importance, rendering sweeping Europe *versus* US comparisons problematic. This point is best illustrated by the case of the United Kingdom, a nation which explicitly and self-consciously distinguishes itself from continental Europe in many of its writings and other contexts. For a variety of purposes, the UK is lumped together with other English-speaking countries (including the US) as representing Anglo-Saxon culture. The heterogeneity of (continental) Europe is further emphasised by the prevalent use of several well-established regional country clusters within Europe (Scandinavia or the Nordic countries, Southern Europe, former socialist countries, and so on). Even within these more homogeneous clusters, individual countries vary significantly in many ways (for example, Sweden and Norway, or Switzerland and Germany). Of course, the US is not a culturally homogeneous entity either. Individual American states also differ significantly from each other in many ways. Alabama is quite different from North Dakota, New York or California. At the same time, the US does have a shared language, history, and overarching federal political and legal system, the level of internal cultural and socio-political heterogeneity is in no way comparable to that of Europe. Van Swaaningen gets at the heart of the issue by stating: "[...] the similarities between Western European nations are perhaps only evident in terms of their contrast with America" (1997a: x). He continues that "[...] nowhere in the First World does such a diversity occur in such a small geographical area. A multiplicity of nations with differing political systems, legal cultures and social structures exist next to each other" (1997a: x–xi).

European criminology versus American criminology?

If you were to ask an American criminologist to define the essence of the "American" criminological enterprise, s/he may be hard-pressed for an answer. Many will never have thought about it. This may reflect the ethnocentric orientation typical for those who are not brought into daily contact with other cultures. With notable exceptions, American criminologists tend to interact primarily within their own English-speaking world, where there is no need to be explicit about the essence of the "American" criminological enterprise. Not surprisingly, for most American scholars, criminology is *American* criminology. That is what they do, that is what they know. It is reflected in the courses they teach, the publications they read, and the congresses they attend. On the other hand, to speak in terms of "European criminology" is much more precarious. "European criminology" is distinct from criminology in Europe. Although there is no question that criminology as a discipline emerged in Europe (Beirne 1993; Rock 1994), in the past "European criminology" was primarily another way of identifying one or more of the more prominent national developments in Europe (the Italian positivists, or the French environmentalists). This is also the most common approach taken by American textbooks and histories of criminology.

Criminology in Europe has never been entirely constrained by national boundaries, or practised within a country entirely by its own nationals (Shapland 1991: 15). Historically, there have always been some forms of interaction between European criminologists (e.g., the debate between the French-Italian schools a century ago); there never was complete isolation. However, the 1975 publication of *Deviance and Control in Europe* (Bianchi et al.), an edited set of papers from the formative conference of the European Group for the Study of Deviance and Social Control, is an important milestone in the history of the development of a distinct European criminology. There is now in Europe clearly a conscious effort towards the integration of and collaboration with the different national criminological enterprises. This is a natural by-product of the internationalisation of society, possibly also reflecting the belief that this is needed to provide a counterweight to the apparent dominance of American criminology. The vision of a distinctly "European" criminology is apparent in the recent publication, *The New European Criminology: Crime and Social Order in Europe* (Ruggiero et al. 1998); the introduction to the papers is titled "Toward a European Criminological Community." A similar belief in a "European" criminology is expressed by Van Swaaningen (1997: x): "Paradoxically, the importance of *a European criminology* is not in the unity but in the diversity of social, political and cultural situations that occur [emphasis added]." "European criminology" obviously means more than simply the collaborative efforts (on drugs, restorative justice, youth gangs) between researchers and scholars from Europe. In this essay, I will not try to get at the essence of "European criminology." I will simply compare and contrast American criminology with criminology in Europe (as it exists in individual countries).

DIFFERENCES BETWEEN THE USA AND EUROPE WITH REGARD TO THE "CRIMINOLOGICAL ENTERPRISE"

What are the main differences between American criminology and criminology in Europe? As I just mentioned, for purposes of comparison I approach European criminology simply as the sum total of the efforts by those involved in the study of law, social order and crime in Europe. Such broad comparison is not without pitfalls. There exists a wide diversity in the criminological enterprises within Europe; the fact that, in some countries, the American influence is quite pronounced (such as the Netherlands, the UK) further muddles the US/Europe comparison.

History

The history of criminological thought in Europe far predates the US. The systematic and scientific search for the causes of crime and criminality began in Europe in the 1800s, and by the end of the 1800s, the European tradition in criminology was firmly established (Willis et al. 1999: 227; but see Rock (1994) for interpretations that go back much earlier in history). Moreover, and importantly, whereas the US only has one history[3] of the development of criminology, Europe knows multiple histories of the study of crime, law and social order. Each nation has its own history, very much shaped by its unique cultural, social and political conditions (compare Italy and the Netherlands, or the UK and Germany).

Scale

Stated very simply: "Size does matter!" The popular expression that everything is larger in the US has a kernel of truth. The American criminological enterprise is the largest in the world. Measured by the number of people who focus on the study of crime, law and social control, the number of university courses, the number of scholarly and professional publications and books, the number of research projects and the amount of funding, there is no question that the US takes the cake. It is difficult to overestimate the importance of scale and numbers. Since the 1950s an incredible amount of empirical research (observational and quantitative) has been done by American scholars, focusing on problems of crime and criminal justice. Large numbers of data have been collected systematically, often from several similar organisations in different American states (such as police departments). The product of the sum total of these efforts is a huge number of studies (admittedly of varying quality), more so than in any European country where considerably fewer scholars are involved in the study of crime and justice. The recently published overview of the state of criminal justice research published by the (American) National Institute of Justice and the American Society of Criminology (*Criminal Justice* 2000) represents the "cream of the crop" of research and theory in the (English speaking) field. The amount of reviewed research in these four volumes is enormous, most of which has been done by American researchers.

Degree of institutionalisation

European countries differ widely in the degree in which the study of criminology has been institutionalised (Van Swaaningen 2001). Many European countries do have scholars who are involved in the broadly defined criminological enterprise (education, research), but without the American level of crystallisation as a clearly defined and well-institutionalised field of study. A short note on the history of the development of *criminal justice* as an academic discipline in the US is in order to provide a context for this observation (see Bernard and Engel 2001; Haen Marshall 2001). The high level of institutionalisation is the fruit of decades of focused investment by the American national government in higher education and research in the areas of crime and crime control.

Crime and crime control have been a high political priority on the American agenda since the late 1960s, with considerable resources allocated to this issue. The focus of this national investment has been on *criminal justice* education and research. Although there are, of course, other fields which focus on related questions, criminal justice has a key position in the American knowledge infrastructure with regard to crime and crime control. Criminal justice is—in the USA—not the same as criminology; it is broader and explicitly interdisciplinary. The distinction between criminology and criminal justice is not that one is abstract and the other applied, but rather in the scope of its study.[4] The study and higher education with respect to law, crime and crime control in the US is—after several decades of focused development—now deeply and soundly entrenched in universities and research institutes, with large numbers of students, professors and researchers. *Criminal justice* is seen as a respectable and recognised profession, with thousands of Bachelors' degrees, and hundreds of advanced graduate degrees offered by American universities. There exists a clearly defined criminal justice professoriate, with large and active professional organisations, hundreds of peer-reviewed publications, several national and regional annual congresses. Although scholars in European countries focus on many comparable issues related to crime, police, courts, and prisons, there is not—within one single country—a comparable level of crystallisation as a well-defined independent academic field of study.

Accessibility

Often it seems that American criminologists believe that the really significant (recent) works on crime are produced primarily in the US. There may be one simple explanation for that: language! "The spread of English has a great deal to do with this perception of American superiority," so states Pells in his book, *Not Like Us* (1997). Pells writes in more general terms about the mutual intellectual influences of Europe and America. He argues that, for a long time, American academics seemed barely aware of what the Europeans, apart from the British, had written. American scholars, along with their counterparts in Britain, could expect their publications to be read by academics throughout the world, since many scholars are able to read the English language.

However, criminologists in France, Italy, Germany and the Netherlands can expect their books and articles to be read only by scholars in their own country (or a handful of foreign scholars who happened to master multiple languages). Since many foreign language publications are not accessible to Americans, it also means that the flow of information has been heavily biased: Europeans may know what is going on on the other side of the Atlantic, but Americans remain largely ignorant of the activities in the different European criminological enterprises. I am undoubtedly not the first to speculate about the important role of the UK as an intermediary between the US and continental Europe in this regard. The increasing use of English as a world language is likely to increase the accessibility of the body of criminological knowledge to more scholars.

Diversity in theory and method

The history of criminology in Europe may be traced back to a diversity of fields (biology, psychology, history, law, social statistics, and sociology). In the US the theoretical development of criminology drew its inspiration mainly from sociology (Willis et al. 1999: 227). The historical diversity continues to resonate in contemporary times. Although there is no European country in which only one model of criminology exists, there are cultural traditions of criminology "which render its practice and theoretical enquiry different in different countries" (Shapland 1991: 14). Analyses of the nature of the criminological enterprise in particular European countries confirm the diversity of approaches within Europe (see Garland 1994 for the UK, Robert 1991 for France, Van Swaaningen 1997b for the UK, the Netherlands and Belgium). More comprehensive overviews illustrating the heterogeneity in the criminological enterprise in Europe have been provided by Robert and Van Outrive (1993) and Van Swaaningen (1997a). A recent publication by *le Groupe Européen de Recherche sur les Normativités* (GERN) represents one of the most current efforts to provide an overview of the criminological enterprise in a number of European countries (Van Outrive and Robert 1999).

In the United States, there are a relatively large number of individuals and organisations which focus on the study of crime and justice, but they operate within the boundaries of a relatively narrow range of theoretical perspectives and methods. Allowing for a certain amount of bias, the American critical criminologist Currie seems to get at the essence of the American criminological enterprise:

> there is a large, rather technocratic, "middle" contingent, the "mainstream," which often produces quite useful work, but is only rarely engaged in the public arena and shies away from sticking its neck out; there is the small but extremely effective right wing that has an extraordinary amount of presence and influence, less within the profession than in the media and among politicians [...]; and there is a self-defined "radical" contingent, complete with its own separate organizations and subsections of organizations [...] (Currie 1999: 17–18)

Bernard and Engel (2001: 14) state that large-scale quantitative studies have become "the bread and butter" of criminal justice research (in the US). The point is not that there is no diversity within American criminology, but rather, that there is, proportionally, dominance of the sociological approach (with some role for biological and psychological factors), with a methodological emphasis on sophisticated quantitative analysis of large data sets.

Critical and self-reflexive stance

This point—although already referred to in Currie's characterisation of the American criminological enterprise—deserves to be singled out. European countries differ significantly in the extent to which their study of law, crime and social control is characterised by a critical, self-reflexive stance (for example, compare France and the UK with the Netherlands, see Van Swaaningen 1997a). A comparative perspective (which is more likely to be taken by European scholars because of the context in which they operate) tends to be more conducive to the development of a critical, macro-level view on law and social control. This is one possible explanation. Another explanation may be found in the presumed American disdain for the importance of abstract speculation (discussed in the next section). It goes beyond the boundaries of this essay to delve any deeper into this very complicated matter. The reality is that—although American scholars do play a role in the critical, self-reflexive branch of the criminological enterprise—proportionally, it represents a relatively unimportant and marginalised approach in the USA.

Focal research questions

A recent overview of the criminological enterprise in nine Western European countries (Van Outrive and Robert 1999) suggests that a large number of the research topics (victims, public and private police, judicial decision-making, juvenile delinquency, organised crime) are similar to those studied in the US (often using similar methods). There is no doubt that many questions related to crime and law transcend national boundaries. Yet, the particular intensity and focus is shaped by the unique national context. For Europe, this has been documented, among others, by Van Swaaningen (1997a), and the authors contributing to the GERN publication (Van Outrive and Robert 1999). The following section provides a brief interpretative analysis of how the American intellectual context has shaped both the method and the focus of the criminological enterprise in the USA.

The American way of "doing science"

I have already alluded to the notion of American exceptionalism. Literally thousands of scholarly and literary works have attempted to get at the essence of the American identity. Shafter's analysis presented in the book *Is America Different?* (1991) may serve as a fairly typical illustration of what the "American model" entails. In his view, the American model is characterized by four central themes: populism, individualism, democratisation, and market-making (233). *Populism* is the doctrine that all members of society should be conceived of as social equals. *Individualism* is the doctrine that the single and independent members of society have a right to construct their personal lives according to their own preferences. *Democratisation* is the notion that major social institutions should be run so as to be directly responsive to the wishes of the public. Finally, *market-making* is the notion that organized alternatives—in products and services, but also in occupations, entertainments, and even lifestyles—ought to appear or disappear as there is (or is not) sufficient demand to sustain them (Shafter 1991: 234–235). These themes, closely interwoven with a host of other historical, intellectual, political and social influences, have provided the context for the "American model" of science (including the study of law, crime and social control).[5]

A well-accepted view among sociologists of knowledge and historians of science is that America from its very beginnings has been "permeated by the culture of science" (Goetzman 1992: 414). One important point of disagreement centres around the question as to whether this "culture of science" makes a distinction between theory and practical technology (Goetzman 1992: 414). *Pragmatism* is one of the key themes of American scientific culture. Scholars have attempted to associate pragmatism with a package of characteristic American traits (Moyer 1992: 206).[6] Pragmatism is important because it reflects "Americans' preconceptions about and aspirations for a modern, scientific culture" (Moyer 1992: 207). It has often been interpreted to mean the (vulgarised) image of "the practical-minded 'Yankee-tinkerer'" (Goetzman 1992: 414). "Pragmatic" and "pragmatism" are often used to refer to "a 'see-if-it-works' suspicion of dogma, of doctrine, and of the rigid adherence to abstract principles and theories [...]", so concludes the American philosopher Hollinger (1985: 24).

Foreign observers (but Americans also) have typified the historical American attitude toward science and scientific research with the so-called "indifference theme" (Glick 1987: 6). Thus, while there was a great deal of activity devoted to inventions and the creation of practical implements, Americans were indifferent to basic science and basic research (Glick 1987: 5), or so it was argued. A later reinterpretation is that—rather than doing pure or fundamental research as a search for knowledge for its own sake—Americans tended to do pure research for economic profit, practical application, and technological progress. A main element of pragmatism is its fixation on "the process of inquiry itself rather than the actual acquisition of knowledge" (Moyer 1992: 207). The "scientific habit of mind" was supposed to rescue civilisation from detrimental trends (Moyer 1992: 207). The pragmatic principle tends to accentuate the scientific method of inquiry. Thus, the American pragmatists (Peirce, James, and Dewey) all proclaimed in one form or another "the scientific method itself, unfettered by traditional absolutes, as the ideal guide to a public philosophy for the nation" (Goetzman 1992: 414). This has lead to the characterisation of a "scientistic" America.

The mainstay of American scientific thought is very much coloured by pragmatism. The Frenchman Crozier cites the frequently heard statement that "nothing is more practical than a good theory" as a typical American way of justifying theoretical work (which is only important in as much as it has practical consequences). Crozier writes that, in his view, for Americans, theories also have to be simple: "[...] say what you have to say, but say it quickly. Any true theory can hold up on the strength of a phrase and three equations, even in the social sciences. The rest is just wordy preface, useless formality, digression, and decadent European flourish [...]" (1984: 23). In the view of many interpreters, Americans often have been hostile to theory, be it in literature, philosophy or science. A case in point is the recently published account of the philosophical and literary "theory wars" (between the French and the Americans) (Mathy 2000). In order to interpret the cross-Atlantic tensions, Mathy makes reference to Hofstadter's (1970) often-cited "anti-intellectualism" in the United States, and its implied resistance to theory in particular in American culture.[7]

In *Essays on American Intellectual History*, Smith (1975) defines the three focal beliefs through which the American philosophical spirit over the last 100 years can be articulated. His summary provides an excellent backdrop for a comparative understanding of the American approach to the study of law, crime and social control. Firstly, the belief that thinking is primarily an activity in response to a concrete situation and that this activity is aimed at solving problems. Secondly, the belief that ideas and theories must have a "cutting edge" or must make a difference in the conduct of people who hold them and in the situation in which they live. This feature has long been regarded as the essence of the American character (Smith 1975: 476). According to Smith, two basic ideas are involved: one is that thinking should be focused not on the general, universal and "timeless" problems, but rather on difficulties arising here and now; the second is that the power of ideas to shape the course of events depends directly on the extent to which they are acted upon and used to guide the conduct of men (476). Americans believe that their total intellectual energy should be focused on "here and now" issues and that there is no time for dealing with problems of a generalized nature which have no clear focal point in time (Smith 1975: 476).[8] Closely connected with this focus on specific problems is the belief that intellectual activity is justified to the extent to which its results are translated into action. Ideas that make a difference are those upon which people act. The practical orientation so often associated with American life and thought is most evident at this point according to Smith:

> an idea is a "mere" idea unless we can see how a situation is changed through the medium of that idea. If, after having the idea, everything remains the same as it was before, then the idea makes no difference—it is without a cutting edge. (Smith 1975: 476)

Thirdly, the American belief that the earth can be civilised and obstacles to progress overcome by the application of knowledge.

In sum, American intellectual thought embodies the primary importance of the scientific method, a practical problem focus (rather than on abstract issues), and a need for ideas (theories) with practical implications. The particular American way of "doing science" finds its reflection in the American criminological enterprise. Besides the scientific culture of a country, there are many other political and socio-cultural factors which shape the way law, crime and social control are studied. Of central importance are those aspects of society which have a direct (substantive) impact on the criminological enterprise: namely, the administration of justice (including the legal tradition on which these practices are based) and the nature of the crime problem.

The American way of "doing justice"

Legal factors—both principles and practices—are of critical importance in shaping the nature of the criminological enterprise. Since the mainstay of American intellectual thought is a pragmatist problem- and-action orientation, it is to be expected that perceived problems related to law and justice have guided American criminology and criminal justice studies.

Many scholarly works have analysed the differences between the American common law system, which differs from most of Europe with the continental (or inquisitorial) system (Reichel 1996, Terrill 1999). That is not the only—or even the main—difference, however; after all, the British (among others) obviously also have a common law tradition, that is where the Americans got it from. It seems that the role of law in American society differs significantly from the European (including the British) situation. The characteristics of the adversarial system of common law are pushed to the extreme in the United States. "The part played by law and by the courts of justice is probably more important in the American society than in any others [...]. No foreign observer could help being struck by the place of law and the judiciary in the United States" (Tunc 1968: 198). The Frenchman Crozier confirms this observation: "No Frenchman or any other European can ever really feel at home with the extraordinary juridical ideology with which the whole of American society is imbued, and which can be summed up in two words—due process" (Crozier 1984: 98).[9] The juridical principle: absolute respect for the rules of procedure is a basic principle governing American life; due process is not just an ideological substrate of American life; it expresses itself in a number of concrete practices and procedures (Crozier 1984: 103). The American emphasis on due process results in greater litigiousness, as well as more formal and extensive efforts to enforce the law. The US is the most litigious society known to the world, it has more lawyers per capita than any other developed country, including all the predominantly English-speaking common law ones (Lipset 1991: 33).

The American "due process model" has been contrasted with the "crime control model" more common in Europe, which focuses on the maintenance of law and order and is less protective of the rights of the accused and of individuals generally (Lipset 1991: 33). Contrasting the American (common law) due process model with the European (inquisitorial or continental law) crime control model is one way of looking at the implications of different legal traditions cross-nationally. Ironically, however, *within* the US the friction between the ideal of due process and the reality of crime control has turned out to be the major impetus for the development of criminal justice research and theory in the USA.

In a recent article, "Conceptualizing Criminal Justice Theory," the American criminologists Bernard and Engel (2001) provide a most interesting interpretative analysis of the historical development of the academic field of criminal justice in the US. One important point is that the scholarly focus on the functioning of the criminal law in the US was initiated in the 1950s by a practical concern of "reform commissions" who were concerned with bringing the "law in practice" into greater conformity with "the law on the books." The realisation that there was a gap between the ideal and the real in criminal justice runs like a connecting thread through much of the criminal justice research in the US. The single event most responsible for the development of criminal justice as an academic field was the realisation, based on several observational studies in the 1960s, that pervasive discretion—although often conflicting with the requirements of due process expressed in the "law on the books"—was an inevitable reality in the daily "law in practice." The field began to acknowledge that a certain amount of legitimate exercise of discretion was not necessarily incompatible with the notion of due process. Gradually, criminal justice research shifted from qualitative (observational) to quantitative and systematic large-scale studies, examining contextual influences on individual decision-making and focusing entirely on describing and explaining what criminal justice agents were actually doing (Bernard and Engel 2001: 13). The research implicitly compares the practice of criminal justice against a normative ideal (equality, due process). These studies focused strongly on the effects of race, gender, class and demeanour—that is, non-legal, and therefore unacceptable factors conflicting with the due process model—on decisions in the criminal justice process. Because of the unique role that "race" and "ethnicity" play in the US, a very large number of empirical studies focusing on the role of race in criminal justice administration (such as police shootings, arrest practices, convictions and sentencing, and so on) now exist. The most recent focus is on racial profiling, race-bias in the use of force by the police, and the link between the war on drugs and race. Perhaps the best illustration of the exceptionalism of the United States, reflecting its strong belief in the importance of due process, combined with a "scienticist" confidence that careful empirical inquiry can provide answers to the most hairy issues, is the extensive body of sophisticated quantitative empirical research focusing on the possibility of (racial) discrimination in the application of capital punishment.

Another characteristic of the American system of justice is its relative harshness and punitiveness, and its reliance on the criminal law (incarceration) as a means to maintain social control. Because of the enormous growth of the police, prosecution, and correctional system over the last several decades, the logistic management problems of the increasingly sluggish apparatus have become an urgent problem (Simon and Feeley: 166; Haen Marshall 1999: 34). Concern about growing prison populations and market-thinking focus on effectiveness and efficiency have inspired many studies on the incapacitating effects of incarceration, as well as the deterrent effect of punishment. Crime control and safety is now "big business" in the US; the market-based approach is reflected in the application of business management principles in the streamlining of criminal justice processing, as well as institutionalised scientific evaluation of processes and results. This type of research provides the "bread and butter" of an ever-growing number of private and public research and training institutes in the USA.

Bernard and Engel (2001: 25) conclude their interpretative analysis of the historical development of the academic discipline of criminal justice in the US with the observation that

> [C]riminal justice [as an academic field] [...] originated as descriptive research, in which theory, insofar as it existed at all, was highly specific and focused on the particular topic at hand. Over the last 50 years, criminal justice [as an academic discipline] has been working its way, with difficulty, towards theory.

They contrast this with the development of criminological theory (in the US): "criminology originated as sweepingly discursive general theories [...] and has worked its way, with difficulty, towards phrasing these theories in such a way that research could test them adequately" (25). The pragmatic resistance toward abstract theorizing notwithstanding, American scholars have indeed developed several discursive (middle range), abstract crime theories.[10] It is very clear, however, that the focus and content of these theories reflect the practical problems which America experiences with crime. This is briefly discussed in the next section.

The American way of "doing crime"

Crime—in particular, serious violent crime—has been defined as one of the major social problems in the US since the 1960s. Countless observers have noted that the US—compared to Europe—suffers much higher crime rates. This difference has begun to level off during the last few years (Blumstein and Wallman 2000). This recent decline, in conjunction with the high levels of violence in Eastern Europe over the last several years, challenges the popular view of the USA as the most violent nation in the industrialised world. Still, serious (gun-related) violence continues to be a problem in the US. On the positive side, crime and crime control have been a major concern for academics in the US for several decades, considerable funding for crime-related research has been available, and a lot of knowledge has been developed. Some of this knowledge may be transferable to Europe, whereas some of which may be tied to uniquely American conditions.

The focus of criminological theorizing and research reflects—to a large degree—the realities of the American crime problem. Allowing for a certain degree of media-hype and social construction of criminality, it cannot be denied that there have been *real* problems with street crime, the central theme of American criminological theory. The most influential early sociological American theories of crime (the social ecology theory developed by Shaw and McKay in 1942; the anomie theory developed by Merton in 1938) focus on street crime, in particular by urban lower-class young males.[11] Sutherland's (1924) differential association and differential social organisation theory was intended to apply to all delinquency, but is best known for its application to young male delinquents.

Violence, in particular gun-related violence, has also ranked high on the agenda of American criminologists (e.g., Wolfgang and Ferracutti's subculture of violence, 1967). With the rise of the serious inner-city violence in the mid-1980s, the link between drugs, guns, and violence became a central concern (e.g., Blumstein and Wallman 2000). The focus on street crime, drugs and violence has placed the role of race and ethnicity in the American crime picture centre stage (Sampson and Wilson 1995; Short 1997). White collar crime has also been a focus of American scholarly inquiry, albeit in much lesser degree (e.g., Sutherland 1940; Coleman 1989; Shover and Bryant 1993). This is not surprising in view of the fact that the US is a capitalist society *par excellence*, with a well-documented problem with corporate and occupational crime. The problems with organised crime in the US have also, quite understandably, been the subject of scholarly exploration (Albini 1971; Ianni 1973; Abadinsky 1981; Block and Chambliss 1981; Ianni and Reuss-Reuter et al. 1983; Jacobs and Gouldin 1999). This is but a handful of the more obvious examples of the problem-based focus of the American criminological enterprise. A note of caution: The link between practical crime problems and scientific development is not straightforward and self-evident; it is easy to oversimplify. A case in point is the absence of an apparent direct link to America's crime problems and the important theoretical contributions by Becker (1963), Lemert (1951) and other American symbolic interactionists (see Rock and Downes 1998).

Theoretical explanations of crime in the US typically have been tied to American exceptionalism, both by American and non-American scholars. Large-scale crime is seen as a natural by-product of American culture (Bell 1953; Lipset 1991). A few examples will suffice. To use the best-known American theory, Merton explicitly stated that his theory was meant to explain crime in the US. He viewed the USA as an anomic society because of the disjunction between cultural goals of material success and structural impediments to these goals. A recent example of this line of reasoning is Messner and Rosenfeld's *Crime and the American Dream* (1997). Explanations of white collar crime have made reference to the extreme and unbridled American competitive culture (Coleman 1989). The high level of violence in the US is typically explained by reference to the American "culture of violence." The American "culture of violence" is viewed as a natural product of America's unique violent history: the frontier tradition, the influence of slavery, lynchings, the Indian Wars (see Butterfield 1995; Brown 1991). It is assumed that America's violent history has formed the essence of the modern American identity, a violent identity. Criminal violence is viewed as a spillover of socially accepted violence. The accessibility of firearms is an essential component of this violent culture. Virtually any (English-language) comparative discussion of criminological theory asserts that most criminological theories are American theories, reflecting American culture and structure (Willis et al. 1999).

Inspired by practical issues or not, there is no question that American scholars have contributed important theoretical insights to the field of criminology. However, it seems that the heydays of creative criminological (sociological) theory development in the US are long gone. A large number of very competent American researchers are now attempting to test and further refine the traditional criminological theories (e.g., Agnew 1992; Bursik and Grasmick 1995), often with a heavy emphasis on advanced methodological techniques. The current focus on crime prevention and risk management together with deep dissatisfaction about the practical utility of (sociological) crime theories has resulted in a gradual turning away from trying to develop etiological theories of crime. Efforts to develop so-called integrated theories are an important exception to this trend (e.g., Sampson and Laub 1993; Vila 1994; Tittle 1995; Bernard and Snipes 1996). The relatively new kid on the block, life course and developmental crime theory, with its focus on identification of risk factors and implications for crime prevention, is the product of collaborative efforts between American researchers and researchers from other countries (see Farrington 1994). Last, and least (from the perspective of contribution to criminological theory), is the popular perspective based on routine activity theory, often called situational crime prevention. Although the theoretical promise of the routine activity has been substantial (Cohen and Felson 1979), in its current form expressed in terms of situational crime prevention (see e.g., Felson 1998, 2000) it lacks theoretical lustre.[12]

CONCLUSION

Although there is a growing criminology in Latin America, South Africa, India, and other parts of the world (see Willis et al. 1999; Del Olmo 1999; Shank 1999), the criminological enterprise remains—for the time being at least—eurocentric.[13] Criminologists in Europe, the United States, Canada, Australia, and New Zealand all use what the philosopher Richard Rorty has called "the conversation of the West."[4] Focusing on the uniqueness or "exceptionalism" of (the criminological enterprise of) the United States compared to what is going on in Europe has the danger of overlooking the fact that intellectual life in America is a part of a larger civilisation that encompasses the national cultures of European countries as well as that of the United States (Hollinger 1985: 176). "[...] the intellectual history of the United States is in many crucial respects a province of the intellectual history of Europe [...]" (Hollinger 1985: 182). The picture gets even more muddled because of the important influence of European intellectuals on American thought and science, before and during the Second World War (Pells 1997). Influences continue to go both ways across the Atlantic, presumably ever faster and faster.

American criminology is a powerful influence in Europe, although "the particular variety dominant at any time has never managed to stifle the heterogeneity in Europe" (Shapland 1991: 16). There may be a tendency to overestimate the importance of American criminology, because of the dominance of English-language publications. The dominance may be particularly overstated by American criminologists. Since it is more likely that English-language publications focus on American criminology (rather than on criminology produced in Europe), it is to be expected that this impression is confirmed. The picture of American dominance is likely to be somewhat different if one uses (implied) assessments by Europeans (in non-English publications). For example, in one of the leading German textbooks, *Kriminologie* (Schneider 1987), a total of 48 names are listed as pioneers in criminology, only 11 of which resided in the US at one point.

American criminology has made many positive contributions to the field of the study of law, crime and social control, and it continues to do so. However, if one defines the essence of American criminology as being policy-oriented, methodologically-driven, and lacking theoretical lustre, diversity, and short of a critical edge, then the fear of "Americanisation" of European criminology is well-placed. "Americanisation" refers to fundamental developments of modernity as cultural homogenisation ("McDonaldisation"), and degeneration. "America so conceived may exist outside of the United States and involve no actual Americans [...]" (Ceasar 1997: 2). It is no longer the criminological enterprise of the US per se, but rather an idea or symbol, called "Americanisation" which is really at issue here. If increasing cultural (including legal) convergence and homogenisation across the countries of the world means growing American dominance (and it should be noted that there are conflicting views on this issue, see Held et al. 1999), then it is reasonable to speculate that American criminology will gain more applicability in "Americanised" Europe. However, regional criminologies will always retain their significance (Haen Marshall 1998). Furthermore, the growing realisation that many different and valuable ways of thinking about crime, law and social control exist outside North America and Western Europe is bound to enrich the conceptual and methodological toolbox of the criminological enterprise (Willis et al. 1999).

A final thought: Internationalisation of crime and crime control makes it inevitable that the future of the criminological enterprise will centre more and more around questions that transcend national boundaries. The need for a transnational or global criminology is no longer to be denied (Findlay 1999). Such worldwide criminology can only prosper through the joint efforts of criminologists from all the continents and regions of the world.

NOTES

[1] The term "criminological enterprise" was—to my knowledge—coined by the American criminologist Don Gibbons (1979). It is a very "American" term by its explicit reference to the market-principle involved. Since the study of crime, law and social control is done by people from many different backgrounds and disciplines in different parts of the world (only a small fraction refer to themselves as "criminologists"), I will use "criminological enterprise" and "criminology" as umbrella terms for all individuals and institutions in some way engaged in the study of law, crime, and social control.

[2] There is a clear problem in using "America" to refer exclusively to the United States. The word designates "the entire landmass of the New World, which comprises North, Central and South America as well as the Caribbean islands" (Ceasar 1997: 15). "North America" includes both the United States and Canada. The Canadian criminological enterprise is distinct and different from that of the United States; it may be characterised as less narrow and more open to foreign influences than the United States.

[3] It is debatable whether it is possible to have an objective history of criminology (cf. Garland 1994).

[4] *Criminal justice* is meant to provide a bridge between criminology and practice. Although it focuses on the practical functioning of criminal justice organisations, it does attempt to be theoretical. After all, there are important theoretical issues related to the functioning of criminal justice organisations. *Criminology* focuses on the nature of crime (individual criminal behaviour, the rates and distributions of criminal behaviour in social units, and the behaviour of criminal law) (Bernard and Snipes quoted in Bernard and Engel 2001: 25). *Criminal justice*, on the other hand, focuses on the individual behaviour of criminal justice agents, the behaviour of criminal justice organisations, and the characteristics of the overall criminal justice system and its components (Bernard and Engel 2001: 5). Sometimes these two terms are used interchangeably; sometimes *criminal justice* is defined as including criminology. For example, Michigan State University, School of Criminal Justice defines *criminal justice* as "the study of the etiology of crime and its control, the decision network devoted to crime control, and the administration of the many public and private agencies involved in the processing of criminal offenders...."

[5] Science as a culture has its own institutions, languages, ideas, values, methods, symbols and recognisable practitioners (Goetzman 1992: 414).

[6] In its pure form, the pragmatist thesis is that the practical context of thought sets all the conditions for judging the validity of the ideas and theories which result from rational activity (Smith 1975: 475). The main founders are Charles Peirce, William James, and John Dewey.

[7] Richard Hofstadter wrote *Anti-Intellectualism in American Life* (1970) as an historical account of what he referred to as America's "national disrespect for mind."

[8] The pragmatist Dewey expressed this point very well when he said that all our efforts should be aimed at eliminating *the evils* of human life, but that we have no time to speculate about *the problem of evil* (Smith 1975: 476).

[9] Crozier titles one of his chapters "The Delirium of Due Process."

[10] American criminological theory is characterized by a low level of formalisation, and problematic empirical testability. For a more extensive discussion, see Meier (1985); Bernard (1990); Bernard and Ritti (1990); and Gibbons (1994).

[11] For an excellent interpretative analysis of the historical development of sociological criminology, see Downes and Rock (1998).

[12] It should be noted that situational crime prevention (together with social control theory) are most influential in shaping crime policy in the Netherlands and the UK.

[13] Conform Goonatilake (1998) describes the general scientific enterprise as eurocentric.

[14] Richard Rorty, *Philosophy and the Mirror of Nature* (Princeton, New Jersey, 1980), cited in Hollinger 1985: 182.

REFERENCES

Albini, J.L. 1971. *The American Mafia: Genesis of a Legend*. New York: Irvington.

Agnew, R. 1992. "Foundation for a General Strain Theory of Crime and Delinquency." *Criminology* 30: 47–87.

Beirne, P. 1993. *Inventing Criminology*. New York: State University of New York.

Bell, D. 1953. "Crime as an American Way of Life." *The Antioch Review* 13: 131–54.

Bell, D. 1991. "The 'Hegelian Secret': Civil Society and American Exceptionalism." Pp. 46–70 in *Is America Different? A New Look at American Exceptionalism*, edited by B.E. Shafter. Oxford: Clarendon Press.

Bernard, T.J. 1990. "Twenty Years of Testing Theories: What Have We Learned and Why?" *Journal of Research in Crime and Delinquency* 27: 325–47.

Bernard, T.J. and R.S. Engel. 2001. "Conceptualizing Criminal Justice Theory." *Justice Quarterly* 18: 1–30.

Bernard, T.J. and R.R. Ritti. 1990. "The Role of Theory in Scientific Research." Pp. 1–20 in *Measurement Issues in Criminology*, edited by K. Kempf. New York: Springer-Verlag.

Bernard, T.J. and J.B. Snipes. 1996. "Theoretical Integration in Criminology." Pp. 301–48 in *Crime and Justice: A Review of Research*, edited by M. Tonry. Chicago: University of Chicago Press.

Bianchi, H., M. Simondi, and I. Taylor (Eds.). 1975. *Deviance and Control in Europe*. London: John Wiley & Sons.

Blok, A.A. and W.J. Chambliss. 1981. *Organizing Crime*. New York: Elsevier North Holland.

Blumstein, A. and J. Wallman. 2000. *The Crime Drop in America*. Cambridge: Cambridge University Press.

Brown, R.M. 1991. *No Duty to Retreat: Violence and Values in American History and Society*. New York/Oxford: Oxford University Press.

Bursik, R.J. and H.G. Grasmick. 1995. "Neighborhood-Based Networks and the Control of Crime and Delinquency." Pp. 107–30 in *Crime and Public Policy: Putting Theory to Work*, edited by H.D. Barlow. Boulder, CO: Westview.

Butterfield, F. 1995. *All God's Children: The Bosket Family and the American Tradition of Violence.* New York: Alfred A. Knopf.

Ceaser, J.W. 1997. *Reconstructing America: The Symbol of America in Modern Thought.* New Haven/London: Yale University Press.

Cohen, L.E. and M. Felson. 1979. "Social Change and Crime Rate Trends: A Routine Activity Approach." *American Sociological Review* 4: 588–608.

Coleman, J.W. 1989. *The Criminal Elite: The Sociology of White-Collar Crime,* 3rd ed. New York: St. Martin's Press.

Crozier, M. 1984. *The Trouble with America.* Berkeley: University of California Press.

Currie, E. 1999. "Radical Criminology—Or Just Criminology—Then, and Now." *Social Justice* 26(2): 16–18.

Del Olmo, R. 1999. "The Development of Criminology in Latin America." *Social Justice* 26(2): 19–45.

Downes, D. and P. Rock. 1998. *Understanding Deviance: A Guide to the Sociology of Crime and Rule-Breaking.* 3rd ed. Oxford: Oxford University Press.

Felson, M. 1998. *Crime and Everyday Life,* 2nd ed. Thousand Oaks, CA: Pine Forge.

Felson, M. 2000. "The Routine Activity Approach as a General Crime Theory." Pp. 205–15 in *Of Crime and Criminality,* edited by S.S. Simpson. Thousand Oaks, CA: Pine Forge.

Findlay, M. 1999. *The Globalisation of Crime: Understanding Transnational Relationships in Context.* Cambridge: Cambridge University Press.

Garland, D. 1994. "Of Crime and Criminals: The Development of Criminology in Britain." Pp. 17-68 in *The Oxford Handbook of Criminology,* edited by M. Maguire, R. Morgan, and R. Reiner. Oxford: Clarendon Press.

Gibbons, D. 1979. *The Criminological Enterprise.* Englewood-Cliffs, NJ: Prentice Hall.

Gibbons, D.C. 1994. "Causal Explanations and Theories in Criminology." Pp. 69–95 in *Talking about Crime and Criminals. Problems and Issues in Theory Development in Criminology,* edited by D.C. Gibbons. Englewood Cliffs, NJ: Prentice Hall.

Glick, T.F. (Ed.). 1987. *The Comparative Reception of Relativity.* Boston: D. Reidel Publishing.

Goetzmann, W.H. 1992. "Exploration and the Culture of Science: The Long Good-bye of the Twentieth Century." Pp. 413–31 in *Making America: The Society and Culture of the United States,* edited by L.S. Luedtke. Chapel Hill: University of North Carolina Press.

Goonatilake, S. 1998. *Toward a Global Science: Mining Civilizational Knowledge.* Bloomington: Indiana University Press.

Haen Marshall, I. 1998. "Internationalisering van de Criminologie." *Tijdschrift voor criminologie* 40: 176–84.

Haen Marshall, I. 1999. "Steeds meer 'Amerikaanse toestanden' in Nederland? Het zal wel me-evallen!" Pp. 19–42 in *Vooruitzichten in de criminologie,* edited by G.J.N. Bruinsma, H.G. van de Bunt, and G.B. Rovers. Amsterdam: Vrije Universiteit.

Haen Marshall, I. 2001. "Onderwijs en Onderzoek in de Verenigde Staten." Working paper prepared for the Commissie Verkenning Criminaliteit, Adviesraad Wetenschap en Technologie Beleid, The Hague.

Held, D., A. McGrew, D. Goldblatt, and J. Perraton. 1999. *Global Transformations: Politics, Economics and Culture*. Stanford: Stanford University Press.

Hofstadter, R. 1970. *Anti-Intellectualism in American Life*. New York: Alfred A. Knopf.

Hollinger, D.A. 1985. *In the American Province: Studies in the History and Historiography of Ideas*. Bloomington: Indiana University Press.

Ianni, F.A.J. and E. Reuss-Ianni. 1973. *A Family Business: Kinship and Social Control in Organized Crime*. New York: New American Library.

Jacobs, J.B. and L.P. Gouldin. 1999. "Cosa Nostra: The Final Chapter?" Pp. 129–90 in *Crime and Justice: A Review of Research*, vol. 25, edited by M. Tonry. Chicago: University of Chicago Press.

Kirk, R. 1993. *America's British Culture*. New Brunswick: Transaction Publishers.

Lipset, S.M. 1991. "American Exceptionalism Reaffirmed." Pp. 1–45 in *Is America Different? A New Look at American Exceptionalism*, edited by B.E. Shafter. Oxford: Clarendon Press.

Mathy, J. 2000. *French Resistance: The French–American Culture Wars*. Minneapolis/London: University of Minnesota Press.

Meier, R. 1985. *Theoretical Methods in Criminology*. Beverly Hills: Sage.

Messner, S.F. and R. Rosenfeld. 1997. *Crime and the American Dream*. 2nd ed. Wadsworth.

Moyer, A.E. 1992. *A Scientist's Voice in American Culture: Simon Newcomb and the Rhetoric of Scientific Method*. Berkeley: University of California Press.

Pells, R. 1997. *Not Like Us: How Europeans Have Loved, Hated, and Transformed American Culture since World War II*. New York: Basic Books.

Reichel, P.L. 1994. *Comparative Criminal Justice Systems: A Topical Approach*. Englewood Cliffs, NJ: Prentice Hall.

Reuter, P., J. Rubenstein and S. Wynn. 1983. *Racketeering in Legitate Industries: Two Case Studies*. Washington, DC: National Institute of Justice.

Robert, P. 1991. "The Sociology of Crime and Deviance in France." *British Journal of Criminology* 31: 27–38.

Robert, P., L. van Outrive, T. Jefferson and J. Shapland (Eds). 1995. *Research, Crime, and Justice in Europe: An Assessment and Some Recommendations*. Sheffield: Centre for Criminological Research.

Rock, P. (Ed.). 1994. *History of Criminology*. Brookfield, VT: Dartmouth.

Ruggiero, V., N. South and I. Taylor (Eds). 1998. *The New European Criminology: Crime and Social Order in Europe*. London: Routledge.

Sampson, R.J. and J.H. Laub. 1993. *Crime in the Making: Pathways and Turning Points Through Life*. Cambridge, Massachusetts: Harvard University Press.

Sampson, R.J. and W. Wilson 1995. "Toward a Theory of Race, Crime and Urban Inequality." Pp. 37–54 in *Crime and Inequality*, edited by J. Hagan and R. Peterson. Stanford: Stanford University Press.

Schneider, H-J. 1987. *Kriminologie*. Berlin: Walter de Gruyter.

Shafter, B.E. 1991. "What is the American Way? Four Themes in Search of Their Next Incarnation." Pp. 222–61 in *Is America Different? A New Look at American Exceptionalism*, edited by B.E. Shafter. Oxford: Clarendon Press.

Shank, G. 1999. "Looking Back: Radical Criminology and Social Movements." *Social Justice* 26(2): 114–34.

Shapland, J. 1991. "Criminology in Europe." Pp. 14–23 in *Crime in Europe*, edited by F. Heidensohn and M. Farrell. London: Routledge.

Short, J.F., Jr. 1997. *Poverty, Ethnicity and Violent Crime*. Boulder, CO: Westview Press.

Shover, N. and K.M. Bryant. 1993. "Theoretical Explanations of Corporate Crime." Pp. 141–76 in *Understanding Corporate Criminality*, edited by M.B. Blankenship. New York: Garland.

Smith, W. 1975. "The Spirit of American Philosophy." Pp. 473–79 in *Essays in American Intellectual History*, edited by W. Smith. Hinsdale, Illinois: The Dryden Press.

Terrill, R.J. 1999. *World Criminal Justice Systems: A Survey*. Cincinnati, Ohio: Anderson.

Tittle, C. 1995. *Control Balance: Toward a General Theory of Deviance*. Boulder, CO: Westview Press.

Tunc, A. 1968. "Law and Judicial System." Pp. 198–223 in *American Civilisation: An Introduction*, edited by A.N.J. den Hollander and S. Skard. London: Longman.

Van Outrive, L. and P. Robert. 1999. "Un tableau d'ensemble." Pp. 13–24 in *Crime et justice en Europe depuis 1990: Etat des recherches, évaluations et recommandations*, edited by L. Van Outrive and P. Robert. Paris: l'Harmattan.

Van Swaaningen, R. 1995. "Sociale controle met een structureel tekort: Pleidooi voor een sociaal rechtvaardig veiligheidsbeleid." *Justitiële verkenningen* 21: 63–87.

Van Swaaningen, R. 1997a. *Critical Criminology: Visions from Europe*. London: Sage.

Van Swaaningen, R. 1997b. "De positie van de criminologie aan Nederlandse universiteiten in vergelijking met België en Engeland." *Nieuws voor criminologen* 8: 5–23.

Vila, B. 1994. "A General Paradigm for Understanding Criminal Behavior: Extending Evolutionary Ecological Theory." *Criminology* 32: 311–60.

Willis, C., T.D. Evans, and R.L. LaGrange. 1999. "'Down Home' Criminology: The Place of Indigenous Theories of Crime." *Journal of Criminal Justice* 27: 227–38.

Wolfgang. M.E. and F. Ferracuti. 1967. *The Subculture of Violence: Towards an Integrated Theory in Criminology*. Beverly Hills: Sage

CHAPTER STUDY QUESTIONS

- What are the distinctive features of "American criminology" in contrast to those of "European criminology"? How can one account for the similarities and differences between American and European criminology?

- One could make the argument that a distinctly "European criminology," separate from "American criminology," is impossible. Do you agree with this argument? Explain. Can this argument also be applied in contrasting American criminology with the criminological enterprise in other countries or regions of the world?

- If you do not currently live in the United States, how does the "criminological enterprise" in your country or region of the world compare with Haen Marshall's description of American criminology? If you do reside in the US, do you agree with Haen Marshall's description of the American "criminological enterprise"? Why or why not?

- What is Haen Marshall's view of the different effects of the influence of American criminology on the development and state of criminology in other countries? Do you agree with her view? Why or why not?

RELATED WEB LINKS

The American Society of Criminology
http://www.asc41.com/
> This is the official website of the American Society of Criminology, described as "an international organization concerned with criminology, embracing scholarly, scientific, and professional knowledge concerning the etiology, prevention, control, and treatment of crime and delinquency."

European Society of Criminology
http://www.esc-eurocrim.org/workgroups.shtml
> The official website of the European Society of Criminology describes established research working groups and provides information on items including membership, conferences, and the Society's journal, *The European Journal of Criminology*, published since 2004.

American Pragmatism
http://radicalacademy.com/amphilosophy7.htm
> This site from the Radical Academy (a project of the Center for Applied Philosophy) describes the essential features of the philosophical movement of American pragmatism developed in the United States by leading thinkers such as Charles Sanders Peirce (1839-1914), William James (1842-1910), and John Dewey (1859-1952).

Archive of European Integration AEI
http://aei.pitt.edu/
> This is an electronic repository and archive for research materials on the topic of European integration and unification made available by the University of Pittsburgh.

Chapter 3

TROUBLE IN PARADISE: CRIME AND COLLAPSED STATES IN THE AGE OF GLOBALIZATION

JEAN-GERMAIN GROS

A TALE OF TWO COUNTRIES, ONE WORLD

One morning in 1998 a small plane from South America entered Haitian airspace in the south-eastern part of the country and began to drop some packets. Some residents, acting perhaps on knowledge of what was happening, immediately created a fracas; they pounced on the packages (if not to mention each other) and opened their content, whereupon they made away with their find. Others—not the most discerning ones, it turned out—ran to tell local authorities. The latter, upon arriving on the scene where the "manna" had been dropped, began to beat up the residents, including the ones who were naïve (or law-abiding) enough to alert them to what had happened. Having emptied the place, these officers of the peace then collected the remaining packages, took them to their office for "inspection," and the rest, as they say, is history. It was revealed later that the incident was the outcome of a drug deal gone awry. But this particular drug deal came with a twist, maybe two: the transaction was international in scope, and the people who were officially sworn to protect Haiti from narcotics trafficking were intimately involved in it, which explains why they mistreated their compatriots so unmercifully. Simply put, the police officers-turned-crooks were upset that they were being outwitted, at least for one day, by civilian crooks, who soon realized that there is nothing more harmful than stealing from armed agents of the state. Meanwhile, in a much bigger and politically significant country—i.e., Russia—some $4bn provided by the International Monetary Fund to support an ailing economy and prevent the meltdown of the rouble "evaporated" literally overnight. Apparently, international money was more combustible than the Russian currency it was intended to save. In other words, Russian government officials, working in concert with the oligarchic *nouveaux riches* of post-communism, had been too fast and clever for the bureaucrats of the Bretton Woods institutions.

The thread connecting these seemingly disparate events is the subject of this chapter: the institutional foundations of global criminality in the post-Cold War era. Specifically, the article will contend that the so-called failed state is the principal actor in the criminalization of the world economy, while globalization is a pre-eminent member of the supporting cast. A point of clarification is in order here: I am expunging violent acts, such as civil homicides, rapes, armed robberies, kidnappings, politically-motivated assassinations and terrorism, from the sordid list of criminal behaviour, except when they are perpetrated to facilitate the economic enrichment of elites (De Brie 1999).[1] Bluntly put, crooks are of greater interest here than thugs, although drawing a line between the two requires a certain amount of arbitrariness.

THE FAILED STATE AND CRIME

What are failed states? If one thinks of the state in electrical and concentric terms, wherein state power starts at the centre (i.e., the capital city) and radiates out to the periphery (i.e., the hinterland), with the sum-total of centralized and peripheral power making up what James C. Scott (1998) calls the power grid of the state, then it becomes possible to visualize the failed state. Failed states are those whose power grids have experienced sustained and massive break-down, or political brownout, wherein state authorities are no longer able to project power either at the centre or at the periphery, and are subsequently, if temporarily, replaced by non-state generators of social power (e.g., NGOs and warlords). It is important to point out, however, that even when modern states fail to generate power, they continue to pretend that they do, and the international sorority of states generally goes along with the *trompe l'oeuil*.[2]

The connection between the failed state and crime in the post-Cold War world is simply this: the failed state, for reasons that will be explored immediately, is a magnet for criminal elements both inside and outside its borders. In other words, the failed state is both a perpetrator and a victim of international crime. How so? First of all, the failed state is likely to lack territorial span of control. In other words, it can only account for activities, licit or illicit, that take place in very limited areas, usually the capital city and sometimes not even that. As a result, criminals may find it relatively easy to set up camp in the hinterland, where they are safely out of reach. They may find an ally in the terrain if it consists of jungles, mountains, swamps or any ecological condition that hinders the movement of armed troops.

When states fail it is not only their territorial span of control that has been severed, thereby rendering their hold on territory and society extremely tenuous; their hierarchical span of control also breaks down, and, as a result, they are unable to monitor their agents. In other words, the typical failed state is one in which hierarchical norms are no longer operative; indeed, what is the state but hierarchy inside and among institutions? When states fail subalterns, be they institutions or individuals, they no longer have to account to their superiors. To the extent that there is account-ability, it is of a most dubious kind: collusion. Often there is tacit agreement between "hierarchs" and "lowerarchs," whereby the latter pay tribute to the former in exchange for silence and protec-tion. The propensity of state officials to engage in felonious behaviour is thus greatly enhanced by the fact that they operate in a vacuous environment where cohesion is missing and accountability in the conventional sense is owed no one. This is fodder for what is called impunity.

The third reason the failed state is attractive to criminals is that economic collapse typically accompanies state collapse or follows closely on its heels. So intimate is the connection between the two that a successful and vibrant economy and a collapsed state are almost unthinkable. When the economy collapses, the state, whatever is left of it, is generally the only avenue for private accumulation, or the only one that can facilitate it. To retain their position, members of the economic elite, who under normal circumstances might think of themselves as respectable, may find that they have no choice but to engage in criminal activity. Among other things, they may find that bribery is the only way to get their goods past customs and to market. They may even set up criminal gangs to protect their possessions or pay soldiers to do the same. For their part, state officials may conclude that in an environment where wages are low and often in arrears—which increases the chances that salaries will be reduced by inflation—the only way to keep food on the table is through "extracurricular" activities such as bribery and even open robbery.[3] The attraction becomes all the more irresistible if "everyone is doing it." After all, of what utility is honesty if the road to survival is manned by crooks?

International criminal syndicates are well aware of which states constitute the "weakest links" in the international state system, and they establish their production centres and distribution networks accordingly. The "weakest link" states are usually those where centralized authority and the formal economy have collapsed and there is a ready-made group of indigenous *courtiers*. Thus, the trade in heroin has as one of its routes Afghanistan (a producer country and a failed state), Nigeria (a transit point and a failed state) and western Europe (a destination and consumption point); that of cocaine has many paths, among them Colombia (a producer country and a failed state), Haiti (a transit point and a failed state) and the United States (a destination and consumption point). The case of cocaine transshipment in the Americas is extremely revealing. Puerto Rico used to serve as the transit point between South America and the United States, but after American drug authorities began to crack down in the Commonwealth, drug traffickers descended upon poor Haiti. At first, they found few local accomplices, so Colombian nationals began to crop up around Port-au-Prince and in southern Haiti to do the job themselves. Soon the traffickers found allies in the highest echelons of Haitian society: the Haitian army. This brings up another piece of evidence of the sophistication of certain international crime syndicates: their capacity not only to identify the weakest states in the international system but to penetrate and corrupt legitimate social institutions and networks, which in some cases go back decades if not centuries.

Istanbul, that age-old bridge connecting eastern and western civilizations, is now used as a transit point to smuggle people into the European Union (Jones 2001). Nigerians of Igbo ethnicity are thought to be overly represented in the drug trade as "mules." Their participation has been explained in terms of the legendary trading skills of the Igbos and the familial and kinship links among them all over the world (Bayart 1999). In Cameroon, a similar role is being played by Bamiléké merchants (another entrepreneurial ethnic group) in the smuggling of goods (not drugs) out of Central Africa, although they are said to be displaced increasingly by the Bétis thanks to state protection. In East Africa, Somali lorry drivers transport *kats* (not an illegal substance in Somalia, to the extent illegality can be determined under conditions of anarchy) and cannabis (marijuana) throughout the region.

Fourth, the failed state lacks *esprit de corps* among its officials. This is often brought about by years, if not decades, of corruption, structural adjustment-induced retrenchment, low salary and morale, lack of opportunities for advancement and various forms of social pressure. *Esprit the corps* can be an effective shield against crime, because it creates among civil servants a sense of purpose, professionalism and obligations toward the public interest. When *esprit de corps* is low or non-existent, state officials may not only have very strong material incentives to engage in unlawful activities, they may see nothing morally wrong in doing so. This is likely to happen, says Peter Ekeh, where the state is perceived as a foreign entity whose assets are fair game as long as they are put to the collective benefit of a more significant commons, such as an extended family, a clan or ethnic group, or used to finance social events, such as naming ceremonies, weddings and Christmas parties (Ekeh 1975). The breakdown in *esprit de corps* is just as strong an indicator of state collapse as economic malperformance. A state that no longer has an administrative praetorian guard, that is to say, a group of people looking to protect its integrity, is one that is vulnerable to criminals from within its corridors and from without.

Fifth, failed states are vulnerable to criminal activity because, even though centralized authorization may not have collapsed completely in some cases, the institutional bases upon which it rests may have become irrelevant during the transition from one regime world to another. This is especially true of Eastern Europe and Russia. Criminal activity in Russia is not due to administrative and policing incapacity, much less the scarcity of natural resources (Handelman 1995). Russia, as its leaders never tire of telling the rest of the world (who ignores the reminder at its peril), is a nuclear power. Further, Russia is well endowed in resources and its population very educated. In sum, Russia has the human and natural resources, physical infrastructure and domestic market size to build a strong state and a vibrant economy. The failed nature of the Russian state stems from the fact that new institutions were either not put in place or existed in embryonic form during the transition from Stalinism to capitalism. In other words, the dominant institutions in Russia in the 1990s still harkened back to the 1970s, the corrupt and stagnant period before *perestroika*, *glasnost* and ultimately the end of communism.

What the world saw in Russia in the 1990s was the collapse of an ideology, economy and even regime-world but the continued survival of institutions either in the exact form as before the collapse or as mutations of the "new" into the "old." In this atmosphere of institutional cross-dressing, corrupt state officials, profiteers clad in the garb of capitalist entrepreneurs and Mafia syndicates were able to use the window of opportunity to enrich themselves. State properties were liquidated at absurdly low prices before rules governing how such assets were to be acquired were enacted. Commercial banks were set up before regulatory measures protecting depositors were put in place. Even westerners, eager to partake in Russia's "emerging market," were left out, and those who did get in quickly got out but generally not before losing their shirts. But however depressing Russia is at the moment, and however justifiable the label "failed state" is to define Russia, the future of the state there is much rosier than that of other failed states in the third world.

GLOBALIZATION AND CRIME

First of all, what is globalization? To some, it is the new *bête noire* of North-South relations; to others, globalization is something akin to the second coming. In other words, globalization does not mean the same thing to all people; as a result, there is much confusion surrounding what it is and what it is not, what it does and does not do. In this chapter, globalization is defined as the deregulation of national economies and financial markets, on the one hand, and their international integration under the aegis of free-market ideology on the other. In specific policy terms, globalization entails deregulation of capital flows, eviction of the state from areas that concern production and with that the privatization of former state-owned enterprises without regards to the source(s) of capital, reduction in the size of government and its commitment to the social safety net, in other words, fiscal discipline (usually to qualify for membership in a trading bloc, fight budget deficits, or both), trade liberalization through reduction in tariffs, quotas and other barriers to commerce and the setting up of duty-free zones, protection of patent rights for multinational corporations, the creation of large trading blocs (EU, NAFTA, MERCOSUR, ASEAN) and other pro-free-market measures.

Contrary to what some of its foes believe, globalization is not the product of American conspiracy.[4] Even in the United States, there are forces inside the two parties that dominate American politics that are skeptical of some aspects of globalization, because they entail, in *their view*, a loss of national sovereignty to multilateral institutions such as the World Trade Organization. Thus, ratification of American membership in the WTO was assured only after certain clauses were added that allow unilateral US actions, including withdrawal, by an ostensibly pro-business, Republican-controlled Senate. In the House of Representatives, it was mainly Democrats, under pressure from organized labour, who scuttled former president William Jefferson Clinton's request for "fast track" powers to negotiate a trade agreement with Latin America. In advanced democracies, domestic politics, rather than conspiracy, determine policy choices. Where globalization is concerned, such choices, depending on the coalitions that are formed, will sometimes be in favor of globalization and sometimes against it. In other words, globalization is not static; its content can be shaped by political struggles.[5] In the United States commodities such as sugar continue to defy free trade rules, thanks to the lobbying strength of the sugar industry (Barboza 2001), and in Western Europe farmers receive subsidies and protection from "unfair" competition from abroad. The most significant factor responsible for the current hegemony of globalization is, I believe, ideological in nature: namely, the demise of the socialist regime-world, which for at least 75 years provided an alternative to the capitalist West.

Whoever first coined the phrase "what is good for the goose is good for the gander" could have been a feminist, a naturalist, an astute farmer or perhaps even all three, but she might as well have been an honest international banker. As stated previously, an important article of faith in the globalization gospel is the free flow of capital, specifically monetary capital. Commercial banks, insurance companies, money transferring agencies (e.g., Western Union), brokerage houses, and individual currency traders are able to conduct around the globe foreign exchange transactions worth at least $1.5 trillion, or one-fifth the annual value of world trade, per day. Hence, on any given day a good portion of the world's assets is being traded at the click of a button or "mouse." Officially, this is designed to stimulate investment in "emerging markets" and punish laggard countries with overvalued currencies. The free flow of money, advocates believe, generates world efficiency: money goes exactly where it needs to go, and exits where it is not welcome. Here is the rub, however: whether by design or ignorance, the technologies and the law are not yet in place to distinguish "clean" money from "dirty" money as it flows through the electronic pipelines of international finance. There is always a lag, as red flags are not raised right away, or bankers choose to ignore them.

As Glynn et al. (1997: 12) note, "the emergence of an electronic financial system markedly enhances opportunities for corruption, the difficulty of controlling it, and the potential damage it can inflict." Much as George Soros can move currency around the world, so too could, at least for a while, Pablo Escobar or Omar Bongo. And just as international crime syndicates are able to recognize the opportunity the failed state offers, either as the final destination or transit point for illicit goods, so too are they adroit in realizing that the fluidity of money markets allows for the movement of illicit profits in and out of countries that are at the epicenter of globalization; often those same countries scorn the activities (e.g., drug trafficking, bribes) from which the profits are derived.

In sum, in the international division of labor created by international crime, the failed state is a haven for the production and distribution of illicit "goods" while globalization provides sanctuary for the profits that flow from those "goods". Crime in the age of an electronic financial system that cuts across borders is not only being committed by professional criminals who peddle in illicit activities. Legitimate entrepreneurs and ordinary citizens also perpetrate crime when they set up International Business Corporations (ICBs) and foreign bank accounts for the sole purpose of hiding their wealth to avoid paying taxes at home (Fields and Whitefield 2001). It is in this sense that crime has gone chic, white collar, mainstream. Thanks to globalization, the "barbarians" are no longer at the gate looking in; they are now inside the walls, mingling with the "civilized."

Another mechanism for crime in the age of globalization is the privatization of state owned enterprises. In the semi-industrial countries of the third world and the industrial countries of the former second world, privatization has proved to be a real bonanza for criminals. Deception here takes many forms. State assets may be deliberately undervalued so as to allow relatively cash-poor buyers to acquire them at fantastically low prices (e.g., Russia). State-owned enterprises may be allowed to fall in decrepitude. When the capital necessary for their revitalization is no longer forthcoming from the national treasury, private capital may then be invited or the enterprises sold (e.g., Ghana and Zambia). Impending sale of state-owned enterprises may not be announced in time for competitive bids to be submitted, so buyers with inside information may have an advantage over those without (e.g., Kenya). Finally, buyers of dubious credit worthiness but with strong political connection may be provided state-secured loans to "purchase" enterprises, which they have no intention of keeping open (e.g., Cameroon, Indonesia under Suharto). Such loans are then recorded as "uncollectible" in the ledger of financial institutions, since the enterprises that were used as collateral for loan disbursement have long gone under. This ruse has a double whammy effect: the demise of industrial enterprises and financial institutions.

Along with privatization of state-owned enterprises, globalization entails, as stated earlier, reduction in the size of government and its commitment to the social safety, which, unfortunately, can intensify criminal practices. This outcome is ironic, since smaller government is intended to reduce corruption. When government gets smaller, it is not necessarily the most incompetent and corrupt who are let go. Indeed, because the overriding goal is to save money through reduction in the public payroll, the people targeted are often those who are on the "high" end of the civil service pay scale as well as those close to retirement (but never the aid consultants or civil servants on loans from donor countries who are remunerated at first world salary levels). But it is precisely the better paid and experienced national civil servants who need to be kept, for they are generally a bulwark against criminality.

Administrative crime in developing countries stems in part from low salaries, which have to be complemented by illegal and extralegal activities if status within a social group is to be maintained. Therefore, the way to fight criminality in the civil service is through better salaries, not mass firing of those who earn them or lower salaries for those who are lucky enough to be retained. Further, excellence in administration, as Chester Barnard reminded us long ago, is often based on repeated encounters with certain experiences and the development of a repertoire of responses that in the past have "worked" (Barnard 1938). Therefore, experience in the public administration may be more valuable than academic training (an admission some readers may find puzzling, coming from a professor of public policy administration). When experienced civil servants are released from their duty, there is a gap in administrative competence which cannot be filled immediately. The young Turks have simply not been around long enough to know how to respond to certain challenges, and the old ones have not left any blueprint for their successors to follow, since most of their actions were informed by personal experience and informal networks. The void provides a golden opportunity for malfeasance.

Globalization also advocates user fees to pay for publicly funded services. The trend has been in evidence in the public administration since the 1980s, and it is not necessarily a bad thing. If consumers are willing (and able) to pay for the services they need, there is no reason why they should receive them for "free" simply because government is the provider. Indeed, government-provided services are never free. Consumers may not have to pay for them on the spot, but make no mistake about it, they do pay. Opponents of user fees usually decry the reduction in access they say occurs when consumers with limited financial means are excluded from services, because of the burden cost recovery imposes on them. But this need not be the case. The poor do not have to forego government-provided services for which a fee is charged, if they are given subsidies or are allowed to buy such services at lower cost.

However, cost recovery can increase corruption. When government makes citizens pay directly for the services they receive, another layer of responsibility is added to the duties of civil servants. They are service providers and collectors of funds.[6] The mix is not always a fortuitous one, especially in countries where administrative accountability is wanting. There is no guarantee that (a) the fee being charged for government-provided services is the one mandated by law and (b) the fee will be deposited in government coffers. Indeed, in many countries user fees become a cloak for unscrupulous officials charging what the market will bear, since many citizens do not know what the legally sanctioned fee is. Even when they do, they may find that, to be served, they have to come up with something extra (so-called tea money). Thus, while working in an African country in 1991, I was able to observe public sector veterinarians asking livestock farmers to pay more for services than had been set by the government; worse, the fees collected at the local level were seldom turned over to provincial, much less central, authorities.[7]

When government salaries are cut or the personnel reduced, the technical core in the administration—accountants, scientists, engineers, doctors and veterinarians, agronomists, etc.—often find it more rewarding financially to join the private sector than to remain in government. This is partly because the very agencies that push for government downsizing (World Bank, IMF, EU, USAID) and humanitarian organizations often use the services of these professionals at a much higher rate of remuneration than government. As a result, qualified personnel leave the civil service as soon as there is an opening in the aid "industry" or the private sector proper. But it is precisely these people, especially accountants, who are needed to combat financial crime in the public administration, for they not only have the technical skills to detect fraud, they are often members of local and international professional associations, which have been known to exert strong influence on their members. The contraction of the technical core, an outcome I admit is more incidental to globalization than deliberate, on top of the departure of experienced administrators in the name of cutting costs, can, once again, intensify criminal activity rather than reduce it.

Trade liberalization is another vital component of globalization. It takes many forms: reduction in tariffs and quotas, relaxation of the rules governing foreign investment especially those having to do with profit repatriation by foreign investors, elimination of non-visible barriers to trade (e.g. health safety inspection of goods that does not threaten public health), and creation of internal free-trade zones, which are generally not subject to the same set of laws that apply in other areas. Trade liberalization does have the potential of benefiting consumers, by opening previously closed markets to foreign competition. It can bring about drastic reduction in the prices of consumer goods as local producers no longer enjoy monopoly power. Furthermore, trade liberalization allows a country to "leapfrog" from one technology to another without having to make heavy investment in basic infrastructure. People in the developing world can now use the cellular phone to communicate with each other and with the outside world. All that is needed is investment in cellular and satellite technology, which in the current atmosphere is incurred by foreign investors anyway. In an earlier time, telecommunications required intricate wiring of entire territories, the purchase of switchboards and other heavy equipment, which consumed significant amounts of foreign exchange, only served elites (periodically) and allowed government to eavesdrop easily on citizens and thus control speech. In sum, trade can help to bring about democratization in the widest sense of the term.

At the same time, the misdeeds (i.e., crimes) committed in the name of free trade, or facilitated by it, are probably too numerous to be listed here in their entirety. Some economies are little more than smuggling sanctuaries, although the language of diplomacy finesses the reality by calling them *entrepôt* economies (Bayart 1999). Nigerian traders, instead of shipping industrial spare parts through Lagos, ship them through quasi-private ports in neighboring Benin, whence they are taken overland to Nigeria. The advantage is twofold: Beninois customs agents are apparently not as greedy as their Nigerian counterparts, and ethnic affinity between Nigerian traders and Beninois customs agents help to keep business in the (Yoruba) "family." Meanwhile, neither the Nigerian nor the Benin government is collecting revenue from the trade. Nor do they know what other commodities, in addition to spare parts for the oil industry, are entering their respective territory. Profit-seeking entrepreneurs use their ownership and control of so-called free trade zones to traffic in everything from expired medicines to stolen cars.

Free trade has also destroyed industries in developing countries, and it cannot be assumed that the losses are temporary. For a variety of reasons, not the least the inadequacy of the educational system, developing countries are not as flexible in responding to the vicissitudes of free trade as their developed counterparts. Losses attributable to free trade in one sector are not accompanied by gains in other sectors. Indeed, in many instances job losses occur in the most dynamic sectors, thereby forcing people to go underground. In Haiti the closing of hundreds, perhaps thousands, of independently owned clothing shops coincided with the opening of the Haitian market to second-hand clothes (*pèpè*) from the United States.[8] Further, the removal of protection for rice farmers in the Artibonite valley led to an invasion of the Haitian market by so-called Miami rice *after* the fall of Jean-Claude Duvalier. This had consequences of a criminal nature. In particular, the emiseration of the Haitian peasantry by free trade led to an upsurge in the incidence of people smuggling. Haitians did make a shift from one money-losing industry to another, but not of the type free trade advocates welcome. They shifted from rice-growing to boat-making in hopes of reaching South Florida, but even the most ardent neo-liberal would admit, the free movement of unskilled labour, unlike that of capital, is not part of the globalization bargain.

MAKING THE FAILED STATE LESS VULNERABLE TO CRIMINALITY

A brief recap is necessary at this point, so the reader can connect the proposed solutions to the problems at hand. The failed state and globalization are fertile ground for criminality. The failed state, once again, is one whose power grid, for whatever reason, has either stopped working or works too infrequently to be satisfactory. Typically, the failed state cannot project authority either in space (territory) or among people. In short, the failed state cannot do the one thing all states are supposed to do: impose and maintain social order. On the contrary, the failed state often is a source of disorder, as many of its officials become involved in criminal activity, or as it becomes an easy target for international criminals looking for safe havens, or both. Reducing international crime then will require strengthening the order-maintenance capacity of failed states. This means, first and foremost, improving the security and justice apparatus of the state. In some countries, the size of the police force will have to be increased, so that there is effective state presence at key strategic points (border checkpoints, seaports and airports).

Once the security and justice apparatuses of the state are strengthened, more attention needs to be paid to the delivery of social services. In other words, order maintenance capacity should be followed by administrative capacity in the social services and regulatory areas. These are important for building public confidence in and support for the state. One of the fallacies in the development of administration literature is that administration in developing countries is too centralized. As a result, policy papers tend to recommend one version or other of de-centralization (USAID 1979; World Bank 1975). In the 1970s and 1980s, many donors made decentralization the cornerstone of their giving aid, and decentralization programmes sprouted at major universities throughout the United States. Collapsed states suffer from what might be called decentralization by default. This is in part what makes them vulnerable.

Reform in the civil administration in collapsed states entails recentralization. Decentralization only makes sense in the context of previously successful efforts at centralization. The problem in the failed state is that genuine administrative centralization (not to be confused with politi-cal personalization) was never achieved; therefore, a policy of decentralization, in the absence of strong support for central agencies and authority, is likely to emasculate the state even fur-ther. The point does not contradict what was said earlier about judges, who could be dispatched to the countryside in greater number but would still be accountable to centralized authority. In other words, it is possible to have recentralization and deconcentration at the same time, as the former connects to authority while the latter to space or geography. Deconcentrated personnel can be made answerable to a centre (e.g., the French prefectural system).

Recentralization means revival of the state institutions that have been allowed to deterio- rate after years of corruption, retrenchment and neglect. The contracting out of services previ- ously provided by the state to non-governmental organizations (NGOs) has undermined state power in many countries. All too often in the developing world, NGOs from the North oper- ate without any supervision by the host government. They become, in essence, states within states. When challenged, NGOs, donor agencies and countries typically point out that NGOs have distinct advantages over recipient governments, not least their being closer to the people they serve, more committed to their work and cheaper to work with (Overseas Development Institute 1988). None of these alleged advantages is inherent to NGOs, but the policy tends to become self-fulfilling. Because civil servants are assumed to be distant, uncommitted and expensive, they are pushed aside in favour of NGO "volunteers." As a result, they are left to perform uninteresting work and become demoralized. Among other things, recentralization means restoring certain functions (e.g., public health, education, environmental protection, natural disaster relief) to the state, re-establishing the principle of hierarchy as the cornerstone of public administration, and making top state officials, especially presidents, prime ministers, cabinet ministers and their closest subalterns, accountable. After all, international society rec- ognizes states as representatives of collectivities (i.e., nations), not NGOs.

MAKING GLOBALIZATION LESS VULNERABLE TO CRIMINALITY

Monitoring capital flows

The downsides of globalization were documented earlier, but as was done with collapsed states, a brief recap is necessary. The wheels of criminality under globalization are greased by untrammeled currency flows, privatization and trade liberalization. In light of the Asian Financial Crisis of 1997–98, it is evident that there is value to controlling capital flows, at least in some countries and for some period of time. Even the International Monetary Fund has had to concede, however grudg- ingly, that controls on capital flows may be appropriate under certain circumstances (International Monetary Fund 1999). The idea has been seconded by *The Economist* (*The Economist* 1998). Malaysia's decision to put brakes on how much investors could take out of the country may have limited the impact of the Asian financial meltdown. In other words, Malaysia was able to recover more quickly than most Asian countries because it abandoned laissez-faire dogmas and rediscov- ered that states matter. But the utility of control on capital flows goes beyond monetary and macro- economic stability; the policy allows a country to study more closely the dealings of its financial institutions. This could go some way toward enabling state officials to determine the origins of some transactions, even if they are not able to account for all of them. Further, if politicians have to face the wrath of the people on the street or at the polls when the national currency is in a free fall, it is only fair that they be given the tools to address the problem. Foreign speculators cannot be allowed, in the name of globalization, to bid down (or up) the value of a country's currency, wreak havoc on their financial system and leave it to the politicians to take the blame.

In addition to sensible control on capital flows, closer regulation of banks and other financial institutions and transparency can help in the fight against financial crime. At the moment, commercial banks in many countries do business in relative obscurity. Swiss banks have had to be browbeaten by victims of Nazi atrocities to reveal the origins of some of their deposits. In the name of privacy, banks can shield transactions from government regulators and even their own officials. As a result of congressional hearings in the United States in 1999, it was revealed that multinational banks like Citibank and the Bank of New York have accounts that deliberately omit the name of their owners and the net value of their deposits. Under this circumstance, it is not surprising that officials from these banks, when faced with a barrage of questions from US senators about their practice, could only feign ignorance and contrition about some of their clients. It follows, therefore, that monitoring capital flows should go hand in hand with greater state supervision of financial institutions, greater transparency in the transactions of these institutions, and more intensive use of encryption technologies to ensure that criminals do not take advantage of so-called e-money.

Financial ruses in the age of globalization are not limited to the rich and powerful. An "ordinary" citizen can open an account in a tax haven (e.g., the Cayman Islands) and, using her MasterCard or Visa debit card, conduct business abroad while avoiding paying taxes at home (Fields and Whitefield 2001). This type of shell game might be caught if the card-issuing companies were subject to stringent regulation. Unfortunately, in the United States they are regulated even less stringently than banks, which can of course issue their own cards under the MasterCard and Visa logo. Indeed, the trend in the financial sector has been toward deregulation worldwide. In the United States, insurance companies are now able to provide a wide range of financial services; banks have been allowed to cross state lines, thereby becoming de facto national; and regulators have been streamlined. The financial services industry is not necessarily more corrupt than other industries because of these changes, but the potential for illicit behaviour is there. All it takes is a few bad apples to sour the entire pie (cases in point: BCCI worldwide and the Savings and Loans crisis in the United States in the late 1980s).

Making privatization more transparent

This entails, first and foremost, credible asset valuation assessment. A familiar trick in countries undergoing privatization is to "low ball" the assets to be sold, so the well-connected can buy them. In some countries (e.g., Nigeria), former state-owned enterprises have been sold to the very people responsible for their valuation, or those who may have helped to run them into the ground (Cameroon). Valuation assessment should be made by an authority that does not have a vested interest in the sale of the assets. This is where the law and the market can be made to intersect. The law can stipulate that no one who has helped to determine the value of an asset will be allowed to bid on its sale, or that anyone purchasing a former state-owned enterprise must come up with a significant share of the accepted price on their own.

In the United States, home buyers must either come up with at least 20 per cent of the sales value of the property they are buying or purchase private mortgage insurance (PMI) for a number of years (usually until they have made payments totaling 20 per cent of the value of the property).

This is designed to protect the lender and give the borrower a personal stake in the investment. A similar law could govern the purchase of former state-owned enterprises. To be sure, banks make money by lending, but they seldom do so without collateral or other financial conditions. The Asian financial crisis was precipitated in part by banks making too many loans to the politically well connected for the purchase of assets that turned out to be of little equity value in an economic downturn. When international investors started withdrawing their money en masse, Asian depositors panicked and ultimately there was an old-fashioned bank run (Sugisaki 1999). Malaysia's answer was to limit how much money could be taken out of the country and reform the banking system, but what caused the bubble to burst were certain occult (nontransparent) practices in which banks, well-connected families and industrial assets were entangled.

The bidding process could be made more open. Invitations to bid on former state-owned assets could be made in time for potential buyers, regardless of political connection, to assemble a dossier, identify co-investors and submit their bid. All too often the public knows about the sale of state-owned enterprises after it has occurred. This is especially the case where the asset in question is thought to be important to the national interest—whether in the military or psychic sense—and involves a foreign buyer (e.g., Ashanti Goldfields of Ghana). Rather than stoke public debate and risk losing popular support, state officials have tended to keep privatization secret, thereby depriving local entrepreneurs of an opportunity to partake in the economic affairs of their country. Stealth privatization is not only bad politics, it is also bad business, inasmuch as secret bidding reduces competition among potential buyers, and with that the final price at which former state-owned assets are sold.

Trade liberalization

To be trade-friendly, a country does not have to relinquish the right to inspect what goods are coming into or leaving its territory. Trade liberalization unwittingly aids global criminality because the rush to encourage the trade of licit goods facilitates that of illicit goods. Cocaine has been hidden in the hauls of international vessels, coffee bean bags, banana crates and stomachs of "mules" (people who swallow small cocaine packets and expunge them through their waste after going through customs). Given the ingeniousness of international crime syndicates in hiding their goods, states must be equally creative and strong, if they are to uncover them. A robust state presence is therefore needed at key points where international trade meets sovereignty, national security and law enforcement. These include airports, seaports and transnational boundaries.

Free trade creates winners and losers. Indeed, one reason for the welfare state, says Katzenstein (1985), is that it helps to compensate the victims of international competition. In the developing world, however, the lack of a social safety net often drives people who have been dislocated by free trade into criminality. Prostitution, illegal beer brewing, drug dealing, armed robbery and people smuggling are usually the survival safety valves of the displaced young urban worker. Thus, a progressive free trade compact armed at avoiding some criminal side-effects must involve compensation, which might simply consist of time-limited unemployment income support and worker retraining. An agricultural component might include providing extension services, seeds and fertilizer assistance to farmers, to enable them to be competitive, and, in some cases, shift from illegal crops (e.g., coca) to legal ones.

In addition, in a truly globalized world economy workers should be able to go where the jobs are, just as capital is allowed to operate wherever it is profitable to do so. The decision to limit labor mobility is more political than economic, as evidenced by the fact that when capitalists pressure elected officials in countries like the United States, changes usually follow allowing "guest workers" in specific industries. Malaysia caught a lot of criticism when it imposed limited and temporary controls on capital flows, but the world has remained mum on the myriad ways in which labour flow from the South has been turned into a trickle by the North. According to globalization advocates, decisions regarding where capital goes should be made by the owners of capital without interference from states, but it is considered entirely within the purview of states to regulate the flow of the most important factor of production: labour. They cannot have it both ways: either the world economy will be global (i.e., truly integrated) or it will not be. Further, strong states are not antithetical to globalization. Indeed, if globalization is to be more than crass profiteering on a planetary scale, involving both legitimate entrepreneurs and parasitic criminals, strong states are essential for insuring compliance with the rules of international commerce and alleviating the worst side effects of the liberal order.

TOWARD A NEW GOVERNANCE AGENDA FOR FIGHTING GLOBAL CRIMINALITY

The previous section presented a number of proposals for fighting global criminality. In this section, the focus shifts on how to implement the aforementioned proposals—in other words, to governance. It bears repeating that criminality is transnational in scope; therefore, the fight against it should be transnational as well. Specifically, criminality in the post-Cold War era is one of the symptoms of structural changes in the architecture of the state system on the one hand and the world economy on the other. The fight against global criminality therefore should entail a greater role for international institutions, but the responsibilities should be parcelled out.

No single institution should be given the task of combating criminality, since the problem itself is multifaceted. What is offered here is a tripartite division of labour, based on the functional capacity, real or potential, of specific international bodies. Under the scenario, the United Nations would tackle state collapse; the World Bank, the International Monetary Fund, the World Trade Organization, and regional financial entities, such as the African Development Bank and the InterAmerican Development Bank, would be responsible for globalization-related financial crimes by government officials; Interpol, working with national law enforcement officials, would take the lead in the investigation of globalization-related financial crimes by international criminal syndicates and private citizens. Each of these approaches is examined in turn below.

First of all, why does the revival of collapsed states along the lines explored earlier (i.e., judicial and police reform, recentralization) require external assistance? By definition, failed or collapsed states are those whose internal governance mechanisms (power grids, to use the metaphor used earlier) have ceased to be effective, thereby causing negative externalities; outside assistance is therefore needed to jump-start such states.[9] The UN may be relatively well-placed to deal with state collapse, since it is often called upon to deal with the phenomenon's most visible consequences (e.g., lawlessness, refugee flows, etc.). Further, the UN may be the only international organization whose intervention is unlikely to be labelled neo-imperialist. In spite of its faults, the UN arguably enjoys a greater degree of legitimacy in international society than any other institution. Finally, given the aversion to "nation-building" among policy elites in countries like the United States, politicians might actually breathe a sigh of relief if the task were carried out by the UN.[10]

I recognize that the UN record in dealing with collapsed states in the post-Cold War era does not inspire confidence that the organization could adequately fulfill the above-mentioned role. In the future, if the UN is to play a leading and successful role in the reconstruction of collapsed states, it will need the full backing of the member-states, especially that of the Security Council and its permanent members. This entails, first and foremost, greater financial support. With a peacekeeping budget of US$4bn in 1992, the UN purse was smaller than that of the New York City police and fire departments, which are responsible for 8 million people (Childers and Urquhart 1994). No one should expect an agency with such a niggardly budget with multiple demands placed upon it to be effective. The reconstruction of collapsed states across the globe would be most likely to require the creation of another specialized UN agency, whose mission would be to identify collapsed (or collapsing) states and help them strengthen basic institutions, especially those that relate to order-maintenance (e.g., the police force and judiciary).

Enlightened self-interest should make the existing permanent members of the Security Council more generous toward the UN, but there are other avenues. At the moment, at least four countries (i.e., Germany, Japan, Brazil and India) are vying for a permanent seat on the UN Security Council. These countries need to understand that visibility on the world stage entails greater financial responsibility in helping to resolve world problems. The enlargement of the Security Council, in addition to recognizing that the world has changed since 1945, might be one of the ways to fund a United Nations Agency for State Reconstruction (UNASR). There is a precedent for this: the World Bank—officially the International Bank for Reconstruction and Development—was founded to rebuild the economies of war-torn Europe after World War II. Can there be economies and development without states? And who but the UN is better placed to revive the latter?

Some might object to the proposal on the ground that it violates sovereignty, which is one of the core principles of the international state system (Maya 2000). However, when states torment their own citizens (or allow citizens to do likewise to each other), steal from them without providing any public good, create massive refugee flows, and become launching pads for criminal activities in other states, then sovereignty no longer applies. In other words, when the criminalization of the state threatens the lives of its citizens and the security and stability of its neighbors, a good case for UN intervention can be made (Dowty and Loescher 1996). If collapsed states are to be revived by the international community, diplomatic platitudes must give way to *franc-parler*. When the UN administers a territory directly, or plays a significant role in assisting the officials of a collapsed state with rebuilding basic institutions, sovereignty can no longer be assumed. For all intents and purposes, such "states" and territories become wards (trusts in legal terms) of international society. Sovereignty under this circumstance would be temporarily suspended and held in escrow by the UN, until such time when the state, with international assistance, is decriminalized and able to reassert its authority. In sum, a "new" definition of sovereignty is being called for here, one that that does not see sovereignty as a modern version of divine right (of states, not monarchs), but rather as an *acquis* that states earn and can, therefore, lose. And one of the grounds for losing sovereignty is large-scale, recidivous criminality with spill-over effects that goes unpunished, either because the state will not or cannot prosecute perpetrators.

Where globalization provides the underpinning of criminality, the UN should cede the right of way to institutions that specialize in economic and financial matters. The World Trade Organization, the World Bank, the International Monetary Fund and regional entities, such as the Asian Development Bank and the InterAmerican Development Bank, should play a leading role in helping to reduce certain ruses, especially when they are concocted by state officials. These institutions have the financial clout to achieve compliance with good behaviour (or the pretence thereof). In Kenya, for example, the threat of an aid embargo by the Bretton Woods institutions was instrumental in getting President Moi to appoint a so-called anti-corruption czar (i.e., the paleontologist Richard Leakey). Of course, some of these organizations are often sceptical of non-market instruments (i.e., currency controls). They need to be less doctrinaire in their approach to globalization. They need to understand that markets, like any other institution created by humans, occasionally fail and can be used for purposes other than the efficient allocation of resources. Markets can be used to deceive, corrupt, intoxicate and even kill. Rules have to be put in place to ensure that none of these side effects is experienced, even if such rules "interfere" with market forces. In addition, key countries like the United States and Britain could provide greater public support for the anti-corruption efforts of the International Monetary Fund, the World Bank and other international institutions. Corrupt leaders must not think that they can play one segment of the international community against another, or that all they have to do is wait for the next election in donor countries in the hope that more friendly governments will come to power.

Finally, where criminality involves transnational non-state actors, organizations like Interpol could play a leading role. Unfortunately, Interpol, like the UN, is beset with problems that limit its efficacy. First of all, Interpol suffers from an image problem. A common misinformation, propagated on the web pages and in the chat rooms of extreme right-wing groups, has Interpol officers roaming the globe, nabbing possibly innocent citizens without their government's consent. The truth is, Interpol has no policing powers. Instead, as the former chief of the organization remarked, "it acts as a global clearinghouse for information on crime and maintains vast databases of fingerprints, mug shots, reproductions of missing art, license plate numbers of stolen cars, and more" (Kendall 2001). Second, certain countries, instead of supporting Interpol, which is a multilateral organization with 178 member states, seem to have a preference for bilateral agreements. Thus, the US Federal Bureau of Investigation (FBI) has an agreement with its sister organization in Russia and numerous other countries, but American support for Interpol has not been what it should be. The third problem with Interpol stems directly from the second: the organization is badly understaffed.[11] If Interpol is to be effective in the fight against criminality, there is no question that, like the UN, it will need more robust financial and political support from member states. In addition, Interpol was founded to fight illegality in the transshipment of physical goods, both licit and illicit, and to help apprehend fugitives. With the advent of the Internet and in the soon-to-be world of e-money, Interpol will have to open a second front in the battle against global criminality: in cyberspace.

In conclusion, global criminality is being fuelled by the collapse of the state system in some regions and the fungibility of globalization, which allows criminals to misuse legitimate institutions and technologies to their advantage. What is needed are countermeasures to stay one step ahead of those who choose to subvert the rules to their advantage rather than play by them, or profit from the lack of rules because of state collapse. In addition, nation-states have to band together, instead of trying to solve global crime on their own or bilaterally. In this connection, the recent decision of the Bush administration to abandon global efforts to control money laundering in tax havens was most unfortunate. The administration appears to have been swayed primarily by ideologues within the Republican party, leaving American trading partners, such as the EU, twisting in the wind.[12] Countries have to take a long-term and multinational approach to global crime fighting. Unfortunately, electoral shifts and domestic political pressure will make that difficult. In the end, it would be comforting if the world worked according to the predilection of science fiction writers and Hollywood movie makers, in whose imagination the good guys always win. Thus far, in the fight against global criminality the reverse seems to obtain.

NOTES

[1] Crime is hereby defined as any willfully committed act that runs afoul of either domestic or international law, and in some cases both. Crime here obviously includes corruption, which is the use of public office for private gains, but it is more than that. In this chapter I am as concerned with public officials as I am with legitimate entrepreneurs, professional criminals and ordinary citizens, who knowingly run roughshod over commercial, financial and tax laws. In monetary terms crime probably accounts for at least one fifth of world trade, or $1.5trn annually; in addition, crime encompasses a wide range of activities, from time-tested corrupt practices by state officials—e.g., bribery and outright theft of collected revenues—to strictly commercial transactions in licit goods that evade domestic law (smuggling in cars, cigarettes, Viagra, etc.) and illicit goods that contravene international conventions (trafficking in cocaine, prostitution, child pornography, etc.). The universe of contemporary criminal activities also includes illegal financial transactions, such as the unauthorized printing and minting of money and its laundering, the sale of state-owned enterprises under nontransparent conditions and at artificially low prices, trafficking in humans and their organs, endangered animals, weapons, toxic waste and even nuclear materials, and finally the pilfering of art works and other objects (e.g., bones of extinct species). Other activities, if they are not downright illegal, barely pass muster. They include efforts at evading domestic taxation by establishing tax havens abroad.

[2] [This translates as "the misleading of the eye."] The denial of state collapse seems to be the price the international community is willing to pay, in light of the consequences of a more interventionist policy, which, in the first instance, contravenes prevailing norms of international relations (i.e., sovereignty, respect for territorial integrity, non-interference in

the internal affairs of sister states, etc.). Freezing the political map of the world makes management of the state system easier, at least temporarily, for once the territory and whatever natural resources failed states have are available for easy plunder, there is no telling what the end-game is, which in the soon-to-be world of miniaturized nuclear weapons may blur the difference between winners and losers, successful states and failed ones.

3 At the height of the conflict in Sierra Leone in the 1990s, soldiers became "sobels": soldiers during the day, rebels and robbers at night. In the last days of the Mobutu regime, soldiers were openly urged to help themselves at the expense of the civilian population, in lieu of pay. And under the military regimes that succeeded each other in Haiti between 1986 and 1990, it was an open secret around Port-au-Prince that some off duty soldiers routinely rented their uniforms to civilians, who then had every incentive to capitalize on their investment by forcibly collecting tributes from ordinary citizens.

4 In spite of popular impressions to the contrary (propagated in the United States primarily by journalists), globalization, in the strict sense of capitalist expansion and economic integration, is not new either. Globalization is the latest incarnation of a process that started 500 years ago with mercantilism, the European discovery of the Americas, the trans-Atlantic slave trade, colonialism, decolonization, the nationalist era, the Cold War and ultimately the post-Cold War era. Globalization is the reason why the largest polo ground in the world is located in Kaduna, not Sheffield; it is the reason why Pakistanis, South Africans and Trinidadians play cricket with the same enthusiasm as that displayed by young people all over the world for baggy pants, rap music and American-made movies. The major difference between contemporary globalization efforts and previous instances of the same is that, whereas in the past, integration of hitherto excluded territories into the world economy meant their subordination to more powerful empire-states and regions, nowadays integration is carried out, not in the name of the white man's burden, *mission civilizatrice* and other euphemisms for state-led imperialism, but in terms of the positive sum of free trade (an old idea that goes back to Adam Smith and David Ricardo). As a concept, globalization is a liberal (or neo-liberal) twist on world-system theory.

5 Popular pressure forced NAFTA signatories to include various "side agreements" in the final document. How well these have worked is beside the point being made here, which is: politicians are not totally insensitive to public opinion, especially if the longevity of their tenure depends on it. A well-informed and well-organized public can have an impact on globalization, if only at the margins.

6 To be sure, this need not happen. The people providing services do not have to be the ones collecting fees, especially in urban areas where a relatively well-developed bureaucracy may insure the separation of service delivery from revenue collection. In the countryside, however, a different picture often emerges. Local service providers also collect funds on behalf of the state, and financial accounting is most rudimentary. This situation obviously favors corruption—nay, crime.

7 I continue to do work in the country in question and maintain a professional relationship with some of its officials. Therefore, the name of the country and the ministry in which I made the observation shall remain anonymous.

[8] On the other hand, the invasion of the Haitian market by second-hand clothing from the United States probably drove costs down and allowed Haitians to dress better. A visit to the environs of Port-au-Prince's Iron Market is an occasion for observing numerous violations of fashion etiquette and disregard for climatic conditions—e.g., Haitian beggars wearing wool overcoats in 90-degree weather—but that is a small price to pay in a county where per capita GDP is less than US$300 per year and the unemployment rate is at least 70 per cent.

[9] There is an alternative to reviving failed states, which is to let them collapse completely and redraw the political map of the world. This approach would presumably create new states, which would be either smaller or bigger than the defunct ones. (For an exposé of this view in the African context, see Herbst 2000.) In my view, the redrawing of the world's political map would create problems that are far more vexing than those that currently exist. As a result, my preference is for reviving collapsed states. Further, remapping the political world would probably intensify, not reduce, international community involvement. The case for greater UN participation therefore stands.

[10] Since the nation is an imagined concept, by definition it cannot be built. Thus, when American politicians speak against nation-building, they probably mean state-building. Of course, it is scarcely worth mentioning that the United States has been in the state-building business for a long time, beginning with bringing back the South into the fold after the American Civil War, the reconstruction of Japan and Germany after World War II to avoid their orbiting toward the former Soviet Union, the shoring up of South Korea in the 1950s on the shoulders of 37,000 US servicemen, the debacle in Vietnam, and the Gulf War, in which the United States undertook to reconstruct by military means a state (Kuwait) that had become the nineteenth province of another (Iraq) in a fortnight. The United States is not against state-building in all cases; it is against state-building in some cases (i.e., when American "national interests" are not at stake but American resources are requested by the international community).

[11] In 2000, Interpol had 373 employees and a budget of US$23m. The illegal drug trade alone is a US$400 bn "industry." The mismatch probably disappears if the budgets of national law enforcement agencies are added. However, this is a poor way of comparing the resources of international criminals to those of law enforcement, since, in the absence of bilateral agreements, national law enforcement agencies typically operate on their own. Interpol, by contrast, is designed to be transnational in scope.

[12] This chapter was written before the events of September 11, 2001. Since then there may have been a shift in U.S. attitude toward failed states and globalization. American leaders seem less opposed to "nation-building" now than they were before 9/11, as evidenced by their willingness to train and equip a new Afghan army: (Afghanistan, a failed state par excellence, having been the launching pad for Al Qaeda). In addition, in October 2001 the U.S. Congress did pass, and President George Bush did sign, legislation purporting to crack down on international money laundering in the context of the administration's so called war against terrorism. In sum, while the chapter was almost prescient in its analysis of the root causes of contemporary criminality on a transnational scale (i.e., the failed state and globalization), the events of 9/11 may have served to spur American interest

in reconstructing failed states and imposing greater state control on some aspects of globalization (e.g., capital flows). These are welcome developments for those of us who have been advocating them for years.

REFERENCES

Barboza, D. 2001. "Sugar Rules Defy Free-Trade Logic." *New York Times* (May 6): A1, A40.

Barnard, C. 1938. *The Functions of the Executive.* Cambridge: Harvard University Press.

Bayart, J.-F. 1999. "The 'Social Capital' of the Felonious State." Pp. 32–48 in *The Criminalization of the African State*, edited by J.-F. Bayart, S. Ellis, and B. Hibou. Bloomington: Indiana University Press.

Childers, E. and B. Urquhart. 1994. *Renewing the United Nations System.* Uppsala: Dag Hammarskjold Foundation.

de Brie, C. 1999. "Dans L'Archipel Planétaire de la Criminalité Financière." *Le Monde Diplomatique.*

Dowty, A. and G. Loescher. 1996. "Refugee Flows as Grounds for International Action." *International Security* 21(1): 43–41.

The Economist. 1998. "The Case for Global Finance." September 12.

Ekeh, P. 1975. "Colonialism and the Two Publics in Africa: A Theoretical Statement." *Comparative Studies in Society and History* 17: 91–112.

Fields, G. and M. Whitefield. 2001. "Tax Havens." *Miami Herald,* (April 10).

Clynn, P., S. Kobrin, and M. Naim. 1997. "The Globalization of Corruption." Pp. 7–27 in *Corruption and the Global Economy*, edited by Kimberly Ann Elliot, Washington, DC: Institute for International Economics.

Handelman, S. 1995. *Comrade Criminal: Russia's New Mafia.* New Haven: Yale University Press.

Herbst, J. 2000. *States and Power in Africa.* Princeton, NJ: Princeton University Press.

International Monetary Fund. 1999. *Report on Financial Sector Crisis and Restructuring: Lessons from Asia,* September 25. Washington, DC: IMF

Jones, D. 2001. "Report from Istanbul." *Weekend Edition on Sunday—National Public Radio,* April 29.

Katzenstein, P. 1985. *Small States in World Markets.* Ithaca and London: Cornell University Press.

Kendall, R. 2001. "Meet the World's Top Cop." *Foreign Policy* 122 (January/February): 31–40.

Maya, J. 2000. *World Politics—Progress and Its Limits.* Cambridge, UK: Polity Press.

Overseas Development Institute. 1988. "Development Efforts of NGOs." *Development: Journal of SID* 4: 41–46.

Scott, J.C. 1998. *Seeing Like a State.* New Haven: Yale University Press.

Sugisaki, S. 1999. "The Reform of Global Exchange and Financial Systems Since the Eruption of the Asian Crisis." International Conference on Central Banking, Macau, May 14.

United States Agency for International Development. 1979. *Managing Decentralization.* Washington, DC: US International Development Corporation Agency.

World Bank. 1975. *The Assault on Poverty.* Baltimore: Johns Hopkins University Press.

CHAPTER STUDY QUESTIONS

- What is a "failed state"? Why are failed states vulnerable to criminal activity?

- What is "globalization"? How is globalization implicated in the production of different forms of international economic crime and administrative crime in developing countries?

- What does Gros argue can be done to reduce types of criminality linked to failed states? To what extent do you agree with Gros's view on how failed states can be made less vulnerable to criminality? Why?

- What does Gros argue can be done to reduce types of criminality linked to globalization? To what extent do you agree with Gros's view on how globalization can be made less vulnerable to criminality? Why?

RELATED WEB LINKS

Globalization Studies Network GSN
http://gstudynet.com/
> The purpose of this website of an international network of globalization research centres is to bring together "worldwide scholars and practitioners who all share an interest in studying globalization collaboratively."

Global Policy Forum
http://www.globalpolicy.org/
> Founded in 1993 as a non-profit organization with consultative status at the United Nations, this organization is designed to "monitor policy making at the United Nations, promote accountability of global decisions, educate and mobilize for global citizen participation, and advocate on vital issues of international peace and justice."

Failed States
http://www.globalpolicy.org/nations/sovereign/failedindex.htm
> This site provides an extensive collection of historical and current information on failed states compiled by Global Policy Forum.

Terrorism, Transnational Crime and Corruption Center
http://www.american.edu/traccc/
> The website of this leading research centre on transnational organized crime is hosted by American University, Washington, DC. The site also features an extensive list of web links to information on corruption, money laundering, human trafficking, and terrorism.

PART 2

GLOBAL CRIME:
DEVELOPMENTS AND ISSUES

The chapters included in this section focus attention on important current developments and issues in the emerging field of global criminology and criminal justice. One of the common themes that runs through these chapters is an acknowledgment of the extent to which globalization has spawned many serious forms of global criminality that simply did not exist to the same extent even a few decades ago. While most of the chapters included here provide information on a number of these often new forms of criminality, each chapter focuses primarily on one particular form, explaining its global spread in recent years, elaborating upon specific case studies illustrative of such crimes, and proposing potential solutions to address some of their negative local, national, and global consequences.

In Chapter 4, David O. Friedrichs and Jessica Friedrichs address the issue of whether the actions taken by powerful international governance organizations, such as the World Bank and the International Monetary Fund, in the course of facilitating the implementation of neoliberal economic policies, amount to a new form of global economic crime. Specifically, the authors point to the often devastating effects the implementation of such policies have on those living in less economically developed countries. Like many other recent critics of these global governance institutions, Friedrichs and Friedrichs argue that "international financial institutions such as the World Bank are key players in an increasingly globalized capitalist system." In addition, they summon evidence to support the argument "that at least some of the policies and practices of the World Bank can be validly characterized as criminal." Consistent with the perspective offered by the authors of ensuing chapters in Part 2, Friedrichs and Friedrichs argue that the global "crimes" committed by the World Bank and other international governance institutions "can only be understood in the context of the notion of 'globalization.'" The authors recognize that globalization has not only economic but also political and cultural dimensions. At the same time, they argue it also has "winners" and "losers." Typically, however, the authors claim, "the winners are disproportionately wealthy multinational corporations and the losers are disproportionately poor and disadvantaged peoples, especially indigenous peoples in developing countries." In this way, "[g]lobalization contributes to an overall increase in economic inequality, fostering impoverishment and unemployment for many." As an illustrative case study of the role of the World Bank in perpetrating "crimes of globalization," Friedrichs and Friedrichs document the case of the World Bank's participation in financing the construction of a large hydropower generating dam at Pak Mun Thailand, which had devastating economic and environmental consequences for local villagers. Friedrichs and Friedrichs maintain that the Pak Mun Dam debacle is only one of the many instances in which the World Bank has been complicit in implementing neo-liberal economic development policies and practices that have had "the interests of the advanced industrialized nations and the Wall Street financial community as their highest priority." In addition to offering a case study that documents a current type of global criminality perpetrated by an international governance institution, the authors contend that their account "also serves as a cautionary tale for a globalized future" and as strong justification of the need for a "truly globalized criminology."

In Chapter 5, Michael Gilbert and Steve Russell tackle the growing problem of transnational corporate crime and call for the development of mechanisms of "global justice" in order to protect the public interest against corporations that commit these types of crimes. According to Gilbert and Russell, globalization has created new opportunities for transnational corporate crime, defined broadly as avoidable harms inflicted across national borders for purposes of economic gain. The authors re-examine theories of corporate criminal liability in the transnational context and draw attention to the French codification of corporate criminal liability in the 1990s as model legislation that deals with corporate crime in terms broad enough to encompass the new economic realities of an increasingly globalized world. Finally, they examine the inability of current adjudicative fora, including the Permanent International Court of Justice, ad hoc tribunals, and the new International Criminal Court, to assert jurisdiction effectively over transnational corporations. Gilbert's and Russell's analysis leads them to conclude that "economic globalization has opened opportunities for corporate criminality on a grand scale" while, for the most part, individual nation states have largely ignored this problem in comparison to the attention they have given to combating transnational "street crime" and terrorism. In order to more effectively address the growing problem of transnational corporate crime and foster social justice in the international arena, Gilbert and Russell call for the establishment of "[a]n international court, armed with a penal code tailored to transnational corporate crime and international conventions to provide authoritative jurisdiction over transnational corporate criminal conduct."

Other related issues that have begun to receive increased attention from global criminologists in recent years are the growth of sex tourism and the illegal trafficking of human beings—mainly women—for the purposes of prostitution. These topics are addressed in detail by Nancy Wonders and Raymond Michalowski in Chapter 6, which compares the development of sex tourism in Amsterdam and Havana, and by Peter Mameli in Chapter 7, which examines the role that transnational policing can play in stemming the flow of forced prostitution.

According to Wonders and Michalowski, the application of the term "'[s]ex tourism' highlights the convergence between prostitution and tourism, links the global and the local, and draws attention to both the production and consumption of sexual services." In Chapter 6,

Wonders and Michalowski undertake a critical examination of the "global forces" that have shaped the production and consumption of sex tourism in recent decades, both internationally and within the context of two very different cities, Amsterdam and Havana. By examining sex tourism as a product of global forces, the authors attempt to shift attention from the standard view of individual "prostitutes" as social problems, to "'sex tourism' as a form of global commerce that is transforming sex work, cities, and human relationships." According to Wonders and Michalowski, globalization has contributed to the growth of sex tourism by causing an increase in the movement of people across borders as the poor migrate in search of work or safety and the rich travel the globe as tourists in ever-larger numbers. Among other consequences is the outcome of "facilitating the commodification of both male desire and women's bodies within the global capitalist economy." The authors' first-hand ethnographic research on the operation of sex tourism industries in Amsterdam and Havana demonstrates that, while there are important local differences, patterns of sex tourism in each locale are increasingly over-determined by global economic forces, connecting the practice of sex work in both cities with the broader phenomenon of globalized sex tourism.

In Chapter 7, Peter Mameli examines another key dimension of the global sex industry that is not directly addressed by Wonders and Michalowski. He considers the fact that many of the women involved in the industry have either been enticed by false promises or forced against their will to enter the sex trade. According to Mameli, this is exemplified, in particular, in Eastern Europe, where the transnational sex industry experienced a surge in the 1990s with the break-up of the former Soviet Union. Mameli draws attention to the virtual enslavement of a growing number of women into the global prostitution market from Eastern Europe, a phenomenon that has begun to be documented in an ongoing manner by independent non-governmental organizations that track migration patterns and international criminal activity. He also highlights the increasing attention that national governments and international governmental organizations such as the United Nations are now focusing on the issue from local and global perspectives. In addition, Mameli gives close attention to examining the various roles that transnational police organizations can play, and have been playing, in preventing and investigating activities of the transnational sex industry, particularly in the context of Europe and in the development of increased European police cooperation through the agencies of Interpol and Europol. After sketching the scope of the problem, identifying players of interest, and examining the roles that they have been performing to date, Mameli offers recommendations for strengthening the response of police organizations to illegal human trafficking for the global sex industry. Mameli argues that as a first important step in this effort, "Interpol and Europol must actively participate in the United Nations Global Programme Against Trafficking in Human Beings in order to flesh out the full range of problems associated with trafficking and fully identify the role and characteristics of globalization in this area, including the complete range of its winners and losers."

Chapter 4

THE WORLD BANK AND CRIMES OF GLOBALIZATION: A CASE STUDY

DAVID O. FRIEDRICHS AND JESSICA FRIEDRICHS

INTRODUCTION

The basic issue addressed in this chapter can be concisely stated: Are the policies and practices of an international financial institution (the World Bank), arising in the context of an accelerated globalization, usefully characterized as a form of crime and a criminological phenomenon? What kinds of strategies and actions are available in response to the harm caused by these policies and practices?[1] International financial institutions such as the World Bank are key players in an increasingly globalized capitalist system. The claim that capitalism itself is a criminal enterprise is, of course, an enduring thesis of Marxist thought (e.g., Buchanan 1983).[2] Moreover, some contemporary critics of globalization—as a transnational expansion of capitalist free markets—seem to suggest that globalization per se is a criminal enterprise that ought to be challenged on every level. We do not propose to pursue such sweeping claims here. Rather, we address the narrower claim that at least some of the policies and practices of the World Bank can be validly characterized as criminal. To support our case, we provide a case history of a World Bank-financed dam in Thailand.

A PERSPECTIVE ON GLOBALIZATION

The policies and practices of international financial institutions such as the World Bank, the World Trade Organization, and the International Monetary Fund can only be understood in the context of the notion of "globalization." The invocation of that term has become ubiquitous, and the literature on globalization has expanded exponentially in the recent era, although its meaning is far from settled (Chase-Dunn et al. 2000; Dunne 1999: 20; Hay and Marsh 2000).[3] The term "globalization" has been in wide use since the 1960s (Busch 2000: 22). In one sense, globalization is hardly a new phenomenon, if one means by it the emergence of international trade and a transnational economic order.[4] Yet globalization has become a buzzword of the transition into the era of the new century due to the widely perceived intensification of certain developments (Mazlish 1999: 5).[5] It is not simply an economic phenomenon, although it is most readily thought of in such terms.[6] Globalization also has important political and cultural dimensions (Chase-Dunn et al. 2000; Mazlish 1999: 7).[7] The phenomenal growth in the importance and influence of transnational corporations, nongovernmental organizations, intergovernmental organizations, international financial institutions, and special interest groups is a conspicuous dimension of contemporary globalization (Mazlish 1999; Shapiro and Brilmayer 1999; Valaskakis 1999).[8] Ordinary people lose control over their economic destiny (Greider 1997). World markets increasingly overshadow national markets, barriers to trade are reduced, and instant tele- and cyber-transactions are becoming the norm (Blackett 1998; Chase-Dunn et al. 2000; Jackson 2000; Scheuerman 1999). In the broadest possible terms, globalization today refers to the dramatic compression of time and space across the globe.

We accept here the view that globalization as a phenomenon is endlessly complex, is characterized by various contradictory tendencies and ambiguities, and is best seen as a dynamic process as opposed to a static state of affairs (McCorquodale with Fairbrother 1999: 733).[9] The contemporary discourse on globalization is quite contentious, characterized by claims about the effects of globalization that are often directly at odds with each other (Busch 2000). On the one hand, certain aspects of globalization—such as increasing global communication and interaction—are surely inevitable. On the other hand, the mission and policy choices of international financial institutions, in relation to the globalized economy, are hardly preordained and are very much open to challenge. Some commentators argue that globalization has basically increased living standards in much of the world and that countries experiencing a rise in standards of living have done so by linking up with a globalized economy (Amsden 2000; Easterlin 2000; Zakaria 1999). No one should dispute the claim that there are many "winners" in the move toward an increasingly globalized economy. However, we strongly agree with those who allege that the winners are disproportionately wealthy multinational corporations and the losers are disproportionately poor and disadvantaged peoples, especially indigenous peoples in developing countries (Frank 2000).[10] Globalization contributes to an overall increase in economic inequality, fostering impoverishment and unemployment for many (Carrasco 1996; George 2000; Kahn 2000b; McCorquodale with Fairbrother 1999: 747; Shapiro and Brilmayer 1999: 2).[11] It has been characterized as a new form of the ancient practice of colonization (Dunne 1999: 22).[12] Falk (1993) argues that the logic of globalization is dictated by the well-being of capital rather than of people. Altogether, globalization is affecting human society in many different ways.[13]

Globalization has many dimensions, but the following are most pertinent to the thesis of this chapter:

1. The growing global dominance and reach of neoliberalism and a free-market capitalist system that disproportionately benefits wealthy and powerful organizations and individuals;
2. The increasing vulnerability of indigenous people with a traditional way of life to the forces of globalized capitalism;
3. The growing influence and impact of international financial institutions (such as the World Bank) and the related relative decline of power of local or state-based institutions; and

4. The nondemocratic operation of international financial institutions, taking the form of globalization from above instead of globalization from below.

THE ROLE OF THE WORLD BANK IN A GLOBAL ECONOMY

The international financial institutions that play such a central role in contemporary global-ization have become prime targets for criticism for their policies and practices in the global economy. These international financial institutions include the World Trade Organization, the International Monetary Fund, and the World Bank. Each entity has a different key mis-sion, with the World Trade Organization primarily focused on fostering trade, the International Monetary Fund on maximizing financial stability, and the World Bank on promoting develop-ment (Stiglitz 2001). Of course, these institutions have many ties with each other, and the lines of demarcation between their activities can become quite blurred. Collectively, much evidence suggests that they have acted principally in response to the interests of developed countries and their privileged institutions, rather than in the interests of the poor (Phillips 2000; Sjoherg et al. 2001; Smith and Moran 2000; Stiglitz 2001). In this chapter, we focus principally on the activi-ties of one of these institutions, the World Bank, because it played a key role in the particular case addressed here.

The World Bank (formally, the International Bank for Reconstruction and Development, or IBRD) was established at the Bretton Woods Conference in 1944 to help stabilize and rebuild economies ravaged by World War II. Eventually it shifted its focus to an emphasis on aiding developing nations (Johnson 2000). The Bank makes loans to governments of its member na-tions and to private development projects backed by the government. Projects are supposed to benefit the citizens of the country receiving Bank loans, which are made at a favorable rate of interest. The World Bank (2000) generally claims to contribute to the reduction of poverty and improved living standards in developing countries. Today the Bank is a large, international operation, with over 10,000 employees, 180 member states, and annual loans of some 30 billion dollars (Finnegan 2000: 44). Historically, the World Bank itself has been the principal source of information about its operations and programs; inevitably, such internally generated informa-tion can be strongly suspected of being self-serving (Rich 1994).

The World Bank was established (along with the International Monetary Fund) at the be-hest of the dominant Western nations, with little if any real input from the developing countries (Kapstein 1998/1999: 28). It is disproportionately influenced or manipulated by elite economic institutions and has been characterized as an agent of global capital (Greider 2000b: 15). In the developing countries, it deals primarily with the political and economic elites of those coun-tries, with little direct attention to the perspectives and needs of indigenous peoples, a practice for which it has been criticized by U.S. senators (Caulfield 1996: 227; Rich 1994: 145). It has had a record of lending money to ruthless military dictatorships (engaged in murder and torture), after having denied loans to democratic governments overthrown by the military (Rich 1994: 99). It favors strong dictatorships over struggling democracies because it believes that the former are more able to introduce and see through the unpopular reforms its loans require (Caufield

1996: 209). Borrowers of money from the World Bank typically are political elites of developing countries, and their cronies, although the repayment of the debt becomes the responsibility of people in these countries, most of whom do not benefit from the loans.[14] In this reading, then, the privileged benefit disproportionately from dealings with the World Bank, relative to the poor.[15]

CRIMINOLOGY AND CRIMES OF GLOBALIZATION

Most criminologists have paid little if any attention to the phenomenon of globalization and international financial institutions such as the World Bank, although some prominent criminologists have called for more attention to globalization as a new context within which crime must be understood.[16] Progressive or critical criminologists—writing in journals such as *Social Justice* and *Crime, Law, and Social Change*—have been especially attuned to the relevance of an evolving global economy to understanding crime and criminal justice issues.[17] A criminology of the 21st century must address immensely consequential forms of crime being committed in an evolving new global order.

If we claim here that it is useful to view at least some of the activities of the World Bank as criminal, an operative definition of crime must be established. First, we adopt the view that a valid definition of crime need not be limited to those actions clearly defined as crime by state law.[18] Some attempts to define crime have broken completely with a legalistic framework, on any level.[19] A core argument of those who reject the purely legalistic definition of crime is that criminologists should not restrict their study of crime to that which is defined by state law as crime, insofar as state-defined crime is ideologically biased and fails to address a wide range of objectively identifiable forms of harm.[20]

That powerful entities (including international financial institutions) are in a strong position to influence national (and international) law has long been recognized (Passas, 1999: 401). In an increasingly globalized world, we need to adopt conceptions of crime that transcend limitations of traditional state-based law. Crime itself is increasingly a transnational or global phenomenon. Nikos Passas (2000: 17–18) offers the following definition of transnational crime: "... cross-border misconduct that entails avoidable and unnecessary harm to society, is serious enough to warrant state intervention, and is similar to other kinds of acts criminalized in the countries concerned or by international law." Such a definition offers a specific starting point for a conception of crime that transcends the limitations of conventional, legalistic definitions within a state-based context. For our purposes here, if international financial institutions adopt policies and practices that violate the provisions of international human rights accords and covenants, they may be said to be complicit in a form of crime. The United Nations International Covenant on Economic, Social, and Cultural Rights (1966), for example, holds that:

> All peoples have the right of self-determination. By virtue of the right they freely determine their political status and freely pursue their economic, social, and cultural development.... In no case may a people be deprived of its own means of subsistence. (United Nations 1966: 225)

Because they are not states, international financial institutions such as the World Bank are not technically bound by this U.N. covenant, but the states to which they have made loans have generally ratified the covenant (Stark 2000: 536–537). Even if these states have done little, if anything, to enforce the economic covenant, willful failures by the international financial institutions and the states to comply with these standards may be regarded as crimes in terms of the conception offered above. Accordingly, if the policies and practices of an international financial institution such as the World Bank result in avoidable, unnecessary harm to an identifiable population, and if these policies lead to violation of widely recognized human rights and international covenants, then crime in a meaningful sense has occurred, whether or not specific violations of international or state law are involved. The failure to characterize the forms of harm perpetrated by international financial institutions as crime tends to dilute the seriousness of such activity.

EXTENDING CRIME TYPOLOGIES TO ENCOMPASS CRIMES OF GLOBALIZATION

The most readily recognized categories of criminal activity include violent personal crime, conventional crime, organized crime, professional crime, and public order—or victimless—crime. Although Sutherland's call for more attention to white-collar crime was not widely embraced for several decades, for some time now the categories of corporate crime and occupational crime have been accepted in some form by professional criminologists, the media, and the public. The senior author has argued elsewhere that certain hybrid or marginal types of white-collar crime—such as state-corporate crime, finance crime, technocrime, enterprise crime, contrepreneurial crime, and avocational crime—merit wider recognition (Friedrichs 1996). Although, in one sense, state crime (e.g., genocide) and political white-collar crime (e.g., accepting bribes) have been long recognized, these forms of crime have been largely slighted by criminologists and viewed by the public and the media as fundamentally disconnected from "the crime problem." A number of criminologists have recently called for more attention to state crime in particular as a significant criminological phenomenon (e.g., Friedrichs 1998; Ross 1995; Kauzlarich and Kramer 1998; Green and Ward 2000). The form of crime addressed here does not fit neatly into any of the existing categories, however. It incorporates elements of state crime, political white-collar crime, state-corporate crime, and finance crime, in particular.[21] In addition, it suggests the need to adapt existing, widely adopted typologies of crime to encompass such activities, prospectively labeled global or transnational state-finance crime. Such crime involves cooperative endeavors between international financial institutions, transnational corporations, and state or political entities that engage in demonstrably harmful activities in violation of international law or international human rights conventions.

If some of the policies and activities of the international financial institutions are specifically characterized as a form of crime, this provides a conceptual framework for systematically exploring parallels and differences, as well as interconnections, with other forms of crime. It facilitates the application of criminological knowledge to this form of crime and contributes to the development of a truly globalized criminology.

A CASE STUDY: THE DANI AT PAK MUN (THAILAND)

> The villagers are not against development. We are against violating rights.
> We're against organizations using their power over the governments of the
> people so that the people don't have a place to live or food to eat.—Mae
> Sompong, villager affected by Pak Mun Dam (in Vienchang 2000: 49)

From December 2000 to April 2001, the junior author lived intermittently at the Assembly of
the Poor Pak Mun (Moon) dam protest village just outside Ubon Ratchatani, Northeastern
Thailand.[22] During this time, she acted as a participant-observer in daily village meetings,
various protests, and marches throughout the country. She interviewed five villagers in great
depth about their experiences with the dam. Interviews were also conducted with local Energy
Generating Authority of Thailand officials, World Bank representatives, international and Thai
nongovernmental organization workers involved in dam or development issues, and Thai academics researching the subject. As an observer, she noted the daily futility of fishing in the Mun
River, as well as the severe economic hardship faced by the villagers. Statistics and other data
related to the issue were obtained from the "World Commission on Dams Report for 2000," the
Bangkok Post newspaper, International Rivers Network publications, and World Bank sources.
At the time of the protest, Thai academics as well as World Bank and government officials
were becoming increasingly aware of the need to weigh affected villagers' concerns as heavily
as environmental and socioeconomic data. In the following case study, dam-affected villagers
present their concerns about the Pak Mun project. Factual data supports their claims. The
project history covers the environmental and socioeconomic damage caused by the dam, and
the protest history outlines the villagers' response to the dam. The entire study centers on the
role and responsibility of the World Bank in this controversy.

History of the project

The World Bank became involved in hydropower dam projects in the late 1970s and 1980s
as part of structural adjustment policies that fostered production industries. The World Bank
approved the Pak Mun dam loan in 1991 to support a shift in Thailand's economy toward export-oriented industrialization (Tyler 2000: 14, 23). Classified as a large dam, it was originally
slated to produce 150 megawatts of energy; since its completion in 1994, however, it has not
generated more than 40 megawatts over a given peak period. Construction costs soared from an
original estimate of U.S. $135 million to an actual cost of U.S. $233 million (World Commission
on Dams 2000). The World Bank contributed a $23 million loan and was involved in many
facets of the project from the beginning (Tyler 2000:14). The Electricity Generating Authority
of Thailand (EGAT) oversaw the project and consulted with the Thai government throughout construction. Among the original goals of the dam were energy generation, irrigation for
nearby farmland, and an increase in fisheries, but the latter have been adversely affected. More

important, the entire process, from loan to construction to operation, took place without input from the many fishing communities along the river. Today, these villagers have lost their livelihood and community due to the dam's destruction of the river ecosystem.

The Mun River is a large tributary of the mighty Mekong River, which snakes through much of Southeast Asia. For generations, villagers living in the rural plateau area of Northeast Thailand along the Mun River sustained their communities through fishing, using fish to barter for rice from farmers nearby. Villagers depended on the complex system of rapids, watershed, and forest for everything in their lives. Yet when TEAM, a World Bank-approved group, conducted the first Environmental Impact Assessments (EIAs) for dam construction in 1982, villagers were not even made aware of the impending plans. One villager did not learn of the dam until 1985, when the construction plans that would affect her entire community and future were announced on the radio. Early on, the villagers were concerned about the effect the dam would have on their livelihoods, but government officials and EGAT and World Bank representatives never addressed their concerns (Vienchang 2000: 18). The EIA itself has been highly criticized. Dams by nature create detrimental effects on the watershed environment surrounding a river, including flooding farmland with reservoirs, submerging natural forests, and preventing the natural migration of fish upstream. In the case of Pak Mun, these issues were magnified by the lack of proper EIAs and pre-construction studies, and the push to complete the project quickly regardless of villagers concerns.

Environmental damage

The EIA at Pak Mun was carried out in 1982 when the World Bank accepted EGAT's proposal to allow TEAM to conduct the studies. Since the consultants were chosen and hired through the Office of Environmental Planning and Policy, a Thai Government body, the developer institution can apply pressure to ensure the EIA is to their liking (Vallabhaneni 2000: 8). This issue, compounded with simple logistics, made for problematic EIAs in the case of Pak Mun. Logistically, the EIA discovered that the original dam site would flood a large portion of national forest, so they proposed to move the dam a few kilometers upstream and lower the dam's overall height. They saw no reason to conduct a new EIA after making these changes because any changes based on environmental concerns alone were considered a major accomplishment within the bank. After completion, the dam's new position was discovered to have serious effects on river life.

First, the dam still flooded a portion of forestland (community forest), violating the bank's own policies on the destruction of cultural property. The World Commission on Dams (2000: 4) report—an independent global evaluation of dams—estimates that at least 40 edible plants, 45 mushroom species, and 10 bamboo species harvested by locals for subsistence and household meals were lost. These plants, overlooked by almost all EIA reports, provided income at local markets and had medicinal usages.

From previous dam experiences, the EIA TEAM group knew the stagnant water created by the dam's reservoir would affect the health of local people. Therefore, the EIA made provisions for parasitic river fluke mitigation, but fewer than 30 per cent of the plans for monitoring the disease have been implemented (Vallabhaneni 2000: 10). Water plants such as hyacinth, which choke up the river, have collected around the dam site, and villagers living in the area are experiencing adverse health effects when they use the river. Traditionally, villagers used river water for most of their daily needs—drinking, bathing, and washing laundry—but today the villagers complain of skin rashes whenever they try to use it.

The blasting of the river's natural rapids, particularly a large one named Geng Supurr that now trickles by uneventfully, is another major concern of the villagers. The World Commission on Dams (2000: 4) reports that more than 50 of Pak Mun's natural rapids have been permanently submerged. Villagers know that the rapids are responsible for oxygenating the water and serve as pools of energy for the fish system. The blasting of rapids around the dam site was extremely questionable since the rapids are technically part of protected forest. The rapids were known to be the habitats of some 20 species of fish, but since no baseline data on fish populations were collected, we cannot be sure of the economic loss due to decline in fish.

The severe decline in fish population that has plagued the surrounding community and ecosystem since the dam's completion was the most devastating effect on the Mun River environment. Peak fish migration, when fish swim upstream to spawn, takes place at the start of the rainy season (May to July), a period in which the dam's flood gates are rarely opened. Due to the blockage of the dam, fish species have declined in the last few years from the 265 species recorded in the Mun watershed before 1994 to only 96 species found upstream of the dam. Therefore, the dam has affected 169 species of fish, with 56 vanishing through extinction. The annihilation of the way of life of these indigenous fishermen, who depended on the abundant fish for food and income, followed. According to the Project for Ecological Recovery, the number of families obtaining income from Mun River fisheries has declined by 75 per cent and the average daily fish catches for family subsistence have decreased by 30 per cent (Vallabhaneni 2000: 9). One villager remembers being able to catch 40 to 50 fish, weighing many kilograms, just by laying her nets in the river only a few years ago. The junior author's observation of villagers in 1999 found them spending an entire day fishing, only to come home with two tiny fish. The World Commission on Dams Report (2000: 7) notes that the 1981 EIA produced inadequate baseline information because studies should have covered different seasons over a two-year time frame and natural fluctuations in abundance of fish should have been monitored. Socioeconomically, the study should have identified the dependency of the local population on fisheries.

Social harm

For fishermen who had relied on the river their entire lives, the environmental damage created by the dam was dramatic. The problems were compounded by the Thai government, EGAT, and the World Bank's unjust handling of resettlement issues. The World Bank's operational directive on involuntary resettlement stresses that potential resettlement issues should be dispatched with early in the evaluation process. Yet qualitative issues of right to livelihood, sustainable economy, and community structure can often be manipulated to suit the project design, since they are inherently much more difficult to define. At Pak Mun, the physical resettlement of villagers who lost their land to flooding was appraised, and compensation was supplied to those affected, but the figures regarding the meaning of "affected" are hotly disputed. World Bank reports claimed 989 families would lose some land and housing, but only 200 would have to resettle because of the dam (Vallabhaneni 2000: 12). The World Commission on Dams (2000: 3) reported on predictions that the dam and reservoir would affect 31 villages, with a direct impact on 241 households. Yet it found that 1,700 households actually lost a house, land, or both. Their figures are much higher because they account for houses affected by the loss of fishing income upstream and downstream of the dam. Beyond flooding and loss of income, the overflow of water from the dam has surrounded some villages, creating difficulties for transportation, farming, and general access through their communities. Further, those building and funding the dam have made culturally insensitive arrangements for those truly dislodged by it. For example, in Ban Hoi Hay, a strip of 11 houses built as "compensation" along a patch of highway far from the river, the one-room houses, which are stacked up on stilts, fail to provide for the traditional Thai family (including extended relatives) living under one roof. Water, previously obtained from the nearby river, now comes through unreliable pipes, leaving the villagers without options if the supply is disrupted.

History of the protest

Villagers along the river witnessed the disintegration of their communities as fish populations declined and difficulties in finding basic sustenance mounted. Able-bodied family members, including young children, left school and the community to find work in big cities like Bangkok. With little formal education, the employment choices of the former fishermen were limited to the most undesirable jobs, such as searching through landfills for recyclable materials. Dissatisfied villagers demanded more for the loss of their land and houses, and after participating in the Assembly of the Poor protest for 99 days in Bangkok, they received some monetary compensation. Yet, as villagers told the junior author, the money was destructive to their community because they were not familiar with managing it. Without land for planting rice or rivers to fish, it was useless. The ideology guiding World Bank development projects such as dams that export energy is that they create a better, more secure future for villagers. Yet, without consultation, villagers are rapidly thrust into a money economy in areas not structured to absorb new employees, such as the rural northeastern area of Thailand around the Mun River.

As the money ran out, villagers became more aware of the struggles they faced due to the lack of fish, inundated farmland, and disintegrating communities. A group of over 5,000 people came together in March 1999 to set up a protest community beside the dam. Between then and March 2000, various villagers from nearby dams came to protest alongside them, and four protest villages were created in response to other dam issues. Instead of compensation, villagers demanded that the dam gates be opened to allow fish to spawn in the river

Throughout the process, the government marginalized and often misled villagers on the future. The original announcement of the dam, one villager recalls, claimed they would be able to plant two or three rice crops a year (instead of the typical one), although this dam never had irrigation capabilities (World Commission Dams 2000: 1). No villagers the junior author spoke with remember being warned of the negative consequences. Villagers who spoke out against the dam early on (in the form of protest) were physically attacked and restricted by government-hired neighbors.

> The World Bank, you have a lot of money, but wherever you invest there is destruction. I want you, if you are building, or developing, or investing in some underdeveloped country, I want you to see the humanity, to not violate the rights of people, to not violate the environment of those who live with nature. You adversely affect their lives, their communities, and cause their culture to crumble. What you have done already, you must fix. Whatever you have destroyed of ours, you must cure it. (Mae Sompong, villager affected by Pak Mun dam, in Vienchang 2000: 48)

A postscript

On July 17, 2000, Thai police under Prime Minister Chuan Leekpai forcibly removed Assembly of the Poor protesters from the area around Government House in Bangkok and arrested 200 of them (South-East Asia Rivers Network 2000). The villagers responded with a mass hunger strike, and both parties met on numerous occasions to discuss the opening of the dam gates, with no resolution. By spring of 2001, a new prime minister had been elected and talks seemed more promising. On May 26, 2001, Prime Minister Thanksin Sninawarta promised to open the Pak Mun gates for a four-month trial period, to determine the impact on fishing. Although representatives from the World Bank visited the dam site and protest village in the spring of 2000, the World Bank has played no role in addressing villagers concerns to date.

THE WORLD BANK AND CRIMES OF GLOBALIZATION

The World Bank has been criticized for being paternalistic, secretive, and counterproductive in terms of any claimed goal of improving people's lives. Specifically, it has been charged with being complicit in policies with genocidal consequences, with exacerbating ethnic conflict, with increasing the gap between rich and poor, with fostering immense ecological and environmental damage, and with the callous displacement of vast numbers of indigenous people in developing countries from their original homes and communities (Rich 1994: xii, 16, 30, 93, 151). Critics claim that many of the less-developed countries that received World Bank loans are worse off today in terms of poverty, and that the severe austerity measures imposed on borrowing countries, deemed necessary to maximize the chances of Bank loans being repaid, most heavily affect the poorest and most vulnerable segments of the population (Johnson 2000).

The most favored World Bank project has been the building of dams, but even its own experts concede that millions of people have been displaced because of these projects (Caufield 1996: 12, 73). In many of these projects, resettlement plans have been nonexistent—violating the Bank's own guidelines—or have been inadequately implemented. In a notorious case from the 1970s, in which antidam protesters in Guatemala were massacred by the military, the World Bank report on the project failed to directly mention the atrocity (Caufield 1996: 207–208, 263). Given such circumstances, claims of criminality have been leveled against the World Bank. At a 1988 World Bank meeting in Berlin, protesters called for the establishment of a Permanent People's Tribunal to try the World Bank (and the International Monetary Fund) for "crimes against humanity" (Rich 1994: 9). An American anthropologist characterized the forced resettlement of people in dam-related projects as the worst crime against them, short of killing them (Caufield 1996: 262). An American biologist characterized the World Bank's report on the environmental impact of one of its dam projects in a developing country as "fraudulent" and "criminal" (Rich 1994: 11–12). These allegations are certainly applicable to the Pak Mun dam discussed here.

The World Bank's complicity in the crimes outlined above is best understood in terms of its criminogenic structure and organization. The historical charge of its charter called upon it to focus on economic developments and considerations, not the other consequences of its policies and practices (Rich 1994: 199). Throughout its history, it has thus avoided addressing or taking a strong stand on human rights issues (Caufield 1996: 206). Its focus on a less than well-defined mission of promoting "long-term sustainable growth" has served as a rationale for imposing much short-term suffering and economic losses (Rich 1994: 189). This orientation has led the World Bank to adopt and apply somewhat one-dimensional economic models to its project-related analyses, with insufficient attention to many other considerations and potentially useful insights from other disciplines (Rich 1994: 195). Once the projects are initiated, they tend to develop a momentum of their own that often marginalizes or negates any real adjustments in response to reports indicating negative environmental or social effects (Vallabhaneni 2000: 11). The underlying incentive structure at the Bank encourages "success" with large, costly projects. Bank employees are pressured to make the environmental (as well as social) conditions fit. Like other international financial institutions, the World Bank is structured so that it rewards its personnel for technical proficiency rather than for concerning themselves with the perspectives and needs of the ordinary people of developing countries (Bradlow 1996: 75).[23]

In terms of their career interests, World Bank officials are rewarded for making loans and moving large amounts of money, rather than relative to any human consequences of these loans. Furthermore, World Bank personnel have not been held accountable for the tragic human consequences of their projects (Rich 1994: 91, 307). All of these institutional factors contribute to a criminogenic environment.

Insofar as the World Bank is not a signatory to international human rights treaties, it has manifested relatively little concern with human rights abuses (Bradlow 1996: 63). International financial institutions are, however, subject to the imperatives of international law and, at a minimum, are obliged to insure that they do not exacerbate conditions impinging on human rights. Most of the countries with which they have dealings have ratified the U.N.'s Economic Covenants, and accordingly should be bound by its provisions.

Our claim is not that the World Bank adopts policies or makes loan-related decisions with the intent or objective of causing harm. The case can be made that at least some World Bank policymakers sincerely hope to achieve positive results, to foster development and reduce the scope of poverty (Caufield 1996; Rich 1994). Furthermore, voices within the World Bank during the recent era have questioned or challenged some World Bank policies and practices that appear to have had harmful consequences. Policies are being examined now through the Bank's internal departments that will more clearly define the Bank's influence (or lack of it) after a project has been completed. This influence may be monetary, such as providing compensation for mistakes made. It may also be based on leverage to pressure governments to take responsibility for a project, leverage that propelled these projects from the start. However, many critics—and even the former chief economist of the World Bank, Joseph Stiglitz (2000, 2001)—contend that the policies and practices of the World Bank and other international financial institutions have adopted the interests of the advanced industrialized nations and the Wall Street financial community as their highest priority. Without checks in the Bank's procedures, it can continue to encourage, fund, and assess development projects that do not support the goals of a country's people (yet continuously prop up powerful government and big business). Ideologically, the World Bank creates and contributes to the general concept of "development" by funding only a certain kind of development. For the past 50 years, the World Bank has invested in large, export-oriented projects such as pipelines and dams that cause severe environmental upheaval and penalize the very people they claim they wish to help: the poor.

A characteristic of significant forms of white-collar crime (including much corporate crime) is that the harm involved is a consequence, not a specific objective, of certain policy choices and practices. As with other forms of white-collar crime, the harmful (or illegal) activity associated with the crimes of international financial institutions occurs within the context of productive, legal activity; it is a byproduct of efforts to achieve gain, avoid loss, or advance some other legitimate organizational objective, with such objectives taking precedence over other considerations. Legitimate organizations do respond at times to claims that they are engaging in harmful (or illegal) activities, as in the case of the World Bank. Yet such responses may simply be cynical (purely for public relations purposes), strategic (to maximize chances of achieving major objectives), political (in deference to internal coalitions, or as necessary compromises), or sincere (authentically concerned with pursuing the most morally and ethically defensible policies). With organizations such as the World Bank, a complex combination of responses is surely involved.

In sum, we do not contend that the specific intent and purpose of the policies of the World Bank is to do harm. However, we hold that the World Bank's mode of operation is intrinsically criminogenic and that it functions undemocratically; its key deliberations are carried out behind a veil of secrecy, and it is insufficiently accountable to any truly independent entity. At a minimum, the World Bank is criminally negligent when it: (1) fails to adequately explore or take into account the impact of its loans for major projects on indigenous peoples; (2) adopts and implements policies specifically at odds with the protocols of the *Universal Declaration of Human Rights* and subsequent covenants; or (3) operates in a manner at least hypothetically at odds with international and state law.

THE SOCIAL MOVEMENT AGAINST INTERNATIONAL FINANCIAL INSTITUTIONS

The anti-globalization movement has targeted the World Bank, the WTO, and the IMF. The movement includes a broad range of constituencies—"an effervescent and troublesome cauldron of peasants, women, environmentalists, human rights activists, indigenous people, religious activists, and other individuals" (Rajagopal 2000: 539). Each has a somewhat different agenda. Some protesters have invoked the notion of "crime" in an attempt to characterize the activities of the international financial institutions.[24] In general, though, the anti-globalization protests in Seattle, Washington, D.C., Prague, and Quebec have been animated by a concern with the alleged harmful consequences of globalization and the activities of the international financial institutions, rather than with claims of criminality. Our premise is that successfully imposing a label of "criminal" on some activities of international financial institutions could broaden the appeal of the anti-globalization movement and lend support to the case for formally adjudicating these claims in an appropriate international body.

The anti-globalization protest movement may have influenced international financial institutions to undertake internal reforms and to incorporate matters such as poverty and environmental protection into their agendas (Gitlin 2000; Rajagopal 2000). Evidence from recent news stories suggests that protests in Seattle, Washington, D.C., and elsewhere have had an impact.[25] Globalization and its effects were the top agenda item in the Millennium Meeting of world leaders at the United Nations in September 2000 (Crossette 2000b).[26] It remained to be seen, however, whether the powerful nations of the world would seriously attempt to address the criminality inherent in the activities of the international financial institutions, or would principally direct their efforts toward deflecting and confronting protests against such activity.

CONCLUSION

Globalization, as defined here, is an increasingly important dimension of the context within which crime of all types occurs. We have argued that the World Bank can be viewed as engaging in a noteworthy form of criminal activity and that it is necessary and useful to view some of its policies and practices this way. Raising consciousness about the criminal dimensions of the activities of international financial institutions ideally fosters the application of comparative criminological frameworks to these phenomena and directs activist responses to it on behalf of those most harmed by present trends.

The term "globalization" is elusive and multifaceted; although globalization is a real and dramatic intensification of existing international patterns, we need not accept its current direction as inevitable. Critics of present global developments call for the development of popular accountability on the part of national and global institutions, for more public control over these institutions, for a true internationalism, and for just alternatives to the criminal activities of international financial institutions (Crossette 2000a; Frank 2000: 16, 19; Hutton and Giddens 2000; Lemisch 2000: 10). Ideally, external pressures on international financial institutions such as the World Bank will lead to substantive internal reforms, or to the demise of such institutions.

What is the role of law in responding to the crimes of globalization? Although law and legal forms play a central role in facilitating the global exchange of persons, capital, and culture, the place of justice in this world order is not clear (Silbey 1997). Advancing human rights demands its own law, one that is independent of national law and sometimes deliberately at odds with states (Teubner 1997; Williams 1990: 660). A movement on behalf of indigenous peoples seeks to establish a universal declaration of such rights, quite independent of the law established by conquering colonial powers. The United States (along with other leading Western powers) has claimed a commitment to human rights and has challenged other countries on human rights issues, but this posture is hypocritical given its own dismal historical record on the implementation of such rights (Hahnel 2000: 41). In a parallel vein, global business and finance engage in hypocrisy by campaigning against many forms of regulatory law in Western developed nations, while calling for adherence to "the rule of law" in developing nations (Greider 1997: 34). The World Bank's perspective on law has been market-focused and has failed to recognize the protection of human rights and of settled indigenous communities as legitimate purposes of law (McCorquodale and Fairbrother 1999: 755).

In one interpretation, the rule of law can play a role in allowing the disadvantaged to protect themselves from abuse. Law can thus serve a positive function by insisting that human rights be incorporated into government policies and those of international financial institutions, demanding the inclusion of human rights in international treaties, and requiring transnational corporations to conduct themselves in line with international human rights law (McCorquodale and Fairbrother 1999: 753, 766). Legal prohibitions could be imposed on World Bank loans for projects with demonstrably harmful consequences (Greider 2000a). Americans have the sovereign power to reform legislation at state and national levels, to impose codes of conduct on corporations, and to impose rules on U.S.-based transnationals (Greider 2000b). Law, then, can be seen as part of the problem or part of the solution in connection with the oppressive and exploitative dimensions of globalization.

This account of the suffering of the Pak Mun dam protesters documents the criminality claim directed at the World Bank; it also serves as a cautionary tale for a globalized future. Demonstrably harmful policies and practices of the World Bank can be appropriately labeled as crime, more fully understood by applying a criminological perspective, and responded to by activist protest and engagement.

NOTES

[1] This article was inspired by a juxtaposition of the authors' intellectual and activist concerns. The senior author was influenced by the progressive political initiatives that emerged in the 1960s and by activist experiences during that era (i.e., the Civil Rights campaign in Mississippi in 1964 and antiwar protests from 1965 on). His most recent intellectual, or scholarly, interests have focused on white-collar crime, state crime, state/corporate crime,

genocide, and elite deviance. The junior author has been strongly influenced by a summer in China and eight months living in Thailand (with trips to Cambodia and Laos). During her time in Thailand, she lived among and became actively involved with anti-dam protesters, landfill scavengers, and traditional fishermen. She has participated in anti-globalization demonstrations in Washington, D.C., and Philadelphia, and has produced an honors thesis on the ACORN antipoverty movement, with which she worked.

[2] [More] recently, in the context of his magisterial exploration of the role of law in a globalized world, Boaventura de Sousa Santos (1995: 359) has called for bringing historical capitalism to trial before a world tribunal, to be held accountable for its complicity in the massive violation of human rights.

[3] For an especially broad, current survey of the issues surrounding globalization, see Held and McGrew (2000).

[4] In the most inclusive sense, globalization is many centuries old, going back at least to the 15th-century voyages of discovery and the gradual emergence of a world economic system (Hay and Marsh 2000; Valaskakis 1999). If one adopts a more restrictive conception of globalization, to refer to the establishment of formal, international institutions to coordinate international trade, finance, and economic activity, such institutions were established in the first half of the 20th century (Thurow 2000). In another interpretation, globalization truly begins from the 1970s on, with the ending of the cooperative economic system established by the Bretton Woods Conference after World War II and with the liberalization of world financial markets (Hay and Marsh 2000: 14, *fn.* 2).

[5] Theorists of globalization are somewhat divided on the extent to which recent developments do or do not establish a fundamentally new institutional order in the world (Dunne 1999: 18). For a thorough discussion of globalization very much in line with our own views, see Greider (1997). In the final section of the book, Greider (1997: 335) observes, "... the global system tears at the social fabric—upending the peasantry in Thailand, attacking the social state of Germany, suppressing human freedoms on behalf of commerce in Indonesia or China, threatening the foundations of social cohesion of Japan, deepening the social deterioration in the United States and elsewhere."

[6] Chase-Dunn et al. (2000: 78) observe that "*economic globalization* means greater integration in the organization of production, distribution, and consumption of commodities in the world economy.... *Political globalization* is conceptualized as the institutional form of global and interregional political/military organizations (including 'economic' ones such as the World Bank and the International Monetary Fund) and their strengths relative to the strengths of national states and other smaller political actors in the world-system."

[7] Globalization leads to homogenization, polarization, and hybridization, with the cultural consequences of globalization being diverse and complex (Holton 2000; Mazlich 1999).

[8] One commentator suggests that the most striking feature of contemporary globalization is the runaway quality of global finance, which appears remarkably independent of traditional constraints of information transfer, national regulation, industrial productivity, or "real" wealth in any particular society, country, or region (Appadurai 1999).

[9] Among the most pertinent general questions and themes pertaining to globalization are: (1) Can poorer countries be helped without compelling them to raise standards on wages, working conditions, and the environment? (2) Can high wages and full employment be maintained in more affluent countries without hindering the economic development of poorer countries? (3) Is protectionism—in either the richer or the poorer countries—ever justified? (4) Can the inherent conflict between economic growth and environmental protection be satisfactorily resolved? (5) Is the notion of effective international regulation of corporations and investors realistic? (6) Should the World Trade Organization, the World Bank, and the International Monetary Fund be reformed or abolished? (Landy 2000: 13).

[10] Critics of globalization must be sensitive to paternalistic attacks on policies and practices that appear to be repugnant in Western terms, but that may be experienced as a "lesser evil" by poor people in developing countries. For example, conditions in developing country sweatshops producing products such as upscale clothing for affluent Americans are often miserable, with wages of 60 cents an hour, but the alternative for sweatshop laborers may be no work, or even more oppressive working conditions, such as prostitution (Kristof and WuDunn 2000; Kaufman and Gonzalez 2001). It does not necessarily follow from consciousness of such realities, however, that one should refrain from exposing and criticizing policies and practices that are inherently unjust and harmful.

[11] The World Bank itself reports that the number of people living on less than a dollar a day had increased to 200 million in the 1990s, and that over 80 countries suffered a decline in per capita income in the recent era (Levinson 1999: 21).

[12] Silbey (1997: 219) regards "globalization as a form of postmodern colonialism, where the worldwide distribution and consumption of cultural products removed from the contexts of their production and interpretation is organized through legal devices to constitute a form of domination." McDonald's is an especially conspicuous symbol of this new form of domination. Similarly, Santos (1998) suggests that globalization is best thought of as the imposition of the agendas of particular entities and countries upon the rest of the globe, rather than authentic globalization. Neumann (2000: 89–90) observes, "our current global system is a process of colonization. It not only creates organizations like the WTO that replace national sovereignty with corporate interests, it also displaces human ways of relating to each other and substitutes monetary relationships in which human worth is measured in dollars."

[13] A number of presidents of sociological associations have recently used their presidential addresses to call for more sociological attention to globalization and to some of the harms attendant to it. Susan Silbey (1997: 209), in a Presidential Address to the Law & Society Association, called for a sociology of globalization. She observed, "while it is clear that law occupies a prominent place in the global society—because most of the global exchange of persons, capital, and culture is managed through legal forms—it is not clear where the place of justice is in this new world order." Francesca M. Cancian (1996), in a Presidential Address to the Pacific Sociological Association, called for a sociological commitment to reducing inequality, a renewal of the commitment of earlier sociologists to social reform, and a more activist research agenda addressing nonacademic audiences and their con-

cerns. Too much present sociology, she stated, follows a pure science model. Evelyn Glenn (2000: 16), in a 1999 Presidential Address to the Society for the Study of Social Problems, noted the great impact of globalization on social existence and the need for sociologists to address new forms of inequality that result, with justice now having to be challenged on a transnational level. Glenn highlighted the role of supranational entities such as the World Trade Organization, the World Bank, and the International Monetary Fund in contributing to conditions of deprivation and inequality on a global scale: "... [T]he new global economy is contributing to new forms of race, class, and gender inequality by widening economic disparities, displacing people from land which provided self-sufficiency and eroding accustomed ways of life that can't be addressed in a strictly domestic context. Struggles for economic justice and human rights thus need to be moved to the transnational level." Pamela Roby (1998), in her 1997 Society for the Study of Social Problems Presidential Address, also argued that sociologists must become actively engaged in promoting movement toward a just world.

[14] As Noam Chomsky (2000: 29) has observed, "debt is not valid if it's essentially imposed by force. The Third World debt is odious debt."

[15] For Caufield (1996: 338), "there is much truth in the saying that development—at least in the monopolistic, formulaic, foreign-dominated, arrogant, and failed form that we have known—is largely a matter of poor people in rich countries giving money to rich people in poor countries."

[16] Freda Adler (1995), in her 1995 Presidential Address to the American Society of Criminology, observed that new paradigms are called for within the global village and in the information age. Margaret Zahn (1999), in her 1998 Presidential Address to the American Society of Criminology, calls for criminology to expand it scope, testing its propositions in new contexts. She noted that the international community requires increasing attention, and that it has established standards based on principles of human rights that may transcend national laws. William McDonald (1997: 7) has called for a global criminology, separate from a comparative and international criminology. He suggests that "the phrase, global criminology, should be reserved for ... the study of crime and justice problems related to the compression of the globe." Mark Findlay (1999), in *The Globalization of Crime*, argues that the globalized economy of today has produced a new context within which the issue of crime must be understood.

[17] Recent issues of *Social Justice*, for example, have explored the intersections between globalization, neoliberalism, militarism, crime, and criminal justice (Weiss 2000; Kirk and Okazawa Rey 2000). Ian Taylor (1999), writing in a recent issue of *Crime, Law, and Social Change*, argues that the rise of the (free) market society provides a new context for a critical criminology.

[18] The familiar term "crime" has been defined in quite different ways, and an ongoing debate within criminology has focused on the most appropriate way to define this key term. E.H. Sutherland's (1940) conception of white-collar crime—incorporating violations of civil and administrative, as well as criminal law—was one influential challenge to more traditional legalistic definitions of crime.

[19] Herman Schwendinger and Julia Schwendinger (1970, 1977) and Larry Tifft and Dennis Sullivan (1980, 1998) have promoted a humanistic conception of crime—as social harm, as a violation of human rights—while Stanley Cohen (1993) has characterized crime somewhat more narrowly as directly harmful violations of widely recognized human rights. Still others—e.g., Raymond Michalowski and Ronald Kramer (1987) and David Kauzlarich, Ronald Kramer, and Brian Smith (1992)—have advanced conceptions of crime based upon United Nations codes or international law.

[20] Conservative and mainstream criminologists have largely dismissed or ignored this call for an alternative approach to defining crime, but even some of those with a progressive orientation contend that stretching the definition of crime as broadly as the Schwendingers propose to do is either counterproductive and unhelpful, or transforms criminology into a moral crusade (Cohen 1993; Green and Ward 2000). Braithwaite (1985) has criticized humanistic definitions of crime as irrelevant to people who do not share the applicable morality.

[21] State-corporate crime is crime committed as a cooperative endeavor between the state and private-sector corporations, such as exploitation by multinational corporations in developing countries. Finance crime is crime committed on behalf of, or in the context of, major financial institutions, such as frauds by thrifts and manipulations of securities markets.

[22] The pronunciation of the river is Pak Moon, although in most of the literature it is spelled Pak Mun.

[23] In the case of Thailand, the government elite adopted a policy to deliberately undermine rural peasants. "The World Bank supported this strategy with development loans to finance infrastructure—roads, dams, electrical generation—and the industrialization of agricultural production" (Greider 1997: 352).

[24] Conversely, a small number of protesters in Seattle engaged in vandalism and were accordingly accused of engaging in criminal activity. In response, an activist collective communiqué states: "We contend that property destruction is not a violent activity unless it destroys lives or causes pain in the process. Private property, especially corporate private property, is in itself infinitely more violent than any action taken against it" (Neumann 2000: 91).

[25] For example, some headlines include the following: "World Trade Officials Pledging to Step Up Efforts Against AIDS: Growing Sensitivity to Criticism as Protests Ebb" (Kahn and Kifner 2000); "World Bank Criticizes Itself over Chinese Project Near Tibet" (Sanger and Kahn 2000); "World Bank Cites Itself in Study of Africa's Bleak Performance" (Kahn 2000c); and "I.M.F. Is Expected to Ease Demands on Debtor Nations" (Kahn 2000d).

[26] U.N. Secretary General Kofi Annan (Crossette 2000b: 4) observes, "it has been said that arguing against globalization is like arguing against the laws of gravity. But that does not mean we should accept a law that allows only heavyweights to survive. On the contrary: We must make globalization an engine that lifts people out of hardship and misery, not a force that holds them down." It is not unreasonable to suppose that the concerns expressed by Mr. Annan and surely shared by many world leaders, have been influenced or activated by the protests. Yet some anti-WTO activists have expressed concern with the U.N's own vulnerability to manipulation by corporations and other elite powers. The U.N. is certain to be buffeted by countervailing pressures on the globalization issue in the years ahead.

REFERENCES

Adler, F. 1995. "Our American Society of Criminology, the World, and the State of the Art—The American Society of Criminology 1995 Presidential Address." *Criminology* 34: 1–9.

Amsden, A.H. 2000. "Ending Isolationism." *Dissent* (Spring): 13–16.

Appadurai, A. 1999. "Globalization and the Research Imagination." *International Social Science Journal* 160: 229–38.

Blackett, A. 1998. "Globalization and Its Ambiguities: Implications for Law School Curricular Reform." *Columbia Journal of Transnational Law* 37: 57–79.

Bradlow, D.D. 1996. "The World Bank, the IMF, and Human Rights." *Transnational Law & Contemporary Problems* 6: 47–90.

Braithwaite, J. 1985. "White Collar Crime." Pp. 1-25 in *Annual Review of Sociology*, edited by R.H. Turner and J.F. Short, Jr. Palo Alto, CA: Annual Reviews, Inc.

Buchanan, A.E. 1983. *Marx and Justice: The Radical Critique of Liberalism.* Totowa, NJ: Rowman & Littlefield.

Busch, A. 2000. "Unpacking the Globalization Debate: Approaches, Evidence and Data." Pp. 21-48 in *Demystifying Globalization*, edited by C. Hay and D. Marsh. New York: St. Martin's Press.

Cancian, F.M. 1995. "Truth and Goodness: Does the Sociology of Inequality Promote Social Betterment?" *Sociological Perspectives* 38: 339–56.

Carrasco, E.R. 1996. "Critical Issues Facing the Bretton Woods System: Can the IMF, World Bank, and the GATT/WTO Promote an Enabling Environment for Social Development?" *Transnational Law and Contemporary Problems* 6: i–xx.

Caufield, C. 1996. *Masters of Illusion: The World Bank and the Poverty of Nations.* New York: Henry Holt and Co.

Chase-Dunn, C., Y. Kawano, and B. Brewer. 2000. "Trade Globalization since 1795: Waves of Integration in the World-System." *American Sociological Review* 65: 77–95.

Chomsky, N. 2000. "Talking 'Anarchy' with Chomsky." *The Nation* (April 24): 28–30.

Cohen, S. 1993. "Human Rights and Crimes of the State: The Culture of Denial." *Australian and New Zealand Journal of Criminology* 26: 97–115.

Crossette, B. 2000a. "Making Room for the Poor in a Global Economy." *New York Times* (April 16): 4.

Crossette, B. 2000b. "Globalization Tops 3-Day UX Agenda for World Leaders." *New York Times* (September 3): A1.

Dunne, T. 1999. "The Spectre of Globalization." *Indiana Journal of Global Legal Studies* 7: 17–34.

Easterlin, R. 2000. "The Globalization of Human Development." *The Annals* 570: 32–48.

Falk, R. 1993. "The Making of Global Citizenship." Pp. 39–52 in *Beyond the New World Order*, edited by J. Brecher, J.-B. Childs, and J. Cutler. Boston: South End Press.

Findlay, M. 1999. *The Globalization of Crime: Understanding Transitional Relationships in Context.* Cambridge: Cambridge University Press.

Finnegan, W. 2000. "After Seattle." *The New Yorker* (April 17): 40–51.

Frank, E. 2000. "Global Democratization: Spotlight on the United States." *New Politics* 8: 14.

Friedrichs, D. 1996. *Trusted Criminals: White Collar Crime in Contemporary Society.* Belmont, CA: Wadsworth Publishing Co.

Friedrichs, D. (Ed.). 1998. *State Crime.* 2 vols. Aldershot, UK: Ashgate/Dartmouth.

George, S. 2000. "Carte Blanche, Bête Noire." *Dissent* (Winter): 13–15.

Gitlin. T. 2000. "Shouts Bring Murmurs, and That Works." *Washington Post* (April 16): B1.

Glenn, E. 2000. "Citizenship and Inequality: Historical and Global Perspectives." *Social Problems* 47: 1–20.

Green, P. and T. Ward. 2000. "State Crime, Human Rights, and the Limits of Criminology." *Social Justice* 27 (1): 101–16.

Greider, W. 1997. *One World, Ready or Not: The Manic Logic of Global Capitalism.* New York: A Touchstone Book.

Grieder, W. 2000a. "Global Agenda." *The Nation* (January 31): 11–16.

Grieder, W. 2000b. "Time to Rein in Global Finance." *The Nation* (April 24): 13–20.

Hahnel, R. 2000. "Globalization: Beyond Reaction, Thinking Ahead." *New Politics* 8: 31–42.

Hay, C. and D. Marsh. (Eds.). 2000. *Demystifying Globalization.* New York: St. Martin's Press.

Held, D. and A. McGrew. (Eds.). 2000. *The Global Transformations Reader.* Cambridge: Polity Press.

Holton, R. 2000. "Globalization's Cultural Consequences." *The Annals* 570: 140–52.

Hutton, W. and A. Giddens. 2000. "Is Globalization Americanization?" *Dissent* (Summer): 58–63.

Jackson, J. 2000. *The Jurisprudence of GATT and the WTO.* Cambridge: Cambridge University Press.

Johnson, B. 2000. "The World Bank Does Not Provide Effective Development Programs." Pp. 116–22 in *The Third World—Opposing Viewpoints*, edited by L. Egendorf. San Diego: Greenhaven Press.

Kahn, J. 2000a . "Globalization Unifies Its Many-Striped Foes." *New York Times* (April 15): A7.

Kahn, J. 2000b. "Globalization: Unspeakable, Yes. But Is It Really Evil?" *New York Times* (May 7): A4.

Kahn, J. 2000c. "World Bank Cites Itself in Study of Africa's Bleak Performance." *New York Times* (June 1): A9.

Kahn, J. 2000d. "I.M.F. Is Expected to Ease Demands on Debtor Nations." *New York Times* (June 30): C2.

Kalm, J. and J. Kifner. 2000. "World Trade Officials Pledging to Step Up Effort Against AIDS." *New York Times* (April 18): A1.

Kapstein, E. 1998/1999. "A Global Third Way: Social Justice and the World Economy." *World Policy Journal* 15: 23–35.

Kaufman, L. and D. Gonzalez. 2001. "Labor Standards Clash with Global Reality." *New York Times* (April 24): A1.

Kauzlarich, D. and R. Kramer. 1998. *Crimes of the American Nuclear State: At Home and Abroad.* Boston: Northeastern University Press.

Kauzlarich, D., R. Kramer, and B. Smith. 1992. "Towards the Study of Governmental Crime: Nuclear Weapons, Foreign Intervention, and International Law." *Humanity and Society* 16: 543–63.

Kirk, G. and M. Okazaw-Rey. 2000."Neoliberalism, Militarism, and Armed Conflict: An Introduction." *Social Justice* 27: 1–17.

Kristof, N. and S. Wu Dunn. 2000. "Two Cheers for Sweatshops." *New York Times Magazine* (September 24): 70–71.

Landy, J. 2000. "Symposium on Globalization: Hard Questions for the Left." *New Politics* 8: 12–13.

Leinisch, J. 2000. "A Movement Begins: The Washington Protests Against IMF/World Bank." *New Politics* 8: 5–11.

Levinson, M. "Who's in Charge Here?" *Dissent* (Fall): 21–23.

Mazlish, B. 1999. "A Tour of Globalization." *Indiana Journal of Global Legal Education* 7: 5–16.

McCorquodale, R. and R. Fairbrother. 1999. "Globalization and Human Rights." *Human Rights Quarterly* 21: 735–66.

McDonald, W. (Ed.). 1997. *Crime and Law Enforcement in the Global Village.* Cincinnati, OH: Anderson Publishing Co.

Michalowski, R. and R. Kramer. 1987. "The Space Between the Laws: The Problem of Corporate Crime in a Transnational Context." *Social Problems* 34: 34–53.

Neumann, R. 2000. "A Place for Rage." *Dissent* (Spring): 89–92.

Passas, N. 1999. "Globalization, Criminogenic Asymmetries, and Economic Crime." *European Journal of Law Reform* 1: 399–423.

Passas, N. 2000. "Global Anomie, Dysnomie, and Economic Crime: Hidden Consequences of Neoliberalism and Globalization in Russia and Around the World." *Social Justice* 27: 16–44.

Phillips, P. 2000. "Seattle Awakens Working People to the Dangers of Globalization." *Social Policy* (Spring): 34–40.

Rajagopal, B. 2000. "From Resistance to Renewal: The Third World, Social Movements, and the Expansion of International Institutions." *Harvard International Law Journal* 41: 529–78.

Rich, B. 1994. *Mortgaging the Earth: The World Bank, Environmental Impoverishment, and the Crisis of Development.* Boston: Beacon Press.

Roby, P.A. 1998. "Creating a Just World: Leadership for the Twenty-First Century." *Social Problems* 45: 1–20.

Ross, J.I. (Ed.). 1995. *Controlling State Crime.* New York: Garland.

Sanger, D.E. and J. Kahn. 2000. "World Bank Criticizes Itself over Chinese Project Near Tibet." *New York Times* (June 27): A7.

Santos, B. de Sousa. 1995. *Toward a New Common Sense: Law, Science, and Politics in the Paradigmatic Transition.* New York: Routledge.

Scheuerman, W.E. 1999. "Economic Globalization and the Rule of Law." *Constellations* 6: 3–25.

Schwendinger, H. and J. Schwendinger. 1970. "Defenders of Order or Guardians of Human Rights?" *Issues in Criminology* 5: 123–57.

Schwendinger, H. and J. Schwendinger. 1977. "Social Class and the Definition of Crime." *Crime and Social Justice* 7: 4–13.

Shapiro, I. and L. Brilmayer. (Eds.). 1999. *Global Justice.* New York: New York University Press.

Silbey, S. 1997. "'Let Them Eat Cake': Globalization, Postmodern Colonialism, and the Possibilities of Justice." *Law & Society* 31: 207–35.

Sjoberg, G., E.A. Gill, and N. Williams. 2001. "A Sociology of Human Rights." *Social Problems* 48: 11–47.

Smith, J. and T.P. Moran. 2000. "WTO 101: Myths About the World Trade Organization." *Dissent* (Spring): 66–70.

South-East Asia Rivers Network. 2000. "Thai Government Denying Human Rights! Arrest of 200 Villagers at Government House." E-mail Transmission (July 17).

Stark, B. 2000. "Women and Globalization: The Failure and Postmodern Possibilities of International Law." *Vanderbilt Journal of Transnational Law* 33: 503–71.

Stiglitz, J. 2000. "The Insider." *The New Republic* (April 17–24): 56–61.

Stiglitz, J. 2001. "Globalization and Its Discontents." Henry George Lecture, University of Scranton (April 26).

Sullivan, D. and L. Tifft. 1998. "Criminology as Peace-Making: A Peace-Oriented Perspective on Crime, Punishment, and Justice That Takes into Account the Needs of All." *The Justice Professional* 11: 5–34.

Sutherland, E.H. 1940. "White Collar Criminality." *American Sociological Review* 10: 132–39.

Taylor, I. 1999. "Criminology Post-Maastricht." *Crime, Law and Social Change* 30: 333–46.

Teubner, G. 1997. "The King's Many Bodies: The Self-Deconstruction of Law's Hierarchy." *Law & Society Review* 31: 763–88.

Thurow, L. 2000. "Globalization: The Product of a Knowledge-Based Economy." *The Annals* 570: 19–31.

Tifft, L. and D. Sullivan. 1980. *The Struggle to Be Human: Crime, Criminology and Anarchism.* Sanday, Orkney, UK: Cienfuegos Press.

Tyler, C. 2000. *The Pak Mun Dam: A Case Study of a Large Development Project in Thailand.* Honors thesis. University Park, PA: Pennsylvania State University.

United Nations. 1966. *International Covenant on Economic, Social, and Cultural Rights.* Reprinted in *Human Rights Reader,* edited by W. Laquer and B. Rubin, pp. 225–33. New York: New American Library, 1989.

Valaskakis, K. 1999. "Globalization as Theatre." *International Social Science Journal* 160: 153–64.

Vallabhaneni, S. 2000. *Inertia of Change in the World Bank: The Pak Mun Dam Project as a Case Study.* Honors thesis. Providence, RI: Brown University.

Vienchang, M.S. 2000. *Voice of the River: One Thai Villager's Story of the Pak Moon Dam.* Edited by J. Friedrichs, S. Olson, K. Peterson, and L. Shula. Translated by D. Streckfuss and A. Chupkhunthod. Koen Kaen, Thailand: CIEE.

Weiss, R.P. 2000. "Introduction: Criminal Justice and Globalization in the New Millenium." *Social Justice* 27 (2): 1–15.

Williams, R.A., Jr. 1990. "Encounters on the Frontiers of International Human Rights Law: Redefining the Terms of Indigenous Peoples' Survival in the World." *Duke Law Journal* 4: 660–704.

World Bank. 2000. "The World Bank Provides Effective Development Programs." Pp. 107–15 in *The Third World—Opposing Viewpoints*, edited by L.K. Egendorf. San Diego: Greenhaven Press.

World Commission on Dams. 2000. *Pak Mun Case Study Final Report—Executive Summary*, http://www.dains.org/studies/th/thfinalscopesect3-4.ltm.

Zahn, M. 1999. "Thoughts on the Future of Criminology—The American Society of Criminology 1998 Presidential Address." *Criminology* 37: 1-15.

Zakaria, F. 1999. "After the Storm Passes." *Newsweek* (December 13): 40.

CHAPTER STUDY QUESTIONS

- What are the arguments that have been presented for and against economic globalization? According to Friedrichs and Friedrichs, who are typically the "winners" and the "losers" in the process of globalization?

- What is the World Bank, how did it develop, and what role has it played in the global economy? Why are Friedrichs and Friedrichs critical of the World Bank and other international financial institutions that are involved in promoting global economic development?

- How do Friedrichs and Friedrichs define the concept of transnational crime? What is their argument regarding why some of the policies and practices of the World Bank can be viewed as forms of transnational crime?

- Describe the various forms of environmental and social harm that resulted from the construction of the Pak Mun Dam in Thailand. According to Friedrichs and Friedrichs, who was responsible for causing these avoidable harms? How does the concept of "global or transnational state-finance crime" fit this case study?

RELATED WEB LINKS

International Political Economy: Links to Relevant Resources on the World Wide Web
http://faculty.maxwell.syr.edu/merupert/Teaching/753links.htm

> This site from a faculty member of Syracuse University provides links to the official websites of the World Bank, International Monetary Fund, United Nations, and World Trade Organization (institutions representing "globalization from above") as well as those of numerous grassroots anti-globalization organizations (representing "globalization from below").

Greenpeace International
http://www.greenpeace.org/international/

> This global organization is dedicated to addressing the most crucial worldwide threats to the biodiversity and environment of the planet.

Environmental Investigation Agency (EIA)
http://www.eia-international.org/
> This private non-profit organization, founded in 1984, has a commitment to investigating and exposing environmental crime. The site provides information and updates on EIA's current campaigns.

Interpol—Environmental Crime—Links
http://www.interpol.int/Public/EnvironmentalCrime/Links/Default.asp
> This page provides links to the websites of a range of international organizations concerned with addressing the problem of international environmental crime.

Chapter 5

GLOBALIZATION OF CRIMINAL JUSTICE IN THE CORPORATE CONTEXT

MICHAEL J. GILBERT AND STEVE RUSSELL

INTRODUCTION

Crime in the *streets* is easier to perceive as crime than crime in the *suites* (Pepinsky and Jesilow 1984; Reiman 1998) in spite of the fact that corporate crimes easily fit the paradigm created in the Model Penal Code primarily for crimes by individuals (Russell and Gilbert 1999). The image of a criminal as a human being, often differing from decision-makers by class or race, and often armed, plays into the "war on crime" rhetoric that fuels American incarceration (Irwin and Austin 1997) and execution rates (Stinchcomb and Fox 1999: 619–25).

Our purpose is to call attention to how private economic power is, or more often, is not controlled and held accountable for its excesses, particularly when corporate actions kill or injure people, destroy property, pollute across national borders or exploit vulnerable nations with unfair trade practices. It is also to call attention to the need for formal international social control structures to provide mechanisms by which corporate entities can be regulated, controlled, and, if necessary, sanctioned by criminal law to protect public interests. If globalized economic integration is to realize its promise of global peace, then it must contain some mechanism for global justice.

We are aware that criminal law is neither the only nor the most efficacious means for controlling human behavior. Corporate criminal liability has long been more controversial than individual criminal liability, and it remains subject to dispute even in jurisdictions where it is well established (Khanna 1996, 1999). We are also aware of theoretical perspectives on globalization that might be characterized as the 21st century iteration of Adam Smith's "invisible hand" where global markets punish extreme corporate deviance (Smith 1952). Finally, there is a great and growing body of international environmental law that attempts to address some of the issues we raise, and the argument that "the analogy to domestic law is false" is a point well taken. We understand criminal law, like tort law and law generally, to be only one of an array of social control mechanisms that must be recast in global terms. We will claim, however, that the analogy to domestic law is correct when it describes some behavior of transnational corporations as "criminal," or, put another way, worthy of criminal sanctions if not a "war on crime."

On the international level, the idea of a "war on crime" gains an ironic twist. The concept of transnational crime adjudicated by an international tribunal was born after World War II at Nuremberg. For the prisoners in the dock, the war crimes tribunal represented victor's justice, a violation of the bedrock principle *nulla poena sin lege*[1] (Taylor 1992).

While the defendants at Nuremburg were not allowed to probe Allied misconduct (McCoubrey and White 1992) and there was little legal precedent for their trials, the United States was instrumental in planting at Nuremberg the seed of the idea of international legality. Ironically, the United States has expended a great deal of effort since 1946 to stop that seed from growing. In Richard Falk's (1999: 696) metaphor, "[t]he United States is both the principal originator of the Nuremberg ethos, and also the lion that is currently blocking the path to its consistent application and evolution since 1946." It is perhaps the lion's fear that the lambs may demand justice that keeps the superpowers wary of any sanctions that cannot be thwarted by Security Council veto. As Russia had Afghanistan and has Chechnya, as China has Tibet, the United States had Vietnam (Taylor 1970) and has its surviving indigenous people (Russell 1999). Some might characterize these barriers to universalizing the Nuremberg ethos as moral; nation-states tend to see them as cultural (Binder 1999; van der Vyver 1998). The search for legal principles that can cross cultural barriers to promote social justice as well as criminal justice is real. However, that reality can be overlooked behind the obvious hypocrisies of American treatment of indigenous peoples (Wunder 1994; Deloria 1969; Debo 1940) and the ebb and flow of legality in American foreign policy (van der Vyver 1998; Taylor 1970).

Every legal system must meet this fundamental crisis of legitimacy: how shall the powerless have redress against the depredations of the powerful? This crisis of legitimacy is more obvious in municipal law[2] than in the law of nations, but attempts to institutionalize legality over raw force on the international level must also resolve it. This difficulty is a barrier to international criminal law, but not a realistic argument against international legal order any more than it would be a realistic argument against a national legal order.

Creation of an international legal order has been slow going. Political will is hostage to public opinion, and on the international level public opinion has so far responded to only the most atrocious conduct. Constant efforts by the United Nations and various non-governmental organizations and intermittent efforts by some governments to promote social justice have borne less fruit than efforts by the World Trade Organization to institutionalize one view of economic justice, a view that in a free market all values find their "natural" level. The ability to deal with harmful, persistent, and egregious corporate behavior nationally and internationally remains an important problem for the 21st century to manage. With the end of the Cold War and the globalization of the economic playing field there will be a dramatic expansion in the need for control of corporate conduct when harms cross national borders. The political desire to answer the need will increase with the number of victims.

CRIMINAL OPPORTUNITIES IN THE GLOBAL VILLAGE

The emerging transnational nature of corporate crime

On January 30, 2000 a cyanide spill from the Aural gold mining operation in Baia-Mare, Romania contaminated the Tisza and the Danube rivers in Eastern Europe. These transnational rivers are among the most important waterways in Europe, from economic and ecological standpoints. The spill occurred when a holding pond containing a cyanide solution burst after heavy rains and runoff from the snow pack. A spokesperson for the World Wide Fund for Nature stated that "... this spill has, in practical terms, eradicated all life ... rehabilitation of the river will take decades" (Associated Press 2000: A12). Although the Romanian government owned 40 per cent of the mine, the majority owner was Esmeralda, Ltd. of Australia, which denied any responsibility for the damage caused by the cyanide spill (Reuters 2000: A8). This is only one of many instances when corporate entities based in one nation produced goods or services in another country and their corporate practices harmed the environment, people, and property in a third (or more) country. The most egregious harms usually occur in countries, like Romania, where the economy is weak, wages are low, local officials are desperate for investment capital and there are ineffective controls over corporate behavior (Brown and Chiang 1995: 45–49; Friederichs 1996: 68, 72, 76–77; Rosoff, Pontell, and Tillman 1998: 96–99; Simon 1996: 176–93). We define transnational corporate crime as conduct by corporate entities (i.e., juristic persons), doing business in two or more nations that creates avoidable harms in at least one nation, which may or may not be the site of corporate activity. These corporate actions either violate existing criminal, civil, or regulatory law or are manifestly harmful to persons, property, indigenous cultures, or the environment. This type of corporate conduct is carried out with the knowledge or support of the corporation's owners, executives, or key managers. The conduct is intended to provide financial advantage to the organization or maintain and extend its power and privilege (Brown and Chiang 1995: 32; Friedrichs 1996: 10; Russell and Gilbert 1999). Transnational corporate crime is economically or instrumentally rational from the perspective of the corporation, harmful, and not necessarily limited to violations of established law in the country in which harms are produced.

In the global economy, transnational corporations have ascended to the pinnacle of world economic power. The annual earnings of some transnational corporations exceed the gross national product of many developing nations. Such corporations often adopt practices that exploit legal, structural, economic, and political weaknesses to shape national laws and public policies as well as to influence international law and treaties to serve private interests. This is accomplished through relationship networks between legislators and executives, special interest groups, and government bureaucrats (Benvenisti 1999; Reiman 1998; Simon 1996). The effect is to provide a business environment in which corporations shop for jurisdictions with low wages, few regulations, few duties, and greatest protection from liability for their actions (Benvenisti 1999).

Recent efforts by groups such as the World Trade Organization, the International Monetary Fund, and the World Bank have promoted free trade policies and development of market based economic systems. These efforts have opened illegitimate, as well as legitimate, business opportunities to transnational corporations. The illegitimate opportunities include dumping of unsafe products in developing nations (Braithwaite 1984; Gerber and Short 1986), illegal disposal of toxic wastes (Leonard 1993; The Global Poison Trade 1988; Porterfield and Weir 1987), use of child labor (Hindman and Smith 1999), failure to pay a living wage (Woods 1998), production of defective products (Brobeck and Averyt 1983; Mokhiber 1988), hiding corporate income (Kerry 1991), exposure of uninformed and unprotected workers to toxic chemicals or dangerous working conditions (Jones 1988; Shrivastava 1987), manipulation of markets (Truell and Gurwin 1992), money laundering (Thornburgh 1990), price gouging, and other financial crimes (Clinard 1990). These actions may be compatible with the competitive values of private enterprise, but they are also avoidable harms and would be transnational corporate crime if the victims or any governmental entity had the power to ascribe the harms to criminal activity rather than mere aggressive competition.

Concerns about such corporate behaviors resulted in massive public demonstrations between November 30 and December 3, 1999 at the World Trade Organization (WTO) meetings in Seattle. Activists representing a variety of non-governmental organizations and labour unions, as well as environmental, human rights, and nationalist interests, demonstrated and disrupted the WTO meetings. Their message conveyed a growing concern that the globalization of business reflects only the interests of economic and political elites without sufficient respect or concern for the lives of those negatively affected by its policies, practices, and actions. From the demonstrators' perspective, free trade policies and activities by transnational corporations produce considerable harm by damaging the environment, undercutting the livelihood of ordinary people, showing insensitivity to indigenous cultures, and eroding national sovereignty. Furthermore, the policies of the World Trade Organization, World Bank, and the International Monetary Fund are seen as undemocratic in that their policies override national laws and local public interest concerns. They argue that such considerations are largely irrelevant to these organizations in the high stakes world of international commerce (Postman 1999; Dunphy 1999a, 1999b; Postman and Mapes 1999; Seattle Times Company 1999a, 1999b; Thurber 2000). Gary Chamberlain, a professor of ethics at Seattle University, succinctly expressed these concerns (cited in Postman and Mapes 1999: 5):

> Until they open the doors at the WTO, what do people have but the streets?
> People sense there aren't any rules to this global economy and that what
> rules there are, are being made by corporations. The WTO is setting the
> rules, but in whose favor?

It is an open question whether the protestors' concerns were heard or understood by the WTO. Two weeks after the Seattle conference was disrupted, the member states struck down, by unanimous consent, an agenda item that would have required that the WTO examine the lessons learned from Seattle at its next meeting in Geneva (*Los Angeles Times* and The Associated Press 1999).

Two years later, similar anti-globalization demonstrations disrupted the *Summit of the Americas* held in Quebec City, Quebec from April 20–22, 2001. The central theme presented by demonstrators was once again that economic policy decisions made by summit participants were undemocratic because they did not effectively consider the concerns of common people about the harms associated with globalization. They argued that inequitable distribution of wealth, erosion of local markets, human rights abuses, destruction of the environment, insufficient protection for the right of workers to organize, weak standards for occupational safety, threats to indigenous populations, and threats to national sovereignty were left out of the debate among summit participants (Boshra 2001; Dougherty 2001; Hanes 2001). Demonstrators at meetings dealing with globalization of trade continue to point out the kind of harms created by powerful economic interests that are of concern in this chapter (Headden 1998).

Enforcement of national law to control transnational corporate crime

The globalization of enterprise and the emergence of transnational corporations that produce avoidable harms across national borders present difficult problems for enforcement of national law. Municipal law enforcement activities are limited to the boundaries of a single nation. By definition, transnational corporate crime involves activities that cross national borders. A crime "occurs" where a prohibited act, a prohibited result, or sometimes a prohibited "criminal" agreement took place. The prohibitions defined in penal codes vary from nation to nation and even within nations—province to province, state to state (Robinson, Cahill, and Mohammad 2000). A crime in one nation may be defined differently or may not be a crime at all in another nation. The principle of sovereignty holds that only national leaders have the authority to define the crimes listed in national penal codes and, consequently, the criminal laws of nations cannot be dictated from outside national borders (Bossard 1990: 5–6).

Criminal laws address only harms that have been legally defined as crimes prior to the acts. This fundamental principle is problematic in the transnational context. Assume for a moment that the Australian mining company Esmeralda Ltd. had obeyed every Romanian statute and regulation in its operation of the mine. There would be no corporate criminal violation in Romania where the mine was operated and the harm originated. The cyanide spill would simply be an accident. The downstream victims, even if their statutes contained a criminal prohibition, would have difficulty in assuming jurisdiction over the "person" of an Australian corporation.

A toxic spill of this nature would lead to civil tort actions in United States' courts and corporate criminal liability would not be far removed. The general requirements for corporate criminal liability are:

- a crime, the intent to harm (*mens rea*) and a criminal act to cause harm (*actus reus*), by a corporate agent,
- acting within the scope of the corporate agent's employment, and
- with intent to benefit the corporation (Russell and Gilbert 1999).

Pollution offenses in the United States are typically strict liability crimes, with no *mens rea* required, but in much of the world strict liability of a corporation—or any liability of the corporation—is not accepted as a principle of criminal law. Traditional criminal liability was developed primarily to deal with crimes by natural persons against other natural persons or their property (Reiman 1998: 61–70). In the cyanide spill example it is difficult, perhaps impossible, to demonstrate that any of the executives of the corporation or any of the lower level employees at the mine intended to harm anyone or anything. Criminal intent is very difficult to establish where the defendant is a corporation because there is no clear intent to harm and corporate documents often describe procedures and practices to avoid harms. This problem is compounded when the harms are small or widely diffused among large numbers of people. Consequently, imposing criminal liability on corporations when victimization is uncertain or without proof of intent is politically difficult for a developing nation that cannot afford to see jobs and infrastructure taken elsewhere.

Although law in the United States allows corporations to be charged criminally, many other nations have not taken that path (Russell and Gilbert 1999). Opposition to corporate criminal liability involves the issue of *mens rea* ("guilty mind"). The basic argument is that corporations have neither a "mind" nor independence of action (agency) apart from the decisions and actions of the human beings involved. Therefore, corporations cannot form criminal intent, cannot act and cannot be meaningfully held criminally liable. The concept of a corporate person (i.e., juristic person) is a legal fiction. Under this view, only people can form criminal intent and act upon that intent. Therefore, only those individuals within corporations who perform criminal acts on behalf of themselves or the corporation and decision makers who induce others to commit criminal acts in the service of corporate interests should be charged as individuals under criminal law (Cressey 1989; Khanna, 1996, 1999; Parker 1997). Under these views there is almost no role for criminal sanctions of corporations. This disagreement about the legal principles to be applied to corporate behavior compounds the problem of controlling transnational corporate crime with enforcement of national laws.

As corporations increase their ability to do harm, more nations are beginning to respond with criminal sanctions. Recent changes to French law now permit corporations to be charged with criminal offenses under a new penal code governing corporate entities (Orland and Cachera 1995). In The Netherlands, a series of case law decisions since 1948 has resulted in corporations being declared eligible for criminal liability (Jorg 1997: 107–111). These changes demonstrate that criminal liability concepts and laws can be restructured in an effort to control corporate crime and that some European nations are beginning to perceive that such restructuring is necessary. These changes in the legal foundations for corporate criminal liability may reflect a growing public awareness and understanding of the nature, scope, and seriousness of harms associated with corporate crime.

Corporate criminal liability: Between agency and structure models

The arguments about applying criminal liability to corporations seem to fall along a continuum, starting with those who recognize only individual agency at one end. Scholars who take this view simply deny that there is any utility in the concept of corporate criminal liability (Cressey 1989; Khanna 1996, 1999; Parker 1997). They seek to hold individual actors associated with the corporation criminally liable rather than the corporation itself. At the other extreme are those who see corporate crime as the product of internal structural dynamics. From their point of view, there is very little utility to individual sanctions because the goal is to change the conduct of organizations. Advocates of this position seek first to prevent corporate crime through collaboration and negotiation with corporations to develop voluntary compliance strategies and monitoring techniques that ensure compliance. Public shaming of corporations would serve as a primary enforcement tool (Braithwaite and Fisse 1995; Lofquist 1997). Between these extremes lie various perspectives that modify or blend the extreme agency and structure models of corporate criminal liability.

Corporations are more than a collection of individual actors who carry out the functions assigned to them as members of units that compose the organization as shown on a chart (Barnard 1982; Drucker 1974; Etzioni 1964; McGregor 1996; Simon 1976). Perhaps one of the most important distinctions is that corporations are immortal while individuals are not (Russell and Gilbert 1999). This immortality is important—owners may die and executives may be fired or incarcerated or they may resign; yet, the juristic person lives on indefinitely. In some industries, such as insurance, immortality is indispensable: without corporate immortality insurance could not be sold, except to the extremely gullible.

Mortal individuals may be kind, loving, decent, respectful, polite, moral, and honest in their personal lives but still function in an amoral manner when at work within the immortal corporate structure. As Punch (1996) notes, personal values and standards may be left at the company door each day as employees arrive at work. He argues that this phenomenon is due to a number of factors:

- the secretive, competitive, and proprietary nature of business;
- informal operational codes related to broadly accepted patterns of thought and action (i.e., corporate culture) that prescribe how things actually get done. Such operational codes often deviate substantially from formal written policies and procedures that prescribe how things ought to be done;
- internal corporate pressures, expectations, and practices that often require employees to simultaneously function in the *world of appearances* (the way things ought to be) and the *world of reality* (to get things done and succeed within the corporate culture);
- the extent to which illegitimate opportunities are available within the industry;
- the extent to which high rewards are associated with "success" while corporate executives demonstrate little regard for the legality, morality, or ethics of the means used;
- the extent to which the corporate culture romanticizes competition, idolizes and rewards risk takers as heroes, employs stereotypes to dehumanize and discredit outsiders, and portrays business as war and their competitors as the enemy, enables individuals within the corporation to separate themselves from the consequences of their actions; and,
- the financial health of the corporation within its industry.

In the corporate context, individuals may function very differently at work than they would at home. It has long been noted that individuals come and go within a corporation but the patterns of values, norms, and expectations that characterize the organization (*organizational culture*) often remain unchanged (Barnard 1982; Simon 1976; Trice and Beyer 1996). To a large extent, this is because the relationships between formal hierarchical structures and networks of supportive social relationships among employees (*the informal organization*) within the organization have remained unchanged. Typically, the larger the organization the more difficult it is to change. When change does occur, new ways gradually replace old ways until the old procedures are forgotten and the new ones become tradition. Such changes typically remain in effect long after the individuals associated with the decision have left the organization. These are some of the ways in which a corporation is more than the sum of its owners, executives, supervisors, and line workers.

Jorg (1997: 101) distinguishes between natural reality and social reality. Natural reality involves the physical world. Corporations are social creations and reside in the social reality of our lives rather than in the physical reality. The behavior of corporations is therefore different than the physical behaviors of individuals. Corporate behavior reflects formal policy, procedures, and rules as well as the informal dynamics of corporate culture. Jorg classifies corporate behavior as *conduct* and the behavior of individuals as *acts*. Thus, corporations conduct business through individuals who carry out specific acts on its behalf. The formal or informal policies that serve corporate interests also influence how individuals within the corporation act. Corporate conduct is the product of consultation and decision-making and requires that the corporation respond to legal obligations incurred in the process of conducting business. If you have health or life insurance, you probably expect the insurance company, rather than the agent who sold you the policy, to pay the benefits authorized. The legal obligation to live up to the terms of an insurance policy is held by the corporation not the agent. As Jorg (1997: 102) states: "... a corporation is a social entity, with the capacity of conduct; it is a social actor." The corporation has a "life" of its own apart from the people who act as its agents.

A corporation does not, in the physical sense, have a brain with which to form intent or the ability to act required for traditional criminal liability. However, it does have a nerve center composed of decision-making processes that govern corporate conduct and make legally binding decisions. Jorg (1997: 102) argues that, to understand corporate intent, it is crucial to determine actual corporate policy. Actual policy refers to the conduct demonstrated by the corporation. Official corporate policy stated in writing may have been designed solely for public consumption and be very different from actual corporate policy in operation. Determining actual policy requires a comparison of corporate objectives as expressed in the corporate charter and mission statement with operational goals expressed in management documents, the allocation of resources, the action(s) of its agents, whether the action(s) were authorized, and whether inappropriate or criminal behavior has been routinely tolerated. Once it is clear that the conduct in question emanates from the central decision-making structures and processes, the conduct ought to be considered intentional corporate conduct. In this sense, the corporate conduct in question is not simply an act by an individual employee but patterned behavior based on corporate dynamics that serve corporate interests. Further, the United States federal courts have developed a number of legal strategies for imputing knowledge and action to corporations instead of individuals (Carrasco and Dupee 1999: 454–57). These strategies include:

- *Collective Knowledge*—where the sum of the knowledge and competencies of employees is imputed to a corporation for liability purposes when no single employee is at fault.
- *Willful Blindness*—when corporate executives show a deliberate disregard for criminal activity within the corporation after discovery because of business or liability concerns.
- *Conspiracies*—when two or more corporate agents agree to commit an offense on behalf of the corporation and one or more of those involved take steps to further the illegal goals of the conspiracy.
- *Misprison of Felony*—when a corporate principal (i.e., owner, senior executive) commits a felony that becomes known within the corporation, and corporate conduct and resources are used to conceal or attempt to conceal the offense.

Thus, a corporation can be seen as a *moral actor*. Through corporate decision-making structures and processes, it has institutional knowledge of the law and is able to distinguish right from wrong. Through internal risk assessment and management, it is able to identify potential harms and assess relative risks. The corporation has the ability to formulate policies that ensure its business is conducted in a manner consistent with this knowledge. It can also identify and understand the interests and points of view of others. It can weigh the potential benefits and potential harms associated against various corporate decisions and express a coherent rationale for its decisions and conduct (Jorg 1997: 104). The recent publication of documents from within the tobacco industry demonstrate, beyond a doubt, the calculated rationality of the industry's strategy to hide what it knew about the addictive and carcinogenic properties of nicotine and tobacco smoke from the public (Kluger 1996; Morales 1998). These corporations understood the law as well as the dangers associated with use of their products. They understood the weakness of their position if the true nature of their business were revealed. They repeatedly made corporate decisions that favored corporate interests at the expense of the health and lives of those who smoked or were exposed to their products. These companies circumvented the law whenever it suited their interests. These documents show that industry executives lied before Congress when they were asked if smoking tobacco was addictive because of nicotine (Morales 1998: 3–5). Industry wide, the corporate intent was to hide the harmful effects of their products to continue a lucrative business.

Unlike crimes by natural persons that involve direct harms to other natural persons or property ("one-on-one harm"), corporate crime involves "indirect harms" in which many people are victimized by the same act (Reiman 1998: 63–64). Aside from the recently established French criminal code for corporate entities, we are unaware of any other nation in which indirect harms by corporations are explicitly addressed by a distinct penal code. Most nations are able to deal with genuine accidents and incidents involving human error through civil litigation, but they are largely unprepared to deal with deliberate, persistent deviant national and transnational corporate crime and the indirect harms produced by such corporate behavior.

Substantive control of transnational corporate crime

An important element in developing a criminal law mechanism for substantive control of transnational corporate crime is the creation of national penal codes like the Nouveau Code Penal in France (Orland and Cachera 1995). The new French penal code specifically deals with criminal responsibility of juristic persons ("personnes morales" or moral persons). The proliferation of comparable national penal codes should lead to common understandings of the nature and extent of corporate crime. These shared understandings may show the way for subsequent multilateral agreements, and it is quite likely that the Nouveau Code Penal of France will inform the development of similar penal codes in other nations. With this understanding about corporate crimes, prosecution of corporations for transnational crime in national fora will be easier. From these foundations, an international forum may be created.

In Russell and Gilbert (1999), we discuss the control of corporate crime within the United States in light of the chartering of corporations by state governments. We note the "race to the bottom" by corporations seeking to charter themselves in jurisdictions that offer corporate management the most legal protection and the fewest duties to shareholders and to the public. International readers may understand this tendency in the maritime custom of flying "flags of convenience," a custom that makes Liberia and Panama appear to have major merchant fleets just as Delaware and South Dakota in the United States appear to be major centers of commerce.

In addition to the "race to the bottom" in search of low taxes and favorable rules of corporate behavior, there is a parallel fluidity in location of corporate economic activities. Principally in manufacturing, corporations seek places where labor is less organized and the externalities imposed upon corporate decision-making by, for example, water and air quality standards are minimized.

Both races to the bottom and the ability of corporations to disadvantage both the communities they leave and those to which they move have been widely noted in the popular news media. Over a four-week period in November 1998, *Time* magazine produced a series of in-depth articles titled "Corporate Welfare" (Bartlett and Steele 1998a–1998h). These articles documented how corporations strategically apply their economic and political influence to gain lucrative tax abatements, public service concessions and tax funded infrastructure improvements. The manipulative techniques used draw heavily on threatening the loss of jobs in the jurisdiction where a company currently operates while promising jobs in other states and cities if they relocate. In this way, corporations whipsaw one jurisdiction against another to leverage economic concessions that amount to public subsidies from communities.

Globalization of the economy has exacerbated the economic race to the bottom by minimizing the inconvenience and expense of crossing national borders in pursuit of economic gain. We suggest now that the international community faces the prospect of replicating the race to the bottom in search of legal advantage. In the global economy, transnational corporations are free to move management responsibilities, assets, and production facilities around the globe in search of low costs, strong property protection, strictly enforced financial privacy rules, weak regulatory systems, and fewest social obligations.

This use of economic power exploits economically desperate nations through political corruption, low wages, unsafe production practices, unsafe disposal of hazardous wastes, and many other forms of conduct that produce avoidable harms. As more countries begin to encounter abuses of corporate power and respond within their municipal legal systems, we anticipate a flight of corporate activity to jurisdictions that have not responded, a flight that would pose no international issue were it not for the transnational character of the potential harms.

In the long term, international law solutions will become necessary. For now, the fundamental concept of corporate criminal responsibility must spread. In Russell and Gilbert (1999) we demonstrated that corporate crimes are comparable to crimes by natural persons under the American Law Institute Model Penal Code and proposed a regime of sanctions building upon the United States Sentencing Commission Guidelines for organizations. The following sections of this chapter draw on this work and the sophisticated approach from the continental legal tradition embodied in the French Nouveau Code Penal to suggest a set of substantive rules within municipal law to address transnational corporate crime and resolve the crisis of legitimacy by providing a means of redress for the powerless against the powerful. Social justice in an era of economic globalization reasserts the dominance of natural persons over juristic persons.

The Nouveau Code Penal: General principles

The Nouveau Code Penal (translation by Orland and Cachera 1995) includes a list of legal principles that establish a foundation upon which offense categories and sanctions are constructed. These principles include (Orland and Cachera 1995: 127–28, 147–50):

- an exclusive focus on *non-state organizational entities* which are for-profit commercial enterprises, non-profit enterprises, and government controlled enterprises (e.g., utilities);
- an inclusion of both national and foreign corporations doing business within France;
- the criminalization of regulatory offenses (primarily dealing with health and safety issues);
- the recognition of offenses committed on behalf of the organization by its agents or organizational units;
- an explicit recognition that criminal prosecution of a corporation does not preclude criminal prosecution of natural persons involved in the offense for the same conduct and under the same statute;
- an understanding that a corporation may be held criminally liable even when criminal responsibility of the natural person has not been established;
- a recognition that lower ranking officials in other regions or subordinate units should be held responsible only for offenses committed in the course of their assigned responsibilities;
- protection from corporate criminal liability when an employee acts solely on individual initiative or solely in his own interests, even if the corporation benefits from the offense;
- allowing the corporation to be charged and tried as either the main perpetrator or as an accomplice (i.e., a corporate executive instructs someone other than an employee to burglarize the offices of a competitor to steal trade secrets); and,

- a standard of establishing corporate criminal intent *before* corporate criminal liability can be found; however, the corporation may be found criminally liable when negligence or imprudence (recklessness) in the failure to comply with established safety standards and regulations results in death or injury.

The Nouveau Code Penal: Corporate crimes

The following examples from the Nouveau Code Penal suggest the types of corporate crimes that could be codified and how they might be defined (Orland and Cachera 1995: 128–29):

> *Article 221–6.* Causing death, by lack of skill, imprudence, carelessness, negligence, or failure to observe safety or prudence required by law or regulations, constitutes involuntary homicide punished by imprisonment for three years and by a fine of 300,000 francs.
> In the case of deliberate failure to observe safety or prudence required by law or regulations, incurred penalties are increased up to five years of prison and up to 500,000 francs for the fine.
> *Article 222–19.* Causing, by lack of skills, imprudence, lack of attention, negligence, or failure to observe safety or prudence required by law or regulations, a total incapacity to work for more than three months is punished by imprisonment for two years and by a fine of 200,000 francs.

In case of deliberate failure to observe safety or prudence required by law or regulations, incurred penalties are increased up to three years of prison and to 300,000 francs for the fine.

> *Article 223–1.* Directly exposing another to an immediate risk of death or injuries which would cause mutilation or permanent disability, by a manifest and a deliberate violation of a special requirement of safety or prudence required by law or regulations, is punished by imprisonment for one year and by a fine of 100,000 francs.

Book II of the Nouveau Code Penal specifies corporate criminal liability for crimes against humanity, drug trafficking, money laundering, exposure to risk of death, unlawful medical experimentation, discrimination, labor conditions or housing conditions inconsistent with human dignity, violations of privacy, misrepresentation, and violations of civil rights (Orland and Cachera 1995: 141–43). Book III specifies corporate criminal liability for theft of property, extortion and blackmail, swindling, fraudulent abuse of vulnerable people (i.e., the elderly and mentally infirm), trust abuse, embezzlement, fraudulent bankruptcy, receiving and transferring stolen goods, and destruction, disruption, deterioration of property including computer systems (Orland and Cachera 1995: 143–45). Other laws provide for corporate criminal liability for pollution, price fixing, corruption, and deceitful accounting practices.

The Nouveau Code Penal: Range of corporate sanctions

A variety of traditional and non-traditional corporate sanctions are provided under the Nouveau Code Penal (Penalties, Section II, Subsection 1). The more traditional sanctions include fines (up to five times the maximum allowed to natural persons charged under the same statute), organizational probation (for up to five years) and confiscation of objects and property used in the offense or gained as a result of the offense. The non-traditional sanctions include:

- corporate dissolution (revocation of the corporate charter and liquidation of assets for the most serious corporate offenses or chronic reoffending);
- permanent or temporary prohibition from performing professional or social activities;
- permanent or temporary closing of one or more establishments of the corporation that were used in committing the offense;
- preclusion from bidding on public projects for up to five years,
- permanent or temporary prohibition from selling stock or bonds to raise capital;
- prohibition from making payments by corporate check (unless by automatic withdrawal or certified check/money order);
- public humiliation by broadcasting a public notice for a two month period in print and/or telecommunication outlets, at the expense of the convicted corporation, indicating the offense and the sentence imposed;
- enhancements for subsequent re-offending by the same corporation raising the penalties to ten times the penalty allowed by law.

These traditional and non-traditional sanctions are consistent with the sanctions regime we presented in Russell and Gilbert (1999). We suggested an array of sanctions appropriate to juristic persons, which could not easily be shifted by corporate executives to innocent bystanders to recoup losses.[3] Several of these sanctions do not appear in the Nouveau Code Penal. Under the general category of *restitution* the following sanctions were suggested: *notice to victims* (known, probable, and unknown), an *apology* to victims, *community service*, *monetary restitution* to victims for damages, and *remedial orders* to repair past harms and prevent future harms. Two types of *fines* were suggested: *day fines* (i.e., the profit on a particular good or service for a single day) and *equity fines* (i.e., court ordered issuance of stock, up to a prescribed value, held in a state controlled fund for victims compensation) (Braithwaite 1984: 333–34; Coffee 1981; Schlegel 1990: 30–34, 166–71). Finally, we provided a *confinement* sanction for corporations. In the corporate sense, confinement is *receivership* in which the juristic person is placed under day-to-day operational supervision of a special master selected and supervised by the sentencing court—thus replacing the top management decision making structure and removing its autonomy as an enterprise.

Sentencing a transnational corporation presupposes an authority with the puissance to impose criminal sanctions upon an entity that may be economically more robust than the nation-state in which the criminal harm occurred and, eventually, international conventions to prevent fleeing across national borders to evade sanctions. Similar conventions were developed to establish the International Criminal Police Organization (INTERPOL) to deal with transnational street criminals (Bossard 1990). An international court, armed with a penal code tailored to transnational corporate crime and international conventions to provide authoritative jurisdiction over transnational corporate criminal conduct, is an essential element of an effective strategy to control transnational corporate conduct, prevent avoidable harms, and foster social justice. National governments, focused on the positive aspects of a globalized economy, have not yet focused attention on harmful conduct that, even when a law proscribes it, is without an effective adjudicative forum.

ADJUDICATIVE FORA

Permanent International Court of Justice

The Permanent International Court of Justice (PICJ) sits in The Hague and has the primary duty of adjudicating disputes between the sovereign states that are signatories to the multilateral agreement creating the court. Like most courts, the PICJ commands no armies or police forces, but unlike municipal fora, it also lacks a social consensus regarding submission to the court or to the principle of legality. What is legal in international relations may or may not be expedient in terms of the domestic politics of countries with business before the PICJ.

Compare, for example, the positions taken by the United States in two fairly recent PICJ cases, *United States v. Iran* (1981 I.C.J. 45); *Nicaragua v. United States of America (Military and Paramilitary Activities in and against Nicaragua)* (1986 I.C.J. 4); *Nicaragua v. United States* [Merits] (1996 I.C.J. 14). On December 15, 1979, the Permanent International Court of Justice ordered the Government of the Islamic Republic of Iran to ensure the immediate release of American hostages taken by a mob of Iranian civilians (Order Indicating Provisional Measures, 1979 I.C.J. 7). The United States, having invoked the jurisdiction of the Court over Iranian objections, stood on the principle of international legality. When, just five years later, the United States was sued in the same Court for alleged unlawful acts against Nicaragua (principally mining Nicaraguan harbors in peacetime), it found itself asserting national sovereignty in much the same fashion as Iran had done. An attempt to "domesticate" the judgment of the PICJ against the United States failed in *Committee of United States Citizens Living in Nicaragua v. Reagan*, 859 F2d 929 (DC cir. 1988), on the issue of standing but consistent with a long tradition of U.S. Courts refusing to address the merits when litigation calls American foreign policy into question.

In a subsequent incident during the Gulf War when an American warship shot down an Iranian civil airliner, the United States successfully resisted jurisdiction even of U.S. courts. While the government did make compensatory payments to the next of kin (Gibney 1997: 277–78), the resistance to any judicial review of the legality of military actions indicates not only an American obsession with but also an extremely narrow interpretation of national interests.

There is no national interest in shooting down a civilian aircraft. If there was a mistake and the mistake was reasonable, there is no war crime. The national interest is being defined as an interest in judging ourselves. That is, no American national should ever have to answer for his conduct of American policy in a neutral forum.

Resort to law rather than resort to force presupposes recognition that the rule of law may, in at least some cases, trump the national interest. The United States is not alone in its tendency to retreat into the haven of national sovereignty, but it is vulnerable to the accusation of hypocrisy for its convenient and selective use of the principle. The United States has advocated respect for national sovereignty when its own (broadly defined) national interests were threatened and ignored the principle when expedient. The meaning of "national interest" and its relationship to "national sovereignty" is situational and defined politically. In the context of transnational business, the purported national interest that leads to the invocation of sovereignty is often a proxy for corporate interests. Thus the sovereignty shelter is also an obstacle to criminal prosecution of corporate persons in an international forum.

Benvenisti's "transnational conflict paradigm" (1999: 169) points out that:

> States are not monolithic entities, and many of the pervasive conflicts of interest are in fact more internal than external, stemming from the heterogeneity within, rather than among, states. Indeed, the transnational conflict paradigm shows how domestic interest groups often cooperate with similarly situated foreign interest groups in order to impose externalities on rival domestic groups. The better-organized, and hence more politically effective, domestic interest groups—usually producers, employers, and service suppliers—cooperate with similar interests in different states to exploit less organized groups such as consumers, employees, and environmentally vulnerable citizens. Thus, the transnational conflict paradigm attributes many global collective action failures to conflicts among warring domestic groups rather than international competition among states.

If this description sounds familiar to American scholars, it is because the United States federal system is often hostage to the same forces. The power to regulate environmental protection, labor relations, and consumer protection on the national level has been clear since the New Deal's early constitutional crises. However, national regulations that cannot effectively proceed on a state level are blocked or watered down at the national level in Congress, where corporate interests masquerade as state interests.

Most of the current body of international environmental law *assumes* that private interests will be asserted as state interests. O'Connell (1992: 315) has noted that "standing is probably the most serious current barrier to environmental litigation in domestic courts." She is probably correct, and the same can be said of much environmental litigation in the PICJ. There is no end to political reasons why a state with standing to complain in the PICJ might not do so, beginning with economic domination by transnational corporations and continuing with policy exigencies having nothing to do with the environment. Therefore, for example, when the Chernobyl nuclear accident in the former Soviet Union spread a cloud of radioactive contamination across Europe in violation of existing treaties, the obstacle to liability on the international level was not primarily negligence, if any, committed by a state enterprise. States could sue the U.S.S.R. in the PICJ. The obstacle was that the governments in the damaged countries were supportive of Mikhail Gorbachev's efforts to end the Cold War. Action against the Soviet government or even against a newly privatized enterprise on that scale would have been a threat to Gorbachev's then-fragile reforms (O'Connell 1992, 1995).

Globalization of corporate activity and interests means that, as long as national policies can be captured and shrouded in the mantle of sovereignty by corporate actors, the principle of international legality will remain vulnerable to the assertions of self-interest (real or imagined) that have limited the utility of the PICJ. The principle of international legality has been able to subvert the principle of national sovereignty with regard to genocide, crimes against humanity, and war crimes—crimes so horrible that they call out for redress without regard to national borders.

Ad hoc tribunals

World opinion is sometimes not enough to secure compliance with decisions of the PICJ, but it is enough at other times to demand criminal sanctions for the most outrageous forms of outlawry. It was world opinion, what Richard Falk (1999) calls "global civil society," that drove the creation of ad hoc tribunals to sort out the carnage in Rwanda (U.N. Doc. S/RES/955, 1994) and the former Yugoslavia (U.N. Doc. S/RES/827, 1993) in an attempt to fix responsibility for genocide and other crimes against humanity. While the world has not yet found the political will to develop an international legal system to address transnational corporate crime, it has found the will to develop rudimentary legal systems to deal with crimes of war.

The slaughter of noncombatants draws world attention and makes the need for legality across borders apparent from the racial, religious, or ethnic hatreds exposed. The need cuts both ways. Serbs and Croats and Muslims need to be tried, as do Hutus and Tutsis, but they all need to be tried fairly. The courts in The Hague and in Arusha, Tanzania sort out ethnic atrocities to protect the innocent as well as to punish the guilty. These tribunals, like the military tribunals that judged German and Japanese war crimes, are limited in jurisdiction to acts that would challenge the very limits of horror. It is only at these limits that the most powerful nations can summon the will to admit some exception to sovereignty, the principle that the king can do no wrong. However, even when crimes against humanity and war crimes are considered, the idea of a permanent international criminal court remains controversial.

Rome Statute of the International Criminal Court

On July 17, 1998, the international community adopted, by a non-recorded electronic vote, the Rome Statute of the International Criminal Court (U.N. Doc. A/CONF.183/9) (hereinafter, "Rome Statute"), a proposed multilateral treaty creating a permanent forum for the prosecution of "the most serious crimes of concern to the International community as a whole." The permanent court would be complementary to national criminal jurisdictions (Rome Statute, preamble). The vote was 120 in favor, 7 against, with 21 abstentions. The only nations known to be among the dissenting seven were China, Israel, and the United States (Brown 1999).

Jurisdiction of the court would be limited to four international "street crimes": genocide, crimes against humanity, war crimes, and the crime of aggression by states (Rome Statute, Article 5, §1). Within the Rome Statute, "crimes against humanity" are defined to include rape, forced pregnancy, forced sterilization and other sexual oppression when practiced in a systematic manner (Rome Statute, Article 7, §1 [g]). Recent incidences of rape and sexual oppression as official policy drove this specific prohibition (Moshan 1998).

Perhaps anticipating the political hurdles facing the Rome Statute, the treaty establishes the Rule of Lenity: "The definition of a crime shall be strictly construed and shall not be extended by analogy. In case of ambiguity, the definition shall be interpreted in favour of the person being investigated, prosecuted or convicted" (Rome Statute, Article 22, §2).

The jurisdiction of the court explicitly is limited to natural persons (Rome Statute, Article 25). It is predictable that nations might be even more protective of their corporate citizens than of their natural citizens, but a more likely reason for this result is that the Rome Statute defines crimes generally identified with individuals who pursue national policies with excessive zeal. This may be a failure of diplomatic imagination. "Crimes against humanity" are defined to include "enslavement" (Rome Statute, Article 7 [1] [c]); the memory of German corporations taking advantage of Jewish slave labor during World War II cannot have entirely faded. Is it such a great leap to suppose that the Korean "comfort women" could have been enslaved and raped by a corporate entity for military convenience?

The artificial person likely to be responsible for the crimes set out in the Rome Statute is not the corporation, but the nation-state. However,

> ... the world's major powers, selective as they have been in establishing ad hoc bodies to investigate certain international crimes, nevertheless progressively have recognized the aspirations of world public opinion for the establishment of an impartial and fair system of international criminal justice. But in the course of the historical evolution that took place, only the concept of individual criminal responsibility was recognized, while that of state criminal responsibility has been rejected (Bassiouni 1995: 53).

This concept of *enterprise responsibility*, whether the enterprise is a corporation or a nation-state, is at the root of American objections to the Rome Statute. It is also a barrier to accountability for transnational corporations for avoidable harms.

The principle expressed by the American objection to the Rome Statute is the fear that American nationals will be subjected to frivolous and politically motivated criminal charges (Brown 1999; David 1999). It is of course possible that a criminal process could be used in an attempt (probably fruitless) to put American foreign policy on trial. In fact, there were many attempted obstructions of the Vietnam War wherein the "Nuremberg defense" was attempted in municipal courts without success.

It is tempting to observe that both Vietnam and the United States would be better off if U.S. courts had recognized the Nuremberg defense and therefore ruled upon the legality of the Vietnam debacle. If the Rome Statute had been in place, perhaps a trial for the crime of aggression, even without a conviction, would have moved American public opinion more in line with world opinion. It should be sufficient to protect legitimate United States interests that any military action taken pursuant to a United Nations Security Council resolution would be effectively insulated from prosecution as aggression, and the definition of "war crimes" in Article 8 of the Rome Statute really codifies existing treaty obligations rather than creating new ones.

It is not our purpose to argue that the United States should submit itself to the Rome Statute and the jurisdiction of the International Criminal Court. Others have ably engaged that task (Brown 1999; David 1999; O'Connor 1999; Penrose 2000), President Clinton signed the treaty as one of his last acts in office, and President Bush subsequently nullified President Clinton's signature to withdraw the United States from the treaty (Gossman 2002). Our concern is for the broader issues of social justice in dealing with preventable harms by corporate entities that escape the effective grasp of national justice systems, in particular environmental harms (Drumbl 1998). The argument that the Rome Statute might become a viable remedy for environmental damage recognized as a human rights violation (Sharp 1999) hopes for much more than is apparent on the face of the statute, which (in addition to lacking applicability against corporate persons) is aimed at a less esoteric understanding of human rights at the level of street crimes. International street crime, as it has been exposed from the Nuremberg Tribunal to the Rome Statute, is important but rare compared to the existing threat of social, economic, environmental, or human damage from entities commanding huge economic resources.

CONCLUSION AND RECOMMENDATIONS

Enabling avoidable harms by juristic persons, like common crimes by natural persons, to be reachable under criminal law is a matter of simple social justice and consistent with "corporate personhood." Corporations have the capacity to formulate intent through formal decision-making structures and processes and conduct to carry out its operational policies through actions by human agents of the corporation. In this way, corporations are moral actors, responsible for the consequences of their conduct. At the national level, criminal law will be needed to reach corporate crime within sub-national jurisdictions. Similarly, at the global level, multilateral agreements on both the substantive definition of criminal conduct and the procedures to be followed will be needed to reach corporate crime that originates in one nation but does harm in other nations. It is clear from the United States' position on the Rome Statute that the world in general, and Americans in particular, have a long way to come before a global consensus will be possible.

We have suggested that economic globalization has opened opportunities for corporate criminality on a grand scale, and an international criminal code should be directed toward controlling corporate behavior along with instances of transnational "street crime" and terrorism. The French Nouveau Code Penal is a hopeful sign from Europe that the danger from crime in the suites may be placed on national agendas. At some point, before chemical poisons or purposeful economic collapse or radioactive contamination make the case in the court of world opinion, we hope to see the problem of transnational corporate crime control discussed in international fora.

The present political will of nations to control international crime has almost exclusively focused on control of international street crime through INTERPOL, tribunals in Arusha, Tanzania and The Hague investigating war crimes, and the Rome Statute. All the while, avoidable harms (often of equivalent or greater magnitude) by transnational corporations are ignored. Yet, real people are injured and die as a result of unscrupulous corporate conduct.

In the 1970s and 1980s, the Swiss-based Nestlé Corporation aggressively marketed infant formula in the developing nations of Africa, South America and the Caribbean. They persuaded millions of impoverished and illiterate mothers to stop breast feeding and switch to infant formula. Most of these mothers could not read the instructions and lacked access to clean water, refrigeration, or sterilization for bottles and nipples, facts known to the corporation during its marketing frenzy (Gerber and Short 1986: 197–198). As a result of Nestle's corporate irresponsibility, millions of children suffered dysentery or died of dehydration or malnutrition from contaminated or diluted infant formula. Mothers who tried to return to breast feeding were often unable to do so (Gerber and Short 1986: 197–200). In response, the World Health Organization established an *International Code of Marketing of Breast-milk Substitutes* (World Health Organization 1981). However, at the end of the century misuse of breast-milk substitutes continues to claim the lives of millions of infants in developing countries each year (World Health Organization 1998).

Corporate marketing practices, like that of the Nestlé Corporation, have resulted in a greater annual pediatric body count than the wars in Rwanda and the former Yugoslavia combined. The deaths and injuries of children are no less abhorrent because they were the result of corporate power rather than wars or street thugs. We have pointed out that the few halting steps toward social justice through transnational law enforcement are focused on relatively uncomplicated horrors, "international street crime," and horror appears necessary to summon the political will to transcend the legal paradigm of nation-states in the name of social justice.

The political will to establish international legal protocols is reactive. It will probably take many more incidents like the cyanide spill at Baia-Mare, Romania by Esmeralda Ltd. and the deaths of children from contaminated baby formula before the means to apply criminal sanctions to transnational corporate crime are developed and implemented. This is the price victims must pay to turn the attention of global civil society from crime in the streets to the avoidable harms of crime in the suites.

NOTES

[1] The Latin term refers to the fundamental legal principle that there can be *no punishment without law.*

[2] Within the international law context, the term "municipal law" refers to national laws.

[3] Common risk shifting strategies employed by corporations to recoup losses include increasing prices, claiming losses as tax deductible business expenses, laying off employees, raising capital through stock or bond offerings, etc. Risk shifting strategies adopted by a corporate enterprise after conviction might be considered as a new offense and prosecuted separately.

REFERENCES

Associated Press. 2000. "U.N. Starts Sampling Danube after Romanian Cyanide Spill." *New York Times* (February 16): A12.

Bassiouni, M.C. 1995. "Establishing an International Criminal Court: Historical Survey." *Military Law Review* 149: 49–63.

Barnard, C.I. 1982. *The Functions of the Executive.* Cambridge: Harvard University Press.

Bartlett, D.L. and J.B. Steele. 1998a. "Corporate Welfare." *Time* (November 9): 36+.

Bartlett, D.L. and J.B. Steele. 1998b. "The Scramble for Jobs: Playing the Zero Sum Game." *Time* (November 9).

Bartlett, D.L. and J.B. Steele. 1998c. "States at War." *Time* (November 9): 40+.

Bartlett, D.L. and J.B. Steele. 1998d. "Durant, Mississippi: Where It All Began." *Time* (November 9).

Bartlett, D.L. and J.B. Steele. 1998e. "Fantasy Islands: And Other Perfectly Legal Ways That Big Companies Manage to Avoid Billions in Federal Taxes." *Time* (November 16): 79+.

Bartlett, D.L. and J.B. Steele. 1998f. "Searle & Co.: A Case Study." *Time* (November 16).

Bartlett, D.L. and J.B. Steele. 1998g. "Arizona: What's that Rotten Smell in Phoenix." *Time* (November 23): 72+.

Bartlett, D.L. and J.B. Steele. 1998h. "The Empire of the Pigs." *Time* (November 30): 52+.

Benvenisti, E. 1999. "Exit and Voice in the Age of Globalization." *Michigan Law Review* 98: 167–212.

Binder, G. 1999. "Cultural Relativism and Cultural Imperialism in Human Rights Law." *Buffalo Human Rights Law Journal* 5: 211–21.

Bossard, A. 1990. *Transnational Crime and Criminal Law.* Chicago: Office of International Criminal Justice, University of Illinois at Chicago.

Boshra, B. 2001. "That Was Then: But the Kids Are All Right, Protestors of '60s Say." *Montreal Gazette* (April 16).

Braithwaite, J. 1984. *Corporate Crime and the Pharmaceutical Industry.* London: Routledge & Kegan Paul.

Braithwaite, J. and B. Fisse. 1995. "On the Plausibility of Corporate Crime Control." Pp. 432–49 in *White Collar Crime: Classic and Contemporary Views,* 3rd ed., edited by G. Geis, R.R. Meier, and L.M. Salinger. New York: Free Press.

Brobeck, S. and A.C. Averyt. 1983. *Product Safety Book: The Ultimate Consumer Guide to Product Hazards.* New York: Dutton.

Brown, B.S. 1999. "U.S. Objections to the Statute of the International Criminal Court: A Brief Response." *New York University Journal of International Law and Politics* 31: 855–91.

Brown, S.E. and C. Chiang. 1995. "Defining Corporate Crime: A Critique of Traditional Parameters." Pp. 29–55 in *Understanding Corporate Criminality*, edited by M.B. Blankenship. New York: Garland Publishing.

Carrasco, C.E. and M.K. Dupee. 1999. "Corporate Criminal Liability." *American Criminal Law Review* 36: 445–74.

Clinard, M.B. 1990. *Corporate Corruption: The Abuse of Power*. New York: Praeger.

Coffee, J.C., Jr. 1981. "'No Soul to Damn: No Body to Kick': An Unscandalized Inquiry into the Problem of Corporate Punishment." *Michigan Law Review* 79: 386–59.

Cressey, D.R. 1989. "The Poverty of Theory in Corporate Crime Research." Pp. 31–53 in *Advances in Criminological Theory*, vol. 1, edited by W.S. Laufer and F. Adler. New Brunswick, NJ: Transaction Books.

David, M. 1999. "Grotius Repudiated: The American Objections to the International Criminal Court and the Commitment to International Law." *Michigan Journal of International Law* 20: 337–411.

Debo, A. 1940. *And Still the Waters Run: The Betrayal of the Five Civilized Tribes*. Princeton: Princeton University Press.

Deloria, V., Jr. 1969. *Custer Died for Your Sins: An Indian Manifesto*. New York: Macmillan.

Dougherty, K. 2001. "Accord at Summit: Despite Weekend of Violent Protests, Leaders of 34 Countries Agree to Pursue Trade, Fight Poverty and Improve Education, Health Care." *Montreal Gazette* (April 23).

Drucker, P.F. 1974. *Management: Tasks, Responsibilities, Practices*. New York: Harper & Row.

Drumbl, M.A. 1998. "Waging War Against the World: The Need to Move from War Crimes to Environmental Crimes." *Fordham International Law Journal* 22: 122–53.

Dunphy, S.H. 1999a. "WTO Agenda Unfinished, But Protesters Have Drawn Battle Lines." *Seattle Times* (November 28).

Dunphy, S.H. 1999b. "Unions Press WTO for Labor Rights." *Seattle Times* (November 29).

Etzioni, A. 1964. *Modern Organizations*. Englewood Cliffs, NJ: Prentice-Hall.

Falk, R. 1999. "Telford Taylor and the Legacy of Nuremberg." *Columbia Journal of Transnational Law* 37: 693–723.

Friedrichs, D.O. 1996. *Trusted Criminals: White Collar Crime in Contemporary Society*. Belmont, CA: Wadsworth Publishing.

Gerber, J. and J.F. Short. 1986. "Publicity and the Control of Corporate Behavior: The Case of Infant Formula." *Deviant Behavior* 7: 195–216.

Gibney, M. 1997. "Human Rights Litigation in U.S. Courts: A Hypocritical Approach." *Buffalo Journal of International Law* 3: 261–88.

Gossman, M. 2002. "American Foreign Policy and the International Criminal Court." Remarks to the Center for Strategic and International Studies by the Under Secretary of State for Public Affairs, May 6, http://www.state.gov/p/us/rm/9949.htm.

Hanes, A. 2001. "Internet Links Anti-Globalists." *Montreal Gazette* (March 28).

Headden, S. 1998. "The Marlboro Man Lives: Restrained at Home, Tobacco Firms Step Up Their Marketing Overseas." *U.S. News and World Report* (Sept. 21): 58–59.

Hindman, H.D. and C.G. Smith. 1999. "Cross-Cultural Ethics and the Child Labor Problem." *Journal of Business Ethics* 19: 21–33.

Irwin, J. and J. Austin. 1997. *It's About Time: America's Imprisonment Binge*, 2nd ed. Belmont, CA: Wadsworth Publishing.

Jones, T. 1988. *Corporate Killing: Bhopals Will Happen*. London: Free Association Books.

Jorg, N. 1997. "The Promise and Limitations of Corporate Criminal Liability." Pp. 99–116 in *Debating Corporate Crime*, edited by W.S. Lofquist, M.A. Cohen, and G.A. Rabe. Cincinnati: Anderson Publishing.

Kerry, J. 1991. "Where is the S&L Money?" *USA Today Magazine* (September): 20–21.

Khanna, V.S. 1999. "Is the Notion of Corporate Fault a Faulty Notion?: The Case of Corporate Mens Rea." *Boston University Law Review* 79: 355–415.

Khanna, V.S. 1996. "Corporate Criminal Liability: What Purpose Does it Serve?" *Harvard Law Review* 109: 1477–534.

Kluger, R. 1996. *Ashes to Ashes: America's Hundred-Year Cigarette War, the Public Health, and Unabashed Triumph of Philip Morris*. New York: Alfred A. Knopf.

Leonard, A. 1993. "Poison Fields." *Multinational Monitor* (April): 14–18.

Lofquist, W. 1997. "A Framework for Analysis of the Theories and Issues in Corporate Crime." Pp. 1–29 in *Debating Corporate Crime*, edited by W.S. Lofquist, M.A. Cohen, and G.A. Rabe. Cincinnati: Anderson Publishing.

Los Angeles Times & The Associated Press. 1999. "WTO Refuses to Discuss What Went Wrong, Lessons to be Learned from Seattle." *Seattle Times* (December 18).

McCoubrey, H. and N.D. White. 1992. *International Law and Armed Conflict*. Brookfield, MA: Dartmouth Publishing.

McGregor, D.M. 1996. "The Human Side of Enterprise." Pp. 176–82 in *Classics of Organization Theory*, 4th ed., edited by J.M. Shafritz and J.S. Ott. Fort Worth: Harcourt Brace College Publishers.

Mokhiber, R. 1988. *Corporate Crime and Violence: Big Business Power and the Abuse of Public Trust*. San Francisco: Sierra Club Books.

Morales, D. 1998. *The Texas Tobacco Lawsuit Victory: What it Means to the People of Texas*. Austin: Office of the Attorney General.

Moshan, B.S. 1998. "Women, War, and Words: The Gender Component in the Permanent International Criminal Court's Definition of Crimes Against Humanity." *Fordham International Law Journal* 22: 154–84.

O'Connell, M.E. 1992. "Enforcing the New International Law of the Environment." *German Yearbook of International Law* 35: 293–332.

O'Connell, M.E. 1995. "Enforcement and the Success of International Environmental Law." *Indiana Journal of Global Legal Studies* 3: 47–64.

O'Conner, G.E. 1999. "The Pursuit of Justice and Accountability: Why the United States Should Support the Establishment of an International Criminal Court." *Hofstra Law Review* 27: 927–77.

Orland, L. and C. Cachera. 1995. "Corporate Crime and Punishment in France: Criminal Responsibility of Legal Entities (Personnes Morales) Under the New French Criminal Code (Nouveau Code Penal)." *Connecticut Journal of International Law* 11: 111–68.

Parker, J.S. 1997. "The Blunt Instrument." Pp. 71–97 in *Debating Corporate Crime*, edited by W.S. Lofquist, M.A. Cohen, and G.A. Rabe. Cincinnati: Anderson Publishing.

Penrose, M.M. 2000. "Lest We Fail: The Importance of Enforcement in International Criminal Law." *American University International Law Review* 15: 321–94.

Pepinsky, H.E. and P. Jesilow. 1984. *Myths that Cause Crime*. Cabin John, MD: Seven Locks Press.

Porterfeld, A. and D. Weir. 1987. "The Export of U.S. Toxic Wastes." *The Nation* (October): 325, 341–44.

Postman, D. 1999. "WTO in Seattle: Everyone Has an Agenda, Including the Turtles." *Seattle Times* (November 28).

Postman, D. and L.V. Mapes. 1999. "Why WTO United So Many Foes." *Seattle Times* (December 6).

Punch, M. 1996. *Dirty Business: Exploring Corporate Misconduct*. Thousand Oaks: Sage.

Reiman, J. 1998. *The Rich Get Richer and the Poor Get Prison*, 5th ed. Needham Heights, MA: Allyn and Bacon.

Reuters. 2000. "Cyanide Spill Kills Danube Fish." *New York Times* (February 14): A8.

Robinson, P.H., M.T. Cahill, and U. Mohammad. 2000. "The Five Worst (and Five Best) American Criminal Codes." *Northwestern University Law Review* 95: 1–89.

Rosoff, S.M., H.N. Pontell and R. Tillman. 1998. *Profit Without Honor: White-Collar Crime and the Looting of America*. Upper Saddle River, NJ: Prentice Hall.

Russell, S. and M.J. Gilbert. 1999. "Truman's Revenge: Social Control and Corporate Crime." *Crime, Law and Social Change* 32: 59–82.

Russell, S. 1999. "A Black and White Issue: The Invisibility of American Indians in Racial Policy Discourse." *Georgetown Public Policy Review* 4: 129–47.

Schlegel, K. 1990. *Just Desserts for Corporate Criminals*. Boston: Northeastern University Press.

Seattle Times Company. 1999a. "Schedule of Events." *Seattle Times* (November 29).

Seattle Times Company. 1999b. "Schedule of Events." *Seattle Times* (November 30).

Sharp, P. 1999. "Prospects for Environmental Liability in the International Criminal Court." *Virginia Environmental Law Journal* 18: 217–43.

Shrivastava, P. 1987. *Bhopal: Anatomy of a Crisis*. Cambridge, MA: Ballinger.

Simon, D.R. 1996. *Elite Deviance*, 5th ed. Boston: Allyn and Bacon.

Simon, H.A. 1976. *Administrative Behavior: A Study of Decision-Making Processes in Administrative Organization*, 3rd ed. New York: Free Press.

Smith, A. 1952. *An Inquiry into the Nature and Causes of the Wealth of Nations*. Chicago: Encyclopaedia Britannica. Originally published in 1776.

Stinchcomb, J.B. and V.B. Fox. 1999. *Introduction to Corrections*, 5th ed. Upper Saddle River, NJ: Prentice Hall.

Taylor, T. 1970. *Nuremberg and Vietnam: An American Tragedy*. Chicago: Quadrangle Books.

Taylor, T. 1992. *The Anatomy of the Nuremberg Trials*. New York: Alfred A. Knopf.

"The Global Poison Trade." 1988. *Newsweek* (November 7): 66–68.

Thornburgh, R. 1990. "Money Laundering." *Vital Speeches of the Day* 56: 578–80.

Thurber, D. 2000. "For Richer, Poorer Nations, Divisions Linger at Trade Conference." *Seattle Times* (February 14).

Trice, H.M. and J.M. Beyer. 1996. "Changing Organizational Cultures." Pp. 473–84 in *Classics of Organization Theory*, 4th ed., edited by J.M. Shafritz and J.S. Ott. Fort Worth: Harcourt Brace College Publishers.

Truell, P. and L. Gurwin. 1992. *False Profits: The Inside Story of BCCI, The World's Most Corrupt Financial Empire*. New York: Houghton Mifflin.

van der Vyver, J.D. 1998. "Universality and Relativity of Human Rights: American Relativism." *Buffalo Human Rights Law Journal* 4: 43–78.

Woods, A. 1998. "Globalisation and the Rise of Labor Market Inequalities." *The Economic Journal* 108: 450, 1463–1482.

World Health Organization. 1981. *International Code of Marketing of Breast-milk Substitutes*. Geneva: World Health Organization.

World Health Organization. 1998. Address to the XXII International Congress of Paediatrics Global Trends in Child Health in Amsterdam, Netherlands by Dr. Gro Harlem Brundtland, Director General, World Health Organization (August 10). Geneva: World Health Organization.

Wunder, J.R. 1994. *"Retained by the People"*: *A History of American Indians and the Bill of Rights*. New York: Oxford University Press.

CHAPTER STUDY QUESTIONS

- What is transnational corporate crime? What is the role played by the globalization of the economic playing field and international free trade practices in the growth of different forms of transnational corporate crime?

- Gilbert and Russell argue that "[a]s corporations increase their ability to do harm, more nations are beginning to respond with criminal sanctions." What steps have been taken in France in this direction? Do you agree with Gilbert and Russell that the French Nouveau Code Penal is a form of model legislation that other countries would be wise to emulate? Explain.

- According to Gilbert and Russell, why are the Permanent International Court of Justice and the new International Criminal Court created through the Rome Statute both incapable of serving as an effective international court for prosecuting cases of transnational corporate crime? In considering this question, give attention to the often incompatible concepts of "international legality" and "national sovereignty."

- Gilbert and Russell call for the establishment of "[a]n international court, armed with a penal code tailored to transnational corporate crime and international conventions to provide authoritative jurisdiction over transnational corporate criminal conduct" in order to more effectively address the growing problem of transnational corporate crime and foster social justice in the international arena. Do you agree with Gilbert and Russell's argument? In your view, what would be some of the major obstacles that might stand in the way of creating the kind of international criminal justice system proposed by Gilbert and Russell?

RELATED WEB LINKS

National White Collar Crime Center
http://www.nw3c.org/

> This US congressionally funded, non-profit corporation is dedicated to helping law enforcement agencies better understand and utilize tools to combat economic and high-tech crime. This website provides access to numerous publications, reports, and recent law enforcement initiatives focused on combating white collar crime.

Corporate Crime Reporter
http://www.corporatecrimereporter.com/

> This site provides access to reports and documents on recent, publicized cases of white collar and corporate crime, along with commentaries and interviews on issues related to the prosecution of white collar and corporate crime.

Global Issues That Affect Everyone
http://www.globalissues.org/

> This site is devoted to providing access to information on global issues, including economic, geopolitical, human rights, environmental, and health issues. The site also contains information and links to other websites dealing with corporations and the International Criminal Court.

Economic Policy Institute
http://www.epi.org/

> This non-profit organization is dedicated to undertaking research and educational initiatives aimed at promoting a prosperous, fair, and sustainable economy. It provides access to publications and reports on globalization and economic trade liberalization.

Chapter 6

BODIES, BORDERS, AND SEX TOURISM IN A GLOBALIZED WORLD: A TALE OF TWO CITIES—AMSTERDAM AND HAVANA

NANCY A. WONDERS AND RAYMOND MICHALOWSKI

The great drama of the last quarter of the 20th century was the collapse of socialism and the subsequent attempt to refashion the world into a single capitalist system managed and controlled from a small core of "global cities" scattered around the world (Amin 1990, 1997; Greider 1997; Hoogvelt 1997; Mander and Goldsmith 1996; Sassen 1996, 1998, 2000a). This process of integrating the world into a single capitalist system—typically termed "globalization"—is often cast as an unprecedented political-economic development (Karliner 1997; Korten 1995). Others suggest that today's "globalization" is essentially a contemporary expression of the historical project of creating a worldwide capitalist system, a project that extends roughly from the rise of mercantile capitalism in the 1400s to the present (Friedman 1999; Hirst 1996). Whether it represents a novel form of political-economy or is just a resumption of the pre-socialist urge of capitalism to command the globe, the current era of globalization is characterized by unprecedented movement of material, information, finance, and bodies across borders.

In this chapter, we examine how globalization facilitates the growth of sex tourism, as well as the particular character of sex tourism in different locales. As others have already detailed (Opperman 1998), "sex tourism" is a protean term that attempts to capture varieties of leisure travel that have as a part of their purpose the purchase of sexual services. Clearly the concepts of "prostitution" and "tourism" are both central to an analysis of sex tourism, but neither term captures the full meaning of sex tourism. "Sex tourism" highlights the convergence between prostitution and tourism, links the global and the local, and draws attention to both the production and consumption of sexual services. The growth in sex tourism over the last two decades is well established (Kempadoo and Doezema 1998; Opperman 1998). In this chapter, we focus specifically on how the global forces shaping this growth connect the practice of sex work in two disparate cities with globalized sex tourism.

Our analysis of sex tourism has two closely related goals. First, we explore the *global forces* that shape the production and consumption of sex tourism. We argue that global forces influence the production of globalized sex tourism via the increased movement of bodies associated with migration and tourism. Global forces also shape the consumption of sexual services by fostering tourism as an industry aimed at those who have the resources to travel and purchase what they desire, thus, facilitating the commodification of both male desire and women's bodies within the global capitalist economy.

By examining sex tourism as a product of global forces, we hope to shift attention from individual "prostitutes" as social problems to "sex tourism" as a form of global commerce that is transforming sex work, cities, and human relationships. Most writings on the sex trade take prostitutes as the starting point for an analysis of sex work. This leads to an overemphasis on individuals, particularly women, as deviant or pathological for their participation in the sex trade.[1] It is our view that an adequate analysis of contemporary sex tourism must consider how the meshing of the supply and demand curves for sex creates a transnational business like any other.

A second goal of our analysis is to foreground cities as strategic sites of globalization and further, to identify some of the mediating institutions that connect cities to the global forces shaping sex tourism. As Sassen (2000a: 143) points out, "Large cities in the highly developed world are the places where globalization processes assume concrete, localized forms. These localized forms are, in good part, what globalization is about." The exchanges of money, ideas, and commands that comprise globalization must always take place *somewhere*, and the modern city is that somewhere, the place where "key global processes ranging from international finance to immigration" are constituted (Sassen 1996: 131). When analyzing a single city, however, it can be difficult to assess the extent to which the locale is shaped by larger, global forces. Comparative work such as ours makes it possible to observe the way that global forces serve to create *global connections* between practices in disparate places. In this chapter, we explore the global connections between sex tourism and two cities with very different histories: Amsterdam and Havana. As our analysis will evidence, although sex tourism differs in each city, the impact of globalization is evident in the changing character of a variety of common mediating institutions that link each city to the global economy and to globalized sex tourism. Because sex work always occurs in a localized context, it is typically treated as an individual adjustment to local economies and local cultures. We contend, however, that in some places global forces increasingly over-determine the localized experience of sex work.

In pursuing the goals outlined above, our approach to sex tourism is both theoretical and ethnographic. Employing political-economic, feminist, and postmodern theoretical perspectives, we seek to further understand the relationship between sex tourism and the emerging global capitalist order. We do this by utilizing the methodology of "global ethnography," as outlined by Burawoy, et al. (2000). Global ethnography combines traditional ethnography with ethno-historical information as a strategy to analyze the impact of globalization.[2] Because globalization operates across time and space, traditional ethnographic methods, which tend to be place-bound, must be supplemented with information linking the particular research moment to the broader historical context, and the particular research site to the broader transnational forces and processes that constitute the global. Global ethnography describes a set of strategies for combining abstract, theoretical insights about globalization with concrete, historically contextualized, geographically situated practices.

Global ethnographic approaches have several features, but the two characteristics most salient for our research are 1) the focus on external global *forces* and 2) the emphasis placed on global *connections* between geographical sites (Burawoy et al. 2000). The term "global forces" refers to the broad trends typically associated with globalization, including (but not limited to) global capital flows, globalized labor markets and industries, mass migration as a result of local economic displacement, growing disparities of wealth and income, and the emergence of global cities. "Global connections" refer to the linkages between particular places created by the impact of global forces on localized environments and vice versa. As Burawoy et al. (2000: 5) emphasize, "Within any field, whether it had global reach or was bounded by a community or nation, our fieldwork had to assemble a picture of the whole by recognizing diverse perspectives from the parts, from singular but connected sites." Thus, global connections reference the process by which local sites and localized practices become connected to the global.

Global ethnography employs the extended case study method to explore global forces and connections by "extending from observer to participant, extending observations over time and place, extending from process to external forces, and extending theory" (Burawoy et al. 2000: 28). Global ethnography recognizes that it is not enough to assert that global forces exist at an abstract level. Global ethnography requires concrete, ethnographic, and localized knowledge about how global forces operate to create connections that cross space and time boundaries.

Our strategy in analyzing sex tourism in two cities closely follows this model. First, we ground our research in broader theoretical and historical insights about the global forces shaping the growth and character of sex tourism, focusing particular attention on those global forces linked to the production and consumption of sex tourism. To do this, we weave together literatures that rarely converse, including work on globalization, feminist research on gender and sex work, and literature addressing consumption, leisure, and tourism. We then explore the way that global forces have impacted two particular cities, Amsterdam and Havana. Drawing on our own fieldwork experiences,[3] we combine ethnographic data with ethno-historical information about each city in order to understand global sex tourism as it appears in each local context. Our analysis focuses on several local institutions that are impacted by global forces, thus mediating between the global and the local: the tourism industry, labor markets, localized sex work, and law and policy. These mediating institutions create global connections that link sex work in these two cities to globalized sex tourism.

There are several limitations associated with our theoretical and methodological approach that should be mentioned. First, although we recognize that there is a growing body of literature addressing male sex workers, female sex tourists, and gay and lesbian sex tourism, our analysis focuses on the modal practice of sex tourism, which involves male customers and female providers of sexual services. While analysis of other variations of sex tourism is important, it is beyond the scope of the current project. Additionally, we acknowledge limitations in the global ethnographic approach we have outlined. Interpreting another culture is always risky. Although our understanding of both Amsterdam and Havana was enhanced by our experiences of living and working in these cultures, and by ethnographic and historical research, our work is not thickly descriptive in the mode of interpretive anthropology (Geertz 1983). At some level, we remain global tourists ourselves. Given our research focus, however, we believe that this vantage point has its advantages.

GLOBAL FORCES: THE PRODUCTION AND CONSUMPTION OF

GLOBALIZED SEX TOURISM

Globalization has wrought many changes, but two are particularly salient for understanding the emergence of sex tourism as a significant form of economic activity. One significant global force shaping sex tourism is the worldwide movement of bodies across borders, whether for business, war, or pleasure. The movement of bodies takes many forms, but two of the most significant are migration and tourism. Migration typically involves bodies from less developed or less stable nations moving across borders into more developed or stable ones in an attempt to improve economic options, or to escape life-threatening conflicts including genocide, war, and famine. Cross-border tourism typically reverses this pattern as privileged bodies from industrialized nations cross into less developed ones in search of exotic pleasures and a little (highly controlled) danger. These increases in tourism and migration have fostered heightened opportunities for sex work as these global forces expand the pools of both potential sex consumers and potential sex workers.

The second global force affecting sex tourism is the shift from a worldwide economic system based on expanding production to one whose central engine of growth is expanding *consumption* (Lury 1996). Globalized capitalism demands the continual development of new commodity forms. The consequence is that many elements of social life that once remained outside the realm of commodity exchange must now be commodified in order to create new markets and to protect or expand profits (Friedman 1999). This, in turn, introduces new forms of labor and new forms of consumption into the global marketplace, of which the expansion of sex tourism is but one example. In the analysis that follows, we argue that sex tourism both fosters and is fostered by the global commodification of (primarily male) desire and (primarily women's) bodies as new markets in ways that transcend and shape local institutions and discourses.

The production of sex tourism: Global inequality, bodies, and border crossings

A great deal has been written in recent years detailing the economic, social, and physical dislocation of people caught in the tide of globalization. Some emphasize that this movement of humanity is largely a response to profound inequality between countries due to the growing concentration and centralization of wealth under globalization (Burbach, Nuiez, and Kargarlitsky 1997; Dougherty and Holthouse 1998). Others suggest that this heightened transnational flow of bodies is not necessarily negative, since people often move in search of higher standards of living, work, or just to enjoy travel and white sandy beaches (Davidow and Malone 1992; Friedman 1999). What is not in dispute, however, is that two of the most significant waves of human movement today are migrants and tourists. While their immediate motivations differ, both tourists and migrants travel because they desire something better than what their current home has to offer.

The intersection of tourism and migration in the globalized world system facilitates the production of sex tourism by bringing together mobile sex workers with mobile sex consumers.

This increased mobility has two vectors. On the one hand, increased concentrations of wealth within industrialized nations means that more people—mostly men, but also some women—can afford to travel as tourists in foreign lands where they can enjoy "exotic" sights, sounds, and in some cases, "otherly" bodies. On the other hand, as global capital disrupts established patterns of economic survival in less developed nations, unemployment, urban migration, and national out-migration rise (Wonders and Danner 2002). This push toward migration was clearly visible in the International Labor Organization's (ILO) estimate that around *thirty percent* of the world's labor force is "unemployed and unable to sustain a minimum standard of living" (Chomsky 1994: 188, emphasis added).

Not all social groups are affected equally by economic displacement. Wonders and Danner (1999: 3) make the point that "globalization has engendered profound change because it is itself gendered." As a 1996 ILO report noted, "the feminization" of international labor migration is "one of the most striking economic and social phenomena of recent times" (Kempadoo and Doezema 1998: 17). Among other consequences, the feminization of migration brings growing numbers of women into geographical and social environments where their best (and in some cases, only) option for economic survival and social advancement is sex work. This is true not only in developing countries where economic options are bleak for the majority, but it is increasingly so in industrialized countries that have thrown up employment barriers to intentionally discourage migration. As Wijers (1998: 72) points out, such restrictions on employment create a situation where "almost the only work migrant women are allowed to do is in the entertainment section or sex industry, whether this is the official policy, as in Switzerland, or just everyday practice, as in the Netherlands."

The growth of tourism as a result of the expanding global economy constitutes one of the most significant engines fueling the increase in commercial sex. As an area of employment, tourism is both large and growing. The World Trade and Tourism Council (WTTC) estimates that between 1989 and 1992 employment in all tourism—international and internal—grew by 20 percent (ILO 1998). In 1996, "the industry's gross output was estimated to be US $3.6 trillion, 10 percent of all consumer spending. The travel and tourism industry is the world's largest employer, with 255 million jobs, or almost 11 percent of all employees. This industry is the world's leading industrial contributor, producing over 10 percent of the world gross domestic product (Theobald 1998: 4). While most of this tourism does not involve the production or consumption of sexual services, an important and growing proportion does. Pietila and Vickers (1994: 121) argue that "prostitution has become big business, and 'traffic in persons' has taken on new and more sophisticated forms and extended on an unforeseen scale to become an international trade ... massive expansion of intercontinental tourism, coupled with the deteriorating situation of women in many developing countries, has made sex holidays an ever flourishing phenomenon." Echoing this perspective, Herman (1995: 5) calls sex tourism "one of the booming markets in the New World Order—a multi-billion dollar industry with finders, brokers, syndicate operations and pimp 'managers' at the scene of action." Even conservative business publications have noted the growing strength and globalization of the sex "industry"; *The Economist* (1998: 23) estimates that the global sex industry is worth "at least $20 billion a year and probably many times that."

Although sex tourism can take many forms, sex tourists are overwhelming men with resources, while sex workers are overwhelming poor women of color (Richter 1998). This has
led many researchers to contend that most global sex tourism—both North-South and North-
North—arises from the linkage between the political-economic advantage enjoyed by affluent
men from developed countries and the widespread cultural fantasy in those nations that dusky-
skinned "others" from exotic southern lands are liberated from the sexual/emotional inhibi-
tions characteristic of women (and/or men) in their own societies (Kempadoo and Doezema
1998; Sanchez Taylor 2000). For advantaged men from the developed world, sex tourism provides an opportunity, not only to experience fantasized sexual freedom with imagined unin-
hibited women, but also the opportunity to experience—in their bodies—their own privilege.
As Skrobanek et al. (1997: viii) write of sex tourism in Thailand, "Thailand is like a stage where
men from around the world come to perform their role of male supremacy over women and
their white supremacy over Thai people." The gendered and racialized patterns of sex tourism
characterized by Skrobanek, and found in the ILO case studies in Southeast Asia, are not
unique to these countries. Rather, as our case studies of Amsterdam and Havana will show, they
are local patterns that are structured by broader global forces.

The consumption of globalized sex tourism:
Commodification of bodies and desire

Global economic forces not only facilitate the production of sex tourism, they also facilitate its
consumption. In the global economic search for new markets, the process of commodification
has gone beyond material goods to all social life. One book title—*Consuming People* (Firat and
Dholakia 1998)—plays out a double entendre that accurately reflects the contemporary global
situation. Today people are constantly consuming, not only material goods, but other people
as well, via the purchase of human services, relational experiences, and sexual encounters.
Indeed, "consumption ... may be the most important force that unites the contemporary world"
(Firat and Dholakia 1998: 103).

The recognition that consumption is an important engine of global and local economic
growth requires that we analyze the production of sex tourism in terms of the behavior and
preferences of sex consumers, not just sex providers. In the global capitalist marketplace, the
desires of those with resources, particularly privileged male consumers, have become prime
targets for producers and retailers of all types of goods and services. As a number of researchers on gender and leisure note, white, male desire has itself been commodified in the global
production of leisure services, including sex tourism (Adkins 1995; Craik 1997). In their quest
for markets and money, creative entrepreneurs develop products and services designed to both
fulfill and shape male desire. Thus, male desire facilitates the production of commodified
services at the same time as service providers in leisure industries seek to commodify male
desire. This interrelationship is necessitated, in part, because of the close proximity of the
production of leisure services to their consumption; "this proximity is thought to mean that
cultural practices, especially the cultural expectations of consumers, act to significantly de-

termine the social relations of production" (Adkins 1995: 7). As primary providers of a range of leisure activities, including sex work, women are expected to tailor the services they provide to consumer expectations, particularly the expectations of their primarily male clientele. In a study of leisure services in England, Adkins (1995), for example, notes that all of the female service workers in two major hotel and entertainment parks were expected to undertake emotional and sensual work as a regular part of their jobs. As primarily male customers voiced their desires, female service workers were expected to immediately respond to expectations. Thus, customers shaped the services they received in a relational fashion. This relational understanding of work in the service sector is taken to an extreme in sex work, since the sexual services sold by prostitutes are largely shaped in the moment, as customers express their desires (Zatz 1997). Thus, the particular form of sex work provided both reflects and (re)constitutes (primarily) male desire. For example, some research shows that the desire expressed by some male sex consumers for emotional and sensual labor to accompany sexual labor shapes the character of sex work for some prostitutes (see the growing body of writings by female sex workers on this point; e.g., Chapkis 1997; Nagle 1997). In this regard, it is crucial to point out that sex tourism is similar to other forms of tourism in that "the cultural experiences offered by tourism are consumed in terms of prior knowledge, expectations, fantasies and mythologies generated in the tourist's origin culture, rather than by the cultural offerings of the destination" (Craik 1997: 118). The expectations and desires of those with resources influence what "others" try to sell to them; in essence, privileged desire influences what options "others" have as they seek wages in the globalized economy (O'Connell Davidson 1998; Richter 1998).

The objectification of bodies, particularly women's bodies, is well documented as a primary source of the commodification of bodies under capitalism (Bordo 1993). But to fully understand the commodification of bodies under globalization, we need to link the process of objectification to the more general disembodiment of workers within the capitalist economy. For Marx, all workers under capitalism are alienated; they are symbolically disembodied as they sell their labor power to employers for a wage in order to survive (Marx [1887] 1958: 207–08). For women in both industrialized and developing countries, however, reasonably remunerative wage labor associated with commodity production is increasingly difficult to secure. This is particularly true for migrant women of color. Under these circumstances, some women do not sell their bodily labor to produce a commodity; instead, their *bodies* become commodities. It is important to emphasize here that we are not positing sex itself as inherently exploitative or problematic, but we do problematize the commodification of bodies in order to make a living wage. As newly industrializing countries struggle to find commodity niches in the globalized economy, they frequently find many of the best product niches taken. As a consequence, in some countries, sex tourism becomes a significant market fostering of both national economic development and international capital accumulation (Enloe 1989; Kempadoo and Doczcma 1998; Lean Lim 1998; Truong 1990). In these countries and in many other parts of the globalized world, sex work is a tolerated "choice" for women for whom it appears the best option for supporting themselves and their families (see selections in Chapkis 1997 or Nagle 1997). In this way, sex work reveals "the gendered organization of the 'economic': of the ways in which social identities available to men and women in the workplace, for instance, relate to the gendered nature of the very fabric of society—to (gendered) economic relations" (Adkins 1995: 52).

As we noted above, the rise of mass tourism is one of the major transformations of the contemporary period. Although other scholars have already made the point, we wish to join the voices emphasizing the gendered character of tourism (Craig-Smith and French 1994; Craik 1997; Richter 1998). As Richter (1998: 392) argues, "Travel has had a different *contextual* meaning for men than for women...." For men, tourism and travel are more often defined as adventure and constant change, as distance and escape from the routine and familiar. This sense of tourism, along with the idea that leisure for the tourist takes place beyond (some might say "against") the home reflects a historically male interpretation of pleasure. While selling sexual services is an old commerce, and leisure travel has long been common for the wealthy, both have changed in ways that increasingly parallel the globalized economy and the desires of privileged male tourists. Increasingly, women are themselves viewed as a tourist destination. Sex and bodies are viewed as commodities that can be packaged, advertised, displayed, and sold on a global scale. Rojec and Urry (1997: 17) argue that "Travel and tourism can be thought of as a search for difference ... Women are the embodiment of difference. The act of leaving home to travel involves, for men, sexual adventure, finding a woman." Craik (1997: 116) emphasizes "the manufacture of simulacra (or 'as if' experiences) as the basis of the contemporary tourist experience." Whether prostitutes are displayed in windows (like clothes on mannequins) or appear in hotel lobbies (as though they are complementary beverages), bodies increasingly are used as simulacra to represent "something else" to the leisure tourist; prostitutes appear as "minor wives," "girlfriends," "exotic others," or "sex toys"—whatever the tourist needs them to be to achieve the experience he desires. In this sense, both tourists and tourist sites engage in a kind of performance where each pretends to meet the "other's" expectations as a way to simulate the desired experience (see Chapkis 1997; Nagle 1997; Rojec and Urry 1997).

Not only is the desire for new experiences commodified in the globalized economy but so, too, is the desire to experiment with different identities. Increasingly, scholars have come to understand all identities as *fluid*, changeable, social constructions (Ferrante and Brown 1998; Wonders 2000). Much of the tourist and consumer experience involves buying products, services, and experiences that create the illusion of becoming someone else. MacCannell (1999) suggests that this opportunity to become someone else is an important reason why many tourists travel in the first place. Travel to other countries facilitates the fluidity of identity because we typically leave behind the signposts and people associated with our present identity, making it easier to adopt new ones. Similarly, tourists feel free to experience the identity of "others" by sampling cultural products, experiences, bodies, and identities. But this sampling is rarely without judgment, since the tourist brings along cultural assumptions and biases on every trip. In the case of sex tourism, expectations and assumptions about other cultures and racial groups often result in racist payment schedules for sexual services; this serves to perpetuate racial hierarchies among sex workers (Kempadoo and Doezema 1998; Pettman 1997), as well as racist laws and regulatory policies directed at particular categories of prostitutes (Bell 1994). Our own ethnographic research confirms that reality.

In this section, we have outlined some of the key global forces shaping the growth and character of sex tourism. Specifically, we suggest that the production of sex tourism is facilitated by the worldwide movement of bodies across borders as a result of expanding migration and tourism, while its consumption is facilitated by the commodification of bodies and desire. In the next section, we investigate the ways that these seemingly abstract global forces come to ground in two diverse cities: Amsterdam and Havana.

GLOBAL CONNECTIONS: A TALE OF TWO CITIES

Research provides compelling evidence that cities are strategic sites for observing the effects of globalization (Sassen 1998, 2000a, 2000b; Sassen and Roost 1997). In our analysis, we detail the way that the global forces shaping the production and consumption of sex tourism impact two very different cities: Amsterdam and Havana. We explore the global connections that link sex work in these two cities with the forces associated with globalized sex tourism. Specifically, we argue that global forces impact sex work in both cities through four mediating institutions 1) the tourism industry, 2) labor markets, 3) the localized sex industry, and 4) law and policy. As mediating institutions in these cities adjusted to the impact of global forces, they created opportunities for sex tourism to flourish.

It is important to our analysis that Amsterdam and Havana are very different cities. Many argue that global forces are easily discerned in "global cities" like Amsterdam (Sassen 2000a, 1998). Global cities are strategically positioned at the center of the global capitalist system as command points, key locations, and marketplaces for leading industries, and major sites of production; they are "strategic sites for the management of the global economy and the production of the most advanced services and financial operations" (Sassen 2000a: 21). Within these cities, the impact of globalization has been documented to be far-reaching (Sassen 1998, 2000a; Sassen and Roost 1997).

In contrast, Havana is located in Cuba, one of the last self-identified socialist states in the world. Cuba is a developing island nation struggling to find a foothold in the new global capitalist economy that will enable it to grow economically, while preserving its socialist accomplishments in health, education, and social welfare (Dello Buono and Lara 1997). Within Cuba, Havana occupies a central role and is best characterized as a "primate city," that is, one which accounts "for a disproportionate share of population, employment, and gross national product (GNP)" within a country (Sassen 2000a: 34). Not surprisingly, "the Caribbean has a long history of urban primacy" (Sassen 2000a: 39). Rarely viewed as a central site of globalization, primate cities are affected by globalization nevertheless, since global forces first come to ground in a country with a primate urban system by impacting these cities (Sassen 2000a).

Despite their differences, we illustrate that globalization's reach is evident in both Amsterdam and Havana. The specific responses to global forces differ, but comparison between these two cities reveals the impact of significant global connections on sex work in both locations.

Shopping for bodies in Amsterdam

In Amsterdam, the commodification of bodies has been perfected to the level of an art form. The red light district resembles the modern open-air shopping mall in the United States. Relatively clean streets, little crime, a neon atmosphere, and windows and windows of women to choose from—every size, shape, and color (though not in equal amounts). The red light district seems designed to be a sex tourist's Mecca. The range of services for the leisure traveler includes sex clubs, sex shows, lingerie, and S&M clothing shops, condomories, and a sprinkling of porno stores. But the character of Amsterdam's red light district is different from most other sex tourist locations because it is centered in an historic district between the Oude Kerk (Old Church) and de Waag (an old weighing station)—two of the most spectacular cultural tourist sites in the city—and it is surrounded by an old, well established residential neighborhood. Indeed, walking through the red light district in the daytime is not so different from walking down any other shopping street in the city, though the area takes on a festival atmosphere at night. Crowds of men walk the street, stopping to gaze at the living merchandise in the window. The routine among men is much like the routine observed among women shopping for clothes, with plentiful commentary on the size, shape, color, and cost of the women on display. The smorgasbord of languages rising through the air reveals the international character of those shopping for bodies.

In describing the Amsterdam scene, it is important to make clear that women sex workers are far from passive in the shopping interaction. On quieter evenings and in the daytime, it is common for women to hover near the doorways of their small window booths, hooting and calling at men to "come here!" in a number of different languages. In an odd role reversal, one male friend commented to me after a walk through the district that: "I've never felt so objectified in my life. I felt like a piece of meat walking through there."

Historical and cultural background: Dutch tolerance and sex "work"

[As in] ... other Western industrialized cities, prostitution has a long history in Amsterdam. Indeed, in the Netherlands, "it has never been forbidden to prostitute oneself" (Boutellier 1991: 209). Although most citizens stigmatize prostitutes, the Dutch have long viewed prostitution as one among many social problems to be minimized, but not criminalized. The goal of Dutch policy toward sex work primarily focuses on reducing the adverse impact of prostitution on local citizens and neighborhoods, what one writer calls "regulated tolerance" (Brants 1998). Thus, officially, there is no national policy toward sex work; rather, each municipality controls policies toward prostitution.

The concept of tolerance plays an important role in preventing and managing conflict in this small, heavily populated country built on religious and cultural difference (Rochon 1999). The Netherlands is often regarded as a liberal country politically, primarily because of its extensive social welfare system and its progressive, "tolerant" attitude toward social problems that other countries tend to criminalize, such as prostitution and drug use. What is little known to outsiders is that much of the country's apparently liberal policy emerges from compromise, particularly among relatively conservative religious groups, rather than broad consensus (Cox 1993). This is the foundation of Dutch pragmatism and tolerance. In practice, tolerance has historically meant that the law is rarely used to regulate social problems, such as prostitution, since compromise is difficult to reach around controversial moral questions (Brants 1998; Haen Marshall 1993). Instead, until recently, local responses to prostitution typically reflected a complex and shifting interplay between prostitutes, authorities, and the concerns of local citizens.

During the 1960s and 1970s, attitudes toward prostitution began to change, reflecting cultural changes taking place in most industrialized Western countries. The women's movement facilitated a sexual revolution that helped to bring greater legitimacy to sex work, largely through the work of women's organizations, but also in conjunction with other organized interests. In 1961, the Mr. A. de Graaf Foundation was created, a non-profit organization whose objectives include "research, policy development, advice, documentation, and public information" regarding prostitution (Mr. A. de Graaf Foundation 1997). Importantly, this organization has played a pivotal role in arguing for "removing prostitution from the sphere of the penal code, and, via a phased introduction of worker's rights, making the legal position of prostitutes identical to that of workers in other (legal) industries" (van der Pod 1995). Without question, the Netherlands has been a leader in the international organization of sex work. It was host to the first international Whore's Conference, and, in the 1980s, The Red Thread (De Rood Draad), a prostitute's rights organization, was formed which also facilitated the redefinition of prostitution as sex "work." Although this redefinition did not dramatically reduce the stigma attached to prostitution (though citizen attitudes toward prostitution probably improved a bit after Dutch prostitutes were required to pay taxes), it did facilitate the decriminalization of sex work. This enabled Dutch prostitutes to seek health care, social service support, and law enforcement protection, benefits rarely available to sex workers in other industrialized countries. It was primarily as a result of this combination of Dutch tolerance and sexual emancipation that the "world famous red light district of Amsterdam grew into a free zone for sex industries" (Boutellier 1991: 205).

Tourism: Amsterdam as a tourist destination

It has been well established that tourism, as a global force, has affected all of Western Europe. As Williams and Shaw (1998: 20) note, "Europe dominates international movements of tourists ... Between 1950 and 1990, the number of international tourists in Europe increased 16 times." There is strong competition among European countries for international tourists, since they tend to spend more money than domestic tourists; additionally, starting in the 1970s, "international tourism income grew considerably faster than international merchandise trade" making it a market worth pursuing (Williams and Shaw 1998: 36).

The Netherlands as a country has not fared particularly well in the race for tourists; tourism receipts to GDP as a result of international tourism are 1.4 per cent in contrast to Spain, Portugal, and Greece, which run closer to 4 per cent, and Austria, where international tourism contributes 6 per cent to GDP. Indeed, given the expenditures the country makes to attract international tourists, the Netherlands is running a deficit with respect to international tourism (Pinder 1998).

But the situation is quite different when cities are the point of comparison. Amsterdam was among the top ten most popular European cities for tourism throughout the 1990s, currently ranking seventh (Dahles 1998). Amsterdam's positioning as a major tourist destination may be surprising to some. Although the city is filled with tree-studded canals and quaint narrow buildings, it lacks the tourist attractions characteristic of other tourist destinations in Europe; there is no cathedral, tower, or monument to draw visitors to the city. Yet, as one writer has noted, "foreign tourists have been attracted to the Netherlands in increasing numbers" and, within the country, "Amsterdam is overwhelmingly the dominant target for visitors from abroad. 1.7 million foreigners stayed in the city in 1995, one-third of them from outside Europe" (Pinder 1998: 307). Dahles (1998: 55) argues that "The image of Amsterdam as a tourism destination is based on two major themes. The first is the image of the city as being dominated by the urban town design of the early modern period ... The second is the current popular image of Amsterdam, which was formed in the late 60s and is based on a youth culture of sexual liberation and narcotic indulgence." Pinder (1998: 310) agrees with this assessment and adds that "The city is renowned for the ready availability of soft drugs, and tolerance has also underpinned the rise of sex tourism as a niche market." He goes on to detail that "... visitor attractions based on the sex industry have gained a firm foothold. Almost half a million people visited the *Venutempel* sex museum in 1995, and 158,000 the Erotic Gallery. Both figures had risen by one-fifth in just two years" (Pinder 1998: 310). The increase in sex tourism and the sex industry as a share of Amsterdam's tourist market is related, in part, to declines in tourism dollars from more traditional tourist sites. As tourism directed toward Amsterdam's cultural heritage stagnates, sex tourism plays an increasingly important role in keeping tourism dollars—and related tourism industry jobs—within the city. It is not the case that the Dutch government or Amsterdam city officials openly embrace the marketing of sex tourism or Amsterdam's image as a liberal city, but a variety of mediating institutions, including the tourism industry, have adjusted to global forces in ways that create opportunities for sex tourism to expand.

Labor markets: Globalization and migration

By the late 1970s and 1980s, the reach of globalization became evident within the Netherlands in other ways as well, particularly in Amsterdam. Clearly, one of the most important global forces affecting sex work in the country was migration. Migration to the Netherlands during this period came from several sources. First, there was an influx of migrants from former Dutch colonies, particularly from Suriname and the Caribbean Islands. Additionally, like many other European countries, the Netherlands was affected by a surge of migrant guest workers from the Mediterranean area, most of whom were directed toward employment in undesirable, low-paying service sector jobs. Later in the 1980s and 1990s, another group of migrants arrived, including those escaping economic hardship in South America and Africa and the former Soviet bloc countries (Bruinsma and Meershock 1999; de Haan 1997). Importantly, most of these migrant populations settled in the major Dutch cities, including Amsterdam. Almost half of the population of Amsterdam now consists of non-native Dutch residents making it, literally, a global city.

The presence of relatively large numbers of migrants within the city plays an important role in shaping local labor markets and the current character of the sex trade. For many female migrants, sex work is virtually the only employment available, particularly given the relatively high unemployment rate for ethnic minorities within the Netherlands (de Haan 1997). As Visser (1997b) notes, " ... the numbers are beginning to get so big that these migrant prostitutes can no longer be considered as a detail." One estimate put the current number of foreign prostitutes to be approximately 60 per cent of all sex workers in the city (Haen Marshall 1993), and "a repeated count by the Amsterdam police in 1994 and 1995 indicated that about 75 per cent of all prostitutes behind windows in the Red Light District, De Wallen, are foreigners and that 80 per cent of all foreign prostitutes are in the country illegally" (Bruinsma and Meershock 1999: 107).

Although prostitution in the Netherlands preceded this mass migration, it is apparent that migration has both increased the number of sex workers and changed the character of the sex industry. According to the Mr. A. de Graaf Foundation (1997: 2), "in the Netherlands, the total number of professional prostitutes is estimated at 20,000"; however, this is clearly a low estimate given the large number of sex workers who are not considered "professional," including a large number of illegal immigrants. Another source puts the number closer to 25,000 and notes that survey research by the Dutch Foundation Against Trafficking has found that female sex workers represent at least 32 different countries of origin (Hughes 2000). In the last two decades, the growth of sex workers accompanying the rise of migration spawned a more complex sex industry within the city (Brants 1998; Haen Marshall 1993). While the window brothels are the most visible form of prostitution in Amsterdam, and according to some sources, workers here are among the most highly paid (see Reiland 1996), this form of prostitution is only one version of sex work in the city. Other forms of sex work include clubs, private houses, escort services, and street prostitution (Meulenbelt 1993). In the majority of these forms of sex work, however, bodies are highly commodified. Sexed bodies are put on display for purchase. Even in the case of sexual services that are delivered to your door, advertisements in local papers hawk the physical characteristics of the bodies for sale. Although emotional labor can be purchased in the Netherlands for those willing to pay the price, many sex workers prefer to simply sell their bodies and keep their emotions to themselves (Chapkis 1997).

Localized sex work: The shift to a sex "industry"

Over the last two decades there has been an important shift within the city from a focus on the individual providers of sexual services, "prostitutes," to a focus on the sex "industry." Although this shift is partly due to local circumstances, it is also partly a response to the global forces associated with the production and consumption of sex tourism. This shift is reflected in two areas: 1) organizational changes that reflect the growth of sex tourism as an industry and 2) the globalized character of sex tourists and sex workers.

In her analysis of prostitution policy in Amsterdam, Brants (1998: 627) describes these changes in some detail:

As conditions changed and opportunities for making money from the sex industry increased, ever more power became concentrated in the hands of a few not particularly law abiding citizens. Some of the pimps who had once controlled part of traditional window prostitution now also owned highly lucrative sex clubs and sex theaters. Prostitution had become big business with a huge and partly invisible turnover that was reinvested in gambling halls, sex tourism and more sex clubs.

This concentration of economic interests combined with consumer interest to create several organizations devoted to supporting sex tourism. Interestingly, some Dutch customers developed an organization to support the interests of the clients of prostitution; this organization is called the Men/Women and Prostitution Foundation. Although the number of active members in this organization is small (personal conversation with a member), it is symbolically important in legitimizing the sex industry as an important "industry" serving consumer desires. Members write articles that articulate client interests and the social benefits of prostitution (ten Kate 1995) and collaborate with other organizations interested in greater acceptance of prostitution.

In 1991, the owners of sex businesses organized, forming an association called the Association of Operators of Relaxation Businesses (Verening Exploitanten van Relaxbedrijven). This organization helped to bring legitimacy to the organized business interests behind sex tourism in the city; this legitimacy is particularly important given the historically strong link between the proprietors of sex businesses and brothels and organized crime (Brants 1998). This organization plays an increasingly important role in policy discussions within the city. Although numbers are hard to come by, everyone agrees that the sex industry represents a substantial commercial activity within the city and, importantly, business owners are now organized to protect their economic interests.

Another organization that facilitates the sex trade is the Prostitute Information Centre (PIC). The Center, which is located in the heart of the red-light district, serves as an information service for both tourists and prostitutes. Run by a former prostitute, the goals of the center are diverse—education around STD and AIDS prevention, information about prices for sex work, courses to prepare newcomers for sex work, and information about how and where to sell sexual labor. For the casual tourist, the most amazing aspect of the PIC is its symbolic character and the way that it resembles a cross between a museum and a sex industry Chamber of Commerce, complete with a sample window brothel to tour (for an extra fee of course), copies of the local Sex Guide, and postcards to purchase. When asked why there were no windows with men in them (despite a large female and gay population in the city, and the presence of male prostitutes), one worker at the center explained that at one time there had been some experimentation with such windows, but the experiment was short-lived; apparently, the windows with men became a public nuisance as women crowded around the booths to enjoy the spectacle. Interestingly, women in large crowds gazing and gawking at men's bodies was defined as a public nuisance, but when men engage in similar behavior, it is not viewed as problematic. Citizens in the West accept the objectification of women's bodies as normal behavior; when men's bodies become objectified—a spectacle—it is a public nuisance. The smooth operation of the sex industry within the city required that male prostitutes be restricted from sitting in windows.

A second global force shaping the sex industry in Amsterdam is the wide variety of sex tourists visiting the city. Currently, the sex industry is amazingly global in character; not just in terms of the providers of sexual services, but also in terms of the consumers. Sex tourists come to Amsterdam from around the world and vary depending, in part, on national holidays. The local *Pleasure Guide* notes, for example, that Italians are common in August. Although Dutch men are common customers, it appears that the Red Light District exists primarily to fulfill the desires of foreign, male, leisure travelers, often executives conducting business in this global city. Unlike tourists, Dutch consumers of the sex trade can frequent the mostly white women in window brothels down less known side streets, or they can utilize the listings in the paper and obtain door-to-door service. It is important to appreciate that foreign tourists do not just pay for sex; they pay for accommodations, to eat at nice restaurants, and to attend cultural events. Indeed, the consumer behavior of sex tourists visiting this city helps to ensure that there will be many organized interests facilitating the continuation of sex tourism within the city.

Public policy and law: Facilitating sex tourism and stratification of sex workers

As might be expected, policies within Amsterdam are also changing in ways that reflect broader global forces associated with the production and consumption of sex tourism. Despite the growth of organized business interests in the sex industry, the city's economic benefit from sex tourists, and the greater legitimacy accorded sex work, current policy does not appear to be strengthening the hand of sex workers. It appears that the full package of worker's rights is withheld from prostitutes for a variety of reasons (Brants 1998; van der Pod 1995).

The presence of drug-addicted prostitutes makes it difficult for those advocating rights for prostitutes to argue for respectability. Perhaps, more importantly, the large and growing presence of non-native Dutch sex workers leads to local hostility toward sex work. One consequence of Dutch participation in the global economy is the inability of the state to continue to provide the extensive social welfare benefits it has provided to its citizens since the 1960s (de Haan 1997). As welfare rights are restricted for citizens, social services continue to be extended to migrants, creating substantial anger toward immigration. Restrictive policies are creeping up everywhere, including in the sex industry. At least one motivation for this greater regulation is to restrict migrant women from engaging in sexual labor. As Raymond (1998: 5) points out, "Third World and Eastern European immigrant women in the Netherlands, Germany, and other regulationist countries lower the prostitution market value of local Dutch and German women. The price of immigrant prostitution is so low that local women's prices go down, reducing the pimps and brothels cuts. To the extent that regulation is designed to keep non-native Dutch women out of sex work, it fosters a two-tiered hierarchy of sex work within the city that leads to even greater impoverishment and risk for migrant women.

Thus, the twin forces of greater organization among sex industry owners and clients and the reduced power of sex workers as a result of the growing hostility toward migrant and drug dependent sex workers have led to efforts to define sex tourism as a "business," rather than as a form of individual self-employment. Significantly, legislation legalizing brothels was approved by the Dutch Parliament and Senate in 1999 (Brewis and Linstead 2000); this is a radical move in the Netherlands, where sex workers were historically only considered "workers" when "self-employed." Until recently, third party involvement in sex work was considered a crime resulting in the oppression and even enslavement of sex workers. Some argue that the legalization of brothels is a first step toward their ultimate regulation, a situation that could improve the working conditions for some sex workers (Brants 1998; Visser 1997a). However, it seems that the focus of regulation is increasingly on improving the "merchandising" environment for the sex industry and for consumers, and reducing disruption to local citizens. Currently, local officials are attempting to identify who owns the buildings that house window brothels and sex clubs so that some standards can be imposed on facilities where sex is sold. Brothels that pass government inspection would receive special certification, serving as a kind of quality control for sex tourists (Visser 1997a). Regulations are growing and include strange new guidelines that limit how long clients can be tied up during purchased sadomasochistic acts. A new "red light district manager" will facilitate the implementation of the new regulations. To many, including De Rode Draad, the rights of sex workers have taken a back burner (Visser 1997a). The proliferation of new regulations has caused some to argue that the red light district is becoming "the red tape district" (Reiland 1996: 29).

Although some regulation seems, at first appearance, to improve the situation of sex workers, it also serves to divide them and institutionalize stratification in the sex industry. For example, Amsterdam spent $1.8 million of taxpayers money to create the Tipplezone, primarily as a way to respond to public order problems caused by drug dependent prostitutes (bodies not so easy to neatly package and commodify) (Forbes 1996). The Tipplezone can be likened to a fast food restaurant—the focus is on speed, efficiency, and easy access by car. The zone is located outside of the city center and rates are typically cheaper for sex acquired there, in part because sex acts occur in the client's car so more acts can be performed in an hour. The Tipplezone has made conditions safer for sex workers (and, importantly, for customers) in the city center, but it is less clear that it has drastically improved the lot of sex workers who are drug dependent. What it has done is segregate the most vulnerable workers, including workers with drug problems, transsexuals, and other marginalized workers, from the safest parts of the city.

Along the same lines, it is interesting to note current proposals to impose price controls on the sex industry. At first glance, this policy appears to be a move toward protecting the wages of sex workers. However, it also serves primarily as a way to discourage price-cutting by illegal immigrants engaged in the sex trade (a common practice since so many other avenues of employment are unavailable, given protectionist Dutch employment policies). This policy is reflective of growing Dutch concern about immigration; like many other European countries under global migration pressures, the Dutch tend to close doors to gainful employment by outsiders rather than open them.

At least one Dutch scholar, Chrisje Brants (1998), believes that the new rules and restrictions, including the legalization of brothels, will continue to facilitate the creation of sex tourism as an industry, since small brothel owners and individual prostitutes are unlikely to be able to compete with the resources of organized crime and proprietors of large sex clubs. As she puts it "the prostitution business will be professionalized, but with the greater scale that is the inevitable result, will come greater concentrations of power and money." In the end, "prostitutes who find themselves unable to compete economically will simply disappear into illegality... (Brants 1998: 633).

In this description of sex tourism and current policy trends in Amsterdam, it is important not to lose sight of the enormously positive public health consequences of current Dutch policy as compared to most other countries. HIV rates are extremely low among prostitutes in the Netherlands, and sex workers clearly have more rights than in most countries worldwide. Still, it is also evident that globalization has changed, and will continue to change the character of sex tourism in this global city. It is important to appreciate that the Netherlands is not unique in this regard. As Raymond (1998: 5) writes,

> The reality is that during the 1980s, as the sex industry in several European countries underwent notable development, commercialization, *and* legitimation through regulationist legislation, it also became an international business.

In Amsterdam, global migration has meant that sex work within the city is a significant form of employment (particularly for migrant women), and there is little effort to generate jobs for migrant women that can compete with the structural advantages now accorded the sex trade by the city and the forces of global tourism. In Amsterdam, [as in] ... other parts of the world, the sex industry has become an important commercial activity, attracting wealthy sex tourists from around the world and increasingly lining the pocketbooks of those with the money to take advantage of cheap labor. Whether intentionally or not, Dutch policy (particularly in the city of Amsterdam) is changing in ways that are likely to facilitate the global production and consumption of sex tourism. To say this is not to take a moral position. It is to describe a global phenomenon that this city only illustrates.

Globalization and the commodification of emotional labor in Havana

Havana, like so many other places in the Caribbean, is a sensuous and social city. Warm nights, humid sea breezes laden with the complex perfume of flowers, diesel exhaust, and restaurant odors, music everywhere, bodies unencumbered by layers of cold-weather clothing, and a culture of public interaction that brings tourists and locals into easy contact. This is the context for Havana's particular soft-sell sex trade. Since the reemergence of sex tourism in the 1990s, the following scene has become relatively common in Havana's tourist districts: A woman, usually decades younger than the object of her immediate interest, approaches a foreign tourist. Brandishing a cigarette, she asks for a light, or maybe points to her wrist and asks for the time. The opening gambit leads to other questions: Where are you from? Where are you going? For a walk? Would you like me to walk with you? Have you been to such-and-such disco? Would you like me to take you there? If the mark seems interested, the woman turns the subject to sex, describing the pleasures she can give, often with no mention of price unless the man asks. If they agree to go off to a disco or for a drink, the subject of sex may not even be openly discussed. Instead, both the *jinetera* and her mark proceed as if they are on a date. Who knows? Maybe this one will be around for a few days, a week, even a month, providing steady work and freedom from having to continually find new customers. Whether the liaison lasts for a night or a month, the tourist will leave something to be remembered by—maybe money or a few nice new dresses, perhaps some jewellery—something that makes the sex and the attention provided worth the effort. This is not the hard sell of commodified bodies typical of sex tourism in Amsterdam. This is a more subtle trade. A trade where local, rather than immigrant women, make themselves available as sex partners and companions to privileged men from North America and Europe who can give them access to the currency of globalization, US dollars.

Historical and cultural background

In recent years, the visible presence of sex workers in Havana who are willing to provide tourists with sexual access for material compensation in the form of cash, gifts, or other benefits has received considerable attention from social analysts.[4] This is not because the sex trade in Havana is comparable in size to what can be found in major international sex tourist destinations such as Amsterdam or Bangkok (Kempadoo and Dozeman 1998). Rather, many analysts see sex tourism in Havana as a demonstration that the forces of globalization are so far-reaching that they are being felt even in a socialist society that was once able to claim the elimination of prostitution and the reorientation of prostitutes to non-sexual labor as one of its earliest revolutionary accomplishments (Elizalde 1996: 19). Or, as Aleida Guevara (1998: A5), a Cuban pediatrician and the daughter of Che Guevara, commented, "Just a few prostitutes in a country that had none before have created quite a scandal." Nor is it only a "scandal" in the eyes of foreign observers. Cuban sociologist Aurelio Alonso (1998: 1) notes that prostitution is "shocking for us because we were used to seeing a society without prostitutes on the street."

Cuban tourism has always centered on Havana, and the relationship between globalization and the reemergence of sex tourism in that city cannot be appreciated without placing Cuba in the context of its pre-revolutionary and revolutionary history. In the 1950s, Cuba led the first wave of mass tourism in the Caribbean. The number of hotel rooms in Havana grew from 3,000 in 1952 to 5,500 in 1958, making it the single largest tourist destination in the region. In 1957, Havana accounted for twenty-one percent of *all* visitors to the Caribbean, with eighty-six percent of these visitors coming from the United States. By comparison, the next two largest tourist destinations, the Bahamas and Puerto Rico, accounted for fifteen percent of all Caribbean tourism each (Villalba 1993).

This growth in tourism had its destructive side, however. Reflecting on Havana of the 1950s, Arthur Schlesinger Jr. (1996: 323–24) described it as a "lovely city ... being debased into a great casino and brothel for U.S. businessmen over for a big weekend from Miami." There was certainly much more to Havana in the 1950s than the hotel/casino district serving foreign tourists. Nevertheless, in the eyes of many potential tourists in the 1950s, the estimated 270 brothels and as many as 100,000 prostitutes who operated there, defined Havana (Elizade 1996).[5]

The Cuban Revolution that triumphed on January 1, 1959 was not initially committed to ending Havana's role as a tourist center for Americans. To the contrary, in 1959, Fidel Castro told the American Society of Tourist Agents annual convention in Havana that the Revolution hoped to establish Cuba as "the best and most important tourist center in the world" (Castro 1993: 262). Soon, however, the unwillingness of revolutionary leaders to enter into corrupt relationships with casino owners, deteriorating US-Cuban relations, and the U.S. embargo of Cuba initiated by President Eisenhower at the end of 1960 began to take its toll. Cuban tourism dropped from a pre-revolutionary high of 272,491 visitors in 1957 to 86,491 by 1960. In 1963, President John F. Kennedy invoked the *Trading with the Enemy Act* against Cuba, prohibiting U.S. citizens or businesses from engaging in commercial exchanges there, and thus bringing to an end Havana's role as a freewheeling tourist destination (Thomas 1998).

The tourism industry: Cuba in the Caribbean

In the late 1960s, the emergence of relatively affordable jet service created a new era of Caribbean island vacations (Patullo 1996: 16). Between 1970 and 1994, the number of stay-over visits to Caribbean islands increased six-fold (Caribbean Tourism Organization 1995). Just as this boom in Caribbean tourism was beginning, the US embargo against Cuba sent Cuban tourism into a steep decline that bottomed out with a mere 15,000 visitors in 1974. From that point forward, however, Cuba began to reorient its development plans to include investments in the tourist industry (Mesa-Lago 1981). Although some development was focused on internal tourism by Cubans, by 1979, foreign tourism had grown to 130,000 stay-over visits. A decade later, 300,000 foreign tourists visited the island, more than in any year prior to the Revolution (Triana 1995). Moreover, only 18 percent of these tourists were from Soviet-bloc countries. Forty percent came from Canada, 15 percent from Western Europe, 15 percent from Latin America, and—despite the embargo—another 12 percent from the United States (Miller and Henthorne 1997: 8).

The most spectacular growth in Cuban tourism came in the 1990s (Robinson 1998). During this period, the Cuban government intensified its investment in tourism as part of a broader search for development strategies that would enable the country to survive in the face of post-Soviet economic and political forces determined by a now-worldwide capitalist market (Castro 1999). Between 1994 and 1999, Cuba doubled the number of hotel rooms from 23,500 to just under 50,000 (Miller and Henthorne 1997: 98). This translated into a five-fold increase in the number of stay-over visits from 300,000 in 1989 to an estimated 1.7 million in 2000. Revenue gains were even greater. Between 1990 and 1998, gross revenue from tourism increased seven-fold, from 243 million in 1990 to 1.8 billion, while the share of the country's GDP contributed by tourism grew from 1.1 per cent to 6.9 percent. This growth made Cuba, once again, a significant force in Caribbean tourism. At 1.8 billion dollars, Cuba's tourism earnings for 1998 were second only to the 2.1 billion tourism dollars earned by the Dominican Republic, and well ahead of the Bahamas and Jamaica, which respectively earned 1.4 billion and 1.1 billion in tourist revenues (Association of Caribbean States 2001).

Some of Cuba's tourism growth has taken place in tourist-oriented beach resorts such as Varadero and Cayo Largo. As Cuba's primate city, however, Havana remains the centerpiece of Cuban tourism, accounting for 75 to 80 per cent of all stay-over visits (Miller and Henthorne 1997). As Sassen (2000a) notes, primate cities such as Havana are linked to "cross-border circuits" in ways that differentiate them from the rest of their country. Thus, while tourist sections of Havana are significantly shaped by the need to meet the desires of foreign tourists, daily life in much of the rest of the city and country is less affected by these global forces and continues to be more nationally than internationally oriented.

Labor markets: Cuban tourism in a globalized world order

Many Habañeros today look back on the 1980s as the "good old days" of growth and development. During the early 1980s, the Cuban Gross Domestic Product (GDP) *grew* by almost 23 per cent at a time when the combined GDP of Latin America *fell* by 9 per cent under the impact of accumulating foreign debt and structural adjustments mandated by the IMF and the World Bank (Budhoo 1994). As the 1980s continued, however, economic development in Cuba began to slow, and, by the decade's end, growth had stalled. As the socialist world crumbled between 1989 and 1993, Cuba underwent a dramatic reversal of fortune that forced a radical reorganization of economic life (Azicri 1992; Landau and Starratt 1994). The disappearance of Cuba's socialist trading partners created what Cuban sociologist Elena Diaz Gonzalez (1997a) characterized as the worst crisis in the history of Cuban socialism. Between 1989 and 1993, the Cuban GDP fell between 35 and 50 percent, importation of Soviet oil declined by 62 percent, overall imports fell by 75 percent, and the domestic manufacture of consumer goods fell by 83 percent (Diaz Gonzalez 1997a; Espinosa 1999).

As Cuba struggled to reconstruct its trade and financial relations to meet the hard-currency demands of the new capitalist world order, many Cubans found themselves facing a significantly altered labor market (Eckstein 1997). As in other former socialist bloc countries, the Cuban government could no longer provide the extensive employment and social-welfare package it once sought to establish as a universal birthright for all Cubans (Koont 1998; Verdcry 1996). By 1999, although Cubans continued to benefit from state subsidies in the areas of food, housing, transportation, healthcare, and education, many desired goods could increasingly only be purchased in dollar stores for prices roughly equivalent to those found in the United States for the same goods (Michalowski 1998). It was at this very moment that international tourism to Havana began to increase significantly, with a concomitant growth in tourist-sector jobs—jobs where it was possible to earn at least some portion of one's salary in hard currency. As a consequence, a growing number of high school and college students in Havana began orienting themselves toward tourist-sector employment rather than state sector jobs, while some Habañeros already employed in professional careers abandoned them to work in tourism as well (Randall 1996).

The impact of expanding tourism in a city with a shrinking state-sector labor market was also cultural. As youth in Havana were increasingly exposed to the growing number of tourist-oriented nightclubs, restaurants, and beachside hotels, and the clothes, jewelry, and the new model rental cars enjoyed by foreign visitors, some began to feel dissatisfied with their own lack of access to these luxuries. Faced with declining returns from routine labor and rising material desires, some Cuban women (and a smaller number of Cuban men) began making themselves sexually available to foreign tourists. By the late 1990s, a sex worker in Havana could earn forty dollars for providing one night of sex and companionship—double the *monthly* salary of a Cuban university professor (Michalowski 1998). While most young Cubans resisted the temptations created by such disparities, enough succumbed to create a pool of available bodies to serve the desires of sex tourists (Diaz Gonzalez 1997b).

It takes more than buyers and sellers, however, to create viable markets. Markets also require facilitative infrastructures. This is why, although tourism to Cuba had been growing since the 1980s, significant sex tourism did not re-emerge in Havana until the 1990s.

Public policy and law: The contradictions of market freedom

Although Cuba has had a significant number of foreign tourists since the late 1970s, the state-centered structure of life in Havana was not well suited to serving them. The array of small private restaurants and shops many European and North American tourists expect when they travel was absent in a city where most retail transactions took place in standardized, state-run enterprises. There was also concern that lively trade between Cubans and affluent foreigners might weaken public commitment to the collective pursuit of social equality. As a result, international tourism in Cuba during the 1980s was organized around self-contained hotels filled with consumer amenities for foreign visitors, but normally off-limits to Cubans. It proved impossible, however, to maintain a sharp divide between tourists and Cubans, particularly in Havana. It was soon breached by an energetic currency black market offering tourists exchange rates four to five times the official one, and by a domestic commodity black market where Cubans sold goods that were purchased illegally (or in some cases stolen) from tourist shops (Michalowski 1995; Michalowski and Zatz 1989). After attempts to suppress these emerging illegal markets during the 1980s and early 1990s, the Cuban government reversed course, and rather than increasing the penalization of these offenses, began legalizing, controlling, and taxing the developing linkages between tourists and Cubans.

In 1993, the government legalized the possession of foreign currency and began allowing citizens to legally exchange dollars for *pesos* at banks and government-run street kiosks known as *cadecas*. Between 1992 and 1994, the Cuban government promulgated a number of other legal changes that would indirectly help create an infrastructure for sex tourism in Havana. These included 1) permitting the private rental of rooms, apartments, and houses; 2) expanding the arena of self-employment; 3) legalizing the establishment of privately owned restaurants, colloquially known as *paladares*; 4) expanding the licensing of private vehicles as taxi-cabs; and 5) opening "dollar" stores where Cubans could purchase a broad range of items including food, appliances, furniture, clothes, jewelry, and many other items for US currency (Gordon 1997).

Structurally, these changes facilitated sex-tourism in several ways. The legalization of the US dollar meant that sex workers could obtain hard currency payment from foreign clients without violation of currency laws, and the opening of dollar stores meant they could spend their earnings without having to enter into black market exchanges. Legalizing the rental of private rooms and houses created new opportunities for commercial sexual transaction by eliminating the rules that required tourists to stay in hotels, while prohibiting Cubans from visiting foreigners in their hotel rooms. The legalization of private restaurants provided places where sex workers and tourists could meet and spend non-sex time. Meanwhile, the legalization of private taxis became an important conduit through which some cab drivers could help sex tourists find their way to prime locations for meeting sex workers, or work as pimps by directing their fares to specific sex workers.

Sex work in Havana: Commodifying bodies and emotions

Although the growth of Havana's tourist industry resulted in a subsidiary increase in sex tourism to the island, so far, this sex trade has not become the province of the organized syndicates—whether legal or illegal—that typically control sex work in many other nations. During her fieldwork in Cuba in 1995, O'Connell Davidson (1996: 40) observed that there was "no network of brothels, no organized system of bar prostitution: in fact, third party involvement in the organization of prostitution is rare ... Most women and girls are prostituting themselves independently and have no contractual obligations to a third party." What O'Connell Davidson saw in 1995 was still in evidence in 1999. While some Habañeros serving sex tourists, particularly younger girls or recent migrants to Havana, were fronted by pimps, and some relied on more fluid third-party arrangements with landlords or taxi-cab drivers, the predominant form of tourist-oriented sex work in Havana involved women and girls engaging in a variety of independent approaches to male tourists on streets and in clubs.

Even though the practice of prostituting for sex tourists in Havana is largely independent and entrepreneurial, it is nevertheless embedded in a globalized market for sex services. To compete in a worldwide capitalist marketplace, every local industry needs a global market niche. The sale of what Hochschild (1983) termed "emotional labor" to accompany a sexually commodified body is that niche for many of Havana's *jineteras* serving the male tourist trade. For many male sex tourists from Italy, Spain, England, and Canada, the particular attraction of Cuba is their expectation that *jineteras* will treat them not as customers but as pseudo-boyfriends. This means acting as a dinner "date" in a restaurant or a dance partner at a disco, serving as a local (and seemingly loving) guide on sightseeing tours, or perhaps spending a few days or even weeks at a seaside resort as bedmate, playmate, and companion.

One Italian sex tourist summarized his attraction to Cuban *jineteras* by saying he came to Cuba because "the women here are really sweet. They make you feel like they really care. They are always trying to do whatever makes you feel good, not just sex, but everything else too." A pair of ex-patriot American men currently living in Costa Rica echoed this sentiment: "The Cuban women don't act like professional whores, 'Here's the sex, now give me the money.' They are really kind. They want to spend time with you, be your friend." As experienced sexual tourists, they bemoaned the growth of sex tourism in Costa Rica because it "ruined" Costa Rican sex workers: "Now they act just like whores in the States. They just do it for the money and when it's over, they want to move on to the next customer. It wasn't like that in the 60s when there were hardly any tourists. Then they were really nice like the Cuban women are today. Things will probably change here [in Cuba], too. So we thought we'd enjoy it while it lasts."[6] In the complicated world of emotional simulacra, sex tourists like these experience the consumption of emotions that sex workers are rarely actually providing. Yet, as long as sex workers give their customers the time and kind of attention that sex tourists in Cuba believe to be signifiers of "caring," the desires that brought them to the island are met.

Another appeal of sex tourism in Havana is its price. In 1999, a sex tourist could spend as little as ten dollars for a quick sexual encounter, and between thirty and forty dollars for a companion for the entire evening. This means that for between one hundred and two hundred dollars a day, including the meals, the tours, and other "gifts," European, Canadian, and American men in Havana can spend days or even weeks in the company of young, seemingly exotic women who appear to be providing them with loving attention, all at a price they can afford. In this way, for a short time, they can enjoy a level of class privilege available only to wealthier men in their home countries.

There are several other important elements of the emotional simulacra consumed by sex tourists in Havana that draw them there. Although too complex to analyze at length here, they need to be mentioned. One is the opportunity that sex tourism in Havana provides for men who are forty, fifty, or older to receive both sex and sexualized companionship from women thirty or more years younger than themselves. This gratifies the Western male sexual ideal of continuing access to the bodies of young women, regardless of one's own age. Another is the appeal of gaining sexual access to the body of the non-white "other." In the racialized world of the North American and European male sexual fantasy, mixed-race Cuban women provide the ideal, the fetishized combination of the imaginary "hot" Latin and the equally imaginary sexually insatiable African (O'Connell Davidson 1996; Sanchez Taylor 2000). Thus, it is little surprise that the majority of the women visibly searching for clients in the tourist areas of Havana in 1999, were typically of the "café" or "carmelita" skin tones signifying this highly desired racialized "other."

The characteristics of *jineteras* in Havana—young, often mixed-race, and seemingly emotionally attentive—connect them to the cross-border circuits of sexual fantasies in Europe and North America. These connections ensure that the sex worker in Havana will have access to a pool of customers from the North who can use their privilege to travel to Cuba where they will purchase for a small fraction of their weekly incomes at home, sexual, and seeming emotional access to young, exotic "others" who appear to desire them.[7]

SEX TOURISM IN A GLOBALIZED WORLD

Policy-makers, scholars, and ordinary citizens tend to see prostitution as a problem caused by prostitutes. Similarly, there is a tendency to view sex tourism as a problem belonging to other nations, a problem that originates primarily with poor Third World women who choose to deviate from "good" women by selling their sexuality. But prostitutes do not cause prostitution any more than poor people cause poverty, or poor nations cause global inequality. We contend that the contemporary growth and character of sex tourism is intimately linked to significant global forces.

These global forces, which include tourism, migration, and commodification, are not just abstract concepts; they can be observed within grounded contexts as a variety of local mediating institutions respond to global pressures. In the cases of Amsterdam and Havana, our research suggests that global forces have altered particular institutions in these cities in ways that expand the possibilities for sex tourism. Our work supports Sassen's (1998) view of cities as strategic sites for globalization. Furthermore, in the cases we studied, this is true regardless of whether the city is a global city, like Amsterdam, or a primate city, like Havana. At a theoretical level, we contend that the global forces of tourism and migration stimulate the production of sex workers, while the increasing commodification of bodies ensures a steady stream of clients who desire to consume sexual services. Within the cities we analyzed, these global forces find concrete expression at the institutional level, specifically in the changing character of the tourism industries, labor markets, sex work, and laws and policies.

As we have described in some detail, in both Amsterdam and Havana, the tourism industry has become a noticeable sector of the local economy as a by-product of efforts by these cities to secure a share of the burgeoning market created by global tourism. This competition is necessitated by a world in which global markets dominate and determine local fortunes for countries and cities. Additionally, in both of the cities we analyzed, labor markets changed in ways that increased the attractiveness and, for some women, the necessity of sex work. This is particularly true among certain populations of women, such as immigrants in Amsterdam seeking jobs in an environment hostile to migrant workers or young Cuban women in Havana for whom globalization has meant that they can earn more dollars and go to more exciting places by selling sex and companionship than they can through more routine employment. Although sex work existed in both cities prior to the current period of globalization, it is evident that the global forces associated with consumption shaped the character of sex work in each city in significant ways. In Amsterdam, sex work became more organized, more stratified, and more like an "industry," while in Havana, tourist-oriented sex work not only re-emerged, but reconstituted in ways that reflect tourist desires for emotional labor and "otherly" bodies. Consumption practices alone do not cause these changes, but the desires of privileged consumers do shape the particular expression and organization of sex work in each city. Finally, in both cities, laws and policies affecting sex tourism increasingly reflect local accommodation to global forces originating outside of the country. In Havana, efforts to find a political-economic niche in a globalized world economy shaped numerous laws and policies, ranging from changing currency regulations to more freedom for local taxicab drivers. In Amsterdam, efforts to make the city more attractive for privileged consumers and to deal with the problem of migration have led to laws and policies ranging from the legalization of brothels to regulating S&M practices. Despite the efforts of these cities to maintain internal control, their mediating institutions evolved in response to global forces, creating the foundation for globally structured, though geographically localized, sex tourism. What is new and noteworthy about global sex tourism is not "sex," "sex work," or even the commodification of bodies, but the extent to which sex work in specific locales is over-determined by broader global forces. This is what has changed significantly in the contemporary period. Thus, local infrastructures that shape the possibilities for sex tourism in Amsterdam and Havana increasingly reflect global, rather than local forces. To the extent that local institutions are increasingly responsive to global forces, city and national governments find it increasingly difficult to exert control over localized practices of sex work (Boyer and Drache 1996). Like most consequences of globalization, sex tourism is a global social problem, even though its expression is locally constituted within cities.

Although sex tourism is growing and changing as a result of the impact of global forces on local structures, it is important to also note that our research reveals that the actual practice of sex work reflects the positionality of each city within the global economy. Amsterdam, a highly developed global city in an advanced capitalist nation, manifests a highly organized and stratified form of sex tourism based on the commodification of the "otherly" bodies of migrant women. In Cuba, the pattern is more characteristic of a developing nation as a primary producer. That is, sex tourism in Cuba involves the exploitation and consumption by foreigners of a local resource, in this case, Cuban women. Thus, although we theorize that global forces affect most major cities, our research also demonstrated that they would be affected differently depending upon their position in the global economic order and the unique character of local infrastructures and cultural histories.

Our analysis suggests that the forces subsumed under the term globalization are reshaping local contexts, whether their histories are capitalist or socialist, and often doing so in ways that cannot be anticipated. In the cities we analyzed, there is a high probability that local institutions will increasingly privilege the economic interests associated with "tourism" as a way to ensure one more niche in the global marketplace. Whether intentionally or as a by-product of local responses to global forces, the growth of tourism will likely increase tourist-oriented commercial sex, often at the expense of the health and welfare of those who provide the sexual services wealthy tourists demand. In their struggle to stay afloat as the global tide comes their way, cities and nations need not embrace or endorse sex tourism in order to become the beneficiaries of the consumer dollars it generates. Thus, sex tourism in Amsterdam and Havana and, presumably, in many other cities, is increasingly structured by global forces, connecting sex work in cities around the world with the broader, more abstract phenomena of globalized sex tourism. Imagining localized sex tourism as a consequence of global forces and connections is an important first step toward understanding and responding to this social problem.

NOTES

[1] This focus on "prostitutes" has led to lengthy debates over the character of prostitution. Because these debates are covered in detail elsewhere (e.g., Chapkis 1997), we do not reproduce them here. Our goal, instead, is to transcend the dichotomy between sex work as a form of oppression versus an employment choice. Our ethnographic work indicates that for many women it is *both*.

2 For more detailed discussions of the ethnographic methods we employ, see also Aggar (1986), Clifford and Marcus (1986), Dubisch (1996), Michalowski (1996), and Van Maanen (1988).

3 The ethnographic knowledge of sex tourism in Amsterdam was gathered by Nancy Wonders and spans a six-year time period; however, the primary fieldwork for this project was conducted during a six-month period in 1997 while she was a Visiting Scholar at the University of Amsterdam. Her fieldwork involved in-depth conversations and interviews with sex workers, sex consumers, public officials associated with advocating for sex workers, academic faculty, and ordinary citizens about sex tourism, as well as extensive research in local libraries, bookstores, and government offices. The ethnographic information reported for Cuba is part of a larger study of social adaptations to the intersection of political-economy and law in a transforming Cuba that has been ongoing since 1985 (Michalowski 1996). The data on current patterns of sex tourism and *jineterismo* are based on fieldwork in 1998 and 1999. During these trips, Ray Michalowski discussed the changing face of social life in Havana with state-sector professionals, faculty from the University of Havana, members of the Cuban legal community, and professionals working in Cuba's emerging private-sector economy. The information acquired from these exchanges was cross-compiled with that obtained from unscheduled interviews with an opportunity sample of male sex tourists, *jineteras*, long-tem professional prostitutes, pimps, and taxi drivers encountered in hotels and other tourist sites in the city. All conversations and interviews were conducted with full disclosure of the research nature of the exchange. As ethnographers, we spent significant time just living in these locales in order to understand and know the cultural context, however imperfectly. As gendered researchers, however, our access to information was also gendered. Ray could more easily fall into conversation with male sex tourists, and could enter into conversations with sex workers and pimps as a result of their initial interest in him as a possible customer. Nancy could more easily interact with formal associations linked to sex work without being questioned as a voyeur or potential client. Although we note these differences as an important statement of reflexivity about our work, we found that our fieldwork yielded roughly comparable case studies, particularly when our ethnographic knowledge was combined with available ethnohistorical literature about each city.

4 See, for example, Cahezas (1998); Diaz Gonzalez (1997b); Elizalde (1996); Fernandez (1999); Fusco (1996); Hodge and Ahiodun (2001); O'Connell Davidson (1996, 1998); Paternostro (2000); Randall (1996); Sanchez Taylor (2000); Strout (1995).

5 An estimate of 100,000 prostitutes operating in Havana is often quoted in discussions of pre-revolutionary sex tourism. This figure, however, includes a significant proportion of prostitutes who served Cuban men. Even at the height of pre-revolutionary tourism in Cuba, there were only 270,000 tourists visiting the island, far too few to account for 100,000 prostitutes.

6 See Contreras (2001) for a similar description of the sex trade in Costa Rica.

7 During a January 1999 speech commemorating the founding of the National Revolutionary Police, Fidel Castro called for a crackdown on uses of Cuba's emerging private sector to

facilitate sex tourism. By February of that year, *jineteras* had become less visible and more subtle in marketing their services, a trend which continued into the following year (see Paternostro 2000).

REFERENCES

Adkins, L. 1995. *Gendered Work: Sexuality, Family, and the Labour Market.* Philadelphia: Open University Press.

Aggar, M. 1986. *Speaking of Ethnography.* Beverly Hills: Sage.

Alonso, A. 1998. Quoted in P. Grogg, "Prostitution Re-emerges on the Heels of Economic Crisis." *Interpress Service* (October 30).

Amin, S. 1990. *Maldevelopment: Anatomy of a Global Failure.* Tokyo: United Nations University Press.

Amin, S. 1997. *Empire of Chaos.* New York: Monthly Review Press.

Association of Caribbean States. 2001. *Statistical Database.* Port of Spain: ACS. Available at www.acs-aec.orglTradefDBaselDBase_engldbaseindex_eng.htm.

Azicri, M. 1992. "The Rectification Process Revisited: Cuba's Defense of Traditional Marxism-Leninism." Pp. 37–54 in *Cuba in Transition: Crisis and Transformation,* edited by S. Halebsky and J.M. Kirk. Boulder, CO: Westview.

Bell, L., J. Pulido Escandell, and C. Pulido Escandell. 1997. *Vision Desde Leuba.* Madrid: SODePAZ.

Bell, S. 1994. *Reading, Writing, and Rewriting the Prostitute Body.* Bloomington, TN: Indiana University Press.

Bordo, S. 1993. *Unbearable Weight: Feminism, Western Culture and the Body.* Los Angeles: University of California Press.

Boutellier, J. 1991. "Prostitution, Criminal Law and Morality in The Netherlands." *Crime, Law and Social Change* 15: 201–11.

Boyer, R. and D. Drache (Eds.). 1996. *States Against Markets: The Limits of Globalization.* NY: Routledge.

Brants, C. 1998. "The Fine Art of Regulated Tolerance: Prostitution in Amsterdam." *Journal of Law and Society* 25(4): 6211–235.

Brewis, J. and S. Linstead. 2000. *Sex, Work and Sex Work: Eroticizing Organization.* London: Routledge.

Bruinsma, G. and G. Meershoek. 1999. "Organized Crime and Trafficking in Women from Eastern Europe in The Netherlands." Pp. 105–18 in *Illegal Immigration and Commercial Sex: The New Slave Trade,* edited by Phil Williams. London: Frank Cass.

Budhoo, D. 1994. "IMF/World Bank Wreaks Havoc on the Third World." Pp. 20–23 in *50 Years Is Enough: The Case against the World Bank and the International Monetary Fund,* edited by K. Danahei. Boston: South End Press.

Burawoy, M., J.A. Blum, S. George, Z. Gille, T. Gowan, L. Haney, M. Klawiter, S.H. Lopez, S.O. Riain, and M. Thayer. 2000. *Global Ethnography: Forces, Connections and Imaginations in a Postmodern World.* Berkeley: University of California Press.

Burbach, R., O. Núñez, and B. Kagarlitsky. 1997. *Globalization and its Discontents: The Rise of Postmodern Socialisms.* Chicago: Pluto Press.

Cabezas, A.L. 1998. "Discourses of Prostitution: The Case of Cuba." Pp. 79–86 in *Global Sex Workers: Rights, Resistance and Redefinition,* edited by K. Kempadoo and J. Doezema. London: Routledge.

Caribbean Tourism Organization. 1995. *Statistical Report: 1994 Edition.* Barbados, WI: Caribbean Tourism Organization.

Castro, F. 1993. Quoted in G. Villalba. *Cuba y el Turismo.* Havana: Editorial de Ciencias Sociales.

Castro, F. 1999. *Neoliberal Globalization and the Global Economic Crisis.* Havana: Publications Office of the Council of State.

Chapkis, W. 1997. *Live Sex Acts: Women Performing Erotic Labor.* New York: Routledge.

Chomsky, N. 1994. *World Orders Old and New.* New York: Columbia University Press.

Clifford, J. and G.F. Marcus. 1986. *Writing Culture: The Poetics and Politics of Ethnography.* Berkeley: University of California Press.

Contreras, J. 2001. "The Dark Tourists." *Newsweek International* (April 30): 20.

Cox, R.H. 1993. *The Development of the Dutch Welfare State: From Workers' Insurance to Universal Entitlement.* Pittsburgh: University of Pittsburgh Press.

Craig-Smith, S., and C. French. 1994. *Learning to Live with Tourism.* Melbourne: Pitman Publishing.

Craik, J. 1997. "The Culture of Tourism." Pp. 113–136 in *Touring Cultures: Transformations of Travel and Theory,* edited by C. Rojec and J. Urry. London: Routledge.

Dahies, H. 1998. "Redefining Amsterdam as a Tourist Destination." *Annals of Tourism Research* 25: 55–69.

Davidow, W.H. and M. Malone. 1992. *The Virtual Corporation: Structuring and Revitalizing the Corporation for the 21st Century.* New York: Harper Collins.

de Haan, W. 1997. "Minorities, Crime and Criminal Justice in The Netherlands." Pp. 198–223 in *Minorities, Migrants and Crime: Diversity and Similarity across Europe and the United States,* edited by Ineke Haen-Marshall. Thousand Oaks: Sage.

Dello Buono, R.A. and J. Bell Lara (Eds.). 1997. *Carta Cuba: Essays on the Potential and Contradictions of Cuban Development.* La Habana: FLACSO-Programa Cuba.

Diaz Gonzalez, E. 1997a. "Introduction." Pp. 3–8 in *Cuba, Impacto de las Crises en Grupos Vulnerables: Mujer, Familia, Infancia,* edited by E. Diaz, T. Carmen León, E. Fernández Zegueira, S. Perro Mendoza, and M. del Carmen Abala Argueller. Habana: Universidad de La Habana.

Diaz Gonzalez, E. 1997b. "Turismo y Prostitución en Cuba." Pp. 3–8 in *Cuba, Impacto de las Crises en Grupos Vulnerables: Mujer, Familia, Infancia,* edited by E. Diaz, T. Carmen León, E. Fernández Zegueira, S. Perro Mendoza, and M. del Carmen Abala Argueller. Habana: Universidad de La Habana.

Dougherty, J. and D. Hoithouse. 1998. "Nogales Nightmare: Life in the Maquiladora Industry Borders on Exploitation." *Tucson Weekly* (November 19).

Dubisch, J. 1996. *In a Different Place: Sex, Gender and Fieldwork at a Greek Shrine.* Princeton: Princeton University Press.

Eckstein, S. 1997. "The Limits of Socialism in a Capitalist World Economy: Cuba Since the Collapse of the Soviet Bloc." Pp. 135–50 in *Toward a New Cuba?: Legacies of a Revolution*, edited by M. Centeno and M. Font. Boulder, CO: Lynne Rienner Publishers.

Elizalde, R. 1996. *Flores Desechables: Prostitiución en Cuba?* Havana: Casa Editoria, Abril.

Enloe, C. 1989. *Bananas, Beaches and Bases: Making Feminist Sense of International Politics.* Los Angeles: University of California Press.

Espinosa, L. 1999. "Globalización y la Economía de Cuba." Interview, Havana, January 23.

Fernandez, N. 1999. "Back to the Future: Women, Race and Tourism in Cuba." Pp. 81–92 in *Sun, Sex, and Gold: Tourism and Sex Work in the Caribbean*, edited by K. Kempadoo. Lanham, MD: Rowman and Littlefield Publishers.

Ferrante, J. and P. Brown, Jr. 1998. *The Social Construction of Race and Ethnicity in the United States.* New York: Longman.

Firat, A. Fuat and N. Dholakia. 1998. *Consuming People: From Political Economy to Theaters of Consumption.* London: Routledge.

Forbes Magazine. 1996. "A Letter from the Tipplezone." 157 (12): 120.

Friedman, D. 1999. *The Lexus and the Olive Tree.* New York: Farrar, Straus, Giroux.

Fusco, C. 1996. "Hustling for Dollars." *Ms. Magazine* 7 (2): 62–70.

Geertz, C. 1983. *Local Knowledge: Further Essays in Interpretive Anthropology.* New York: Basic Books.

Gordon, J. 1997. "Cuba's Entrepreneurial Socialism." *The Atlantic Monthly* 279 (1): 18–30.

Greider, W. 1997. *One World, Ready or Not: The Manic Logic of Global Capitalism.* New York: Simon and Schuster.

Guevara, A. 1998. Quoted in Irwin Block, "Much Work To Be Done: Cuban Revolution Hasn't Brought Full Emancipation of Women." *Montreal Gazette* (March 24): A5.

Haen Marshall, I. 1993. "Prostitution in the Netherlands: It's Just Another Job!" Pp. 225–48 in *Female Criminality*, edited by C. Cullive and C. Marshall. New York: Garland.

Herman, E.S. 1995. *Triumph of the Market: Essays on Economics, Politics and the Media.* Boston: South End Press.

Hirst, P. 1996. *Globalization in Question: The International Economy and the Possibilities of Governance.* Cambridge, MA: Blackwell Publishers.

Hochschild, A.R. 1983. *The Managed Heart: Commercialization of Human Feeling.* Berkeley: University of California Press.

Hodge, D.G. and H. Abiodun. 2001. "The Colonization of the Cuban Body." *NACLA Report on the Americas* 34 (15): 20–30.

Hoogvelt, A. 1997. *Globalization and the Postcolonial World: The New Political Economy of Development.* Houndmills, Basingstoke, Hampshire: Macmillan.

Hughes, D. 2000. "The Transnational Shadow Market of Trafficking in Women." *Journal of International Affairs* 53: 625–651.

International Labor Organization (ILO). 1998. "Sex Industry Assuming Massive Proportions in Southeast Asia." *ILO Press Release* (August 19). Geneva: International Labor Organization.

Karliner, J. 1997. *The Corporate Planet: Ecology and Politics in the Age of Globalization.* San Francisco: Sierra Club Books.

Kempadoo, K. and J. Doezema (Eds.). 1998. *Global Sex Workers: Rights, Resistance and Redefinition*. London: Routledge.

Koont, S. 1998. "Cuba's Unique Structural Adjustment." Unpublished paper presented at the Latin American Studies Association annual meeting, Chicago.

Korten, D.C. 1995. *When Corporations Rule the World*. West Hartford, CT: Kumerian Press.

Landau, S. and D. Starratt. 1994. "Cuba's Economic Slide." *Multinational Monitor* 10 (November 15): 7–13.

Lean Lim, L. 1998. *The Sex Sector: The Economic and Social Bases of Prostitution in Southeast Asia*. Geneva: International Labor Office.

Lucy, C. 1996. *Consumer Culture*. New Brunswick, NJ: Rutgers University Press.

MacCannell, D. 1999. *The Tourist: A New Theory of the Leisure Class*. 2nd ed. Berkeley: University of California Press.

Mander, J. and E. Goldsmith. 1996. *The Case Against the Global Economy and for a Turn Toward the Local*. San Francisco: Sierra Club Books.

Marx, K. [1887] 1958. *Capital*, Vol. 1. Translated by S. Moore and E. Aveling Moscow: Progress Publishers.

Mesa-Lago, C. 1981. *The Economy of Socialist Cuba*. Albuquerque: University of New Mexico Press.

Meulenbelt, E.B. 1993. De Verdiensten van Prostitutie. Doctoraal Scriptie Sociologie, Amsterdam.

Michalowski, R. 1995. "Between Citizens and the Socialist State: The Negotiation of Legal Practice in Socialist Cuba." *Law and Society Review* 29: 65–101.

Michalowski, R. 1996. "Ethnography and Anxiety: Fieldwork and Reflexivity in the Vortex of U.S. Cuban Relations." *Qualitative Sociology* 19: 59–82.

Michalowski, R. 1998. "Market Spaces and Socialist Places: Cubans Talk About Life in the Post-Soviet World." Unpublished paper presented at the Latin American Studies Association annual conference, Chicago.

Michalowski, R. and M. Zatz. 1989. "The Second Economy in Cuba: Nothing Fails Like Success." Pp. 101–21 in *Second Economies in Marxist States*, edited by M. Los. London: MacMillan.

Miller, M. and T. Henthorne. 1997. *Investment in the New Cuban Tourist Industry: A Guide to Entrepreneurial Opportunities*. Westport, CT: Quorum Books.

Mr. A. de Graaf Foundation. 1997. "Between the Lines." *Newsletter of the Mr. A. de Graaf Foundation, Institute for Prostitution Issues*. Amsterdam, The Netherlands.

Nagle, J. 1997. *Whores and Other Feminists*. New York: Routledge.

O'Connell Davidson, J. 1996. "Sex Tourism in Cuba." *Race and Class* 38: 39–48.

O'Connell Davidson, J. 1998. *Prostitution, Power and Freedom*. Ann Arbor, MI: University of Michigan Press.

O'Connell Davidson, J. and J. Sanchez Taylor. 1998. "Fantasy Islands: Exploring the Demand for Sex Tourism." Pp. 37–54 in *Sun, Sex, and Gold: Tourism and Sex Work in the Caribbean*, edited by K. Kempadoo. Lanham, MD: Rowman and Littlefield Publishers.

Opperman, M. 1998. *Sex Tourism and Prostitution: Aspects of Leisure, Recreation, and Work*. New York: Cognizant Communication Corporation.

Paternostro, S. 2000. "Communism vs. Prostitution." *The New Republic* (July 10): 18–22.

Patuilo, P. 1996. *Last Resorts: The Cost of Tourism in the Caribbean*. London: Cassell.

Pettman, J. 1997. "Body Politics: International Sex Tourism." *Third World Quarterly* 18: 93–108.

Pietila, H. and J. Vickers. 1994. *Making Women Matter: The Role of the United Nations*. London: Zed Books.

Pinder, D. 1998. "Tourism in The Netherlands: Resource Development, Regional Impacts and Issues." Pp. 301–323 in *Tourism and Economic Development: European Experiences*, edited by A. Williams and G. Shaw. New York: John Wiley and Sons.

Randall, M. 1996. "Cuban Women and the U.S. Blockade." *Sojourner* 22: 10–11.

Raymond, J. 1998. "Violence Against Women: NGO Stonewalling in Beijing and Elsewhere." *Women's Studies International Forum* 21: 1–9.

Reiland, R. 1996. "Amsterdam's Taxing Issue: Wages of Sin." *Insight on the News* (June) 12 (21): 29.

Richter, L. 1998. "Exploring the Political Role of Gender in Tourism Research." Pp. 391–404 in *Global Tourism*, edited by W. Theobald. Oxford: Butterworth-Heinemann.

Robinson, L. 1998. "Castro Gives Tourism A Try: The Pope and 1.4 Million Other People are Expected to Visit Cuba This Year." *U.S. News and World Report* 124 (1): 32–36.

Rochon, T. 1999. *The Netherlands: Negotiating Sovereignty in an Interdependent World*. Boulder, CO: Westview Press.

Rojec, C. and J. Urry. 1997. *Touring Cultures: Transformations of Travel and Theory*. London: Routledge.

Sanchez Taylor, J. 2000. "Tourism and 'Embodied' Commodities: Sex Tourism in the Caribbean." Pp. 41–53 in *Tourism and Sex: Culture, Commerce, and Coercion*, edited by S. Clift and S. Carter. New York: Pinter.

Sassen, S. 1996. "Identity in the Global City: Economic and Cultural Encasements." Pp. 131–51 in *The Geography of Identity*, edited by P. Yaeger. Ann Arbor, MI: University of Michigan Press.

Sassen, S. 1998. *Globalization and its Discontents: Essays on the New Mobility of People and Money*. New York: The New Press.

Sassen, S. 2000a. *Cities in a World Economy*. Thousand Oaks, CA: Pine Forge Press.

Sassen, S. 2000b. "Women's Burden: Counter-Geographies of Globalization and the Feminization of Survival." *Journal of International Affairs* 53: 503–24.

Sassen, S. and F. Roost. 1997. "The City: Strategic Site for the Global Entertainment Industry." Pp. 143–54 in *The Tourist City*, edited by D. Judd and S. Fainstein. New Haven, CT: Yale University Press.

Schlesinger, A., Jr. 1996. Quoted in Robert E. Quirk. *Fidel Castro*. New York: W.W. Norton.

Skrobanek, S., N. Boonpakdee, and C. Jantateero. 1997. *The Traffic in Women: Human Realities of the International Sex Trade*. London: Zed Books.

Strout, J. 1995. "Women, the Politics of Sexuality, and Cuba's Economic Crisis." *Socialist Review* 25: 5–16.

ten Kate, N. 1995. "Prostitution: A Really Valuable Asset." Paper distributed by the Mr. A. de GraafStichting. Amsterdam: The Netherlands.

The Economist. 1998. "The Sex Industry: Giving The Customer What He Wants." (February 14): 23–25.

Theobald, W. 1998. *Global Tourism.* Oxford: Butterworth-Heinemann.

Thomas, H. 1998. *Cuba: Or, The Pursuit of Freedom.* Updated ed. New York: Da Capo Press.

Triana, J. 1995. "Consolidation of the Economic Reanimation." *Cuban Foreign Trade* 1: 17–24.

Truong, T.-D. 1990. *Sex, Money and Morality: Prostitution and Tourism in Southeast Asia.* London: Zed Books.

van der Pod, S. 1995. "Solidarity as Boomerang: The Fiasco of Prostitutes' Rights Movements in The Netherlands." *Crime, Law, and Social Change* 23: 41–65.

Van Maanen, J. 1988. *Tales of the Field: On Writing Ethnography.* Chicago: University of Chicago Press.

Verdery, K. 1996. *What Was Socialism, and What Comes Next?* Princeton: Princeton University Press.

Villalba, G. 1993. *Cuba y el Turismo.* Havana: Editorial de Ciencias Sociales.

Visser, J. 1997a. "Dutch Preparations For A Different Prostitution Policy." Mr. A. de Graaf Foundation: Institute for Prostitution Research. Amsterdam, The Netherlands (January).

Visser, J. 1997b. "The Dutch Law Proposal on Prostitution: Text and Explanation." Mr. A. de Graaf Foundation: Institute for Prostitution Research. Amsterdam, The Netherlands (July).

Wijers, M. 1998. "Women, Labor, Migration: The Position of Trafficked Women and Strategies For Support." Pp. 69–78 in *Global Sex Workers: Rights, Resistance and Redefinition*, edited by K. Kempadoo and J. Doezema. London: Routledge.

Williams, A. and G. Shaw. 1998. *Tourism and Economic Development: European Experiences.* New York: John Wiley and Sons.

Wonders, N. 2000. "Conceptualizing Difference." Pp. 11–26 in *Investigating Difference: Human and Cultural Relations in Criminal Justice*, edited by The Criminal Justice Collective of Northern Arizona. Boston: Allyn and Bacon.

Wonders, N. and M. Danner. 1999. "(En)Gendering Globalization: International Women's Rights and Criminology." Unpublished paper presented at the annual meeting of the American Society of Criminology (November). Toronto, Canada.

Wonders, N. and M. Danner. 2002. "Globalization, State-Corporate Crime, and Women: The Strategic Role of Women's NGOs in the New World Order." Pp. 165–184 in *Controversies in White Collar Crime*, edited by G. Potter. Cincinnati: Anderson.

Zatz, N. 1997. "Sex Work/Sex Act: Law, Labor, and Desire in Constructions of Prostitution." *Signs* 22 (21): 277–308.

CHAPTER STUDY QUESTIONS

- Wonders and Michalowski conclude from their comparative study that "globalization facilitates the growth of sex tourism, as well as the particular character of sex tourism in different locales." According to Wonders and Michalowski, what are the global forces that have contributed in shaping the local production and consumption of sex tourism in recent years?

- According to Wonders and Michalowski, what have been the effects of "migration" and "cross-border tourism" on the production and consumption of sex tourism? Based on their research findings, what grounds are there for arguing that the growth of globalized sex tourism is typically associated with the increased exploitation of lower class, visible minority, and immigrant women?

- What is involved in the research methodology referred to as "global ethnography"? How do Wonders and Michalowski use this research method in their comparative study of sex tourism in Amsterdam and Havana?

- According to Wonders and Michalowski, "[p]olicy-makers, scholars, and ordinary citizens tend to see prostitution as a problem caused by prostitutes" while there is a similar "tendency to view sex tourism as a problem belonging to other nations, a problem that originates primarily with poor Third World women who choose to deviate from 'good' women by selling their sexuality." How do the findings of Wonders and Michalowski's comparative study of sex tourism in Amsterdam and Havana bring these traditional views into serious question?

RELATED WEB LINKS

Amsterdam Hotspots
http://www.amsterdamhotspots.nl/
> This is an online guide to Amsterdam tourist hotspots, with links to information on red light businesses and sex tours.

Third World Women's Health – Prostitution and Sex Tourism
http://haneydaw.myweb.uga.edu/twwh/traf.html
> This website provides information on the effects of prostitution and sex tourism on women's health in Third World countries along with suggestions on possible solutions to the problem.

The UC Atlas of Global Inequality
http://ucatlas.ucsc.edu/
> This website provides information relevant to issues of global inequality using online, downloadable maps and graphics.

Women and Globalization
http://www.unpac.ca/economy/introglob.html

> This website provides information on the effects of globalization on the role of women in the economy, with particular attention to migrant workers, domestic labour, farm labour, and the increasing involvement of women in prostitution and the international sex trade.

Chapter 7

STOPPING THE ILLEGAL TRAFFICKING OF HUMAN BEINGS: HOW TRANSNATIONAL POLICE WORK CAN STEM THE FLOW OF FORCED PROSTITUTION

PETER A. MAMELI

GLOBALIZATION AND THE TRANSNATIONAL SEX INDUSTRY

Illegally trafficking human beings for the purpose of forced prostitution in the transnational sex industry expanded at the close of the twentieth century as a direct result of globalization processes and other influences (*The Economist* 1998: 21; United Nations Office for Drug Control and Crime Prevention 1999; O'Neill-Richard 2000).[1] Increased ability to travel and communicate raised the demand for, and supply of, this commodity among interested parties. Where illegal trafficking for the purposes of prostitution was concerned, large organized crime syndicates were often involved with the coordination and/or protection of the process. These syndicates frequently took advantage of structural dislocations within countries due to economic crises or conflicts in order to establish flow routes and recruit/kidnap individuals for placement into the transnational sex industry. Additionally, in all states, corruption of government officials has served to further the success of these operations. Those suffering the brunt of the illegal traffickers' growth were the "[i]ncreasing number of women and girl children from developing countries and from some countries with economies in transition" (United Nations 1997).

This pattern of activity continues today and its influence is growing. Unfortunately, the problem of illegally trafficked women and girls for the transnational sex industry remains poorly defined in terms of scope. Both the raw numbers of events taking place, as well as when and where they are occurring are yet to be fully identified with any degree of assurance. Further, the operational structures of the organized crime syndicates responsible for conducting substantial portions of the trade remain in the shadows, and there is insufficient knowledge as to the range and patterns of global traffic flows. Finally, the need for intergovernmental, cross-level, and cross-cultural cooperation remains difficult to actualize. However, some positive action is taking place.

At the international, national and local levels of political response, governments are now attempting to assess the problem with better record and statistics keeping, identification and analysis of best practices, and partnering regionally and internationally with relevant international governmental and non-governmental bodies to strengthen their efforts at control and accountability. There has also been movement towards accurately defining the problems that are being confronted in the area of illegally trafficking women and children so that the issue can begin to be productively researched.

One useful definition of trafficking in women and children was recently provided by the United States' President's Interagency Council on Women. For the purposes of this chapter, the aspect of the definition relating to sexual slavery is of central importance. The definition reads:

> Trafficking is all acts involved in the recruitment, abduction, transport, harboring, transfer, sale or receipt of persons; within national or across international borders; through force, coercion, fraud or deception; to place persons in situations of slavery-like conditions, forced labor services, such as prostitution or sexual services, domestic servitude, bonded sweatshop labor or other debt bondage.[2]

Another thorough definition has been constructed by the European Union. It reads:

> "Traffic in human beings" means subjection of a person to the real and illegal sway of other persons by using violence or menaces or by abuse of authority or intrigue with a view to the exploitation of prostitution, forms of sexual exploitation and assault of minors or trade in abandoned children. (Europol Convention 1998)[3]

While a universal working definition of trafficking in women and children is fast being developed, a satisfactory explanation of globalization, the primary engine for the transnational sex industry's growth, is still struggled with. Importantly, some of the elements that have been difficult to capture in a definition of globalization relate directly to the discussion of trafficking in human beings.

In recent years, the general study of globalization has become of central concern to many scholars in the social sciences (Schott 1994; Krasner 1994; Storper 1992; Thrift 1992; Riggs 1999). Yet, as Harris notes "[t]erminology in this whole area seems designed for obfuscation" (Harris 1993: 757). A basic definition provided by MacEwan (1994: 1) describes the phenomenon as "[t]he international spread of capitalist exchange and production relationships." While this definition does expose some of the powerful players and structures at the heart of the globalization explosion (capitalists and capitalism), it doesn't completely cover the matter. Held and McGrew (1993: 262) offer deeper insight with the following comments:

> On the one hand, the concept of globalization defines a universal process or set of processes which generate a multiplicity of linkages and interconnections which transcend the states and societies which make up the

modern world system: the concept therefore has a spatial connotation. On the other hand, globalization also implies an intensification in the levels of interaction, interconnectedness or interdependence between the states and societies which constitute the modern world community.

Many of these writers have made significant headway in coming to terms with what globalization in fact is. For the most part, capitalists and national power elites are identified as the practitioners (and essentially the winners) of globalization in civil society and government circles. However, few people seem terribly concerned with negative aspects of globalization such as the growth in the trafficking of human beings, the increased dispersion of diseases such as the Human Immunodeficiency Virus/Acquired Immune Deficiency Syndrome (HIV/AIDS), or who globalization's winners in uncivil society are. Further still, even fewer people seem to care about who have become the losers in this global experiment, or what they have been experiencing. To fully understand the problem of illegally trafficking human beings for the transnational sex industry, these components of globalization must be probed as well, and the explanation of globalization's strengths must be wed to its weaknesses.

Beyond defining the problem and its causes, additional options open to law enforcement and public authorities must also be evaluated. To date, three primary areas of action have been generally identified and accepted. First, developing methods to prevent women and children from being drawn into trafficking schemes—often through public awareness campaigns. Second, enhancing the effective investigation and prosecution of these crimes. Third, protecting victim's rights (Stoeker 2000: 137). This chapter will examine several possible options for action relating to the broad areas of prevention and investigation. It will also examine the unique role that transnational police organizations such as the European Police Organization (Europol) and the international police organization (Interpol) can play in redressing the global spread of this criminal activity.

EUROPE'S EXPERIENCE WITH THE TRANSNATIONAL SEX INDUSTRY

The impact of globalization on Europe can be seen in many areas. From the overall regionalizing of its governance and economic structures to those within civil society who are capitalizing on new opportunities presented by emerging technologies and weakening nation-state borders, its presence is evident. However, globalization's effects are not limited to governmental actors, or those within civil society. Elements of uncivil society are taking advantage of the processes of globalization as well. These changes have had a direct impact on the European sex industry and the trafficking of human beings within Europe.

As markets have become more open and fluid through globalization processes in the 1990s, the mobility of sex workers in the European Union (EU) has increased dramatically, creating a migrant class of sex worker that can be found operating to some degree in any EU country. Contributing to this development has been post Soviet Union economic instability in Eastern Europe during the 1990s. As a result of precarious financial times, some desperate (and some entrepreneurial) individuals from the Newly Independent States saw sex work as a means of survival that offered a chance to move to more economically comfortable Western European countries. The development of this migratory class left some of these individuals vulnerable to transnational organized crime syndicates, who themselves had independently become encouraged to enhance trafficking within their portfolios as they sought to take advantage of structural disruptions within the region (Brussa 1996: 193-94).[4] However, beyond women who might have been selecting migratory sex work as a profession, there were many women and girls from the Newly Independent States who did not intend to go into sex services of any kind, but rather were seeking travel, education, and/or were interested in migrating to the West for more standard forms of employment. Unfortunately, many of these individuals were manipulated, lied to and/or kidnapped into the transnational sex industry by criminal elements (Pope 1997; Global Survival Network 1997). With this unwilling source of labor from the East, the illegal trafficking of women and girls to the EU reached new heights in terms of numbers and technique by the turn of the century.

While these patterns were taking shape, international non-governmental and international governmental organizations were not blind to these new developments. Of particular note for Europe is the work of the International Organization for Migration (IOM). During the mid to late 1990s, IOM catalogued trends and events relating to trafficking in migrants (for sexual and other purposes) in a monthly newsletter. Country specific and regional tracking was conducted to the best of IOM's ability with the limited information available, and European countries were often commented on or spotlighted in specific reports on trafficking abuses. At the same time, the United Nations has been profiling the issue of trafficking at international conferences, in international legislation and through the United Nations Drug Control Program. All in all, the topic of trafficking was clearly placed on both government and civil society agendas.

Within the EU specifically, beyond erecting new legal infrastructure to enhance response to trafficking incidents, several approaches were employed to address the growing problem. Among the earliest was investing in Europol a clear mandate to pursue the trafficking in human beings issue in 1994. The task of documenting, researching, and developing strategies for response to trafficking human beings to, and within, the EU was to be carried out by the Europol Drugs Unit (Europol 2000a).[5] While Europol's efforts to date have been considered more rhetoric than substance by critics, the fruits of this investment are becoming more obvious as its work in this area is coming to light.

At the end of the 1990s, Europol estimated that roughly several thousand individuals were being trafficked into the EU each year for the transnational sex industry. Of this estimated number, 90 per cent of trafficking victims in the EU were believed to be originating from Central and Eastern European states. The main countries contributing to trafficking in human beings into the EU were identified as Ukraine, Hungary, Czech Republic, Bulgaria, Poland, Romania, Russia and Albania. Source countries outside of Europe where human beings were being trafficked into the EU from included Thailand, China, Vietnam, Ghana, Morocco, Nigeria, Sierra Leone, Brazil, Columbia, and the Dominican Republic. Europol notes that the victims it has observed are almost exclusively women between 18 years of age and 30 years of age. However, girls 13 and 14 and young boys have also been trafficked (Europol 1998a).

Beyond research and documentation, Europol has been involved with coordinating two "expert meetings" in 1998 to support on-going investigations, as well as engaging in developing means to stop the trafficking of child pornography over the Internet and sharing its expertise with academic research projects in the EU. Additionally, Europol organized its first seminar for representatives of non-EU states and organizations to start defining means and opportunities for future cooperative activities (Europol 1998a; Europol 2000b).

Two other approaches to the trafficking problem that ... [were] underway in the EU in the late 1990s and that ... intersected with Europol's activities, include the "Incentive and Exchange Programme for Persons Responsible for Combating Trade in Human Beings and the Sexual Exploitation of Children (STOP)," established by the European Commission, and the "Daphne Programme," also established by the Commission. These programs ... [were] both supported by Europol.

The STOP program [sought] to further establish a means of exchanging information between Member States by encouraging training, exchange programs, multidisciplinary meetings, and the conducting of studies and research by professionals responsible for combating this phenomenon (judges, public prosecutors, police departments, civil servants, public services concerned with immigration and border controls, etc.) (European Union 1996). The Daphne Programme [sought] to develop productive relationships between non-governmental and other organizations, including public authorities, where they work together to combat violence against women and children (including trafficking) and to provide effective means of raising public awareness on these topics (European Union 1997). [Note from the editors: These have since been replaced by follow-up "STOP II" and "Daphne II" Programmes, which represent a continuation of European Union member state cooperation in combating trade in human beings and all forms of sexual exploitation (European Union 2000).]

THE TRANSNATIONAL SEX INDUSTRY BEYOND EUROPE

In the late twentieth century, the notion of illegally trafficking women and children into the sex industry was considered primarily an Asian problem. Focus on the topic was seldom conducted with the intense scrutiny it has achieved today with the recognition that globalization has had a hand in vastly expanding the enterprise. In fact, even today, some still focus on Southeast Asia, in particular, as ground zero in the globalization of the sex industry, and consider it the epicenter of today's developments (Kuo 2000). Others record and examine the industry's development within a distinctively Asian context (Leuchtag 1995; Law 1999).

Given that this perspective has been the dominant one to date, the law enforcement organization (other than those indigenous to countries) that would likely have been involved with addressing this issue would have been Interpol. However, there is little documentation that speaks to the efforts of Interpol in this area.

Interpol's history dates back to its birth in Europe in the early 1900s. Its efforts and membership have grown to worldwide proportion since that time.[6] While Interpol is not an international police "force," so to speak, it is a conduit among the world's nation-state police forces.

As such, it can help to coordinate investigations among Member states, provide training, and support Member states efforts in police actions. In the area of trafficking, it seems that the bulk of Interpol's efforts have been aimed at reducing child prostitution. Operation Cathedral is an example of Interpol's ongoing efforts to coordinate police action in this area (see www.interpol.int). [More] recently, with the death of 58 Chinese immigrants illegally smuggled into England in 2000, Interpol and Europol became focused on trafficking in humans beyond the purposes of sex work (Elliot 2000). However, this type of engagement can only serve to strengthen the involvement of both organizations in the effort to curb the transnational sex industry as well, and is a welcome development. As with Europol, Interpol has a unique position that allows it to provide a transnational perspective on transnational crime as well as a means of investigation and intervention. Its use of "notice programs" to identify differing types of criminals and victims on an international scale serves as only one means of establishing effective communications between police forces (Imhoff and Cutler 1998). What is of potentially greater use in the future is Interpol's capacity to partner with differing law enforcement organizations around the world in order to build capacity for identifying, investigating, and intervening in the activities of the transnational sex industry.

OPTIONS AND OPPORTUNITIES

Interpol and Europol must actively participate in the United Nations Global Programme Against Trafficking in Human Beings in order to flesh out the full range of problems associated with trafficking and fully identify the role and characteristics of globalization in this area, including the complete range of its winners and losers.

At the international, national, and regional levels of political response, Interpol and Europol need to continue to encourage relationships with a wide range of states and international governmental and non-governmental organizations in order to be able to structure effective intervention and public awareness campaigns on trafficking in both supply and demand countries.

Interpol and Europol should consider encouraging local law enforcement agencies and sex workers operating outside of the trafficking industry to find mutual ground upon which to build a working trust, perhaps through the auspices of non-governmental intermediaries.

The current mandate of Europol allows for the prevention and combating of trafficking in human beings, including child pornography, through facilitating data exchange among EU states, providing operational analysis to Member States, and providing expertise and technical support for investigations and operations carried out by Member States' law enforcement agencies. Envisioned future roles for Europol where trafficking and other crimes are concerned involve enabling the organization to facilitate and encourage cooperation among Member States, extending to the creation of joint teams of professionals to conduct specific investigations. Additionally, Europol is expected to develop specific area expertise that will be put at the disposal of Member States. Further, Europol is expected to promote liaison agreements between prosecuting/investigating officials involved in fighting organized crime. Finally, Europol is expected to establish a research, documentation, and statistical network on cross-border crime in the EU (Europol 2000a). Interpol is already engaged in many of these same activities. As the perceived future of Europol and Interpol places a heavy emphasis on coordinated action with other actors, it seems likely that partnership scenarios would be a wise investment for responding to the trafficking dilemma in Europe and the world. However, encouraging and facilitating partnerships must take place at the international, regional, national, and local levels simultaneously if success is to be cultivated. Further, such partnerships need to be multi-sectoral in nature and able to span and link multiple policy areas when warranted.

At the international level, Interpol and Europol have to become more deeply ingrained in the global efforts of the UN to address trafficking in human beings. In particular, commitments need to be made to support and work with the United Nations Centre for International Crime Prevention (CICP) and the United Nations Interregional Crime and Justice Research Institute (UNICRI) as they implement the Global Programme Against Trafficking in Human Beings (United Nations Office for Drug Control and Crime Prevention 2000: 8–9). The program's goals are to assess regional and inter-regional trends, collect best practices, and initiate pilot projects. If the effort to fully define the trafficking issue area, assess the impact of globalization on governance and criminality, and move analysis of this topic to even broader ground is to be taken seriously, this project must be supported.

On the regional and national levels, partnerships need to be encouraged between law enforcement and a variety of players. Non-member states, states outside of regions of a country's specific interest, non-governmental organizations, international governmental organizations, and agencies within countries that are not likely to be currently interacting in regard to this topic need to be coaxed into developing supportive relationships.

As part of the problem of trafficking in human beings is the demand from citizens in affluent Western states for these services, awareness campaigns that not only point out the human rights violations associated with forced sex work via trafficking but that also key on criminal penalties and the potential for transmission of diseases such as HIV/AIDS are essential elements in fortifying a framework for disrupting the desire of a population for this commodity. Such awareness campaigns do not need to be structured as fear inducing or blame laying campaigns, ultimately aimed at the women caught in the transnational sex industry, but rather as information providing campaigns designed to highlight their plight and display how they are kept away from the resources necessary to protect both themselves and their clients. Explicit awareness campaigns can educate the public as to what to look for in regard to the conditions these operations conduct their business under, thereby educating potential clients as to what they are actually dealing with when confronted with certain environmental surroundings. However, to construct such campaigns effectively, Interpol and Europol officials, along with national law enforcement authorities, must work closely with public health authorities in the field so as not to create a general backlash of fear against sex workers outside of the trafficking issue area that would serve to drive this population away from HIV/AIDS public health services.

Regarding identifying and examining where trafficking is occurring and who is involved with it, a special project could be undertaken by Interpol and Europol to complement their efforts to train law enforcement personnel to understand what they are looking for in regard to the environmental conditions of trafficking. This special project could be to train law enforcement to partner with relevant non-governmental organizations in developing working relationships with sex workers and sex worker unions in various states. Establishing a mutually beneficial rapport, where sex workers rights are protected (within the realm of their currently criminalized capacity) and law enforcement ... [is] made aware of environmental changes that threaten the well being of all involved, would benefit all.

Police are only at ground zero within government circles and civil society. Sex workers themselves (local and migratory) are at ground zero in uncivil society. As such, it is they who will see the activities of the transnational sex industry on the ground first. Due to decreased market share, gossip among themselves, and knowledge obtained from clients, local sex workers are likely to know when trafficking situations are developing before anybody else. The question becomes, "Is there room for a partnership to develop between law enforcement, sex workers, and sex worker unions that would enable tapping into this information cache at local, national, regional and international levels?" Recent experience does indicate that possibilities for progress in this area exist, although one would assume that skepticism about such a partnership would deservedly be high.

The Transnational AIDS/STD Prevention Among Migrant Prostitutes in Europe Project (TAMPEP) began in 1993 and is an effort that combines active intervention with the direct involvement of sex workers (European Network for HIV/STD Prevention in Prostitution 2000).

The central mission of the project is to provide culturally relevant HIV/STD education to migrant sex workers. It also examines their working conditions through fieldwork. TAMPEP has documented an increase in migrant sex work, particularly into Western Europe from Eastern and Central Europe. Additionally, there is an internal migration from Eastern Europe into Central Europe noted (European Network for HIV/STD Prevention in Prostitution 2000). In addition to TAMPEP, the European Intervention Projects, AIDS Prevention for Prostitutes (EUROPAP) program also works to assess and provide workable intervention on HIV/AIDS issues to sex workers (European Network for HIV/STD Prevention in Prostitution 2000). These two organizations merged and became the European Network for HIV/STD Prevention in Prostitution in 1996. Certain elements of their work offer interesting insights into how the trafficking problem might be approached in tandem by law enforcement, NGOs and sex workers.

Of particular importance to this chapter's theme is the potential for partnership that organizations like TAMPEP and EUROPAP might have with the EU state's law enforcement personnel, and how these partnerships might aid in reducing the illegal trafficking of human beings and [the] concurrent threat of increased HIV/AIDS transmission. Although common logic indicates that sex workers would be unlikely to trust law enforcement due to the stories of abuse of power by police over sex workers that circulate in many circles regardless of country, and police would likely not consider sex workers as partners in crime prevention, there is one recent compelling example of cooperation between the two parties that emerged from a EUROPAP project in Dublin which raises a variety of interesting possibilities for future activities.

> The project in Dublin organized a two-day seminar for members of the Gardai (police), and the liaison which resulted led to a female Garda coming to the project every month to give advice to sex workers on reporting assaults and to build confidence between the women and the Gardai.

> This initiative has been much appreciated by project users, with increasing numbers seeking Garda support. (European Network for HIV/STD Prevention in Prostitution 2000)

While opening a channel of productive communication with sex workers is a far cry from having them provide information on those who are trafficking in human beings for the transnational sex industry, even this humble effort is a start down a path others would have thought completely closed off. As such, it opens the possibility of greater pay back if explored beyond its current parameters.

Although it is impossible to know if such a venture would ever provide the type of results that would be necessary to help law enforcement deal with its trafficking problems, it is an avenue that could be examined in greater depth. Interpol and Europol could begin such an effort by reaching out to NGOs in Europe and abroad about the possibilities that exist for future activities in this area. At the very least, local police forces should be informed that such a development has occurred in Ireland and that they too may be able to produce a similar partnership if the prospect is appropriately pursued.

CONCLUSION: DO WE NEED A WORLD POLICE FORCE IN THE TWENTY-FIRST CENTURY?

The processes of globalization are complex, and their results varied. One of the unfortunate negative results of these developments has been an expansion in the transnational sex industry, as well as [in] the activities of organized (and unorganized) crime groups across the globe. Europe's response to these conditions has been to create their own transnational law enforcement organization, Europol, that would facilitate and coordinate Member State activities where such problems exist. [Given that Europol is] patterned off Interpol, the questions arise, are these types of law enforcement organizations the wave of future police work, and when will they move from being support organizations to actual police forces themselves?

In a recently heralded article on the dangers of new technologies, Bill Joy sounded a warning that genetic engineering, nanotechnology and robotics were advancing without adequate controls and could easily fall into the wrong hands, thus being turned into new types of weapons of mass destruction (Joy 2000a).[7] While Joy does not address topics as mundane as the transnational sex industry, the elements of the equation he is sketching hold true in this environment as well. Globalizing knowledge and ability favors both those in civil and uncivil society. In response to Joy's ideas, Attali and Fukyama (2000: 6–7) note that:

> We need a world police, and it cannot be only an American one, to control rogue states or, mainly, rogue non-state groups and individuals who will be the pirates along the new routes of the future.

Clearly, today the pirates are starting to show their faces as criminal activity takes on a more global character than we have seen to date. To this end, the transnational sex industry is but one example of this emergence. In response, we see a regionalized group of nation-states moving to create a transnational law enforcement entity that will help to coordinate their police actions against transnational crime. While it is too early to say that Joy's fears will come true, or that Attali and Fukyama's concerns will need to be actualized, we are seeing glimmers of both of their prognostications as the world lurches forward into this new millennium.

NOTES

[1] Beyond globalization processes, gender roles and cultural norms that relegate women to second class status need to be analyzed to fully define this problem.

[2] Definition provided in O'Neill-Richard (2000: v). The author also offers useful definitions of "Force or Coercion" and "Organized Criminal Groups."

[3] Europol is the European Union's law enforcement agency established to support Member States by facilitating data exchanges, providing operational analysis, and providing expertise and technical support for investigations and ongoing operations. [For more information on the organizational structure and operation of Europol, see the chapter by Hartmut Aden in this volume.]

[4] Additionally, for a further discussion of the development and characteristics of global organized crime, see Mittleman (2000).

[5] Fact Sheet 3 from the Europol website describes the history of these developments: "The establishment of Europol was agreed to in the Maastricht Treaty on European Union of 7 February 1992. Based in The Hague, The Netherlands, Europol started limited operations on 3 January 1994 in the form of the Europol Drugs Unit with the fight against drugs and progressively added other important areas of criminality. The Europol Convention was ratified by all Member States and came into force on 1 October 1998. Following a number of legal acts related to the Convention, Europol took up its full activities on 1 July, 1999." Available from: http://www.europol.eu.int. Additionally, as Mittelman (2000: 27) notes, Europol itself is a state-centered reaction to globalization. The creation of transnational police forces such as Europol seeks to manage globalization's negative impacts by providing the state a means of monitoring and reacting to illegal disruptions.

[6] See Imhoff and Cutler (1999) and Muth (2000) for background as to the history and activities of Interpol.

[7] The topic is taken further in Joy (2000b).

REFERENCES

Attali, J. and F. Fukuyama. 2000. "The Beginning of a New History." *New Perspectives Quarterly* (Summer): 6–7.

Brussa, L. 1996. "Transnational AIDS/STD Prevention Among Migrant Prostitutes in Europe." Pp. 193–94 in *Crossing Borders: Migration, Ethnicity and AIDS*, edited by M. Haour-Knipe and R. Rector. London: Taylor and Francis.

Elliot, F. 2000. "MI6 Ordered to Track Down the Snakeheads." *The Scotsman* (June 25).

European Network for HIV/STD Prevention in Prostitution. 2000. *EUROPAP*, http://www.med. ic.ac.uk/df/dfhm/europap/tampep/index.htm.

European Union. 1996. "Incentive and exchange programme for persons responsible for combating trade in human beings and the sexual exploitation of children (STOP)." *Europa: Activities of the European Union–Summaries of Legislation*, http://www.europa. eu /scadplus/ leg/en/1vb/133015.htm.

European Union. 1997. "The Daphne Programme." *Europa: European Union—Justice and Home Affairs*, http:europa.eu.int/comm./justice_home/project/daphne/en/index.htm.

European Union. 2000. "Stop II." *Europa: Justice and Home Affairs—Funding*, http://ec.europa. eu/justice_home/funding/stop/funding_stop_en.htm

Europol. 1998a. "Public Summary on Trafficking in Women."

Europol. 1998b. "Report on the Activities of the Europol Drugs Unit/Europol 1998." *EUROPOL: European Law Enforcement Cooperation*, http://www.europol.eu.int.

Europol. 2000a. "Fact Sheet 3." *EUROPOL: European Law Enforcement Cooperation*, http:// www.europol.eu.int.

Europol. 2000b. "Green Light to Europol for Cooperation with Non-EU States and Bodies in Fighting International Organized Crime!" *EUROPOL Press Release* (April 27).

Europol Convention. 1998. *EUROPOL: European Law Enforcement Cooperation*, http://www. europol.eu.int/index.asp?page=legalconv

Global Survival Network. 1997. *Crime and Servitude: An Exposé of the Traffic in Women for Prostitution from the Newly Independent States*. Washington, DC: Global Survival Network.

Harris, R. 1993. "Globalization, Trade, and Income." *Canadian Journal of Economics* 26: 755–76.

Held, D. and A. McGrew. 1993. "Globalization and the Liberal Democratic State." *Government and Opposition* 28 (2): 261–88.

Imhoff, J. and S. Cutler. 1998. "Extending Law Enforcement's Reach Around the World." *FBI Law Enforcement Bulletin* (December): 10–16.

Imhoff, J. and S. Cutler. 1999. "Helping Police Around the World." *Law & Order* (March).

Interpol. "Homepage." *Interpol*, http://www.interpol.int/

Joy, B. 2000a. "Why the Future Doesn't Need Us." *Wired* (April), http://www.wired.com.

Joy, B. 2000b. "Act Now to Keep New Technologies Out of Destructive Hands." *New Perspectives Quarterly* (Summer): 12–14.

Krasner, S. 1994. "International Political Economy: Abiding Discord." *Review of International Political Economy* 1: 13–19.

Kuo, M. 2000. "Asia's Dirty Secret: Prostitution and Sex Trafficking in Southeast Asia." *Harvard International Review* 22: 42–45.

Law, L. 1999. "The Traffic in Women." *Journal of Southeast Asian Studies* 30: 409–410.

Leuchtag, A. 1995. "Merchants of Flesh: International Prostitution and the War on Women's Rights." *The Humanist* (March/April): 11–16.

MacEwan, A. 1994. "Globalization and Stagnation." *Monthly Review* 45: 1–16.

Mittelman, J. 2000. *The Globalization Syndrome: Transformation and Resistance.* Princeton: Princeton University Press.

Muth, M. 2000. "Your Best Resources for International Investigations." *Sheriff* (March/April).

O'Neill-Richard, A. 2000. "International Trafficking in Women in the Untied States: A Contemporary Manifestation of Slavery and Organized Crime." *Center for the Study of Intelligence* (April): 1–2, 27–28.

Pope, V. 1997. "Trafficking in Women: Procuring Russians for Sex Abroad—Even in America." *U.S. News and World Report* (April 17): 38–44.

Riggs, F. 1999. "Globalization—An Inquiry About Meaning." *PA Times* (October).

Schott, T. 1994. "Collaboration in the Invention of Technology: Globalization, Regions and Centers." *Social Science Research* 23: 23–56.

Stoeker, S. 2000. "The Rise in Human Trafficking and the Role of Organized Crime." *Demokratizatsiya: The Journal of Post-Soviet Democratization* 8: 129–31.

Storper, M. 1992. "The Limits to Globalization: Technology Districts and International Trade." *Economic Geography* 68: 60–92.

The Economist. 1998. "The Sex Industry: Giving The Customer What He Wants." (February 14): 23–25.

Thrift, N. 1992. "Muddling Through: World Orders and Globalization." *The Professional Geographer* 44: 3–7.

United Nations General Assembly. 1997. *Traffic in Women and Girls: Report of the Secretary General.* September 17, A/52/355. New York: United Nations.

United Nations Office for Drug Control and Crime Prevention. 1999. *Global Programme Against Trafficking in Human Beings: An Outline for Action.* Vienna: United Nations. Available from http://www.uncjin.org/CICP/traff_e.pdf.

United Nations Office for Drug Control and Crime Prevention. 2000. *Update: Trafficking in Human Beings.* Vienna: United Nations. Available from http://www.unodc.org/pdf/newsletter_2000-01-31_1.pdf.

CHAPTER STUDY QUESTIONS

- According to Mameli, the study of the process of globalization is important to fully understand the problem of illegally trafficking human beings for the transnational sex industry. Do you agree with this argument? Explain.

- Mameli notes that until recently "the notion of illegally trafficking women and children into the sex industry was considered primarily an Asian problem." What evidence does Mameli introduce in his discussion to show that the illegal trafficking of human beings for the sex industry is no longer a problem mainly confined to Asian countries?

- Mameli contends that, although "the problem of illegally trafficked women and girls for the transnational sex industry remains poorly defined in terms of scope," some positive action is taking place with regard to combating this form of transnational organized crime. What are some of the positive international developments in this regard outlined by Mameli that involve increased cross-national governmental and law enforcement cooperation?

- According to Mameli, Interpol and Europol have a unique position that allows them to take a leading role in the international effort to stop illegal trafficking for the purposes of prostitution. In Mameli's view, what are the available options and opportunities that these international police organizations should pursue in this regard?

RELATED WEB LINKS

Humantrafficking.org
http://www.humantrafficking.org/publications/211
  This is a web resource for combating human trafficking.

European Commission—Trafficking in Human Beings
http://ec.europa.eu/justice_home/fsj/crime/trafficking/fsj_crime_human_trafficking_en.htm
  This website outlines the steps being taken by European Union (EU) Member States through the European Commission to combat the problem of the trafficking in human beings.

United Nations Office on Drugs and Crime—Report on Trafficking in Human Beings: Global Patterns
http://www.unodc.org/unodc/trafficking_human_beings.html
  This is a detailed (128-page) report on global patterns of trafficking in human beings.

Interpol—Trafficking in Women
http://www.interpol.int/Public/THB/Women/Default.asp
  This site describes the efforts being undertaken by Interpol to increase and improve international law enforcement co-operation in order to help combat the problem of the trafficking of women for sexual exploitation.

PART 3

GLOBAL TRENDS IN POLICING AND SECURITY

Transnational policing represents one of, and the most important, and controversial issues in the globalization of criminal justice for several reasons. Although international cooperation between the police agencies of different nation-states has been common for at least 100 years, the rapid globalization that has characterized the past two decades has frequently blurred the distinction between internal and external security for many states. For example, the fact that the European Union has dismantled passport controls and other overt symbols of national sovereignty means that the security of any member nation is increasingly vulnerable to weaknesses in the security efforts of other members. Similar parallels can be drawn in North America with respect to the largely undefended border between Canada and the United States. Although this situation has existed for the past several decades, it has become particularly important in the aftermath of increased terrorist activities such as the Madrid train bombings and the destruction of the World Trade Center. Further, the rapid spread of free trade agreements and the growing power of multinational corporations have contributed to the development of a "global economy" that has facilitated the growth of transnational organized crime and white collar crime. It has also precipitated the emergence of transnational social and legal problems, such as illegal immigration, and the increased international migration of legal workers who attempt to follow better paying jobs around the globe.

All of these issues underscore the need for increased information sharing and other forms of cooperation between the police of different countries, and the new global situation has contributed to the development of what some analysts refer to as a trend towards "transnational" policing. Although many analysts consider this trend both inevitable and positive, it has not developed smoothly or without controversy. Aside from the obvious problems that arise from attempting to mesh the different legal standards and operational procedures of different countries, there is a very real concern over the loss of sovereignty that results from transnational policing. Further, human rights activists in Canada, Britain, the United States, and many European countries have argued that a significant potential for human rights abuses arises from

189

cooperating with police forces that do not operate under the same due process constraints that exist in most Western democracies. Although this latter problem is not entirely new, it is much more significant in an era of transnational policing. The chapters included in this part provide detailed discussions of selected aspects of the challenges facing police and policing in a world characterized by increased globalization.

In "Convergence of Policing Policies and Transnational Policing in Europe," Hartmut Aden addresses five key issues with respect to transnational policing. First, he argues that modern police agencies are characterized by as much similarity as diversity. Although he notes that many police agencies were originally created to impose and reinforce state power, he argues that the roles of police agencies have converged over time to focus on the protection of the public. Thus, while there is considerable diversity in the specific practices and organization of police agencies around the world, most modern police agencies carry out the three interrelated roles of criminal investigation, order maintenance, and traffic regulation. Further, while this convergence is partly due to the rise of Western democracy, Aden suggests that it can also be attributed to increased international cooperation. While Aden generally interprets this process in a positive light, he notes that most international cooperation is elitist insofar as it involves communication and high-level agreements between high-ranking officers and criminal investigation specialists, rather than day-to-day police cooperation. Although these elitist forms of international police cooperation are important because they contribute to everyday cooperation, Aden argues that more formal procedures must be developed to guide and facilitate the increasingly routine forms of transnational and cross-border police work.

Aden further argues that there is an increased need to legitimate transnational police work and that this is being carried out by means of both public discourses on the dangers that need to be combated as well as the creation of specific legal frameworks to justify existing forms of transnational policing and international cooperation. In terms of public discourses, debates over such issues as immigration control, transnational organized crime, and the new criminal opportunities created by the abolition of border controls have all been used to justify increased international cooperation and cross-border police operations. However, Aden argues that this increased cooperation also needs legal frameworks to legitimate such activities—beyond the executive authority granted to high-level police executives—and to establish minimum standards for transnational police operations. This formal legal legitimacy is particularly crucial with respect to cross-border activities in which police agencies actually operate in other countries. Aden notes that the Europol and Schengen conventions create a detailed body of rules that outline the authority for European police agencies to operate on foreign territory. He also notes that the European Convention on Human Rights establishes the minimum standards that all European police officers and agencies have to respect during transnational operations. Aden concludes his discussion by arguing that transnational policing actually constitutes a form of multi-level and multi-actor governance dominated by police leaders, and he speculates that the legal frameworks created to justify it may be the prelude to a European state.

The next chapter in Part 3 discusses the policing of migration as it relates to the enforcement of immigration laws and the control of immigrant groups in the broadest sense. In "Policing Migration: A Framework for Investigating the Regulation of Global Mobility," Leanne Weber and Benjamin Bowling analyse the development of migration policing in Britain and propose a "sites of enforcement" framework to guide further analysis of immigration control. Weber and Bowling start from the premise that, although Britain has always been concerned with the control of immigrant groups, this concern has intensified in recent decades because globalization has fuelled political and economic crises in the less developed world. They argue that these crises have precipitated increased migration, as the populations of developing countries attempt to find refuge in stable, more affluent parts of the world. However, the resulting migration flows are viewed by developed countries as threats to their way of life, and many developed countries have enacted containment policies aimed at stemming the tide of unwelcome asylum seekers and potential new immigrants. Weber and Bowling note that concern over migration flows has heightened considerably after the terrorist attacks on the World Trade Center. This concern has led to the passage of tougher immigration provisions in Britain and the United States, provisions that effectively designate all asylum seekers, and particularly Muslim, Middle Eastern, and South Asian men, as "suspect" populations.

In developing their "sites of enforcement" model, Weber and Bowling note that while migration policing always has been a transnational process, recent developments have intensified the degree and scope of the international cooperation that occurs. These changes have also lead to a restructuring of immigration control to include more involvement by the regular police, as well as a shifting of border controls outside the geographical limits of Britain. They argue that a complete analysis of migration control can be achieved only by examining a range of enforcement sites that include pre-entry controls, border checks, and in-country enforcement. In addition, an increase in generalized surveillance, as represented by the establishment of a public hotline to report "suspected" violators and the imposition of sanctions against employers who fail to check the immigration status of job applicants, further redefines the status of immigrants as a suspect population. And finally, they argue, such policies as the harmonization of asylum policies and of sanctions against airlines and other public carriers liable for transporting passengers without adequate documentation reinforces a "Fortress Europe" or "Global Apartheid" mentality. Weber and Bowling conclude their discussion by arguing that the involvement of regular police in migration control activities has contributed to mistrust and hostility between the police and minority groups. They further suggest that the increased power of immigration officers to interrogate and detain asylum seekers and other immigrants has given rise to a host of human rights concerns that require further scrutiny.

In "The Transformation of Policing? Understanding Current Trends in Policing Systems," Trevor Jones and Tim Newburn assess the validity of recent arguments that policing is undergoing a dramatic transformation worldwide. In particular, they question the validity of the "transformation thesis" postulated by Bayley and Shearing, which argues there has been an end to the monopoly of public policing, coupled with an increased re-evaluation of the role of the police, often by the police themselves. Although Jones and Newburn agree that there has been a fragmentation of policing as evidenced by a significant increase in private security and citizen involvement in crime prevention activities, they argue that this does not amount to the dramatic transformation outlined by Bayley and Shearing. Instead, they point out, these activities have existed for many years, and it is doubtful that a public monopoly ever existed to the extent envisioned by the transformation thesis. They further argue that changes in the character of policing, such as increased managerialism and civilianism, have occurred gradually in Britain. In any case, Jones and Newbury contend that these events constitute a restructuring of the "forms of social control not directly connected to formal policing" rather than a transformation of public policing.

Jones and Newburn further develop their arguments regarding the formalization of non-policing social control by distinguishing between primary, secondary, and tertiary social control. They define primary social control as "policing" activities carried out by police, commercial security, and other formal agents of social control. In contrast, secondary social control consists of activities carried out by teachers, bus conductors, railway guards, and those in other similar occupations, whereas tertiary social control is carried out by work groups, churches, community groups, and the like. They argue that the decline in the effectiveness of secondary and tertiary social controls has contributed to the growth of formal policing, both public and private (i.e., commercial security), rather than the growth of commercial security at the expense of the public police. In conclusion, Jones and Newburn suggest that many current analyses of policing trends exaggerate the degree of change occurring, while under-emphasizing the amount of continuity in policing. They also argue that there is insufficient evidence to conclude that many of the trends identified in the literature are global in scope and that Bayley's and Shearing's analysis clearly applies much more to North America than it does to other developed countries such as Britain.

The final chapter in this section discusses the accountability of transnational police organizations, using Interpol as an example. In "The Accountability of Transnational Policing Institutions: Interpol," James Sheptycki argues that the recent academic focus on transnational policing is motivated partly by concerns about the changing natures of sovereignty, legality, and the rule of law during a period of increased globalization. Much of this interest has focused on the need to develop mechanisms of accountability to constrain the operations of transnational police agencies. Sheptycki commences his analysis by arguing that accountability is more complex than simple command relationships and outlines a four-fold typology of accountability that includes formal versus informal and internal versus external mechanisms for achieving accountability. He notes that, because Interpol was not established by treaties between governments, it occupies a unique position in international law as a nongovernmental organization (NGO) that is frequently treated as an intergovernmental organization (IGO) by the United Nations and many sovereign states. In terms of internal accountability, Sheptycki notes that Interpol's constitution outlines a clear system of governance and well-defined rules of accountability. In terms of external accountability, however, he argues that, although Interpol has an external supervisory board, its membership is largely controlled by Interpol itself. For this reason, Sheptycki contends that Interpol is virtually immune from formal external accountability requirements, and thus operates constitutionally as an autonomous transnational organization.

Despite the apparent lack of a formal external accountability mechanism, Sheptycki notes that Interpol is subject to considerable transnational accountability from a practical perspective. This accountability stems from the fact that the day-to-day operations of Interpol are carried out through a network of National Central Bureaus, each of which is bound by the laws and operational culture of its host nation. Sheptycki notes that the efficiency of this network depends on a number of factors, including financial resources, the internal police politics in different member nations, and the external political dynamics between member nations. Insofar as the latter is concerned, Sheptycki observes that one of the most important sources of political friction between member-states centres on the distinction between "ordinary law crimes" and "political crimes." In an attempt to maintain political neutrality, Interpol has always limited its operations to ordinary law crimes; however, member nations disagree significantly over the exact definition of a political crime. In past practice, most of the controversy over this issue has involved terrorist acts, and Interpol has generally refused to get involved in events such as the attack on the Israeli athletes in Munich. However, increasing terrorism has gradually led to a narrowing of the political crime exception, and Sheptycki argues that the events of September 11 may well eliminate it entirely. Sheptycki concludes his analysis by suggesting that Interpol's unique accountability mechanisms provide academic criminology with insight into the emerging questions about the accountability of other transnational policing organizations. For this reason, he claims, Interpol must be held accountable to the "global commonweal."

Chapter 8

CONVERGENCE OF POLICING POLICIES AND TRANSNATIONAL POLICING IN EUROPE

HARTMUT ADEN

Transnational policing has many faces. Besides institutions such as Interpol, the Schengen group, and Europol, a patchwork including working groups and information institutions for police cooperation in Europe was set up during the 20th century.[1] This chapter analyses the common framework of these widespread phenomena as well as the interconnections between the different geographical levels of police organisations and of policing. Five hypotheses structure the following analysis: (1) The reality and the difficulties of transnational policing are characterised by the diversity of national policing, but also by convergent tendencies. (2) Elitist forms of cooperation which only concern a small number of high-ranking specialists in criminal investigation are predominant. Forms of everyday cooperation in border regions are getting more important where border controls have been abolished. (3) With the intensification of transnational policing, the need of legitimacy has grown. Legitimating discourses and the attempt to create legitimacy by a legal framework for transnational policing are the main answers to this growing need. (4) The structures for transnational policing are today a special mix of multi-level government and governance as well as of multi-actor government and governance. (5) Finally, European police cooperation may under certain conditions be interpreted as an element of a future European state.

DIVERSITY AND CONVERGENCE OF NATIONAL POLICING AS A BACKGROUND OF TRANSNATIONAL POLICING

The general framework of transnational policing is characterised by the diversity of national and regional police organisations and policing and, at the same time, by parallels in their historical evolution and by convergent tendencies of policing during the past few decades.

Comparative historical research on policing has shown that centralised national police units have in many cases been created to impose a national state against violent resistance (Bayley 1985: 69–72). Some police organisations have developed from military forces. The forms of policing developed by the French regimes in the early 19th century largely influenced the

Western European countries conquered by Napoleon (Fijnaut 1979). Professionalisation characterises the evolution of many police organisations. The setting up of more and more specialised police departments, for example, for investigations into special forms of crime, has led in most industrialised countries to complex, highly differentiated police organisations.

In spite of these common roots neither police organisations nor their daily actions are uniform in all western industrialised countries. Some countries have rather centralised, others rather decentralised police structures. Some countries have one single police organisation, others several.[2] The division of authority between general and specialised police units, between police and military, between police units and secret services and also between police units and social workers differs in an important way. While some countries have a strict separation of policing and military forces, in other countries, parts of the police organisations belong to the military and depend on the defence ministry, for example, France. Secret services and police forces are strictly separated in some countries, for example in Germany, where the abuse of police forces for political suppression was a characteristic of the Nazi state. Even if the German criminal police have special units to investigate political crime, the separation from the political secret service (*Verfassungsschutz*) is still an important principle for democratic policing. In other countries which have not experienced similar forms of abuse, the political secret service is a part of the general police, for example, France (*Police Nationale*) (Monet 1993: 71-147; Bayley 1985; Aden 1998b).

Despite this diversity, convergence of police organisations and of policing does not only result from similar historical roots but ... [is] mainly due to similar functions that police organisations and their work have in different societies and political systems. They all have more or less specialised units for criminal investigation. Traffic regulation and the maintenance of public order [are] also among the tasks fulfilled by most police organisations and by their specialised subdivisions. National and regional police organisations mostly have anti-riot units.

Recent trends in policing and policing policies can be observed in many industrialised countries, especially the shift from the production of the state's security to individual safety in the legitimising discourses for policing. While many national police forces were originally created to ensure political power, this function became less and less important in western democratic countries during the 20th century. This has become even truer since the end of the cold war and the east-west conflict because combating internal political enemies for democratic political systems is no longer the most important police task. Generally, national police forces were not reduced after having lost their old internal enemies, but shifted to combating general crime or to special programs which focused on the citizens' individual security. The importance which has been given to crime prevention in most European countries since the 1980s[3] is another point of convergence. It has led to new forms of cooperation between police forces and social workers, two groups of professionals which before had been more or less hostile to each other because of their different approach to crime and the reasons for crime.

In some cases, convergence of policing is directly linked to international cooperation. Investigation strategies are an important example. Undercover investigation has been repeatedly promoted by international cooperation agencies. Avant-garde countries for undercover policing, especially the USA (Nadelmann 1993) and to lesser degree Germany, have used international circles and organisations to promote or even to impose their concepts for policing. Common operations, for example in cases of international drug trafficking, have led to standards for the steering of investigations by undercover means. Police cooperation circles not only diffuse the knowledge about undercover policing, but they also play a coordinating role. International "controlled deliveries" of illegal drugs have been organised by the US Drug Enforcement Agency and by European agencies since the 1970s, in order to get more evidence about the structures of drug trafficking organisations (Busch 1999: 238–84; Nadelman 1993; Bevers and Joubert 1996: 202–07). In the late 1980s and in the 1990s, many countries formally legalised this investigation strategy (Bevers and Joubert 1996). Europol is now coordinating controlled deliveries, also of other illegal goods (Europol 2000: 16).

International cooperation has also set standards for police technology. This is not only the case for the centralised databases, which have been built up for Interpol, Schengen, and Europol.[4] The cooperating states were obliged to harmonise their data standards in order to make them compatible for international use. Other forms of police techniques have been harmonised by specialised working groups in order to improve the general standard of technical police equipment or simply to save money by using technical inventions produced in other countries. This has been the case since the 1970s in the TREVI group, an informal cooperation network set up in the 1970s to combat terrorism, radicalism, extremism, and violence (Busch 1995: 306–319), and continued in the 1990s in the Schengen group as well as in the working structures of the third pillar of the European Union (Aden 1998b: 109-111).

ELITIST VERSUS EVERYDAY POLICE COOPERATION AND THEIR INSTITUTIONAL FRAMEWORK

In order to understand the institutional framework of transnational policing it is useful, in a first step, to differentiate between elitist and everyday forms of cooperation and to show, in a second step, the interconnections between these two forms. The existing forms of police cooperation and their institutional framework reflect these two fundamental types of transnational police work.

In some ways international police cooperation has always been and is still elitist in the sense that it only concerns a small part of the police officers in the countries which take part in it. A small group of specialists is highly involved in international police cooperation, most of them in criminal investigation departments. But the huge majority of policemen have rarely or never had anything to do with transnational policing.

From this point of view, the border regions are an exception. Here the limit of the territory for daily policing constitutes a major concern, for both police leaders and policemen in basic units. What I call *everyday police cooperation* can be observed more and more in border regions. Police leaders in the densely populated Dutch-Belgian-German region around Aachen and Maastricht were the pioneers for this form of everyday cross-border cooperation. They did not have a large political support when they established a private association in 1979 (Brammertz, De Vreese, and Thys 1993; Aden 1998b: 74–76). Daily police work in such a region can easily lead to a situation in which a quick understanding with colleagues from the other side of the border is necessary. The hot pursuit after a bank robbery is the most cited example. A research project on the Dutch-Belgian-German border region, carried out by several Dutch and Belgian university departments in the early 1990s, has shown that different legal bases of everyday policing, differences in administrative organisation and police techniques, as well as the communication in a foreign language are major practical obstacles for everyday cooperation (Hofstede, Van Twuyver, Kapp, and De Vries 1993; Renault and Derriks 1994; Brammertz et al. 1993). The Schengen Complementary Convention established in the 1990s a general legal framework for the cooperation in border regions, including hot pursuit and observation on foreign territory (Bevers and Joubert 1996). Since then, Schengen member states have concluded a lot of bilateral treaties in order to complement the Schengen facilities by more concrete dispositions.[5] The French-German Police and Customs Cooperation Centre, set up in the late 1990s at Offenburg in southern Germany, is a concrete result of such a bilateral agreement. For the custom agencies, whose work directly depends on the borders between states, everyday cooperation with their colleagues from the other side of the border has always been more evident.

The elitist forms of police cooperation can mainly be found in the sector in criminal investigation, which has seen the institutionalisation of several forms of coordination and cooperation during the 20th century. Interpol, the oldest one, has always been a "policemen's club," dominated by police leaders and specialists for criminal investigation (Bresler 1993; Greilsamer 1997). With the creation of Europol in the 1990s, an even more elitist agency for criminal investigation in Europe appeared. These forms of cooperation are elitist under two aspects. They only involve a relatively small number of high ranking or highly specialised police officers. And they are far removed from the concerns of daily police work. Other coordinating structures are elitist under the aspect that they only consist of small groups of high ranking police officers who meet more or less regularly to discuss common strategies. Political decision makers tend to delegate the elaboration of policing strategies to such circles. In 1999, the European Council meeting at Tampere called for the establishment of a *European Police Chiefs' Operational Task Force* "to exchange, in cooperation with Europol, experience, best practices and information on current trends in cross-border crime and contribute to the planning of operative actions" (European Council 1999: no. 44). This new institution continues the activities of more informal coordinating circles which had been working in the TREVI group, the Vienna group, the Police Working Group on Terrorism and other informal circles since the 1970s.[6] The integration of the major part of these activities into the third pillar European Union in the 1990s was already a first step to more formal and institutional structures.

Elitist and everyday police cooperation do not exist without taking notice of each other. They have important interconnections. Negotiations concerning the general framework of everyday cooperation often take place in elitist coordination structures. This is, for example, the case in the Schengen treaties which have been negotiated in rather elitist circles of representatives of national ministries and police forces and which have established a general framework for everyday cooperation in border regions. In these cases, improvements for everyday cooperation are, at least, a side effect of elitist cooperation. Elitist cooperation projects such as Europol interfere with local or regional policing when they coordinate decentralised police action or provide support for concrete cases of investigation. Generally, high-level cooperation units provide intelligence (mainly data from their electronic data bases such as the Schengen Information System or the future Europol Information System), coordination, and technical support.[7] A third kind of interference between elitist and everyday policing concerns the security measures around major events, for example international football championships, demonstrations with an international public, or other major events, for example, world exhibitions. Elitist circles of high ranking police officers coordinate the police tactics for these events, including early exchange of information, and they support local police forces, for example by sending liaison officers. Since the TREVI projects of the 1980s, liaison officers from the home countries of the public that usually meet at football championships or other major events are sent to the place to give advice to the local police services or to intervene in conflicts in which their compatriots are involved.

LEGITIMATING DISCOURSES AND LEGITIMACY BY A LEGAL FRAMEWORK

The construction of legitimacy is another important aspect of the framework of transnational policing. The legitimacy of cross-border police work is a major topic of public debates during the periods in which institutions of international policing such as Interpol, Schengen, and Europol are being installed, enlarged, or given more authority. Legitimating transnational police work requires different components. On the one hand, the public discourses on the dangers and evils to combat by means of new structures of transnational policing. And on the other hand, the legitimisation of the installed cooperation structures by means of a legal framework.

Discourses justifying the necessity of transnational police cooperation

The justification discourse of transnational policing is not uniform, and it has changed with the "dangers" and "insecurities" which have been publicly visible or at least debated in different periods (Bigo 1996; Aden 1998a). In the early period of Interpol, pickpockets who used the growing mobility to move to other countries were a major concern (Bresler 1993: 28). In the 1950s and the 1960s, the search for authors of serious crime who had fled to foreign countries dominated international police work. In the 1970s, the different forms of violence subsumed under the term of terrorism led to new forms of cooperation, but at a low level of formal legitimacy.

In the 1980s, three new major scenarios of "dangers" to combat occurred: The new opportunities for cross-border crime caused by the abolition of border controls in the European single market countries, illegal immigration, and the different forms of serious crime resumed under the term of *organised crime*.

The new opportunities which the abolition of border controls were supposed to bring for criminals were the major arguments for the necessity of *compensatory measures* in the form of intensified police cooperation, in the border regions as well as at higher, more elitist levels of criminal investigation. The empirical justification of the demand for compensatory measures has been intensively debated. The argument that border controls are a filter preventing cross-border crime or helping to catch criminals is empirically founded only for certain cases, as for example, small quantities of drug trafficking (Bigo 1996; Busch 1995).

During the preparation of the Schengen Complementary Convention in the late 1980s, *immigration control* became the most important argument to justify compensatory measures for the abolition of border controls. Only the combination of policing and immigration arguments made it possible to mobilise financial resources, namely for the Schengen Information System (SIS). The practical implementation of the SIS and the intensified police controls in the border regions have shown since then that immigration control is the most important aspect under which the Schengen cooperation has had practical impacts. The refusal to (re-)enter the Schengen territory is the primary reason for registration in the SIS. Immediately after the official start of the SIS in 1995, Germany entered the data of more than 416,000 third country foreigners (Article 96 of the Schengen Complementary Convention, mainly refused asylum seekers) into the central database, France more than 74,000. In total 507,000 of the 569,000 individuals initially registered in the SIS were article 96 cases (Schengen Central Group 1996).

Organised crime is the third argument newly used since the 1980s to justify more police cooperation in Europe. Established in the US since the 1960s, when the Katzenbach Commission presented the *Task Force Report: Organized Crime* (The President's Commission on Law Enforcement and Administration of Justice 1967), this term comprises different forms of serious crime such as drug trafficking, certain forms of corruption, or even terrorism under one single term. In the 1980s, the term showed itself to be useful by convincing political decision makers and a larger public of the necessity to react by undercover policing and by international police cooperation. Even if it was very difficult to harmonise the definitions of what should be understood under *organised crime* at an international level (Aden 1998b: 136–145), combating it has stayed a favourite argument justifying international police cooperation. The setting-up phase for Europol in the early 1990s was largely dominated by the debate [about] whether organised crime was going to spread in Europe (Fijnaut 1991). Even in a national legal framework, the term is difficult to define and consequently stays rather vague.[8] In spite of this vagueness, the term is being officially used in the EU primary law (Articles 29 and 31 EU).

Legitimating transnational policing by a legal framework

Legitimating transnational policing has a second component: the installation of a legal framework. Some forms of elitist cooperation work easily without any legal framework, because most governments have enough executive autonomy to participate in international cooperation circles without a formal legal base. It has always been possible to bring together small groups of specialists on terrorism or other forms of crime without any Member of Parliament or journalists taking notice of their meeting. But the forms of transnational police cooperation which set standards for policing at national or even regional level or which involve a larger number of policemen have shown a growing need of legitimacy. This need becomes even more urgent when policemen cross the border in order to continue their work in the territory of another country.

Consequently Schengen, Europol, and the regional forms of cross-border cooperation have produced a more or less detailed legal framework, including restricted authority to act in the foreign territory in cases of hot pursuit, cross-border observation, etc. While Interpol is working on the basis of relatively broad statutes,[9] the Schengen Complementary Convention is a comprehensive body of rules for the abolition of internal border controls and for compensatory measures (German Bundesgesetzblatt 1993: 1010). The Amsterdam Treaty has integrated the content of the Schengen conventions into the European Union (German Bundesgesetzblatt 1998: 429). The Europol Convention is a relatively detailed legal base on the organisation and authority of the European police office. At this point, the concept of legitimacy follows the classical German idea of a *Rechtsstaat* (Aden 1998b: 255–260) in which executive intrusions on individual rights are only legitimised if they are allowed by a legal base, normally by a parliamentary law. The European Convention on Human Rights is an important reference for these treaties (Bevers and Joubert 1996). The individual rights guaranteed by the Human Rights Convention constitute, at least in theory, the minimum standard which police officers from all European countries have to respect when they cooperate.

The legitimacy of executive action on foreign territory is another function that these bi- and multilateral treaties on police cooperation fulfil. As the Schengen Complementary Convention only outlines a general framework for everyday cooperation in border regions, many bilateral treaties have been concluded and adapted to the special situation in each region (Statewatch 1998). Besides their legitimating functions, international treaties on police cooperation also fix the results and the compromises concluded during the political and administrative negotiations which precede an international treaty (Aden 1998b: 306–48).

After being concluded, these treaties produce secondary effects on the legal framework of national policing. An important example is the enlarged authority for identity controls in border regions which were attributed to many police organisations after the abolition of border controls in the Schengen area. Also the authority for undercover operations has been enlarged as a result of international standard setting (Bevers and Jobert 1996: 308–21, 187–42). Europol regularly makes use of the authority to coordinate operations of trans-border surveillance (Europol 2000: 13–14).

In return, debating transnational police cooperation and preparing treaties for this purpose is a subject which easily fills international meetings and European summits which would otherwise end without any result. This is one factor which explains why transnational policing has become a favourite subject for international politics.

TRANSNATIONAL POLICING AS AN EXAMPLE OF MULTI-LEVEL AND MULTI-ACTOR GOVERNMENT AND GOVERNANCE

Transnational policing and its interconnections with national, regional and local policing is a special case of multi-level and of multi-actor governance mixed with major elements of traditional government. The ambiguous term *governance*[10] is here being used to analyse forms of international norm making and steering or control mechanisms which develop independently from international organisations and traditional forms of international public law.[11]

Transnational policing between government and governance

Taking into account the absence of international governmental authorities, transnational policing cannot be interpreted as a classical form of government, in which police organisations are a
central means to assure political power and depend directly on governments' hierarchical command. Transnational policing has produced special arrangements negotiating and implementing cooperation in more or less binding regimes. The special form of governance in the field
of policing can be explained by a model of inner and outer circles, in which the inner circles
produce relatively binding forms of govern*ment* limited in their geographical extent, while the
outer circles produce less binding forms of gover*nance* of a larger geographical extent.

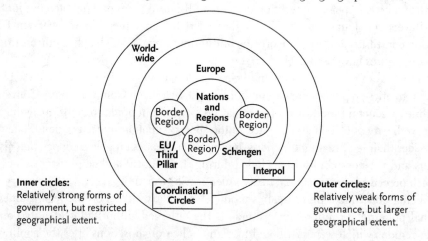

Figure 1. Transnational policing in Europe as a multi-level government and governance system.

   The national governments, in federal states also the regional governments, form the inner circle which produces binding executive measures based on a strong legal framework but
limited to the national or regional territory. Cooperation in border regions produces a relatively
strong regime of rules for concrete cooperation, but limited to a small territory. European cooperation is based on a more general institutional and legal framework, but coordinates policing in a larger territory. Worldwide coordination structures are limited to producing a general
framework of knowledge and rules. The implementation mostly depends on the good will of the
participating actors. They form the outer circle of the system of police cooperation governance,
in which informal meetings of police leaders play a role as well as international organisations
setting crime problems on their political agenda, for example the OECD (Zürn 1998) and the
summit of industrial countries (G 7/G 8).
   Establishing transnational police work in international or European institutions such as
Interpol, Europol, or the Schengen Information System leads to a more binding framework
than simple coordination circles.
   Interconnections between the different levels of regimes are main characteristics of multi-
level governance. The outer circles of international regimes for policing with their patchwork

of more or less institutionalised cooperation circles depend largely on the classical forms of national government in the inner circles. Policing is still based for a major part on the concept of law enforcement, which in democratic systems would not work without a strong framework of penal law at the national (or sub-national) level. For this reason, the national (and sub-national) level stays a central point of orientation for international cooperation regimes in this field. In this point of view, the political priorities and the legal framework of countries which are able to impose their concepts ... [on] others are particularly important. But there is also a major interconnection in the other direction. Cooperation regimes produce standards for national policing. Even if these standards are usually not binding, they are a point of orientation for national governments. Governments should take into account these international standards if they want to play a role in the development of the international cooperation regimes.

Multi-actor governance dominated by police leaders

A look at the actors who influence the concrete decision making for transnational policing shows a system of multi-actor governance largely dominated by police leaders. Police leaders and their national and international networking form the inner circle of actors influencing the governance for this policy.

High-ranking police officers have played a central role for the political agenda setting and for the implementation of transnational policing. They produced the concepts that political decision makers later established by international conventions. The dominant role that high ranking police officers have played in the setting up of Interpol as a "policemen's club" in the 1920s is an early example of the role that police officers themselves have played in the internationalisation of their work. Confronted with cases of offenders using the growing mobility that became possible in the second half of the 19th century, policemen looked for contacts to foreign colleagues, even in states which had been enemies in wars a short time before. Governments played only a minor role in the setting up of this structure (Greilsamer 1997; Bresler 1993).

Figure 2. Actors influencing transnational policing in Europe.

For the European cooperation projects which were installed in the 1980s and the 1990s, high ranking police officers played a crucial role by defining necessities for cross-border police work. In the 1970s, new formal and informal cooperation circles at the level of high-ranking police officers had emerged but had stayed in a grey zone of executive cooperation without parliamentary consent. In the 1980s, cross-border policing reached an extent which could no longer stay at a clandestine level. Intensifying police cooperation as a compensatory measure for the opening of internal borders became a subject of larger public debates. Police leaders used these debates to demand new structures for an intensified cooperation. They diffused their propositions in specialised police revues as well as in larger public debates on Europe without internal borders (Aden 1998b: 185–95). Political decision makers answered positively by mobilising an important budget and a legal framework for new cooperation projects.

The specialists in regional and national governments provide the framework (money, legal bases, international negotiations) for regional, national, and international policing, in further reaching cases approved by national parliaments. Policemen involved in elitist transnational coordination groups participate in the outer circle, in which transnational standards for policing are being negotiated. The European Home Affairs and Justice Council is a central actor for police cooperation in Europe. In the 1970s and the 1980s, the TREVI group worked as an informal structure parallel to the Council. The ministers provide the general framework for European police cooperation and decide how far practice can go in the concrete situation: This is the precondition for a relative autonomy which characterises the European police leaders' daily cooperation. This autonomy is stronger than the influence that police agents generally have on policing policy because of their advantage of experience with handling crime problems in practice.[12]

The European Commission and the European Parliament only play a marginal role. The EP repeatedly demands more democratic control of transnational policing. But European police cooperation has always been dominated by administrative bodies.

Different from other polices (for example, environment or consumers rights), interest groups in general do not formally participate in political decision making for policing. But under two aspects they play a major role in the system of multi-actor governance. On the one hand, policemen's interest groups (unions, associations of police leaders) play a central role in the constitution of networks in which future standards for international policing are being prepared, discussed, and diffused. On the other hand, economical interest groups support policing, at least in as much … [as they contribute] to a stable economical framework. Consequently, economical interest groups have a major interest in transnational policing, which contributes to providing stable conditions for investment in foreign countries and for international trade. This explains why *organised crime* and corruption in countries such as Russia or China have become a major topic for international policing policy.

CONCLUSION: TRANSNATIONAL POLICING AND EUROPEAN INTEGRATION—TOWARDS A EUROPEAN STATE?

Up to now, transnational policing has been closely related to governmental law enforcement at the national level. International police cooperation has reached a major extent in a context of governance without government.

Following Max Weber's state theory, the monopoly on the use of force is a main characteristic of a state (Weber [1921] 1972). The developing international police cooperation regimes show that the direct inversion of this argument is not possible. Institutions coordinating the use of force at international levels exist without the formal framework of a state. Furthermore, the question can be raised ... [whether] the international governance structures in the field of policing and internal security are preliminary structures for a future state. This question is even more justified in Europe (Bunyan 1993), where political integration has reached a high extent since the treaties concluded during the 1990s, in Maastricht and Amsterdam. The existence of European institutions in the security field is another indication for the development of the European Union from intergovernmental cooperation to an institution that is getting more and more similar to a state. Consequently, transnational policing raises the problem that institutions for a possible future state are being set up in a phase characterised by feeble democratic legitimacy. Once established, international bureaucratic institutions such as Europol will leave little scope to be reshaped by democratic institutions.

Policing will not become totally uniform all over the world, or in Europe. But the extending forms of transnational policing are producing international standards which largely influence national and regional policing, even everyday work at the local level. The major influence that policemen themselves have on transnational policing makes policing policy relatively independent from changing political decision makers and parliamentary majorities.

NOTES

[1] This chapter will not ... [detail] the history of transnational policing in Europe. See for details on the history of transnational policing Aden (1998: 65–101) with further references. [Also, see Chapter 11 in this volume by J. Sheptycki.]

[2] See Bayley (1985: 38–52); on the history of specialisation of German police forces in the 19th century, see Funk (1986: 240–311).

[3] Comparative analysis in Hebberecht and Sack (1997); see also Bayley (1994: 102-120).

[4] See Aden 1998: 324–341; on the Europol Information System, see Europol (2000) and Manske (2001: 105–108).

[5] Schengen Working Group 1 on Police and Security, *Report on Agreements on Police Cooperation at the Internal Borders of the Schengen Area* (Brussels, 26 May 1998), documented in Statewatch (1998).

[6] For more details, see Aden (1998: 76–84).

7 See Articles 7–9 of the Europol Convention; details on the setting up are in Manske (2001) and
       Europol (2000).
8 See, for example, the critique by Albrecht (1997).
9 Documented, for example, by Greilsamer (1997: 299–304).
10 On the ambiguity of the term, see Kooiman (1999).
11 On this concept of governance, see Roseneau (1997: 144–152).
12 Monjardet (1996: 88) calls this the *inversion of hierarchy.*

REFERENCES

Aden, H. 1998a. "Europäische Polizeikooperation. Konstruktion und Wandel von
       Legitimationsfiguren." Pp. 65–78 in *Inszenierung: Innere Sicherheit: Daten und Diskurse,*
       edited by R. Hitzler and H. Peters. Wiesbaden: Opladen.

Aden, H. 1998b. *Polizeipolitik in Europa. Eine interdisziplinäre Studie über die Polizeiarbeit
       in Europa am Beispiel Deutschlands, Frankreichs und der Niederlande.* Wiesbaden:
       Opladen.

Albrecht, P.A. 1997. "Organisierte Kriminalität: Das Kriminaljustizsystem und seine konstrui-
       erten Realitäten." *Kritische Vierteljahresschrift für Gesetzgebung und Rechtswissenschaft*
       80: 299–304.

Bayley, D.H. 1985. *Patterns of Policing.* New Brunswick, NJ: Rutgers University Press.

Bayley, D.H. 1994. *Police for the Future.* Oxford: Oxford University Press.

Bevers, H. and C. Joubert. 1996. *Schengen Investigated. A Comparative Interpretation of the
       Schengen Provisions on International Police Cooperation in the Light of the European
       Convention on Human Rights.* Den Haag: Kluwer.

Bigo, D. 1996. *Polices en Réseaux: L'expérience Européenne.* Paris: Presses de la Fondation
       Nationale des Sciences Politiques.

Brammertz, S., S. De Vreese, and J. Thys. 1993. *Internationale Politiesamenwerking: Onderzoek
       naar de modaliteiten voor Belgische participatie in internationale politiesamenwerkingspro-
       jecten van regionale omvang.* Brussels: Politeia.

Bresler, F. 1993. *Interpol: A History and Examination of 70 Years of Crime Solving.* London:
       Penguin Books.

Bunyan, T. 1993. "Trevi, Europol and the New European State." Pp. 15–36 in *Statewatching the
       New Europe,* edited by T. Bunyan. London: Statewatch Publications.

Busch, H. 1995. *Grenzenlose Polizei? Neue Grenzen und polizeiliche Zusammenarbeit in Europa.*
       Münster: Westfäli.

Busch, H. 1999. *Polizeiliche Drogenbekämpfung – eine internationale Verstrickung.* Münster: Westfäli.

European Council. 1999. *Tampere European Council 15 and 16 October 1999: Presidency
       Conclusions.* Luxembourg: European Parliament.

Europol. 2000. *Annual Report for 1999.* The Hague: Europol.

Fijnaut, C. 1979. *Opdat de macht een toevlucht zij? Een historische studie van het politieapparaat
       als een politieke instelling.* Antwerp: Arnhem.

Fijnaut, C. 1991. "Organized Crime and Anti-Organized Crime Efforts in Western Europe: An Overview." Pp. 15–33 in *Organized Crime and its Containment: A Transatlantic Initiative,* edited by C. Fijnaut and J. Jacobs. Boston: Deventer.

Funk, A. 1986. *Polizei und Rechtsstaat.* Frankfurt, M: Campus.

German Bundesgesetzblatt II. 1993. [Germany's official gazette of federal law]

German Bundesgesetzblatt II. 1998. *Amsterdam Protocol on the integration of the Schengen acquis into the European Union.* [Germany's official gazette of federal law]

Greilsamer, L. 1997. *INTERPOL: Policiers sans frontières.* Paris: Fayard.

Hebberecht, P. and F. Sack (Eds.). 1997. *La prévention de la délinquance en Europe. Nouvelles stratégies.* Paris: Harmattan.

Hofstede G., M. Van Twuyver, B. Kapp, and H. De Vries. 1993. *Coopération Policière Transfrontalière entre la Belgique, l'Allemagne et les Pays-Bas avec une Attention Particulière pour l'Eurégion Meuse-Rhin.* Maastricht: Maastricht University Press.

Kooiman, J. 1999. "Social-Political Governance: Overview, Reflections and Design." *Public Management: an International Journal of Research and Theory* 1: 67–92.

Manske, M. 2001. "Das 'Europol-Informations-System' (Europol-IS): Eine Herausforderung für die nationalen polizeilichen IT-Systeme." *Kriminalistik* 55: 105–08.

Monet, J.C. 1993. *Polices et Sociétés en Europe.* Paris: La Documentation Française.

Monjardet, D. 1996. *Ce Que Fait la Police: Sociologie de la Force Publique.* Paris: La Découverte.

Nadelmann, E.A. 1993. *Cops across Borders: The Internationalization of US Criminal Law Enforcement.* University Park, PN: Pennsylvania State University Press.

Renault, G. and E. Derriks. 1994. *La Collaboration Policière Transfrontalière: Les Obstacles Législatifs.* Brussels: Politeia.

Rosenau, J.N. 1997. *Along the Domestic-foreign Frontier: Exploring Governance in a Turbulent World.* Cambridge: Cambridge University Press.

Schengen Central Group. 1996. *Jahresbericht über die Anwendung des Durchführungsübereinkommens im Zeitraum vom 26 März 1995–25 März 1996* (Annual Report on the implementation of the SIC). Brussels 26.3.96, SCH/C (96) 17 rev.

Statewatch. 1998. *European Monitor* 1 (1): 30–31.

The President's Commission on Law Enforcement and Administration of Justice. 1967. *Task Force Report: Organized Crime.* Washington, DC: US Government Printing Office.

Weber, M. [1921] 1972 *Wirtschaft und Gesellschaft.* 5th ed. Tübingen: Mohr.

Zürn, M. 1998. "Gesellschaftliche Denationalisierung und Regieren in der OECD-Welt" Pp. 91–120 in *Regieren in entgrenzten Räumen, PVS-Sonderheft No. 29,* edited by B. Kohler-Koch. Wiesbaden: Opladen.

CHAPTER STUDY QUESTIONS

- According to Aden, transnational policing does not emerge naturally on its own, but, instead, it must be justified and legitimated. Do you agree with this argument? Why? Why not?

• Aden argues that transnational policing in Europe is mainly a development of the 1990s. Discuss some of the legal mechanisms that legitimated transnational policing to the extent that police forces can operate in foreign territory. Do you think that these mechanisms would be effective in the North American context? Explain.

• Transnational policing has been described as "a multi-level government and governance system." Outline the main features of this system. What are the implications of the growth of this type of policing system for national sovereignty and police accountability?

• Aden argues that the "construction of legitimacy" is crucial to the success of cross-border policing and other forms of transnational police cooperation. Outline at least 2 or 3 discourses that have been used to justify transnational policing.

RELATED WEB LINKS

Canadian Transnational Crime Working Group
http://ww2.psepc-sppcc.gc.ca/Publications/Policing/TransCrime_e.pdf
> This website accesses a detailed report by the Canadian Transnational Crime Working Group on alternate approaches to combating transnational crime.

Sourcewatch
http://www.sourcewatch.org/index.php?title=Transnational_organized_crime
> This website focuses on policing transnational organized crime as the key international policy issue of the twenty-first century. Information is provided on many other topics relevant to transnational social control, and links are provided to many other related organizations.

Europol
http://www.ex.ac.uk/~watupman/undergrad/pollard/index.htm
> This website deals entirely with Europol. It provides concise descriptions of the history, role, crimes units, and the future of transnational policing in the European context.

Association of Southeast Asian Nations (ASEAN)
http://www.aseansec.org/4964.htm
> This website provides information on many issues relevant to transnational crime and terrorism from the perspective of nations in Southeast Asia. Links are also provided to the main ASEAN website which provides information on many other transnational issues.

Chapter 9

POLICING MIGRATION: A FRAMEWORK FOR INVESTIGATING THE REGULATION OF GLOBAL MOBILITY

LEANNE WEBER AND BENJAMIN BOWLING

Criminologists are increasingly pointing to new forms of control that are associated with the regulatory-yet-punitive states of late modernity. This chapter starts from the premise that the policing of global population movements is an example of an emerging punitive regulatory system that demands urgent attention by criminologists. It articulates an agenda for the critical examination of "migration policing" in Britain set against the backdrop of the historical inclusion and exclusion of immigrant groups, and proposes a "sites of enforcement" framework that is intended to guide further empirical investigations into the operation of immigration control networks.

Mass population movements are occurring at a time when modes of governance and definitions of citizenship are themselves shifting. Increasingly free movement of capital is being accompanied by increased spending on police, prisons, and migration control. The "policing" of migration is considered here in the sense of direct police involvement in the enforcement of immigration law and the control of "immigrant" communities, and in the wider sense of the police-like activities of immigration authorities and other agencies that are acquiring new coercive powers.

Our intention is to draw all these enforcement activities together under the umbrella of "migration policing." This terminology acknowledges that modes of regulation are diversifying and can no longer be contained within the discrete boundaries of criminal justice agencies that tend to shape the thinking of criminologists and limit the scope of empirical research. This chapter builds on a piece written for an anthology that explored the impact of the September 11 events on law enforcement and other aspects of public life (Weber and Bowling 2002).[1] It expands on that discussion by outlining a conceptual framework for investigating the policing of migration that was first presented at the British Society of Criminology in Keele in 2002 and also provides some historical context that could not be included in the September 11 collection.[2]

A HISTORY OF EXCLUSION

Migrants have been seen as "trouble" for England and its rulers since the time of Queen Elizabeth I's famous declaration that "all blackamores" should be "sent forth of the realme"

(Fryer 1984: 10–12). Throughout England's history, certain migrant groups—including Irish, European Jews, Roma and populations from Cyprus, Malta, the Indian Subcontinent, the West Indies, and Africa—have been subjected to surveillance and control by the state because of their designated status as a "problem." At times, hostility to specific groups has led to them being repelled, harassed, and abused by the native population (Fryer 1984; Holmes 1988; Bowling 1999; Bowling and Phillips 2002). Backlashes against minority communities have often been sparked by conditions of political or economic insecurity following periods of economic growth and relative tolerance.[3] During times of repression, the most undesirable of aliens have been defined or re-defined as "illegal," excluded from entry, and subjected to detention and deportation. Ultimately, it has been the role of the tithingman, constable, or the modern-day immigration officer to detect and exclude the "undesirable aliens" from the territory.

The beginnings of a modern, bureaucratic approach to immigration control were apparent by the end of the nineteenth century, when alarm about the rising number of Jewish immigrants from Russia and Poland led to a series of Parliamentary Select Committee reports. The last of these recommended the setting up of an Immigration Department "whose officers would have the power to make whatever inquiries necessary ... to determine whether persons were criminals, prostitutes, persons of 'notoriously bad character,' lunatics, idiots or persons 'likely to become a charge on the public funds'" (Shah 2000: 33; Royal Commission on Alien Immigration 1903). The proposals were controversial but, after several abortive attempts, the Aliens Act 1905 was passed. The Act enshrined in law a definition of "undesirable aliens" based on the principles outlined above, charged immigration officers with the task of refusing entry and detaining individuals judged to fit these criteria, and established measures for controlling aliens who succeeded in gaining entry (Shah 2000).

In the latter half of the twentieth century, the drama of inclusion and exclusion has been played out most noticeably in the public and official reaction to two distinct waves of migration: immigration to Britain from the "New Commonwealth" during the 1950s and 1960s (see Hall et al. 1978; Holmes 1988; Solomos 1993), followed by the arrival of the "New Asylum Seekers" in Europe after the 1980s (Martin 1988; Gibney 1994). Although laws intended to restrict and control these populations were publicly justified in terms of *numbers*, the *origins* of these groups were central to the perception of them as a problem. Uncontrolled non-white immigration embodied public fears about the diminution of national sovereignty arising from loss of Empire and the encroachment of the European Union (EU).

Since then, the globalizing trends which have helped to fuel life-threatening economic and political crises in the less developed world have also provided unprecedented access to information and new opportunities to seek refuge in the few remaining pockets of order and affluence. This has given rise to a renewed moral panic about mass population flows into these secure havens, despite the fact that the vast majority of refugees and displaced people are restricted to neighbouring countries that are equally poor and troubled.[4] At the same time, within affluent societies, individual mobility has become an indicator of global inclusion and a personal expression of "life ambitions" (Bauman 2000). Alongside these developments, Braithwaite (2000) argues that the "globalizing logic of risk management" has sparked a proliferation of public and private regulatory agencies, a blurring of boundaries between the state and civil society, and reliance on means of social control which are increasingly automated and asocial.[5] According to Rose (2000: 326), these new forms of control operate through a variety of "switch point(s) to be passed in order to access the benefits of liberty."

Nowhere is this more apparent than in contemporary efforts to control global population movements. Tens of millions of people travel annually through the world's seaports, airports, and other nodal points in transport systems, and while they are on the move they are repeatedly checked, subjected to human and technical surveillance systems, documented and sometimes detained. British Immigration and Nationality Department annual reports reveal the increasing pressure at ports in the United Kingdom during the 1990s to deal efficiently with the massively increased business and tourist traffic, while performing an effective gatekeeping function in relation to less welcome visitors. Although people applying for asylum at ports form only around 0.03 per cent of arriving passengers, and are outnumbered by a factor of more than five hundred to one by arriving EU nationals who are potentially able to work and claim entitlements in Britain, it is asylum applicants who are likely to be defined as "immigration problems" and blamed for administrative overload at ports.[6] This relates to the widespread perception among immigration officers that the disorderly and unauthorized manner of their arrival undermines the operation of immigration controls, and has a practical basis in the disproportionate administrative workload their applications generate (see Weber and Landman 2002: Chapter 2).

Furthermore, virtually without exception, the states of the developed world have assessed the spectre of uncontrolled migration from the less developed world as a threat to their way of life. What is seen to be at stake is "nothing less than a question of sovereignty" as the power to control borders is one of the few remaining prerogatives of the declining nation-state (Joly 1996: 17). Governments have reacted to dramatic increases in asylum seeking with policies aimed at containment rather than protection (Shacknove 1993) and erected what amounts to a system of "global apartheid" (Richmond 1994). This network of visa restrictions, carrier sanctions, and extra-territorial controls serves to shore up the unequal global distribution of risk while ensuring the "extraterritoriality of the new global elite and the forced territoriality of the rest" (Bauman 2000). Migration researchers have pointed to the "involuntary immobility" of aspiring migrants, whose ability to realize their need or desire to relocate is increasingly thwarted by these restrictive immigration policies (Caning 2002).

The political rhetoric about "bogus asylum seekers" and "illegal immigrants," which has accompanied coercive measures such as indefinite detention and forced deportations, can also be seen as a sustained programme of criminalization (Weber 2002) whereby the very act of seeking asylum has been construed as a "crime of arrival" (Webber 1996; Weber 2002). These defensive policies have forced thousands of people into the hands of organized people-smugglers and sparked an explosion in the use of false passports and irregular modes of travel (Morrison and Crosland 2001). This, in turn, has served to heighten suspicions about the identity and intentions of the massive numbers of desperate people currently circling the globe in search of security, through a process which criminologists will recognize as deviancy amplification. The perception of refugees and immigrants as threats to national security has been further intensified by the events of September 11, which emulated within the developed world the conditions of life-threatening insecurity that have been the legacy of global apartheid for much of the world's population.

New British legislation hastily enacted after the atrocity further conflates the categories of "asylum seeker" and "terrorist", and potentially casts all asylum seekers as "suspect" populations.[7] Soon after this legislation came into force, Amnesty International released an expression of concern over arrests made by immigration authorities and police under the new powers, describing the process as "a shadow criminal justice system in which the normal safeguards protecting the rights to liberty and fair trial are being eroded" (Amnesty International 2001). In the United States, where the reaction to the heightened perception of threat following September 11 was even more pronounced, the immigration system has reportedly been used as a key investigative tool by the Federal Bureau of Investigation, and it has been argued that the government has "chosen to assume individuals with immigration violations, particularly Muslim, Middle Eastern, or South Asian men, are terrorists until proven otherwise" (Salyer 2002: 62).[8]

AN OVERVIEW OF MIGRATION POLICING

"Migration policing" is developing at a time when the work that police do is becoming an increasingly global enterprise (Sheptycki 2002). Policing has historically been tied to the nation state (whether centralized or decentralized), its powers arising from the state's possession of the monopoly of coercive force within a geographical territory (Bittner 1970). Despite the inevitable local focus of most policing activity, there is no doubt that contemporary police work frequently transcends national borders and involves police officers from overseas. In addition to well-established agencies such as the International Criminal Police Organization (INTERPOL), national police agencies—especially from the United States, Canada, and European countries—increasingly post liaison officers overseas, supply advisers, fund training (in-country and overseas), and provide information technology.

There are a number of factors driving the development of transnational policing. The "growing threat" of global crime, drug supply, and terrorism is frequently cited as *the* explanation for increased international cooperation in crime investigation. There is a growing belief within government and police services that international cooperation is an essential component of the response to transnational organized crime (House of Commons 1995: Sheptycki 2002). More skeptical commentators have wondered whether increasingly expensive national and international policing agencies have sought to justify their existence by reference to a band of new global "folk devils" (Sheptycki 2002). As might be predicted, broader institutions of global governance such as the United Nations and the EU have also taken a strong interest in the development of international policing structures. For example, in December 2000, the United Nations Convention Against Organized Crime was signed in Palermo, Italy, calling for extensive transnational police cooperation. This is an important development because domestic laws are introduced in the wake of international agreements (Anderson et al. 1995). Already there exists a complex web of bilateral and multilateral arrangements for the sharing of information about crimes and criminals and conducting joint investigations. This development clearly has implications for policing in general and the policing of migration in particular.

Policing forms a significant element in maintaining social stability through the "governance of crime" both locally (Crawford 1997) and globally (Sheptycki 2000), but policing is a paradoxical occupation. As numerous commentators have noted (e.g., Klockars 1980, "The Dirty Harry Problem," cited in Kleinig 1996), in order to achieve the laudable goals of preventing and detecting crime and detaining criminals and maintaining public order, police officers must engage in the morally dubious practices of using physical coercive force and intruding into the individuals' private lives through the use of surveillance, undercover officers, and informers. Although the research in this sphere is underdeveloped, it seems likely that transnational policing will tend towards the covert, intrusive, and coercive end of the spectrum of policing (Bowling and Foster 2002: McLaughlin 1992: 483; Kraska 2001).

Migration policing is—by its very nature—a transnational enterprise. Its ambit is defined by the control of movement of people between nation-states, arriving and departing through geographical spaces as well as the surveillance of "migrant populations," groups of people defined by their extraterritoriality. While the mechanisms of global apartheid are aimed at *physically* excluding asylum seekers and unwanted immigrants from national territories, punitive policies such as detention and the withdrawal of cash benefits *socially* exclude those who reach foreign shores, and serve as a second line of defence. Those who remain are likely to be subjected to extensive surveillance by way of identity cards, databases, and intelligence systems. The policing of migration therefore mobilizes a range of enforcement agencies such as Police, Immigration and Customs, and—in line with predictions about the new forms of the regulatory state—has begun to draw in an ever-expanding range of private actors and commercial bodies. At the same time, the concept of physical borders—the ultimate switch point governing movements between nation-states—is being reinterpreted and manipulated by governments. In Britain, resources have been shifted and controls expanded both inwards and outwards, effectively moving much of the decision making about entry away from borders in ways that will be discussed further below. This has been accompanied by government rhetoric that seeks to reinforce the *symbolic* importance of border protection as an expression of national sovereignty and a core political value.

At the national level, the respective roles of agencies involved in the policing of migration have changed over time as the balance between internal, external, and extra-territorial controls has shifted. Historically, the police role has been twofold. Police have been charged with the function of securing territory through the identification and exclusion of known international criminals or other threats to national security, and assisting in the expulsion of those deemed to be undesirable. This role has expanded with the construction of border threats as matters of national security and organized crime requiring specialist policing responses. Police have also been involved in the ongoing surveillance of existing "suspect populations." For some people being a "migrant" or "immigrant" is not so much a matter of being on the move but a designation of their permanent status.

Unlike police officers, immigration officers are specialists in the enforcement of immigration law. They have traditionally been associated with border controls, but their roles and powers have overlapped with police and shifted over time. During the Cold War, Soviet defectors were few in number and were initially held at police stations for security checks prior to being interviewed by an immigration officer in relation to their asylum claim.[9] An immigration officer interviewed by one of the authors recounted feeling "very honoured being asked to go to the police station where a defecting Eastern European person had turned up" (Weber 2002:

20). Since then, a huge bureaucratic machinery has developed for dealing with asylum seek-ers—many of whom lodge their applications at ports.[10] Police may still be expected to deal ini-tially with clandestine entrants who are found in lorries or present themselves at police stations, but newly arrived asylum seekers are no longer considered primarily "police property."

On the other hand, the emergence of protracted bureaucratic procedures to deal with the greatly increased numbers of applications, and the political emphasis on the removal of "failed applicants"—often after long periods spent in the community, has led to a convergence of the police and immigration roles. Police have been increasingly involved as participants and advis-ers in the so-called "snatch squads," comprising both police and immigration officers who carry out these forced removals. Additional police-like powers of search, seizure, and arrest have also been granted to immigration officers to enable them to operate independently of police in some circumstances.[11] This reflects a worrying trend for coercive powers to "migrate," so to speak, from the criminal justice system into agencies that are generally regarded as administrative and where due process safeguards are less likely to apply.

There are other examples of blurred boundaries between the criminal and administrative spheres in the policing of migration. Immigration officers have reported using their extensive powers of administrative detention at times to allow Special Branch police at ports additional time to make checks about suspect individuals. Even more controversially, Immigration Act detention powers are sometimes used pre-emptively as a crime prevention measure—a usage that was of-ficially sanctioned under bail provisions that were enacted in the 1999 Immigration and Asylum Act, but never implemented. Both these practices extend well beyond the administrative purpose for which Immigration Act detention powers were created and are recognized by some immigra-tion officers as leading them onto "dangerous ground" (see Weber and Gelsthorpe 2000: 15–16).

SITES OF ENFORCEMENT

The discussion so far has pointed to a proliferation of sites at which immigration law is enforced and immigrant communities regulated. We have also argued that a variety of agencies armed with a complex, and at times controversial, mix of criminal and administrative powers have been drawn into this network. Figure 1 is an attempt to represent the multiple sites, both within and outside Britain, at which the policing of migration takes place, and to identify the functions performed by the various agencies involved.

The central plank of immigration control in Britain is border checks—indicated in the cen-tre of the diagram in Figure 1 by the presence of the Immigration Service (Ports), Special Branch police, and, to a lesser extent, Customs.[12] The diagram also reflects the spread of mi-gration policing into internal controls operated by the enforcement arm of the Immigration Service (IS) and various branches of the metropolitan and regional police services, working either independently or in conjunction with immigration authorities. Looking further afield, the model incorporates offshore controls which include pre-boarding checks, conducted by IS liaison officers posted at overseas airports, and visa regimes operated by Foreign Office and Immigration Service staff working from overseas diplomatic missions.

However, this deterrence-based programme has failed to produce the lasting reduction in asylum applications that policy makers have sought.[13] Faced with relentlessly rising workloads, legal changes were introduced in 1999 aimed at further streamlining the processing of "desirable" passengers at ports. Guild (2000) argues that section 3A of the Immigration and Asylum Act 1999 effectively shifted the legal act of entry from the time of arrival at the border to the moment a visa is granted at an overseas mission, leaving very little room for decisions about eligibility for entry to be made at ports. This produces the interesting paradox that, from a legal perspective, the holder of a British visa may be simultaneously present in two different places on the globe. The idea of a non-geographical or "virtual" border has been further developed in proposals for "juxtaposed controls" to be conducted by British immigration officials at selected French ports, which are said by the British Refugee Council to "effectively shift border controls from England to France."[14]

Furthermore, as visas have become the key to negotiating the "switch points" of entry to Britain, it is not surprising that their availability has been increasingly restricted. Organizations supporting immigrants have long complained about the difficulties experienced by overseas relatives trying to make family visits. In June 2003, a number of legal rights organizations reportedly wrote to the government demanding an explanation for the "massive increase" in refusals of family visit visas observed in the latter half of 2002.[15] In a further clampdown on the granting of visas, the Home Office announced on 9 July 2003 that all Sri Lankan applicants for visitors' visas would be required to provide fingerprints as part of a trial programme to tackle "immigration and asylum abuse."[16]

Moving further out in both directions on the "sites of enforcement" model, we see an ever-widening participation in this network of enforcement. Within Britain this already encompasses private security firms involved in detaining and transporting asylum seekers and "immigration offender,"[17] public and private employers required by law to check the immigration status of job applicants,[18] haulage companies liable to criminal sanctions for transporting clandestine entrants across the English Channel, airlines subject to fines under the Carrier's Liability Act 1987 for allowing passengers to board flights bound for Britain with "inadequate" documentation, and the population at large who are increasingly being encouraged to act as the eyes and ears of the police and Immigration Service.[19]

Figure 1. Migration policing: sites of enforcement.

Externally, we see the development of pan-European structures and legal agreements such as Europol and the Dublin Convention. Loader (2002: 125) has argued that the threat of the "migrant other" has been one of the justifications used by European governments for the extension of what he calls "an enhanced policing capacity—one comprising a complex, ever-shifting mix of informal professional networks, inter-governmental co-operation, and nascent supranational institutions (notably Europol)." With the abandonment of internal borders through the Schengen Agreement, the nations of Western Europe have exhorted countries at the perimeter to exercise greater control over entry to "Fortress Europe" (King 1994). The prospect of EU expansion has created further opportunities to extend this *cordon sanitaire* by exerting pressure on hopeful new members to stem the flow of asylum seekers and immigrants at points even further to the east as part of the process of defining the contours of a new European identity (Green and Grewcock 2002).

The media have also reported the prospect of a paramilitary style border police to patrol the external frontiers of the EU. An article in *Statewatch* magazine reports that, although no agreement has yet been reached on these proposals, a feasibility plan for "European border management" has been developed which includes a liaison officer network at international airports, exchange of information and personnel, coordinated criminal investigations, shared "risk assessment" procedures, and a joint rapid response unit (Statewatch 2002). These developments are particularly significant for Britain, which has opted out of the Schengen Agreement and elected to maintain its own border controls, while *also* embracing these beyond-border measures. In the wake of September 11, and the furore over disruptions to train services in the Channel Tunnel, there were calls for a specialist Anglo-French force to prevent incursions by asylum seekers into the tunnel.[20]

It is our hope that the "sites of enforcement" framework will help us to understand the dynamics of these developments in migration policing and to formulate a number of questions about the roles of domestic police, immigration officials, and other actors. Further research will be needed to understand the full range of activities that are already taking place, those that are planned for the future, or those that are emerging out of existing practice. The remainder of this discussion concentrates on what we can say at this point about the roles of the police and immigration services in Britain.

THE CHANGING ROLE OF POLICE

The 1971 Immigration Act introduced border controls against groups that had not previously been subject to entry restrictions, and prompted a major recruitment drive for new immigration officers to work at ports. At the same time, the legislation stimulated the creation of internal immigration controls, or "pass laws," for people of African, Caribbean, and Asian descent resident in Britain (Sivanadan 1982: 135; Gordon 1984). Police and immigration authorities were given considerable powers to detain and question people who were suspected of being in breach of immigration law, for example, by entering illegally or overstaying terms of entry (Gordon 1984).

Studies during this period provided evidence that ordinary policing often involved checks of immigration status, for instance when people from ethnic minorities reported crimes of which they had been the victim. These tactics can be understood as opportunistic—as police using the new and highly flexible provisions of the Immigration Act as a resource to achieve other policing aims. However, more systematic activities were also documented, for example by the covert Illegal Immigration Intelligence Unit in London, the purpose of which was to "receive, collate, evaluate, and disseminate information relating to known or *suspected* offenders" (cited by Gordon 1984: 35, emphasis added). Throughout the 1970s, these inquiries included major passport raids at workplaces and homes that amounted to a "witch hunt" of African, Caribbean, and Asian communities (Gordon 1984: 35–36). Consequently, this form of migration policing became a major source of suspicion and mistrust between the police and minority communities, and was labelled "sus 2" by the Institute of Race Relations (1987).

Despite the waning of the moral panic about the arrival and settlement of African, Caribbean, and Asian people in the United Kingdom, migration policing remained contentious throughout the 1990s. The renewed hysteria about "bogus asylum seekers" led to a further wave of immigration legislation—the 1993 Asylum and Immigration (Appeals) Act, the 1996 Asylum and Immigration Act and the 1999 Immigration and Asylum Act—which increased the range of immigration offences, particularly in relation to those who employed or facilitated the entry of illegal entrants. Commentators tended to view the introduction and strengthening of criminal provisions against individual immigrants as largely symbolic, since the sweeping *administrative* powers to detain and expel that are exercised by the Immigration Service remain considerably more flexible than the corresponding criminal powers. However, much criticism was directed towards the employer sanctions that were expected to have a detrimental effect on race relations and to impact adversely on established residents from ethnic minorities.[21]

It was predicted that the signaling of a "tough stance" on immigration would prompt a wave of vigorous migration policing. Reports suggested that the police increasingly asked for identification documents and evidence of immigration status from black and "foreign-looking" people they encountered during routine traffic stops, or who were witnesses to an accident or crime (Institute of Race Relations 1987). Police also became increasingly involved in joint enforcement operations with the Immigration Service where police powers of search and arrest were needed. Their activities included large-scale employer raids and forced deportation actions, some of which have resulted in deaths and attracted national and international criticism (see Chigwada-Bailey 1997: 34).[22] Police involvement in this work has proved to be controversial and has not always been welcomed by senior police who fear a detrimental impact on police-community relations.[23]

The intensification of internal immigration controls has also drawn the police into more routine activities that have clearly been viewed by the affected forces as "rubbish"—draining police resources and unlikely to lead to any result in terms of prosecution or crime control. For example, the Metropolitan Police Service declined to continue its role in monitoring asylum applicants who were required by the Immigration Service to report regularly to a police station, and various regional forces have indicated their reluctance to deal with clandestine entrants found emerging from lorries on major arterial roads. The use of police cells for immigration detainees where Immigration Service detention space is unavailable has also reportedly been discouraged, if not discontinued, in most parts of the country (Weber and Gelsthorpe 2000: 47). Determining who is ultimately responsible for the security of immigration detainees held in privately run detention centres has also been problematic at times. When several asylum seekers escaped from the detention centre at Oakington soon after it was opened, Cambridgeshire police announced to the local press that they would not pursue the escapees unless they committed a criminal offence. And when the Yarl's Wood detention centre in nearby Bedfordshire was burnt to the ground, Lloyd's syndicate, representing Group 4, lodged a writ against Bedfordshire Police Authority under the Riot Damages Act 1886 in a move to sue for almost £97 million damages.[24]

Police have also been drawn, more willingly it seems, into those aspects of border control that hold out the prospect of serious criminal prosecutions. The creation of a market for people-smuggling in response to visa regimes is said to have attracted organized criminal networks that were previously engaged in less lucrative smuggling enterprises. This has been met by intelligence-driven policing tactics originally designed to deal with other forms of cross-border crime. For a number of years, Special Branch officers have been routinely deployed at major ports of entry, charged with the detection and prosecution of the facilitators of illegal migration. The nature of their activities and their interface with Immigration Service personnel requires more investigation. However, frontline immigration officers interviewed in 1999 reported some cooperation and exchange of intelligence between themselves and the Special Branch police (Weber and Gelsthorpe 2000: 15–16). A specialist unit, the Organised Immigration Crime Section (OICS), has now been established within the National Criminal Intelligence Service (NCIS) to coordinate the intelligence response to organized illegal immigration. A combined intelligence cell has also been set up at Hounslow, comprised of seconded Metropolitan Police officers, NCIS intelligence officers, and Immigration Service officers, with the stated purpose of targeting human trafficking networks, abuse of immigration and asylum procedures, and employment of illegal entrants.[25]

THE EXPANDING ROLE OF THE IMMIGRATION SERVICE

Many of today's senior immigration officers were recruited in the 1970s to work at ports following the introduction of new controls through the 1971 Immigration Act. Since then, a notable shift of resources has occurred away from border controls towards in-country enforcement and the processing of asylum applications by Home Office officials (Crawley 1999), and separate Enforcement and Ports Directorates were established to carry out these different functions. At the same time, there has been a proliferation of centralized units to oversee the increasingly complex legal and administrative system of immigration controls and manage the burgeoning detention estate.

For traditionally minded immigration officers, the identification and subsequent removal of individuals who are considered not to meet United Kingdom entry requirements is seen as their core function (Weber and Landman 2002). Notwithstanding the new visa procedures described earlier, immigration officers stationed at ports have considerable discretion to refuse entry to arriving passengers either on technical grounds (because they do not have the required documentation) or on "credibility" grounds (because they are considered likely—often on minimal evidence—to breach the terms of their entry). Dealing with asylum seekers is generally seen by border officials as time-consuming and frustrating, offering no likelihood of a "result" since the 1951 United Nations Convention on the Status of Refugees prohibits their summary expulsion pending consideration of their asylum claims.

By contrast, after-entry operations aimed at the removal of rejected asylum applicants or the detection and deportation of "immigration offenders"[26] are directed towards a clear, if not always attainable, outcome. For this reason, enforcement work appears to be popular among immigration officers who are bored with the routine stamping of passports, demoralized by significantly increased workloads, and frustrated by the perceived abandonment of political commitment to border controls (Weber and Landman 2002: Chapter 2). The number of people subjected to enforcement action has increased sharply in recent years—from 3,200 in 1986 to 22,890 in 1999 (Jackson and McGregor 2000). Still, critics of Britain as a "soft touch" have demanded more efficient removal of "undesirable aliens," prompting a more than doubling of the level of arrests, detentions and removals to over 50,000 in the year 2000. Not satisfied with this, in the summer of 2001 the government announced the goal of a sixfold increase in removal targets (Home Office 2001). The opening of two new immigration detention centres during that year at Dungavel and Yarl's Wood, and the expansion of the existing facility at Harmondsworth, provided 1,500 new detention spaces to facilitate this programme of expulsion.[27] Moreover, the White Paper that preceded the 2002 Nationality and Immigration Act suggests that the government aims to establish four new accommodation centres with 750 bed spaces each (Home Office 2002).[28]

Another crucial element in the attempt to meet political targets has been the granting of increased powers for immigration officers coupled with training in policing techniques. The Metropolitan Police Service has been used to train immigration officers in arrest procedures and has entered into a joint protocol aimed at enabling the bulk of enforcement actions to take place without police involvement.[29] It could be argued that a new kind of police force is being created within the Immigration Service with the full range of coercive and intrusive powers. However, the applicability of the 1984 Police and Criminal Evidence Act and other constraints on discretion is unclear. An increasingly intelligence-led approach based on established policing techniques is also apparent in the operations of the Immigration Service at ports. For example, detention is used systematically on arrival in response to patterns of "abuse" that have been identified by intelligence analysts (Weber and Gelsthorpe 2000: 21). There are also indications that interviews with asylum applicants conducted at ports are increasingly directed towards gathering intelligence about facilitators and travel routes, rather than details about the individual's need for protection (Weber and Landman 2002: 88; Crawley 1999: 68).

The increasingly "police-like" powers being granted to immigration officers do not necessarily align with individual officers' perceptions of their role. Interviews with officers based at ports in 1999 indicated an internal division between those who see themselves as a distinct and elite group of specialist law enforcers and those who identify more generally as professional civil servants (Weber 2003). When asked about a possible shift in the use of detention for asylum seekers away from the time of arrival towards the point of removal, many immigration officers who saw themselves primarily as administrators said they feared the development of a more heavy-handed approach if forced removals were stepped up (Weber and Gelsthorpe 2000: 91–94). The indications of increasingly coercive tactics were already apparent in the mid-1990s, by which time Immigration Service officers had been implicated in several "balcony deaths."[30]

At the same time as the expansion of enforcement activities, pre-entry checks by immigration officers posted overseas have been intensified and selectively targeted against potential asylum applicants. A controversial exemption to the 2000 Race Relations (Amendment) Act allows immigration officers to discriminate against nationalities (and, indirectly, against particular ethnic groups) that are named in "authorizations" promulgated by the Home Secretary (Dummett 2001). These targeted categories are identified through intelligence information that links certain nationalities or ethnic groups to "systematic abuse" of asylum procedures. Czech Roma prevented by United Kingdom immigration officials from boarding flights at Prague Airport were one of the first reported targets of these selective offshore controls.[31] These moves towards more directed, supposedly intelligence-led, controls, although motivated in large part by a desire to improve efficiency at ports, clearly have discriminatory outcomes. These practices also pave the way for further pre-emptive targeting of groups who could be broadly identified as threats in light of the ongoing "war against terror."

CONCLUSION

When civil regulatory agencies acquire "police-like" powers of search and arrest, quasi-judicial functions including the power to detain for prolonged periods, and the use of an extensive secure estate of prisons and detention centres, some fascinating and deeply troubling questions emerge. These questions have a practical, human rights dimension, and a relevance to academic criminology. What does it mean, for example, to conceptualize the system of regulating migration as being based on criminalization and deterrence? How does this "migration-crime-control" model equate to the dominant "law and order" discourse, and to what extent does it have a counterbalancing "due process" (Packer 1968), "human rights" (Ashworth 1998) or "freedom" (Sanders and Young 2000) model as outlined by criminologists?

On a practical level, emphasizing the continuity of traditional policing with other emerging "police-like" activities helps us challenge official claims that these practices are merely administrative and therefore benign, and not requiring the more intensive scrutiny that is demanded, although not always delivered, in relation to the police. The involvement of police in migration policing also demands a re-evaluation of their role in a society that is not only multicultural but also globally interconnected. Governments often argue that tough immigration policies are a pre-requisite for stability within multicultural societies, but the harsh enforcement of immigration controls inevitably impacts on relations between minorities and the police and therefore their relationship with the state more broadly.

The granting of police-like powers to immigration officers, the secondment of police officers to the Immigration Service, and the use of police to train immigration enforcement officers suggest that the policing of migration in Britain will share many of the characteristics of domestic policing. Conceiving of the wide spectrum of immigration control as linked under the umbrella of "migration policing" opens up the possibility that the research techniques and bodies of theory developed after half a century of police research can be called upon to create an integrated understanding that cuts across organizational boundaries. One crucial area for further study will be understanding the factors that shape the exercise of discretion by the various actors involved at the coalface of migration policing.[32] The task of applying and adapting this body of theory to the policing of migration still lies ahead.

NOTES

[1] Thanks to Phil Scraton for permission to reproduce passages published in his edited collection *Beyond September 11th: An Anthology of Dissent* (Scraton 2002).

[2] The authors would like to thank Jasmine Chadha for providing valuable assistance with the research and editing of this chapter.

[3] See Panayi (1996) for various historical examples of British reactions to minority communities; Mayall (1995) for an historical analysis of the state response to English Gypsies; and Goldhagen (1996) on the intensification of anti-Jewish sentiment in Germany prior to the Holocaust.

[4] At the end of 2001, Asia hosted the largest refugee population (48.3%), followed by Africa (27.5%), Europe (18.3%), North America (5%), Oceania (0.6%), and Latin America and the Caribbean (0.3%) (Source: UNHCR Population Statistics (Provisional), 7 June 2002. Available online at www.unhcr.org).

[5] See almost any contribution to the special edition of the *British Journal of Criminology* (Vol. 40, no. 2, Spring 2000) for a development of these themes.

[6] The source for these estimates is statistics on arrivals at UK ports from 1998 to 2001 from Tables 1.1 and 2.1 of *Home Office Statistical Bulletin* 11/02, Control of Immigration: Statistics United Kingdom, 2001.

[7] See Part 4 of the 2001 Anti-terrorism Crime and Security Act.

[8] The page number cited is the page within the printed format of this article, as accessed from the electronic version of the journal.

[9] Although they were formally interviewed by immigration officers, the grant of asylum was virtually a formality and was not characterised by the "culture of disbelief" that prevails today.

[10] Between 1992 and 2001, the proportion of asylum applications in Britain that were lodged on arrival fluctuated between one-half and one-third (source: www.homeoffice.gov.uk/rds).

[11] E.g., Part VII, ss.128–146 of the 1999 Immigration and Asylum Act creates powers for immigration officers to arrest and search certain persons; and Part VII, ss.152–156 of the 2002 Nationality and Immigration Act strengthens immigration officers' powers to enter business premises to search for and arrest "immigration offenders."

[12] We acknowledge that the role of customs officers in migration policing has not been given adequate consideration here and requires further research.

[13] Most refugees will not be in a position to seek pre-entry clearance into Britain before their departure (and may not even know their final destination) and are not likely to be granted a visa even if they are able to apply.

[14] Source: "Refugee Council's response to Home Office Consultation on Juxtaposed Controls Implementation, Dover-Calais, November 2002." Available online at www.rcfugeecouncil.org.uk.

[15] Reported in Siti Altaf Deviyati, "Denial of visitor visas for families," 18 June 2003—a news item available online at www.irr.org.uk.

[16] Source: Home Office press release 196/2003, 8 July 2003. Available online at www.homeoffice.gov.uk/pressreleases.asp.

[17] Loader (2002, citing Johnston) has pointed to the growing involvement of commercial security concerns *at a global level* in the detection of illegal migrants. The supra-national aspect of their activities is not adequately represented in the "sites of enforcement" model as it stands at present.

[18] S.8 of the 1996 Asylum and Immigration Act and Part 7, s. 147 of the 2002 Nationality and Immigration Act.

[19] E.g., the Home Office has issued press releases calling on British residents living in coastal areas to be alert for unauthorised boat arrivals, and a telephone hotline to enable members of the public to report suspected "immigration offenders" was proposed in the 2002 White Paper (Home Office 2002). On 24 March 2003, the Institute of Race Relations electronic news service reported that library staff in Plymouth had refused a police request to log Internet activities by asylum seekers living in the town, which was reportedly prompted by a public complaint about use of the library Internet facilities by a "foreign student" which had proven to be unfounded (Arun Kundnani "Libraries rebuff police surveillance of asylum seekers." Available online at www.irr.org.uk).

[20] The status of this particular proposal is not known, but the Refugee Council document on Juxtaposed Controls, referred to in ... [endnote 14] above does not refer to the existence of such a force in its list of measures aimed at preventing the arrival of "illegal immigrants" in Britain.

[21] See the report of the Glidewell Panel (1996), which documents a range of concerns surrounding the 1996 legislation.

[22] The most notorious case is that of Joy Gardener, a woman of Jamaican origin, who died in 1993 as a result of police restraint. She was visited by the (now disbanded) Metropolitan Police Alien Deportation Group, had her wrists handcuffed to a leather strap around her waist, was bound by a second belt across her thighs and a third one around her ankles. As she lay on the floor, 13 feet of adhesive tape were wound around her head and face. Mrs Gardner collapsed and died in hospital a few hours later.

[23] "Met frets over drive against migrants," *Guardian*, 19 October 2001; "Met warns Blunkett of deportation risks," *Guardian*, 30 August 2001.

[24] Under this legislation, the police can be held liable for damages caused during civil disturbances. According to press reports at the time, fire crews claimed, in fact, that detention centre staff prevented them from accessing the building for fear of allowing detainees to escape.

[25] From www.ncis.gov.uk.

[26] This term includes those who have entered illegally or breached the terms of their entry by working or overstaying, and should not include "failed" asylum seekers who have been granted temporary admission while their claims are considered.

[27] The subsequent failure to meet the 2002 removal targets was blamed in part on the destruction of the Yarl's Wood facility.

[28] Part 2, s. 16 of the 2002 Nationality and Immigration Act outlines the setting up of accommodation centres, but does not provide a limit on the number of centres or number of places.

[29] Immigration Service/Association of Chief Police Officers (2001), Joint Protocol between the Immigration Service and the Police Service for the Removal of Immigration Offenders.

[30] On 27 April 1994, Kwanele Eldah Siziba fell 150 feet to her death as she attempted to flee from what she believed to be immigration officials coming to deport her. On 23 October 1994, Joseph Nnalue died after falling from his second floor flat in Stockwell, South London, when police and immigration officials called to question him regarding his immigration status. On 15 March 1996, Noorjahan Begum died after falling 30 feet from the balcony of a flat in Stepney, East London. Two immigration officers called at the flat early on the morning of her death. On Sunday, 25 November 2001, two police officers and two immigration officials raided a third floor flat in Streatham, Southwest London. One person fell to his death from the balcony trying to escape.

[31] See the item entitled "The Czech and British Governments" in the round-up section of the August 2001 edition of *iNexile*, the newsletter of the British Refugee Council.

[32] Established findings from police research include the legal and organisational framework (Dixon 1997); the occupational culture and its norms, values and recipes for action (Holdaway 1983; Chan 1997); the influence of politicians and other interest groups (Grimshaw and Jefferson 1987); wider societal values and expectations of police (Chan 1997); and structural factors such as the social divisions of age, gender, class, and ethnicity (Scraton 1987).

REFERENCES

Amnesty International. 2001 "United Kingdom: Concern over Anti-Terrorist Arrests." *News Flash* December 19 (AI Index: EUR 45/028/2001), http://web.amnesty.org/library/index/engeur450282001.

Anderson, M., M. den Boer, P. Cullen, W. Gilmore, C. Raab, and N. Walker. 1995. *Policing the European Union: Theory, Law and Practice*. Oxford: Oxford University Press.

Ashworth, A. 1998. *The Criminal Process: An Evaluative Study*. Oxford: Oxford University Press.

Bauman, Z. 2000. "Social Issues of Law and Order." *British Journal of Criminology* 40: 205–21.

Bittner, E. 1970. *The Functions of Police in Modern Society*. Chevy Chase, MD: National Institute of Mental Health.

Bowling, B. 1999. *Violent Racism: Victimization, Policing and Social Context*. Oxford: Clarendon Press.

Bowling, B. and J. Foster. 2002. "Policing and the Police." Pp. 980–1033 in *The Oxford Handbook of Criminology*, 3rd ed., edited by M. Maguire, R. Morgan, and R. Reiner. Oxford: Oxford University Press.

Bowling, B. and C. Phillips. 2002. *Racism, Crime and Justice*. London: Pearson.

Braithwaite, J. 2000. "The New Regulatory State and the Transformation of Criminology." *British Journal of Criminology* 40: 222–38.

Caning, J. 2002. "Migration in the Age of Involuntary Immobility: Theoretical Reflections and Cape Verdean Experiences." *Journal of Ethnic and Migration Studies* 20: 5–42.

Chan, J. 1997. *Changing Police Culture: Policing in a Multicultural Society*. Cambridge: Cambridge University Press.

Chigwada-Bailey, R. 1997. *Black Women's Experiences of Criminal Justice: A Discourse on Disadvantage*. Winchester: Waterside Press.

Crawford, A. 1997. *The Local Governance of Crime*. Oxford: Oxford University Press.

Crawley, H. 1999. *Breaking Down the Barriers: A Report on the Conduct of Asylum Interviews at Ports*. London: Immigration Law Practitioners' Association.

Dixon, D. 1997. *Law in Policing: Legal Regulation and Police Practices*. Oxford: Oxford University Press.

Dummett, A. 2001. *Ministerial Statements: The Immigration Exemption in the Race Relations (Amendment) Act 2000*. London: Immigration Law Practitioners' Association.

Fryer, P. 1984. *Staying Power: The History of Black People in Britain*. London: Pluto.

Gibney, M. 1994. "Refugees and Immigrants in the New Europe." Pp. 157–73 in *Human Rights in the New Europe: Problems and Progress*, edited by D. Forsythe. Lincoln, NB: University of Nebraska Press.

Glidewell Panel. 1996. *The Report from an Independent Enquiry into the Implications and Effects of The Asylum and Immigration Bill 1995 and Related Social Security Measures*. London: Glidewell Panel.

Goldhagen, D.J. 1996. *Hitler's Willing Executioners: Ordinary Germans and the Holocaust*. London: Little, Brown & Co.

Gordon, P. 1984. *White Law: Racism in the Police, Courts and Prisons*. London: Pluto.

Green, P. and M. Grewcock. 2002. "The War Against Illegal Immigration: State Crime and the Construction of European Identity." *Current Issues in Criminal Justice* 14: 87–101.

Grimshaw, R. and T. Jefferson, T. 1987. *Interpreting Police Work*. London: Unwin.

Guild, E. 2000. "Entry into the UK: The Changing Nature of National Borders." *Immigration and Nationality Law and Practice* 14: 227–38.

Hall, S., C. Critcher, T. Jefferson, J. Clarke, and B. Roberts. 1978. *Policing the Crisis: Mugging, the State, and Law and Order*. London: MacMillan.

Holdaway, S. 1983. *Inside the British Police*. London: Basil Blackwell.

Holmes, C. 1988. *John Bull's Island: Immigration and British Society, 1871–1971*. Basingstoke: MacMillan.

Home Office. 2001. "Control of Immigration Statistics: United Kingdom 2000." *Home Office Statistical Bulletin* 14 (1) August.

Home Office. 2002. *Secure Borders, Safe Haven: Integration with Diversity in Modern Britain*. London: HMSO.

House of Commons Home Affairs Committee. 1995. *Organised Crime*. London: HMSO.

Institute of Race Relations. 1987. *Policing Against Black People*. London: IRE.

Jackson, K. and R. McGregor. 2000. *Control of Immigration: Statistics United Kingdom, First Half 2000*. London: Home Office.

Joly, D. 1996. *Haven or Hell? Asylum Policies and Refugees in Europe*. Basingstoke: Macmillan.

King, M. 1994. "*Fortress Europe*": The Inclusion and Exclusion of Migrants, Asylum Seekers and Refugees. Leicester: Centre for the Study of Public Order.

Kleinig J. 1996. *The Ethics of Policing*. Cambridge: Cambridge University Press.

Klockars, C. 1980. "The Dirty Harry Problem." *The Annals* 452 (November): 33–47.

Kraska, P. (Ed.). 2001. *Militarizing the American Criminal Justice System*. New York: New York University Press.

Loader, I. 2002. "Policing, Securitization and Democratization in Europe." *Criminal Justice* 2: 125–53.

Martin, D. (Ed.). 1988. *The New Asylum-Seekers*. Dordrecht: Nijhoff.

Mayall, D. 1995. *English Gypsies and State Policies*. Hatfield: University of Hertfordshire Press.

McLaughlin, E. 1992. "The Democratic Deficit: European Unity and the Accountability of the British Police." *British Journal of Criminology* 32: 473–87.

Morrison, J. and B. Crosland. 2001. *The Trafficking and Smuggling of Refugees: The End Game in European Asylum Policy?* Geneva: UNHCR.

Packer, H. 1968. *The Limits of the Criminal Sanction*. Stanford: Stanford University Press.

Panayi, P. 1996. *Racial Violence in Britain during the Nineteenth and Twentieth Centuries*. London: Leicester University Press.

Richmond, A.H. 1994. *Global Apartheid: Refugees, Racism and the New World Order*. Oxford: Oxford University Press.

Rose, N. 2000. "Government and Control." *British Journal of Criminology* 40: 321–39.

Royal Commission on Alien Immigration. 1903. *Report of the Royal Commission on Alien Immigration* (Cmnd 1741, 1903, Vols I–IV). London: HMSO.

Salyer, J.C. 2002. "Abuse of immigration detainees: Before and after September 11." *Criminal Justice Ethics*. 21: 2, 61–63.

Sanders, A. and R. Young. 2000. *Criminal Justice*. London: Butterworths.

Scraton, P. (Ed.). 1987. *Law, Order and the Authoritarian State*. Milton Keynes: Open University Press.

Scraton, P. (Ed.). 2002. *Beyond September 11th: An Anthology of Dissent*. London: Pluto.

Shacknove, A. 1993. "From Asylum to Containment." *International Journal of Refugee Law* 5: 516–533.

Shah, P. 2000. *Refugees, Race and the Legal Concept of Asylum in Britain*. London: Cavendish.

Sheptycki, J. (Ed.). 2000. *Issues in Transnational Policing*. London: Routledge.

Sheptycki, J. 2002. *In Search of Transnational Policing: Towards a Sociology of Global Policing*. Burlington, VT: Ashgate.

Sivanandan, A. 1982. *A Different Hunger: Writings on Black Resistance*. London: Pluto.

Solomos, J. 1993. *Race and Racism in Britain*. Basingstoke: MacMillan.

Statewatch. 2002. "European Border Police, Developing by Stealth?" *Statewatch* 12 (5): 20–21.

Webber, F. 1996. *Crimes of Arrival: Immigrants and Asylum-Seekers in the New Europe*. London: Statewatch.

Weber, L. 2002. "The Detention Of Asylum Seekers: 20 Reasons Why Criminologists Should Care." *Current Issues in Criminal Justice* 14: 9–30.

Weber, L. 2003. "Decisions to Detain Asylum Seekers: Routine, Duty or Individual Choice?" Pp. 164–85 in *Exercising Discretion: Decision-making in the Criminal Justice System and Beyond*, edited by L. Gelsthorpe and N. Padfield. Uffculme: Wiflan.

Weber, L. and L. Gelsthorpe. 2000. *Deciding to Detain: How Decisions to Detain Asylum Seekers are Made at Ports of Entry*. Cambridge: Institute of Criminology, University of Cambridge.

Weber, L. and B. Bowling. 2002. "The Policing of Immigration in the New World Disorder." Pp. 123–29 in *Beyond September 11: An Anthology of Dissent*, edited by P. Scraton. London: Pluto.

Weber, L. and T. Landman. 2002. *Deciding to Detain: The Organisational Context for Decisions to Detain Asylum Seekers at UK Ports*. Colchester: Human Rights Centre, University of Essex.

CHAPTER STUDY QUESTIONS

- The policing of global population movements is an example of an emerging punitive regulatory system that demands urgent attention by criminologists. Do you agree with this argument? Explain.

- According to Weber and Bowling, recent years have witnessed the development of a system of "global apartheid" aimed at containing the international flow of immigrants and asylum seekers. What are the concerns raised by Weber and Bowling about this system? Do you agree with their arguments? Why or why not?

- Identify the different levels of enforcement activities outlined in the Weber and Bowling "sites of enforcement" model of migration policing. What are the political and administrative problems associated with many of the specific control policies they identify?

RELATED WEB LINKS

Journal of Mediterranean Politics
http://www.gcsp.ch/e/publications/Issues_Institutions/ME_Med/Academic_Papers/
Lutterbeck-Med_Politics-March06.pdf
> This website accesses an informative article on policing migration in the Mediterranean region.

Columbia University
http://www.columbia.edu/cu/lweb/indiv/lehman/guides/pop.html#Columbia
> This website accesses a resource listing established by the Lehman Social Sciences Library at Columbia University. It provides a bibliography as well as links to individual articles and other websites that deal with transnational migration and refugees.

Copenhagen Consensus 2004
http://www.copenhagenconsensus.com/Default.aspx?ID=226
> This website provides access to a major paper on migration and immigration control. It discusses a range of possible issues including barriers to migration, guest worker programs, and the costs and benefits of population migration. Access is also provided to two rebuttal papers.

USAF Air University
http://www.au.af.mil/au/aul/bibs/illegalim.htm#doc
> This website is maintained by the USAF Air University. It provides access to a wide range of papers and articles (many of which are full-text) on the topic of illegal immigration into the US. Links are also provided to other organizations active on the topic.

Chapter 10

THE TRANSFORMATION OF POLICING? UNDERSTANDING CURRENT TRENDS IN POLICING SYSTEMS

TREVOR JONES AND TIM NEWBURN

> Modern democratic countries like the United States, Britain and Canada have reached a watershed in the evolution of their systems of crime control and law enforcement. Future generations will look back on our era as a time when one system of policing ended and another took its place. (Bayley and Shearing 1996: 585)

In recent years, there has been growing consensus that the policing systems of Western industrial societies are experiencing profound changes. Authors have highlighted a range of developments, including the expansion of private security (Shearing and Stenning 1987; Johnston 1992; Jones and Newburn 1998; Loader 1999), the growing importance of "transnational" policing organizations and practices (Anderson et al. 1995; Sheptycki 1997), changes in the organization and management of public police forces (Chatterton et al. 1996; Johnston 1996), the impact of new technologies upon policing and crime control (Marx 1988), and the emergence of new "risk-based" policing strategies (Feeley and Simon 1992; Ericson and Haggerty 1997). Such changes are clearly crucially important to a deeper understanding of policing systems in Western industrial countries as we move into the twenty-first century. However, it has further been suggested that we are currently seeing a transformation in policing of a magnitude at least as great as occurred with the introduction of the New Police in the early nineteenth century. This transformation has been variously described as "post-Keynesian policing" (O'Malley and Palmer 1996), "'pick 'n mix' policing for a postmodern age" (Reiner 1997) and, even, the "End of Public Policing" (McLaughlin and Murji 1995).

In this chapter, we aim to address some of the broader issues relating to the interpretation of current trends by focusing upon one particular example within this "transformation" literature in policing. In 1996, two of the most distinguished academic criminologists, David Bayley and Clifford Shearing, published an article entitled "The Future of Policing" in the journal *Law and Society Review* (Bayley and Shearing 1996). In the article, they made a series of sweeping claims about the significant changes they perceived to be taking place in developed democratic societies. Whilst we must begin by saying that we concur with many of their observations, there are also some key points at which our respective views of both the history of policing and, consequently, the future of policing, diverge. In particular, we question the degree to which current developments in policing should be interpreted as a qualitative break with the past. Here, we begin by setting out the central elements advanced by Bayley and Shearing in their article and then move on to discuss these key points of divergence. We argue that the article, and some of the other writing in the field, whilst identifying some important developments in modern policing, tends to overstate the novelty and the "epochal" nature of current trends. Furthermore, we feel in general that what we will refer to as the "transformation thesis" fails to take sufficient account of important differences between the nature and form of policing in North America and that in other countries, such as Britain.[1] Finally, we suggest that rather than seeing current changes as a fragmentation of policing, they are better viewed as an ongoing process of formalization of social control.

THE TRANSFORMATION THESIS

Bayley and Shearing open by making clear the radical nature of the focus of their paper. Their concern is with "the watershed in the evolution" of the systems of crime control and law enforcement in the United States, Britain, and Canada. They forcefully argue that that "[f]uture generations will look back on our era as a time when one system of policing ended and another took its place" (1996: 585). This epochal change is characterized by two developments:

- The pluralizing of policing—or as they put it "the end of a monopoly" by the public police and
- The search for identity by the public police.

Before exploring each of these in greater detail, they make the important point that the focus of their concerns is with *policing*, not just the *police*. They are interested in "all explicit efforts to create visible agents of crime control, whether by government or by non-governmental institutions" (1996: 586). The reason for emphasizing explicit efforts is to distinguish the "elephant of social control" from the "breadbox of policing."

The end of a monopoly

The core of Bayley and Shearing's thesis is that "in the past 30 years the state's monopoly on policing has been broken by the creation of a host of private and community-based agencies that prevent crime, deter criminality, catch law-breakers, investigate offences, and stop conflict" (1996: 586). As a result, they argue, the police and policing have become increasingly distinct. Their conceptualization of the "pluralization of policing" can be broken down into the following main points:

- There used to be a state monopoly on policing, but this has been fractured during the past 30 years (i.e., since the mid-1960s);

- Evidence for this is to be found in the fact that there are now *three times* as many private as public police in the United States and *twice* as many "private security agents" than public police officers in the UK; in addition, the private security sector is growing faster than public policing;
- Citizen policing—in the form of car and foot patrols, neighbourhood watches, crime prevention associations, protective escort services, and monitors around schools, malls, and public parks—have been "transformed in less than a generation" (1996: 587) from something that would have previously been viewed as "vigilantism" but is now so common that the "police are no longer the primary crime-deterrent presence in society."

Searching for identity

Alongside the increasing pluralization of policing, the other major element in the restructuring that is taking place in developed democracies is the increasing questioning of the role of the police—particularly by the service itself. "This is attributable," Bayley and Shearing (1996: 588) argue, "to growing doubts about the effectiveness of their traditional strategies in safeguarding the public from crime." There are numerous components to this:

- The "visible deterrent" of patrol has declined as the police have been gradually swamped by the need to respond to emergency calls;
- Clear-up rates remain extremely low;
- There is therefore a search for "new approaches"—these have included "community policing" and "order maintenance policing" (a hybrid of "community-oriented and crime-oriented policing");
- The increasing sale by the police of the protective services they used to provide without charge;
- The hiring of police officers as private security guards;
- The increasing civilianization of public policing—including the use of Special Constables or other auxiliaries; and
- The increasingly rigorous supervision of the police by governmental and non-governmental agencies.

Although Bayley and Shearing focus on the search for a new identity, other authors have, in a similar way, highlighted qualitative shifts in the nature of police activity. In particular, although Bayley and Shearing do not mention this specifically, one might include under this point the shifts towards new policing functions identified by writers such as Feeley and Simon (1996) and Ericson (1994). Feeley and Simon argue that the police (and the criminal justice system in general) are increasingly adopting "actuarial" rather than "disciplinary" approaches. These techniques are characterized by a pragmatic emphasis on the management of risky populations, rather than aiming to reform, punish or deter individuals. A related point is made by Ericson and Haggerty's (1997) analysis of the transformation of policing functions in developed societies. They argue that the public police role is no longer primarily concerned with law enforcement and peacekeeping, but has moved towards "information brokering" within a wider patchwork of organizations and individuals concerned with the promotion of security.

Taken together, it is this raft of changes which has been interpreted by some authors as constituting a transformation to a fundamentally new kind of policing system. For example, Bayley and Shearing's (1996: 591) conclusion runs as follows: "the pluralizing of policing and the search by the public police for a new role and methodology mean that not only has government's monopoly on policing been broken in the late 20th century, but the police monopoly on expertise within its own sphere of activity has ended. Policing now belongs to everybody—in activity, in responsibility, and in oversight."

As we have already indicated, there is much in these arguments with which we would not argue, particularly in relation to some of the changes taking place in the police organization (see Jones and Newburn 1997). However, particularly in relation to what we have elsewhere referred to as the "policing division of labour" (Jones and Newburn 1998), it is our view that Bayley and Shearing both overstate the degree of novelty attributable to the changes taking place and posit an "over-globalized" view of the world. They lose sight of the important continuities in policing systems and, further, fail to make sufficient allowance for the important differences between, for example, North America and the UK. It is to this we turn next.

HOW STRONG IS THE EVIDENCE?

For the purposes of empirical examination, we will consider three distinct elements of what we have termed the "transformation thesis": the "end of monopoly"; "the pluralization of policing provision"; and "the changing character of, and the search for a new identity for, the public police."

The end of monopoly?

How "policing" or "the police" are best characterized has been the subject of considerable academic debate. Most attempts to define or distinguish the police from other policing organizations have focused either on functions or on legal capacities. Neither approach is entirely adequate (see the criticisms contained in Johnston 1992 and Jones and Newburn 1998). A functional focus tends to equate the police with policing assuming, implicitly or otherwise, that the two are effectively the same. In response to this, several authors have argued that what distinguishes policing from other activities is the capacity to apply the "legitimate use of force." Indeed, the best known of these, Egon Bittner, went further and argued that this was in fact the distinguishing characteristic of *the police* (Bittner 1974, 1980). It is this capacity that is often being referred to when the idea of a "public monopoly" of policing is used.

The term "monopoly" is defined by economists as the condition that exists when a firm or individual produces and sells the entire output of a commodity or service. The monopolist has total power in the market place to set prices and prevent the entry of new competitors. If all that is meant by "monopoly" is that the public police were the sole repositories of state-backed coercive power, then the public police monopoly continues today. In Britain, at least, it is the public police who retain the legal power to arrest, detain, and charge on behalf of the state (backed, if necessary, by the use *of legitimate force*), and there is strong resistance to providing such special legal powers to other bodies, and especially to private security guards.

In relation to policing, however, the term "monopoly" tends to be used in a broader sense to describe a perceived functional, spatial, and, above all, symbolic dominance over policing by the public police. In this sense, it is clear that the symbolic monopoly that equated "policing" with the activities of the public police has fractured in the past 20 years or so. The period most associated with a public police monopoly, especially in Britain, is the two decades immediately following the Second World War. However, although the 1950s still tend to be presented as the "golden age" of public policing, Reiner (1992b) has persuasively argued that this was as much a matter of image as of substance. Relatively low rates of crime and disorder overall and high police popularity ratings of the post-war years might be better explained with reference to wider social and economic conditions than by anything the police were actually doing at the time. Even during the height of the "golden era," police relationships with certain elements of the population remained difficult and conflictual, and there is no evidence that police malpractice was less common during this period (in fact, there are good reasons to suppose that levels of police deviance may well have been substantially higher than [in] the present day, see Reiner 1992b). The main point here is that the height of the symbolic "monopoly" of public policing was an era in which low crime rates and relative social harmony were produced by a wide variety of structural influences which underpinned a more effective network of informal social controls. It is the breakdown of these more effective informal controls that ... [has] been a primary contributor to the growing demands upon public policing services and the increasing soul-searching of state police forces. In an important sense, then, the public "monopoly" over policing was always a fiction, the idea that sovereign states could guarantee crime control to their subjects was always a myth, albeit a powerful one (Garland 1996). The crucial change in the current era is that the myth is increasingly explicitly recognized as such, even by those state agencies tasked with dealing with crime.

The pluralization of policing

We deal with two major elements under this heading: first, *the growth of private security* and second, *the emergence of other policing bodies* (not part of constabularies or the private security sector). Bayley and Shearing argue that private security growth far outstrips [that of the] public police in both the United States and the UK, [and has been] growing faster than the public sector [since] the 1960s. They further argue that there has been a growth of *citizen policing* (we return to this below)—automobile and foot patrols, neighbourhood watches, crime prevention associations, and so on have been "transformed in less than a generation" from something that would have previously been viewed as "vigilantism" into a primary crime-deterrent presence. Other authors (see for example, Johnston 1992, 1996) have highlighted the activities of a range of other policing bodies—including the regulatory and investigatory bodies attached to national and local government—as part of a growing fragmentation of policing provision.

The growth of private security

In pure numerical terms, and reinforcing our argument above, it is clear that a "monopoly" in the field of security provision has never really existed. Data from both the US and the UK suggest that, whilst significant changes have certainly taken place in the policing division of labour, the idea of the end of a "monopoly" is difficult to support. According to Bayley and Shearing, the "rebirth" of private security occurred sometime around the 1960s. However, the Rand report (Kakalik and Wuldhorn 1972), which provides the best historical picture of private security in the United States, found that in 1950 there were approximately half as many private security guards as public police staff. This is approximately a decade and a half *before* the "rebirth" of private security is alleged to have taken place. Similarly, in Britain, the 1951 census of population estimates about 66,000 private security employees compared with approximately 85,000 police officers.[2] At the very least, therefore, the argument that a public monopoly has been broken in the past 30 years is impossible to sustain. Was there ever a public monopoly? This is also doubtful. In Britain, commercial provision (and other "private" forms) of policing continued throughout the nineteenth century, despite the introduction and expansion of the New Police, and the early twentieth century contains many examples of private provision, including the development of the guarding industry in the inter-war period (Johnston 1992). What is clearly true is that the private security industry has become more important since the 1950s, both in absolute terms and relative to public policing. However, we feel that it is important to emphasize that, although the empirical evidence is limited, what there is suggests that the private security industry was relatively well established even during the height of the "monopoly" era for the public police. In our view, current developments are perhaps therefore better presented as the continuation of a long-term trend extending back several decades rather than [as] a seismic shift occurring in the dying years of the twentieth century. Put another way, there is considerable *continuity* as well as *change*.

Of course, employment estimates alone cannot adequately measure the expanding influence of commercial forms of policing provision. A number of other factors have contributed to the growing visibility of commercial policing. First, there has been a long-term trend within business organizations towards the contracting-out of non-core tasks, such as security. Thus, whereas many of the people working in security and related occupations in the 1950s and 1960s would have been employed in-house, increasingly companies contract in security services from specialist providers (Jones and Newburn 1998). Second, the functional remit of commercial policing has expanded in recent years, with the private sector undertaking tasks previously viewed as the preserve of state bodies, such as prisoner escort, court guarding, and the patrol of public places. Finally, the spatial remit of commercial policing has arguably grown, with the emergence of private patrols in public spaces (see McManus 1995; Noaks 2000) and also the growth of "mass private property" in the form of large shopping centres, private theme parks, etc. However, the available evidence suggests that such changes have been considerably less extensive in Britain than is the case in the USA (Jones and Newburn 1999a).

The growth of other forms of policing

Another important aspect of the "pluralization" of policing (although not an element upon which Bayley and Shearing focus a great deal in their article) concerns the activities of what Johnston (1992) has termed "hybrid" policing bodies, such as Environmental Health Officers and Health and Safety Inspectors. However, as we have pointed out elsewhere (Jones and Newburn 1998) it is rather misleading to consider these bodies as though they are part of a relatively recent "fragmentation" of policing organizations. In the United States, and certainly in Britain, regulatory and investigatory bodies attached to national and local government have been undertaking "policing" activities for over a century. The fact that criminologists have only recently taken an interest in these perhaps reflects the general assumption, widely held until comparatively recently, that "policing" can be equated with "what public constabularies do."

During the mid to late 1800s in England and Wales, it was local constabularies that delivered services such as inspecting weights and measures, inspections under the Diseases of Animals Act, and inspections of dairies and shops (Critchley 1967). It was not until the late nineteenth century, beginning with the Local Government Acts of 1888, and the early twentieth century that local government began to undertake these "policing" functions itself. The post-war expansion of the welfare state introduced new "policing" functions which were undertaken by public bodies outside of the police (for example, benefit fraud investigation). As Bayley and Shearing correctly point out, many police forces in Britain and North America are currently seeking to divest themselves of what have increasingly been seen as "ancillary" functions, part of which has involved withdrawal from regulatory activity such as licensing bars, parking regulations and so on. However, in the light of the longer history of the policing of such activities, this is far from a novel development. Rather, it is the latest of a series of functional shifts between different policing bodies. For the large part of the twentieth century, policing functions have been undertaken by this mix of bodies, with the balance shifting between the different elements from time to time. For example, Taylor's (1999) fascinating analysis of policing in England and Wales in the early part of the twentieth century explains a dramatic fall in prosecutions for non-indictable offences such as vandalism and begging by reference to such a functional shift:

> [The Home Office's] argument that society had suddenly civilized to the extent that wife-beating, assaults, truancy, drunkenness, immorality, begging, child cruelty, vandalism and other similar "minor" offences had really fallen by two-thirds between the first world war and 1931 was unbelievable. Instead, many of these offences must have continued to be committed but were probably dealt with by agencies or departments of government other than the police ...

Notwithstanding these functional shifts, over the longer period from the mid-1800s to the mid-1950s it seems that the public police gradually obtained pre-eminence within the complex of policing bodies, in terms of staffing numbers, functions, and spatial operation, but particularly in symbolic terms. However, it is clear that they never achieved anything even approaching a total "monopoly" over the provision of policing services (except possibly—and very briefly—at a symbolic level). This, however, is not to deny the fact that, since this time, the balance has shifted significantly again, and the dominance of the public police has declined. What is less clear is that the current era, rather than any other (for example, the 1890s or the inter-war years) represents a dramatic move into a completely new system of policing.

In fact, taking a longer historical perspective suggests that, on one level, policing provision has become less rather than more fragmented. In particular, repeated reorganization over the nineteenth and twentieth centuries has seen a massive decline in the total number of constabu-laries and bodies of constables. Thus, out of the mixture of formal, semi-formal and informal policing "bodies" that existed in the eighteenth and nineteenth centuries, there emerged the "New Police." Beginning with the Metropolitan Police in 1829, these public policing bodies expanded rapidly in the nineteenth century, to the point where, by 1870, there were over 220 constabularies in England and Wales. From this point until, arguably, the 1960s, a process of centralization and formalization existed—albeit alongside other changes taking place. The number of constabularies was reduced by the Police Act 1946 to 131. Further amalgamations reduced the number of provincial forces to 117 by the early 1960s. In 1966 they were further reduced to 49 and, most recently, the Local Government Act 1972 reduced the number of provincial forces to 41. The Police and Magistrates' Courts Act 1994 gave increased powers to the Home Secretary to amalgamate forces without the need to consult publicly, and such amalgamations may well occur in the future.[3]

The changing character of the public police

This relates to the view that public policing organizations have somehow fundamentally changed in character as a result of the various pressures under which they have been placed. Bayley and Shearing concentrate on the police drive for improved effectiveness and the application of perfor-mance monitoring. As we have suggested, other authors have argued that the basic functions of public policing have now shifted to new actuarial and information-brokering roles. The question for us here is how far such changes represent a transformation towards a qualitatively different form of policing. We shall focus on three particular elements that have been linked with the changing character of public policing: the growth of managerialism and quasi-markets, civilian-ization, and the emergence of citizen-led forms of policing and crime control.

Managerialism and quasi-markets

The growth of managerialism has undoubtedly been one of the most significant changes in policing of the past 20 years or so. These changes have been widely documented elsewhere, and there is not the space here to analyse these developments in detail. Nevertheless, whilst not doubting their significance, we would argue that these changes, in Britain at least, have not yet been of such a degree as to constitute the transformation to a new policing system. Once again, the work of Howard Taylor (1999) highlights the danger of assuming the novelty of current trends. He has demonstrated how concerns about expenditure on policing and the promotion of effective use of police resources was a central feature of British policing during the years following the First World War. At this time, centrally driven management targets were applied to a number of aspects of police work. This is not to deny that the police service in Britain in recent years has again been significantly affected by another, perhaps more vigorous, form of managerialism. As part of the general trend towards "new public management," the police have been required [to] publish objectives, measure performance against these objectives, charge fees for some services, introduce devolved management structures, and link resources to performance (Jones and Newburn 1997). Clearly, this is a significant development, and one that could fundamentally subvert the nature of policing as a collectively purchased public service, should it be taken to the extreme. However, we would argue that, at the present at least, public policing in Britain remains a "public" service in several crucial ways, and clearly distinguishable from commercial private security. The police remain overwhelmingly (and increasingly) funded by a combination of national and local taxation. The vast majority of their workforce is made up of full-time publicly employed officials. Recent developments have clearly tried to heighten the privatization mentality. For example, section 24 of the Police and Magistrates Courts Act allows local authorities and health authorities to contract with police authorities and pay for extra constables for their areas. To date, however, few developments have been noted. Police forces are increasingly encouraged to charge for services where possible, for example, for providing security at rock concerts or at football matches. Although this has grown significantly in recent years, legal provision for this was first made in England and Wales in the 1964 Police Act.

One further difficulty in applying Bayley and Shearing's thesis to, say, the UK, concerns its very particular North American focus (despite their claims to be talking about broader global changes). Thus, they additionally refer to two aspects of the "privatization mentality" which apply in North America and Canada which do not apply to Britain. The first involves "moonlighting" by sworn police officers who may take employment as private security guards. Such activities are forbidden by police regulations in Britain. Second, they refer to the internal market of policing services in Canada, where local authorities may choose between a range of competing public sector providers in a quasi-market. These developments go substantially further than the current situation in Britain. Though the "transformation thesis" rightly identifies many changes taking place in British policing, it also tends to exaggerate them. It will require the emergence of a significantly more competitive internal market in British policing, for example, before Bayley and Shearing's picture appears an accurate one.

Civilianization

Another key feature of the fracturing of the public police identity crisis has involved the increasing involvement of civilians within the public police service, both in ancillary roles within the police organization and in undertaking voluntary duties as "special" constables or police auxiliaries. We do not currently have data for the US or Canada on these trends. However, the data that are available in Britain do not tend to support the notion of dramatic growth in the involvement of police auxiliaries over the past decade or so. In fact, the available data suggest the opposite, with substantially fewer special constables operating in Britain than was the case in the early and mid-twentieth century.

The civilianization of key posts within the police service was an important element of policy encouraged by successive Conservative administrations during the 1980s. Forces were encouraged, by various funding incentives, to replace with civilian employees relatively expensive police officers in posts not directly requiring police powers, training, or experience (such as traffic depot managers, force finance officers, administrative functions). Undoubtedly, the main drive to civilianization came after 1980, with up to a third of total police strength in the UK now accounted for by civilian employees. However, as we showed in an earlier study (Jones et al. 1994) the employment of civilians in the police service has a long history dating back to the early years of this century. Although there was a rapid expansion in civilian employment in the police during the 1980s, this expansion has now levelled off.

Turning to the Special Constabulary in Britain there have been various government initiatives aimed at expanding the role (and number) of Special Constables in British police forces, particularly since 1980. Encouragement of the Special Constabulary has been an important priority for governments keen to promote wider public involvement in policing and crime prevention activity. However, taking a longer-term perspective, we can see that, despite an expansion of the Special Constabulary over recent decades, total numbers of Specials remain substantially lower than has been the case for the majority of the post-war period. The figures below (which have been rounded to the nearest thousand) illustrate the general trend.

The growth of citizen-led policing

Bayley and Shearing (among numerous others) focus on the significant expansion of citizen involvement in "policing" activities in the form of neighbourhood watch, citizen patrols, and other community-led crime prevention and policing initiatives. It is clear that these are very significant developments. The growth of neighbourhood watch, as an explicit public policy, is a relatively recent phenomenon both in North America and Britain and is generally agreed to date from the early 1980s. Since the 1980s, governments in most industrial democracies have been engaged in what Garland (1996) calls "responsibilization strategies" whereby individuals and organizations outside of the state apparatus are encouraged to take responsibility for crime prevention and security. We agree that this is a key aspect of the changes that are currently occurring in policing. However, we are less sure that this can be accurately represented as a part of a shift from public monopoly to mixed economy of policing provision. It is clear that private citizens and organizations are now more involved in organized self-conscious activities aimed at order maintenance, crime prevention, and control. However, although much of the current debate focuses upon the growth of private and self-policing mechanisms, purportedly at the expense of an increasingly beleaguered public police service, we offer here a slightly different interpretation.

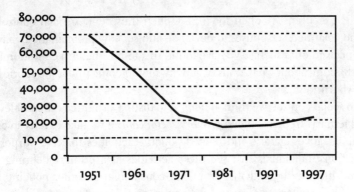

Figure 1. Special Constabulary strength (England and Wales).
Source: Derived from Leon (1991) and recent Home Office figures.

Part of the problem for the public police is that citizens in general have been increasingly, rather than decreasingly, taking matters to them for resolution. Calls to the police, reported crime, and disorder incidents have grown exponentially across all Western countries (Smith 1996). Since the demand for formalized policing services has so far outstripped the ability of public police organizations to respond, commercial security and citizen-led approaches have unsurprisingly seen a major growth. But we would suggest that rather than see these developments as a fragmentation of "policing," with non-state provision benefiting at the expense of public constabularies, what we are seeing is a general trend towards the formalization of social control. In particular, we would argue that the current growth in alternative forms of policing is related to a restructuring in forms of social control not directly connected to formal "policing," private or public.

We have so far considered some of the changes taking place within public policing together with those occurring in the broader policing division of labour. In thinking through current trends in policing systems, this is only part of the picture however. We now want to move on to consider changes in the broader context of policing and social control, changes that we take to have been central to the developments taking place since the Second World War.

THE FORMALIZATION OF POLICING AND CHANGES IN SOCIAL CONTROL

A large body of literature has linked current trends in crime control and penal systems to wider structural developments in capitalist societies in the late twentieth and early twenty-first centuries (see, for example, Johnston 1996; Bottoms 1983; Garland 2000). There is not the space here to provide a detailed examination of this large body of literature. However, we will highlight just some examples of changes in the nature of wider social control systems that we think may prove helpful to a deeper understanding of what is happening to policing.

As Cohen noted, there is a danger that the term "social control" can be defined so broadly as to be meaningless, covering "all social processes to induce conformity, from infant socialization to public execution" (Cohen 1985: 2). Cohen thus defines social control in terms of "organized" and "planned" responses to deviance and socially problematic behaviour "which are actually conceived of as such." We have found this to be a helpful definition in beginning the process of thinking about what kinds of activity should come under the rubric of "policing" (Jones and Newburn 1998).

Returning to social control, we think it helpful to distinguish three different levels: primary, secondary, and tertiary. In this context, *primary social control* we take to refer to crime prevention, peacekeeping, investigatory, and related policing activities that are purposively carried out by organizations/individuals that see these activities as a primary defining part of their role. This would include the activities of public constabularies, other policing bodies, such as inspectorates or regulatory bodies, and the commercial security sector. Thus, in our terms, primary social control covers those activities that we have previously described as "policing" (Jones and Newburn 1998). By contrast, *secondary social controls* may be said to be exerted by functionaries for whom social control activities are not a primary part of their role, but where, nevertheless, social control is an important secondary aspect of what they do. We would therefore include within this group teachers, park-keepers, caretakers, railway guards, bus conductors, and a range of other similar occupations. What such occupations have in common, in our view, is a very clear social control function, but one that is not a primary defining part of their role. This leaves the third category: *tertiary social control.* This corresponds to Cohen's wider concept of social control and includes the informal social controls exerted by "intermediate" groups within local communities, including workgroups, churches, trade unions, clubs and societies, and community groups.

Our categorization of social control activities shares some characteristics with Hunter's (1995) work on developments in urban space. There, Hunter categorizes three different kinds of "order": the *public*, the *parochial*, and the *private*, each with its particular institutional and spatial domain. The private order is based upon the family and informal "primary groups" including interpersonal friendship networks and the institutions of kinship. The parochial order arises from the interlocking of these networks and local institutions which service the "sustenance" needs of local residential community, such as local stores, schools, churches, and community associations. These correspond to the "intermediate level" institutions outlined above. Finally, the public social order is found mainly in the bureaucratic agencies of the state: the "public order" related to the state and its monopoly over the legitimate use of force. Hunter argues that growing crime and fear of crime has led to overwhelming demands on the police and criminal justice system. However, we should look to the private and parochial orders for the fundamental sources of this overload. Stronger parochial orders are a prerequisite for more effective social control activities along with the state and the private order. The limitations of the private order in terms of wider social control can be addressed by linking such networks through parochial institutions such as schools, churches, and youth clubs.

Several authors have highlighted this apparent decline in informal bases of social control in many Western societies, corresponding roughly to our tertiary level outlined above. For example, Giddens (1990) discussed what he termed "disembedding," whereby social relations are removed from local contexts due to the increasing mobility of people, of capital, and of information. Authors such as Etzioni (1993), Putnam (2000), and Sennett (2000) have highlighted the fact that, increasingly, the decline of participation in "intermediate" level institutions such as community groups, secure employment, trade unions, churches and local societies and organizations, has meant that citizens are more likely to relate to the social world as individuals.

In this connection, we would wish to argue that current trends in policing can be related to the decline of more indirect (and arguably more effective) sources of social control. This is not just in the general sense of a decline of social bonds and indirect (tertiary) controls connected with the parochial sphere, but also with the decline of "secondary" social control activities. There has been a marked decrease in employment in a range of occupations providing "natural surveillance" and other low level controls as a corollary to their primary functions. In part, this has been a consequence of the development and spread of new labour-saving technologies such as self-purchasing ticket machines and automatic barriers, CCIV, and automated access control. The spread and impact of such technologies was underpinned and encouraged by neo-liberal public policies which sought to maximize profit, often through reductions in labour costs via "downsizing." Much criminological literature has assumed that the "rise" of private security has been on the back of reductions in (or, at least, restrictions on the growth of) public policing. Whilst there may be a small element of truth in this, in our view, it is the decline of "secondary social control occupations" which is much more significant. In our own local case study of the policing of a London borough, we found that commercial security was carrying out activities that were previously undertaken not by public police officers, but by caretakers, receptionists, teachers, prefects, and park-keepers. Thus, the decline in such occupations as bus conductors, railway station masters, train guards, ticket inspectors, park-keepers, etc. has removed an important source of secondary social control (Jones and Newburn 1998; see also Smith and Clarke 2000: 177–178). To what extent is it possible to show that this has been a long-term national trend?

The table below is derived from census figures for 1951, 1971, and 1991. The figures should be taken as approximate indicators only, given that, in all cases (bar 1951) occupational estimates for the GB are based on a 10 per cent sample only. Furthermore, changes in occupational classifications over the years make comparison over time more difficult. Nonetheless, the figures are reasonably robust and, given the absence of any other reliable longitudinal data, provide the most accurate picture to date of this particular area of occupational change.

As the table indicates, there has been a sharp increase in the security and related occupations (i.e., what is often talked of as "private security") over the past 40 years. In addition to noting that this covers a longer time period than that outlined by Bayley and Shearing, the census data show that, as far back as 1951, the size of this sector was substantial. Indeed, in the first decade after the Second World War, the numbers of people employed in the sector represented the equivalent of four fifths of those employed in public constabularies. As we have shown elsewhere, by the early 1960s, the sector employed greater numbers than did the public police (Jones and Newburn 1998). Over the past 50 years, there has also been a large increase in the numbers of public police officers, though the extent of the increase has not been as great. The conclusion to draw from this, it seems to us, is not that the well-documented increase in private security reflects a process of transfer of functions and responsibilities from the public to the private police, though there may be some elements of this. Rather, and more fundamentally, it is better understood as a formalization of "secondary" social control activities. More particularly, we think it is more accurate to see the declining visibility of occupations with a secondary social control element as being a key contributor to the growth of "primary" forms of social control—i.e., private and public policing. Only a limited number of such occupations can be estimated from census data, but four key examples are illustrated below. Taking what the census generally classifies as "roundsmen/women"—the house-to-house delivery of milk, bread and other goods—there has been a significant decrease in these kinds of occupations since 1951, with numbers approximately halving. Census figures suggest that there has been a very sharp decrease in the number of bus and tram conductors. In 1951, the census estimated over 96,000 people in such occupations. In stark contrast, the 1991 census estimated only about 2,500 in Great Britain. There has also been a sharp decrease in census estimates of the numbers employed as rail ticket inspectors or train guards. This declined from 35,715 in 1951 to 15,642 in 1991. Even though these figures are approximations, they do suggest a quite dramatic fall in some of these occupations with secondary social control effects in public space, whilst policing, both private and public, has expanded.

Table 1 *Primary and secondary social control occupations in Britain*

	1951	1971	1991
Police officers	84,585	115,170	149,964
Security guards and related	66,950	129,670	159,704
"Roundsmen/roundswomen"	98,143	48,360	49,182
Bus (& train) conductors	96,558	57,550	2,471
Rail ticket inspectors/guards	35,715	46,800	15,642

Source: Occupational estimates from the 1951, 1971, 1991 *Census of Population* (GB)

The decline—and in some cases the almost complete disappearance—of each of these occupations is important in its own right, given the implications they have for both the perception and the reality of safety and security in local neighbourhoods, on buses and trains (and in bus and railway stations), and, no doubt, in other places too. It is the decline in such occupations that has been explicitly recognized and addressed by new forms of "municipal" policing such as the employment of uniformed patrollers by some local authorities in Britain (see Johnston 2000) and similar developments in the Netherlands (see Hauber et al. 1996). Collectively, however, the very rapid transformation in this key set of occupations has, we believe, had an impact wider than simply the formalization of social control—important though that is. Though we have not the space to develop the argument here, it seems plausible to us that the marked decline of "secondary social control occupations" that has taken place in England and Wales since the war is linked not only to changes in the formal policing division of labour, but is also implicated in the rising levels of crime during the same period. In explaining the rapid rise in levels of reported crime over the past half century, authors have focused on numerous changes in contemporary forms of (particularly urban) life: the unintended consequences of urban renewal (Jacobs 1992), the dispersal of routine activities (Felson 1998), the rise of market society (Currie 1997; Taylor 1999), and the "exclusionary" nature of late modernity (Young 1999), to list but a few. Each of these, in different ways, has something important to offer in our attempt to understand post-war social change. Yet each, in our view, would be enhanced if it also contained a focus on the important role played by the decline of secondary social control occupations in the period.

CONCLUSION

In short, our argument here has three major elements. First, in our view, much current criminology tends to exaggerate the degree of change, and underplay the extent of continuity, in seeking to explain the transformations taking place in contemporary policing systems. More particularly, we are unsure to what extent it is realistic to present current developments as an "epochal" change in policing.[4] Some of the changes are undeniably far-reaching. Consequently, it is understandable that commentators should wish to focus on what is novel. It is clearly the case that new institutional forms of policing, outside of nation state boundaries, are developing quickly. Similarly, both the form and content of public policing is changing (though perhaps less radically than some would have us believe), as is the commercial sector. Our concern is that, in focusing on such changes, important as they are, it is all too easy to exaggerate their extent, either by failing to recognize the consistencies and continuities that exist or by misrepresenting what it is supposed used to exist but is now disappearing (e.g., the mythical "public monopoly" in policing).

Secondly, we are concerned that many current theoretical analyses of policing transformation pay insufficient attention to variation between nation states. Thus, for example, there is a tendency to assume that the changes (believed to be) taking place within North America are, in large part, identical to those affecting other developed economies. Whilst we accept that there are indeed some important commonalities and continuities, nonetheless, there are also some extremely important points of departure: the nature, timing and reasons for the growth of the commercial security sector to name but three. To date, such differences have remained largely resistant to academic scrutiny. In part, this is due to the relative absence of comparative research. In this regard, it is particularly ironic that we should be critical in this article of one of the few scholars in the policing field to have undertaken comparative analyses of policing systems: David Bayley. In such work, he has talked persuasively of some of the general lessons that can be learned from policing systems around the world (e.g., Bayley 1994). As we have suggested, we have no difficulty with Bayley and Shearing's proposition that there are some quite strong common elements to the changes taking place in policing systems in many developed economies. However, it is clearly also the case that not all countries exhibit the same degree of change in their policing systems. More importantly, in our view there is no inevitability about the future direction or degree of change that will affect policing systems in these countries. That is, we should not assume that the policing systems of different countries are all moving in the same direction for the same reasons.

Finally, it is our view that the set of changes taking place "within" policing can profitably be set within a wider context. It is certainly the case that changes within one part of the "policing division of labour" can, and do, have effects on other parts—and it is important for us to seek to develop an understanding of such changes. Nonetheless, there is, we think, a broader social transformation taking place (at least in the UK). It is our view that, rather than seeing current changes simply as indicative of a process of fragmentation of policing, ... they are better viewed as part of a long-term process of formalization of social control. In particular, we highlighted in this article a shift that appears to have taken place between what we have termed *primary* and *secondary* social control activities. More particularly, there is clear evidence that, during the last half century, there has been a significant decline in certain key *secondary social control occupations*. It is this set of changes, we argue, at least as much as the changes affecting public policing bodies, that has had a profound impact on the size and visibility of the commercial policing (and particularly guarding) sector. Moreover, we think it plausible that these important changes in the labour market have also played an important role in the rise in recorded crime rates since the Second World War.

NOTES

[1] We have noted a similar problem of ethnocentrism in the literature on developments in private security (see Jones and Newborn 1999).

[2] Due to changes in occupational classifications and census estimates, these figures are approximations and should be taken as general indicators rather than exact measurements. However, the estimates for numbers of police officers compare reasonably well with official figures, and it is fair to say that these are currently the best available figures to examine change over time.

[3] See, for example, what has happened recently to the probation service in England and Wales.

[4] David Wall (1997: 225) notes how the discourse of transformation and "new age policing" is far from new. It has emerged at various points during the history of policing in Britain, most notably during the early years of the twentieth century when police commentators envisaged the revolutionary impacts that new technologies would have upon the police role.

REFERENCES

Anderson, M., M. Den Boer, P. Cullen, W.C. Gilmore, C.D. Raab, and N. Walker. 1995. *Policing the European Union: Theory, Law, and Practice*. Oxford: Clarendon Press.

Bayley, D. 1994. *Police for the Future*. Oxford: Oxford University Press.

Bayley, D. and C. Shearing. 1996. "The Future of Policing." *Law and Society Review* 30: 585–606.

Bittner, E. 1974. "Florence Nightingale in Pursuit of Willie Sutton: A Theory of the Police." Pp. 17–44 in *The Potential for Reform of Criminal Justice*, edited by H. Jacob. Newbury Park, CA: Sage.

Bittner, E. 1980. *The Function of the Police in Modern Society*. Cambridge, MA: Oelgeschlager, Gunn and Ham.

Bottoms, A. E. 1983. "Neglected Features of Contemporary Penal Systems." Pp. 166–202 in *The Power to Punish: Contemporary Penalty and Social Analysis*, edited by D. Garland and P. Young. Aldershot: Ashgate.

Chatterton, M., C. Humphrey, and A.J. Watson. 1996. *On the Budgetary Beat*. London: Chartered Institute of Management Accountants.

Cohen, S. 1985. *Visions of Social Control*. Cambridge: Polity Press.

Critchley, T. A. 1967. *A History of Police in England and Wales, 1900–1966*. London: Constable.

Currie, E. 1997. "Market, Crime, and Community: Toward a Mid-Range Theory of Post-Industrial Society." *Theoretical Criminology* 1: 147–72.

Emsley, C. 1996. *The English Police: A Political and Social History*. Harlow: Longman.

Ericson, R. 1994. "The Division of Expert Knowledge in Policing and Security." *British Journal of Sociology* 45: 149-75.

Ericson, R. and K. Haggerty. 1997. *Policing the Risk Society*. Oxford: Clarendon Press.

Etzioni, A. 1993. *The Spirit of Community: Rights, Responsibilities and the Communitarian Agenda*. New York: Simon and Schuster.

Feeley, M. and J. Simon. 1992. "The New Penology: Notes on the Emerging Strategy of Corrections and Its Implications." *Criminology* 30: 452–74.

Feeley, M. and J. Simon. 1996. "Actuarial Justice: The Emerging New Criminal Law" Pp. 173–201 in *The Futures of Criminology*, edited by D. Nelken. London: Sage.

Felson, M. 1998. *Crime and Everyday Life*. Thousand Oaks, CA: Pine Forge Press.

Garland, D. 1996. "The Limits of the Sovereign State." *British Journal of Criminology* 36: 445–71.

Garland, D. 2000. "The Culture of High Crime Societies: Some Preconditions of Recent 'Law and Order' Policies." *British Journal of Criminology* 40: 347–75.

Giddens, A. 1990. *The Consequences of Modernity*. Cambridge: Polity Press.

Hauber, A., B. Hofstra, L. Toornvliet, and A. Zandrergen. 1996. "Some New Forms of Functional Social Control in the Netherlands and Their Effects." *British Journal of Criminology* 36: 199–219.

Hunter, A. 1995. "Private, Parochial, and Public Social Orders: The Problem of Crime and Incivility in Urban Communities." Pp. 209–25 in *Metropolis: Centre and Symbol of Our Times*, edited by R. Kasinitz. Basingstoke: Macmillan.

Jacobs, J. 1992. *The Death and Life of Great American Cities*. New York: Vintage.

Johnston, L. 1992. *The Rebirth of Private Policing*. London: Routledge.

Johnston, L. 1996. "Policing Diversity: The Impact of the Public-Private Complex in Policing." Pp. 54–70 in *Core Issues in Policing*, edited by F. Leishman, B. Loveday, and S. Savage. Harlow: Longman.

Johnston, L. 2000. *Policing Britain: Risk, Security and Governance*. Harlow: Pearson Education.

Jones, T. and T. Newburn. 1997. *Policing after the Act: Police Governance after the Police and Magistrates' Courts Act 1994*. London: PSI.

Jones, T. and T. Newburn. 1998. *Private Security and Public Policing*. Oxford: Clarendon Press.

Jones, T. and T. Newburn. 1999a. "Policing Public and Private Space in Late Modern Britain." Pp. 99-119 in *Crime Unlimited: Questions for the Twenty-First Century*, edited by P. Carlen and R. Morgan. Basingstoke: Macmillan.

Jones, T. and T. Newburn. 1999b. "Urban Change and Policing: Mass Private Property Reconsidered." *European Journal on Criminal Policy and Research* 7: 225–244.

Jones, T., T. Newburn, and D. Smith. 1994. *Democracy and Policing.* London: PSI.

Kakalik, J.S. and S. Wildhorn. 1972. *Private Police in the United States.* Rand Report, 4 vols. Washington: US Department of Justice.

Leon, C. 1991. *Special Constables: An Historical and Contemporary Survey.* Unpublished doctoral thesis. Bath, UK: University of Bath School of Humanities and Social Sciences.

Loader, I. 1999. "Consumer Culture and the Commodification of Policing and Security." *Sociology* 33: 373–92.

Mclaughlin, E. and K. Murji. 1995. "The End of Public Policing? Police Reform and the "'New Managerialism.'" Pp. 110-27 in *Contemporary Issues in Criminology,* edited by L. Noaks, M. Levi, and M. Maguire. Cardiff: Cardiff University Press.

McManus, M. 1995. *From Fate to Choice: Private Bobbies, Public Beats.* Aldershot: Avebury.

Marx, G. 1988. *Undercover: Police Surveillance in America.* Berkeley, CA: University of California Press.

Noaks, L. 2000. "Private Cops on the Block: A Review of the Role of Private Security in Residential Communities." *Policing and Society* 10: 143–61.

O'Malley, P. and D. Palmer. 1996. "Post-Keynesian Policing." *Economy and Society* 25: 137–55.

Putnam, R. D. 2000. *Bowling Alone: The Collapse and Revival of American Community.* New York: Simon and Schuster.

Reiner, R. 1992a. *The Politics of the Police.* 2nd ed. Hemel Hempstead: Harvester Wheatsheaf.

Reiner, R. 1992b. "Policing a Postmodern Society." *Modern Law Review* 55: 761–81.

Reiner, R. 1997. "Policing and the Police." Pp. 980–1033 in *The Oxford Handbook of Criminology,* edited by M. Maguire, R. Morgan, and R. Reiner. Oxford: Clarendon Press.

Sennett, R. 2000. *The Corrosion of Character: The Personal Consequences of Work in the New Capitalism.* New York: W.W. Norton and Co.

Shearing, C. and P. Stenning. 1987. "Say Cheese! The Disney Order that Is Not so Mickey Mouse." Pp. 317–23 in *Private Policing,* edited by C. Shearing and P. Stenning. Newbury Park, CA: Sage.

Sheptycki, J. 1997. "Transnational Policing and the Makings of a Postmodern State." *British Journal of Criminology* 35: 613–35.

Smith, D. J. 1996. *Explaining Crime Trends.* Companion volume to *Themes in Contemporary Policing,* edited by W. Saulsbury, J. Mott, and T. Newburn. London: PSI.

Smith, M. J. and R. V. Clarke. 2000. "Crime and Public Transport." Pp. 169–233 in *Crime and Justice: A Review of Research,* vol. 20, edited by M. Tonry. Chicago: University of Chicago Press.

Taylor, H. 1999. "Forging the Job: A Crisis of 'Modernization' or Redundancy for the Police in England and Wales, 1900–1939." *British Journal of Criminology* 39: 113–35.

Taylor, I. 1999. *Crime in Context: A Critical Criminology of Market Societies.* Cambridge: Polity.

CHAPTER STUDY QUESTIONS

- Policing systems in Western industrial countries are currently undergoing radical change. Do you agree with this argument? Why? How can current transnational trends in policing systems be explained?

- Outline the "transformation thesis" by which Bayley and Shearing explain current trends in policing systems. What are the criticisms that have been made of this thesis? Do you agree with these criticisms? Why?

- Current trends in policing can be understood more fully when looked at within the context of changes in wider social control systems. What arguments and evidence do Jones and Newburn present in support of this view? What are the implications of this view for future comparative research on policing?

- What do Jones and Newburn mean by the term "secondary" social control? How has the decline in secondary social control affected the transformation of public policing and the development of commercial policing?

RELATED WEB LINKS

NCRJS
http://www.ncjrs.gov/pdffiles1/nij/187083.pdf
> This website provides a link to a subsequent report written by Bayley and Shearing (2001) for the US National Institute of Justice entitled "The New Structure of Policing: Description, Conceptualization, and Research Agenda."

Vera Institute of Justice
http://www.vera.org/section9/section9_3.asp
> This website provides access to research and publications on policing and security issues. It also includes many full-text publications on issues related to the reform and transformation of criminal justice and police agencies.

Institute for Security Studies
http://www.iss.co.za/Pubs/Papers/42/Paper42.html
> This website accesses an occasional paper discussing the challenges facing the development of community policing in South Africa. It focuses on a specific police reform issue in a nation that has recently emerged from a long period of racially motivated oppression.

The Serco Institute
http://www.serco.com/instituteresource/market/Justice/suppser/index.asp
> This website provides access to a variety of resources dealing with the transformation and modernization of policing. Many of these resources are full-text reports and occasional papers that discuss the modernization of policing in many different countries, including Canada, South Africa, the United States and the United Kingdom.

Chapter 11

THE ACCOUNTABILITY OF TRANSNATIONAL POLICING INSTITUTIONS: THE STRANGE CASE OF INTERPOL

JAMES SHEPTYCKI

At the historical heart of the "standard paradigm" of policing accountability lies the archetypal Big City Police Department. In the evolution of the standard paradigm, the emphasis has been on questions as to how such agencies might be made democratically accountable to the citizenry, and the key to this has been understood to lie in systems of public law administration based on principles of liberal democracy and the rule of law.[1] Initially, the focus was on those agencies that were elements of the state *qua* state, but a key development in the paradigm concerned the implications of the public-private divide in security provision and the consequences of the "marketisation" of social control for systems of accountability. Although tangential to the discussion pursued here, which concerns the accountability of Interpol, it is fair to point out that this evolutionary offshoot of the standard paradigm has thrown up some astonishing evidence regarding the increasingly centralised nature of private transnational security conglomerates such as Wackenhut, Intelligarde, and Securicor (Johnston 2000; Jones and Newburn 1998; Rigakos 2002).[2]

The jurisdictional reductionism evident in the standard paradigm for policing accountability is understandable since, up until quite recently, it has been easy to assume that the operational reach of most important institutions of governance, criminal justice agencies in particular, has been territorially limited. It is only within the last decade or so that attention has come to focus on transnational practices.[3] Academic attention given to transnational policing is symptomatic of wider developments and concerns about the changing nature of sovereignty in a globalising world, the changing nature of legality and the rule of law under conditions of globalisation, and even the possibilities for "global governance".[4] This interest has arisen out of the recognition of a rise in the prominence of transnational practices undertaken through virtually every social institution. Human action and interaction is no longer bounded by the territorial limitations of an earlier age; the world stage is no longer the exclusive preserve of Heads of State and their diplomatic representatives; and many social, political, economic, and cultural practices have become transnational. At the cusp of the 21st century, questions came to be asked about the future of democratic principles in an era where global forces had turned the nation-state system inside out, transforming it into the transnational-state-system.[5]

By looking at the practices of transnational policing, we come to better understand the political form of the emergent transnational-state-system (Sheptycki 2003). The standard paradigm for policing accountability has done much to both theoretically illuminate the nature of modern governance and to practically regulate the institutions responsible for such. This chapter sets out to discuss the problematic of accountability for transnational policing, and it does so by reference to Interpol, the only existing and formally constituted global transnational policing institution funded by taxpayers' money.[6] Examining the curious nature of Interpol's accountability framework illuminates questions about the accountability of transnational institutions more generally.

The chapter proceeds in several stages. In the next section, some terminological consideration will be given to the concepts of both "accountability" and of "globalisation." Neither term is so simple that it can be taken as read, but the central problem—which asks how transnational institutions may be rendered democratically accountable—can be made plain. This naturally leads to a discussion of the accountability framework for Interpol, which pays particular attention to how the organisation came to be treated as if it were an intergovernmental organisation. It will be shown that Interpol is not without an accountability framework, but that this is complicated because of its transnational nature and the peculiarities of its history. The politics of accountability for Interpol will also be discussed. This will focus primarily on changing interpretations of Articles 2 and 3 of the organisation's Constitution. Like most issues of global governance, transnational police work is a matter of hot political contestation. Concomitantly, difficulties arise regarding systems of accountability and control. Asking questions about "policing the world" is to reflect in fundamental ways about the political character of the "global system" (Anderson 1989; Sklair 1991).

SOME KEY CONCEPTS

Philip Stenning has done as much to clarify what we mean by "accountability" as anyone. "Fundamentally," he tells us, "accountability is about no more nor less than requirements to give accounts" (Stenning 1995). Accountability may be rooted in formal legal requirements and rules, or it may be rooted in custom or power relations. In short, it may be formal or informal. In liberal democracies, the ideal has been that, while working systems of accountability involve all of these elements in different measure, the requirement to give account is, at its most basic, a requirement to make matters of institutional and individual practice *transparent*. The key questions that arise are transparent to whom, when, how, and about what? Understanding the answers to these questions as they relate to criminal justice institutions is particularly revealing because this type of agency is so central to social ordering. Of all the institutions of governance, this is the one that most impacts on people's safety and freedom. It is when the accountability stakes are highest that we have the best opportunity, and the strongest motive, to understand what accountability is.

Richard Ericson famously coined the term "account-ability" as a way of showing that relationships of accountability are not simple command relationships between the sub and super-ordinate. Even in organisations such as the police, which are ostensibly rank-structured bureaucracies, accountability is not the same as control. That is because systems of account-ability provide tools to those who are being held to account at the same time that they provide tools to those who require accounts. Accountability mechanisms are resources in the hands of officials who use them to construct, explain, and justify actions in ways that, perhaps ironically, often preclude effective scrutiny and control by outsiders (Nelken 2003). Further, David Bayley, among others, has drawn the distinction between internal and external accountability. The trend toward establishing citizen review boards to oversee the work and policy of municipal police departments (as well as other systems of external accountability for police agencies) (Goldsmith 1991; Goldsmith and Lewis 2000), prompted Bayley to observe that systems of external accountability exist alongside internal mechanisms of accountability. The contradic-tory effect of an over-reliance on external oversight might be to foster indifference and even resistance within the organisation under scrutiny, thereby weakening internal systems of ac-countability. Internal mechanisms of accountability thus weakened, the degree of external con-trol over a given police organisation and its members (or any other type of institution for that matter) may actually decline.

The reader will have already seen that the distinctions drawn between accountability and account-ability, between formal and informal, and between internal and external accountabil-ity have something to do with the question of control. At least in the democratic societies of the West, accountability systems create relations between different social actors who use those mechanisms as tools in a complex interplay of power relations. In considering governmental practice, the nexus of control and accountability includes many players who have recourse to these enabling devices. Moreover, as the scale of institutional action increases, as the number of actors multiplies, the functional ambit grows, and the division of labour complexifies, sys-tems of accountability become more attenuated and the interplay between the various actors who interact on the basis of established accountability mechanisms becomes more complex. Paradoxically therefore, although systems of accountability ostensibly aim at making institu-tional action transparent, ultimately such systems tend towards opacity.

This problem is further amplified in contemporary debates which emphasise the account-ability not of police, but of policing. Observing the growth of private security providers, and the development of subterranean networks of policing agents that form bridges between the great variety of agencies that comprise the police sector, scholars have suggested that regula-tion should focus on networks of security rather than on being limited to specific organisations (Rigakos 2002; Law Commission of Canada 2002; Shearing 2001). In Shearing's formulation, when policing networks are made the focus of accountability what becomes requisite is a net-work of participatory "nodes"—each with authority, capacity and knowledge that together pro-vide for the governance of security. That being the case, the arrangements for regulation and oversight of policing networks (and, indeed, for their funding) are destined to replay all of the tensions made explicit through the conceptual distinctions made between formal and informal accountability, and internal and external accountability. Only now, the problems of control exposed through the notion of "account-ability" become even more fraught because networks may be less circumscribed and easy to pin down than formally constituted agencies. Shearing's answer to this is that individual "nodes" of governance should be founded on the basis of local knowledge and capacity. The implicit view is that public support for—as well as the legitimacy of—security provisions are dependent on the localised basis of governance.

This terminology is complicated. One way of simplifying the issues at stake is by reference to the typology laid out in the following table.

A Typology of Accountability

	Internal Accountability Mechanisms	External Accountability Mechanisms
Formal Accountability Mechanisms	Chain of Command	Civilian Review; Parliamentary Scrutiny
Informal Accountability Mechanisms	Sub-cultural "ways and means"	Public legitimacy & consent

In bureaucracies, the internal and formal means for achieving the accountability of governmental agents rely on relationships of sub- and super-ordinance. They depend on a "chain of command" and the ability to identify "where the buck stops." This seems much harder to achieve with regard to networks where command relations may be supplanted by the need for co-operation and, even more importantly, organisational boundaries and responsibilities may be difficult to define with precision. Consequently networks seem more likely to be held to account, if at all, via informal and sub-cultural means. When formal accountability mechanisms imply some element of external scrutiny such as can be found in Policing Boards and various types of Parliamentary oversight, it is considered important to ensure that external oversight works in harmony with internal accountability mechanisms, for example police-on-police or "internal affairs" forms of enquiry. It is here that the pragmatics of accountability are manifestly political. The nature of policing subculture(s) depends, at least partly, on the commensurability of formal and informal accountability ties. But such subcultures also rest on the way in which the mission is defined; the difference between policing and mere law enforcement being the clearest example of how sub-cultural values are shaped by the definition of the mission. The way that particular policing organisations and their agents relate to the policed population (both as individuals and as categories of population) is a microcosm of the relations between governmental practitioners and the governed population or, in an older parlance, the state and civil society. This relation may be achieved via many means, including but not limited to media typifications and campaigning by groups in civil society. The character of these interactions is indicative and partially determinative of the overall degree of public legitimacy and consent given to the governmental enterprise.

Relations of social power in democratic societies are seldom so simple that a description of them in mechanical terms can count as an explanation as to their workings. In the democratic societies of the West, our understanding of issues relating to accountability and control is bound up with normative conceptions about the legitimate exercise of social, political, and economic power. Accountability is a cultural construct as much as a technique of government. It is not the simple imposition of a mechanistic set of auditing requirements, but rests rather on notions of what is right, just, fair, and proper. In short, it rests on shared cultural understandings about the legitimacy of governmental power and its mode of exercise. The literature on accountability has taught us that control over major social institutions, and especially those institutions that are responsible for social ordering through the mechanisms of criminal law enforcement, involves broad cultural traditions regarding the conduct of politics and the constitutional rules and conventions that apply in *particular* jurisdictions. For that reason, Philip Stenning cautioned students of governance that "comparative scholarship on the accountability of such agencies [i.e., criminal justice agencies] is bound to be misleading if it does not take the variability of these more general traditions of governance and accountability into account" (1995: 12). On this view it is both possible and necessary to compare and contrast the political traditions of, for example, the Netherlands and Belgium, in order to understand the relative effectiveness of different strategies and mechanisms that aim to achieve higher standards of democratic accountability in different jurisdictions (Sheptycki 1999). Broadly speaking, that has been the aim in much of the literature on police accountability.

Historically, modern systems of governance—including within them systems, mechanisms, and traditions of accountability—have been nested in a particular institutional form, that being the nation-state. Each such state has most often been thought of as a hermetically sealed holistic system. That assumption is what has made cross-national comparison both possible and plausible. In the contemporary period we are confronted with a host of institutions (e.g., the WTO, IMF, OECD, WIPO—the alphabet soup of transnational government) that operate at a level seemingly above that of nation-states and beyond their control while the actions of both sub-state and non-state actors transgress state boundaries.[7] Globalisation is the term used to describe this state of affairs, but it is an ill-understood word. It is an abstract analytical category that serves a wide variety of purposes simultaneously. Partly a category of fear, it is also a social science term used to describe supposedly worldwide social, cultural, political and, above all, economic changes. Frequently, it is averred that the processes of globalisation have greatly weakened the nation-state. This is especially so in the economic sphere because global financial flows seem to have largely escaped the capacity of states to control or direct them.

However, it is inescapable that states remain significant actors on the global stage. What has changed is that formally designated representatives of states now share that stage with many other actors. Some of these actors are non-state actors—some of whom can be relatively quite powerful, for example large multinational companies, religious organisations, and a variety of non-governmental organisations. Other actors on the global stage are in fact sub-state agents, that is, persons formally in the employ of particular states but who are not necessarily formally mandated to act internationally by the ministry or other governmental office responsible for foreign affairs (police agents are a good example of this). Then too, in the contemporary period, there are supranational entities and international organisations that participate in the action taking place on the global stage. "The politics of global governance," David Held and Anthony McGrew observe, "is thus significantly differentiated (...) [r]ather than a monolithic and unitary system, it is best understood as multidimensional; (...) [i]n addition to being multilayered and multidimensional, global governance is a multi-actor complex in which diverse agencies participate in the formulation and conduct of global public policy" (Held and McGrew 2002: 67). Importantly, in Held and McGrew's account the hegemony of "powerful states" (the OECD countries or members of the G8 and perhaps one or two others, but especially the United States) remains a key feature of the global system. However, that is not the same as saying that the dynamics of the present world order remain the same as they were fifty or even twenty years ago. The complex global system that they describe involves the transnational practices of state, sub-state and non-state actors. In other words, it is not a simple "balance of power system." The ability of a multitude of sub-state and non-state actors to act transnationally has altered the conditions of global relations. So, at the same time that the state-system has come to be buttressed and supported by transnational co-ordination and regulation, the divergent interests of corporate, national, technocratic, and cosmopolitan elites have been sutured together at the transnational level as well. The foreign policy choices of state actors are conditioned by the transnational activities of non-state, sub-state, and even supra-state agents in a way that was inconceivable in an earlier age. A *fortiori*, the domestic activities of sovereign state actors are profoundly affected by transnational interplay. The nation-state system has become the transnational-state-system.

The advent of the transnational-state-system has many consequences, but possibly the most profound has to do with our conceptions of democratic governance and accountability. In democratic countries not so long ago, it was possible to try to pursue or shift policy goals relating to the actions of governmental agencies by mobilising the citizenry. Within the confines of demarcated jurisdictions, major institutions of governance (such as criminal justice agencies) could, in theory if not wholly in practice, be held in check by demands for accountability. The Police Citizen Review Board is one example of this logic. In the contemporary period, when policing has superseded police, we may have Policing Boards and a "nodal" conception of the relations between security providers (Shearing 2001). But when we foreground the processes of transnationalisation in our thinking and consider the consequences that this has for the governability of governance, this localised approach seems a rather too limited strategy. This has partly to do with the global scale of the institutional relations in question, partly to do with the complexity of relations between the various actors involved and partly to do with the complex interplay between different policy areas. Configuring a system of democratic accountability for the transnational-state-system across all nodes and at every level is as theoretically challenging as it is practically difficult. The project of cosmopolitan democracy advocated by Held and McGrew, among others, is an attempt to discover the possibility of rendering the transnational-state-system democratically accountable. Scholars of policing and criminal justice agencies have contributed greatly to both the theory and practice of democratic governance. They have done so by looking at policing in particular (not to say parochial) jurisdictions, and the lessons drawn from comparative study have had a global impact. Thinking globally and focusing attention on the accountability of Interpol (a unique transnational policing organisation), therefore, is a useful further contribution to the literature on both policing accountability and global governance.

A DEVELOPMENTAL CHRONOLOGY OF INTERPOL

Historical context is important for understanding accountability issues. The history of Interpol is already quite long, and, at certain transitional moments, the story is complicated. In a short chapter such as this, it is very difficult to do justice to the complexities of this institutional history, so a simple chronology will have to suffice. The aim here is to give the reader a sense of the trajectory of development of Interpol up to the present in order to situate discussion of its accountability framework.

In the long list of international organisations, Interpol occupies a very unusual position. It lacks a treaty basis and yet, ultimately, it is funded with taxpayers' money. Over time, it has come to achieve legally recognised roles in transnational police and judicial co-operation and has acquired something like customary recognition in international law as an Intergovernmental Organisation (IGO). The idea for the organisation can be traced back to just prior to World War One, but it was not until that conflagration had passed that it was actually established as a working organisation. Much has been written about Interpol since then, but little is of scholarly value. The following account draws on the best of these contributions (Anderson 1992; Deflem 2000; Deflem 2002a, 2002b; Fooner 1989; Sheptycki 1995).[8]

Prognostications prior to the Great War about the need for an international congress of criminal police aside, the historical genesis of Interpol came in 1923. At that time, the head of the Austrian state police, Dr. Johan Schober, sought to reconstitute the influence and reach of the Austrian police beyond the vestigial rump of the Austro-Hungarian Empire established by the Treaty of Saint-Germain.[9] From those early days, and to the present, the organisation has essentially been a network of police officials facilitating police-to-police contact across international boundaries.

One way to view the subsequent development of Interpol during the 20th century is that it was a transnational organisational entity that was "captured" by certain specific states' interests and that the really significant signposts of its chronology are moments when the captive status was transferred. It seems fairly clear that, in the early period, the organisation acted partly, if not solely, as an arm of the Austrian State police. To paraphrase Anderson, the old habits of the Habsburg police of maintaining international contact to keep track of political radicals and subversives probably constituted the "hidden motives" behind Schober's moves (Anderson 1989). Upon the capture of Vienna in 1938 the organisation entered its period of "nazification" (Deflem 2002a, 2002b). From the 1940s until 1986, Interpol was under almost total French influence (Fooner 1989). In 1986, the period of "Anglo-American hegemony" commenced (Bresler 1992). However, the pure simplicity of the "pass the baton" history of Interpol lost some of its grounds for plausibility during the latter years of the century.

Partly because of the agency's non-operability with regard to domestic European terrorism, it was during the 1970s that a host of other transnational police networks were developed in the region. The police working group on terrorism (PWGOT), the TREVI system and latter Schengen and Europol all sprang up on Europe's fertile ground. Thus, when in 1986 French suzerainty over the organisation was supplanted by a new Anglo-American hegemony, Europe was a field crowded with transnational policing agents. It was during the latter half of the 1980s that Interpol was given a radical overhaul of its information and communications systems, moving directly from communication by Morse code to communication by email "almost overnight" (Sheptycki 1995). For most of its institutional history, Interpol had been primarily a European-based police network, but by the dawn of the 21st century its centrality in that region had been displaced. The primacy it lost in Europe was partly compensated for by its expanded presence in other regions, most notably in the Caribbean. However, the fantastic growth in transnational policing, and especially the internationalisation of American police power, has meant that, even globally, Interpol has no monopoly on the many tasks that require cross-border police co-operation.[10]

In the contemporary period, Interpol functions as part of the complex web of global policing. It facilitates the transnational police mission by providing channels of communication between police agencies in its 181 member countries. Interpol itself has no operational role. The man from Interpol never arrested anyone (Sheptycki 1995). Having no operational capacity, it cannot initiate investigations or undertake judicial enquiries on its own behalf. Interpol's primary role is facilitating the exchange of messages—for example requests for information about a given person's criminal history or requests that enquiries be undertaken—between police and judicial authorities of the member countries. The organisation uses a system of coloured "notices" to facilitate police-to-police communication. Red notices amount to a worldwide diffusion of national arrest warrants and could therefore be viewed as a semi-official international arrest warrant. Blue notices request information on named persons. Green notices circulate information on suspected criminals and their activities. Yellow notices relate to missing persons, and black notices relate to unidentified dead bodies. Additionally, there is the circulation of information about stolen goods and other materials and things of interest, and about the *modus operandi* of criminals.

From the mid-1980s onwards, Interpol developed and maintained large electronic databanks based on information created by these exchanges. Interpol has begun to mine this accumulated data for the purposes of crime analysis, but there is no way to know with precision what this has resulted in. It cultivates a low public profile with respect to its operation, but claims to have a high impact. Occasionally, stories emerge in the press which indicate that Interpol has played a role in a police operation, but it is seldom clear from the press accounts precisely what Interpol contributed.[11] Interpol is also active in the organisation of conferences on a multitude of criminal matters, including the sexual exploitation of children, counterfeiting, drug markets, money laundering, and terrorism. Thus, although there are many participants in transnational policing, Interpol is in a powerful position to shape its contours, both symbolically and practically. The network of policing communications of which it is a part is productive of information (data) which practically shapes expectations of what policing consists ... [of], from the local to the transnational level. The Interpol *marque*, along with the symbols of a handful of other policing-type agencies, is recognised worldwide, and therefore the image of the policing mission it projects has important consequences for the nature of policing globally. Interpol's communications nodes are an important part of the global policing network. As such it plays an important role, not only in helping to orchestrate policing operations but also in the symbolic representation of policing (both globally and locally).

THE LEGAL ACCOUNTABILITY OF INTERPOL

To whom or what is Interpol externally accountable? It has been often assumed that Interpol is an Intergovernmental Organisation (IGO), but this is not fully accurate.[12] IGO status is achieved with respect of the United Nations. Thus, according to the UN Economic and Social Council, "[e]very international organization which is not created by means of intergovernmental agreements shall be considered as a non-governmental organization" (Economic and Social Council 1950). One view of the system of global governance would place the United Nations at its centre with three concentric rings wrapped around it (Held and McGrew 2002).[13] At the centre of this model are the core bodies of the UN, including the Security Council, ECOSOC, the International Court of Justice, the Office of the Secretary General, and the General Assembly. In the first concentric ring are the UN programs themselves. Examples of these that would be of more that tangential interest to scholars of criminal justice agencies would include the United Nations Drug Control Program (UNDCP), the UN High Commissioner for Refugees (UNHCR), and the Office of the High Commissioner for Human Rights (OHCHR). There are, of course, many others in different policy domains, but, obviously, Interpol does not belong among this class of agencies. In the second concentric ring are specialised agencies as defined by Article 57 of the United Nations Charter. According to the Charter, such agencies are "established by intergovernmental agreement, and having wide international responsibilities, as defined in their basic instruments (...) [they] shall be brought into relationship with the United Nations (...)" (Held and McGrew 2002: 61). It is this unequivocal status as an intergovernmental organisation (IGO) that has been erroneously attributed to Interpol.[14]

Interpol was not initially constituted by treaty or any other similar legal agreement. On this point it is interesting to note that, in 1977, the MP for Southampton (Brian Gould, Labour) asked the United Kingdom Home Office by way of a written question "whether there is any formal signed agreement under which the United Kingdom is a member of Interpol." The reply was that "Membership of the International Criminal Police Organisation (Interpol) is not obtained by an intergovernmental treaty or agreement. The question of a formal signed agreement by the United Kingdom does not therefore arise" (U.K. House of Commons 1977). In point of fact, precisely who or what is a member of the organisation is a somewhat ambiguous matter. The precise wording of Article 4 of the Interpol Constitution states that "[a]ny country may delegate as a Member to the Organisation any official police body whose functions come within the framework of activities of the Organisation." Further, "[t]he request for membership shall be submitted to the Secretary General by the appropriate governmental authority."[15] The use of the word "country" and not "state" should give pause for consideration, and the clear implication that it is police agencies and not "countries" that constitute the membership can be interpreted as an attempt to divorce the organisation from national and international politics. Ultimately then, it is the RCMP that is a member of Interpol and not the government of Canada. This fact seems to place Interpol in the third ring, the zone inhabited by organisations described as non-profit citizen's voluntary organisations or non-governmental organisations (NGOs).[16] Examples of other agencies that inhabit this space include Greenpeace and the International Olympic Committee, neither of which are formally externally accountable to any other institution.

The matter might be deemed to rest there. However, during the second half of the 20th century, Interpol gradually acquired customary status as an IGO. The first step on this path took place in 1947 when the agency applied to ECOSOC for recognition as an NGO. This was turned down initially because UN officials could not understand how an organisation of police officials (who are usually thought of as an essential arm of the state and firmly integrated into states' administrations) could be considered nongovernmental. Later that year status as an NGO was granted. However, this was always awkward not only because the agents of the organisation were police officials but also since the organisation very quickly gained consultancy status as part of the UN drug control strategy (Anderson 1989). The position of Interpol as an NGO was reviewed in 1954 and again in 1969 but it was not until 1971 that any change was made. It was at this time, and after what Fenton Bresler (1992) described as some "de Gaulle-like posturing" by the then Interpol Secretary General Jean Népote, that a new "special relationship" was constituted between the UN and Interpol. This was done by means of a Special Arrangement in which Interpol would, under certain circumstances, be treated *as if* it were an intergovernmental organisation (Economic and Social Council 1971). This resolution approved co-operation between the two organisations for the purposes of the prevention and repression of commonly recognised crimes. It allowed for the exchange of information, documentation, observers at meetings and some collaboration. In a legal opinion written on behalf of the organisation concerning the legal problems of Interpol's constitution, the distinguished international lawyer Paul Reuter regarded this resolution as, in effect, a treaty between the two organisations.[17] André Bossard, who followed Népote in the office of Interpol Secretary General, was later to say that "[i]t is true that this arrangement did not officially modify Interpol's status, but it did constitute recognition of the fact that Interpol differed from the other non-governmental organisations having consultative status with ECOSOC" (Yalleix 1984). Since Interpol had over this period attained recognition from other organisations active in the transnational sphere (for example, the Customs Co-operation Council and the International Civil Aviation Organisation), any ambivalence due to its lack of a treaty basis was gradually disregarded. Interpol accrued something like customary status as an IGO.

Because it lacks an unambiguous and formal treaty basis, the historically somewhat awkward position of Interpol vis-à-vis the UN was also manifest in its relation to individual sovereign states. Indeed, until Interpol signed its first Headquarters Agreement with the government of France in 1972, the organisation had not been officially recognised by the government of the country in which its headquarters had been based for the previous 25 years. The 1972 agreement endowed the organisation with a recognised legal status in France, which was later enhanced by the second Headquarters Agreement in 1982. In many ways the 1982 Headquarters Agreement consolidated the organisation (or at least its headquarters) as one that was largely free from external accountability to interested states or, by way of private court action, to private individuals. The legal immunities granted in the 1982 agreement are extensive. Personnel working for the organisation have effective full diplomatic immunity—even after they have ceased to work for the organisation—as does the organisation itself (Anderson 1989; Fooner 1989). Historically, financial accounts were kept secret, and it was not until 1990 that Interpol changed its practice in this regard.[18]

During this same period, equally important developments were taking place in the United States. There, between 1978 and 1981, four federal court cases mounted by private parties fundamentally challenged Interpol's working relationship with US law enforcement agencies. The basis of these legal challenges was that Interpol was a kind of world police agency and that US co-operation with it, insofar as it involved law enforcement actions with respect to US citizens, was an infringement of the sovereign status of the US Constitution. As Anderson (1989) put it, "this is mythology which appeals to imaginations prone to conspiracy theories" but the court cases nevertheless represented a serious threat to US participation in Interpol. On June 16, 1983, US President Ronald Reagan signed Executive Order 12425 designating Interpol "a public international organization entitled to enjoy the privileges, exemptions, and immunities of the International Organizations Immunities Act" (Fooner 1989: 184). Of course, such immunity can be withdrawn. However, the immunities conferred by Executive Order 12425 were one more way in which the formal ties of external accountability were loosened.

Regarding the organisation's external accountability, the real acid test concerned data protection and criminal intelligence exchange. In most contemporary police organisations, information flow is the lifeblood, and so it is with Interpol. However, "it was not until 1982 that information dissemination became subject to rules and supervision originating outside of the organization" (Fooner 1989: 77). The impetus for this came after the passage of new data protection legislation in France in 1978, legislation that was intended to protect individuals from abuse of privacy and civil rights and to prohibit unwarranted disclosure of personal information. This law would have imposed the scrutiny of the French government on Interpol's use and exchange of information and was viewed by many inside the organisation as antithetical to its operations. Eventually, a compromise was devised and a supervisory board was constituted by an exchange of letters included in an appendix to the 1982 Headquarters Agreement. The board thus created is comprised of five members, three of whom are selected because of expertise in data protection issues. Of these three, one is appointed by the French government and one by Interpol, and these two choose the third who serves as the Chair of the Supervisory Board. The fourth member is from Interpol's Executive Committee and the fifth is selected by the Chair from a list of five data protection/computer security experts submitted by Interpol. Initially, the French government chose the then head of the French data protection agency the *Commission nationale de l'informatique et des libertés* (CNIL). What cannot escape notice is that only one member of the board is not directly appointed by Interpol or chosen from a list pre-selected by that organisation. Malcolm Anderson (1989: 66) observed that "both in the composition of the Board and its terms of reference, the compromise seemed to lean towards the Interpol rather than the French government's position." In other words, supervision of Interpol's use and transfer of criminal intelligence remains largely a matter for its own officials, and the supervisory board is only superficially a mechanism of external accountability. Some European states continue to find the data protection measures adopted by Interpol to be wanting, and scholars generally recognise that "the issue of data protection is likely to be a continuing problem which can only be definitively settled by formal treaty provisions" (Anderson et al. 1995: 52).[19]

In terms of external accountability, then, the legal position of Interpol is one which seems to grant it a considerable degree of latitude, and hence little incentive to adopt the techniques of account-ability in any routinised sense. Interpol's 1956 Constitution, supplemented by some subsequent resolutions of the annual General Assembly, sets out the organisation's internal lines of accountability. The General Assembly is the organisation's controlling body. It admits new members and may sanction existing members if they fail to comply with the rules set out in the organisation's statutes, although this is extremely rare. The General Assembly elects the Executive Committee, which consists of thirteen members: a president, three vice-presidents, and nine delegates. This committee draws up the agenda for the General Assembly, plans Interpol's activities, and oversees the work of the Secretariat-General. The latter is responsible for daily management and is not formally held to account by any government of any member state. This suggests that the Secretary General of Interpol is independent, "rather like the UN Secretary General" (Anderson et al. 1995: 51).[20] Constitutionally, then, Interpol functions as an autonomous transnational organisation subject only to its own internal accountability regime.

THE PRACTICAL ACCOUNTABILITY OF INTERPOL

There is a long-standing debate in socio-legal scholarship regarding the relationship between legal frameworks, rules, and prescriptive norms for accountability systems, on the one hand, and the practical working relationships of accountability on the other. Legal scholars tend to assume that clarification of legal prescriptions, or the imposition of rules, will have the effect of tightening accountability structures. Social scientists tend to focus on practical working relationships as the embodiment of real accountability (Stenning 1995). In the previous section, the formal legal framework for the accountability of Interpol was discussed. It was shown that, by virtue of its curious status in international law, Interpol seems largely insulated from the external accountability requirements of sovereign states. Because of its peculiar transnational character, it is certainly not externally accountable in any sense to the global civil society whose interests it putatively aims to serve.

This section examines the way that the Interpol system functions. It will be seen that, in spite of the loose accountability framework that Interpol is wrapped in transnationally, its day-to-day working remains subject to national sovereignty claims. While Interpol's General Assembly and General Secretariat operate in ways that seem virtually unfettered by the external accountability requirements, National Central Bureaus (NCBs) cannot be obliged to comply with any directive issued centrally by the organisation and remain effectively bound by the operational context of the policing establishment in the host country. That is to say, although the General Assembly and the General Secretariat are formally sovereign in all matters affecting the organisation, a basic reality of Interpol's workings is that national sovereignty prevails (Fooner 1989).

The practical day-to-day functioning of Interpol takes place through the system of National Central Bureaus (NCBs). It is the bureaus that are the workhorses of Interpol. Each participating country establishes its own NCB, which is supposed to facilitate communications between police agents in the host country and police agencies elsewhere. It is expected that the NCB in each country should receive formal appointment by its respective government and that this will usually be made by either the executive or legislative authority. NCBs facilitate enquiries on behalf of requesting member police agencies. Each Interpol NCB operates as an independent unit within the structure of Interpol. No NCB is bound by treaty or international convention to send information to other NCBs, or to act on their behalf. Neither are they required to communicate with Interpol Headquarters in Lyon or to act on its behalf. The workings of individual NCBs, and the interactions between them, ultimately define the operations of the Interpol system. These relationships are essentially about the international trade in "police information," which is broadly defined in Interpol's Rules on International Police Co-operation (the currently operating version of which came into force in 1984) as pertaining to "ordinary law crimes." Under these operating rules, all information in the Interpol network is declared to be subject to the internal controls of the organisation and is not subject to the legislation of any nation. However, nominally, individual member police agencies do retain control over the usage of information put into the Interpol system and can withdraw information from the Interpol archives (Bresler 1992).[21]

There are wide differences in the functional capacity of different NCBs. Although the organisation itself is *de jure* mandated by its charter instruments to facilitate co-operation between member police agencies, any country's *de facto* co-operation is dependent on the way its own police authority is constituted, distributed and directed. Few countries have unified police structures. The policing division of labour in any given country—and the rivalries that this may foster—has important consequences for how individual NCBs fit into the transnational police mission. The configuration of the police sector within a specific jurisdiction and the priorities set thereby affect the operability of Interpol within a specific jurisdiction and its interoperability with partner police agencies abroad. Moreover, co-operation between Interpol members is also conditioned by the general level of cordiality between governments.

To illustrate, Michael Fooner explained in 1989 how the American NCB developed from something close to an institutional non-entity in the early 1970s to the largest and most financially well endowed in the Interpol network by the end of the 1980s. This came during a period when the American government was amplifying its own international policing capacity.[22] It also came during the same period that the National Law Enforcement Telecommunications System (NLETS)—facilitating information exchange between the roughly 20,000 law enforcement agencies operating within the United States—had its greatest growth spurt.[23] In the United States, state and local law enforcement agencies can contact each other and the Washington NCB through the NLETS. It is through the NLETS that local US police agencies request investigative assistance from Interpol members. Thus, in 1990, an interface between the NLETS system and the Canadian Police Information Centre (CPIC) went fully operational, thereby enabling police patrol officers in either country access to their respective national criminal databases on a 24-hour basis (Sheptycki 1998). Enquiry response times using this interface are said to range between three and five minutes. Information exchanged includes driver vehicle license details, criminal records, sex offenders registers, and much else. The need to enhance the "interoperability" of policing intelligence and information systems on a worldwide basis was a key theme in a speech given by RCMP Commissioner Giuliano Zaccardelli to the 71st Interpol General Assembly in October 2002.[24] But the speech also acknowledged, albeit in an oblique manner, that the public was not well informed about the steps being taken: "in our culture that is traditionally secretive, public involvement is a major challenge for all of us." While Zaccardelli suggested that such secrecy was not optimal in terms of police legitimacy, he had no answer for his own question: "How do we keep citizens informed without compromising national security or the rights of our citizens?" Zaccardelli's rhetorical question is symptomatic of the lack of transparency that has characterised the transnationalisation of policing intelligence and information systems.

Further, according to Fooner, by the last decade of the 20th century not only was the Washington NCB especially well-manned and financially supported, it had significantly enlarged its transnational capacity by establishing and maintaining a sub-bureau in San Juan, Puerto Rico. Fooner reported that "upon creation of the San Juan sub-bureau, the United Nations agreed to finance an Interpol telecommunications system in the Caribbean/Central American region, through the fund provided for drug abuse control" (Fooner 1989: 123–24). This project was used to create a police communications network that spanned the Caribbean basin. It was, moreover, an important element of the substantially expanded international presence of US law enforcement in the region. In the NAFTA region and the Caribbean, then, transnational policing activity may be undertaken under the auspices of Interpol, but it is substantially underwritten by the political will of participating states, and, in the contemporary period, especially that of the United States.[25]

Interpol NCBs in the countries of Western Europe are similarly technically sophisticated. These operate in close proximity to other transnational police communications nodes (specifically those of the Schengen Information System). Then too, Interpol operates alongside Europol and within the context of complex formal and informal liaison officer networks (which include police agents and personnel from other policing-type agencies including customs, immigration and counter terrorism). It is not always easy to empirically disentangle the different routes of bi-lateral and multi-lateral transnational police communications.[26] Long-standing doubts regarding the security of Interpol communications channels and remarks about its inefficiency have tended to ensure that transnational police work within the European sphere has been undertaken via these other networks. This is especially so with regard to counter-terrorism. According to the London Metropolitan Police Special Branch, "Interpol staff are not experienced in affording the proper protection to classified material, do not possess the requisite security clearances, and the politics and motives are, to say the least, questionable in this context."[27] Interpol channels are notoriously slow, and, consequently, transnational policing in the European region is more likely to make use of the other communications routes (Benyon et al. 1993; Sheptycki 2002). The sheer complexity of transnational policing networks in Europe means that the accountability of pan-European policing is by no means clear (den Boer 2002). The sub-text to the establishment of Europol in the early 1990s is partly about the lack of accountability and control that various European governments had over police co-operation in the Euro-region. Thus, observing that no international oversight mechanism exists over Interpol, that it is accountable to no one, and that there is no representative structure for governance of the management and operations of Interpol, Cyrille Fijnaut explained that Interpol was not—and could not be—given a European mandate in response to organised crime or terrorism (Fijnaut 1993). Then, too, problems of administrative inefficiency have historically been widely expressed by practitioners. Thus, in the European context, Interpol suffered from (and continues to suffer from) lack of support from both its paymasters and its customers.

Looking further afield, it is reasonably clear that the NCBs operating in most of Africa, the Middle East, and many other parts of the developing world operate at a level far below the technical sophistication of those in Europe and North America. Thus, although the organisation officially had 181 members in 2000, only about 50 per cent of those had access to Internet-based communications (Interpol 2000, 2001). The functional capacity of individual NCBs is dependent on several interrelated factors: financial resources, their placement within the national structure of a specific country's policing system, the cordiality of relations between specific countries, and the nature of proximate allied communications nodes within the national and transnational network of police communications. As the history of the NCB system up to the present well illustrates, when the political will is lacking for an NCB to function within a specific national context (or with respect to specific issues), it can be institutionally side-lined, financially under-funded, or otherwise derogated, so that its practical workings are stunted. Conversely, it is by well situating their NCBs within both the national and transnational policing architecture that participating countries gain influence over the workings of the organisation. The practical accountability of the Interpol network is grounded in the technicalities and functioning of its communications infrastructure. The extent to which particular member countries develop their own international presence and maintain their own national central bureaus for linking into the transnational network that is Interpol determines, in large measure, their practical ability both to participate in the organisation and to hold it to account. In certain practical respects, then, Interpol is beholden to states' interests. It is therefore unsurprising to find that there remain clear political differences regarding at least some of the work carried out through Interpol channels.

THE POLITICS OF ACCOUNTABILITY IN INTERPOL

The current Constitution of Interpol was laid down and adopted in 1956. Subsequently, there were concerted efforts to revise the document, beginning in 1986, but these were abandoned in 1993 because of significant differences of opinion among the Members. The original 1956 constitution was drafted in both English and French, which has created some problems of interpretation.[28] In terms of the politics of accountability for Interpol, perhaps the most important of the articles are those which stipulate the parameters of its mission. Article 2 states the aims of the organisation:

> A) to ensure and promote the widest possible mutual assistance between all criminal police authorities within the limits of the laws existing in the different countries and in the spirit of the Universal Declaration of Human Rights;
> B) to establish and develop all institutions likely to contribute effectively to the prevention and suppression of ordinary law crimes.

The concept of "ordinary law crime" is important, but its meaning is by no means clear cut. In French, the term is *"criminalité de droit commun,"* but the term is not particularly common parlance in either language. The focus on "ordinary law crime" is intended to bracket off those sorts of illegalities that are "political" in nature. This point is further emphasised in Article 3, which stipulates that "it is strictly forbidden for the Organisation to undertake any intervention or activities of a political, military, religious or racial character."

Again, there are differences between the French and English versions. The French version of Article 3 states, "Toute activité ou intervention dans des questions ou affaires présentant un caractère politique, militaire, religieux ou racial est rigoureusement interdite à l'Organisation."

The difference between the English and French versions is significant, because the political and otherwise nature do not relate to the same thing. In the English version, it relates to activities of the organisation itself, which are forbidden if and when they acquire these characteristics. In the French version, it is the matters which the organisation might be called on to intervene in which are the object. The difference of meaning is a source of uncertainty that is unhelpful in enunciating the mission of Interpol. In practice, it is the French version which seems to be operative. Debates over the meaning of "political crime" and what can be loaded into the meaning of "ordinary law crime" have shaped the politics of accountability within Interpol in important ways during the last half of the 20th century. The former term is evocative of concerns about infringement of states' sovereignty. The latter is reflective of a sub-culturally defined law enforcement mission.

There are many chapters in the history of the debates surrounding the "political crime" concept. Three instances have been selected for brief mention here because they well illustrate what has been considered to be at stake. The first of these examples concerns the hijacking of a Czechoslovak plane in March 1950. The Czechoslovak government, then under communist rule, requested that the hijackers be repatriated from whence they had sought refuge, which happened to be an American airbase in West Germany. The Czechoslovakian NCB issued red notices and, in so doing, argued that the offences of kidnapping and hijacking were "ordinary law crimes." Indignant that the organisation should be used to further the ends of a communist government, J. Edgar Hoover opined that the offence was "political" in the sense laid down in the Interpol constitution. Hoover's view was not shared by the Interpol General Secretariat, and the red notices were issued. The red notices proved to be a dead letter and extradition never happened. Nevertheless, Hoover severed FBI relations with Interpol, citing this incident as one of the principal reasons for doing so.[29] The second example concerns the refusal of a request made by the Cuban NCB to the General Secretariat in 1959 to issue a red notice pertaining to senior police officers of the Batista regime that formerly ruled Cuba. In arguing the case, the head of the Cuban NCB stated that Batista's police, who had been notorious for their violence and corruption, were "really thieves and criminals pretending to be police" and that they were "offenders against ordinary criminal law" (Breslar 1992: 127). Various members of the Secretariat spoke out in a General Assembly arguing that the request had "a political motive," and a red notice was never issued. The third example concerns the attack by Black September at the Munich Olympics on September 5th, 1972. To most observers at the time, this was clearly a terrorist attack, but the Interpol Secretariat refused to involve the organisation in the matter on the grounds that terrorism is politically motivated and therefore, under Article 3, could not properly be considered part of the organisation's mission.[30]

It can be seen from the above examples that the distinction between what might be considered an "ordinary law crime" and a "political crime" has been contested when the circumstances impinge on matters of perceived national interest, when the political stakes seem especially high, or when the political rhetoric is especially heated. In the context of the politics of Interpol's accountability framework, attempts to smooth over any contradictions or tensions that arise rest on the assumption that limiting the scope of Interpol's mission to "ordinary law crimes" is an essential aspect of its political neutrality. Subsequent jurisprudence pertaining to the "political crime" category turned on the notion of "preponderance" (initially formulated in 1951) and the "doctrine of the conflict area" (formulated in the mid-1980s). It has also been informed by international developments in extradition law, which has also taken account of the concept of "political offence."

To take the latter point first: the concept of "political offence" had a stubborn presence in extradition law from the late eighteenth century onwards. Early on in the development of liberal democracy, it became the practice to exclude offences of a political nature when considering the extradition of fugitive offenders. Thus, with regard to "common crimes" such as murder or arson, extradition could be refused if it established that the offence was of a "political character." This exception was thought necessary for a number of reasons, but two stand out. The first was that it removed from adjudication by the courts matters which concern diplomatic relations and foreign policy—thus eliminating, or at least limiting, the possibility of warfare by judicial means. The second was that the political offence exception created the possibility of providing sanctuary to the victims of oppressive laws. It has been explained that liberal democratic theory contains within it "the notion that individuals have the right to engage in revolutionary political activity in pursuit of liberty" (Abraham Soafer, Legal Advisor to the US Department of State, quoted in Anderson et al. 1995: 227) Given this, democracies have been loath to surrender to foreign despots persons exercising the right to resistance and protest.

This position was expressed in paragraph 1 of the 1957 European Convention on Extradition, which states that "extradition shall not be granted if the offence in respect of which it is requested is regarded by the requested party as a political offence or as an offence connected with a political offence." But the term "political offence" was not defined in the text; instead, this determination was left to the requested party to decide on a case-by-case basis, a reflection of near universal practice. Moreover, Article 3(2) of the Convention provided that extradition "shall be refused if the requested party has substantial grounds for believing that a request for extradition for an ordinary criminal offence has been made for the purpose of prosecuting or punishing a person on account of his race, religion, nationality, or political opinion, or that that person's position may be prejudiced for any of these reasons." Chapter I of the Second Additional Protocol (1978) restricted the political offence exception, so that crimes against humanity and war crimes were not considered under it, but this did not immediately gain wide acceptance. The European Convention on the Suppression of Terrorism seemed initially to augur a significant change to the political offence exception since it defined as non-political a list of specified offences "of the type used by violent terrorists." However, Article 13 of the Convention provided a series of exceptions, including the political offence exception—which continued to feature in extradition law in Europe—even in cases of terrorism. As the end of the millennium approached, it seemed that this state of play would be maintained. But all of this was swept aside in the aftermath of 9-11 with the advent of the European Arrest Warrant, which effectively abolished the political offence exception in the territory of the European Union and, quite possibly, globally.[31]

The stunning events of September 11, 2001 changed the nature of extradition law forever, but it is still too early to say precisely how that will affect the politics of accountability in Interpol. It may therefore be instructive to look to the changing interpretative understanding of Articles 2 and 3 of Interpol's constitution over this period. Following the hijacking of the Czech airliner in 1951, the Interpol General Assembly adopted Resolution AGN/20/RES/11. This established the principle of predominance and stated that no request should be made in connection with offences of a predominantly political, racial, or religious character even if the facts amount to an offence against ordinary criminal law in the requesting country. The adoption of the predominance theory seemed to confirm the principle of total non-intervention in political cases, as evidenced by Interpol's non-action in the wake of the Munich attacks. The significant change came in 1984. By this time, the second Headquarters Agreement with the government of France had been signed, and the customary status of Interpol as an independent IGO was sufficiently well established such that the organisation could successfully re-articulate its position with regard to the numerous international conventions on terrorism.

The re-articulation came in the form of Resolutions AGN/53/RES/6 and AGN/53/RES/7 the *raison d'être* of which was to provide the possibility to intervene in matters previously barred under Article 3. Interpol Resolution AGN/53/RES/6 used the term "terrorism" for the first time and Resolution AGN/53/RES/7 confirmed the principle of predominance set out in the 1951 resolution; indeed it went even further by giving a list of offences which were political in nature. Where the 1984 resolutions really broke new ground was with the "doctrine of the conflict area." Henceforth, in determining the ordinary-law predominance of a case, the existence or otherwise of links between the offenders' aims and their victims would be taken into account. This was to be done with reference to the location of the crime, the status of the victims, and the seriousness of the offence. The location of a terrorist act became the preponderant consideration among these three criteria. This meant that the ban on co-operation could be lifted when the acts were committed outside the "conflict area." Offences committed by persons with definite political motives but outside the territory where the conflict pertains, or when the offences committed had no direct connection with the political life of the offender's country, could not be brought under the scope of Article 3.

With the doctrine of the conflict area, the issue of national sovereignty was sidestepped. As Raymond Kendal, Interpol Secretary General from 1985 to 1999, explained it "what goes on in a particular conflict area would not be of interest to us for international police co-operation while it remains in that conflict area. On the other hand, if a Jordanian comes to Paris and shoots the Israeli Ambassador, then it does become our concern because it is outside of the strict conflict area" (Bresler 1992: 184). In a globalising world, where crime and terrorism had gone transnational, Interpol seemed ready to intervene in political crimes defined as terrorism. Astute observers might well have asked questions about how the changing doctrine might affect other forms of transnational crime, such as crimes against the environment—the dumping of hazardous or toxic waste on the high seas for example—which also transcend the boundaries of particular jurisdictions. And yet, the issue of national sovereignty remained. Among the principles articulated in AGN/53/RES/7 and AGN/53/RES/7 it was stated that

> Although Member states have the inherent right as sovereign nations to determine the political character of an offence, their rights do not impede the Organization from ensuring that the provisions of its constitution are respected. Similarly, the Organization's right to interpret its constitution is not to be construed as limiting the Member's ability to reach a contrary decision with respect to the political character of an offence.

The continuing and underlying presence of the doctrine of national sovereignty meant that member countries retained the right to decide whether and how they would make use of Interpol's infrastructure when acts of terrorism (or other crimes defined as "political") are concerned. It also meant that they were free to use any other channels available to them in the event that political considerations meant that the organisation refused to process their requests. The coincidence of the doctrine of the conflict area alongside the principle of national sovereignty was an attempt to create a legal balance by which the organisation could maintain the appearance of political neutrality. This balance, and the appearance of neutrality it projects, obscures a paradox. In principle political power (i.e., policing power) should only be exercised within the limits of the law—including international law—but ultimately it has to be admitted that there are contingencies when the exercise of such power has escaped legal purview.

DISCUSSION AND CONCLUSION

This chapter has set out to extend the standard paradigm regarding the accountability of police and policing by giving consideration to the accountability of Interpol. It was argued that this very special case could hold general lessons for understanding the character of the "global system." Understanding the curious nature of Interpol's accountability framework offers general lessons about a world where transnational actors and forces cut across the boundaries of national communities in diverse ways and where questions about who is accountable to whom, and on what basis, are not easy to answer. Regional and global interaction networks of policing agents are developing and strengthening, and they have variable and multiple impacts across different countries. This is not to say that national sovereignty has been subverted. Rather, sovereignty has been transformed. It has been displaced as an illimitable, indivisible, and exclusive form of public power—as, for example, exhibited by the traditional image and capacities of the "public police"—and embedded in a system of multiple, overlapping networks of policing that extend from the parochial domain to the transnational.

What the discrete history of Interpol reveals is a story of sub-state actors being elevated to the level of transnational actors. Manned by self-styled "international civil servants" (Bresler

1992: 189–190) who, in accountability terms, are routinely only loosely bound by the particular interests of the major players in the transnational-state-system and cloaked by the stereo-typifications of the sub-culturally defined nature of the law enforcement mission, Interpol is a policing brand-name with worldwide recognition, even if its day-to-day operations remain a mystery to most people. Although admittedly it is difficult to measure precisely, the image of the transnational policing mission that has been constructed around the Interpol *marque* has consequences for policing everywhere. For this reason, if for no other, we would want to ensure that Interpol is accountable to the global commonweal.

The Interpol network exists within a broader web of policing communications. Transnational policing is played out in conditions that resemble a global State of Nature where the G8 Leviathans walk amidst stout competition. Such a state of affairs can, all too easily, give rise to a sense of fatalism. If the more powerful geo-political forces are not to settle these pressing matters with reference to their own objectives and by virtue of their own power, then existing structures of accountability for transnational policing need to be reconsidered, The developing "nodal conception of governance" can be stretched to consider how transnational policing agents may be brought to account via democratic means. But we are still a long way off cosmopolitan democracy. What ever else an examination of accountability for Interpol teaches us, it is that multi-level nodal governance can be exceedingly undemocratic.

Contemporary transformations in policing and security are partly underwritten by the development of new, transnational, developments in insecurity. Policing is becoming transnationalised, and so we need to think about transnational accountability. In the absence of a court with universal jurisdiction over all transnational policing work, and in the absence of an executive power with responsibility for this kind of security function globally, there remains much work, both theoretical and practical, to be done. As with transnational governance generally, calling for the development of a democratic framework of accountability for Interpol can hardly be expected to provide an instant solution. However, to label this call as utopian is to cleave to a cynical obsession with brute power. Democratic accountability for transnational policing sounds naïve, but the alternative is simply depressing.

NOTES

[1] The standard paradigm for the accountability of police and other criminal justice agencies is articulated in a number of excellent books, see in particular Goldsmith (1991), Goldsmith and Lewis (2000), Newburn and Jones (1997), and Stenning (1995).

[2] See also Sheptycki (1995) for a discussion of the "marketisation" of security and policing.

[3] Key studies here include Anderson (1995), Den Boer (2002), Nadelmann (1993), and Sheptycki (2000, 2002).

[4] Some interesting perspectives on globalisation and governance can be found in a collection of essays edited by Ericson and Stehr (2000). See also Held (1995) and Held and McGrew (2002). Gessner and Budak (1998) provide a wide-ranging collection of essays on the changing nature of legality under conditions of globalisation. The report of the Commission on

Global Governance (1995) offers considered proposals to promote the security of peoples worldwide, equitably manage the global economy, and strengthen the Rule of Law globally.

[5] Mark (2000) provides a strong theoretical disquisition regarding constitutional democracy under conditions of globalisation. The concept of the "transnational-state-system" is discussed with regard to policing in Sheptycki (1997).

[6] Interpol's global stature invites comparison with its regional competitor Europol. The relationship will be touched upon at relevant points throughout the paper.

[7] See Sheptycki (2003), especially the introduction. See also Sheptycki (2002).

[8] As good as this work is, none of it can claim to illuminate in any detail how Interpol actually functions on a day-to-day basis. Unlike most of the important democratic police agencies in the West, no researcher has ever actually studied its working methods at first hand. This is a call for the kind of field study perhaps best exemplified by the pioneering work of Michael Banton and William Westley. Indeed, it is possible to argue that the first step on the road to democratic accountability for Interpol would be just the sort of research access that Banton and Westley obtained in their studies of municipal police departments in the United Kingdom and the United States almost forty years ago. See Banton (1964) and Westley (1970).

[9] The Treaty of Versailles is often, but erroneously, said to be the treaty that ended the First World War, but, in truth, it is only the treaty that consolidated peace between Germany and the Allies. The treaty that set the peace terms between the Allies and Austro-Hungary was the lesser-known Treaty of Saint-Germain (Hobsbawm 1995).

[10] On the internationalisation of US law enforcement, see Nadelmann (1993). As Fooner (1989: 117) explains, when it comes to international police work, agencies often have recourse to other-than-Interpol channels. Thus US federal agencies "have their own external networks of agents: the FBI has legal attachés resident in a number of foreign embassies, the Drug Enforcement Administration, the Secret Service and other departments have agents assigned to foreign locations and reporting to their own departmental chiefs in Washington." As it is with the USA, so it is with other countries that are active in transnational police co-operation.

[11] For example, in 2002, a member of the Greek terrorist group November 17 was apprehended after an accidental explosion. This turned out to be the first step in bringing to an end an almost 30-year-long history of terrorism which claimed the lives of many people, including the CIA station chief in Athens (in 1975) and a British Brigadier General who was a military attaché there (in 2002). Following interrogation of the detainee, Interpol became involved in the international traffic in intelligence about the group. Because officials from both countries had been assassinated, British and American police were already involved in the search for other members of the group. On July 7, 2002, *The Daily Telegraph* lead on the story announced that "Greece has credited Scotland Yard with the success of an operation against November 17, a terrorist group that has [had] the attention of agencies such as Interpol and the FBI for 30 years." A spokesperson for the Greek government explained that their police strategy had been directed by British detectives. "We sealed off the area

and conducted the search according to Scotland Yard methods (...) we have worked with FBI but Scotland Yard are better because of their experience with the IRA."

[12] See, for example, the following: Anderson (1989), Besler (1992), and Fooner (1989). All of these observers make this claim.

[13] The UN-centric view of global governance is only one model of the global system; see Held and McGrew (2002: 60–61).

[14] So-called Specialised Agencies are linked to the UN by a special accord de liaison, which is rather different than the co-operation agreement between the two organisations. An *accord de liaison* confers powers of *coordination*, whereas a co-operation agreement merely consolidates co-operation. A new co-operation agreement between Interpol and the UN was signed on July 8, 1997 and came into force following its approval by the Interpol General Assembly by virtue of Resolution AGN/66/RES/5 adopted at the 66th session (held in New Delhi in 1997). This replaced the previously existing Special Arrangement concluded with ECOSOC in May of 1971. The current co-operation agreement follows the adoption by the United Nations General Assembly on October 22, 1996 of Resolution A/RES/51/l, which granted Interpol Observer Status in the UN General Assembly. It defines the areas in which the two organisations should co-operate and the conditions for the exchange of information and documents. It opens the way for technical co-operation and joint action, and provides for reciprocal representation at meetings held by each organisation.

[15] Interpol, *ICPO–Interpol Constitution and General Regulations*, http://www.interpol.int/Public/ICPO/LegalMaterials/constitution/constitutionGenReg/constitution.asp.

[16] That is precisely where Held and McGrew (2002: 60) place them.

[17] P. Reuter, *Legal Problems concerning the ICPO-JNTERPOL Constitution: Preliminary Observations* (n.d.) [unpublished legal opinion, English Translation, archived at Interpol]. Professor Reuter's legal opinion states, in part, that Interpol could "apparently be rightly called an international intergovernmental organisation, and indeed has been recognised as such by the United Nations Secretary General after some degree of understandable hesitation" (manuscript at 1-2). He states further that, while it is true that nearly all IGOs have been set up thorough formal treaties, under the principles of international law, "it is even possible to conceive of an intergovernmental organisation being set up without a single written instrument, merely as the result of a series of precedents created by governments" (ibid. at 3-4). Professor Reuter conceded that this was not a complete answer to the question of Interpol's status because it did not consider the terms of constitutional law in all of the (very numerous) participating countries. However, his view was that, because the various parties to the Interpol organisation had "been applying its provisions for many years without ever having claimed that their commitment thereunder was unconstitutional" and because Interpol was "a centre of voluntary cooperation, exercising no powers which would conflict with national sovereignty" it would therefore "ill become a State to claim after so many years of successful activity that its commitment was unconstitutional and therefore invalid" (ibid. at 5-6). Were such questions to be raised, it "would be more legal and more seemly for it [the objecting state] to withdraw from the agreement" (ibid. at 6). Professor Reuter drew his legal opinion to a close by asking if there would be any benefit to

raising Interpol's status to that of a fully fledged and *bona fide* UN Specialised Agency. His answer was that, although the organisation might accrue a greater measure of prestige as a result, this had to be weighed against the loss of independence that this would bring since any such agreement would require full co-ordination with the administrative practices of the United Nations. He averred that participating States "would probably not adopt a unanimous position on such a transformation" (ibid. at 19).

[18] Under the terms of Article 26 of the Constitution, which were adopted in 1990, external auditors are appointed on a three-yearly basis to conduct an external audit of the organisation's accounts and finances. Final drafts of the audit are presented to the Secretary General and the General Assembly.

[19] It might do to note that the efficiency and effectiveness of the CNIL in securing privacy and civil liberties interests of French citizens has also been criticised; see Raab (1994). Owing to an internal debate within Interpol regarding the rules relating to the processing of policing information, new common security rules for Interpol's information system were adopted in 2003 (Cisco 2003).

[20] Except, of course, that the UN Secretary General is almost entirely beholden to the Security Council. As Kofi Annan explained it, the office of UN Secretary General is "invested only with the power that a united Security Council may wish to bestow" (quoted in Shawcross 2000: 19). Further to this point, Anderson (1989: 61) notes that Articles 29 and 30 of the Interpol Constitution establish the independence of the Secretary General. In general, the S-G should represent the organization, not a particular country. The Secretary General should neither solicit nor accept instructions from any government or authority outside the organization and should abstain from any action which might be prejudicial to its international role. Also, under Article 30, each member country is expected to undertake to respect the exclusively international character of the duties of the Secretary General and the staff and abstain from influencing them in the discharge of their duties.

[21] It is not inappropriate to say that member police organisations retain nominal control over information in the Interpol databanks because the security of that information is moot. Some professional police agents have been critical of the inability of Interpol to maintain the integrity and secrecy of information. Thus, regardless of principles of proprietary control, questions have been raised about actual control. There is currently an internal debate within Interpol regarding these operating rules, and there are plans to try to tighten them up, but it is too early to say if changes to the operating rules will significantly alter perceptions.

[22] See Nadelmann (1993) for a full account of the internationalisation of US law enforcement.

[23] For an overview of the National Law Enforcement Telecommunications system, see http://www.nlets.org/ (accessed on January 3, 2003).

[24] The text of this speech is available at http://www.interpol.int/public/ICPO/speeches/Zaccardelli.asp

[25] It is also worth noting that the United Kingdom maintains two sub-bureaus in the Caribbean region, one in Bermuda and the other in Grand Cayman. Also the Kingdom of the Netherlands maintains liaison officers in its dependencies, and Interpol offices maintained in Aruba and the Netherlands Antilles are technically sub-ordinate to Dutch sovereignty.

[26] See Joubert and Bevers (1996). They are especially concerned to examine the extent to which such transnational police communications can be adequately governed by legal principles. See also Bigo (2000). Bigo argues that transnational liaison officers are substantially unaffected by frameworks of legal accountability.

[27] See the report of the U.K. House of Commons (1989–1990: 43). Elsewhere in this report, it is remarked that Interpol's working methods were "bureaucratic and laborious" (vol.1 at xxv).

[28] Malcolm Anderson (1989: 61) states that the ambiguity of the Constitution was a deliberate ploy to ensure the informality of the organisation, and hence insulate it from (inter)national politics.

[29] Interpol continued to liaise with US authorities through the offices of the US Treasury, despite the fact that, at the time, US law designated the FBI as the only official conduit for international police transactions.

[30] For more details on these incidents consult Bresler (1992). On the case of the Czech hijacking, see pages 110–112 and 120–121; on the case of the request of the Cuban NCB for a red notice against former members of the Cuban police establishment, see pages 127–128; and on the Black September attacks at Munich, see pages 149–155. Incidentally, the Cuban instance throws up another possible deficiency of the Interpol Constitution since there is no provision within it to withdraw membership. This is why Cuba remains a member of the organization despite the fact that it has not paid any membership dues since 1959.

[31] See the Statewatch Observatory at http://www.statewatch.org/observatory2.htm for a comprehensive analysis of these issues post 9-11. It is worth noting that the European Arrest Warrant also abolished the concepts of "dual criminality" and "double jeopardy." Indeed, the Eurowarrant does not even include a *habeas corpus* safeguard, prompting Sir Neil MacCormick, a Scottish Nationalist Member of the European Parliament and Professor of Public Law at Edinburgh University, to observe that policy makers in the EU had muddied the waters by equating allegations with hard proof. "They seem to think that prosecutors never make mistakes. Well they do. It's most urgent that we have remedies to prevent abuses of power" (quoted in Ambros Evans-Pritchard, "EU Gets A New Arrest Warrant But Safeguard Is Blocked" *The Daily Telegraph* (7 February 2002). The European Arrest Warrant came into full force in 2004, without the mechanism of the writ of *habeas corpus*.

REFERENCES

Anderson, M. 1989. *Policing the World: Interpol and the Politics of International Police Co-operation*. Oxford: Clarendon.

Anderson, M., M den Boer, P. Cullen, W. Gilmore, C. Raab, and N. Walker. 1995. *Policing the European Union*. Oxford: Clarendon.

Banton, M. 1964. *The Policeman in the Community*. London: Tavistock.

Benyon, J., L. Turnbull, A. Willis, R. Woodward, and A. Beck. 1993. *Police Co-operation in Europe: An Investigation*. University of Leicester: Centre for the Study of Public Order.

Bigo, D. 2000. "Liaison Officers in Europe: New Officers in the European Security Field." Pp. 67–99 in *Issues in Transnational Policing*, edited by J. Sheptycki. London: Routledge.

Bresler, F. 1992. *Interpol*. London: Mandarine.

Cisco. 2003. "Cisco Helps Interpol Create and Deploy Ambitious New Virtual Private Network: I-247: Interpol Bureaus around the World Collaborate over Secure VPNs." *News@Cisco*, http://newsroom.cisco.com/dlls/hd_052003.html.

Commission on Global Governance. 1995. *Our Global Neighbourhood*. Oxford: Oxford University Press.

Deflem, M. 2000. "Bureaucratization and Social Control: Historical Foundations of International Police Cooperation." *Law and Society Review* 34: 739–78.

Deflem, M. 2002a. *Policing World Society; Historical Foundations of International Police Co-operation*. Oxford: Oxford University Press.

Deflem, M. 2002b. "The Logic of Nazification: The Case of the International Criminal Police Commission ('Interpol')." *International Journal of Comparative Sociology* 43: 21–44.

Den Boer, M. (Ed.). 2002. "Special Issue on Policing Accountability in Europe." *Policing and Society* 12: 243–338.

Economic and Social Council. 1950. *Resolution 288 (X)*. 27 February 1950.

Economic and Social Council. 1971. *Resolution 1579 (L)*. 3 June 1971.

Ericson, R. and N. Stehr. (Eds.). 2000. *Governing Modern Societies*. Toronto: University of Toronto Press.

Fijnaut, C. 1993. *The Internationalization of Police Co-operation in Western Europe*. Boston: Kluwer.

Fooner, M. 1989. *Interpol: Issues in World Crime and International Criminal Justice*. New York: Plenum Press.

Gessner, V. and A. Cern Budak. 1998. *Emerging Legal Certainty: Empirical Studies on the Globalisation of Law*. Dartmouth: Ashgate.

Goldsmith, A. 1991. *Complaints Against the Police: The Trend to External Review*. Oxford: Clarendon.

Goldsmith, A. and C. Lewis. 2000. *Civilian Oversight of Policing; Governance, Democracy, and Human Rights*. Oxford: Hart.

Held, D. 1995. *Democracy and the Global Order: From the Modern State to Cosmopolitan Governance*. Cambridge: Polity.

Held, D. and A. McGrew. 2002. *Globalisation/AntiGlobalisation*. Cambridge: Polity.

Hobsbawm, E. 1995. *Age of Extremes: The Short Twentieth Century 1914–1991*. London: Abacus.

Interpol. 2006. *ICPO–Interpol Constitution and General Regulations*, http://www.interpol.int/Public/ICPO/LegalMaterials/constitution/constitutionGenReg/constitution.asp#

Interpol. 2000. *Interpol at Work: Annual Report*. Lyon: Interpol, www.interpol.int.

Interpol. 2001. *Interpol at Work: Annual Report*. Lyon: Interpol, www.interpol.int.

Johnston, L. 2000. *Policing Britain: Risk, Security, and Governance*. Harlow: Longman.

Jones, T. and T. Newburn. 1998. *Private Security and Public Policing*. Oxford: Clarendon.

Joubert, C. and H. Bevers. 1996. *Schengen Investigated*. The Hague: Kluwer.

Law Commission of Canada. 2002. *In Search of Security: The Roles of Public Police and Private Agencies* (discussion paper). Ottawa: Law Commission of Canada.

Marks, S. 2000. *The Riddle of All Constitutions*. Oxford: Oxford University Press.

Nadelmann, E. 1993. *Cops Across Borders: The Internationalization of US Criminal Law Enforcement*. University Park, PA: Pennsylvania State University Press.

Newburn, T. and T. Jones. 1997. *Policing After the Act: Police Governance After the Police and Magistrates' Courts Act 1994.* London: Policy Studies Institute.

Raab, C. 1994. "Police Co-operation: The Prospects for Privacy." Pp. 121–36 in *Policing Across National Boundaries,* edited by M. Anderson and M. den Boer. London: Pinter.

Rigakos, G. 2002. *The New Parapolice: Risk Markets and Commodified Social Control.* Toronto: Toronto University Press.

Shawcross, W. 2000. *Deliver Us From Evil: Warlords and Peacekeepers in a World of Endless Conflict.* London: Bloomsbury.

Shearing, C. 2001. "A Nodal Conception of Governance: Thoughts on a Policing Commission." *Policing and Society* 11: 259–72.

Sheptycki, J.W.E. 1995. "Transnational Policing and the Makings of a Postmodern State." *British Journal of Criminology* 35: 613–35.

Sheptycki, J.W.E. 1997. "Transnationalism, Crime Control, and the European State System: A Review of the Literature." *International Criminal Justice Review* 7: 130–140.

Sheptycki, J.W.E. 1998. "Policing, Postmodernism and Transnationalisation." *British Journal of Criminology* 38: 485–503.

Sheptycki, J.W.E. 1999. "Political Culture and Structures of Social Control: Police Related Scandal in Low Countries in Comparative Perspective." *Policing and Society* 9: 1–31.

Sheptycki, J. (Ed.). 2000. *Issues in Transnational Policing.* London: Routledge.

Sheptycki, J. 2002. "Accountability Across the Policing Field: Towards a General Cartography of Accountability for Post-Modern Policing." *Policing and Society* 12: 323–338.

Sheptycki, J. 2003. *In Search of Transnational Policing.* Aldershot: Avebury.

Sklair, L. 1991. *Sociology of the Global System.* New York: Harvester Wheatsheaf.

Stenning, P. (Ed.) 1995. *Accountability for Criminal Justice: Selected Essays.* Toronto: Toronto University Press.

U.K. House of Commons. 1977. *House of Commons Daily Debates (21 January 1977).* Hansard. Vol. 924, col. 344.

U.K. House of Commons. 1989–1990. "Home Affairs Committee Report on Practical Police Co-operation in the European Community." 7th report, HC 363-1 Vol. 2:43.

Yalleix, C. 1984. "Interpol." *Revue Générale de Droit International Public* 8(3): 621–652.

Westley, W. 1970. *Violence and the Police: A Sociological Study of Law, Custom, and Morality.* Cambridge, MA: MIT Press.

Zaccardelli, G. 2002. "Law Enforcement in the Third Millennium." Speech given at the 71st Interpol General Assembly, October 21-24, Yaoundé, Cameroon. Available at http://www.interpol.int/Public/ICPO/speeches/Zaccardelli.asp

CHAPTER STUDY QUESTIONS

- Sheptycki argues that the "nation-state system has become the transnational-state-system." Why does he make this argument? What are its ramifications for the autonomy of nation-states and their ability to control police agencies within their own borders?

- Sheptycki argues that accountability is not the same as control. Why does he make this argument? How can external accountability be strengthened without weakening internal control mechanisms?

- Describe the internal and external accountability and control mechanisms that govern the day-to-day operations of Interpol. Outline the advantages and disadvantages that exist with respect to both categories. Overall, how would you rate the effectiveness of Interpol's external accountability mechanisms?

- Identify several issues that "politicize" external accountability with respect to Interpol. Which of these issues do you consider most serious? How have the events of September 11, 2001 altered many of these issues?

RELATED WEB LINKS

Interpol
http://www.interpol.int/
> This, the main website of Interpol, provides the organization's history and other background information.

Intelligarde
http://www.intelligarde.com/home.html
> This is the main website of Intelligarde, one of the largest of the private security conglomerates referred to by Sheptycki.

Social Sciences Research Network
http://papers.ssrn.com/sol3/papers.cfm?abstract_id=875451
> This website provides access to a full-text article on the difficulties of organizing and legitimating police undercover work involving more than one country.

Europa
http://europa.eu/scadplus/leg/en/s22007.htm
> This website is devoted to police and customs cooperation in Europe. It provides access to a wide range of reports and legislative summaries and analyses on topics related to transnational policing, including an analysis of the legislative basis for the control and accountability of Europol.

PART 4

SYSTEMS OF CRIMINAL PROSECUTION, THE COURTS, AND SOCIAL CONTROL

The operation of the courts, as exemplified by the prosecutorial and judicial processes, constitutes a crucial link in the evolution and application of social control policies. Criminal justice systems are frequently viewed as continuums that include legislatures, police, courts, and corrections, with the different components operating in relative isolation from each other. While all components are expected to adhere to accepted standards of integrity and fairness, the prosecution and judiciary are entrusted with special responsibility for upholding due process and safeguarding the constitutional rights of accused persons during all stages of the criminal justice process. Thus, although the enactment of laws by legislatures necessarily involves a highly political process, the application of these laws by the courts should be as free from political influence as possible. In this respect, it is frequently argued that an autonomous and independent judiciary is essential to the administration of justice and that political and other forms of harassment aimed at judicial officials severely weakens due process, and may even render constitutional protections meaningless.

The role of the courts is becoming increasingly important in a globalizing world as increased interaction and cooperation will inevitably lead to conflict among interest groups from countries that follow very different court procedures. Although most contemporary Western legal and criminal justice systems attempt to insulate the courts from direct political influence, many regions of the world do not consider such independence essential or even desirable. In much of the Third World, political corruption is endemic and routinely involves all aspects of the criminal justice system, including the courts. In this case, attempting to implement an independent judicial system would run counter to an entrenched political culture that sees the courts as an extension of the political process, to be used at the whim of economic and political elites. In Islamic societies, on the other hand, religious figures and tribal elders frequently carry out the prosecutorial and judicial functions. Under Islamic law, these authorities are simply carrying out the will of Allah, and an independent judiciary would represent a contradiction that undermines religious authority. And finally, in socialist legal systems, the role of the law is

275

considered subordinate to government policy, and, by limiting state power, a truly independent judiciary would threaten the goal of creating a perfect socialist state. Thus, there is clearly a great deal of diversity in how the global community views the pivotal role of the courts.[1] Despite this diversity, however, it is equally clear that the global community must find a way to achieve the degree of cooperation necessary to ensure that the global community continues to develop economically, politically, and socially.

The chapters included in Part 4 discuss the role of the courts from a variety of different perspectives and in systems that represent Western, Islamic, and socialist approaches to social control. In "Prosecutorial Discretion and Plea Bargaining in the United States, France, Germany and Italy: A Comparative Perspective," Yue Ma conducts a comparative analysis of recent changes to prosecutorial practices in the United States and France, Germany, and Italy. He commences his analysis by arguing that prosecutors in the United States exercise virtually unlimited discretion regarding the charging process and that this unchecked discretion affords them enormous power to decide the fate of defendants based on whatever criteria they choose. Ma further notes that this power is used to control the plea bargaining process that is considered essential to the administration of justice in the United States. Although plea bargaining is intended to expedite the flow of cases by offering defendants lower charges and penalties in return for guilty pleas, Ma argues that it is hardly an equal bargaining process given the enormous discretion wielded by prosecutors and that prosecutors frequently use such tactics as overcharging and electing to use penalty enhancing provisions to force defendants to enter guilty pleas. He concludes his discussion of US prosecutors by arguing that the widespread use of such tactics can result in discrimination that actually threatens the equality provisions in the US constitution.

Ma commences his discussion of continental prosecutorial practices by noting that not all European countries follow the same charging practices. He notes that the major distinction is between countries that follow the legality principle, which mandates prosecution in all cases where sufficient evidence exists, and countries that follow the expediency principle, which allows prosecutors to consider the greater public good in deciding whether to prosecute. He analyses these differences with reference to prosecutorial practices in France, which follows the expediency principle, and Germany and Italy, which follow the legality principle. Ma argues that French prosecutors are classed as members of the judiciary and are expected to seek an outcome that is just and fair, rather than simply pursuing the heaviest sentence possible. Further, they are not required to prosecute, even in cases where sufficient evidence exists to obtain a conviction. Although serious cases are sent to an examining magistrate, and prosecutors lose control of them at this point, prosecutors can avoid this by reducing the charges below the level that requires an Assize Court trial. Ma argues, however, that these decisions are not predicated on a confession or guilty plea and instead are based on the principle of the "greater public good." Ma concludes his discussion of French prosecutorial practices by arguing that balance is brought to the process by the fact that victims can either join existing proceedings or initiate their own proceedings if they feel that charges were dropped inappropriately.

In discussing prosecutorial practices in Germany and Italy, Ma notes that the practice of compulsory prosecution has started to break down and plea bargaining has started to develop in both countries. However, he argues that the practice of plea bargaining contains more safeguards for the defence in both Germany and Italy than exist in the US court system. In Germany, for example, plea bargaining arises from the prosecutor's power to dismiss minor cases and settle other cases without a full trial. Although, in this regard, the German and US systems are similar, Ma argues that the German system differs in that the defence also possesses significant bargaining power to influence the process. Further, any deals must be approved by the judge, who can also initiate plea negotiations if she or he feels they are warranted. These factors, combined with the fact that a defendant's refusal to accept a deal does not automatically result in a more severe sentence, significantly limit the prosecutor's ability to force guilty pleas from defendants. Similar provisions for judicial review exist in Italy, where judges are required to provide written reasons for all decisions, including those that accept a plea bargain deal. In addition, Italian prosecutors must agree to a maximum sentence of two years in all plea bargains and also must provide written reasons when they refuse to agree to a sentencing deal requested by a defendant. Ma argues that these safeguards significantly constrain prosecutorial discretion and limit the abuses that are so common in the US system.

The second chapter in Part 4 presents a view of French pre-trial procedures that casts some doubt on the positive picture outlined in Ma's chapter. In "The Police, the Prosecutor and the Juge D'Instruction: Judicial Supervision in France, Theory and Practice," Jacqueline Hodgson argues that French pre-trial procedures are premised on the principle that judicial supervision of police activity during the pre-trial phase of criminal investigations will best facilitate the pursuit of justice. Both the prosecutor (procureur) and the juge d'instruction (examining magistrate) are members of the judiciary and are expected to conduct an impartial search for the truth that does not favour either side. Under this model, the police are always under the supervision of either the prosecutor or the juge d'instruction and derive most of their investigatory power by delegation from these two judicial officers. The prosecutor is generally considered central to the process and decides whether to proceed with charges and whether referring the case to a juge d'instruction is warranted. Since only the most serious cases are referred to juges d'instruction (approximately 8 per cent), the prosecutor clearly plays a much greater role than the juge in pre-trial screening. However, the juge d'instruction enjoys greater judicial independence and is expected to supervise the police more closely than the prosecutor.

Although the French model theoretically presents a more balanced approach to the pre-trial process than occurs under an adversarial model, Hodgson argues that it does not always guarantee a balanced and objective investigation in practice. According to Hodgson, part of the problem arises because both prosecutors and juges d'instruction are overloaded and are thus unable or unwilling to supervise police activities closely. This limited supervision allows the police wide latitude to conduct investigations as they see fit, so violence and coerced confessions are commonplace. Further, Hodgson notes that an attitude that all detained persons are guilty permeates the occupational culture of the prosecutors and juges d'instruction and that they almost always side with the police when allegations of police misconduct arise. These factors are compounded by the minor role assigned to defence lawyers and the relatively weak due process protections that exist under French law. Hodgson argues that lax supervision of investigations and weak checks on police, judicial, and prosecutorial power preclude an opportunity to mount a defence in the sense envisioned by adversarial systems while also failing to guarantee that the rights of the defendant will be adequately protected by a judicially supervised pre-trial investigation. Ultimately, however, she concludes that, despite the weaknesses of the French system, judicial supervision of the pre-trial process should not be rejected out of hand and that exploration of alternate models is necessary.

The third chapter in this part deals with the judicial processes that have developed in Iran after the 1979 revolution that overthrew the Shah. In "Iranian Criminal Justice under the Islamization Project," Hassan Rezaei argues that the Islamic power structure that emerged in Iran after the revolution immediately dismantled the Western style of criminal justice that existed and replaced it with one based on Islamic law. Although the first step was to create a constitution that appeared to retain some human rights protections, these were clearly subordinate to Islamic principles, as were most other legal provisions. Other developments included the replacement of the previous system of classifying crimes according to their seriousness with a strict Islamic classification system and the abolition of the prosecution as a separate entity. This latter provision was particularly problematic because the prosecution functions were transferred to the tribunals, and thus the judiciary effectively carries out the judicial and prosecution roles in the same case. This situation creates obvious due process issues for Western jurists, and the problem is exacerbated because many judges are poorly trained for their judicial function and individual rights are clearly subordinate to the interests of the state.

In concluding his discussion of Iranian legal developments following the 1979 revolution, Rezaei asserts that any assessment of the Iranian Islamic legal system must take into account the fact that Islam is a theory of government as well as a system of religious and moral principles. Thus, while the Islamization project was ostensibly motivated by a desire to bring criminal justice into accordance with Islamic principles, it was actually motivated by the interests of the *political* clergy in Iran. He also argues that the decision to base the Iranian criminal justice system on a very "literal and traditional" interpretation of Islamic teachings has lead to the creation of a very authoritarian criminal justice system that has clear conflicts with international standards of human rights. The resulting system is also incompatible with many important teachings of Islam. As a result, a new reformist movement has evolved that is advocating a complete revision of the constitution. Rezaei notes that the dominant discourse favours the "modernization and democratization of criminal justice within the context of an Islamic society." Such a system, he argues, would likely meet international standards and would also facilitate the integration of Islam and secularization.

The fourth chapter discusses justice and human rights in post-war Afghanistan. In "Building a Post-War Justice System in Afghanistan," Ali Wardak argues that, while the formal Afghan criminal justice system had largely disintegrated by the end of the war that ousted the Taliban, the legal culture in Afghanistan contains many important elements that could be incorporated into a post-war justice system. He notes that four dimensions are part of the post-war justice system in Afghanistan. These dimensions include Islamic law (Shari'a), customary law (jirga/maraka/shura), the interim legal framework and current criminal justice system, and the fundamental principles of human rights and transitional justice. He argues that the current justice system is faced with several serious problems that can be traced to the previous formal justice system and the series of wars that took place over the past twenty years. One of the most serious of these problems is that the past wars created a "culture of abuse" and that many of the worst abusers of human rights have not only gone unpunished but also remain in positions of power. This factor is exacerbated because the formal criminal justice system is extremely uncoordinated and many police agencies are actually under the control of local warlords who use them to commit further abuses on the population.

In response to these problems, Wardak proposes an integrated model of criminal justice that explicitly incorporates a popular, non-sectarian version of shari'a (Islamic law) and jirga (customary law) as central elements. According to Wardak, popular Islam is so central in the daily lives of most Afghans that it must occupy a central role in any system of justice. He also argues that dispute resolution based on customary law is still widely used and would serve a reintegrative function, as well as simplify the administration of justice and make it more accessible to common people. In order to accommodate Afghanistan's increasing integration into the global community, Wardak proposes that that these two "internal" dimensions be integrated into a formal justice system that makes explicit provision for the protection of human rights. Thus, he advocates the establishment of "human rights units" at the district level that would carry out a myriad of roles, including education regarding human rights issues and the investigation and resolution of current complaints. The human rights units would also have the authority to investigate and report past abuses to a Special Court of Human Rights and to monitor local government officials for abuses. Wardak concludes that Afghanistan provides an opportunity for developing a justice system that is democratic and respectful of existing cultural and religious norms, while also meeting international standards for the protection of human rights.

The final chapter in Part 4 compares Chinese social control policies to those in the West in several dimensions. In "Social and Legal Control in China: A Comparative Approach," Xiaoming Chen argues that the cultural context of Chinese social control incorporates a much more positive conception of human nature than exists in Western societies. This view of human nature assumes that people are essentially good and that their antisocial tendencies can be cured by education and reintegration into the community. In order to accomplish reintegration, Chinese society de-emphasizes individual autonomy and emphasizes group interests. These group interests are used to justify community intervention at the first sign of non-conformity by utilizing informal mechanisms that operate at the neighbourhood level. These informal mechanisms are integrated into networks of powerful neighbourhood committees that exercise enormous power and are actually formally constituted as government-controlled entities, despite Western tendencies to view them as low-level volunteer organizations. Chen argues that this approach creates a social control net that is very different from anything that exists in the West. The resulting emphasis on crime prevention and education also extends to the police and corrections. In this respect, the police largely assume a non-penal role and may even help offenders find employment. Similarly, the correctional system takes a paternalistic approach that emphasizes rehabilitation over punishment and is similar to the doctrine of *parens patriae*, which once served as the philosophical basis of juvenile justice in many Western countries.

Although he presents the Chinese system of social control in a generally positive light, Chen notes that it would almost certainly clash with many Western value systems. He further notes that there are several philosophical and legal problems even within the Chinese context. From a philosophical perspective, Chen argues that the emphasis on "order over freedom, duties over rights, and group interests over individual ones" can lead to situations where relatively trivial incidents can be used to stifle individual expression and stigmatize offenders in ways that clearly limit future opportunities. At the practical legal level, the virtually unlimited discretion afforded to the police and judiciary severely limit protections for individual rights well below a level that would be tolerated in the West. Chen notes that China has made considerable progress towards developing protections for individual rights based on a rule of law; however, he cautions that this should not be interpreted as a movement towards Western values and ideals. He argues that the emphasis of Chinese social control remains focused on mass participation and that group interests still override individual rights. He also points out that any emphasis on using the law to solve crime problems is connected to specific political goals, which may be far removed from the specific problems being addressed. Chen concludes that despite their many philosophical and legal differences, Chinese and Western social control policies are starting to converge, with China emphasizing greater legalism and Western societies adopting a more community-based approach. However, he suggests that it is not yet clear whether such hybrid systems will be effective in either society.

NOTE

[1] Interestingly enough, the United States, often considered a bastion of due process, provides for the direct election of both prosecutors and judges at the state level. Although this approach may appear to run contrary to the goal of limiting political interference, some theorists argue that it grants both judges and prosecutors a level of political autonomy that they would not otherwise enjoy and also raises their political roles to a much more transparent level that inhibits corruption and undue influence.

Chapter 12

PROSECUTORIAL DISCRETION AND PLEA BARGAINING IN THE UNITED STATES, FRANCE, GERMANY, AND ITALY: A COMPARATIVE PERSPECTIVE

YUE MA

Prosecutorial discretion has long been a point of controversy in the United States. Prosecutors, as the central figure in the administration of American criminal justice, make perhaps the most crucial decisions in the daily administration of justice. Prosecutors face the task of choosing, from a mass of overlapping criminal statutes, which of them best fits the facts presented by the police. The responsibility of prosecutors, however, is not limited to demonstrating their legal expertise in fitting charges to different fact situations. In making charging decisions, they are expected to take into consideration a broad range of factors, including evidentiary sufficiency, the extent of the harm caused by the offense, the disproportion of the authorized punishment in relation to the particular offense or the offender, cooperation of the accused in the apprehension or conviction of others, and the cost of prosecution to the criminal justice system (American Bar Association 1986).

Given the complex nature of prosecutorial decision making, it is well recognized that prosecutors must be afforded a certain degree of discretion. Even commentators who are most critical of American prosecutorial discretion agree that discretionary power when properly exercised facilitates rather than hinders the cause of justice (Davis 1969; Vorenberg 1981). What concerns the critics is prosecutors' overly broad and essentially unchecked discretion. More than 60 years ago, then Attorney General and later U.S. Supreme Court Justice Robert Jackson described the prosecutor as having "more control over life, liberty, and reputation than any other person in America" (Jackson 1940: 18). Jackson warned that, because the prosecutor stands a fair chance of finding at least a technical violation of some act on the part of almost anyone, the prosecuting power, if not properly exercised, is susceptible to the greatest danger of abuse. Another early commentator, Thurman Arnold, also cautioned about the great potential of prosecutorial abuse. Arnold opined that "the idea that a prosecuting attorney should be permitted to use his discretion concerning the laws which he will enforce and those which he will disregard appears to the ordinary citizens to border on anarchy" (Arnold 1932: 7).

Despite the concerns raised by the early commentators, in the ensuing years, neither legislatures nor courts have taken serious steps to restrain prosecutorial discretion. The past 30 years have actually witnessed a dramatic expansion of the power and prestige of prosecutors (Currie 1998; Gershman 1992; Walker 1993). With the transition from a due-process-oriented criminal justice model to a model that attaches overriding emphasis on crime control, and with the rise of the mentality of winning the "war on crime" at all costs, instead of restraining prosecutorial discretion, legislatures have granted even more power to prosecutors (Gordon 1994). As legislatures have armed prosecutors with broad new weapons such as RICO, sentencing guidelines, the Violent Crime Control and Law Enforcement Act, three-strikes laws, and truth-in-sentencing laws, the courts have cooperated in the efforts by taking an increasingly passive stance in providing supervision over prosecutors. The expanded power of the prosecutor, coupled with the relaxed judicial supervision, has made the prosecutor truly the most preeminent figure in the administration of criminal justice in America. Commentators who are critical of the continuing expansion of prosecutorial power argue that the current scope of discretion is unjustifiably broad in terms of the principles of fairness, equity, and accountability on which the American criminal justice system is based, and it creates a potential for prosecutorial abuse greater than ever before (Ely 1980; Gershman 1992; Ohlin and Remington 1993; Uviller 1999; Vorenberg 1981).

In debating whether and how prosecutorial discretion should be restrained, reform-minded commentators have time and again turned their attention to continental European countries' practices and experience, believing that the continental law models may offer cures for several troublesome aspects of the American system of justice (Davis 1969; Langbein 1974, 1977, 1979, 1981; Schlesinger 1977; Weigend 1980). In the 1970s, as the American system turned increasingly to plea bargaining as the way of resolving criminal cases, advocates of American law reform spoke with great admiration of the lack of plea bargaining in continental law countries and suggested that the American system be reformed on the model of "the land without plea bargaining" (Langbein 1979: 224). Other commentators, skeptical of the claim that continental countries had succeeded in running a smooth system without resource to bargaining justice, argued that the nonexistence of plea bargaining in Europe was more a myth than a reality. They maintained that plea bargaining was by no means an American phenomenon and that analogues of plea bargaining existed in continental countries as well. In their view, continental systems in substance operated not much differently from the way the American system operated; there was therefore little to gain in attempting reforms on continental models (Goldstein and Marcus 1977). The debate in the 1970s produced few conclusions and virtually no reform efforts.

Since the early 1990s, there seems to be a rekindled interest in referring to foreign experience as a source of ideas and inspiration for American law reform (Dubber 1997; Frase 1990; Frase and Weigend 1995; Van Kessel 1992). However, continental law systems in the past 30 years have undergone significant changes. In the context of prosecutorial practice, nothing illustrates the extent of the changes better than the emergence of plea bargaining and the gradual expansion of prosecutors' autonomy. Nevertheless, a careful analysis of continental and American prosecutorial systems reveals that—the recent expansion of prosecutorial autonomy in continental law countries notwithstanding—American prosecutors still stand virtually alone in their overly broad and largely unchecked discretion. Though plea bargaining has emerged in continental law countries, it remains a unique American feature that prosecutors are allowed to gain such an overwhelming dominance in the bargaining process that they can exact highly pressurized pleas from defendants. It is in this context that continental models may still offer valuable lessons in fashioning reforms of the American system.

This chapter seeks to provide readers with a comparative analysis of the prosecutorial practices in the United States and in three continental European countries. The three European countries included in the study, France, Germany, and Italy, are traditionally regarded as preeminent continental law countries (Merryman 1985; Zweigert and Kötz 1987). The selection of the three countries is further justified on the ground that comparative legal scholars in most instances include criminal procedures of the three countries in their exploration of the possibilities of American law reform on continental models (Davis 1969; Goldstein and Marcus 1977; Langbein 1974, 1977, 1979, 1981; Weigend 1980). Discussion of the prosecutorial practices in these three countries therefore offers a better reference point for American readers. The article introduces to readers the recent developments in both the United States and the three continental countries, such as the vast accretion of prosecutorial power in the United States and the various forms of plea bargaining in the three continental countries. Attention will be given especially to the differences between the American and continental prosecutorial practices and to those aspects that the American system may borrow from the continental systems.

PROSECUTORIAL DISCRETION AND PLEA BARGAINING IN THE UNITED STATES

Charging and plea bargaining are at the core of prosecutors' power. A prosecutor's first formal duty is to determine whether a defendant should be charged with a crime and, if so, what charge should be brought. But what makes American prosecutors such powerful figures in the administration of justice is not their power to charge but rather their power *not* to prosecute further, even in the face of sufficient evidence. Prosecutors' absolute power to dismiss a case can be traced to the old common law doctrine *nolle prosequi*. Although the power of *nolle prosequi* is commonly justified on the ground that prosecutors' discretion not to act is a form of leniency, commentators have long warned that the power to be lenient is the power to discriminate. Through decisions about whether and what to charge, prosecutors hold the power to decide who will undergo the expense, anxiety, and embarrassment of criminal proceedings and who will face society's most fundamental sanctions. Injustice may easily result from the improper exercise of the discretion to be or not to be lenient (Davis 1969; Vorenberg 1981).

While prosecutors' discretion to engage in selective enforcement has been heavily criticized, their power to do so has been repeatedly upheld by appellate courts. The judicial reluctance to interfere with prosecutors' charging authority is perhaps best explained by then Judge of the U.S. Court of Appeals for the District of Columbia and later Chief Justice of the U.S. Supreme Court Warren Burger. Burger stated that "few subjects are less adapted to judicial review than the exercise by the Executive of his discretion in deciding when and whether to institute criminal proceedings, or what precise charge should be made, or whether to dismiss a proceeding once brought" (*Newman v. United States* 1967: 480). Today, with more than 90 per cent of criminal cases in the American system being disposed of by way of guilty pleas, the full display of American prosecutors' discretionary power probably can be best seen in the process of plea bargaining.

Thirty years ago, when the U.S. Supreme Court recognized the legality of plea bargaining, it justified the acceptance of the bargaining of justice largely on economic grounds. The Court reasoned that "if every criminal charge were subject to a full scale trial, the states and the Federal Government would need to multiply by many times the number of judges and court facilities." Based on this concern, the Court described plea bargaining as "an essential component of the administration of justice" and held that "properly administered, it is to be encouraged" (*Santobello v. New York* 1971: 261). Although the Court justified plea bargaining on economic grounds, it assumed at the same time that the bargaining process would be a fair give-and-take process. The Court assumed that the defendant, represented by counsel and protected by procedural safeguards, would be capable of "intelligent choice in response to prosecutorial persuasion" (*Bordenkircher v. Hayes* 1978: 363). Commentators, however, are quick to note the radically skewed balance of advantage in the bargaining process. They point out that plea bargaining is far from a process in which defendants enter into consensual agreements with prosecutors after adversarial negotiations. Defendants, in many cases, must simply choose between pleading guilty and getting mercy, on the one hand, or proceeding to trial and facing the risk of receiving a much more severe penalty, on the other. Commentators therefore characterize plea bargaining as prosecutors' unilateral determination of the level of defendants' criminal culpability and the appropriate punishment for defendants (Alschuler 1983; Gifford 1983).

If the playing field was tilted in favor of prosecutors when the Court first sanctioned the practice three decades ago, today, with the vastly expanded prosecutorial power, the inherent inequality in the bargaining process has only intensified, making the idea of adversarial negotiation between the defense and the prosecution almost obsolete (Gershman 1992; Uviller 1999). Though plea bargaining has now become the most prevalent form of resolving criminal cases, the U.S. Supreme Court, relative to its case law on trial adjudication, has not developed clear constitutional limitations on the guilty plea process. The Court, in principle, maintains the basic voluntariness standard for accepting guilty pleas. It has held that a guilty plea that is compelled by the government is unconstitutional because it violates the Fifth Amendment protection against self-incrimination (*Brady v. United States* 1970). It has further held that punishing a defendant for his exercise of his legal rights is "a due process violation of the most basic sort" (*Bordenkircher v. Hayes* 1978: 363). In the context of plea bargaining, however, the Court has placed very few limitations on the types of inducements that prosecutors may use to obtain guilty pleas. Prosecutors today, with their vastly expanded power, have greater leverage than ever to compel plea bargaining and to force cooperation. A fundamental issue raised by the current bargaining practice is that, with prosecutors having the power to coerce defendants into pleading guilty by threatening draconian penalties for non-cooperation, it becomes highly questionable whether the guilty pleas agreed upon by defendants can be considered to truly rest on voluntariness.

The coercive nature of American plea bargaining is well illustrated in various tactics that prosecutors may use in the bargaining process. "Overcharging" is a tactic often employed by prosecutors to augment leverage in bargaining. Overcharging is an ambiguous term and may include both unlawful and lawful but ethically inappropriate prosecutorial decision making.

The basic legal criterion that prosecutors meet in making a charging decision is that charges filed must be supported by probable cause (*Bordenkircher v. Hayes* 1978). However, prosecutors may deliberately file charges that are not supported by probable cause as a bargaining strategy. The strategy, though it is unlawful, can be a successful one. Because American law does not require prosecutors to open their entire file for inspection by the defense, the defense may well be kept in the dark as to the true strength of the prosecutor's case against the defendant.

Charging defendants with offenses without the support of probable cause is clearly unlawful, but a more difficult issue is whether all charging decisions that are supported by probable cause should be considered appropriate. Legally speaking, prosecutors' charging decisions are not in violation of law so long as the charges are supported by probable cause. In reality, however, if the goal of filing the charges is to secure convictions at trial, no cautious and responsible prosecutor would charge a defendant with crimes that are supported only by probable cause. The prosecutor must be confident that evidence is strong enough to meet the trial standard of proof beyond a reasonable doubt. But prosecutors may well decide to file charges that are only supported by probable cause in order to gain bargaining leverage. Because American prosecutors enjoy literally unlimited power to drop charges at later stages, they never have to suffer the embarrassment that the charges cannot be proven at trial. They can drop the weak charges and go to trial with only charges that are supported by stronger evidence. Considering that prosecutors bear an ethical duty to "seek justice, not merely to convict" (American Bar Association 1986: 36), filing multiple charges with the intent to compel plea bargaining, though not unlawful, is arguably in violation of prosecutors' ethical duty not to be mere partisan advocates.

Apart from filing multiple charges, another powerful weapon available to prosecutors is charging defendants under penalty-enhancing statutes. Penalty-enhancing statutes authorize enhanced punishments for offenders who have a certain number of prior convictions or who have committed offenses with certain aggravating circumstances. If a defendant is convicted under these statutes, the defendant cannot escape the minimum mandatory sentences stipulated in the statutes. Prosecutors, however, maintain the discretion to charge a defendant with offenses that would trigger the enhancement. Prosecutors' freedom to charge or not to charge under penalty-enhancing statutes therefore provides a powerful leverage to pressure defendants to accept deals desired by prosecutors.

Prosecutors' ability to influence the penalty of defendants is further strengthened by the adoption of federal and state sentencing guidelines. Sentencing guidelines are adopted in the name of curtailing sentencing judges' discretion in order to avoid sentencing disparity. The guidelines, however, have hardly solved the problem of sentencing disparity. Although they have greatly reduced sentencing judges' discretion, the guidelines have made no attempt to restrict prosecutors' charging decisions. Prosecutors' decision making on whether and what to charge has therefore become the most crucial factor in determining the length of defendants' sentences.

One of the most disturbing aspects of sentencing guidelines is the granting of prosecutorial power to request that defendants be punished for crimes of which they were not convicted. Under most sentencing guidelines, prosecutors are allowed to introduce at the sentencing phase far more serious but unproven crimes in order to enhance defendants' punishment. Because at the sentencing stage courts follow a more lenient standard in determining whether unproven crimes should be admitted as a factor in determining defendants' sentences, a tactic that prosecutors may use is to charge defendants with crimes of which they are confident of conviction and to save the weaker but possibly more serious charges to be introduced at the sentencing hearings as aggravating factors to enhance defendants' penalty. Using this tactic, prosecutors in many cases have succeeded in imposing on defendants sentences that are far more severe than the sentences that are stipulated for the crimes of which the defendants were convicted.

The accretion of prosecutorial power is also seen in the effect of the "federalization" of crime. In the past several decades, the federal government has become increasingly involved in regulating criminal conduct that was traditionally regarded as matters for states. The federal expansion into the criminal law arena has created a vast area of concurrent federal and state jurisdiction. This dual jurisdiction is best illustrated in the area of illegal drugs. Because of generally more severe penalties provided in federal statutes for similar offenses, the mere prospect of being prosecuted in the federal system, rather than in the state system, constitutes a potent threat to defendants.

To be fair to prosecutors, as legislatures have created new crimes without providing the resources for trial and punishment of all those who could be convicted, prosecutors have increasingly been forced to allocate resources by exercising discretion to decide whether to charge and whether to offer leniency in exchange for guilty pleas. Plea bargaining undoubtedly plays an important role in conserving the limited criminal justice resources. Nevertheless, considering that what prosecutors try to persuade defendants to give up is [the] defendants' constitutionally protected right to trial, it is quite reasonable to insist that everything be done to ensure that the bargaining process is a fair and just one. The current practice of providing prosecutors with such great power to compel guilty pleas and to force cooperation can hardly be said to have met this fairness standard. To allow prosecutors to threaten defendants with such enormous sentencing differential between pleading guilty and proceeding to trial serves only to underscore the discrepancy between promise and performance in the American criminal justice system and its hypocrisy vis-à-vis the constitutionally guaranteed right to a jury trial.

Prosecutors' power, though broad, is not totally unconstrained. The U.S. Supreme Court has long held that the exercise of prosecutorial discretion is subject to constitutional constraints. The Supreme Court first addressed the issue of selective prosecution in the seminal decision of *Yick Wo v. Hopkins* (1886). In that case, the Court overturned Yick Wo's conviction on the grounds of improper exercise of prosecutorial discretion. A San Francisco ordinance prohibited operating a laundry in a wooden building without the consent of the Board of Supervisors. The Board routinely granted permits to Caucasian but not to Chinese applicants. In invalidating the prosecutor's decision, the Court stated that even though the law is fair and impartial on its face, if it is "applied and administered by public authority with an evil eye and an unequal hand, so as practically to make unjust and illegal discriminations between persons in similar circumstances, material to their rights, the denial of equal justice is still within the prohibition of the Constitution" *(Yick Wo v. Hopkins* 1886: 373–74). The Court in later cases, however, made it clear that not all forms of arbitrary prosecution are prohibited by the Constitution. The Constitution prohibits selective prosecution on such grounds as race, gender, religion, and the exercise of First Amendment rights *(Oyler v. Boles* 1962; *Wayte v. United States* 1985).

Although the modern Court still upholds the position that prosecutors are prohibited from filing prosecution on constitutionally impermissible grounds, it has set a high evidentiary threshold for proving such improper exercise of prosecutorial discretion. The modern Court takes the position that mere discriminatory effect does not suffice to show a constitutional violation. To prevail in a claim on equal protection grounds, a party must provide evidence to show discriminatory purpose (*Washington v. Davis* 1976). In challenging improper exercise of prosecutorial discretion, defendants therefore must show impermissible motive on the part of prosecutors. The problems involved in showing such motive are enormous. A prosecutor would rarely admit that the charging decision was based on constitutionally impermissible grounds. The Court, meanwhile, is reluctant to make other means available for defendants to prove prosecutors' motive. The Court's recent decision in *United States v. Armstrong* (1996) provides the best example to illustrate the difficulty that the Court has created for defendants in such an attempt.

The *Armstrong* case involves a challenge to a prosecuting decision based on race. The respondents in *Armstrong* were all blacks, and they were indicted on crack cocaine and federal firearms charges. The respondents filed a motion for discovery, alleging that they were improperly selected for prosecution in the federal court in the crack cases. Based on statistical evidence showing that nonblacks were disproportionately being prosecuted in state courts, thus facing less severe penalties, the respondents sought a court order to compel the U.S. Attorney's Office to disclose relevant information regarding the selective prosecution of crack cases. The district court issued the order, but the U.S. Supreme Court reversed.

In reversing the discovery order, the Court stated the need to establish a "substantial barrier" to proving selective prosecution claims. The Court held that, before prosecutors can be required to comply with a discovery request regarding selective prosecution, defendants must meet the threshold requirement of a credible showing that there is a different treatment of similarly situated persons. The Court justified its ruling on the grounds of respect for the separation of powers between judicial and executive branches and the interests in facilitating effective law enforcement. The Court reasoned that judicial deference to prosecutorial discretion would serve the purposes of avoiding unnecessary delay in criminal proceedings and protecting the prosecution from being compelled to reveal prosecutorial strategies.

The *Armstrong* case poses hurdles for defendants to overcome. If defendants want to request discovery from the prosecution, they must first demonstrate with credible evidence that similarly situated persons are not prosecuted, but such evidence is usually available only to prosecutors. Without access to such evidence, defendants may never succeed in seeking a discovery order or prevail in a claim challenging the constitutionality of a prosecutorial decision. Given the modern Court's prosecution-oriented approach, one should not be surprised to learn that *Yick Wo* was the first and the last time the Supreme Court struck down a prosecution on the grounds of improper selection of the target by prosecutors.

Setting formidable evidentiary thresholds for defendants seeking discovery is not the only step that the Court has taken to insulate prosecutors from judicial supervision. The Court has also strengthened prosecutors' discretionary power by relaxing the constitutional protections embodied in the exclusionary rule and due process (*New York v. Quarles* 1984; *Nix v. Williams* 1984; *United States v. Leon* 1984) and by interpreting statutory and evidentiary rules in favor of the prosecution (*United States v. Mezzanatto* 1995). The passive stance taken by the Court with respect to judicial supervision over prosecutorial behavior has undoubtedly stimulated a law enforcement mentality that the "end justifies the means." The approach of extreme deference to prosecutorial decision making has created a great incentive on the part of prosecutors to enact bold and aggressive prosecutorial initiatives and to test judicial tolerance for highly offensive law enforcement methods.

PROSECUTORIAL DISCRETION IN CONTINENTAL LAW COUNTRIES

Despite the common perception that all continental law systems operate in more or less the same fashion, there are marked differences in criminal justice practices between continental law systems. In the context of prosecutorial practice, the principle of compulsory prosecution is far from universally accepted. Prosecutorial discretion in filing charges differs among continental law countries, depending on whether a country follows the "expediency principle" or the "legality principle." In countries that follow the expediency principle, prosecutors are allowed a high degree of autonomy in making charging decisions; prosecutors have discretion to consider various public interest factors in deciding whether charges should be filed in a particular case. In countries that follow the legality principle, by contrast, prosecutors are required to file charges whenever sufficient evidence exists to support the guilt of the accused; public interest considerations are irrelevant in prosecutors' decision making (Fionda 1995).

Few countries follow either principle strictly. However, based on the extent to which a country follows one principle or the other, commentators are still able to determine whether a country follows the expediency principle or the legality principle. For instance, the prosecutorial systems in France and the Netherlands are classified as following the expediency principle, whereas the systems in Germany and Italy are categorized as following the legality principle (Fionda 1995; Grande 2000; Verrest 2000).

A noticeable development in recent years is that even in countries that follow the legality principle there are signs of moving away from strict adherence to compulsory prosecution. This trend is probably best seen in the emergence of plea bargaining in Germany and Italy. What is equally noticeable, however, is that, despite the emergence of plea bargaining in continental law countries, no country has allowed prosecutors to gain such bargaining advantage over the accused that they are in a position to exact highly pressurized pleas from the accused. This point is amply illustrated in the following discussion of plea bargaining analogues in France, Germany, and Italy.

France

France follows the expediency principle. The enforcement of the law does not oblige prosecutors to file charges in all cases with a view to obtaining the severest sentences possible. On the contrary, a long-established principle in France is that prosecutors, as members of the judiciary, are not entrusted with the task of securing convictions in all cases. Prosecutors' obligation is rather to determine a just solution to the case and present it to the judge (Sheehan 1975; Vouin 1970). This principle is embodied in the French Code of Penal Procedure. The provision in the Code that defines the responsibility of prosecutors simply provides that "the prosecutor receives complaints and denunciations and decides what to do with them" (Code of Penal Procedure, Article 40). This language is interpreted to permit prosecutors not to prosecute even when sufficient evidence exists to prove the guilt of an accused. Available statistics indicate that in France, as in the United States, the majority of cases reported to prosecutors do not end with a criminal trial. It is estimated that between 50 per cent and 80 per cent of cases brought to the attention of prosecutors in France are disposed of by no-further-proceeding (Frase 1990; Verrest 2000; West, Desdevises, Fenet, Gaurier, and Heussaff 1993).

French law classifies criminal offenses into three categories: *contraventions* (minor offenses), *délits* (intermediate offenses), and *crimes* (serious offenses). Corresponding to the three types of offenses, there are three first-instance trial courts. *Contraventions* are tried in the Police Court; *délits* are tried in the Correctional Court; and *crimes* are tried in the Assize Court (Terrill 1999). The pretrial screening process differs depending on the type of offense involved and the court in which the prosecution is to be instituted. The law mandates a stringent pretrial screening for cases to be tried as *crimes* in the Assize Court. Once a decision is made that a case is to be tried in the Assize Court, the prosecutor must send the case to the examining magistrate for a judicial investigation. If the magistrate finds sufficient evidence to bind the case over for trial, the case must be sent to the indicting chamber for further screening. The role of prosecutors is quite limited in cases that involve a judicial investigation. Prosecutors have the discretion to make the initial decision whether to refer the case to the examining magistrate, but once the case is sent to the magistrate, prosecutors lose control over the case. At the completion of the magistrate's investigation, prosecutors must follow the magistrate's recommendation for disposition (Frase 1990; Tomlinson 1983; West et al. 1993).

In contrast to the stringent pretrial screening for cases to be tried in the Assize Court, French law requires no pretrial screening of any kind for cases to be tried in the Correctional Court or the Police Court. Prosecutors have the sole authority to decide whether a case should be prosecuted or dismissed. Because of the cumbersome procedures involved in prosecuting a case in the Assize Court, prosecutors understandably view with distaste the prospect of trying all *crimes* in the Assize Court. Although the law requires that all *crimes* be tried in the Assize Court, prosecutors may circumvent this limitation by charging an offender who has committed a *crime* with only a *délit* or a *contravention*. The prosecutors' power to reduce charges is known as *correctionalization*. It is this power of correctionalization that is referred to by American commentators as the French analogue of plea bargaining (Frase 1990; Goldstein and Marcus 1977; Tomlinson 1983).

The correctionalization of a *crime* to a *délit* or a *contravention* is undoubtedly similar to the charge reduction used by American prosecutors. The varied reasons cited by French prosecutors for correctionalizing a *crime* are also similar to those given by American prosecutors for reducing charges. French prosecutors may correctionalize a *crime* to avoid subjecting defendants to the possibility of more severe penalties imposed by the Assize Court. There are times that, though an offense is technically a *crime*, the prosecutor may feel that, under the particular circumstances, it is not appropriate to subject the defendant to the harsh punishment that is spelled out for the offense. The prosecutor may then charge the defendant with a less serious offense to avoid the harsh penalty. Prosecutors may also use correctionalization as a means to alleviate the congested calendar in the Assize Court (Frase 1990; Leigh and Zedner 1992; Tomlinson 1983).

The similarities between American plea bargaining and French correctionalization, however, end here. In France, there is no evidence indicating that the reduction of charges or the decision to correctionalize a *crime* is a result of bargains and negotiations between prosecutors and the defense. The decision to correctionalize a case is the unilateral decision of prosecutors. The only role that defendants play is their right to reject a prosecutor's decision to correctionalize a *crime* to a *délit* or a *contravention*. Because defendants enjoy more elaborate procedural protections if their cases are tried in the Assize Court, if defendants are willing to risk more severe penalties in case of conviction, they have the right to insist that their cases be tried in the Assize Court. In reality, however, few defendants choose to challenge prosecutors' decisions to correctionalize a *crime* to a *délit* or a *contravention* (Frase 1990; Tomlinson 1983).

In the American system, a prosecutor's promise to reduce charges is usually made on the condition that the defendant makes a full and irrevocable confession of guilt. By contrast, a French prosecutor's decision to correctionalize a *crime* is not dependent on whether a confession is made by the accused. Relative to the procedural protections granted to suspects by American law, French law grants suspects very limited protections at the police investigative stage. Under French law, the accused has the right to remain silent, but police bear no obligation to inform. A limited right to counsel at the police inquiry was not introduced into the French criminal procedure until 1993. Under the amended law, suspects have the right to seek legal consultation only after the first 20 hours of detention have expired (Field and West 1995; Hatchard, Huber, and Volger 1996). During the first 20 hours, police are therefore given the opportunity to interrogate suspects without informing them of their right to remain silent or providing them with legal representation. Because suspects at this stage are not represented by counsel, it is unlikely that their confessions are made with the expectation that the confessions will lead to prosecutors deciding to reduce their offenses to less serious ones.

Furthermore, under French law a defendant's admission of guilt does not replace trial, and a confession is never irrevocable. Even after an admission of guilt, a defendant still has to go through a trial. A defendant's decision not to contest his guilt, however, will make the trial shorter. A defendant may retract the confession at any time, either before or during the trial. The defendant's retraction, however, would not prevent the confession from being introduced at trial. The defendant's confession, retracted or not, will be introduced to court for consideration. The only effect of a retraction is that the prosecutor in such a case will introduce to court both the defendant's confession and the fact that it was retracted (West et al. 1993).

Unlike American prosecutors, who have unlimited power to drop charges before and after they are filed with the court, French prosecutors' broad charging authority is confined to the initial decision whether to file a charge with the court. Once prosecutors file charges with the examining magistrate or the court, they cannot drop the charges without the approval of the magistrate or the court (Frase 1990; Tomlinson 1983). French prosecutors' inability to drop charges at post-filing makes it impossible for them to use overcharging as a means to coerce cooperation from the accused. Because prosecutors cannot drop charges once they are filed, if the charges are not supported by sufficient evidence they can only be rejected by the magistrate or the court (Frase 1990; West et al. 1993). From the prosecutor's point of view, to file charges that would be rejected by the court or the magistrate as inadequately supported by the evidence could serve no purpose and would negatively reflect on the prosecutor's professional ability. It is hard to imagine that cautious prosecutors would be willing to risk their professional reputation for the doubtful advantage of using overcharging as a means to induce cooperation from the accused.

Charging defendants with multiple offenses is another powerful weapon available to American prosecutors. What makes multiple-offense charges a potent threat is the likelihood that defendants may be subject to multiple consecutive sentences if convicted. French prosecutors, with their broad charging discretion, can certainly decide to charge an accused with multiple offenses. Under the French sentencing law, however, it is unlikely that such a move would provide prosecutors with powerful leverage to induce cooperation from the accused. French law prohibits the imposition of multiple consecutive sentences in multiple-offense cases. This means that, even though an accused is convicted of multiple offenses, only one sentence for the most serious offense can be pronounced. The maximum sentence for the most serious offense cannot be enhanced on the ground that the accused was also convicted of collateral offenses (Frase 1990; West et al. 1993).

Prosecutorial discretion in France can also be constrained by victims. French law provides several means for victims to challenge prosecutors' decision not to prosecute. French law also recognizes the right of victims to seek compensation by joining the criminal proceedings as a civil party. The law stipulates two ways in which victims may do this. Victims may make a request to be joined as a party to criminal proceedings already instituted by prosecutors. However, if prosecutors decline to prosecute a case, victims may open the proceedings for compensation in a criminal court by themselves. If a victim chooses to open the proceedings for compensation in a criminal court, the prosecutor is then obligated to prosecute the case, even though prosecution was initially declined (Terrill 1999; West et al. 1993).

Victims also have the power to prevent prosecutors from correctionalizing a *crime* to a *délit* or a *contravention*. If victims wish to seek a more severe penalty than the Correctional Court or Police Court can impose, they may file a complaint directly with the examining magistrate and request that the magistrate commence a judicial inquiry into the case. The reference of a case to the magistrate by a victim has the same effect as the reference of a case by prosecutors. Once the case is referred to the magistrate, prosecutors are no longer in control of the case. The magistrate, upon finding sufficient evidence, may order prosecutors to prosecute the case in the Assize Court (Tomlinson 1983; West et al. 1993; Zauberman 1991).

It should be noted that correctionalization is not the only means available to French prosecutors to avoid lengthy trials in the Assize Court. Since the early 1980s, there has been a steady increase in the number of criminal offenses in France. To allow prosecutors to dispose of the dramatically increased number of cases in a timely fashion, French law makes available to them several options of settling cases. In minor offense cases, instead of prosecuting, the prosecutor may give an order to the police to issue an official warning to the offender. In cases of vandalism and petty theft, the prosecutor may ask the offender to repair the damage or compensate the loss suffered by the victim as a condition to dismiss the case. The prosecutor can also settle a case through mediation. If a mediation agreement can be reached by the victim and the offender, the prosecutor may decide to dismiss the case on the condition that the offender follow through on the terms of the agreement (e.g., pay damages to the victim) (Verrest 2000).

For offenses that arc punishable by no more than seven years' imprisonment, the law also permits prosecutors, with the consent of the accused, to process the case through speeded-up trial proceedings (*comparution immédiate*). These proceedings are most commonly used in cases where offenders are caught red-handed. In the speeded-up trial proceedings, suspects, after a brief meeting with their lawyers, are brought to trial immediately. Prosecutors, however, do not have the sole control over the proceedings. The court has the final authority to decide whether the speeded-up proceedings are appropriate. The court can decide to postpone dealing with the case and refer it back to the prosecutor if it feels that the case was insufficiently investigated (Verrest 2000).

Germany

The appeal of the German prosecutorial system to American law reformers lies largely in the principle of compulsory prosecution. Many American readers believe that, under the rule of compulsory prosecution, prosecutors are allowed no discretion and are required to prosecute all cases that are supported by the evidence. This view, however, does not represent a correct understanding of the rule. The rule of compulsory prosecution was incorporated into the German Code of Criminal Procedure in 1877 when the Code was first drawn up (Fionda 1995). The aim of incorporating the rule into the Code was to achieve an equal application of law and to prevent the possibility that prosecutors would use law enforcement power to persecute political opponents (Schramm 1970). Since 1877, a variety of new provisions aimed at widening prosecutors' discretion have been incorporated into the Code. These new provisions have led to a gradual erosion of the principle of mandatory prosecution.

The celebrated rule of compulsory prosecution is prescribed in Section 152 (II) of the Code of Criminal Procedure. The Section provides that prosecutors must "take action against all prosecutable offenses, to the extent that there is sufficient factual basis." The Code, however, contains several exceptions to the rule. A major exception is provided in Section 153a. This section, which was added to the Code in 1975, authorizes prosecutors to refrain from prosecuting any minor offenses on the condition that the accused agrees to pay a sum of money to a charitable organization or to the state. The section, when it was enacted, was designed to limit prosecutorial discretion to misdemeanor cases only. It was further expected that prosecutors, guided by the rule of compulsory prosecution, would exercise the power of dismissal only in trivial misdemeanor cases (Langbein 1979).

Implementation since the section's enactment, however, shows that prosecutors have used the section to dismiss both petty and serious crimes. The exceptions to the rule of compulsory prosecution have provided opportunities for the development of plea bargaining in Germany.

The origin of plea bargaining in Germany can be traced back to the early 1970s. Initially, the bargaining practice was limited in scope and restricted to minor offenses. By the mid-1970s, with the increase in prosecutions against white-collar crimes and drug offenses, plea bargaining became more prevalent. Since the 1990s, the rise in popularity of plea bargaining is attributable directly to the sharp increase in white-collar crimes, economic crimes, drug offenses, and the increased caseload brought about by German reunification. Plea bargaining, as noted by the commentators, occurs most frequently in cases involving white-collar crimes, tax evasion, drug offenses, and crimes against the environment (Dubber 1997; Frase and Weigend 1995; Herrmann 1992; Swenson 1995).

Plea bargaining in Germany takes different forms. The most commonly identified forms are (a) diversion bargains under Section 153a, (b) bargains over penal orders, and (c) bargains over confessions. Section 153a permits the prosecutor to conditionally dismiss cases when the crime is minor and the public interest does not require prosecution. Under the section, prosecutors may refrain from prosecuting on condition that the offender either provides some form of compensation to the victim or makes payment to a charity or to the Treasury. Since its enactment in 1975, Section 153a has opened up the possibility for the prosecutor and the defense to negotiate as to whether a case should be settled.

In complicated cases, if prosecutors believe that further investigation may occupy too much time, they may offer to settle the case under the section. To induce defendants to settle, prosecutors may make it clear to the defense counsel that the offer is a one-time offer, and, if it is refused, there will be no further chance for negotiation. Defense counsel may also influence prosecutorial decision making on whether to settle a case. Under German law, defense counsel at trial has the right to make motions to request that the judge consider additional evidence favorable to the accused. To induce prosecutors to settle the case before the case goes to trial, defense counsel may threaten to make numerous motions requesting the court to examine additional evidence. Concerned that such moves may delay the trial, prosecutors may agree to settle the case under Section 153a (Albrecht 2000; Frase and Weigend 1995; Herrmann 1992).

The second form of plea bargaining originates from the penal order procedure. The penal order is a document prepared by the prosecutor, which contains the accused's offense and the punishment for the offense. Punishments in the penal order include day fines, a suspended prison sentence of up to one year, suspension of a driving license, and forfeiture of the profits of the crime. The prosecutor must obtain the consent from a judge to make the order legally binding. Once judicial authorization is obtained, the prosecutor dispatches the order to the accused. The accused has 14 days to decide whether to accept the order or to request a trial in court.

The attractiveness of the penal order for the accused lies in less severe penalties contained in the order compared to the potential sentences that could be imposed if the accused were convicted at trial. In the vast majority of cases, the penalty contained in the penal order is a monetary fine. By paying the fine, the accused avoids embarrassment, publicity, and the costs of trial. Under the penal order procedure, though there is a possibility that the accused may receive more severe penalties by choosing to go to trial, a higher sentence is not an automatic consequence of the accused's rejection of the penal order. If the court were to increase the severity of the accused's penalty after a trial, the judge must indicate the reasons for such a decision. Rejection of the penal order alone is not sufficient grounds to increase the severity of the penalty to be imposed on the accused. There is therefore no evidence showing that prosecutors use the possible higher sentences to pressure the accused to accept a penal order (Frase and Weigend 1995; Herrmann 1992).

The third form of plea bargaining is bargaining over confessions. In Germany, as in France, an accused's confession and guilty plea do not replace the trial. The advantage for the prosecutor in obtaining a confession is that an accused's admission of guilt could shorten the length of the trial. A noticeable distinction between German bargaining over confessions and American plea bargaining is the role of the judge in the bargaining process. Plea bargaining in the United States is typically a negotiation between prosecutor and defense counsel. The judge is not an active participant in the bargaining. In Germany, before a formal charge is filed with the court, the prosecutor plays a major part in negotiating with defense counsel regarding the prospect of an accused's confession; the prosecutor may offer to charge the accused with fewer offenses than the accused is alleged to have committed or to move for a lenient sentence at trial. Once the charge is filed with the court, however, the judge may become an active participant in the plea negotiation.

A judge who is faced with a backlog on the docket may contact defense counsel and inquire whether the accused would be willing to make a confession at the beginning of the trial. To encourage the accused to confess, the judge may indicate an upper sentencing limit that might be imposed. Under German law, the judge cannot make a definite settlement of the case until after the trial. The understanding reached between judge and defense counsel is therefore *de jure* nonbinding. In most cases, however, if the accused agrees to make a confession, the sentence that the accused eventually receives will be below the upper limit indicated by the judge. Negotiations could also occur during the trial. For instance, defense counsel may agree not to call additional evidence or promise not to bring an appeal in exchange for sentencing concessions from the judge (Dubber 1997; Herrmann 1992; Swenson 1995).

The increased popularity of plea bargaining in Germany, a country once praised as a land without plea bargaining, unquestionably represents one of the most significant developments in prosecutorial practices in continental law countries. German plea bargaining, however, differs in several aspects from the bargaining practice in the United States. In Germany, defendants' decisions to plead guilty after negotiating with prosecutors are usually well informed. In the German system, defense counsel at the pretrial stage has the right to inspect the prosecutor's file in its entirety. In negotiations with the prosecutor, the defense attorney would have the full knowledge of the strength of the prosecutor's evidence. This broad pretrial discovery right not only makes it easier for defense attorneys to provide well-informed advice to defendants, it also makes it difficult for prosecutors to resort to tactics such as overcharging or charging the accused with offenses that are not supported by evidence (Frase and Weigend 1995; Swenson 1995).

German prosecutors may indeed use the tactic of dropping collateral charges as leverage to encourage the accused to admit guilt. This charge bargain nevertheless is not conducted in a highly pressurized fashion. In Germany, although a prosecutor's offer to drop collateral charges may provide incentives on the part of the accused to cooperate, prosecutors are not in a position to drastically increase the severity of the penalty to be imposed on the accused in multiple-offense cases. German law does not permit the imposition of multiple consecutive sentences. Prosecutors therefore cannot expect that a threat to charge the accused with multiple crimes would create pressure on the accused to plead guilty or cooperate with the government (Pram and Weigend 1995; Swenson 1995).

In Germany, the prosecutor's discretionary power is also constrained by victims. In contrast to victims' powerless position in the American system, victims in Germany may take several courses of action to influence prosecutors' charging decisions. If a victim is not satisfied with the prosecutor's decision not to prosecute, the victim may file a formal complaint with a chief prosecutor. The chief prosecutor must internally review the dismissal decision and decide whether a prosecution should be ordered. If the chief prosecutor upholds the decision to dismiss, the victim has the right to request an appellate court judge to review the case. The victim's right to request judicial review, however, is limited to cases in which the prosecutor's decision to dismiss is made on evidentiary grounds. In those cases, if the judge finds evidence to be sufficient for prosecution, the prosecutor can be ordered to prosecute. The victim has no right to ask the court to review the prosecutor's decision of non-prosecution if the prosecutor's decision rests on policy grounds (for instance, the prosecutor's belief that the public interest does not require prosecution) (Albrecht 2000; Fionda 1995).

The German system imposes more restrictions on the exercise of prosecutorial discretion, but the system is by no means perfect. The German prosecutorial service is organized at the state level instead of nationally. This fragmented organizational structure makes it difficult to maintain consistent prosecutorial decision making throughout the system. There are usually guidelines in local prosecutors' offices to aid individual prosecutors in their decision making. These guidelines, however, differ from office to office. The statutory criteria for non-prosecution, such as lack of public interest and the seriousness of the offense, are often subject to different interpretations. To reduce these discrepancies, some states have attempted to impose statewide rules. These rules, nevertheless, tend to be short and lacking in detail, making them unlikely to harness the use of prosecutorial discretion effectively (Fionda 1995). The weaknesses notwithstanding, one aspect of the German system that may have made German prosecutors more accountable than their American counterparts is the requirement that prosecutors provide written reasons for their disposal of cases. Such requirements undoubtedly encourage prosecutors to consider their decisions more carefully and to rest them on defensible grounds.

Italy

Comparative legal scholars in the past several decades have noted the trend of convergence between civil and common law systems (Frase and Weigend 1995; Glendon 1984; Zweigert and Kötz 1987). Recent changes in the Italian criminal justice system probably offer the best example of trends in the convergence between the two systems. Italy's adoption of the new Criminal Procedure Code in 1989 has attracted wide attention from the world legal community. One of the most noticeable features of the new code is its introduction of adversarial elements into Italy's deep-rooted inquisitorial trial proceedings (Fassler 1991; Pizzi and Marafioti 1992). In the context of prosecutorial practice, what is equally noticeable is the new code's introduction of plea bargaining analogues into the Italian criminal justice system.

Before the adoption of the new code, Italy was one of the few countries that followed the legality principle in its strictest sense. The strict adherence to the principle had resulted in a tremendous judicial backlog. Because no trial avoidance mechanisms were available in the Italian procedure, the system relied principally on regularly granted amnesties as a way to alleviate overcrowded courts. The amnesties, however, were far from a solution to the problem. Finding ways to solve the problem of congested courts thus became a primary task of the drafters of the new code. The new code does not use the language of plea bargaining, but it contains two trial avoidance procedures that allow the imposition of sentences on the accused without a full trial. These special procedures have become known as Italy's plea bargaining analogues (Boari 1997; Grande 2000; Mack 1996; Miller 1990; Van Cleave 1997).

The two trial avoidance procedures are: (a) party-agreed sentences, and (b) abbreviated or summary trials. The procedure of party-agreed sentences means that the prosecutor and the defense may enter into an agreement as to the appropriate sentence to be imposed on the defendant without going through a trial. The statutory requirement for the two parties to enter into such an agreement is that the final punishment cannot exceed two years of imprisonment. This statutory requirement does not prohibit the procedure from being used in crimes that are punishable by more than two years of imprisonment. It simply means that, after considering all the circumstances surrounding the case, if the prosecutor and the defense attorney agree that the final sentence would not exceed two years of imprisonment, the procedure can then be applied (Grande 2000; Van Cleave 1997).

The agreement entered into by the prosecutor and the defense attorney is subject to judicial review. The Code of Criminal Procedure contains the specific standards by which the judge is to evaluate the party-agreed sentences. The judge is required to evaluate whether the parties have correctly determined the nature of the offense and whether the sentence agreed upon by the parties is appropriate in light of the evidence. The judge may reject the agreement if he or she believes that the agreement was inappropriately reached (Code of Penal Procedure Article 444).

In Italy, it is a constitutional requirement that judges give written reasons for all dispositive judicial actions (Italian Constitution Article 102[1]). A controversy that arose after the adoption of the new Criminal Procedure Code was whether judges should give reasons when they are performing the function of evaluating party-agreed sentences. Some argued that the constitutional requirement should not apply to cases where a judge is simply performing the function of accepting party-agreed sentences (Van Cleave 1997). The Italian Constitutional Court, however, rejected this argument, holding that, even when judges are imposing party-agreed sentences, they must still issue written reasons for the sentences (*Decision of March 29. 1993*). The ruling of the Italian Constitutional Court strongly indicates that the Court does not want judges to simply perform a rubber-stamp function and endorse all agreements reached by the parties. Under the ruling of the Court, judges must faithfully execute their judicial duties to ensure that agreements reached by the parties are truly in compliance with the law.

In the United States, in order for a deal to be presented to a judge for approval, there must be an agreed upon deal between prosecution and defense. Prosecutors have total freedom to refuse to offer a deal to a defendant or to stop dealing with the defendant at any time after the initiation of the negotiation. The Italian procedure, by contrast, has not granted prosecutors the absolute power to deny defendants the opportunity to enter into a deal with the government. In party-agreed sentences, prosecutors' consent is required; there is nevertheless a requirement that prosecutors not withhold consent unreasonably (Code of Penal Procedure Article 448[1]). Prosecutors must justify their decision to reject a defendant's request for party-agreed sentences in writing, and the justifications given by prosecutors are subject to judicial evaluation. A prosecutorial rejection of a defendant's request to cut a deal ... will [technically] force the case to trial. However, if the judge at trial determines that the prosecutor unreasonably withheld consent to the defendant's request to settle the case, the judge may grant the defendant the reduced sentence that the defendant originally requested (Boari 1997; Grande 2000; Van Cleave 1997).

Abbreviated trial is another procedure designed to unclog the courts by quickly disposing of cases. In contrast to party-agreed sentences, which can be initiated by either the prosecutor or the defense, abbreviated trial procedure can only be requested by the defendant. At the preliminary hearing, the defendant may request that the court dispose of the case on the basis of the evidence thus far accumulated. Although this procedure cannot be initiated by the prosecutor, the prosecutor's consent is required. If the prosecutor gives consent to the defendant's request, the judge will determine whether it is possible to dispose of the case by using the abbreviated trial. If the judge determines that the case can be so disposed, the judge will issue a sentence of conviction (Code of Penal Procedure Articles 438, 440[1], 442). The incentive given to defendants for availing themselves of this special procedure is that, after being convicted under this special procedure, they will receive a statutorily mandated one-third reduction of the sentence that would have been imposed on them should they have been convicted after a full trial (Code of Penal Procedure Article 442[2]).

An interesting point, once again, is the role of the prosecutor. The prosecutor's consent is required before a case can be settled under the abbreviated trial procedure. But there is a similar requirement that the prosecutor not withhold consent unreasonably (Code of Penal Procedure Article 440[1]). The prosecutor's dissent to a defendant's request to settle the case under the abbreviated trial procedure will have the effect of forcing the case to go to a full trial. If the judge, however, determines that the prosecutor's dissent is unreasonable, the judge may grant the defendant the one-third sentence reduction in disregard of the prosecutor's dissent (Grande 2000; Van Cleave 1997).

There are no explicit provisions in the Italian Code of Criminal Procedure that require prosecutors to provide reasons for their dissent to a defendant's request to settle a case under the abbreviated trial procedure. However, the Italian Constitutional Court has held that it is a constitutional requirement that prosecutors give reasons for not granting consent. The basic reason for the Court to impose such an obligation is to ensure that the courts may evaluate the appropriateness of prosecutors' decisions (*Decision of February 8, 1990; Decision of April 18, 1990; Decision of February 15, 1991*). The Court rested its decisions to subject the prosecutor's dissent to judicial scrutiny on two grounds. The first is the principle of equality between prosecutor and defense. The Court reasoned that, because the prosecutor's dissent would affect the ultimate choice of sentences, the principle of equality calls for a judicial review of the prosecutor's decision. The second reason for the Court's insistence on judicial review is based on the concern that giving prosecutors the unreviewable power to decide who may avail themselves of the abbreviated trial may result in a situation that similarly situated defendants may receive different sentences.

COMPARISON AND OBSERVATIONS

Three decades have passed since the great debate in the 1970s on the merits of reforming the American system based on the continental models. The past 30 years have seen dramatic changes in continental law systems. The emergence of plea bargaining represents one of the most significant changes that have taken place in continental law systems. Today, none of the major continental law countries can still be described as a land without plea bargaining. The recent expansion of prosecutorial autonomy in continental law countries notwithstanding, it remains true that continental prosecutors' discretion is subject to much stricter control and supervision than that enjoyed by their American counterparts. Furthermore, despite the emergence of plea bargaining, no continental law countries have allowed plea bargaining to be conducted in a highly pressurized fashion. If the goal is to narrow the scope of prosecutorial discretion and to subject prosecutorial discretion to more meaningful control and supervision, the American system can still benefit from the experience of continental law countries.

When comparing the inquisitorial and the adversarial systems, it is generally recognized that the inquisitorial system places more emphasis on the search for the substantive truth, whereas the adversarial system focuses more on ensuring procedural fairness for the adversaries (Ehnnann 1976; Meriyman 1985; Van Kessel 1992; Zweigert and Kötz 1987). Philosophical differences regarding the criminal justice process are apparent in the structural differences between the two systems. In the inquisitorial system, the procedures, from investigation to trial, are designed with the aim of facilitating the ascertainment of the substantive truth. Investigators are under the legal obligation to conduct an objective investigation by following all leads that may shed light on the case, regardless of whether they are against or in favor of the accused. At trial, the judge, in the interest of searching for the truth, is obligated to examine all evidence with the same vigor, regardless of whether it points to the accused's guilt or innocence (Frase 1990; Sheehan 1975; Tomlinson 1983; Van Kessel 1992).

Tension may develop, however, between the zeal of searching for the truth and the interest of efficient administration of justice. As illustrated by what happened in Germany and Italy, the growing number of cases may make it difficult for the criminal justice system to handle all cases through formal trials. Continental law countries, therefore, have also turned to plea bargaining as a way to alleviate the burdened system of justice. An examination of various forms of plea bargaining in continental law countries, however, suggests that the bargaining proceedings are designed only to allow prosecutors to encourage the accused to admit guilt. Prosecutors in none of the continental law countries are given the power to threaten the accused with sentencing differentials as a way to compel plea bargaining and force cooperation. In other words, even with their embrace of the bargaining justice, continental law countries have not allowed the interest of efficient administration of criminal justice to unduly outweigh the interest of ascertaining the truth.

Scholars have long criticized the distortive effect of American plea bargaining on the roles of the prosecutor, judge, and defense counsel (Alschuler 1983; Gifford 1983; Misner 1996). The players in the bargaining process in many cases are more interested in working out deals for their respective interests than in searching for the substantive truth. A perplexing aspect of American plea bargaining is that defendants in many jurisdictions are allowed to plead guilty to offenses that do not represent the facts of the cases. Some jurisdictions require the judge who reviews the plea agreement to examine whether there is a factual basis for the plea. Rule II of the Federal Rule of Criminal Procedures prohibits the court from accepting a plea without inquiry into whether there is a factual basis for the plea. Not all jurisdictions, however, require the judge to conduct such an inquiry. In many jurisdictions, defendants are allowed to plead guilty to offenses that include elements that their conduct does not satisfy. In those cases, the truth is apparently allowed to be distorted for the convenience of cutting deals between prosecution and defense.

Truth seeking is also an important concern in the adversarial system. In the United States, prosecutors, in particular, have an obligation to seek the truth. Both the law and professional ethics demand that prosecutors be "something more than a partisan advocate intent on winning cases." Prosecutors bear a special duty "to protect the innocent and to safeguard the rights guaranteed to all, including those who may be guilty" (American Bar Association 1986: 20). In the adversarial system, however, the goal of truth seeking centers on the trial. At trial, detailed rules are developed with the aim of providing the prosecutor and the defense attorney with the fair opportunities to present and debate the evidence that they have each discovered. It is expected that, from the clash of the adversaries, the truth will emerge. But the problem with current American criminal justice administration is that trial procedures—so painstakingly developed in practice—contribute little to the cause of truth seeking when the vast majority of cases are settled not through trials but through guilty pleas. Despite the overwhelming dominance of plea bargaining in the American system, neither legislatures nor courts have shown any interest in developing mechanisms that would ensure that the truth will emerge from the bargaining process.

Although American plea bargaining is criticized, few advocate its abolition. It seems that plea bargaining, as reasoned by the U.S. Supreme Court over 30 years ago, has indeed become "an essential component of the administration of justice" (*Santobello v. New York* 1971: 261). Commentators, however, do believe that there is an urgent need to reform the way in which plea bargaining is currently conducted (Davis 1969; Dubber 1997; Frase 1990; Frase and Weigend 1995; Uviller 1999; Vorenberg 1981). It is in this context that the experience of continental law countries may provide important insights into how the American prosecutorial system may be reformed.

Lower penalties

A look at continental systems suggests several reforms to reduce coercion within the American system of plea bargaining. In comparison with the sentencing laws of continental law countries, American law imposes far more severe penalties on convicted offenders. The availability of long prison terms for a large number of crimes has provided prosecutors with the power to subject defendants to extremely severe penalties by charging multiple offenses or by seeking consecutive sentences. Prosecutors' discretion to decide whether to subject a defendant to the most severe sanction authorized by the penal law provides powerful leverage to coerce defendants to accept deals desired by prosecutors.

American scholars have long engaged in a debate on the relationship between the harshness of criminal sanctions and prosecutorial discretion. It is commonly agreed that a desirable aspect of prosecutorial discretion is that it allows the prosecutor to mitigate the severity of the criminal law and to individualize justice (Goldstein 1981). Some commentators further suggest that an important reason for the legislature's tendency to pass harsh laws is the legislature's belief that prosecutors will play the role of softening the harshness of criminal penalties by fitting them to the circumstances of individual offenders (Pizzi 1993).

There is no evidence indicating whether the harshness of criminal penalties is a cause of broad prosecutorial discretion or an effect of it. Commentators who are critical of broad prosecutorial discretion, however, are against the notion that prosecutors should be allowed to play the role of mitigating the harshness of the penal law. They argue that prosecutors should not be put in a position to overrule the legislature's judgment by dispensing mercy in the face of harsh sentences (Vorenberg 1981). Moreover, arming prosecutors with the power to choose from a wide range of sentences creates a great potential for prosecutors to misuse the power as leverage in coercing deals from defendants.

Broader pretrial discovery rights

A great disadvantage that an American defendant suffers in the bargaining process is a lack of complete knowledge about the prosecutor's case. In the continental criminal justice process, there is usually only one official criminal investigation. The investigation is carried out by either an examining magistrate or a prosecutor, with the assistance of the police. The officer responsible for the investigation is obligated to conduct an objective inquiry into the case, examining both evidence in favor of and against the accused. At the end of the investigation, a dossier is prepared, which contains all of the information gathered during the investigation. The defense has the unlimited right to examine the dossier. The advantage of this open process is that, because the defense is fully aware of the strength of the evidence held by the prosecution, it is unlikely that the prosecutor would use the tactics of overcharging or charging the defendant with unprovable offenses to gain bargaining advantages.

Most defendants in the American system, by contrast, do not know the true strength of the prosecution's case against them. Under present discovery rules, the prosecution has no obligation to reveal all evidence amassed against the defendant. Although the U.S. Supreme Court has held that prosecutors bear a constitutional duty to disclose exculpatory information that is material to the defense (*Brady v. Maryland* 1963), the scope of this prosecutorial duty is quite narrow because of the Court's conservative interpretation of the materiality rule (*Kyles v. Whitley* 1995; *United States v. Agurs* 1976; *United States v. Bagley* 1985). Because defendants have no right to have full access to the prosecutor's file, they are likely to be kept in the dark, during the plea negotiation, as to the strength of the evidence in the charges that prosecutors have filed. Limited pretrial defense discovery rights provide the opportunity and the incentive for prosecutors to overcharge or to charge defendants with unprovable offenses as a bargaining strategy. The introduction of broader discovery rules therefore would reduce prosecutors' incentives to overcharge and would prevent prosecutors from threatening defendants with unprovable charges.

Judicial supervision

Despite the recognized judicial power to constrain prosecutorial excesses, the American judiciary has traditionally played a passive role in providing supervision over the exercise of prosecutorial discretion (Goldstein 1981). It is for this reason that comparative legal scholars long ago observed that prosecutorial discretion in continental law countries is consistently controlled, whereas prosecutorial discretion in the United States is consistently uncontrolled (Davis 1969; Langbein 1979). Today, even with the emergence of plea bargaining and the expansion of prosecutorial discretion in continental law systems, the observation remains true that continental prosecutors are subject to far greater judicial control and supervision than their American counterparts.

Judges play an active role in various bargaining analogues in France, Germany, and Italy. In France, although the prosecutor has the power to correctionalize a *crime* to a *délit* or a *contravention*, a correctionalized case still goes to a regular trial. At trial, the judge must examine whether there is a factual basis for the charge and whether the charge is supported by sufficient evidence. Similarly, in Germany, after a confession agreement is reached between the prosecutor and the defendant, the case must still go to trial and be examined in open court by the judge. Commentators believe that the requirements that the defendant make a public confession and that the judge inquire into the case in open court can serve as a deterrent to prosecutorial overreaching, which in turn would reduce the likelihood of false convictions (Dubber 1997; Herrmann 1992).

In Italy, in both party-agreed sentences and abbreviated trial procedures, the judge is required to vigorously scrutinize the appropriateness of prosecutorial discretion. To ensure that prosecutors would not withhold consent to an accused's request to employ the special procedures, the law provides the judge—rather than the prosecutor—with the final authority to determine whether the benefit provided under the special procedure should be granted to the accused. The strict judicial supervision is designed to ensure that prosecutors exercise their discretion in conformity with the law (Grande 2000; Van Cleave 1997).

The United States boasts of a constitutionalized code of criminal procedure. Because improper exercise of prosecutorial discretion in many cases may implicate citizens' constitutionally protected rights, it seems logical that the courts should be more vigilant in the likelihood of prosecutorial abuse. But the American judiciary plays a much less vigorous role than courts in continental law countries in providing supervision over the exercise of prosecutorial discretion. The U.S. Supreme Court seems to have justified its reluctance to encourage more vigorous judicial supervision over prosecutors on three grounds: the separation of powers, the faith in prosecutors to discharge their duties properly, and the concern that vigorous judicial supervision over prosecutors may produce a chilling effect on law enforcement. Though each of these grounds has its merits, none of them provides sufficient justification for complete judicial deference to prosecutorial discretion.

Separation of powers provides a primary justification for the American judiciary's passive stance in supervising the prosecutorial function. It is reasoned that law enforcement is a function of the executive branch and that the judiciary, therefore, should show deference to prosecutorial decision making. The courts, however, routinely review the appropriateness of the decision making of other executive agencies, and they seldom decline review by citing the separation of powers. Judicial review of police action since the 1960s has imposed numerous new restrictions on law enforcement. The U.S. Supreme Court regularly reviews the appropriateness of police decision making. The issues covered by the Court in its decisions range from the circumstances under which police may establish probable cause and reasonable suspicion (*Florida v. J.L.* 2000; *Illinois v. Gates* 1983; *Illinois v. Wardlow* 2000; *Terry v. Ohio* 1968) to the appropriateness of various law enforcement tactics (*Atwater v. City of Lago Vista* 2001; *Indianapolis v. Edmond* 2001; *Michigan Department of State Police v. Ski* 1990) and the circumstances that may give rise to police civil liability (*Anderson v. Creighton* 1987; *Monroe v. Pape* 1961). Beyond the review of police actions, the Court has similarly determined issues such as school integration (*Alexander v. Holmes County Board of Education* 1969; *Swann v. Charlotte-Mecklenburg Board of Education* 1971) and the adequacy of prisons (*Rhodes v. Chapman*, 1981; *Whitley v. Albers*, 1986) and mental hospitals (*Connecticut Dept. of Income Maintenance. v. Heckler* 1985; *Zinermon v. Burch* 1990).

Because judicial review of executive decision making is commonplace, Davis observed more than 30 years ago that "if separation of powers prevents review of discretion of executive officers, then more than a hundred Supreme Court decisions spread over a century and three quarters will have to be found contrary to the Constitution!" (Davis 1969: 210). It is certainly true that the doctrine of separation of powers prohibits courts from usurping the prosecutor's power to execute the law. But there is a difference between the judiciary stepping into prosecutor's shoes to discharge the duties that should be performed by prosecutors and the judiciary providing necessary supervision to prevent arbitrary and unjustifiable prosecutorial decision making. Separation of powers therefore should not be a justification for the judiciary to withdraw from its obligation to control the abuse or misuse of prosecutorial power (Davis 1969; Goldstein 1981; Vorenberg 1981).

A fundamentally important principle that has repeatedly been upheld by the U.S. Supreme Court is that effective law enforcement cannot be accomplished at the expense of citizens' constitutional rights (*Mapp v. Ohio* 1961; *Miranda v. Arizona* 1966; *Payton v. New York* 1980). If effective law enforcement were the only goal of criminal justice, the Court might well relax judicial scrutiny of law enforcement actions. The Court, however, has never felt comfortable leaving freewheeling powers in the hands of police. Appreciating the special status that the Court has granted to prosecutors requires an examination of the Court's long-held presumption that prosecutors will discharge their duties properly.

The Supreme Court has held, in case after case, that judicial deference to prosecutorial decision making is justified on the presumption that prosecutors, as members of a respected profession, are able to discharge their official duties properly *(United States v. Ash* 1973; *United States v. Bagley* 1985; *United States v. Chemical Foundation Inc.* 1926; *Wayte v. United States* 1985). Although no one should doubt that prosecutors in most cases properly discharge their official duties, there is no reason to disregard the possibility that prosecutorial irregularities may occur. In the American system, the political process has played a significant part in the shaping of the role of the prosecutor, and there is a real possibility that political influence may enter into the prosecutor's decision-making process (Dubber 1997; Gershman 1992; Heller 1997; Vorenberg 1981). Prosecutors may deal with particular individuals harshly or gently for political reasons. It is also possible that race may play a role in prosecutorial decision making. It is for these reasons that Justice Stevens in his dissent in *Armstrong* said, "The possibility that political or racial animosity may infect a decision to institute criminal proceedings cannot be ignored" *(United States v. Armstrong* 1996: 476). This possibility, however, is mostly overlooked by the Court's current approach of insulating prosecutors from judicial review and supervision.

The American judiciary could play a more active role in supervising the exercise of prosecutorial discretion without American judges assuming the roles of continental judges. Prosecutorial accountability can be enhanced without drastically changing the traditional role played by judges in the American system. A modest step toward enhancing prosecutorial accountability through judicial supervision would be to require prosecutors to provide written reasons for prosecutorial decisions. Continental law countries seem to be quite aware of the importance of requiring prosecutors to provide justifications for their decisions. In Germany, prosecutors are required to provide written reasons for their disposition of cases, including their decisions in various forms of plea bargaining. In Italy, prosecutors are similarly required to justify their prosecutorial decisions in writing. Moreover, to ensure that judicial supervision over the newly introduced trial avoidance procedures would not be turned into a mere formality, the law further requires judges to give reasons for their acceptance of bargained agreements reached by prosecutors and defendants.

American prosecutors, in general, are not required to give reasons for their decisions. Courts are willing to accept prosecutors' decisions as constitutionally and legally appropriate without independent inquiry. In *Singer v. United States* (1965), the U.S. Supreme Court ruled that the prosecutor need not articulate reasons for withholding consent to a defendant's waiver of a jury trial. The Court rested its decision on familiar ground, i.e., its "confidence in the integrity of the federal prosecutor" *(Singer v. United States* 1965: 34). The willingness of the Court to tolerate a degree of secrecy in the decision making of one of the most crucial criminal justice agencies is quite inconsistent with the ideal of an open and decent system of justice.

There are multiple advantages to requiring prosecutors to provide justifications for their decisions. Prosecutor's obligation to justify their decisions would certainly compel individual prosecutors to be more careful in their decision making. The requirement would also make it easier for prosecutors' offices to exercise internal supervision. But the most significant advantage of such a requirement is that the written record left by prosecutors would allow courts to better evaluate the appropriateness of prosecutorial decision making. When the appropriateness of a prosecutor's decision is challenged, if the judge finds that the prosecutor's decision making is consistent with fairness and established procedures, the judge would concur with the propriety of the decision. If the prosecutor's decision grossly deviates from general patterns of fairness and law, the prosecutor must be required to furnish a rational basis for the deviation and to convince the court that the deviation is not based on constitutionally or legally impermissible grounds.

In making prosecutorial decisions, prosecutors consider a full range of factors. In addition to evidential sufficiency, prosecutors consider the attitude of the victim, the cost of prosecution to the criminal justice system, the avoidance of undue harm to the suspect, the availability of alternative procedures, the use of civil sanctions, and the willingness of the suspect to cooperate with law enforcement authorities (Miller 1970; Wallace 1995). No one should question the legitimacy of prosecutors' consideration of these factors. Courts under the doctrine of separation of powers indeed should not interfere with prosecutors' decisions as to which factors to consider and how much weight to give to each factor, but courts do have a duty to supervise prosecutors' decision making to ensure that discretion is applied consistently and evenhandedly. Due process demands no less.

CONCLUSION

American prosecutors' overly broad and essentially unchecked discretion remains one of the most distinctive features of American criminal justice. In the past 30 years, courts and legislatures, in the name of enhancing the fairness of American criminal justice and protecting relevant parties' due process rights, have imposed restrictions on the discretionary power of the police, sentencing judges, parole boards, and correctional authorities. Prosecutors, however, have been spared this shrinking of discretionary power. Indeed, as the discretionary authority of other criminal justice officials has contracted, that of prosecutors has expanded. Prosecutors now are truly the most central figures in the administration of justice. They are entrusted with the power to determine on whom penal resources will be spent and against whom society's harshest sanctions will be dispensed, but their decision-making process is, for the most part, insulated from judicial review and supervision. This uncontrolled prosecutorial discretion has created a great potential for abuse.

In contrast to American prosecutors' essentially unchecked power, continental prosecutors' discretion is subject to much stricter control and supervision. Faced with the pressure of handling a growing number of cases with limited resources, continental law countries have also turned to plea bargaining as a means to streamline criminal justice and alleviate overcrowded courts. But they have so far avoided turning plea bargaining into a prosecutor-dominated unilateral process. Their experience seems to indicate that, even though plea bargaining needs to be recognized as a component of the administration of justice, it is possible to have plea bargaining without it being coercive.

Comparative legal scholars have long argued for utilizing comparative criminal justice as a guide to American law reform. Despite the misgivings about the suitability of reforming one nation's legal system on the experience of another, the evolution of the world legal systems shows that there have been frequent migrations of legal institutions from one culture to another. Legal transplants are not only feasible but desirable (Ehrmann 1976; Jackson and Tushnet 1999; Schlesinger, Baade, Herzog, and Wise 1998; Zweigert and Kötz 1987). Today, as the world enters a new era of globalization, people who hold the view that the American system, because of its unique features, can never be reformed on foreign models seem to still be looking at problems from a parochial and self-centered perspective. In today's rapidly shrinking world, to effect meaningful law reforms, American reformers must be willing to look outward to other countries' experience and open up to the possibility that others may have developed approaches and procedures that can serve as a guide to American law reform.

REFERENCES

Albrecht. H.J. 2006. "Criminal Prosecution: Development, Trends and Open Questions in the Federal Republic of Germany." *European Journal of Crime, Criminal Law and Criminal Justice* 8: 245–56.

Alexander v. Holmes County Board of Education. 1969. 396 U.S. 19.

Atschuler, A. 1983. "Implementing the Criminal Defendant's Right to Trial: Alternatives to the Plea Bargaining System." *University of Chicago Law Review* 50: 931–1050.

American Bar Association. 1986. *Standards for Criminal Justice: The Prosecution Function.* Boston: Little Brown.

Anderson v. Creigton. 1987. 483 U.S. 635.

Arnold, T. 1932. "Law Enforcement: An Attempt at Social Discretion." *Yale Law Journal* 42: 1–24.

Atwater v. City of Lago Vista. 2001. 533 U.S. 924.

Boari, N. 1997. "On the Efficiency of Penal Systems: Several Lessons from the Italian Experience." *International Review of Law and Economics* 17: 115–25.

Bordenkircher v. Hayes. 1978. 434 U.S. 357.

Brady v. Maryland. 1963. 373 U.S. 83.

Brady v. United States. 1970. 397 U.S. 742.

Connecticut Department of Income Maintenance v. Heckler. 1985. 471 U.S. 524.

Currie, E. 1998. *Crime and Punishment in America.* New York: Metropolitan Books.

Davis, K.C. 1969. *Discretionary Justice.* Baton Rouge: Louisiana State University Press.

Decision of February 8, 1990. Italian Constitutional Court.

Decision of April 18, 1990. Italian Constitutional Court.

Decision of February 15, 1991. Italian Constitutional Court.

Decision of March 29, 1993. Italian Constitutional Court.

Dubber, M.D. 1997. "American Plea Bargaining, German Lay Judges, and the Crisis of Criminal Procedure." *Stanford Law Review* 49: 547–605.

Ehrmann, H.W. 1976. *Comparative Legal Cultures.* Englewood Cliffs: Prentice-Hill.

Ely, J. 1980. *Democracy and Distrust.* Cambridge: Harvard University Press.

Fassler, L.J. 1991. "The Italian Penal Procedural Code: An Adversarial System of Criminal Procedure in Continental Europe." *Columbia Journal of Transnational Law* 29: 245–78.

Field, S. and A. West. 1995. "A Tale of Two Reformers: French Defense Rights and Police Powers in Transition." *Criminal Law Forum* 6: 473–506.

Fionda, J. 1995. *Public Prosecutors and Discretion: A Comparative Study.* Oxford: Clarendon Press.

Florida v. J.L. 2000. 529 U.S. 266.

Frase. R.S. 1990. "Comparative Criminal Justice as a Guide to American Law Reform: How do the French do it, How Can We Find Out, and Why Should We Care?" *California Law Review* 78: 539–683.

Frase. R.S. and T. Weigend. 1995. "German Criminal Justice as a Guide to American Law Reform: Similar Problems, Better Solutions?" *Boston College International and Comparative Law Review* 18: 317–60.

Gershman, B.L. 1992. "The New Prosecutors." *University of Pittsburgh Law Review* 33: 393–458.

Gifford, D.G. 1983. "Meaningful Reform of Pleas Bargaining: The Control of Prosecutorial Discretion." *University of Illinois Law Review* 1983: 37–98.

Glendon, M.A. 1984. "The Sources of Law in a Changing Legal Order." *Creighton Law Review* 17: 663–91.

Goldstein, A.S. 1981. *The Passive Judiciary: Prosecutorial Discretion and the Guilty Plea.* Baton Rouge: Louisiana State University Press.

Goldstein, B.L. and M. Marcus. 1977. "The Myth of Judicial Supervision in Three 'Inquisitorial' Systems: France, Italy, and Germany." *Yale Law Journal* 87: 240–83.

Gordon, O.R. 1994. *The Return of the Dangerous Classes.* New York: Norton.

Grande, E. 2000. "Italian Criminal Justice: Borrowing and Resistance." *American Journal of Comparative Law* 48: 227–60.

Hatchard, J., B. Huber, and R. Vogler. 1996. *Comparative Criminal Procedure.* London: British Institute of International and Comparative Law.

Heller, R. 1997. "Selective Prosecution and the Federalization of Criminal Law: The Need for Meaningful Judicial Review of Prosecutorial Discretion." *University of Pennsylvania Law Review* 145: 1039–358.

Hermann, J. 1992. "Bargaining Justice: A Bargain for German Criminal Justice?" *University of Pittsburgh Law Review* 53: 755–76.

Illinois v. Gates. 1983. 462 U.S. 213.

Illinois v. Wardlow. 2000. 528 U.S. 119.

Indianapolis v. Edmond. 2001 531 U.S. 32.

Jackson, R.H. 1940. "The Federal Prosecutor." *Journal of American Judicature Society* 24: 18–19.

Jackson, V.C. and P.L. Tushnet. 1999. *Comparative Constitutional Law.* New York: Foundation Press.

Kyles v. Whitley. 1995. 514 U.S. 419.

Langbein, J.H. 1974. "Controlling Prosecutorial Discretion in Germany." *University of Chicago Law Review* 41: 439–61.

Langbein, J.H. 1977. *Comparative Criminal Procedure: Germany.* St. Paul: West.

Langbein, J.H. 1979. "Land Without Plea Bargaining: How the Germans Do It." *Michigan Law Review* 78: 204–25.

Langbein, J.H. 1981. "Mixed Court and Jury Court: Could the Continental Alternative Fill the American Need?" *American Bar Foundation Research Journal* 1981: 195-219.

Leigh, L.H. and L. Zedner. 1992. *The Royal Commission on Criminal Justice: A Report on the Administration of Justice in the Pretrial Phase in France and Germany.* London: HMSO.

Mack, R.L. 1996. "It's Broken So Let's Fix It: Using a Quasi-Inquisitorial Approach to Limit the Impact of Bias in the American Criminal Justice System." *Indiana International & Comparative Law Review* 7: 63–93.

Mapp v. Ohio. 1961. 367 U.S. 643.

Merryman J.H. 1985. *The Civil Law Tradition.* Stanford: Stanford University Press.

Michigan Department of State Police v. Sitz. 1990. 496 U.S. 444.

Miller, F.W. 1970. *Prosecution: The Decision to Charge a Suspect with a Crime.* Barton: Little Brown.

Miller, J.J. 1990. "Plea Bargaining and Its Analogues Under the New Italian Criminal Procedure Code and in the United States: Towards a New Understanding of Comparative Criminal Procedure." *New York University Journal of International Politics* 22: 215–51.

Miranda v. Arizona. 1966. 384 U.S. 436.

Misner, R. 1996. "Recasting Prosecutorial Discretion." *Journal of Criminal Law and Criminology* 86: 717–77.

Monroe v. Pipe. 1961. 365 U.S. 161.

New York v. Quarles. 1984. 467 U.S. 649.

Newman v. United States. 1967. 382 F.2d 479.

Nix v. Williams. 1984. 467 U.S. 431.

Ohlin, L.E. and F.J.Remington. (Eds.). 1993. *Discretion in Criminal Justice: The Tension Between Individualization and Uniformity.* Albany: SUNY Press.

Oyler v. Boles. 1962. 368 U.S. 448.

Payton v. New York. 1980. 445 U.S. 537.

Pizzi, W.T. 1993. "Understanding Prosecutorial Discretion in the United States: Limits of Comparative Criminal Procedure as an Instrument of Reform." *Ohio State Law Journal* 54: 1325–313.

Pizzi, W.T. and L. Marafioti. 1992. "The New Italian Code of Criminal Procedure: The Difficulties of Building an Adversarial System on a Civil Law Foundation." *Yale Journal of International Law* 17: 1–40.

Rhodes v. Chapman. 1981. 452 U.S. 337.

Santobello v. New York. 1911. 404 U.S. 257.

Schlesinger, R. 1911. "Comparative Criminal Procedure: A Plea for Utilizing Foreign Experience." *Buffalo Law Review* 26: 361–85.

Schlesinger, R., H.W. Basde, P.E. Herzog, and E.M. Wise. 1998. *Comparative Law.* New York: Foundation Press.

Schramm, G. 1970. "The Obligation to Prosecute in West Germany." *American Journal of Comparative Law* 18: 627–32.

Sheehan, A.V. 1975. *Criminal Procedure in Scotland and France.* Edinburgh: HMSO.

Singer v. United States. 1965. 380 U.S. 24.

Swann v. Charlotte-Mecklenburg Board of Education. 1971. 402 U.S. 1.

Swenson. T. 1995. "The German Plea Bargaining Debate." *Pace International Law Review* 7: 373–429.

Terrill, R. J. 1999. *World Criminal Justice Systems.* Cincinnati: Anderson.

Terry v. Ohio. 1968. 392 U.S.1.

Tomlinson, E. 1983. "Non-Adversarial Justice: The French Experience." *Maryland Law Review* 42: 131–95.

United States v. Agurs. 1976. 427 U.S. 97.

United States v. Armstrong. 1996. 517 U.S. 456.

United States v. Ash. 1973. 413 U.S. 300.

United States v. Baqley. 1985. 473 U.S. 667.

United States v. Chemical Foundation Inc. 1926. 272 U.S. 1.

United States v. Leon. 1914. 468 U.S. 897.

United States v. Mezzanatto. 1995. 513 U.S. 196.

Uviller, H.R. 1999. *The Tilted Playing Field.* New Haven: Yale University Press.

Van Cleave, R.A. 1997. "An Offer You Can't Refuse? Punishment Without Trial in Italy and the United States: The Search for Truth and an Efficient Criminal Justice System." *Emory International Law Review* 11: 419–69.

Van Kessel, G. 1992. "Adversarial Excesses in the American Criminal Trial." *Notre Dame Law Review* 67: 403–551.

Verrest, P. 2000. "The French Public Prosecution Service." *European Journal of Crime, Criminal Law, and Criminal Justice* 3: 210–44.

Vornberg, J. 1981. "Decent Restraint of Prosecutorial Power." *Harvard Law Review* 94: 1521–573.

Vouin, R. 1970. "The Role of the Prosecutor in French Criminal Trial." *American Journal of Comparative Law* 18: 483–97.

Walker. S. 1993. *Taming the System: The Control of Discretion in Criminal Justice, 1950–1990.* New York: Oxford University Press.

Wallace, H. 1995. "A Prosecutor's Guide to Stalking." *The Prosecutor* 29: 26–30.

Washington v. Davis. 1976. 426 U.S. 229.

Wayte v. United States. 1985. 470 U.S. 598.

Weigend, T. 1980. "Continental Cures for American Ailments: European Criminal Procedure as a Model for Law Reform." *Crime and Justice: An Annual Review of Research* 2: 381–421.

West, A., Y. Deidevises, A. Fenet, D. Gaurier, and M.C. Heussaff. 1993. *The French Legal System.* London: Format Publishing.

Whitley v. Albers. 1916. 475 U.S. 312.

Yick Wo v. Hopkins. 118 U.S. 356.

Zaubemsan, P. 1991. "Victimes en France: Des Positions, Intérêts et Stratégies Diverses." *Déviance et Société* 15: 27–49.

Zinermon v. Burch. 1990. 494 U.S. 113.

Zweigert, K. and Kotz, H. 1987. *Introduction to Comparative Law.* Oxford: Clarendon Press.

CHAPTER STUDY QUESTIONS

- Compare the role and discretionary power of US prosecutors to French, German and Italian prosecutors. How are they similar? How are they different? Does any system offer a clear advantage over the others? Why? Why not?

- Yue Ma argues that plea bargaining is carried out in Europe to a much greater degree than most American legal experts believe happens. However, he argues that the bargaining process is much more equitable to defendants in Europe than in the US. Outline the factors that permit French, German, and Italian prosecutors to engage in plea bargaining. Also, discuss the legal factors that constrain their power to force defendants to plead guilty.

- Compare and contrast the prosecutors' roles in France with those in Germany and Italy. Does the difference between the legality and expediency principles result in large differences in how the law is actually applied?

- What elements from the French, German, and Italian prosecutorial practices do you think could be used to reform the US system? What elements do you think are not applicable to US criminal justice? Why?

RELATED WEB LINKS

British Crown Prosecution Service
http://www.cps.gov.uk/
> This is the website of the British Crown Prosecution Service. It provides information on the organization and working of the CPS and serves as a counterpoint example to the French, German, and Italian systems.

Europa
http://europa.eu/scadplus/leg/en/lvb/l33159.htm
> This website provides information on recent legislative moves towards the establishment of a European Public Prosecutor who would report to the European Parliament.

Federal Judicial Center
http://www.fjc.gov/public/pdf.nsf/lookup/CivilLaw.pdf/$file/CivilLaw.pdf
> This website accesses a full-text "primer" on civil law legal systems. It discusses all aspects of civil law systems including the judicial and prosecutorial systems. Selected countries are used as examples including France, Chile, and Brazil. A brief comparison is made to common law systems.

Euro Justice
http://www.eurojustice.org/
This is the homepage of the organization of European Prosecutors General. Its main purpose is to foster mutual understanding and cooperation among European prosecution services. Links are provided to several other agencies and organizations that are actively promoting "eurojustice."

Chapter 13

THE POLICE, THE PROSECUTOR, AND THE JUGE D'INSTRUCTION: JUDICIAL SUPERVISION IN FRANCE, THEORY AND PRACTICE

JACQUELINE HODGSON

The inquisitorial method of judicial supervision has long been of interest to common law commentators as a possible means of better controlling police discretion in the exercise of their investigatory powers.[1] But in contrast to the wealth of criminal justice research both in the USA and in England and Wales, the debate on this issue continues to be conducted largely in the absence of a clear understanding of the legal framework which might govern judicial supervision, as well as a lack of empirical data on the way in which such supervision operates in practice. In this chapter, I examine the legal provisions regulating the investigation of offences in France and the models of regulation and supervision which they suggest. Then, drawing upon data from my own major empirical study of the French pretrial process, I examine the ways in which these mechanisms of control and accountability are understood by those charged with putting them into practice and the consequences this may have for our understanding of judicial supervision as a form of regulating criminal investigations.

INVESTIGATION: THE LEGAL FRAMEWORK

In Anglo-American systems, the judiciary is quite separate from the lawyers who prosecute and defend, and their role is largely limited to adjudicating in the trial process. In France, however, in common with many other European countries, there is a career judiciary, collectively known as the *magistrature*, whose members exercise the functions of *procureur*,[2] *juge d'instruction* and trial *juge*. They enjoy a common training, and it is possible to move between the three functions. As *magistrats*, the *procureur*, and *juge d'instruction* exercise a judicial role in the pre-trial supervision of investigations — even though the *procureur* is also responsible for the prosecution of offences.[3] The separation of these three functions acts as a series of checks, a guarantee ensuring the protection of the rights of the accused and the careful scrutiny of the dossier of evidence at each stage of the case.

The French *Code de procédure pénale* (CPP) sets out the powers, duties, and responsibilities of the police, and those responsible for the supervision of criminal investigations. The police[4] are responsible for recording crime, gathering evidence, and seeking out those who have committed offences (CPP Article 14), and they must inform the *procureur* of all *crimes*[5] or *flagrant*[6] offences (CPP Article 54). In more serious or complex cases, an *information*[7] is opened on the authority of the *procureur* and the *juge d'instruction* takes responsibility for the investigation. In other instances, the police are under the direction of the *procureur* (CPP Article 12).

The nature of this direction is set out in CPP Article 41. The *procureur* is responsible for the investigation and prosecution of offences, and in carrying out this task, she directs the activity of the police (whose powers she shares) and supervises the detention of suspects in police custody (the *garde à vue*). The initial decision to detain a suspect is made by a senior police officer, but the *procureur* must be informed as soon as possible, and her express authority is required for detention beyond 24 hours (CPP Articles 63, 77).

Since 1993, the *garde à vue* period has been closely regulated, and a number of safeguards are now provided for those detained.[8] A formal record of detention must be kept, detailing interrogation times, rest periods, and the duration of the *garde à vue* (CPP Articles 64, 65). As soon as the suspect is placed in detention, she must be informed of her rights which include having a member of her family or her employer informed of her detention (CPP Article 63-2); to see a doctor (CPP Article 63-3); and to see a lawyer for 30 minutes, 20 hours after the start of the detention period (CPP Article 63-4).[9] The lawyer must be told of the nature of the offence investigated, but not the reason why the suspect has been detained.[10] She is allowed to consult with her client in private, but is not permitted to be present during any interrogation. She may also make written observations on the custody record.

At the close of detention, the *procureur* decides whether to charge or release the suspect, or send the case to the *juge d'instruction* for further investigation. Originals and certified copies of all evidence gathered by the police must be sent to the *procureur* (CPP Article 19). Everything is recorded as a signed statement, a *procès verbal*, and placed in the *dossier*, or case file. The *dossier* attaches to the case through until trial, and it is reviewed by the *juge d'instruction* if appointed, as well as the *juges* at trial. The importance of formal and written procedures, which are easily subject to later review, is implicit in what Damaska (1975: 506) terms a hierarchical model of accountability, and provision is made in the CPP for the exclusion of evidence where these procedural formalities have not been respected, regardless of the substantive impact the breach might have upon the reliability of the evidence.[11]

The *juge d'instruction* supervises the investigation in around 8 percent of cases. This is done by the *procureur* opening an *information*, which is mandatory for *crimes*, the most serious offences,[12] and at the discretion of the *procureur* for *délits* and *contraventions* (CPP Article 79). The *juge d'instruction* is empowered to undertake any lawful investigations which she considers useful in the search for the truth (CPP Article 81). These may include telephone taps or staging a confrontation between witnesses and the accused, as well as interviewing witnesses and gathering expert evidence. These may be done on the *juge's* own initiative or at the request of the *procureur*, the accused, or the victim (CPP Article 82).[13] Other than the questioning of the *mise en examen*[14] and preparation of the report on her background (the *enquête de personnalité*), investigations may be delegated to police officers through the *commission rogatoire* (CPP Article 151), granting them the same powers as the *juge d'instruction* herself (CPP Article 152).

The *mise en examen* may have a lawyer present whenever she is brought before the *juge* for questioning or for a confrontation with another witness, and, through her defence lawyer, she may make written submissions at any point in the investigation which are then placed on the case file (CPP Article 199). The lawyers for both the accused and the victim have access to the dossier of evidence and may make copies for their own use (CPP Article).[15] As well as an investigative role, the *juge* also exercises a purely judicial function in deciding whether to keep the suspect in custody during the period of investigation. This has been widely criticized in France (see, e.g., Commission de justice pénale et droits de l'homme 1991; Commission de réflexion sur la justice 1997), as a confusion of investigative and judicial functions, and the recent reform in June 2000 created a *juge des libertés et de la détention* who will determine the issue of pre-trial detention.

The judicial character with which investigations are imbued also influences the structure of the trial process and the probative value afforded evidence gathered during the investigation. The *dossier* of evidence (even where no *information* has been opened) is regarded not as a police file, but the fruit of a judicially supervised enquiry and written statements may therefore be accepted without the need for oral testimony and cross-examination. In the lowest court, the *Tribunal de Police*, police statements are considered proof of the *contravention* unless the contrary is proved (CPP Article 537). Where cases are investigated by the *juge d'instruction*, any application to exclude evidence because of a procedural irregularity is made, not during the trial itself, but within a month of the close of the investigation (CPP Article 175).[16]

It will be apparent, even from the brief account provided above, that the legal framework governing criminal investigations in France is quite different from that in England and Wales, where the police have sole responsibility both for the investigation of crime and the initial decision whether to charge. The Crown Prosecution Service (CPS) can only react to the police decision re charge and may request, not require, further investigations. This absence of early CPS involvement has contributed to the long-standing criticism that many police files contain insufficient evidence, resulting in charges being downgraded to less serious offences or cases being discontinued altogether. Of greater concern is the way in which investigations have been found to focus prematurely upon a police suspect, with all efforts directed at constructing a case against that individual. Important evidence may be overlooked or suppressed and, ultimately, the wrong person convicted. The now notorious miscarriages of justice, as well as a number of empirical studies, have demonstrated the ways in which this approach is embedded in police culture and practice. The French system, in contrast, anticipates early involvement of the *procureur* or the *juge d'instruction* while the investigation is still ongoing, and the decision whether to charge and with which offence is not that of the police, but the *procureur*. It is this degree of independent direction or oversight of the investigation leading up to prosecution which appeals to many Anglo-American commentators[17] and which I would like to examine more closely.

THE CENTRALITY OF THE PROCUREUR

Just as jury trial and vigorous cross-examination are often regarded as the hallmarks of an adversarial system so the *juge d'instruction* takes on an almost iconic status to common law commentators.[18] But the process of *instruction* in France is almost as exceptional as jury trials in Britain. The law permits, and indeed anticipates, that the vast majority of cases will be investigated by the police under the supervision of the *procureur* qua *magistrat*. The absence of direct judicial investigation in most cases is in exact conformity with the law, and a number of mechanisms (described above) are provided which avoid judicial supervision in its purest form: the appointment of the *juge d'instruction* is mandatory only in cases of *crimes*, and provision is made for virtually all tasks to be delegated to the police through a *commission rogatoire*. Furthermore, even where cases are investigated under the supervision of the *juge d'instruction*, the all important preliminary enquiries, including interrogation of the suspect, will have already been carried out by the police under the responsibility of the *procureur*.

Within the structure of the law itself, it is the *procureur* who occupies the central position of judicial supervision in the criminal process. She must be notified of all *crimes* and *délits* and is responsible for their investigation and prosecution. She supervises the *garde à vue*, deciding whether to authorize and later prolong detention. She possesses broad discretion over both (being able to avoid the mandatory opening of an *information* for *crimes* by proceeding on the basis of a *délit*) and the precise point at which the case is passed on to the *juge d'instruction*. The centrality of the *procureur* has its origins in the nineteenth century when the rise of the *procureur's role* paralleled the huge rise in the number of cases entering the criminal process from a greatly enlarged police force and *gendarmerie* (Lévy 1993). The *juge d'instruction* became overburdened and the response of the *procureur* was to send fewer cases to *instruction* and more cases directly to trial[19] further assisted by a procedure introduced in 1863 authorizing the *procureur* to bring directly before the court those accused of *flagrant* offences. Lévy (1993: 178) describes this as significant, as it "resulted in an increased capacity of the judiciary to deal with cases, thus adapting it to the demands of police 'production' which was growing steadily" and enhanced the importance of the *procureur*, who emerged as "the real official head of judicial investigations."[20]

However, whilst the practice of *procureur*-supervised investigations is not a deviation from the law, it does represent a model of judicial supervision which is different from that provided by the *juge d'instruction*. First, supervision is characterized by the law in different ways. Leigh and Zedner (1992: 3) focus upon the word "*contrôle*" which, they say, is used most often and signifies oversight and accountability, rather than minute direction. This is true of the *garde à vue*, but in the investigation and prosecution of crime the *procureur* is required to direct (*diriger*) police activity (CPP Article 41). However, the nature of this "oversight" and "direction" is left open. There is nothing in the text of the law which anticipates that the *procureur* should be present at the police station for the interviewing of witnesses or the suspect. The police retain the initiative in arresting and detaining a suspect and then reporting to the *procureur*. This practice was reflected in the modification of the requirement to inform the procureur of detentions in *garde à vue* "without delay" to "as soon as possible" (CPP Article 63). According to the explanatory document accompanying the change, this was in recognition that it was not always possible to inform the *procureur* immediately and to allow the *parquet* in each area the freedom to specify how they wished to be notified—for example, by fax.[21]

The *juge d'instruction* is characterized as being more directly involved in the investigation. She is personally required to conduct (*procéder à*) the investigation, and police involvement is by active delegation through the use of *commissions rogatoires*, which represents a significant transfer of power from the *juge* to the police, rather than the regulation or supervision of an existing power.[22] And once an *information* has been opened, the police are no longer permitted to question the *mise en examen*—only the *juge d'instruction* may do this. The level of control and direct supervision suggested by the legal text in the two instances is not the same—indeed, if it were, there would be no logic in having two separate procedures and two different *magistrats*.

Secondly, the *procureur* and the *juge d'instruction* occupy different parts of the institutional structure of the criminal process. On account of France's political history, the role of the state is a constant background feature in all discussions of law (Noreau and Arnaud 1998: 278), and, in the area of criminal justice, this focus is on the relationship between the *magistrature* and the elected government. Under the republican model of government (brought about in France by the 1789 Revolution), the state is said to represent the will of the people and guarantees the rights and freedoms of the individual. The law is a legitimate expression of this political power, and the unelected judiciary must give effect to it, whilst at the same time remaining subordinate to it.[23] The *procureur* represents the public interest and is part of the *ministère public* which is under the direction of the Minister of Justice. The minister may issue national circulars addressing general issues of prosecution policy, may give direct instructions concerning a specific case, and may remove a case from one *procureur* to another. She is also a powerful influence in the process of appointment and promotion of *procureurs*. This creates a tension between the accountability of the *procureur* as part of the *ministère public* representing the public interest and her independent status as a *magistrat*.[24] In contrast to the *procureur*, the *juge d'instruction* is not answerable to a government minister and is free from hierarchical control of this nature. Furthermore, the *juge d'instruction* does not prosecute the case and her role in investigations is cast in more neutral terms than that of the *procureur*: she is charged with searching for the truth,[25] she investigates the offence rather than the accused and looks not simply for evidence on which to prosecute but to *charger* or *décharger*.

This structure of judicial supervision in France also has implications for the role assigned the defence in the pre-trial process, which is often forgotten by those who wistfully imagine transplanting the *juge d'instruction* into English soil.[26] Due process guarantees are assured by the statutory role and independence of the judicial inquirer. They are not (as the adversarial model is regarded by the French) contingent upon the presence or quality of a defence lawyer. In an inquisitorial process, the defence protects the interests of the accused, not through the independent (proactive) construction of a defence case but by (reactively) ensuring that those responsible for gathering evidence and compiling the dossier have respected the procedural formalities which are part of the guarantees of fairness, both in the investigation and the treatment of the suspect.[27] Current reforms seeking to strengthen the presumption of innocence, whilst enlarging the role of the defence lawyer in some respects (for example, allowing earlier access to *garde à vue*), are in no way designed to move towards a more adversarial procedure.[28]

JUDICIAL SUPERVISION IN PRACTICE

Perhaps surprisingly, given the centrality of judicial supervision within the French pre-trial process, little empirical work has been carried out to evaluate its success. Evaluations of the French criminal process by French scholars tend to be most commonly at a broad theoretical level or, less frequently, a narrow empirical one (Renouard 1993).[29] Insights into practice are often the result of writers being academic practitioners,[30] rather than through any systematic collection of data.[31] The empirical work that is carried out is concentrated in state funded research centres, and so the focus is invariably upon law reform and policy, and the results are not well disseminated (Noreau and Arnaud 1998). There are some sociological studies of policing and, more recently, both fear of crime and victimization studies have appeared on the socio-legal horizon. Robert (1991: 32) reports that there are a growing number of historical and sociological accounts, but most work to date has relied heavily upon criminal and judicial statistics.[32] The work of researchers at CESDIP (a CNRS centre which researches crime and criminal justice in France) is no exception, but recent projects, such as Renée Zauberman's (1997) study of the *Gendarmerie*, have also employed interviews and some direct observation.[33]

The accounts of foreign observers have included some empirical work. Goldstein and Marcus, for example, carried out a very limited number of interviews[34] and observed several trials and requests for warrants in each of the three jurisdictions studied.[35] Leigh and Zedner's study for the RCCJ was also based upon interviews rather than observation, but in the absence of information about who they spoke to (police, *procureurs, juges d'instruction*) or how many interviews were conducted, it is difficult to assess the proper weight to attach to their findings.[36]

In my own study of the investigation and prosecution of crime in France, fieldwork was carried out in Paris, two large urban centres, a medium size town and one small area of 170,000 inhabitants during the period 1993–1994 and 1997–1998.[37] Researchers spent between one and four months at each site, located in the offices of *procureurs, juges d'instruction*, police, and *gendarmes*, where we were able to observe the ways in which criminal investigations are directed and supervised on a daily basis, as well as the conduct of pre-trial hearings and the questioning of suspects and witnesses. By being placed in the office of the group being observed, we were able to follow cases through the process and to supplement our observations with discussion of particular cases or decisions and the wider issues which arose out of them. We were also allowed access to case dossiers at each stage of the process. This method (or blend of methods) produced a rich stream of data, allowing for the collection of formally determined categories of information[38] whilst at the same time remaining sufficiently flexible to respond to new issues which emerged once in the field.[39] At the end of the observation period we conducted 20 interviews (primarily with *magistrats*) and received 37 questionnaire responses from *procureurs* and 12 from police. Based upon some of the data from this empirical study, I will examine the legal culture in which judicial supervision is understood and the ways in which it is put into practice.

THE RELATIONSHIP BETWEEN MAGISTRAT AND POLICE

The appeal of judicial supervision to foreign commentators is its potential to ensure a wider investigation, where the police might also follow leads which exculpate, as well as incriminate, the suspect.[40] And although the law does not expressly require it, this is implicit in the wider structure of the criminal process: the status accorded the *dossier* as the product of a judicial en-quiry; the relatively minor role afforded the defence lawyer. But in contrast, the work of both the *procureur* and the *juge d'instruction* is perhaps best characterized as being concerned with the *outcome* and the *form* of the police investigation, rather than the *method*: neither is concerned to monitor closely the work of the police.[41] This is done quite literally by monitoring the output of the investigation and ensuring that procedural safeguards have been complied with: that state-ments are signed and in triplicate; that the *garde à vue* documentation records times, medical visits, and the communication to the suspect of her rights; that the *procureur* has been informed of the suspect's detention[42] and any extension authorized; or that the *commission rogatoire* has been carried out within the time requested. The *magistrat* performs a kind of (necessarily ret-rospective) bureaucratic review of the investigation carried out by the police. Great reliance is placed upon written evidence and authenticity of form is equated with a wider guarantee of legitimacy in relation to how the evidence was obtained. As one *substitut* we observed warned an accused who wished to correct something in his statement taken by the police: "I am paid to read the dossier of evidence. I believe what I read ... This is written and signed."

This characterization is also true of more direct forms of supervision undertaken by the *magistrat*. Although required to direct or carry out the investigation, it was extremely rare for *magistrats* to intervene directly in the police enquiry. The *juge d'instruction's* heavy reliance upon *commissions rogatoires* has been well documented[43] and her caseload is such that, whilst she may discuss the progress and outcomes of investigations with officers, the initiative and di-rection of the case remains with the police. Even the opening of an *information* itself was often at the request of the police in order that their investigation could progress by employing wider powers (typically a phone tap) which only the *juge d'instruction* could authorize. Similarly, *pro-cureurs* were often responsible for the detention of suspects in *garde à vue* across a wide area[44] and had too many cases in progress at any one time to allow for anything more than minimal involvement via telephone or fax.[45] As one *substitut* [D2] [46] told us, "... at times it feels as though you are working on a production line." The new *temps réel* procedure requiring officers to report even minor cases to the *procureur* has the advantage that a decision about the disposition of the case can be taken immediately, but in an environment of stretched resources,[47] it has increased the workload yet further.

However, the disengagement of *magistrats* from the case investigation is not purely a resource issue. It is part of the legal cultural expectations of what constitutes supervision and direction, the context in which these broadly defined legal duties are interpreted by *magistrats* in practice. The legal text is framed such that the *procureur* or the *juge d'instruction* could undertake personally large parts of the investigation, but, for a number of reasons, there is no expectation that this will take place. In part, it is a function of the paradoxical structural relationship between the *magistrat* and the police, in which the *magistrat* is an authority over the police, yet at the same time is dependent upon them.[48] In our questionnaire survey, although most *procureurs* (85 per cent) said that they would never see the police, whatever their rank, as colleagues and 79 per cent described officers as subordinates, there is a recognition that cooperation and trust are more likely to foster a good working relationship than assertions of authority. One *substitut* [E2] told us, "I think that, really, I direct [the investigation], but equally, so do the police ... Fine, you can assert your authority, but that is not an effective way to get things done." Another *substitut* [D1] also explained the importance of trust given the dependence of *magistrats* upon the police: "I think you need to be aware that you cannot work without the police. Then, if you want to do a good job, there needs to be a relationship of trust and mutual respect. Legally, hierarchically, we give them orders, but anyone who thinks that it just needs to be written in the law to work like that is mistaken."

The importance of trust in the *police-procureur* relationship was particularly apparent in the approach of the *parquet* to visits to the police station. On the rare occasions when these were made, they were announced in advance and more likely to be for practical reasons or to enhance relations with the police than to assert authority or to check on those detained in police custody.[49] This was borne out by the police themselves who, far from seeing visits as a form of regulation or monitoring, complained that the *procureur* "never had time to come to the station these days." The consequence of a more surveillance-based approach was explained to us by a *substitut*: "There used to be a woman in the *permanence* who did go down to the police station, and it caused a terrible rumpus. The police were furious that she just turned up. You have to be careful when you go down—so that the police don't think it's because you're suspicious of them."

Similarly, the relationship between *juge d'instruction* and police was consistently characterized to us (both by the *juges* themselves and the police) as being based upon trust, though of a different kind. One group of officers explained their approach to working with the *juge d'instruction* in this way: "We propose the way forward ... we find the leads to follow up ... the *juge* directs the investigation, but we carry it out and keep him informed ... you need to gain his trust and persuade him ... it's not a question of permission, it's a question of trust." The nature of the process of *instruction* is such that the police may be left for weeks or even months before reporting to the *juge*, unlike the initial enquiry, which takes place over a matter of days. As a result, the police may feel more, rather than less, freedom when acting under *commission rogatoire*. One *juge d'instruction* [A5] contrasted her role with that of the *procureur* "[The police] probably see the *juge d'instruction* as a director, someone they have to report to. The *procureur* is seen as someone who keeps a closer eye on them."[50]

But while resources and dependence upon the police dictate the approach of the *magistrat* to some extent, the wide discretion afforded the police is also part of the ideology of the *juge* that the functions of *magistrat* and of police should be kept separate. There is a distance between the two which cannot be bridged. As one *procureur* [D2] put it: "There is a part of [the police's] work that I cannot evaluate. I can only talk of their role in the legal procedure, how they report on the telephone. We inhabit different worlds. They do not know the world of judges, and I do not know the world of nightclubs." This comment was echoed by a senior police officer [D5], who said, when asked about relations with the *parquet*: "Our work is different. They are in their offices and we are outside on the ground." Lévy (1993: 181) explains, " ... there is a professional ideology which opposes the magistrate, incarnation of the law whose hands must remain clean, to the policeman, who inevitably soils himself by contact with the underworld and who must as a result be kept at a distance."

This professional distance between *magistrat* and police has clear functional benefits to the *magistrature*. Whilst the *magistrat* deals with the relative "moral certainties" of legal procedure, distant from the realities of investigation and interrogation, the police are left to do what is necessary to get the evidence the *magistrat* requires to do her job. The *magistrat* is not concerned to look too closely at the methods employed, provided her dossier is complete at the end of the day, but, in the event of a major police transgression, she remains free to condemn the offending officers and to emerge unscathed.

Two contrasting examples illustrate this point. In the first case, the accused appeared before the *substitut* with cuts to his face and nose. He did not contest any of the charges made against him, but protested at the rough treatment he suffered when arrested and claimed that the police had stolen something from him. The *substitut* ignored these complaints without further enquiry and simply told him to "Stop talking rubbish" and to "Tell it to the court." It was left to the defence lawyer to raise an official complaint before the court that day. When asked about his approach to the suspect, the *substitut's* lack of commitment to due process rights was clear: "You have to bear in mind that he has several convictions and does not respect the law, so his word counts for less than that of the police." In the second case, the suspect, a juvenile, was held on suspicion of assaulting a police officer. In the dossier, there was a medical certificate relating to the injuries of the suspect, but not the police. This clear documentary evidence prompted an immediate response from the *substitut* who instructed the police to ask the suspect's father if he wished to lodge a formal complaint, before then instigating an official enquiry into the affair. Although responsible for supervising the police investigation, there is a sense in which the *magistrat* does not want to delve too deeply into "police work" unless compelled to do so. The detention and interrogation of suspects is perhaps the paradigm example of this.

INTERROGATION AND THE SEARCH FOR THE TRUTH

In keeping separate the functions of *magistrat* and police, interrogation is regarded by *magistrats* as "dirty" work best left to the police. It might be argued that, although the *procureur* is responsible only to *contrôle* the *garde à vue*, this relates to the conditions of detention; the actual interrogation of suspects or witnesses is part of the investigation, which she is required to *diriger* or direct. Yet, most *procureurs* never leave their offices. Despite being conscious of the limitations of the kind of supervision that they can provide, such as the risk of being manipulated by the limited accounts given by the police over the telephone or the fact that things might be left out of written statements (there is no tape recording), 87 per cent of our questionnaire respondents said that they rarely or never visited the police station. When asked if she had ever been present during the questioning of a suspect or a witness, one *substitut* [A2] told us, "That would make me ill-at-ease. If I realize that there are questions that should have been asked, I ask the police to put them to the suspect, but I am not actually present. I can go to the scene and make sure all the evidence is seized after a search, yes. But I do not sit in on interviews." For her, this was strictly police work. It fulfilled a necessary function, but one in which she declined to take part: "The *garde à vue* is a constraint which can last 48 hours, or four days for drugs cases. It is to put the pressure on ... With people who resist, it breaks them down."

The reluctance of the *procureur* to visit the police station is all the more interesting given the relatively high number of questionnaire respondents (40 percent) who reported suspecting that violence or excessive pressure had sometimes been used against the suspect during the *garde à vue*. In one area observed, there was concern that suspects were being brought to court bloodstained and untidy. The police were instructed by the *procureur* that this was not acceptable and that it did not look good before the court. No enquiry was made, however, into why suspects arrived in this state. The French police have had the reputation of being violent towards suspects and, although both police and *magistrats* claim that this is a relic of the past, part of the "old ways," serious cases of violence continue to occur, and the 1990s have witnessed the police shooting of a number of suspects both in and outside the police station.[51] Five officers were imprisoned for seriously assaulting two suspected drug traffickers whilst they were held in *garde à vue* in 1991. The victims were beaten about the face, head, body, and genitals with fists and truncheons, threatened with a syringe and a blowtorch, sexually assaulted and urinated on.[52]

While such cases of violence are extreme and will be condemned publicly,[53] there is a general tolerance among *magistrates* of the kinds of pressure that the police might need to exert to make the suspect tell "the truth."[54] And the crime control ideology of the *procureur* means that in most instances, "the truth" is a confession. Suspects in police detention who say little when questioned, or deny the offence, are repeatedly interviewed on the instructions of the *procureur* in order to get "the full story" or "a satisfactory explanation." It is also a common reason for prolonging detention or remanding the person in custody during the *instruction*. As one *procureur* told the police on the telephone, "Let the *garde à vue* do its job. We can always prolong it. Keep interviewing him from time to time to refresh his memory."[55] Another *substitut* from the juvenile section of the *parquet* explained that, "the 48 hours can be used to get him [the suspect] to crack. I systematically prolong the *garde à vue* to ensure this. Frequently, it's the first interview in the morning after they've spent the night in custody that they crack, because they're tired and vulnerable and realize that we will keep them in custody ... It's not an environment where the police hit them—it's more psychological."

Even questioning which might be classed as overbearing or oppressive by a British court is considered acceptable, and at times necessary, to get at "the truth." One *substitut* [D1] told us that when he spent some time at the police station as part of his training, he saw a suspect slapped across the face: "It's not shocking, it was just to move things on. It was a drug case and the officer wanted to know the truth ... I wouldn't call that 'violence.'" Another, very experienced *substitut* [D3] explained, "It's true that the *garde à vue* exerts a certain psychological pressure, and, for some people, that pressure may lead to slightly ill-considered admissions ... But that is not the point of view of a *procureur*—there are no innocents in *garde à vue*." This, he explained, was why cases were frequently kept for up to five days before opening an *information*: "The reason it's five days is because that is the limit for *flagrance*. That way, the police still enjoy wide powers, and we can carry out the investigation ... we want to get the culprit ... The *juge d'instruction* is not going to interview the suspect three or four times, sit across the table from him and say 'Are you going to admit this?' The police station is a hostile environment. It's unpleasant, and the police will use more pressure. And that does not make it unlawful—sometimes you need some pressure."

The *juge d'instruction* also reaps the benefits of the relatively invisible and unregulated conditions of police interrogation. For example, the suspect, once *mise en examen*, may only be interviewed by the *juge d'instruction*, her lawyer is present and has access to the dossier of evidence, and the statement made is meticulously recorded. However, where a suspect emerges once the *information* has been opened and is not yet *mise en examen*, it was common for the *juge* to direct the police to interview her as a witness, avoiding the safeguards of the process of *instruction* and so leaving the police free to prepare the ground. Interviewing a suspect in the relative invisibility of the police station is seen as a valuable and legitimate investigative tool. As one *juge d'instruction* explained when asked why he opposed the safeguard of tape recording of police interrogations, "It's unbelievable! And to think that we might end up doing that here ... You should just leave the police to do their job. When you're dealing with difficult people like drug addicts and hooligans, you need to put the pressure on. I don't mean hitting them, but you have to make them talk."

Although leaving the hard work of interrogation to the police, the *juge d'instruction* had her own ways of putting pressure upon suspects. Typically, evidence against the suspect will be temporarily withheld from the dossier so that the lawyer is denied access to it and the suspect is unaware of it and may "trip up" and contradict it. But perhaps the most important trump card held by the *juge d'instruction* is her power to detain suspects in custody. As with so many things, detention is justified in the eyes of *magistrats* as a necessary tool in the search for the truth. We were frequently told that only "guilty" people were detained.[56] In several instances, detention, or the threat of it, was used against suspects who failed to provide the *juge* with sufficient information or as a means of getting others to talk.[57] One *juge d'instruction* [A5] explained, "I had someone in *garde à vue* who I was going to put in pre-trial detention ... I was alone with him at that point. I told him, 'what I want is for all the information to be in the dossier so that I can make my report. If you just make up anything, then you are at risk....' He confessed ... I was not threatening him with detention, just putting all my cards on the table ... I explained the grounds for pre-trial detention and he quickly got the message." The reform in June 2000 removed this power from the *juge d'instruction* and transferred it to a newly created *juge des libertés et de la détention*. This has been received warmly by lawyers, who hope that this will end the practice of bargaining liberty with confessions.[58]

Unsurprisingly, given the distance from police interrogation which the *parquet* and *juge d'instruction* prefer to keep, a greater role for the defence pre-trial is widely opposed by *magistrats* as likely to hamstring the police in their ability to question the suspect (and obtain admissions) and so to interfere with the effectiveness of the investigation. In contrast to those whose professional standards and ideology are considered beyond reproach as *magistrats* searching out the truth, lawyers as paid partisan representatives of the suspect's interests are considered ill-suited to act in this capacity. Of our questionnaire respondents 97 per cent considered the current arrangement of up to 30 minutes' consultation with a lawyer after 20 hours of detention to be appropriate both to the needs of the accused and of justice. Eighty-four per cent thought that the lawyer should not have access to the suspect at the start of the *garde à vue* (as will soon be the case after the June 2000 reform takes effect) and 89 per cent thought they should not have access to the dossier.[59] The reasons offered for this were that it would undermine the confidentiality and effectiveness of the investigation in searching out the truth, as well as the "spontaneity" of the suspect's remarks. The suspect may collude with her lawyer in giving an account or, worse still, refuse to speak altogether. The presence of an outsider is viewed negatively as it risks interfering with the psychological pressure that detention in *garde à vue* necessarily exerts. For the *magistrats* in an inquisitorial process, the defence lawyer acts not as a participant but as a guarantee of procedural fairness and one which ultimately legitimates the judicial enquiry: "In France, the lawyer is not there to advise the person but to signal any problems in the conditions of the *garde à vue*, not so much to provide legal advice as moral support" [E31]. When asked what the defence brought to the process of *instruction* one *juge d'instruction* told us, "They do not bring anything to the case—it is not their job to. I investigate the affair and their job is primarily to ensure that the correct procedure has been followed and to challenge any irregularities."[60] A greater role for the defence pre-trial would undermine the structure of judicial supervision, where the supervisor can be trusted to guarantee the respect of due process rights because of her status as *magistrat*.

THE MAGISTRAT: SOCIETY'S TRUSTED REPRESENTATIVE

Rooted in their own adversarial legal culture, many foreign commentators imagine the judicial supervisor in adversarial terms, investigating a case which has two sides, representing defence interests which are in opposition to those of the police and prosecution, as well as investigating the guilt of the suspect. But in the French system, there is only one side to the case investigation which the *magistrat* undertakes—that of seeking out the truth—and all other interests, including those of the accused, are subordinated to this. Searching out the truth is not achieved through opposition and conflict, checks and balances: to the French *magistrat* these may stand in the way of obtaining crucial evidence. Instead, it is achieved through a concentration of power in the hands of one person, who represents neither the narrow interests of the defence or prosecution but what are claimed to be the wider interests of society.[61] *Magistrats*, as administrators of the law enacted by the state, give effect to the will of the people. This gives them an authority and a legitimacy which is quite different from the defence lawyer, in particular, who is seen as representing the partisan interests of the accused, working for money rather than for justice.[62] The defense lawyer is less trusted than even the police. A *juge d'instruction* explained that a defence witness statement in court "has less validity than if the statement was taken by a police officer because we do not know the circumstances. It could have been taken with a gun to the witness's head. If taken by the police, we know that it was taken under proper conditions."

Acting in the public interest, it is the *magistrat* who is trusted to define what is in the interests of the investigation and so, in the interests of justice, including decisions which affect the rights and liberties of the individual—whether it be the detention of the suspect, denying her the right to a lawyer, doctor or contact with a family member whilst in *garde à vue*, or placing her in pre-trial custody. Her status as *magistrat* overrides her function as investigator or prosecutor. This is especially true of the *juge d'instruction* whose role is almost one of pre-judgment. In contrast to the adversarial model which carries the conflict through to trial, the French model disposes of issues during the period of investigation. One *juge d'instruction* commented, "In a way, our job is to prepare the case for trial. We establish a dossier of evidence ... In England [rape or incest cases] take a long time to try at court because all the witnesses are heard. We [the *juges d'instruction*] do all that beforehand. The court is not going to start over again when the evidence has already been taken ... what you do at court, we do in my office. It is not done in public" [B1]. The low acquittal rate of cases after *instruction* is taken as proof of their success, and one *juge d'instruction* told us proudly that in ten years, only two of the cases he had sent to trial had resulted in acquittals.

The extent of the *magistrat*'s power in the investigation in contrast to the relatively diminished role of the defense is justified on the basis of the former's independence as a judicial inquirer, her status as a *magistrat*. Yet, we have seen that, in practice, independence does not guarantee neutrality and in particular, the stance of the *procureur* in representing the public interest is predominantly one of crime control. One former *juge d'instruction* entering the *parquet* reflected on her changing role: "For the *parquet*, the question, the aim, is always to charge. They are acting for the public. That will be uppermost in their mind." The rights and interests of the accused are not protected, but redefined within the "interests of the investigation." The guilt of the suspect is presumed and denials are rejected. Evidence of violence committed on the suspect by the police was ignored and left for the defence to raise at court; the word of the victim or of the police was consistently preferred over that of the suspect; serious cases meant an almost automatic request for a remand in custody, even where the evidence was thin. At trial, the most serious charge which the evidence might support was preferred: the public interest demanded that nothing should risk going unpunished.

The *magistrat* as a neutral agent applying the law, someone above personal or partisan interests is a powerful image within the rhetoric of judicial supervision and one which is internalized by the *magistrats* themselves. It permeates all contact between *magistrat* and accused. Explanations of charges, remands in custody, the opening of an *information* or the sentence at court are consistently prefaced with the phrase "I am obliged by the law to ..." or "I am required to ..." The accused is admonished by the state and by the law, not by the individual *magistrat*. As one *substitut* explained: "[Suspects] ask me to take pity on them, but I cannot. I have no other solution but to apply the law ... I have no choice." Decisions are impersonal and non-negotiable, uniform and not discretionary. The fragility of this claim was revealed as the *substitut* qualified her remarks in the following way: "Even so, there is a great deal of latitude ... we are all different. Each *magistrat* has his or her own way of doing things, of applying the law, of being severe or not. The differences are individual, personal." In making judgments about the gravity of the offence or the disposition of the offender, or deciding whether to issue a summons or take a more serious view and send the case to trial that day, appeals to legality allow the *magistrat* to hand out tough decisions behind the veil of the "requirements of the law."[63]

The law allocates quite separate functions to the *procureur*, the *juge d'instruction*, and the trial *juges* in order that each may act as a brake upon the power exercised by the others, but their status as *magistrats* binds them together in significant ways. There is a great deal of formal and informal communication between the three. They are generally housed in the same building, the *Palais de justice*, they may lunch together, and they frequently appear before one another at court or hearings during instruction. This contact has many advantages in that they are not isolated from the consequences of their decisions, and they have a global view of the criminal process. But their sense of working together also leads them to discuss cases with their colleagues in a way which goes beyond, for example, the *juge d'instruction* obtaining a better insight into a case from the *procureur* involved in the original investigation, and risks compromising the independence of the decision made. *Juges d'instruction* (or even *juges délégués*)[64] frequently discussed with the *procureur* whether someone should be placed in pre-trial custody, for example; and the vice-president of the court frequently sat down and discussed the afternoon's cases with the *procureur* to make sure that there were no problems.

Although instruction is a legally separate phase, the practical fact that the *procureur* has followed the case from the outset means that, in many instances, opening an *information* is not a fresh investigation but the continuation of an ongoing one, passed to the *juge* because time has run out or additional powers are required. In some instances, the *procureur* and *juge d'instruction* (and even the police) discussed what charge the *information* was to be opened under and the necessary *commissions rogatoires*. The *procureur* and *juge d'instruction* are in close contact and strategies are often discussed between the two: whether holding the suspect's wife will make him talk; whether placing the suspect in detention will precipitate more information from other witnesses; and in some cases, the suspect is primed by the *procureur* before being passed to the *juge*. One *juge d'instruction* [A2] explained that he felt closer to the *parquet* than to the trial judges: "The *parquet* works on the case before and after me. Our jobs are complementary. When I get a dossier, I always bear in mind that I am working for the *parquet*. The two roles are very complementary. We're on the same wavelength." The *instruction* builds upon what has gone before. Often the same officers will continue the investigation; the evidence collected so far becomes part of the file; and the views of the *parquet* are actively sought out. Aware of this, some police commented to us that they thought fresh officers should be brought to the case once an *information* is opened, to avoid initial case theories prevailing and to allow new perspectives to emerge.

Most *magistrats* saw these close working relationships as unproblematic. Discussion beforehand did not prevent them from playing out their role at the appropriate time: the pre-trial hearing or the trial. It did not undermine the system of checks and balances which the separation of functions is designed to achieve. Others were less sure. One *juge délégué* [65] explained the conflict she felt: "It can be difficult to release somebody if the *juge d'instruction* has worked hard on a case. There is a pressure from being part of the same institution. You want to satisfy your colleagues." Another *juge d'instruction* [B1] questioned whether such discussions undermined their independence and the principle that their functions should be kept separate: "There is a solidarity. We are the same, we come out of the same college, we know each other. It takes a certain strength of character. I have managed to make a distinction between my friendship with a person and their job function ... Sometimes I'm shocked by the way some people talk about cases before and after trial. It encroaches on one's independence ... It's shocking sometimes ... I once heard a trial judge saying "but we have to defend the police." But for most *magistrats*, this culture of cooperation was unproblematic. In contrast to the defence lawyer who is regarded with suspicion, *magistrats* continually point to their status as *juges* as a guarantor of their independence and objectivity. The *juge d'instruction* feels no conflict of interest in her power to place in custody those she is investigating;[66] cases can be discussed freely without the fear of compromising independence. As one *juge d'instruction* [A5] said, "The issue of independence does not mean that you cannot communicate."

CONCLUSION

Supervision of criminal investigations in practice is not the paradigm model of wholly objective direction and supervision, a pre-trial judicial officer with a "clear and publicly proclaimed duty to investigate both sides using the police as his agents" (Devlin 1979: 78). Neither is it a wholly regulatory model like that of the Police and Criminal Evidence Act 1984, where the procedure is regulated by a variety of rules, procedures, and people: custody records, detention reviews, tape recording, custody officers, defence lawyers, standards of fairness in interrogation. Supervision and direction are constituted by a form of bureaucratic review which includes some regulation (for example, the procedural requirements during *garde à vue* or *instruction*) but which relies upon and is principally concerned with the form rather than the content of investigations. *Magistrats* understand themselves to be supervising, directing, orienting, or regulating investigations, and their lack of direct involvement in the enquiry is unproblematic in legal terms. But integral to their understanding and practice of supervision is a reliance upon professional ideologies,[67] trust and hierarchy, and, above all, their status as *magistrats*, rather than a concern with proactive or direct intervention. To be a *magistrat* is to represent and therefore to define what is in the public interest. It is not to be one of two equal and opposing sides, but to be the only side that counts. "Truth" is the *magistrat*'s trump card, which can be played at any time. It justifies and legitimates their actions and resolves any apparent contradictions. The result is a system which structurally and ideologically excludes the defence whilst providing no real guarantee that the accused will be adequately protected by a *magistrature* whose commitment to the search for the truth regards, for example, the exercise of silence or a refusal to confess as being contrary to the needs of the enquiry.

At one level these observations undermine the attractiveness of proposals to introduce some form of judicial control over police investigations. The model of judicial supervision held by many commentators is an ideal-type, represented neither in the text of the law itself nor in practice. But this should not kill off debate around the notion of judicial supervision simply on the grounds that there is not a model ready for easy importation. Such an argument would replicate the narrow and misdirected approach of the Royal Commission on Criminal Justice (1993) which, finding that inquisitorial systems have their problems too, rejected them out of hand. Rather, we need to explore more widely notions of judicial supervision: what they mean within the legal culture in which they exist and the consequences they have for the functioning of other parts of the legal process, be it the role of the defence or the independence of the investigation and prosecution from political influence. Even the failure of something in one legal system does not preclude its consideration and possible adoption in a modified form in another jurisdiction. What I have attempted to do here is to set out a more finely drawn account of one part of French pre-trial justice, a framework which draws upon the history and the rhetoric of the law itself, as well as the ways in which this rhetoric is employed by legal actors working within the process. This suggests a different understanding of the concept of judicial supervision and its associated problems, one which challenges both earlier assertions of deviant practice, as well as the "myths" of many advocates of the judicial supervision of criminal investigations.

NOTES

[1] See, e.g., Langbein and Weinreb (1978), Frase (1990), Cooper (1991), Field (1994), Mansfield and Wardle (1993), and Rose (1996). However, the miscarriages of justice in the 1980s and 90s prompted some debate in the press. See, e.g., Berlins (1990) and "Justice in the Dock" (1990).

[2] The *procureur* and her *substituts* (deputies) are public prosecutors collectively known as the *parquet*.

[3] Compare Goldstein and Marcus (1977) who dismiss the judicial character of the *procureur's* supervision as a fiction, implying that "real" judicial control is provided only by the *juge d'instruction*. Leigh and Zedner's (1992) account also relegates the *procureur* to a simple prosecutor stripped of her judicial office. The role of the *juge d'instruction* is described as being "truer to the ideal of a supervised investigation" (p. 14) and more successful than the *procureur* in filtering out weak cases as "a function of his status as a judge" (p. 21).

[4] References in this paper to the police include the *gendarmerie nationale*.

[5] Offences are classed as *crimes* (the most serious, such as murder), *délits* (such as assault or burglary), and *contraventions* (the least serious). These classifications represent a hierarchy of gravity and will determine the mode of trial for the offence.

[6] Around 85 per cent of offences are *flagrant*. This is defined in CPP Article 53 and, in general, refers to offences which are being, or have recently been, committed. The distinction is important in determining the powers of the police and the length of time the suspect may be detained in custody.

[7] This is the process of passing the case to the *juge d'instruction*. An *information* is opened, and the process of *instruction* begins.

[8] For example, prior to this reform, witnesses who were in no way suspected of being involved in the commission of the offence could be held in police custody. This power was removed in relation to *enquêtes préliminaires* in 1993 and then for *enquêtes flagrantes* in June 2000.

[9] Only juveniles over 13 may be held in *garde à vue*, and those under 16 may consult with a lawyer immediately. The reform of June 2000 requires the interrogation of juveniles to be videotaped. It also allows all suspects, including adults, to consult with their lawyer from the start of detention. For the first time, the police are now required to tell suspects of the nature of the offence for which they are being held, and of their right to silence.

[10] This changed under the June 2000 reform. Since January 2001, lawyers have to be informed by the police of the date and the nature of the offence in connection with which their client is being held.

[11] In France, for example, exclusion will result from the failure to sign and date documents in the dossier or a failure to document that the suspect has been advised of her rights, even though she later exercised them or expressly refused to take them up.

[12] Around 3 per cent of cases going to *instruction* are *crimes*.

[13] The June 2000 reform extended further the right of the parties to request investigative acts.

[14] This is how the suspect has been referred to during the *instruction* since the 1993 reforms. The notion of "being examined" was thought to reflect better the presumption of innocence than the former term *inculpé* which was more suggestive of accusation. The June 2000 reform sought to encourage the *juge d'instruction* to make greater use of the procedure of *temoin assisté* where there is a lesser degree of suspicion.

[15] Interestingly, to ensure the efficacy of this arrangement, there are rules as to how precisely the dossier should be organized. There are five distinct sections which must be classified in a set order, by the *greffier*, the personal legal secretary to the *juge d'instruction*. See the general circular of 1 March 1993, accompanying CPP Article 81.

[16] This was part of the 1993 package of reforms. See Hodgson and Rich (1993) and Trouille (1994).

[17] See, e.g., Devlin (1979, chap. 3) and authors cited in endnote 1.

[18] See recently, for example, the Royal Commission on Criminal Justice (1993), Mansfield and Wardle (1993), and Rose (1996). The dangers of such idealized accounts are compounded when compared (usually favourably) with critical empirical evidence from the commentator's own jurisdiction. See Hodgson (2000).

[19] Between 1831 and 1880, the proportion of cases passed to the *juge d'instruction* fell from 50 per cent to 13 per cent, whereas cases sent directly before the court increased from 13 per cent to 33 per cent (Lévy 1993: 172).

[20] The *Commission justice pénale et droits de l'homme* (1901), chaired by Professor Mireille Delmas-Marty, recommended that the *parquet* be responsible for the investigation of *all* offences. This proposal was rejected.

[21] Compare *Circulaire du 24 août 1993* accompanying the reform of that date, para. 2.1.2. The June 2000 reform required the *procureur* to be informed "at the start of detention," rather than "as soon as possible."

[22] During *instruction*, the authority originates with the *juge d'instruction*. In contrast, the *procureur* enjoys the same powers as the police and was originally an officer of the *police judiciaire*.

[23] It is the role of the *juges* in the fall of the monarchy leading up to the Revolution which continues to colour the way in which they are viewed within France as a potential political power which must be constrained. See Badinter (1995) and Magendie and Gomez (1986).

[24] For further discussion see Badinter (1995). Current legislative reforms seek to weaken the hierarchical control over the *parquet* exercised by the Minister of Justice.

[25] See, for example, CPP Article 81.

[26] See endnote 1.

[27] See also Damaska (1975: 535–538).

[28] The argument that our two systems are "converging" has gained currency in recent years. See, e.g., Markesinis (1994) and Harding et al. (1995). Madame Guigou, the then French Minister of Justice, made clear her views when addressing the *Sénat* in June of 1999: "The adversarial system of justice is by nature unfair and unjust. It favours the strong over the weak. It accentuates social and cultural differences, favouring the rich who are able to engage and pay for the services of one or more lawyers. Our own system is better, both in terms of efficiency and the rights of the individual."

[29] Noreau and Arnaud (1998: 282) note "the importance accorded to theoretical work in France—empirical work is largely swept away both in volume and legitimacy." See also the discussion by Garapon (1995) of the symbolism and the potential of the power of the *juge* or *magistrat* and the need to move towards more nuanced accounts based upon practice.

[30] For example, Jean Pradel, a leading commentator, is a former *juge d'instruction*.

[31] Leigh and Zedner (1992) claim that French scholars are becoming increasingly empirical, but such material is unpublished and they were unable to consult it.

[32] The development of judicial statistics from the early nineteenth century (known as the Davido database, after André Davidovitch who began the work) has provided useful historical information relating to, e.g., trends in prosecution. See Aubusson de Cavarlay et al. (1990) and Lévy (1993).

33 In Zauberman's case, this has enabled analysis to go beyond quantitative measures of clear-up rates and to examine the impact of a changing working culture where, in line with population shifts, *gendarmes* are now increasingly working in suburban settings as well as the tightly knit rural communities of which they have traditionally been a part.

34 In France, three public prosecutors, two defence counsel, two *juges d'instruction*, and two trial judges, all in Paris.

35 Their research examined France, Germany, and Italy.

36 They themselves describe their study as "inevitably impressionistic" (p. 2).

37 A total of 18 months' observational fieldwork was conducted by me and two French colleagues, Ms Brigitte Perroud and Ms Genevieve Rich. I am grateful to the Nuffield Foundation and to the British Academy for funding for the earlier project and to the Leverhulme Trust for funding the latter study.

38 For example, in what ways does the *magistrat* effect supervision of the police in practice?

39 For example, the significance at all stages of the supervisor's status as *magistrat*.

40 See Mansfield and Wardle (1993), Rose (1996), and those [studies] discussed by Field (1994: 120).

41 Leigh and Zedner (1992: 14) note this in relation to the *juge d'instruction*.

42 This requirement is part of the structure of supervision of the *garde à vue*, but the lack of attachment to anything beyond compliance on paper was demonstrated in one area where the *parquet* was informed by fax of the detention, but did not speak to the police until the next day when a decision as to the disposal of the case was required. This systematically excluded the *parquet's* ability to direct the investigation during the detention period.

43 See, for example, the *Commission de justice pénale et de droits de l'homme* (1991).

44 In one urban centre, for example, this included 660 officers supervised for the most part by three *substituts*.

45 The size of an area can be an important variable. In small towns and villages, the *gendarmes* are a part of the local community, and the *procureur* is almost a local dignitary. All public office holders know one another, and even the local defence lawyer may turn out to be the mayor!

46 Where quotations are from interviews, these are identified by a letter (denoting area) and number (denoting the person).

47 This was a constant complaint of all criminal justice personnel interviewed and observed who frequently lack proper secretarial support or even an adequate system of mail distribution. Half of our questionnaire respondents reported that they were "owed" posts and so were working understaffed; e.g., one of the areas observed had only one permanent and one temporary member of the *parquet* instead of three.

48 Although we saw no instances where this issue was problematic in practice, it should also be noted that, whilst responsibility for the conduct of criminal investigations is under the Ministry of Justice (with day-to-day answerability to *magistrats*), the police organization and administrative function (crime prevention, public order, traffic control, political intelligence gathering) is under the Ministry of the Interior. As part of the army, the *gendarmes* have a third master in the Ministry of Defence. This structure of accountability can give

rise to conflicts between judicial and police priorities. "In a difficult inquiry, a police officer is likely to follow the advice of his police boss, rather than that of the magistrates" (Guyomarch, cited in Horton 1995: 36). This was seen quite clearly in an affair in Paris in 1996 when a number of officers, on the orders of the head of judicial police in Paris, refused to follow the orders of a *juge d'instruction* to search the home of Jean Tiberi, a politician and mayor of Paris. As a result, the head of the judicial police, M. Olivier Foll was stripped of his status as a judicial police officer for six months. See *Le Monde*, February 28, 1997.

[49] The June 2000 reform required the *procureur* to visit the police station at least three times a year and to keep a record of these visits. Given the prevailing culture, the likely impact of this is unclear.

[50] This is in stark contrast to the accounts of many common law commentators who suggest that supervision by the *juge d'instruction* represents a "purer" model—e.g., Goldstein and Marcus (1977) and Leigh and Zedner (1992).

[51] In the late 1990s, several officers were *mis en examen* for the murder of a 16-year old who tried to drive through a road block in December 1997. See *Le Monde*, September 8, 1999.

[52] See *Le Monde*, March 31, 1999. The police unions protested at the judgment. They claimed that the injuries were the result of the "turbulent questioning" of the two suspects.

[53] Though not necessarily to the benefit of the accused who falls victim to it. It is rare for evidence to be excluded on such grounds. As Leigh and Zedner (1992: 13) put it, "French law tends to separate the question of brutality from that of the veracity of the confession."

[54] Pradel, cited in Leigh and Zedner (1992: 56), notes that police authors distinguish between lawful torture, such as prolonged interviews resulting in mental disequilibrium and unlawful torture, such as physical violence. Very much absent is any discussion of the general unreliability of confession evidence, in the way that we have witnessed in Britain. See, e.g., the discussion in Belloni and Hodgson (2000: 54–64).

[55] The dedication of the *gendarmes* and their willingness to carry on working through the night, interviewing the suspect to try and elicit an admission and therefore a complete dossier, was praised by several of those interviewed and observed.

[56] This view of guilt appeared to be widely understood beyond the office of the *juge d'instruction*. One *juge* explained that she had to place someone in custody for a serious offence, or this would signal to the trial court that she did not believe the accused to be guilty, and he may escape conviction.

[57] The grounds justifying detention are sufficiently broad to allow this. See CPP Article 144.

[58] See *Le Monde*, July 11, 1997.

[59] The few that thought lawyers should have greater access to the suspect and the dossier were again concerned with procedural advantages: it would ensure that the suspect had been told of her rights.

[60] Compare commentators who highlight the importance of the defence role in stimulating the critical reflexes of the *magistrat* and ensuring the integrity of the procedure in an inquisitorial process: Leigh and Zedner (1992: 73) and Field et al. (1995: 5).

[61] The *procureur's* role in representing the public interest in civil matters underlines this.

[62] One wonders if Michael Mansfield's enthusiasm for things inquisitorial might be blunted by the cynical disregard in which defence lawyers are held, where they are likened to "greengrocers, business people" rather than "officers of justice."

[63] Soulez-Larivière (1995: 53) argues that the recruitment, training and "collective fantasies" of the profession provide the institutional framework for this psychological structure, whereby the judge does not identify with the person being judged, but hides "behind a judicial logic which codifies reality."

[64] Introduced for a short time during 1993 to make the pre-trial detention decision independent of the investigating *juge d'instruction*.

[65] See preceding footnote.

[66] Reforms, including the current one creating a new *juge des libertés et de la détention* to determine pre-trial detention, were widely opposed by the *juges d'instruction*.

[67] See the debate between Goldstein and Marcus (1977, 1978) and Langbein and Weinreb (1978) over the assertion that "in the end these Continental systems rely more on their ideology, and on the assumption that officials adhere to the ideology, than on detailed supervision" (Goldstein and Marcus 1977: 283).

REFERENCES

Aubusson de Cavarlay, B., R. Lévy, and L. Simmat-Durand. 1990. "Dismissal by the Public Prosecutor." *Penal Issues (CESDIP)* 3 (2).

Badinter, R. 1995. "Une Si Longue Défiance." *Pouvoirs* 74: 7–12.

Belloni, F. and J. Hodgson. 2000. *Criminal Injustice: An Evaluation of the Criminal Justice Process in Britain*. London: Macmillan.

Berlins, M. 1990. "Weighing the Evidence." *The Guardian*, 10 January.

Commission de Réflexion sur la Justice. 1997. *Rapport au Président de la République de la commission de réflexion sur la justice*. Commission chaired by Pierre Truche. Paris: La Documentation Française.

Commission de Justice Pénale et Droits de l'homme. 1991. *La mise en état des Affaires Pénales*. Commission chaired by Mireille Delmas-Marty. Paris: La Documentation Française.

Cooper, J. 1991. "Criminal Investigations in France." *New Law Journal* 141: 381–82.

Damaska, M. 1975. "Structures of Authority and Comparative Criminal Procedure." *Yale Law Journal* 84: 480–544.

Devlin, Lord. 1979. *The Judge*. Oxford: Oxford University Press.

Di Frederico, C.D. 1998. "Prosecutorial Independence and the Democratic Requirement of Accountability in Italy." *British Journal of Criminology* 38: 371–87.

Field, S. 1994. "Judicial Supervision and the Pre-Trial Process." *Journal of Law and Society* 21: 119–35.

Field, S., P. Alldridge, and N. Jorg. 1995. "Prosecutors, Examining Judges, and Control of Police Investigations." Pp. 227–49 in *Criminal Justice in Europe: A Comparative Study*, edited by P. Fennell, C. Harding, N. Jorg, and B. Swart. Oxford: Clarendon.

Frase, R.S. 1990. "Comparative Criminal Justice as a Guide to American Law Reform: How Do the French Do It, How Can We Find out, and Why Should We Care?" *California Law Review* 78: 539–683.

Garapon, A. 1995. "La Question du Juge." *Pouvoirs* 74: 13–26.

Goldstein, A. and M. Marcus. 1977. "The Myth of Judicial Supervision in Three 'Inquisitorial' Systems: France, Italy and Germany." *Yale Law Journal* 87: 240–83.

Goldstein, A. and M. Marcus. 1978. "Comment on Continental Criminal Procedure." *Yale Law Journal* 87: 1570–577.

Harding, C., B. Swart, N. Jorg, and P. Fennell. 1995. "Conclusion: Europeanization and Convergence: The Lessons of Comparative Study." Pp. 379–86 in *Criminal Justice in Europe: A Comparative Study*, edited by P. Fennell, C. Harding, N. Jorg, and B. Swart. Oxford: Clarendon.

Hodgson, J. 2000. "Comparing Legal Cultures: The Comparativist as Participant Observer." Pp. 139–56 in *Contrasting Criminal Justice*, edited by D. Nelken. Aldershot: Ashgate.

Hodgson, J. and G. Rich. 1993. "A Criminal Defense for the French?" *New Law Journal* 143: 414.

Horton, C. 1995. *Policing Policy in France*. London: Policy Studies Institute.

"Justice in the Dock." 1990. [Editorial.] *The Guardian*, 13 July.

Langbein, J.H. and L.L. Weinreb. 1978. "Continental Criminal Procedure: Myth and Reality." *Yale Law Journal* 87: 1549–569.

Leigh, L.H. and L. Zedner. 1992. A *Report on the Administration of Criminal Justice in the Pre-Trial Phase in France and Germany*. London: HMSO.

Lévy, R. 1993. "Police and the Judiciary in France since the Nineteenth Century." *British Journal of Criminology* 33: 167–86.

Magendie, J. C. and J. J. Gomez. 1986. *Justices*. Paris: Atlas Economica.

Mansfield, M. and T. Wardle. 1993. *Presumed Guilty*. London: Heinemann.

Markesinis, B. 1994. *The Gradual Convergence: Foreign Ideas, Foreign Influences and English Law on the Eve of the 21st Century*. Oxford: Clarendon.

Noreau, P. and A.J. Arnaud. 1998. "The Sociology of Law in France: Trends and Paradigms." *Journal of Law and Society* 25: 257–83.

Pradel, J. 1989. "Les Pouvoirs de la Police Judiciaire en Droit français." *Revue Juridique Thémis* 23: 319.

Renouard, J. M. 1993. "French Research on Criminal Justice—Appraisal and Synthesis." *Penal Issues (CESDIP* 6 (4).

Robert, P. 1991. "The Sociology of Crime and Deviance in France." *British Journal of Criminology* 31: 27–38.

Rose, D. 1996. *In the Name of the Law*. London: Jonathan Cape.

Royal Commission on Criminal Justice. 1993. Cm 2263. London: HMSO.

Soijlez-Larivière, D. 1990. "Les Nécessités de l'accusatoire." *Pouvoirs, PUF* 55: 65–79.

Trouille, H. 1994. "A Look at French Criminal Procedure." *Criminal Law Review* (October): 735–44.

Zauberman, R. 1997. "The Treatment of Theft and Burglary by the Gendarmerie Nationale." *Penal Issues (CESDIP)* 10 (2).

CHAPTER STUDY QUESTIONS

- The administration of criminal justice in France has been described as a "non-adversarial process." Why? What are the claimed virtues of the French "non-adversarial," criminal justice process compared to the adversarial system that exists in many common law countries?
- The French inquisitorial justice system offers few protections for the rights of accused criminal offenders. Do you agree with this statement? Explain.
- Is the strict judicial supervision of criminal investigations a central aspect of the French inquisitorial justice system? What is the role of the *procureur* in the judicial supervision of criminal investigations in France? Is it the same as the role played by the prosecutor in the criminal justice systems of common law countries? Defend your answer.
- It has been pointed out that members of the judiciary in France view themselves more as legal and administrative technicians rather than autonomous decision makers. Why has this ideology evolved in France? What affect does this shared ideology of French magistrates have on the manner in which pre-trial criminal investigations and criminal trials are carried out in France?

RELATED WEB LINKS

US Department of Justice
http://www.ojp.usdoj.gov/bjs/pub/ascii/wfbcjfra.txt
> This website provides an overview of the French legal, political, and criminal justice systems. It also provides background information on human rights, crime rates, and the judicial and prosecutorial systems.

The Brookings Institution
http://www.brook.edu/fp/cusf/analysis/shapiro20030325.pdf
> This website accesses an article that analyses the importance of judicial systems in fighting terrorism. The article deals specifically with the French judicial systems.

LLRX
http://www.llrx.com/features/frenchlaw.htm
> This website provides a very detailed outline and discussion of all aspects of the French legal system. In addition, links are provided to journals, court decisions, government reports, statutes, and more. It is highly recommended for background information on French law and criminal justice.

International Information Programs
http://usinfo.state.gov/products/pubs/archive/freedom/freedom4.htm#conc
> This website accesses an article on judicial independence. The article primarily compares the French and US judicial systems, although brief reference is also made to other countries, such as Venezuela.

Chapter 14

IRANIAN CRIMINAL JUSTICE UNDER THE ISLAMIZATION PROJECT

HASSAN REZAEI

The Islamic Republic is a system based on belief in:
1. The one God as stated in the phrase "There is no God except Allah," His exclusive sovereignty and right to legislate, and the necessity of submission to His commands;
2. Divine revelation and its fundamental role in setting forth the law;
3. The return to God in the Hereafter and the constructive role of this belief in the course of man's ascent towards God;
4. The justice of God in creation and legislation.

Constitution of the Islamic Republic of Iran, Article 2

Just as the French Revolution of 1789 can be considered as a point of departure from pre-modern religious systems of criminal justice to a modern and secular one in Europe (Kelly 1993; Rousseaux, Bouchat, and Vael 1999), the Iranian Revolution of 1979, almost two centuries later, with the idea of "Islamization" of the criminal justice system, namely the intended revival of pre-modern Islamic law (*Shari'a*), shall be assumed as a thoughtful event in an increasing secular world. By the word "Islamization," we mean changing the existing legal system to be in conformity with Islamic classical law, while *Shari'a* has been defined as "the collection of legal provisions divinely revealed by the Prophet" (Salim al-Awwa 1982: 128).

Islamic law, as a sacred law, is the most typical manifestation of the Islamic way of life and is the kernel of political Islam. The concept of "Justice of Islam," as it has re-emerged in the Islamic countries applying Islamic law in their criminal justice systems, such as Iran, Pakistan, Sudan, Saudi-Arabia, Libya, Kuwait, United Arab Emirates and Afghanistan, seems currently to be a matter of utmost world importance. Contemporary events have again highlighted the importance of a better understanding of Islamic law for world peace and justice. In this context, the victory of the Islamic Revolution of Iran in reviving political Islam in the Islamic world, and its impact in raising interest in Islamic Law in the west, is undeniable.[1]

Moreover, the examination of the Islamization process and its consequences within Iranian society is arguably a good method of evaluating the achievements of political Islam in challenging the exigencies of criminal justice in the modern society.

The Iranian criminal justice system after the Islamic Revolution has witnessed radical changes. As a matter of comparative scholarship and in the quest for an effective criminal justice system, it could be interesting for scholars of criminal justice to observe this different model of legal change. Since the principal aim of drastic changes in the Iranian criminal justice was the application of the divine laws, the features of Iranian criminal justice are different from all other forms of contemporary criminal justice reforms in the west. It may therefore be regarded as a fascinating subject for comparative criminal justice scholars, whose interest is the study of the full range of possible legal phenomena. Besides this, the new desire of Iran to be counted as the most important Islamic participant in the course of dialogue among civilizations is also significant in this context.[2]

This chapter, after a historical overview of the criminal justice system in Iran, particularly in the context of the Constitution, attempts to describe, albeit briefly, the significant aspects of the Iranian Criminal Procedure under the Islamization policy. It seeks to show the manner through which a traditional understanding of Islamic law, as a religious law, constituted the criminal procedure of Iran. The significant aspects of the existing Iranian criminal justice system and its problems in establishing effective and fair criminal justice will be discussed. The main focus of the chapter is on two important statutes of 1994 and 1999, which have fundamentally changed the Iranian criminal justice system.

PRE-REVOLUTIONARY PROCESS OF SECULARIZATION

The legal history of Iran shows that Justice had always been located between two powers: The Shah and the Clergyman (see Figure 1). The modernization of Iranian criminal Justice began from the early 20th century and, astonishingly, throughout this period Iran witnessed two revolutionary movements. During the first one, i.e., the Constitutional Revolution of 1906–1911, modern legal conceptions were introduced to the Iranian customary law. This Revolution resulted in a constitution that laid down for the first time a division of powers.[3] Although the majority of the religious scholars had expected a return to classical Islamic law in its entirety, the waves of the Constitutional Revolution affected a section of the clergy, and they consequently recognized a process of modernization in criminal justice, especially the right to be tried in accordance with due process of law. But, according to the dominant religious culture, it was provided that no legislation shall be contrary to the Islamic law (*Shi'a school*).[4] Under the formulation of Article 2 of the Supplementary Constitution of 1906–1907, a supreme parliamentary committee of five high ranking Islamic jurists (*ulama*) was established. They would determine whether legislation was in conformity with *Shari'a* (Esposito 1991: 85–86).

Ancient Iran	Islamic Conquest	Constitutional Movement Era	Islamic Revolution
(550 BC–652 AD)	(652–1900)	(1900–1979)	(since 1979)
• The King is the source of justice. • The clergymen were acting as his supporters and advisors.	• Two simultaneous systems of justice: • Securlar Courts • Shari`a Courts • Except for several short periods, arbitrary secular courts were active.	• Iran encounters modernity and models of Western law. • 1912: First Iranian Code of Criminal Procedure Based on the French Model 1808).	• Islamization of Criminal Law and Procedure to date. • In recent years the idea of modernistic Islamic Law is developing rapidly.

Figure 1. An overview of Iranian judicial history

Despite Article 2 of the Constitution of 1906–1907, an autocratic process of secularization in the Shah monarchy (both father and son who reigned between 1925–1979) was pursued. In 1910, a department of Public Prosecutions was set up. In 1912, the first Iranian Code of Criminal Procedure entitled "The Temporary Codes of Criminal Trials" was passed by a body of modern lawyers appointed by the Justice Minister. The Code was introduced as a temporary and experimental measure in order to circumvent the opposition of the clergy. This Code, which was very much influenced by the French Code of Criminal Instruction of 1808, with its subsequent amendments, remained as the framework of the Iranian Criminal Procedure until 1994 (Mohammad 1997). This system of criminal procedure, like its French model, was based on the blend of inquisitorial procedure at pre-trial stage and accusatory procedure at trial. As a result, the influence of Islamic law in criminal justice, because of the absence of the clergy from power, was considerably reduced. Later developments thoroughly shook the foundations of classical Islamic law (Amin 1985).

POST-REVOLUTIONARY PROCESS OF ISLAMIZATION

Following the Islamic Revolution of 1979, which was to a large degree a reaction to the Shah's radical secularization program, the first step taken by the new government was the preparation of a new Constitution to legitimize its power. Naturally, the new Constitution had to keep to the new revolutionary goals: "Freedom, Rule of law, and Islamic Government," or in other words, Islamism and Republicanism.

Making a modern and harmonized composition of those idealistic aspects of the Revolution was not an easy task.[5] However, Article 4 of the Constitution of 1979 set the stage for using "Islamization" as a pretext for changing substantive and procedural criminal law in post-revolutionary Iran. It states:

All civil, penal, financial, economic, administrative, cultural, military, political laws and other laws or regulations must be based on Islamic criteria. This principle applies absolutely and generally to all articles of the Constitution as well as to all other laws and regulations and the *fuqahã* (Islamic jurists) of the Council of Guardian are judges in this matter.[6]

As this Article shows, it is the Islamic rulings as determined by Islamic jurists (who, due to Article 110, are to be appointed by the Leader) that in fact constitute the supreme law in Iran (Mayer 1999; Amin 1985: 107). The problem which arises, however, is the varying understandings and interpretations of the "sacred texts" (*Nusũs*), so that, as a consequence of the generality of the Constitution, speaking about the rule of law in its modern concept is very difficult and confusing. For instance, alongside Article 159 of the Constitution, [which] provides the rule of law in administration of justice as *"the courts of justice are the official bodies to which all grievances and complaints are to be referred. The formation of courts and their jurisdiction is to be determined by law,"* there is Article 61, which stipulates *"the function of the judiciary are to be performed by courts of justice, which are to be formed in accordance with the criteria of Islam, and are vested with the authority to examine and settle lawsuits, protect the rights of the public, dispense and enact justice, and implement the Divine limits [al-hud d al-Il hiyyah]"* or Article 167 providing *"The judge is bound to endeavour to judge each case on the basis of the codified law. In case of the absence of such a law, he has to deliver his judgment on the basis of authentic Islamic sources or authoritative fatwãs."* These formulations show very well a structural dualism within the Iranian judicial system, originating from the Constitution.[7] In practice, during the last two decades, many courts have issued judgments, even the death penalty, with reference to the Article 167, which is also repeated in several procedural laws (Gudarz 1999: 95; Lawyers Committee for Human Rights 1997: 28). The problems related to this dualism have developed out of an unusual system of criminal procedure in Iran. Most of the fundamental human rights protected under international law in the Iranian Constitution are qualified by reference to ill-defined "Islamic criteria." This specificity of the Iranian system is due to the special powers entrusted with the unelected Council of Guardians, which has exercised both considerable authority since the Revolution and encroached on the democratic Parliament's legislative functions, with the effect that a serious crisis for the entirety of the Republican principles of the Constitution has developed.[8]

However, the Islamization plan for criminal procedure began very quickly. In June 1979, just four months after the Revolution, the clergy-dominated Council of Revolution, in the absence of the Parliament, passed a draft law which changed the pre-revolutionary court system. The most salient feature of Islamization in this draft law was Article 2, according to which all judgments of the first instance were regarded as final and immediately put into effect (Official Gazette, No. 10094, 18 October 1979).

A week later, in June of 1979, this Revolutionary Council, functioning as a legislator preceding the establishment of the Islamic parliament, established the Islamic Revolutionary Courts in accordance with Imam Khomeini's decree (Official Gazette, No. 10018, 16 July 1979). By virtue of the Regulations, new special courts were created: "the Revolutionary Courts and

Prosecution Offices." The aim of the Revolutionary Courts was to investigate crimes committed by supporters of the Shah regime before the Revolution and to fight against foreign influence and other enemies of the Revolution (Articles 4–10).

The clerics of the Ex-Supreme Judicial Council (substituted by the Head of Judiciary in the Constitutional revision of 1989) were not still satisfied with this amount of Islamization and, in 1982, prepared a draft of a criminal procedure law based on the traditional understandings of *Shari'a* principles and precepts. Islamic Parliament, because of the traffic of legislation, could not pass the draft entirely and accordingly, merely 30 fundamental articles were enacted (Official Gazette, No. 10953, 03 October 1982). Under this Act (which was amended in 1982, 1988, and 1992), the previous system of classification of crimes, adopted from the French Penal Code of 1816, which divided offences according to their seriousness into crimes, misdemeanors, and violations, was abandoned. Instead, Islamic classification, simultaneously based on crime/punishment, was introduced. This consisted of *Hodūd* (determined offences with quantified, mandatory, and fixed punishments based on the Qur'an), *Qesās* (crimes of just retaliation for intentional homicide and battery), *Diyāt* (crimes of compensation for unintentional homicide and battery and as alternative for retaliation), and *T'azirāt* (crimes of discretionary punishments) (Tellenbach 1989; Bassiuoni 1982).

The constant changes in the laws concerning criminal justice show that the Islamic revolutionary law-maker could not easily pass from the pre-revolution system to his Islamic ideal. Whenever he partly changed the procedure code, he was forced a little afterward to make new amendments to the changed one. The clearest example of this is the system of appeal which was changed regularly. The reason was/is the strict conflict between the modern rules of appeal and Islamic traditional adjudication: in accordance with Islamic law, which recognizes the authority of the Islamic judge to issue *fatwa*, revision of the judgment of an Islamic Judge is not allowed, except in cases of claims of non-competence of the judge (morally and legally) by any of the two parties, and in instances where the judgment is considered to be in contradiction to the provisions of the Islamic principles or omission of the judge of *ratio decidendi*. Paradoxically, there is no time limitation in these vague and exceptional cases.[9] Clearly, the ideal model has been the institution of *Qadi's justice* in Islamic traditional law.[10] In *Qadi's justice*, the judges are among fully qualified (morally and scientifically) Islamic jurists and, as the delegates of the Prophet on earth, have general jurisdiction whether it is a civil or criminal case. The court is held with a single judge, and there is no idea of *res judicata* (Liebesney 1975: 240). Seemingly, the Islamic lawmaker believes that there is no contrast between these simple rules of adjudication and modern technical systems of courts and procedure. But after two decades of experience, it has become clear now for many, including the clerics of the Judiciary, that this system does not work. The legislative efforts to introduce the *Qadi's Justice* into the modern context of Iranian criminal justice with its strong secular background was only a simplism, which has left, of course, a dysfunctional system of appellate review procedure for Iran.[11]

Reviewing these developments of Iranian criminal justice reveals that the Judiciary has, in the last decade, done its best to maximize the Islamization project. Distant from academic centres and the ideological attitude of its high officials as well as the majority of the conservative wing of Parliament, an Act was passed in July 1994 that yet again changed the criminal procedure and the judicial system—the so-called "Act of Establishing Public and Revolutionary Courts" (Mohammad 1995). This Act launched heavy protests from lawyers and academics due to its revolutionary measure of abolishing the office of public prosecution. According to the new Act, responsibilities and powers of the prosecutors were transferred to the tribunals.

Following the establishment of the new court system, the Islamic lawmaker was obliged to provide for a new criminal procedure code compatible with the new system. Finally, the code of Criminal Procedure of the Public and Revolutionary Courts passed Parliament on 20 September 1999.

SOME SIGNIFICANT ASPECTS OF THE NEW CRIMINAL JUSTICE

As a result of the above-mentioned process of Islamization, Iran now possesses an unusual criminal justice system, which may be somehow unfamiliar from a comparative criminal law perspective. Some significant aspects of the new criminal procedure are:

1. The abolition of the public prosecutors office.
2. The security approach to criminal proceedings.
3. The introduction of the concept of God's rights, individual rights, and public rights into the criminal process.
4. Moral restrictions on criminal justice.

Abolishment of the public prosecutor's office

It may be surprising that, notwithstanding the orientation of most criminal justice systems of the world (at least those following a democratic tradition) to separate the office of the prosecutor from judicial functions and to emphasize the role of prosecutors in the administration of criminal justice and the establishment of an impartial and fair trial (UN Guidelines on the Role of Prosecutors 1990; Council of Europe 1997), the Islamic Republic of Iran has acted otherwise. When faced with the numerous objections of the Guardian Council declaring the judicial measures of the public prosecutors in conflict with Islamic criteria (Documents of the Islamic Assembly, No. 580, 31.08.1989), the Islamic legislature simplified the problem and, in spite of the opposition of Iranian lawyers and universities, abolished the prosecutor's office in the Public and Revolutionary Courts. However, the question is that if the public prosecution is not in accordance with the Islamic procedure, why such an institution still exists at the Special Court for the Clergy and the Military Tribunals.

In any case, it is assumed that, in accordance to the Islamic law, the court shall have the general authority.

At the moment, in Iran, pursuant to this Act, prosecution, investigation, and trial are carried out by the court itself. A criminal case is directly referred to the judge, and, if he decides so, he can transfer pre-trial measures to the instruction judge or even to law enforcement officers, provided that all judgments shall be issued by the judge alone. The instruction judge has no right to act independently. In fact, the instruction judge and the police replaced the former posts of interrogators and public prosecutors.

Apparently, the difference between the new system and the former is that the prosecution stage was removed from the pre-court to the court stage, so that all judicial measures take place under the supervision of the court, which is allegedly compatible with Islamic criteria. Accordingly, there is no indictment in this system, but the explanation of the charge is regarded as the indictment.

The contradiction of this system with Article 37 of the Constitution of the Islamic Republic is apparent. Article 37 provides, *"Innocence is to be assumed and no one is to be held guilty of a charge unless his or her guilt has been established by a competent court."* The majority of the Iranian people were probably not aware of this problem; however, when the public viewed the broadcast of the trial against the mayor of Teheran, Mr. Karbaschi, in 1999, this great deficiency of the new system was disclosed. Since that time, a common understanding has been established among people that the new court system cannot preserve impartiality. In Iran, the Karbaschi trial is called the "blessed trial" because of its disclosure against the new system.

The efficacy and the legitimacy of the new system is nowadays under intense criticism, and, according to recent reports, the judiciary, which is seriously seeking to re-establish the public prosecutor's office, has offered a reform bill that again would fundamentally change the present system (*The Daily Nowrooz,* 12 July 2001). Interestingly, ... these days, the new Head of Judiciary makes severe criticism of the existing system stating that it is contrary to Islamic law. It is notable that he himself was for many years a cleric member of the Council of Guardians and, during his membership, made no objection to it (IRNA, 18 April 2000).

Security approach to the criminal proceedings

In the new system, there are various signs indicating the security view of the lawmaker of the criminal justice system. As a matter of fact, the concept of security in Iran is often reduced to the security of the government. For instance, in the new Iranian Code of Criminal Procedure, whenever it is felt that the security of government confronts the rights of the defendant, precedence is obviously given to the interests of [the] regime.

Of course, we cannot interpret this approach without the post-revolutionary circumstances. Throughout the last 20 years, the Islamic Republic has witnessed war, terrorism, sabotage, and violence. This social unrest has very likely influenced the lawmakers.

The establishment of the Revolutionary Courts and extending its jurisdiction to all security crimes is an explicit instance for the aforementioned security approach of criminal legislation. These are essentially security courts. Article 5 of the 1994 Act, which determines the jurisdiction of the Revolutionary Courts, is a good example:

> Revolutionary Courts as may be required in number shall be formed in
> each provincial capital and in the districts determined by the head of the
> judiciary and under the administrative supervision and legal authority of
> the judicial districts to investigate the following offences:

1. Any crime against the domestic or foreign security of the Islamic Republic of Iran and decay on earth.
2. Any act amounting to an affront against the founder of the Islamic Republic and/or its leader.
3. Any conspiracy or plot against the Islamic Republic of Iran or any armed uprising, terrorism, or demolition of public buildings or facilities with the aim of confronting the Islamic government of the country.
4. Spying for foreigners.
5. Drug trafficking or related crimes.
6. Suits filed under Article 49 of the Constitution (related to the confiscation of illicitly obtained wealth) (Official Gazette, No. 14383, 23 August 1994).

Rather than being Islamic and fair, the history of the last 20 years shows that these courts are in fact revolutionary and arbitrary. Most of the criticism of the international human rights organizations against Iran is based on the practice of these courts.[12] The judges of these courts are mostly clerics with no, or little, knowledge of legal matters, and, for this reason, they are rarely satisfied with the presence of defence counsel in their proceedings. These Courts created ecclesiastical tribunals having no basis in the law. The procedure of these tribunals also departed from the strict requirements of proof and safeguards for the defence. Initially, the verdicts of these Courts, inspired from the Islamic system of *Qadi justice*, were final and were enforced without any judicial review. It was only in 1988 that a right of appeal was provided (Lawyers Committee for Human Rights 1993: 31). Proceedings have largely taken place in secret, and defendants are rarely given the opportunity to have defence counsel (Amnesty International 1990: 32). As quoted from the Head of Judiciary in March 2001, between the years 1988–2000, more than 8,999 convictions on death penalty for drug offenders alone were pronounced by these courts (Ali-Hossein 2001).

Indications of security considerations are also very clear in the new Code of Criminal Procedure (hereinafter CCP). Article 128 of this Code states,

> In secretive cases or in cases which according to the judge's determination
> the presence of non—defendants causes decay and also in crimes against
> the security of the country, attendance of defence counsel in the investiga-
> tion is permitted, if the courts give permission.

In addition, Article 113 stipulates, "if the public interest necessitates, the court will issue a summons without mentioning the cause of summons and the consequences of not attending the court." Also in Article 104, the control of individual telephones in security cases is allowed, leaving this to the judge's discretion.

Traces of such a security mind are also found in the expansion of compulsory detention. Under Article 35 CCP, in addition to the 12 offences of murder, kidnapping, spraying acid, armed robbery, spreading decay on the earth, fraud, theft, embezzlement, bribery, abuse of confidence, forgery, and using forged documents, the issue of a warrant of detention is obligatory in any case where the penalty is capital punishment or life imprisonment. But the law does not content itself with this, and gives the right of detention to the judge whenever he finds that the liberty of the defendant leads to "decay" (*Fisād*). However, the instances of the term *Fisād* have never been defined by the law, and, as such, it is the right of the judge to determine when and how it applies. Through this Article, which accords to the procedures of *Qadi justice*, the court has gained the power to issue a warrant arbitrarily against every defendant.

Apparently, for the Islamic revolutionary lawmaker, the protection of the theory of the Islamic Government remains above internal security. Using general and vague expressions in laws, such as decay or propaganda against the regime (for instance, Article 500 of the Islamic Penal Code), has proved to be the best way to prosecute any political protest during recent years (Report of Special Representative of the UN Commission on Human Rights in Iran 2001). The Special Courts for the Clergy, which are out of the bounds of the judiciary and remain under the control of the leader, are, according to the regulations of their procedure, empowered to try any dissident cleric. Unfair trials by the Special Court against government critics, including *Shi'a* clerics, journalists, and students, are reported regularly. Critics of the Government have been tried and sentenced in trials in which procedures did not conform to international standards for a fair trial. The Special Court for the Clergy and the Revolutionary Courts apply procedures that are inconsistent in proceedings that are often conducted in a summary way. Public criticism of the special courts is increasing, and they are widely perceived as a mechanism for silencing criticism (Amnesty International 2000, 2001; Afshari 2001).

The rights of God, the individuals (victims), and the public in criminal proceedings

In Islamic law, there are three key notions: God's right, the individual's right and the public's right.[13] But the "individual or public rights" should be understood in the context of Islamic legal tradition, in which human or public rights are defined in the light of "*duties*," unlike modern law which is based on the primacy of *rights*. The language of *Shari'a* is the language of duties, and humanity in the mirror of religion as a duty-bound creature. By comparison with secular law, the main tenet of Islamic law is the concept of God, his exclusive right of lawmaking and the duty of human beings before his absolute sovereignty. Muslims are constantly warned not to overstep the boundaries set by God (*Hodād Allah*) lest they be held responsible and have to suffer the consequences of their trespass. The Islamic law texts state partly the rights of humans, but such passages are not common. For instance, in the Qur'an we read, "*Whoever is killed unjustly, we have appointed to his next-of-kin authority; but let him not exceed in slaying; he shall be helped*" (Qur'an 17: 35). For this reason, it is difficult to speak of human rights in Islamic law (Soroush 2000: 61–64). Observing the difference between the language of modern law under the rubric of rights and the field of Islamic law, which deals with duties, illustrates the depth of the rift between the secular and religious legal theories. Thus the notion of "God's right" in the prosecution of offences and punishment is quite peculiar. The Islamic legal theory expresses to perfection the ideal of a system of law representing the divine command of *Allah*, which as interpreted by Islamic jurists is "to behave properly in this world and to prepare for the world to come" (Coulson 1983: 9).

With the beginning of the Islamization project, the Iranian Islamic lawmaker, in adopting this Islamic doctrine, annulled the previous French-based model of the classification of crimes. For example, since Allah has given the right of prosecution and punishment to the individual in murder, only the family of the victim of a killing or, in the case of bodily harm, the victim himself has the right to press charges for retaliation, to forgive the culprit, or demand compensation for the injury and damage. With this understanding of Islamic law, Iranian society, until 1991, had no legal right to prosecute the murderer who has been forgiven by the heirs of the victim.[14]

The category of a public right, in the sense of social reaction to crimes of homicide and battery, was, at least for *Shi'i* law, to a certain extent new, because *Shi'i* law was historically isolated from government and the concept of public law did not develop. The Islamic Republic as a state, when confronted with the increasingly dangerous consequences of this traditional Islamic formulation, through a new *fatwa* from Ayatollah Khomeini on this matter, tried to introduce the notion of public rights alongside of the two former categories (Ashouri 1997:1975). From then on, however, the Iranian criminal justice system, in its process of Islamization, has constantly tried to establish a meaningful balance between these three categories so that, on the one hand, it could not be accused of secularization and abandonment of *Shari'a* and, on the other hand, it would be able to maintain the public order and security. Whether this development amounts to secularization of Islamic law is a vital question for the future of the Islamization project. In the view of some prominent scholars of Islamic Law trying to bridge the gulf between secular and *Shari'a* institutions of justice would amount to secularism (Schacht 1955: 84).

The new code of criminal procedure, for instance, intentionally seeks to put the scope of public law into the content of Islamic law. Consequently, Article 2 of CCP provides for three kinds of rights:

Kinds of rights / Consequences	God's rights	Individual's rights	Public's rights
Prosecution	Obligatory (exceptional situation in sexual crimes)	Upon the request of the individual	Upon the provisions of the law
Pre-trial detention	Possible	Upon the request of the individual	Possible (in accordance to law)
Proceeding	Only in-parte proceeding	Both ex-parte and in-parte proceeding	Both ex-parte and in-parte proceeding
Compromise	Impossible	Encouraged	Possibility of mitigation of punishment
Confession	Blameworthy (judge may prevent)	Effective	Relating to given law (generallly accepted)
Remission and pardon	Permitted in the case of no eyewitnessed proof after repentance	Absolutely or conditional is permitted	Under the provisions of the law by the leader
Prescription	NO	NO	YES

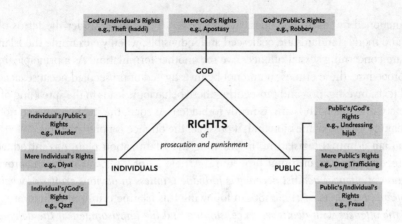

1. God's rights, which cover offences that are considered violations of God's commands as enunciated in the *Qur'an* and sound Tradition (*Sunnah*).[15]
2. Rights of the individual, which includes the rights granted by God to his servants, e.g., the right to ask for retaliation (*Qesās*) or compensation.
3. "Public's rights," based on the duty of the Islamic ruler to maintain public order and security. In the case of murder, for instance, under Article 208 of the Islamic Penal Code of 1991, the offender, apart from the victim's right, will in any case be punished by imprisonment from 3 to 10 years by virtue of the public's right.

The Iranian legislator does not offer specific criteria distinguishing these three sorts of rights, although this classification shapes the whole of criminal procedure. Therefore, the Courts still have problems in new criminal cases in deciding whether the crime/punishment rest upon public or individual rights. In Figures 2 and 3, some main differences between these rights and their consequences in criminal procedure have been illustrated.

MORAL RESTRICTIONS ON CRIMINAL JUSTICE

In Islamic legal theory, making a concrete distinction between law, faith, and morality is very difficult if not impossible, while in secular theories of law, especially in the Western theories, there is a clear-cut distinction between them. Morality relates to the conscience, whether individual or public. Faith and religious beliefs, as a private matter, relate to the human soul and spirit, and the legal system is a man-made system to regulate behaviours of individuals in social life and is not basically concerned with metaphysical standards deriving from religious faith, beliefs, or moral conviction (Coulson 1983: 8). For instance, in the European criminal law tradition, extramarital sexual liaisons may be regarded as immoral, but are not the subject of any criminal prosecution, unless there are aggravating factors, such as the lack of consent, young age of one of the parties, a blood relationship between them, or public indecency. Contrarily, in Islamic law and subsequently in the Iranian law, any sexual relationship outside marriage is not only immoral but is a criminal offence sanctioned by severe penalties. Although, up to this stage, under the terms of Islamic law, legal and moral standards are coalesced and indivisible, when we examine the Islamic rules of procedure concerning sexual offences, we see another formulation. As a principle, in Islamic criminal procedure, these crimes should not be investigated or prosecuted because, according to the sacred texts, investigating and prosecuting these behaviours leads to the spreading of obscene acts in society, and this is, in Islam, is firmly forbidden. As such, the judge is advised not to allow the defendant to make a confession and, if possible, the offence is not to be proved.[16]

The Iranian criminal legislature, in pursuing the Islamization plan, has introduced these Islamic precepts into the criminal procedure. Article 43 of CCP, for instance, provides that *"investigation of offences against decency is forbidden, unless in obvious crimes or when the private complainant requests."* Article 186, in following this Islamic criminal policy very radically, states, '*in the offences with death sentence, stoning and life imprisonment if the defendant does not introduce any private defence and refrains from having a defence counsel, the state shall not determine an attorney for him.*" Hence it should be mentioned that, in Iranian criminal justice, adultery and sodomy which are certainly regarded as offences against decency in Iran, are to be punished by the death penalty.[17]

Another moral aspect of the Iranian criminal procedure is Article 235 of CCP. Under this Article, one of the reasons for reconsideration of the judgment of a first instance court is the claim of a lack of moral competence of the judge. For example, if it is proved that the judge does not pray or fast or does not believe in resurrection, his judgment will be reversed.

FINAL REMARKS

The study of the Iranian criminal justice system is interesting from many points of view. The Islamic Republic is part of a global phenomenon of Islamic revivalism throughout the Middle East, North Africa, and beyond. It is a religious movement seeking comprehensive reform of the Iranian society.

In the view of Imam Khomeini, Islam is not confined to the arena of individual rituals and moralities. Islam is the theory of government and is integral to the conduct of social, economic, legal, and political relationships. The sacred legislation of Islam is the sole legislative power. Islam has precepts for everything which concerns man and society. Islam is essentially political and the Islamic ruler must therefore Islamicize the entire system (Algar 1981: 55). Accordingly, in Iran, the project of Islamization of criminal justice was theoretically adopted to bring the criminal justice system into maximum conformity with the standards of classical Islamic law, but the developments of the Iranian criminal justice over two decades show that it was mainly the interests of the political clergy which determined the guidelines of Islamization, not the ultimate goals of Islamic law.

The radical changes of the Iranian criminal justice system in the name of Islamization became associated with setbacks to the value of rule of law. Since, for a majority of cleric judges with traditional clerical education, the procedural codes and regulations are regarded as roadblocks in the way of implementation of Islamic substantive criminal law, there was always a strong desire by these judges to resort to the classical institution of *Qadi justice* in which the judge has almost unbridled power.

During the past two decades, whenever the Islamic legislature has tried to change the criminal justice system it has faced a lot of practical problems. The radical changes in the criminal justice system, especially the abolition of the Prosecution as an institution, has, according to a literal interpretation of sacred texts, currently exposed a set of serious challenges to the Judiciary in Iran. Much legislation and many practices of the Iranian Judiciary run counter to the teachings and spirit of Islam. These challenges are jeopardizing the legitimacy and efficacy of the Islamic state as a whole. Many Iranian intellectuals and even clerics argue that this literal and traditional understanding of Islamization did not facilitate the establishment of the ideal of Islamic Justice and crime control, but instead damaged the Islamic faith among the Iranian Muslim people. They argued that the plan to implement traditional interpretations of Islamic law was a political decision; its hermeneutical assumptions are very controversial and in practice resulted in a particular authoritarian criminal justice that has obvious conflicts with international human rights standards. Amalgamating the Islamic traditional system of *Qadi justice* with the modern institutions of criminal procedure has proved not only to be incompatible with the ultimate goals of *Shari'a*, but also amounts to conflict, inconsistency, and cruelty in the administration of criminal justice.

The reformists call very clearly for a paradigm shift in the application of Islamic law. The classical understanding of the sacred legal texts regards them as being autonomous from their context, yet these legal texts of Islam, in the first instance, have been revealed to solve the problems of the revelation's time and space. Therefore, they are mostly local rulings of Islam, not universal and permanent. Indeed, they were a very rational and just response to their primary context. In their discussion, the reformists refer mainly to the historical phenomenology of sacred texts and, on this basis, conclude that most of the Islamic criminal precepts were accidental and not the substance of Islam (Shabestari 2000: 45–50).

In Iran today, after enjoying for over two decades implementation of a political-traditional reading of Islamic law, particularly in the scope of criminal justice, both modern clerics and intellectuals clearly demonstrate a concern for the rule of law and judicial development. "Civil Society" is becoming the main agenda for reform in Iranian criminal justice. In the meantime, some scholars strongly argue that since the Constitution fails to give a coherent version of these revolutionary ideals, the clash of Islamists and liberalists about the rule of law will never cease unless there is a total revision of the Constitution in favour of a democratic understanding of Islamic principles or, alternatively, completely in favour of traditional Islam (Schirazi 1997: 291–306; Mayer 1999: 29–30).

Now the dominant discourse is the modernization and democratization of criminal justice within the context of Islamic society, something which seems to be vital for the Islamic revivalists around the world and for their perspectives of modern law. It seems that, through new discourses in Iran, which are based on the theological and philosophical aspects of Islamic law, the Iranian version of Islamic criminal justice in particular can approach the international standards of criminal justice. Surely, this event should be highly appreciated because it could give an indigenous solution to the clash of Islam and secularism. In this process, the moral and virtual aspects of Islamic law can be introduced into the secular systems, thereby enabling Islamic states to share in world peace and to establish a moral system of criminal justice.

NOTES

[1] In this regard, a memory from the prominent scholar of Islamic law, N.J. Coulson, is very expressive. He writes, "On my first visit to the school of U.C.L.A (California) in 1961, my class numbered five. On my latest visit to Harvard in 1979, I found myself faced with a class of 55. For a brief moment I was congratulating myself on my growing personal reputation. But I then realized that my arrival at Harvard had coincided with the arrival in Teheran of the Ayatullah Khomeini." See Coulson (1983: 8).

[2] In November 1998, the General Assembly of the United Nations proclaimed the year 2001 as the "United Nations Year of Dialogue among Civilizations." The resolution GA/RES/53/22, proposed by the Islamic Republic of Iran and supported by a large number of countries, invites "Governments, the United Nations system, including the United Nations Educational, Scientific and Cultural Organization, to plan and implement appropriate cultural, educational, and social programmes to promote the concept of dialogue among civilizations, including organizing conferences and seminars and disseminating information and scholarly material on the subject." A subsequent resolution reaffirmed the provisions of the resolution GA/RES/53/22 in February 2000 (resolution 54/113).

[3] For more details on the Constitutional Revolution and an English translation of the first Constitution, see Brown (1910).

[4] For a full explanation of the Shi'a School, see Momen (1987).

[5] For a critical examination of this Constitution, see Schirazi (1997).

[6] For discussion on this Article, see Mayer (1999).

[7] Considering the criminal procedure as the seismography of the Constitution, one can understand the current situation of the Iranian system better. For discussion on the relationship between the Constitution and criminal procedure, see Roxin (1998).

[8] The Council of Guardians is very similar to the French *Conseil Constitutionnel*, but also there is a very important difference between them. In France, the scrutiny of a law by the *Conseil Constitutionnel* can take place only if requested by the six persons or bodies specified by Article 61, while the scrutiny of the Council of Guardians in Iran is automatic and absolute. Due to Article 94 of the Constitution and its interpretation by the Council itself, all enactments of the Parliament and also the pre-revolution laws shall be submitted to the Council to control whether or not they comply with the Islamic law. If the Council finds the enactments contrary to Islamic rulings, it shall return them to the Parliament for modification. For more discussion, see Mallat (1993: 23–79) and, for details, see Tellenbach (1985: 188).

[9] By virtue of Ayatollah Khomeini's fatwa, "It is not permissible for the verdicts issued by qualified Islamic jurists to be reviewed or subject to appeal" (Rouhollah 1981: 406).

[10] For an exploration of Qadi courts in Islamic traditional law, see Tyan (1975).

[11] Notably, ... because of increasing problems arising from this unusual mixed system of appeal, especially the delay in proceedings, upon the request of the Head of Judiciary, the Expediency Council (and out of the control of the traditional cleric jurists of the Council of Guardians) has passed a decree discarding traditional Islamic law and affirming the positive rules of appeal. The main argument for passing this decree was protecting the public interest. Reported by, Islamic Republic News Agency (IRNA), 6 August 2000.

[12] See Lawyers Committee for Human Rights (1993: 30–36) and the numerous reports of Amnesty International and UN Commission of Human Rights Reports. For more recent [material on the] situation of human rights in the Islamic Republic of Iran, see the Report of Special Representative of the UN Commission on Human Rights A/56/150, 10 August 2001.

[13] For a full description of these notions in the view of Islamic traditional jurists, see *Mousu 'a al-Fiqhiiah* (2000: 8–25).

[14] Articles 9–15 and 43 of Hodud & Qesas Act of 1982, Official Gazette, No. 10988, 16 November 1982. For more details, see Tellenbach (1985: 201–202).

[15] Sunnah in [the] Shia School of Islamic Law means the traditions of the prophet and the 12 holy Imams.

[16] It seems there is a logical relationship between the severity of the punishment and the kind of procedure. See Radzinowicz (1948: 27).

[17] Articles 82, 83, and 110 of Islamic Penal Code of 1991.

REFERENCES

Afshari, Reza. 2001. *Human Rights in Iran: The Abuse of Cultural Relativism*. Philadelphia: University of Pennsylvania Press.

Algar, H. 1981. *Islam and Revolutions: Writings and Declarations of Imam Khomeini*. Berkeley: Mizan Press.

Ali-Hossein, Nadjafi 2001. "La politique criminelle en matière de stupéfiant." *Problèmes Actuels de Science Criminelle* 14: 75.

Amin, S.H. 1985. *Middle East Legal Systems*. Glasgow: Royston.

Ashouri, Mohammad. 1997. *ein-e D drasi- e Keifari Vol. 1 [Criminal Procedure]*, Teheran.

Amnesty International. 1990. *Iran: Violations of Human Rights 1987–1990*. London: Amnesty International.

Amnesty International. 2000. *Country Report: Iran*. London: Amnesty International.

Amnesty International. 2001. *Country Report: Iran*. London: Amnesty International.

Brown, E.G. 1910. *The Persian Revolution*. Cambridge: Mage Publishers.

Coulson, N.J. 1983. "The Islamic Legal System: Its Role in Contemporary Muslim Society." Pp. 7–19 in *Studien zum islamischen Recht*, edited by. N.J. Coulson and F. Schwind. Vienna: Verlag der Akademie Abdulwadoud.

Council of Europe. 1997. *The Role of the Public Prosecution Office in a Democratic Society*. Strasbourg: Council of Europe.

Documents of the Islamic Assembly, No. 580, 31 August 1989.

Esposito, J.L. 1991. *Islam and Politics*. 3rd ed. New York: Oxford University Press.

Gudarz, E.J. 1999. "Asl-e Q_n_ni b_dan-e Jar_yem va Moj_z_th_." [The Principle of Legality of Crimes and Punishments]. *The Journal of Legal Researches* 14 (25–26).

Hodud and Qesas Act. 1982. Articles 9–15 and 43.

Islamic Penal Code. 1991. Articles 82, 83 and 110.

Islamic Republic News Agency (IRNA). 18 April.2000.

Kelly, J.M. 1993. A *Short History of Western Legal Theory*. Oxford: Clarendon Press.

Lawyers Committee for Human Rights. 1993 *The Justice System of the Islamic Republic of Iran*. Washington, DC: Unpublished paper.

Lawyers Committee for Human Rights. 1997. *Islam and Justice*. New York: Unpublished paper.

Liebesney, H.J. 1975. *The Law of the Near and Middle East*. Albany: State University of New York Press.

Mallat, C. 1993. *The Renewal of Islamic Law*. Cambridge: Cambridge University Press.

Mayer, A.E. 1999. *Islam and Human Rights*. 3rd ed. Boulder: University of Colorado Press.

Mohammad, Achouri. 1995. "Quelques réflexions sur la nouvelle loi iranienne relative à l'organisation judiciaire et aux compétences des juridictions répressives (loi du 6 juillet 1994)." *Revue de science criminelle et de droit pénal comparé* 4: 785–794.

Momen, M. 1987. *An Introduction to Shi'a Islam*. New Haven: Yale University Press.

NA. 1990. *Mousu'a al-Fiqhiiah [Encyclopaedia of Islamic Jurisprudence]* 18: 8–25.

Rouhollah, K. 1981. "Tahrir al-Vasileh [Commentary on Shia jurisprudence]." *Qom* 1981: 406.

Rousseaux, X., M.S. Dupont-Bouchat, and C. Vael. 1999. *Revolution and Criminal Justice: French Models and National Traditions 1780–1830*. Paris: L'Harmattan.

Roxin, C. 1998. *Strafverfahrensrecht*. 25th ed. Munich: C.H. Beck.

Salim al-Awwa, M. 1982. "The Basis of Islamic Penal Legislation." Pp. 127–147 in *The Islamic Criminal Justice System*, edited by M.C. Bassiouni. London: Oceana Publications.

Schacht, J. 1955. "The Schools of Law and Later Developments of Jurisprudence." Pp. 57–84 in *Law in the Middle East*, edited by M. Khadduri and H.J. Liebensey. Washington, DC: Middle East Institute.

Schirazi, A. 1997. *The Constitution of Iran: Politics and the State in the Islamic Republic*. Translated by J. O'Kanne. New York: I.B. Tauris.

Shabestari, M.M. 2000. *Naqdi bar Qarāa't-e Rasmi-e Din* [A Critique of the Official Reading of Islam]. Teheran: Tarh-e Naw.

Soroush, Abdolkarim. 2000. *Reason, Freedom, and Democracy in Islam*. Edited and translated by M. Sadri and A. Sadri. Oxford: Oxford University Press.

Tellenbach, S. 1985. *Untersuchungen zur Verfassung der islamischen Republik Iran vom 15 November 1979*. Berlin: K. Schwarz.

Tellenbach, S. 1989. "Zur Re-Islamisierung des Strafrechts in Iran." *ZStW* 101: 188–92.

Tyan, E. 1955. "Judicial Organization." Pp. 237–78 in *Law in the Middle East*, Vol. 1, edited by M. Khadduri and H.J. Liebensey. Washington, DC: Middle East Institute.

United Nations. 1990. *UN Guidelines on the Role of Prosecutors*, E/1990/31-E/AC.57/1990/8.

United Nations. 2001. *Report of Special Representative of the UN Commission on Human Rights*. General Assembly Documents. A/56/150.

CHAPTER STUDY QUESTIONS

- The Iranian constitution contains several provisions for the protection of human rights, yet Iran is noted for human rights abuses on a gargantuan scale. What issues, according to Rezaei, weaken the effect of these constitutional protections? Do you think that it would be possible to strengthen human rights protections without also weakening the influence of Islamic law?

- Rezaei suggests that many judicial practices that were instituted in Iran after the 1979 revolution do not follow Islamic law and may even be "unIslamic." Outline several examples that he uses to illustrate this argument.

- Identify several factors that have led to the creation of an arbitrary and extremely authoritarian criminal justice system in Iran. Can these factors be traced to Islam itself, or are they rooted in other political and cultural practices?

- Rezaei argues that the Islamization project was motivated by factors other than the desire to bring Iranian criminal law into line with Islamic ideals. Outline at least one of these motivations. In reality, how is this situation different from legal developments in democratic countries such as Canada or the United States?

RELATED WEB LINKS

Networking Human Rights Defenders
http://www.fidh.org/rubrique.php3?id_rubrique=228
> This website represents over 140 different human rights organizations around the world. It contains access to articles, court cases, and the reports of governmental agencies and NGOs (e.g., Human Rights Watch and Amnesty International).

Young Muslins Canada-Wide
http://www.youngmuslims.ca/
> This website provides access to articles and other information on Islam, including information on the theory and practice of *Shari'a* justice. (http://www.youngmuslims.ca/online_library/books/shariah_the_way_to_justice/)

Global Law and Justice
http://www.nyulawglobal.org/globalex/Iran.htm
> This website contains a detailed article that describes the history of Iran, its governmental structures and Iranian law. It also provides links to other websites that provide information on such topics as the role of women, sodomy laws in Iran, laws governing commerce, and many other topics.

Ekawaaz-One Voice
http://ekawaaz.wordpress.com/2006/08/29/execution-of-a-teenage-girl-in-iran-under-sharia-law/
        This website provides access to a video depicting the brutal execution of a 16-year-old girl
        for adultery. It also provides access to news articles on Islam and Islamic countries.

Chapter 15

BUILDING A POST-WAR JUSTICE SYSTEM IN AFGHANISTAN

ALI WARDAK

The formal justice system of Afghanistan has been influenced, to varying degrees, by Western (mainly French) legal thought and moderate Islam, radical Marxism, and by radical interpretations of Islam. These influences, by and large, reflected the values, ideologies, and politics of the various governments that Afghanistan has witnessed since its emergence as a politically organized society. In the 1950s and 1960s, the justice system was modernized, and state law, rather than *shari'a*, became the primary source of the justice system. After the military coup in 1978, the Marxist government attempted to introduce a Soviet-style judicial system, but these changes were rejected before they took root. The subsequent *mujaheddin* regime of 1992–1996 declared *shari'a* as the basis of the state, and this was further entrenched by the taliban's regime. While most of these regimes have partly used their systems of justice as tools for achieving their political goals, they have nevertheless contributed to the richness of Afghan legal culture; there is much within these different doctrines and approaches that could be fruitfully used and integrated in a post-war justice system.

It is also important to mention that, as the formal Afghan justice system was elitist, corrupt, and involved long delays (Wardak 2002a; ICG 2003b), many Afghans avoided contacts with it. As a result, many Afghans—particularly in rural areas—continued to use traditional institutions of informal justice such as *jirga*, *maraka*, and *shura* (see endnotes 1 and 2 for a distinction between these concepts). Although the practices of these traditional institutions of popular justice sometimes conflicted with Afghan legal norms and with international standards of human rights, they nevertheless resolved tribal and local conflicts expeditiously and in cost-effective ways (Wardak 2002b).

Since the establishment of the Afghan Interim Administration in December 2001 (and later the Afghan Transitional Authority) and the reinstatement of the 1964 Afghan Constitution and "existing laws," there has been a new emphasis on the need to incorporate international human rights principles into Afghan justice institutions (Decree on the Establishment of Afghan Judicial Commission 2002). The increasing involvement of the international community and the UN in the social, political, and economic reconstruction of Afghanistan appears to necessitate the compatibility of the Afghan justice system with international standards and principles of human rights.

In this paper, key dimensions of the post-war justice system in Afghanistan are examined. These are *shari'a* (Islamic law), traditional informal justice (*jirga*), "existing laws" (interim legal framework), and human rights principles. On the basis of an analysis of the interrelationships among these, an experimental integrated model of the post-war justice system in Afghanistan is proposed. However, first, it is important to place the subject of examination in this paper in the general context of Afghan society and nearly a quarter of a century of conflict in the country.

THE AFGHAN CONTEXT

Afghanistan is a land-locked country that lies at the crossroad between South and Central Asia. To the north and northwest of the country lie the former Soviet republics of Uzbekistan, Tajikistan, and Turkmenistan; to the south and east is Pakistan; to the west of Afghanistan lies Iran and to its northeast is China. It is this strategic geopolitical location of Afghanistan that has made it both a crossroad between civilizations and a battlefield between competing global and regional powers.

The total population of Afghanistan is estimated to be between 20–25 million, composed of various ethnic and tribal groups, most of whom have lived together in the country for centuries. These include Pashtun, Tajik, Hazara, Uzbek, Turkmen, Aimaq, Baluch, Brahui, Nuristani, Pashaie, Pamiri, Kirghiz, Qizilbash, Mongols, Arabs, Gujars, Kohistanis, Wakhis, and Jats. Among these, the Pashtuns constitute the largest ethnic group (estimated around 50 per cent of the total Afghan population), followed by Tajiks, Hazras, and Uzbeks (Dupree 1980; Canfield 1986; Glatzer 1998; Wardak 2004a).

Although these various Afghan groups are generally distinguishable from one another by their members' distinct language (or accent) and ethnic origin, for generations trade and commerce, universities/colleges, government institutions, and cross-regional employment opportunities have pulled thousands of Afghans from different ethnic/tribal backgrounds to live and work side by side. Furthermore, intermarriages, service in the national army and police, and participation in shared cultural, religious, and social activities have strengthened citizenship at the expense of ethnic/tribal affiliations in urban centres and cities. This interaction among Pashtuns, Tajiks, Hazaras, Uzbeks, Turkmen, and other Afghan ethnic and tribal groups has resulted in a cultural fusion among various Afghan ethnic and tribal cultural traditions at the national level. The richness of Afghan national culture owes much to ... [this century-old] multicultural fusion.

However, since the Soviet military intervention in Afghanistan in 1979, the country has been used as a battlefield between competing global and regional powers and groups—a battlefield between the former Communist USSR and the Capitalist West (mainly the USA) in the 1980s; in the 1990s, a battlefield between Pakistan and the Arab Gulf countries, on the one hand, and Iran and Russia on the other; and, more recently, a battlefield between foreign Muslim extremist groups and a right-wing US administration. In this process of rivalry, Afghanistan's main immediate neighbours infiltrated deep into Afghan politics. With competing interests in the country, they created their client factions/warlords and sponsored them militarily, financially, and politically. The factions gradually became so dependent on their foreign sponsors that they saw Afghanistan's interests through the eyes of these foreigners. These neighbours also exploited Afghanistan's existing ethnic and religious composition and justified their interventions on the grounds that they had common religious and ethnic ties with their clients. Thus the armed conflict (which continued for several years even after the defeat of the former Red Army) resulted in the extensive destruction of Afghanistan's economic, political, and social infrastructure. The Western world, particularly the USA, which lured the Soviets to invade Afghanistan (Brezinski 1998; Cooley 2002) and strongly supported the Afghan *mujaheddin*—Islamic warriors—almost completely abandoned the ruined country after the Red Army was defeated.

The destruction of the country's economic infrastructure, in particular, provided opportunities for foreign players and their client Afghan warring factions to exploit the situation, seeking their strategic goals and sectarian interests at the expense of the Afghan population. The almost total collapse of the Afghan pre-war economy gradually resulted in the emergence of a "war economy" (Rubin 1999; Goodhand 2003)—economic conditions that mainly centred on the manufacturing, repair, use and smuggling of weapons and ammunition, on the one hand, and on the smuggling (and production) of illicit drugs and national treasure, on the other. The nearly quarter century-long conflict also resulted in a generation of young people who were largely deprived of the opportunity of gaining educational qualifications and other useful skills. This "war generation" of thousands of young people has been deeply traumatized by the war—many lost their parents, relatives and homes. The various factions were able to recruit their fighters from amongst this war generation, so that the conflict in which they had a stake continued. Fighting for one or another warlord provided these young men with a source of income, social status, and a way of channelling their energies. More importantly, this situation provided the opportunity for foreign Muslim extremist groups—mainly the *al-qa'ada*—to use Afghan soil as headquarters for terrorist activities against other nations. There now exists an increasingly convincing body of evidence, which links the Afghanistan-based *al-qa'ada* to the 11 September terrorist attacks on New York's Twin Towers and on other targets in the United States.

In the wake of the US-led military campaign in Afghanistan that resulted in the collapse of the Taliban regime, the Bonn Agreement of December 2001 was signed among the representatives of Northern Alliance warlords, pro-Zahir Shah (former King of Afghanistan) technocrats/intellectuals, and two other small Afghan groups that were mainly based in Pakistan and Iran. Although the four anti-Taliban groups did not consult (or represent) the people of Afghanistan, the Bonn Agreement, which was signed in a rush, did open the possibility of a new participatory political order for Afghanistan. It provided a framework of state formation processes that aimed at the eventual creation of a "broad-based, multi-ethnic and fully representative" government by 2004. The Agreement, which resulted in the establishment of the Afghan Interim Administration in December 2001, raised hopes among many Afghans that there was an opportunity to end warlordism in Afghanistan and to rebuild the country's social, political, and economic institutions. However, the reinstatement of most warlords as key political and military leaders in the post-Taliban administration, and the US government's emphasis on the "war against terrorism" rather than on rebuilding Afghanistan, has spread disillusion among many Afghans about the prospects of lasting peace. The US's military and financial support for warlords, who may cooperate in hunting down remnants of the *taliban* and *al-qa'ada*, continues to be a major obstacle to the development of national participatory institutions in Afghanistan, and therefore, a major source of increasing instability in the country.

Despite this, the people of Afghanistan still expect the patriotic Afghan leaders/forces and the fair-minded international players to help them lay down the foundations of participatory institutions and lasting peace in the country. Most Afghans see the deployment of the International Security Assistance Force (ISAF), economic reconstruction plans, and the UN-led political stabilization process in Afghanistan as a unique opportunity for rebuilding their country and for its re-integration into the global community. These efforts may, for the first time in the past 25 years, provide common ground between the interests of the international community and the interests of the ordinary Afghan people. Central to political stabilization and to the re-building of social and political order in Afghanistan is the establishment of an effective system of justice in the country. In this paper, key dimensions of a post-war justice system in Afghanistan are identified and discussed. One of the most important of these is *shari'a*.

KEY DIMENSIONS OF POST-WAR JUSTICE IN AFGHANISTAN

I: Shari'a (Islamic law)

As the overwhelming majority of the people of Afghanistan are Muslim, Islamic teachings and *shari'a* permeate various spheres of life in Afghan society. Thus, *shari'a* has strongly influenced the development of Afghan justice since the emergence of Afghanistan as a politically organised society. The population of Afghanistan is mainly divided by their religious following into an estimated 80–85 per cent *sunnis* and 15–20 per cent *shei'ite*. The overwhelming majority of *sunnis* in Afghanistan are followers of the *hanafi* school; Afghan *shei'ite* are, by and large, followers of the *ja'afari* jurisprudential school.

Shari'a is an Arabic word which means "the path to follow"; it is also used to refer to legislation, legitimacy, and legality in modern Arabic literature. However, *shari'a* in a jurisprudential context means Islamic Law. The primary sources of *shari'a* are the *quran* and the *sunnah*. The first refers to the holy book of Islam, and the second to the statements and deeds of the Prophet Mohammed. However, relatively small portions of the verses of the *quran* and the contents of the *sunnah* include legislative material (Lippman et al. 1988). Taken together, the two do not seemingly provide answers to all types of legal issues. However, the *quran* and the *sunnah* do lay down general principles as well as specific rules that are subject to interpretation and analysis. Thus, after the death of the Prophet Mohammed, the *caliphs* (leaders of the Muslim community) and the *sohaba* (the Prophet's associates) appointed consultants to help in the correct interpretation of the *quran* and the *sunnah* and in the extraction of rules (for new situations) that seemingly did not exist in the two primary sources of *shari'a*. As a result, *qiyas* and *ijma* were added as secondary sources of *shari'a*.

Qiyas, in the context of Islamic jurisprudence, means analogical reasoning. That is, cases and questions not seemingly answered by the primary sources are deduced from similar original cases in the *quran* or in the *sunnah* through a process of reasoning by analogy. This process was handled only by those Islamic jurists who met strict criteria relating to their knowledge, piety, and personal integrity; they were also required to fulfil very strict conditions for the kind of cases that were handled by *qiyas*.

The fourth source of *shari'a*, *ijma*, means the consensus of Islamic jurists on a ruling. When qualified Islamic jurists reached a unanimous agreement on the solution to a specific new problem, their opinion became binding with absolute authority. In this way, the outcomes of both *qiyas* and *ijma* were transformed into statements of divine law. This has, in turn, resulted in the documentation and compilation of hundreds of cases and books that are used, today, as references in Islamic jurisprudence (Wardak 2004b).

In the process of the consolidation of the Afghan state institutions, particularly in the early 20th century, the *hanafi* school (alongside traditional customary laws) provided the basis of the Afghan justice system. This version of the *shari'a* existed in symbiotic relationships with Afghan customary laws and with *sunni* "folk Islam" that generally reflected the cultural, social, and economic realities of everyday life of the overwhelming majority of the people of Afghanistan. *Ulama* (Islamic scholars) interpreted this version of Islam and the *shari'a* and also worked as *qadi* (judges) in state courts (Olesen 1995). However, in order to have control over the *ulama* and over their interpretation of Islam and *shari'a*, the government established the official institution of *jami'at -al- ulama* (society of Islamic scholars/jurists) and the state-funded Islamic *madrasas* of *dar -al- o'lume arabi* and *abu hanifa* in Kabul. While *jami'at -al- ulama* members, who were paid very handsome salaries, endorsed the government policies, the two official *madrasas* trained students of Islamic theology and jurisprudence as *qadi*, or state judges.

In the 1950s and 1960s, as Afghanistan's political, economic, and cultural relationships increased with the rest of the world, the rulers started to modernise the Afghan justice system in line with those of the Western world. The justice model that Afghan rulers chose to adopt resembled closely the Egyptian model, which was strongly influenced by the French and Ottoman legal systems (Kamali 1985). In order for the modern Afghan justice system to be run by professional judicial personnel, the faculties of Islamic Law and of Law and Political Science were opened at Kabul University. Thus, the graduates of *dar -al- o'lume arabi* and *abu hanifa* were only eligible to work as judges after they had studied modern positive laws as well as Islamic jurisprudence at the Faculty of *shariat*. Similarly, students at the *qazayee and saranwali* (judiciary and prosecution) branch of the Faculty of Law and Political Science were trained to work as judges mainly in the commercial and administrative sections of the Afghan judiciary. In addition, from the early 1960s, all these graduates had to do a nine-month legal training course (including 3 months on-the-job training) called *kadre qazayee*. Some working legal professionals/judges and lecturers at the faculties of Islamic Law and Law and Political Science were also sent to the USA and Egypt for further legal training. This modernisation process was also accompanied by the codification of many Afghan laws in the 1960s and 1970s.

This process gradually resulted in the relative secularisation of the Afghan justice system, especially in the areas of criminal law, commercial law, and general civil law. Thus state law, rather than *shari'a* became the primary source of the justice system. Nevertheless, *shari'a* remained a secondary source. As Article 69 of the 1964 constitution states, "... In area [s] where no such law exists, the provisions of the *Hanafi* jurisprudence of the *Shariaat* of Islam shall be considered as law." While this justice system appears to have reflected a balance between Islamic *shari'a* and modern legal norms, its administration involved long delays, bribery and corruption. Many Afghans, particularly in rural areas, avoided contact with state judicial institutions (Wardak 2002a).

After the 1978 military coup, the Afghan Marxist government attempted to introduce the (former) Soviet-style judicial system in line with its socialist ideological, political and economic goals. However, since the Marxist totalitarian regime was at odds with both Islam and Afghan traditions, the whole system of governance and its judicial reforms (decrees) were massively rejected. After the collapse of the last Afghan Marxist government, the *mujaheddin* government (1992–1996) declared *shari'a* as the basis of their "Islamic State of Afghanistan." Despite the fact that the various *mujaheddin* groups, which formed the government interpreted Islam in conflicting ways, most of them attempted to impose a totalitarian theocracy of which *shari'a* laws were part and parcel. The *taliban's* theocratic regime (1996–2001) imposed an even more regressive version of *shari'a*, much of which reflected their ignorance of *shari'a*, as well as of a system of justice.

Despite the over (or under) emphasis on the role of *shari'a* in Afghan state institutions by different political regimes, it remains as an important constituent element of post-war Afghan justice. This is recognised by the Bonn Agreement (2001:3), which emphasises that the Afghan Judicial Commission and the UN shall "rebuild the [Afghan] domestic justice system in accordance with Islamic principles, international standards, the rule of law and Afghan legal traditions." Past experiences, indeed, show that it is only that version of *shari'a* that is in harmony with Afghan cultural traditions, existing legal norms, and fundamental principles of human rights that can make important contributions to a credible post-war justice system in Afghanistan.

II: Customary law and jirga

The role of the Afghan central government and its formal institutions of justice (courts, police, corrections, etc.) in maintaining social order in Afghan society has always been limited (Wardak 2002a; ICG 2003b). This particularly applies to rural Afghanistan, where it is estimated that over 80 per cent of the Afghan population live. In some southern and eastern parts of the country, formal institutions of justice have no (or just nominal) existence, and yet there exists a reasonable degree of social order in these areas.

A great many potentially serious disputes, relating to domestic violence, divorce, inheritance and marriage, are normally settled within the "private" sphere of the Afghan extended family without the involvement of local/tribal or state institutions (Wardak 2002a). They are dealt with on the spot before becoming a "public" problem and a burden on other societal institutions. However, those disputes that are considered "public" are resolved by public institutions at local and tribal levels. The main institution that has traditionally operated as a mechanism of dispute settlement (at village and tribe levels) is *jirga/maraka* among the Pashtuns and its approximate equivalent—*shura*[1]—among the non-Pashtuns of Afghanistan (Carter and Conner 1989; Farhadi 2000; Gletzer 1998; Hashemi 2000; Malekyar 2000).

The term *jirga*, according to the *Pashto Descriptive Dictionary* (1978: 1272), is an original Pashto word, which, in its common usage, refers to the gathering of a few or a large number of people; it also means consultation according to this source. The word *jirga* is also used in Persian/Dari. According to *Ghyathul-lughat* (1871: 119) it is derived from *jirg*, which means a "wrestling ring" or "circle," but is commonly used to refer to a gathering of people. Other scholars believe that the word *jirga* originates from Turkish, where it has a very similar meaning (Faiz-zad 1989: 5).

Jirga,[2] in everyday practice, refers to a local/tribal institution of decision-making and dispute settlement that incorporates the prevalent local customary law, institutionalized rituals, and a body of village elders whose collective decision about the resolution of a dispute (or local problem) is binding on the parties involved (Wardak 2002b). Those on the *jirga* combine "traditional authority" (based on personal qualities, social status, and leadership skills) as well as "competent authority" (based on the individual's recognized expertise and skills), which play a central part in achieving a *prikra* (ruling) that is satisfactory to both parties.

One important form of tribal *jirga* is *nanawate*, which means seeking forgiveness/pardon and the obligatory acceptance of a truce offer. This happens when the tribal *jirga* makes a *prikra* (decision) that relatives of the *par* (guilty party) send a "delegation" to the victim's house. This consists of a group of people that include elders, a female relative of the offender holding a copy of the holy *quran*, and a *mullah* (Muslim priest), alongside the offender's other close relatives (and sometimes the offender himself) who bring a sheep and flour to the victim's house. The sheep is often slaughtered at the door of the victim's house. Once inside the house, the delegation seeks pardon on behalf of the offender. As it is against the tribal code of behaviour to reject a *nanawate*, the victim's relatives pardon the offender and the two parties are reconciled. This reconciliation is called *rogha*. Thus, unlike formal state justice, which often labels offenders as different, evil, and excludes them from the community, *nanawate* reintegrates them into the community. Existing criminological knowledge suggests that reintegrative social control is, by and large, more effective in reducing crime than disintegrative social control, normally exercised by formal state institutions (Braithwaite 1989).

The main reasons that Afghan people have preferred *jirga/shura* to formal justice is because the former is conducted by respected elders with established social status and a reputation for piety and fairness. In many cases, the disputants personally know the local elders and trust them. In addition, in the context of *jirga/shura*, elders reach decisions in accordance with accepted local traditions/values (customary law) that are deeply ingrained in the collective conscience of the village/tribe—they have a profound existence in the collective mind of the village and in the minds of its individual members. Also, unlike state courts, *jirga/shura* settle disputes without long delays and without financial costs. Illiteracy plays an important role in discouraging people from using the formal courts—the overwhelming majority of Afghans are unable to make applications, read/understand the laws or complete the paper work.

However, *jirga/shura* has its own problems: in some cases of murder, *jirga* may recommend *badal* (direct vengeance) or the marriage of a woman from the *par*'s tribe to the victim's close relative. Although these practices have become increasingly rare in recent years (Johnson et al. 2003), the first punishment is in direct conflict with the Afghan state laws, and the second one is a clear violation of fundamental human rights. In addition, *jirga/shura* is generally a male-only institution; it sometimes can also be excessively influenced by powerful elders. More important, in areas where warlords exercise direct control over the population, *jirga/shura* decisions are influenced (or undermined) by those with guns and money. However, ... incorporating *jirga/shura* into the new justice system ... would [help it] conform to the norms of the national legal order of post-war ... Afghanistan. This would, in turn, help to make this traditional patriarchal institution more inclusive of both men and women. But a pre-requisite for all this is a secure social environment where, *jirga/shura* and the justice system as a whole could operate without any illegitimate influence by warlords.

III: Interim legal framework and the current justice "system"

The Afghan Interim Administration (AIA), that was established as a result of the Bonn Agreement in December 2001, inherited a justice system devastated by the 25 year-long civil conflict in Afghanistan. However, under the Bonn Agreement, the 1964 Afghan constitution and "existing law" were reinstated with some important modifications. In effect, this constitution and the "existing laws" currently provide an interim legal framework for Afghanistan. This "framework" represents a mixture of *shari'a* and positive laws that were enforced until the Marxist coup d'eta in 1978.

Under the Bonn Agreement, the establishment of an independent Judicial Commission of Afghanistan was authorised. It was envisaged that the Commission (with the assistance of the UN) would provide the opportunity for Afghanistan's best legal scholars and practitioners to review and reform the Afghan domestic justice system. However, in view of the vastly devastated state of the post-war Afghan justice "system," much of it needs rebuilding and even building from scratch. The Judicial Commission, which has a huge and complex task ahead of it, currently focuses on four major areas of Afghan justice system and legal order:
  a. law reform;
  b. assessment and development of technical, logistical, and human resources;
  c. review of the structure and functions of the justice system and the division of labour among its various components;
  d. legal aid and access to justice.

Despite the formal reactivation of the formal Afghan justice "system" throughout the country, it is far from prepared to deliver justice. It is a hugely devastated institution. The devastation not only includes extensive damage to buildings, office furniture, official records, and essential office equipment but also the lack of qualified judges and other justice personnel. Importantly, it is highly fragmented, with little or no interaction among the judiciary, the police, the prosecution, and the prison/correction service (Amnesty International 2003a; Johnson et al. 2003; UNDP 2002). One of the main reasons for the lack of co-operation between the judiciary and the police is that the latter consist predominantly of Northern Alliance militia who are highly dependent on and more loyal to their factional patrons than to the national Afghan Interim Administration. The police, in many ways, are merely an extension of the Northern Alliance's militia, who mainly represent Afghan Tajiks; they have no (or little) basic understanding of policing, and most of the people they police have no trust in them (Amnesty International 2003a; Johnson et al. 2003).

In addition, corrective regimes and rehabilitative programs for both adult and young offenders do not currently exist in Afghanistan. Althougha *dar -al- ta'adeeb* (juvenile correctional institution) is nominally functioning in Kabul, the institution has neither the necessary facilities nor the professional personnel to deal with the serious personal and social problems that young Afghan rule-breakers face today. Thus, the current fragmented Afghan justice "system" is highly ineffective and dysfunctional; it does not operate as a system at all.

Similarly, the Afghan prison/correction "service" has only a very basic existence in the main urban centres; it has no existence at all in many rural districts and some provincial centres (Amnesty International 2003b; Johnson et al. 2003). Although the prison service in Kabul was recently transferred from the Ministry of the Interior to the Ministry of Justice, its personnel has not changed. Many of the inmates are political prisoners who live in very overcrowded conditions and are fed by their relatives and friends. The situation in the prisons is particularly serious in Sheberghan and Herat (Amnesty International 2003b; Physicians for Human Rights 2002). The sources report that these prisoners are treated in inhuman ways, and many of them suffer from illnesses related to malnutrition and overcrowding; dozens have died since their surrender to the US-led Northern Alliance forces in November 2001.

However, Afghanistan has a large body of codified laws including the 1975 Afghan Civil Code, the 1976 Criminal Codes, the amended 1973 Law of Criminal Procedure, and the 1973 Law of Police. Although these laws are currently implemented, they need some important modifications. In addition, as stipulated in the 1964 Constitution, in areas where no law existed, the *hanafi* school of *shari'a* is considered as applicable. These various laws, which currently provide the interim legal framework, are to be used as an important element of the post-war justice system in Afghanistan.

IV: Fundamental principles of human rights and transitional justice

The past 25 years of war have badly brutalized Afghan society as a whole. During this period, serious abuses of human rights and war crimes (by all sides of the conflict) have taken place. These include massacres, looting of houses and property, rapes, revenge killings, illegal imprisonment, the torture and murder of prisoners/POW and assassinations of political opponents (Dehghanpisheh, Barry, and Gutman 2002; Rubin 2003). These abuses of human rights continue to be committed by those with guns and money, many of whom currently occupy very important political and military positions in the country (Amnesty International 2003a; Human Rights Watch 2002a, 2002b, 2003). This legacy of war, poverty, and religious fanaticism have particularly affected Afghan women, who have suffered from both cultural and structural inequalities (and violence) in Afghan society for centuries. The persistence of this situation over the past quarter of a century has produced a "culture of human rights abuses"—patterns of behaviour and practices that are justified and even positively sanctioned in the shadow of warlordism in Afghanistan.

The gravity of this situation has long been recognized by Afghans, the UN, and international human rights organizations. While conformity of post-war justice to "international instruments ratified by Afghanistan" was emphasized by the Bonn Agreement, the issue of past crime was not. The Bonn Agreement (2001: 3), which authorized the establishment of an independent Human Rights Commission for Afghanistan says, "The Interim Administration shall, with the assistance of the United Nations, establish an independent Human Rights Commission whose responsibilities will include human rights monitoring, investigation of violations of human rights, and development of domestic Human Rights institutions." But the Agreement that was concluded in a rush and under heavy pressure from the US and its rediscovered allies in the war against terrorism—the Afghan warlords—remained silent with regard to past crimes and a mechanism for investigating them. The need for this was more clearly reflected in the Secretary-General's report to the Security Council in December 2001, which stated that "The Afghan people and their international partners must commit themselves to addressing the problems of the past by ending impunity and ensuring accountability for past abuses, including gross and systematic violations of human rights" (C/2002/1157, Paragraph 83). However a mechanism for addressing crimes of the past and the role of the "international partners" was not clarified. Several months later, Mary Robinson, the former United Nations High Commissioner for Human Rights, raised the issue more explicitly and proposed that dealing with past crimes needed to be part and parcel of the process of reconstruction and institutional reform in post war Afghanistan:

> We know well from past experience, in Afghanistan and elsewhere, that sustainable peace, reconciliation, reconstruction and development cannot be built upon a foundation of impunity ... There can be no amnesty for perpetrators of war crimes, crimes against humanity, and gross violations of human rights. Just as has been the case in Sierra Leone, East Timor, Cambodia, the Former Yugoslavia, and Rwanda, so it must be the case for Afghanistan. When we speak of accountability, we refer to an Afghan-led and owned process that has different elements. These are justice, truth telling, reconciliation and institutional reform ... All these elements are indispensable. (Robinson 2002)

The lack of political will on the part of key international players and the Afghan warlords who dominate the Afghan Transitional Authority means that this valuable advice has yet to be translated into action. One of the most obvious vehicles for implementing this advice is the Afghan Human Rights Commission. However, since the birth of the Commission (about two years ago), it has had neither the power nor the resources to accomplish most of the tasks it was assigned. The Commission's work-plan to establish regional offices and "working groups" in the main centres of Afghanistan has only been partially implemented. Even the "working groups" that have been established are largely ineffective. The ICG's (International Crisis Group) recent report (2003: 14) says that "The working groups—which were to include human rights education, monitoring and investigations, women's human rights, and transitional justice—have been largely ineffective, hobbled in part by changed assignments for individual members." This raises serious questions about the independence of the "independent" Human Rights Commission of Afghanistan. Indeed, the problem for Afghanistan is that many of those accused of human rights violations and war crimes are key figures in the Afghan Transitional Authority and military power-holders in various regions of the country. Thus, it is not surprising that, since the installation of the Afghan Interim Administration and its successor, the Afghan Transitional Authority, vast-scale human rights violations have taken place (Amnesty International 2003a; 2003b; Human Rights Watch 2002b; 2002c; 2003).

Changing the "culture of human rights abuses" needs, as Mary Robinson proposed, concrete inter-institutional efforts with strong and long-term support and commitment by the intentional community. Co-ordination of the activities of the Afghan Human Rights Commission, justice, [and] educational institutions, at local and national levels, is particularly important. As will be discussed later, with the collaboration of Afghan educational and civil society institutions, the justice system can play an important role both in the successful investigation of past abuses of human rights and in the effective prevention of future violations.

NORMATIVE LOCATION OF KEY DIMENSIONS OF POST-WAR JUSTICE

What has been so far described would seem to indicate that the establishment of a new justice system in post-war Afghanistan is a complex and multidimensional process. Post-war Afghanistan needs an integrated framework of justice that reflects the interplay between *shari'a*, local/tribal institutions of informal justice, the Afghan interim (formal) legal framework, and fundamental principles of human rights. The normative locations of the key dimensions of the post-war justice system in Afghanistan are illustrated in Diagram 1 below.

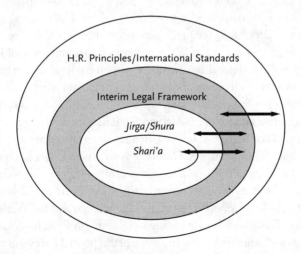

Diagram 1. Normative location of key dimensions of post-war justice in Afghanistan.

Diagram 1 above, shows that, as Islamic *shari'a* permeates different aspects of Afghan society, it constitutes the innermost part of post-war justice and social order in Afghanistan. What is meant by *shari'a*, in this context, is its non-sectarian popular version that is not only part and parcel of the belief system of the overwhelming majority of the people of Afghanistan but also strongly influences the social and cultural life of Afghan society. This version of Islamic teachings and *shari'a* is understood by local people and is closely tied to their daily lives. In order to interpret *shari'a* in ways consistent with the spirit of Islam as well as with the demands of the 21st century, a new body of *jami'at -al- ulama* (society of Islamic scholars/jurists) needs to be established. Comprising Afghanistan's best, well-reputed, and truly independent Islamic scholars/jurists (both *sunni and shei'ite*), the new *jami'at -al- ulama* would also need to be advised by international legal experts—both from Muslim countries and the Western world. Final decisions made and *fatwas* (religious decrees) issued by the Afghan *jami'at -al- ulama* would have a binding effect on all (Muslim) Afghans. This would ensure that *shari'a* is interpreted prudently and in the Afghan context. This would in turn, help strengthen the validity of a moderate and non-sectarian interpretation of *shari'a* at the expense of those "imported" and used by extremist Islamic groups for their own political agendas.

The non-sectarian popular version of *shari'a* has, over the centuries, closely interacted with the institutions of *jirga/shura* and existed in symbiotic relationships with them—the two have influenced one another significantly. Despite the opposition of the Afghan theocratic and Marxist regimes to traditional mechanisms of dispute settlement, *jirga/shura* has been widely used as the main alternative to the formal Afghan justice "system." More recent empirical evidence shows that *jirga/shura* is very commonly used in the resolution of conflicts in the current post-war situation in Afghanistan (Johnson et al. 2003, UNDP 2002; ICG; 2003b). This further confirms that the two internal dimensions of post-war justice in Afghanistan—popular Islam and *jirga/shura*—are located at the heart of the normative order of Afghan society and are central to its justice system. This point is recognized by the Bonn Agreement (2001: 3), which advises the Afghan Judicial Commission and the United Nations to rebuild the post-war Afghan domestic justice system in accordance with "Afghan legal traditions," among other things. The phrase "Afghan legal traditions," in the context of the Bonn Agreement, is elaborated by UNAMA (2002: 5) in this way: "The issue of Afghan legal tradition refers to the customs, values and sense of justice acceptable to and revered by the people of Afghanistan. Justice, in the end, is what the community as a whole accepts as fair and satisfactory in the case of dispute or conflict, not what the rulers perceive it to be." Indeed, justice that is imposed by the state is likely to remain "justice on paper."

With regard to the external dimension, as Afghanistan is increasingly integrated into the international community, the post-war Afghan justice system must be sensitized to international norms and the fundamental principles of human rights. This dimension can no longer be completely separated from the normative order of Afghan society in the 21st century—Afghanistan, today, is as much part of the emerging "global culture" as any other nation in the world. There would, however, be a degree of tension/conflict between some aspects of *shari'a* and *jirga/shura* and the Western conception of human rights principles. This issue relates to the broader discussion about the "clash of civilizations" or "dialogue of civilizations," which is beyond the scope of this paper. However as mentioned earlier, finding solutions to such tension/conflict would be the responsibility of Afghan *jami'at -al-ulama* assisted and advised by international legal experts in the West and in the Islamic world.

In the current situation, it is the Afghan interim legal framework which is the centre of gravity. Located in the middle of the Afghan normative order, it has the formal authority to act as a medium of communication between the demands of the external and internal dimensions of post-war justice in Afghanistan—between the demands of the moral order of the Afghan society and the requirements of living in an increasingly "globalized" international community. It is the future, popularly approved, Afghan constitution and other laws (the "existing laws" in the interim period) that would define the role and limits of Islamic *shari'a* within a formal legal framework. Likewise, informal local/tribal institutions of informal justice would need to be in harmony with the goals of the Afghan national state, its legal order and general principles of human rights. However, no attempt should be made by formal authorities to codify customary law; *jirga/shura* must continue to function as a genuinely local institution representing local people and their values/interests. This is to ensure that local people have the ownership of the justice system and are able to apply customary laws flexibly in various local contexts within which different conflicts are resolved.

In the same vein, it is also the interim legal framework (and a future, popularly approved, Afghan constitution/other laws) that has the responsibility to define human rights in ways that do not violate the cultural and religious sensibilities of the people of Afghanistan. A degree of conflict does exist between the ways some human rights are defined by the Universal Declaration of Human Rights and the ways they are understood in an Islamic cultural context (An-Nai'im 1990). This conflict will not be resolved by a unilateral imposition of a single set of standards by the state and its international supporters. The "universal" would need to be legitimised and properly understood within the "particularistic" and culturally relative context of Afghan society at the grass roots level. Reaching final decisions about such issues would be mainly the responsibility of the Afghan *jami'at -al- ulama* and Human Rights Commission. Post-war Afghanistan would need to learn from the experiences of other Muslim nations, where human rights principles are integrated, to a certain degree, into their domestic laws. This analysis of the interrelationships among the various dimensions of post-war justice in Afghanistan is further translated into an integrated model.

TOWARDS AN INTEGRATED MODEL OF A POST-WAR JUSTICE SYSTEM

The examination of the key elements of post-war justice in Afghanistan shows that a reinstated pre-war Afghan justice system (or a superficially reformed one) will not have the capacity to face the challenges of the post-war situation and meet the demands of the 21st century. It points to the need for the development of a new post-war model of justice—an integrated multi-dimensional model that represents Afghan cultural traditions, religious values, legal norms, and, at the same time, has the capacity to draw on human rights principles. Thus, an experimental model is proposed, which is illustrated in Diagram 2.

Diagram 2 shows that the post-war justice model proposes the establishment of *jirga/shura* and genuinely independent human rights units alongside the existing court of justice (based on *shari'a* and positive law) and their integration into the overall system of justice at the district level. The *jirga/shura* unit would be staffed by one or two full-time paid coordinators based in a fully equipped local office with a *jirga* hall. These local officers would replace the *amer -e- hoquq* (law officer) who is closely connected with the formal justice system and has a reputation for corruption. *Jirga/shura* would be conducted by around half a dozen elected local elders with expertise in traditional dispute settlement and/or legitimate social influence. The elders would be paid only an honorarium (in form of consultancy fees) and travel expenses; the expenses of hosting *jirga/shura* would also be paid from the public purse. Although not illustrated in the diagram, *jirga/shura* would also advise the district administrator in issues relating to local governance.

As Diagram 2 illustrates, the *jirga/shura* unit would mainly deal with minor criminal, and all types of civil incidents at the district level. In the case of civil incidents, people would have the choice to start their cases with either the *jirga/shura* or with the district court of formal justice. However, all serious criminal cases would be dealt with exclusively by the district court of justice, and those cases that *jirga/shura* fail to resolve satisfactorily would be referred back to the formal process of the district justice system. The referral would be based on a joint decision by the *jirga/shura*, the district judge, and the district administrator. While paper work and official procedures must be kept to the minimum, the final *prikra* (ruling) should be communicated to both the district court of justice and the human rights unit to ensure that it is in line with national legal norms and with accepted principles of human rights. In this way, *jirga/shura* would not only significantly reduce the workload of the court of justice; more importantly, the use of this traditional local/tribal institution of dispute settlement would empower ordinary people to have ownership of the justice processes.

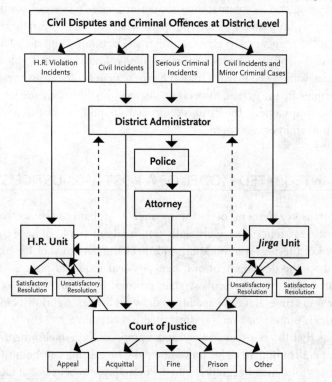

Diagram 2. An integrated model of a post-war justice system (district level) in Afghanistan.

In addition, the processes, rituals, and outcomes of *jirga* as a traditional tribal/local Afghan institution resemble closely the spirit, values and principles of "restorative justice"—one of the most recent paradigms in modern criminology and criminal justice. Although the phrase—"restorative justice"—is defined differently in different social contexts, it proposes a community-based model of justice that places special emphasis on the restoration of dignity, peace, and relationships between offenders and victims; it provides restitution to victims and promotes the reintegration offenders into the community (Braithwaite 2002a; 2002b; 2003; Bottoms 2003; Hudson 2003; Johnston 2001; Van Ness 2003). The theory of restorative justice, which emphasizes informalism and community involvement, is increasingly translated into practice in different parts of the world, especially in Australia, New Zealand, Canada, and South Africa (Daly 2003; Morris and Maxwell 2003; Roberts and Roach 2003; Skelton 2002).

The human rights unit, on the other hand, would be run by two full-time, truly independent, highly educated and well-reputed officials based in well-equipped local offices. In order to counter-balance the male-dominated *jirga* unit, these officers should mainly be female (as far as is practical in the current situation). In the short term, the unit's officials would act as ambassadors of human rights, and their role would be mainly educational. Liaising closely with district level educational institutions, the human rights officials would prepare educational and human rights awareness materials and disseminate them in culturally sensitive ways. They would also organize lectures and seminars given by leading, nationally recognized human rights activists and other Afghan personalities. However, soon after the district human rights unit is fully established at the local level, it would have the power to pro-actively investigate serious past human rights abuses and war crimes; it would liaise closely with the Independent Afghan Human Rights Commission, compiling serious past human rights abuses and war crimes and reporting them to the Special Court of Human Rights of Afghanistan (or the Truth Commission) that Afghanistan would need to establish. The unit would also be the first point of receiving new cases/complaints of human rights abuses, including issues relating to domestic violence (mainly violence against women) and dealing with them in culturally sensitive ways. In addition, the human rights unit would advise the district administrator about local human rights issues, and would have the authority to monitor human rights violations by local government officials as well. It is important to emphasize that the human rights unit must be totally independent from the state, warlords, and other political factions. Otherwise, it will become an ineffective body, and even an instrument in the hands of those with guns, power, and money for staying in positions of power.

The diagram further illustrates complex interrelationships between the district court of justice, the *jirga/shura*, and human rights units: as mentioned earlier, while the final *prikra* (ruling) of *jirga/shura* should be reported to both the district court of justice and to the human rights unit, the latter two would consult the former for its mediatory role in cases that need diversion from the formal justice processes. Likewise, *jirga/maraka* and human rights units would consult the court of justice about cases that may need to be dealt with in more strictly legalistic ways within the criminal justice system. A positive and constructive interaction between the state and local civil society institutions would provide an integrated inter-agency justice system that is effective, accessible and humane. However, such a system of justice is part and parcel of the processes of democratization, institutional reform (and building), disarmament, and the establishment of the rule of law in post-war Afghanistan. It can only, therefore, successfully operate in a social and political environment where the rule of law prevails, not the rule of guns and money.

CONCLUSION

What has been discussed in this chapter shows that, despite the historical fragmentation and the current devastated state of the Afghan justice system, Afghanistan has a rich legal culture that could partly be used as a basis for rebuilding a new post-war justice system. This legal culture also provides important lessons for Afghans to avoid repeating the mistakes of past rulers of the country who mainly used their systems of justice as an instrument of state control. An unfortunate consequence of this has been the development of justice systems that have been elitist, inaccessible, and corrupt, which alienated ordinary people from the state and its formal institutions of justice. This further resulted in the huge lack of communication between the Afghan state and ordinary people, which further widened the "culture gap" between cities and rural areas in Afghanistan. Thus, it has not been a coincidence that ordinary people, especially in rural Afghanistan, have traditionally preferred not to use formal justice institutions for the resolution of their disputes.

The integrated model of a post-war justice system in Afghanistan proposes inter-institutional co-ordination between the Afghan formal justice system, informal justice, educational, and human rights institutions. It is argued that the incorporation of *jirga/shura* into the formal justice system would not only simplify the justice process for ordinary people ... [but,] more importantly, enable them to have its ownership. This, it is maintained, would make the justice system more widely accessible, cost-effective, and expeditious. Likewise, addressing issues relating to the vast violation of human rights during the past 25 years of brutal war and challenging the existing "culture of human rights abuses" effectively need inter-institutional co-ordination. The creation of a truly independent human rights unit, and its incorporation into the justice system, is an effective way of creating awareness about human rights, accounting for past crimes, and preventing future violations of human rights.

More importantly, this inter-institutional interaction between the local justice executive and educational and civil society institutions would provide an important channel of communication between the state and ordinary Afghan citizens. This would gradually result in the inclusion of women and those without guns and money into the political, economic and cultural life of Afghan society. These processes would further pave the way for the gradual replacement of a "culture of human rights abuses" in Afghan society by a culture of respect for human rights and the rule of law. Indeed, communication plays an important role in social integration (Habermas 1987) and in strengthening social solidarity (Durkheim 1984), which Afghanistan badly needs today. However, in order to test the applicability of this model in the real world, it first needs to be thoroughly discussed among Afghan and international legal experts and ordinary people, at the grass roots level, and then piloted in selected districts in Afghanistan.

NOTES

[1] Carter and Connor (1989: 9) operationally define *shura* in this way: "A *shura* is a group of individuals which meets only in response to a specific need in order to decide how to meet the need. In most cases, this need is to resolve a conflict between individuals, families, groups of families, or whole tribes." This description would seem to indicate that *shura* and *jirga* are fundamentally very similar Afghan informal (non-state) mechanisms of conflict resolution that operate in varying social and tribal contexts.

[2] *Jirga* and *maraka* involve very similar processes and the main constituent elements of the two are not fundamentally different from one another. Therefore, the concepts are often used interchangeably. However, the fact that *jirga* deals with serious and important conflicts within the tribe (or between tribes), such as murder, disputes over land, mountain, jungle/woods, and the fact that it operates at a higher level of tribal formation [mean that] its social organization is more structured. *Maraka*, on the other hand, mostly deals with civil and relatively less serious criminal matters at the local village (or inter-village) level, and, therefore, it is loosely structured, and its related rituals are not as elaborate as those of a tribal *jirga*.

REFERENCES

Amnesty International. 2003a. *Afghanistan: Police Reconstruction Essential for Protection of Human Rights* (12 March Report). London: Amnesty International. http://web.amnesty.org/library/Index/ENGASA110032003?open&of=ENG-AFG

Amnesty International. 2003b. *Afghanistan: Crumbling Prison System Desperately in Need of Repair* (1 July Report). London: Amnesty International. http://web.amnesty.org/library/Index/ENGASA110172003?open&of=ENG-AFG

An-Na'im, A. 1990. "Islam, Islamic Law and the Dilemma of Cultural Legitimacy for Universal Human Rights." 31–54 in *Asian Perspectives on Human Rights*, edited by C. Welch and V. Leary. Boulder: Westview Press.

The Bonn Agreement. 2001. *Agreement on Provisional Arrangements in Afghanistan Pending the Re-Establishment of Permanent Government Institutions*. Bonn: United Nations Security Council.

Bottoms, A. 2003. "Some Sociological Reflections on Restorative Justice." Pp. 79–133 in *Restorative Justice and Criminal Justice,* edited *by* A. Hirsch, J. Roberts, A. Bottoms, K. Roach, and M. Schiff. Oxford: Hart Publishing.

Braithwaite, J. 1989. *Crime, Shame and Reintegration*. Cambridge: Cambridge University Press.

Braithwaite, J. 2002a. "Setting Standards for Restorative Justice," *British Journal of Criminology* 42: 563–77.

Braithwaite, J. 2002b. *Restorative Justice and Restorative Regulation*. New York: Oxford University Press.

Braithwaite, J. 2003. "Principles of Restorative Justice." Pp. 1–20 in *Restorative Justice and Criminal Justice*, edited by A. Hirsch, J. Roberts, A. Bottoms, K. Roach, and M. Schiff. Oxford: Hart Publishing.

Brzezinski, Z. 1998. "Les Révélations d'un Ancien Conseiller de Carter." Pp. 15–21 in *Le Nouvel Observateur*, edited by R. Troyer. London: Praeger Press.

Canfield, R. 1996. "Ethnic, Regional, and Sectarian Alignments in Afghanistan." Pp. 75–103 in *The State, Religion and Ethnic Politics: Afghanistan, Iran, Pakistan*, edited by A. Banuazizi and M. Weiner. New York: Syracuse University Press.

Carter, L. and K. Connor. 1989. *A Preliminary Investigation of Contemporary Afghan Councils*. Peshawar: ACBAR.

Constitution of Afghanistan. 1964. Kabul: Education Press.

Cooley, J. 2002. *Unholy Wars*. London: Pluto Press.

Daly, K. 2003. "Mind the Gap: Restorative Justice in Theory and Practice." Pp. 219–36 in *Restorative Justice and Criminal Justice*, edited by A. Hirsch, J. Roberts, A. Bottoms, K. Roach, and M. Schiff. Oxford: Hart Publishing.

Decree on the Establishment of Afghan Judicial Commission. 2002. Kabul: UNAMA.

Dehghanpisheh, B., J. Barry, and R. Gutman. 2002. "The Death Convoy of Afghanistan." *Newsweek* (August 26): 15–25.

Dupree, L. 1980. *Afghanistan*. Princeton: Princeton University Press.

Durkheim, E. 1964. *The Division of Labor in Society*. New York: Free Press.

Faiz-zad, M. 1989. *Jirga Haie Bozorge Milie Afghanistan*. Lahore, Pakistan.

Farhadi, R. 2000. "Tajikane Afghanistan wa Qadamhaie Ashti Bain Aishan" in *Qadamhaie Ashti wa Masauliate ma Afghanistan*, Falls Church, VA: Kabultec.

Gheyathoddin, M. (Ed.). 1871. *Ghyathul-Lughat*. New Delhi: Kanpur Press.

Glatzer, B. 1998. "Is Afghanistan on the Brink of Ethnic and Tribal Disintegration?" Pp. 167–81 in *Fundamentalism Reborn? Afghanistan and the Taliban*, edited by W. Maley. New York: New York University Press.

Goodhand, J. 2003. "From War Economy to Peace Economy?" Presented at the Symposium on State Reconstruction and International Engagement in Afghanistan, May 30–June 1, Bonn, Germany.

Habermas, J. 1984. *The Theory of Communicative Action: Vol. 1, Reason and Rationalisation of Society*. Boston: Beacon Press.

Hashemi, M. "Qadamhaie Asshti Baine Uzbakan" in *Qadamhaie Ashti wa Masauliate ma Afghanha*. Falls Church, VA: Kabultec.

Hudson, B. 2003. "Victims and Offenders." Pp. 177–194 in *Restorative Justice and Criminal Justice*, edited by. A. Hirsch, J. Roberts, A. Bottoms, K. Roach, and M. Schiff. Oxford: Hart Publishing.

Human Rights Watch. 2002a. "Paying for the Taliban's Crimes: Abuses Against Ethnic Pashtuns in Northern Afghanistan." *Human Rights Watch Report* (April) 14 (2).

Human Rights Watch. 2002b. "The Warlords are Plotting a Comeback." *Commentary* (June 10), http://hrw.org/english/docs/2002/06/10/afghan12860.htm

Human Rights Watch. 2002c. "Afghanistan: All Our Hopes are Crashed: Violence and Repression in Western Afghanistan." *Human Rights Watch Report* (October) 14 (7).

Human Rights Watch. 2003. "Killing You is a Very Easy Thing For Us: Human Rights Abuses in Southeast Afghanistan." *Human Rights Watch Report* (July) 15 (5).

International Crisis Group (ICG). 2003a. "Afghanistan: Judicial Reform and Transitional Justice." *Asia Report No. 45.* Brussels: ICG. http://www.crisisgroup.org/home/index. cfm?id=1631&l=1

International Crisis Group (ICG). 2003b. "Peacebuilding in Afghanistan." *Asia Report No. 64.* Brussels: ICG. http://www.crisisgroup.org/home/index.cfm?l=1&id=2293.

Johnson, C., W. Maley, A. Their, and A. Wardak. 2003. *Afghanistan's Political and Constitutional Development.* London: ODI.

Johnston, G. 2001. *Restorative Justice: Ideas, Values, Debates.* Cullompton: Willan.

Kamali, M. 1985. *Law in Afghanistan: A Study of Constitutions, Matrimonial Law and the Judiciary.* Leiden: E.J. Brill.

Malekyar, S. 2000. "Qadamhaie Ashti wa Solh dar Ananaie Hazarahaie Afghanistan" in *Qadamhaie Asshti wa Masauliate ma Afghanha.* Falls Church, VA: Kabultec.

Morris, A. and G. Maxwell. 2003. "Restorative Justice in New Zealand." Pp. 257–72 in *Restorative Justice and Criminal Justice,* edited by A. Hirsch, J. Roberts, A. Bottoms, K. Roach, and M. Schiff. Oxford: Hart Publishing.

Olesen, A. 1995. *Islam and Politics in Afghanistan.* Curzon: Surrey.

Pashto Descriptive Dictionary. 1978. Kabul: The Academy of Sciences of Afghanistan.

Physicians for Human Rights. 2002. *Report on Conditions at Sheberghan Prison, Northern Afghanistan* (January 28). Cambridge, MA: Physicians for Human Rights.

Roberts, J. and K. Roach. 2003. "Restorative Justice in Canada." Pp. 237–56 in *Restorative Justice and Criminal Justice,* edited by A. Hirsch, J. Roberts, A. Bottoms, K. Roach, and M. Schiff. Oxford: Hart Publishing.

Robinson, M. 2002. "In Solidarity with the Afghan People: Towards Implementation of the Human Rights Provisions of the Bonn Agreement." Speech given by the United Nations High Commissioner for Human Rights at the Afghan National Workshop on Human Rights, March 9.

Rubin, B. 1999. "The Political Economy of War and Peace in Afghanistan." Presented at the meeting of the Afghanistan Support Group, Stockholm, Sweden.

Rubin, B. 2003. "Transitional Justice in Afghanistan." *The Anthony Hyman Memorial Lecture.* London: University of London School of Oriental and African Studies.

Skelton, A. 2002. "Restorative Justice as a Framework for Juvenile Justice Reform: A South African Perspective." *British Journal of Criminology* 42: 496–513.

United Nations Assistance Mission in Afghanistan (UNAMA). 2002. *The Judicial Commission: Rebuilding the Justice System.* Kabul: UNAMA.

United Nations Development Programme (UNDP). 2002. *Strategy for Justice System Reform and the Rule of Law.* Kabul: The United Nations.

Van Ness, D. 2003. "Proposed Basic Principles on the Use of Restorative Justice: Recognizing the Aims and Limits of Restorative Justice." Pp. 157–76 in *Restorative Justice and Criminal Justice,* edited by A. Hirsch, J. Roberts, A. Bottoms, K. Roach, and M. Schiff. Oxford: Hart Publishing.

Wardak, A. 2002a. "Structures of Authority and Establishing the Rule of Law in Post-War Afghanistan." Presented at *Establishing the Rule of Law and Governance in Post Conflict*

Societies. Conference organized by Harvard University, the United Nations Association – USA, and Koç University, Istanbul, July 11–14.

Wardak, A. 2002b. *"Jirga*: Power and Traditional Conflict Resolution in Afghanistan." Pp. 187–204 in *Law after Ground Zero,* edited by John Strawson. London: Cavendish.

Wardak, A. 2004a. "The Tribal and Ethnic Composition of Afghan Society" in *Afghanistan: Essential Field Guides to Humanitarian and Conflict Zones,* edited by E. Girardet and J. Walter, 2nd ed. Geneva: Crosslines Ltd.

Wardak, A. 2004b. "Crime and Social Control in Saudi Arabia." Pp. 91–116 in *Transnational and Comparative Criminology,* edited by J. Sheptycki and A. Wardak. London: Cavendish.

CHAPTER STUDY QUESTIONS

- Why does Wardak argue that a "culture of human rights abuses" has existed in Afghanistan over the past 25 years? What elements or events have contributed to this culture? Do you think that a new legal system can remedy this situation in the absence of other changes in Afghan society?

- Outline the four dimensions of Afghanistan's current legal system described by Wardak. Which dimension appears to offer the greatest flexibility in dealing with legal and social disputes? Which one enjoys the greatest public legitimacy and respect?

- Identify at least two issues that limit the ability of Afghanistan's current legal system to deal adequately with human rights issues. What does Wardak argue is necessary to overcome these problems and foster greater respect for human rights?

- Describe the components of Wardak's proposed new legal system. Do you feel that it provides adequate checks and balances to allow it to meet international standards for the protection of human rights? Why? Why not?

RELATED WEB LINKS

Human Rights Watch
http://www.hrw.org/press/2003/07/afghan072903.htm
> This website provides an analysis of the problems still associated with American-backed warlords in Afghanistan. It also provides access to the main Human Rights Watch website and many other articles on Afghanistan and human rights around the world.

Afghanistan Independent Human Rights Commission
http://www.aihrc.org.af/
> This website provides access to many studies and publications carried out by the AIHRC.

UN Office for the Coordination of Humanitarian Affairs
http://www.irinnews.org/report.asp?ReportID=45571&SelectRegion=Asia&SelectCountry=A
FGHANISTAN Yes

> This website provides access to several reports on Afghanistan (and other regions) commissioned and published by the UN office for the Coordination of Humanitarian Affairs.

Center for Humanitarian Dialogue
http://www.hdcentre.org/Rule%20of%20Law%20in%20Afghanistan

> This website provides access to numerous papers and reports on peace and conflict resolution in post-war Afghanistan.

Chapter 16

SOCIAL AND LEGAL CONTROL IN CHINA: A COMPARATIVE PERSPECTIVE

XIAOMING CHEN

Social and legal control takes place in all societies because, in every society, a normative order must be accompanied by institutionalized and noninstitutionalized structures for maintaining this normative order. However, Chinese society exercises a cultural option when it develops a specific way of looking at crime and a characteristic mechanism for controlling it. Because of its unique cultures and traditions, social and legal control in Chinese society generally reflects Chinese cultural values and the ongoing changing political situations. As one of the world's oldest civilizations, China is imbued with a legacy of cultural prescriptions and proscriptions that have produced a strong, normative system.

Chinese society and Western societies may represent two different extremes with respect to the nature of social and legal control. Although each social system establishes its own social norms for governing behavior and its own limits of tolerance for violations of those norms, there undoubtedly exist some cross-cultural commonalities (Wilson 1977: 12). It is hoped that a deeper understanding of different social and legal systems can be developed through a comparative analysis. At the same time, the reader may find something that might be worth trying in China or in Western countries. Limitations of space and knowledge require that the subject be restricted only to those aspects of social and legal control that the author believes to be particularly important, including the nature of humans, the model of social and legal control, the functions of community, early police intervention, and the system of correction. Additionally, given the cultural disparity between the Western and Chinese ways of thinking, theoretical concepts have to be contextualized and explored differently in each culture. Therefore, many ideas may have to be reconceptualized in the process of my analysis.

The term *social and legal control* is used so frequently today that it is often assumed that everyone means the same thing when using it. Yet the definition of social and legal control differs widely in meanings and contents. "Social control (both as a concept and a notion) is currently interpreted in different ways in different academic disciplines, and is utilized for a variety of purposes" (Wardak 2000: 15). Therefore, it is essential to pin down the term *social and legal control* as the term is used in Chinese parlance. As in other countries, there are quite big differences within criminological literature in China. Generally speaking, however, in China, social and legal control is considered a generic term for responding to nonconformity, including both the formal and informal ways society has developed to help ensure conformity to social norms. The term *informal*, as it is used here, has a different meaning from that common in the West. From a strict point of view, it should be considered to be a specific form between formal and informal, which may be more properly called quasi-formal. The theory and practice of Chinese social control indicate that it is not a completely informal system; rather, it is formally invested in less formal structures—in mass groups more than in traditional social institutions. For example, some informal institutions such as neighborhood committees do not form a part of the formal criminal justice system, yet they are established based on certain legal regulations and often are trained by local justice organs or police. In such a way, the Chinese social control system appears to reflect Chinese cultural characteristics. The term *informal* is used to highlight their reliance on volunteers and mass support.

THE NATURE OF HUMANS

China's traditional value system is a complex amalgam of ideas that evolved over centuries and was shaped by Confucianism, Legalism, Daoism, Buddhism, and other influences; however, Confucianism has remained the dominant Chinese philosophy that has influenced Chinese society and provided the basis for social order since the Han dynasty (206 B.C. to 221 A.D.). The Confucian school adhered to the premise that humans are basically good by nature and that their good qualities can be brought out through education and eventually lead to virtue, because people are willing to perfect themselves. Confucius refused any notion that individuals are driven by an uncontrollable force, which would suggest that crime is endemic in human society (Woodward 1984). Nor did Confucian philosophy accept the concepts of original sin and the fallen state of humanity.

Positive thinking about human nature results in the Chinese having strong beliefs that criminal tendencies are not innate and can be cured. The Chinese system of social control is founded on this view. Unlike Western countries, where the individual has been the central focus, in Chinese society, the internal personality dynamics of the individual are not emphasized, and the external environment is regarded as having the greatest responsibility for offence. In this view, the offender is not looked upon as a deficient person but as a victim of certain negative influences in the environment. The proper societal response to such deviations is education, persuasion, and salvation (the official policy). Therefore, education has been the key ingredient for maintaining order in China. Contrarily, punishment did not necessarily make people learn or induce them to be good. The primary aim of education was to cultivate and correct mental attitudes toward social norms. In other words, the offender should be reformed and reintegrated into society as a useful member of that society. However, the Chinese approach may have a drawback because it assumes a rather rigid definition of what is compatible with human nature.

Contrary to the concept of human nature of Confucius, Western people tend to have a more pessimistic view of human nature, which has been influenced by the idea of original sin, based on certain strands of the Judeo-Christian tradition. The emphasis on the principle of utility and hedonism in 19th- and 20th-century Western social thought has been consistent with this vision of human nature as intrinsically self-centered, demanding, and controllable only by commands and prohibitions, punishments, and rewards. Therefore, in the West, human beings are more likely to be viewed as basically selfish and motivated primarily by self-interest, although even the worst of them may have moments of spontaneous generosity. According to a utilitarian view of human nature, people avoid vice in favor of virtue only because they believe that, although vice brings pleasure immediately, it brings pain eventually (Mead 1942: 38). Therefore, Westerners accept as a given that there will always be aberrant behavior; the issue is how it can best be controlled and what specialized agency should deal with it. Based on this belief, Western countries devise criminal justice systems and rely on them for controlling crime. This situation may discourage the public's involvement in crime prevention and the correction of offenders.

MODELS OF SOCIAL AND LEGAL CONTROL

In China, the belief that society is both a cause and a victim of crime confers on society the right and duty to be involved in such matters. Moreover, intrusion into other people's lives is taken for granted and viewed positively. It is perceived as a sign of caring rather than meddling. Many Chinese people are trained in the concept of social duties and obligations rather than self-interest or personal aggrandizement. In addition, the deep-seated interdependency and communitarianism in Chinese society and culture are conducive to public support and enthusiasm for dealing with any problems affecting the community. Dorothy Bracey made the following comments:

> When the Chinese say that crime is a social problem, they are not simply saying that an individual is a product of the social environment and therefore is not totally responsible for his behavior. They are saying that the social group—not an abstract "society" but a village, neighborhood or work group—is both responsible for and a victim of crime. The conclusion they reach is that the social group has the right and duty to intervene in behavior that might lead to crime. (1984: 10)

Therefore, Chinese crime control does not just work from the top down through the formal criminal justice system but, and above all, from the bottom up. Chinese people do not mind only their own business; they prefer to handle minor criminal and civil dispute problems in their neighborhood rather than hand them over to professionals. As a result, almost all members of the society seem to have become active controllers of crime instead of silent observers. They intervene at the first sign of possible trouble. The Chinese experience suggests that many disputes can be handled informally, probably with greater satisfaction on the part of the involved parties. The smaller the deviation and the earlier it is treated, the more confident one can be of success. It follows that the most efficacious treatment results from an early intervention when the offender is young and the offences are trivial. The result is an extensive, proactive social control apparatus.

In the social control mechanisms of contemporary China, mass participation is still regarded as a key tenet. The social order in China is supposed to be maintained by "the capacity of society's members to understand one another and to act in concert in achieving common goals through common rules of behavior" (Johnson 1983: 152–153). Compared with the West, Chinese society has developed a very different model of social control. As Xin Ren, an overseas Chinese scholar, stated,

> The most important distinction, perhaps, is the efforts of the Chinese state
> to control both the behavior and the minds of the people. Social confor-
> mity in the Chinese vocabulary is not limited to behavioral conformity
> with the rule of law but always moralistically identifies with the officially
> endorsed beliefs of social standards and behavioral norms. Perhaps it goes
> against the free-will notion of the classical theory of criminology or per-
> haps it is socialist totalitarianism. Whatever it is, the Chinese tradition
> of so-called "greatest unity" has always attempted to achieve ultimate uni-
> formity of both mind and act within Chinese society. (1997: 6)

Chinese people have a general idea that the anti-social thought occurs before the anti-social behavior, and minor norm violations will develop into full-scale crimes if they are left unchecked. Therefore, when an individual's thoughts or behavior have been detected as deviating from the social norm, initiating thought or behavior reeducation by others will be necessary. In terms of crime control, an approach based on this philosophy would not be reactive but proactive in that it would not wait for criminal behavior to occur but look for incorrect thoughts. It is thus clear that Chinese society, compared with the West, has developed a characteristic model of social control. The heavy emphasis is clearly on informal rather than formal methods of social control.

By contrast, in most Western societies, cultural and legal concepts give less encouragement to the use of these extralegal mechanisms, and a greater scope of personal deviance is tolerated. Informal, proactive social control is often perceived as unacceptable interference or meddling in other people's affairs. Therefore, on one hand, people tend to form a litigious attitude whereby they view all conflicts in legal terms and rely on courts to solve them, and, on the other hand, the criminal justice and other control mechanisms seem to be quite distant from the majority of people in their everyday lives. They appear as large, bureaucratic organizations located in office complexes far from residential neighborhoods. They keep their distance and are not forthcoming with help at the early stages of social deviancy. It is only when a serious deviant behavior has actually occurred that they get involved. This situation weakens the preventive effect of social control, as the experience from different countries suggests that, for crime control to be effective, local citizen involvement in norm formation and enforcement and/or involvement in the formulation of the law is crucial (Adler 1983).

However, there are also some apparent problems and shortcomings in the philosophy of the Chinese model. Both socialist and traditional theories emphasize order over freedom, duties over rights, and group interests over individual ones. Consequently, whenever the social order is perceived by the authorities as being threatened, legal niceties may be set aside. The existence of some loopholes in criminal law also gives the judicial system too much arbitrary power in applying criminal sanctions. The continuing active role of the Communist Party's political and legal committees limits the degree of independence allowed to the judiciary. The severity of punishment is strongly affected by the political situation at the given time.

Moreover, whether a deviance or dispute is relatively trivial, the public's early, informal involvement may not only suppress the offender's individual expression and lead to a loss of privacy but may also bring about a certain degree of damaging stigma. A shame-induced, negative self-image must have a detrimental effect on some offenders. This may persist even though early intervention does not attempt to demean and humiliate offenders but, rather, to emphasize reintegration into the community following treatment at an institution. Once stigmatized with a deviant label, however, offenders usually have fewer opportunities to enter school, find jobs, and even establish a family. Thus, they may experience a sense of injustice at the way they are victimized by agents of social control. This situation may indeed influence some offenders to have more negative attitudes toward society and regard themselves as more delinquent. Under these circumstances, deviance becomes, and is rationalized as, a defensible lifestyle, which is difficult to change. Additionally, appeals to family, neighborhood committees, and other informal social groups in preventing and controlling crime may raise political questions about both the extent of the state's responsibility for the citizens' safety and about its effectiveness and legitimacy in the area of crime control. The Chinese model gives a greater responsibility to individuals and collectivities and a lesser responsibility to the state in controlling crime. Therefore, this situation appears to carry with it its own tensions and contradictions. Moreover, the semiofficial role allotted to the family and other intermediary groups legitimates intense surveillance in society and promotes subordination to the dominant state ideology.

FUNCTIONS OF COMMUNITY

Based on the tradition of the management of social conflict through a combination of popular mediation and discipline sanctions applied through an administrative rather than an adjudicative process, tight control over community organization and neighborhood life has been a characteristic of the Chinese social control system.

Community in the Western world "is both a signifier and referent around which complex and contradictory effects, meanings and definitional struggles coalesce" (Crawford 1995: 98), but in China, it is principally defined in geographical terms. It is usually defined as an area in which a bounded territory is named and identified by residents. The number of households and people in a community fluctuates depending on different factors within a community, such as residential areas, businesses, factories, markets, hotels, and so on.

The strong emphasis on a communal existence with powerful neighborhood committees produces throughout the country a social control net that is much different from that present in Western countries. In China, one of the most apparent differences is that neighborhood committees are both proactive and reactive in identifying potentially troublesome social situations, preventing crime, resolving conflicts, and dealing with offensive behavior. In Western literature, these low-level neighborhood committees tend to be viewed as informal forms of control, but, in reality, they are constituted in China as quite formal institutions of social control. Although they are often referred to as mass organizations, "they are not volunteer associations in the U.S. sense; they are government organized and controlled entities" (Troyer 1989: 27). Therefore, they may be regarded as the first level of the governmental structure or an arm of a higher level of control. Western sociological and criminological literature on crime and delinquency seems to customarily focus on specialized, formal agencies such as police and courts. Undoubtedly, formal institutions are very important; however, informal institutions should not be overlooked. Otherwise, biased results may be produced. Such would certainly be the case for Chinese society today. Social control in Chinese society is so strong that dropping out, becoming invisible, or carving out an area of one's life and declaring it out of bounds to anyone but oneself or one's family seems to be impossible (Simon 1985: 99–100). The extensive participation of the public throughout the entire process of controlling deviancy obviously minimizes the function of formal legal control within Chinese society. According to Black's behavioral theory of law, "law is stronger where other social control is weaker" (1976: 107). Conversely, law is weaker where other forms of social control are stronger. Black's assertion that law varies inversely with other forms of social control is certainly applicable in Chinese society.

This approach is considered beneficial, because few human and material resources need to be invested in the formal criminal system. Perhaps because of the sheer size of China and its population, this is the only practical approach to controlling crime. In China, a primary reliance on the formal criminal justice system in maintaining the social order would not only be socially impractical but also financially unviable. Although the economic reform that started in 1978 did weaken community bonds, the informal organizations will certainly continue to exist and constitute the basis of the social control system.

However, this system may provide insufficient protection for an individual against unfair group actions as well as inadequate means of restraining improper official actions. The lack of perfected formal procedural laws often leads to confusion about rights and obligations and means that there is no sufficient protection of individual rights. Not only may deliberate abuse of power by law enforcement personnel go undetected but also mob lynching can easily take place. Under these circumstances, how is one to be protected against the tyranny of one's group? How can abuse of power by legal officials be restrained? This is especially dangerous when compounded with the awesome discretionary power that law enforcement personnel have. Moreover, this situation also engenders the lack of trained personnel and institutionalized means of carrying out legal work thereby restricting the capacity of the legal system to handle problems more complex than the management of interpersonal affairs. It should be noted, however, that in the past 20 years, there has been a vast improvement in the protection of the individual against state excesses and arbitrary actions in the Chinese criminal justice system, including the promulgation of criminal laws and the formal commitment to procedural protections and citizens' rights all tending to provide accused persons with more opportunities to defend themselves in criminal proceedings.

POLICE EARLY INTERVENTION

Central to the contemporary Chinese legal philosophy is the concept that crime prevention is the most effective form of controlling social behavior. As part of this philosophy, early police intervention is always emphasized. The dependence on mass support and cooperation, combined with the Chinese belief that it is right and necessary to intervene early before minor offences grow into serious crimes, may constitute a unique Chinese policing style. This policing style offers the police opportunities:

> to build durable relationships with the people of the area, provide needed
> services to the ill and the elderly, and have the greatest opportunity to
> display the therapeutic, conciliatory, and compensatory styles that tend to
> garner more goodwill than does the penal approach. (Bracey 1989: 139)

Although the police participate directly in the early intervention, they are not concerned with law and punishment as such but, rather, with helping offenders become law-abiding and useful citizens. Therefore, the characteristic Chinese mode of police response is largely non-penal.

For many people in countries with a heritage of individual rights and civil liberties, the Chinese police may play too many roles compared to the police in their own countries. Moreover, some of the roles may be perceived as not being police business. Indeed, in Western countries, police intervention is mostly limited to situations where they believe that an offence has been committed and an arrest should be made. Otherwise, the intervention may be considered inappropriate. In China, because of the belief in early intervention, the police are expected to respond to minor offences in the early stage and actively participate in such intervention to act in concert with the relevant mass groups. The police not only provide community surveillance but also conduct many education programs at the neighborhood level, such as distributing legal materials and educating the residents in the neighborhood about laws and rights, holding community meetings to discuss justice and social problems, preparing messages involving legal and crime prevention matters, persuading residents of the necessity of rules for public security and individual protection, and visiting offenders and their families to determine what the problem is, [to] seek solutions outside of the criminal justice system, and [to] help them solve such problems as employment. Direct involvement by the police is also intended as a reminder that an arrest can still be affected if the offender strays further from the beaten path. The aim is to put a greater pressure on offenders. In reality, the police prefer not to arrest offenders, and there is no strong expectation that they will make an arrest, either. The mere presence of the police is considered to be able to strengthen the effects of early intervention and has, in fact, become an integral part of it.

Some of these functions may sound similar to those implied by the community policing model in the West, but, in the Chinese context, they involve more direct ideological work and a greater emphasis on penetrating the daily life of the communities policed. A distinct characteristic of early intervention is that it is proactive and continuous. This built-in vigilance not only makes early detection of deviation and early intervention and treatment possible, it also makes for an environment that deters individuals from making illegitimate or illegal material gains, because they would not have the opportunity to enjoy them (Li 1973). The extent and the diversity of activity performed by the Chinese police indicates that the police not only are a prime force in enforcing the criminal law but also play an important role in the elaborate system of informal social control.

SYSTEM OF CORRECTION

The purpose of the unique Chinese system of reforming criminal offenders, based on an unrelenting optimism about human nature, is to reform inmates mainly through labor and education and make them become new people rather than simply to apply punishment to inmates and to make them pay for their crimes. The concept of rehabilitation is still embedded deeply in the present Chinese theory and practice of reforming offenders, although it seems to be declining in Western countries, especially in the United States. Dramatized throughout the Chinese correctional program is the paternalistic dictum that the individual can and should be reasoned with and guided toward positive ends and, therefore, that correctional officials must be to inmates as parents are to their children, as doctors are to patients, and as teachers are to students.

Unlike Western countries where the individual has been the central focus, in Chinese society, the internal personality dynamics of the individual are not emphasized, and the external environment is regarded to have the greatest responsibility for crime. Thus, rehabilitation has been conceptualized within a Marxist context that locates the causes of deviant behavior in the society rather than in the individual. In this view, the offender is not looked upon as a deficient person but as a victim of certain negative influences in the environment. Therefore, the offender should be reformed and reintegrated into society as a useful member of that society.

The use of both formal and informal resources for the correction of offenders is integrated within the system of macro-control to a far greater degree than in Western societies. According to the policy of the state, every correctional institution is established just like a factory, a farm, or a school. A reformed offender means a changed person—a new person. Every institution should help and educate offenders with tangible means and in ways that relate to the environment to which offenders will have to return upon their release. In contrast, the West appears to be disillusioned with its attempts at the rehabilitation of offenders and is in the process of redefining the purpose of sentencing. Based on the assumption that criminal activities result from a deliberate choice, the former stress on social rehabilitation of offenders seems to now be replaced by a renewed emphasis on punishment, deterrence, and incapacitation. The recent interest in community-based sentencing and reintegrative shaming notwithstanding, behavioral compliance, rather than repentance and moral reeducation, are the main goals of the criminal justice system. Although this approach does not interfere with the individual's value system, it is, by the same token, unable to produce any meaningful or lasting change in his or her behavior and attitude toward others. The lesson for the West may therefore lie in the appreciation of the role of the collective and the importance of the sense of belonging. It must, however, be kept in mind that, if carried too far, the belief in the total malleability of human beings may dangerously undermine their autonomy, and an overzealous stress on conformity may clash with Western values.

Perhaps China is not radically different from Western and other societies in terms of problems encountered and the measures employed to handle common crime. However, more than any other country in the world, China puts a special emphasis on the participation of a wide range of people in combating the problem. To the Chinese mind, because offenders come from society and will eventually go back to society, the participation of the whole society in reforming offenders will greatly accelerate the process of socialization of offenders. Therefore, an unusually broad range of citizens and groups are drawn into the process. Different levels of government and other organizations, such as labor unions, the Youth League, women's associations, schools, and communities all assist correctional institutions with reforming offenders.

At the lowest levels, it includes parents and other family members who have the basic responsibility for social order. In contemporary Chinese society, although the family system has undergone significant transformation, including changes in its composition, type, and its role in the life of the individual, family ties still remain relatively strong. The family itself has survived as the key site of education and exercises great mediating influence in a person's relations with the state and the society in general. Furthermore, because Chinese society has developed no other forms of social control that would operate effectively and stably in the absence of family control, the family is still the principal institutional locus for a highly effective form of social control, which Braithwaite (1989), a contemporary Western criminologist, has labeled reintegrative shaming. Reintegrative shaming represents a societal response to deviance that affirms wrongdoing while encouraging the reacceptance of deviants back into society. According to Braithwaite, families are usually the most effective agents of social control precisely because they are oriented toward reintegrative forms of shaming. Societies in which the family is the dominant social institution can therefore be expected to exhibit low overall rates of crime.

In addition, there is a universal assumption in China that parents' behavior and methods of education can contribute to their children's deviance, because parents are their child's first teachers. Therefore, the important role in reforming offenders played by parents is heavily emphasized. As Dutton (1992) stated,

> While the family of the inmate was, in the classical period, treated with suspicion and, at times, outright hostility, such relations have been reordered in the contemporary period. The family is now interpolated into the reform and becomes an instrument of government. This transformation in the role of the family within penal discourse would not have been possible had it not been for the other great changes which had transformed the social function of the family. (260)

Thus, the family has, in fact, become an ally of the state in the penal reform process rather than the co-object of the state's punishment in modern China. Although the positive dimensions of a strong family cannot be denied, the new approach is in some ways a double-edged sword in that it can place extreme pressure on both the offender and his or her family. Parents of inmates are expected to combine several roles: educators of offenders, assistants to correctional institutions, and parents of offenders. Under the watchful eyes of those with whom the offenders have the most frequent daily contact, they are encouraged to reform and develop a sense of social responsibility, which will lead to their reintegration into society.

The great pressure that various organizations exert on the individual to conform to group norms must certainly have an impact on offenders. Also, their active involvement symbolizes reacceptance of offenders while also offering a practical basis for reintegrating offenders. The purpose of all these efforts is to enable inmates to realize that society has not forgotten and deserted them and to strengthen their confidence in returning to society. Mass involvement in reforming offenders is one of the most striking aspects of the Chinese justice system that differentiates it from Western models.

CONCLUSION

The Chinese social control system has endured for more than 2,000 years. Despite the passage of time and the progress of science and technology, ideas and practices associated with the Confucian tradition generally continue to influence Chinese thinking and behavior. This is not to say that modern China is just an extension of the old, traditional society. Rather, there are some cultural continuities.

Obviously, the historical development of social and legal control in China has taken a very different path from that of the West and has produced some different results. For Chinese society, social order was maintained primarily based on moral socialization, not on the deterrence of penal law. For Western society, because of the prevalence of law, the enforcement of moral rules seems to both cover less ground and be less effective. Stanley Lubman (1983: 182–83) summarized four main characteristics of the system of traditional Chinese social and legal control: (a) the dominance of informal means of settling disputes and punishing minor offences; (b) the lack of functional separation between law and bureaucracy; (c) the popular fear and avoidance of the legal system, and (d) the subordination of law to a dominant state philosophy.

Today's China is different from the China of the past. Chinese approaches to social and legal control have been undergoing great changes. The Chinese have realized the limitations of control by the masses and informal procedures; therefore, the trend in the Chinese social and legal control model is toward being more formal and professional to provide equality and to protect individual rights. China has developed an extensive array of coded laws and made a massive effort to strengthen the criminal justice system. Law is now recognized as a principal tool for the achievement of social justice, social stability, and economic development. Nevertheless, this trend cannot be viewed as a phenomenon related to the transition to Western practices. Rather, there are still many fundamental differences.

First, although the West does not deny the existence and importance of groups, its primary concern is with the individual—whether in terms of legal status, religious salvation, or personal fulfillment. Consequently, the Western system stresses individuality, privacy, and diversity.

Chinese society places less importance on the individual and greater emphasis on how he or she functions within the context of a larger group. Thus, although China is engaged in the construction of legalism, it is still emphasizing mass participation and a parallel development of formal and informal social control.

Second, contemporary Chinese laws apparently reflect a combination of traditional and Western influences. They reflect the Chinese cultural tradition and a vast experience accumulated by government agencies and non-government organizations in controlling crime. The Confucian and Legalist heritage, Western influence, and the ideology of the Chinese Communist Party all have had a great impact on the current criminal justice system of China. Despite their differences, with respect to social and legal control, all these philosophies have permeated the current practice of social and legal control. Perhaps the uniqueness of the system of Chinese social and legal control lies in this centralized synthesis of very eclectic elements and influences.

Third, the ongoing changes merely represent the adjustment of an old model to a new social environment. This adjustment is characterized by an attempt at a parallel development of social and legal control systems, which is a part of what the Chinese government called "socialism with Chinese characteristics," intended to meet the new situations of a market economy. Therefore, these changes should be seen more as responses to changing political and economic situations than as shifts in attitudes among the general public.

Finally, China's emphasis on the law as a means of solving social problems such as crime is still closely connected with specific political situations. Therefore, the punishment of offenders in China can be recognized as a political tactic. This seems to be consistent with Foucault's analytic understanding of punishments. According to Foucault (1978: 23–24), the study of punitive mechanisms should not be concentrated on their *repressive* effects alone or on their *punishment* aspects alone. Rather, these mechanisms should be situated in a whole series of their possible *positive* functions, even if these seem marginal at first sight. Thus, punishment is to be regarded as a complex social function. The author can assert that the goals of punishment of offenders in China are not limited simply to reducing crime. Indeed, punishment can be seen as a political tactic that serves the following positive, complex functions: (a) to demonstrate the Chinese government's superior power through open trials and other visual effects, (b) to demonstrate that the social order advocated by the Chinese government is not to be disrupted and that it has the ability to maintain peaceful social order, (c) to announce and demonstrate that the Chinese government can control the direction of political and economic development and can secure the success of, and noninterference with, its modernization policies, (d) to deflect attention from various critiques of the economic and social policies pursued and to satisfy the widespread desire for speedy restoration of social order through clamping down on crime, (e) to demonstrate that the Chinese government is not only the instructor of people but also their guardian through mobilizing the masses to be involved in early intervention, and (f) to demonstrate that the Chinese government, through its emphasis on the functions of punishment, can solve such social problems as crime.

In conclusion, the parallel development of formal and informal mechanisms of social control may be the best way to approach crime. Without law, the basic rights of citizens cannot be protected effectively. The formal laws, after all, embody important principles and provide the framework and safeguards for the exercise of state authority. However, law has its substantial limitations. It provides an excuse for not involving the community in maintaining order by relegating this function to the police and judicial organs. Without the active involvement of other social institutions in addressing crime problems, the law may not gain broad enough community support to guarantee conformity and may be perceived as arbitrary and removed from society. Moreover, the law has become too costly and complex to rely on as the primary method of maintaining social order and resolving disputes.

What is intriguing is that the recent trends of social and legal control in Chinese and Western societies seem to converge. On one hand, to deal with its recent epidemic of crime, China is emphasizing formal legal methods in dealing with offenders. On the other hand, Western countries conduct diversion programs that involve the gradual removal of criminal cases from the general jurisdiction of the courts and entrust them to informal bodies as a better approach to reducing the crime rate. Perhaps only time and further experience will tell whether these hybrid systems can deliver what they promise.

REFERENCES

Adler, F. 1983. *Nations Not Obsessed with Crime*. Littleton, CO: Rothman.

Black, D. 1976. *The Behavior of Law*. New York: Academic Press.

Bracey, D. 1984. "Community Crime Prevention in the People's Republic of China." *The Key: Newsletter of A.S.P.A. Section on Criminal Justice Administration* 10: 3–10.

Bracey, D. 1989. "Policing the People's Republic." Pp. 130–140 in *Social Control in the People's Republic of China*, edited by R. Troyer, J. Clark, and D. Rojek. New York: Praeger.

Braithwaite, J. 1989. *Crime, Shame and Reintegration*. Cambridge, UK: Cambridge University Press.

Crawford, A. 1995. "Appeals to Community and Crime Prevention." *Crime, Law and Social Change* 22: 97–126.

Dutton, M. 1992. *Policing and Punishment in China: From Patriarchy to "The People."* Cambridge, UK: Cambridge University Press.

Foucault, M. 1978. *Discipline and Punishment*. New York: Penguin.

Johnson, E. 1983. "The People's Republic of China: Possibilities for Comparative Criminology." *International Journal of Comparative and Applied Criminal Justice* 7: 151–56.

Li, V. 1973. "Law and Penology: Systems of Reform and Correction. Pp. 144–56 in *China's Developmental Experience*, edited by M. Oksenberg. New York: Praeger.

Lubman, S. 1983. "Comparative Criminal Law and Enforcement: China." Pp. 182–92 in *Encyclopaedia of Crime and Justice*, edited by S. Kadish. New York: Free Press.

Mead, M. 1942. *And Keep Your Powder Dry*. New York: William Morrow.

Ren, X. 1997. *Tradition of the Law and Law of the Tradition*. Westport, CT: Greenwood.

Simon, R. 1985. "A Trip to China." *Justice Quarterly* 2: 99–101.

Troyer, R. 1989. "Chinese Social Organization." Pp. 26–33 in *Social Control in the People's Republic of China*, edited by R. Troyer, J. Clark, and D. Rojek. New York: Praeger.

Wardak, A. 2000. *Social Control and Deviance: A South Asian Community in Scotland*. Aldershot, UK: Ashgate.

Wilson, A. 1977. "Deviance and Social Control in Chinese Society: An Introductory Essay." Pp. 1–13 in *Deviance and Social Control in Chinese Society*, edited by A. Wilson, S. Greenblatt, and S. Wilson. New York: Praeger.

Woodward, K. 1984. "The Soul of Confucius Meets the System of Mao." *Psychology Today* 18: 41–45.

CHAPTER STUDY QUESTIONS

- In China, the criminal justice system is used as a last resort. Which elements from this approach might benefit criminal justice in Canada and the United States? Why?

- The Chinese social control system appears to reflect Chinese cultural characteristics. What are these characteristics, and how do they specifically affect the nature and operation of social control mechanisms in China? Would Westerners tolerate the high level of intrusion into private lives that is part of Chinese social control?

- What is the role of the community in crime prevention and social control in China? To what extent can the Chinese community-based model of social control be replicated in Western countries? Why?

- Chen argues that the Chinese criminal justice system is predicated on the belief that criminal tendencies are not innate and can be cured. As a result, he argues that it focuses on treatment and correction rather than punishment for the sake of punishment. Does this argument seem compatible with the view of China's justice system presented in the Western media, which includes high execution rates, brutality, corruption, and forced confessions? In what ways, if at all, might the West's view of Chinese social control be tainted by ethnocentric biases? What could constitute the source of these biases?

RELATED WEB LINKS

Wikipedia Free Encyclopedia
http://en.wikipedia.org/wiki/Chinese_law

> This encyclopedia provides an overview of basic information about China and the history and philosophical underpinnings of Chinese social control. Links to other websites are also provided.

Yale Law School

http://www.law.yale.edu/documents/pdf/Chinas_Criminal_Justice_System.pdf

> This site provides access to a detailed description and analysis of Chinese criminal justice from a Western perspective.

Restorative Justice Online

www.restorativejustice.org/editions/2005/oct05/china/2005-09-30.6724889539/download

> This website provides access to a dissertation that conducts a detailed analysis of the Chinese criminal justice system from a restorative justice perspective.

Amnesty International Canada

http://www.amnesty.ca/take_action/actions/china_death_penalty.php

> Canada's site provides a detailed analysis of the use of the death penalty in China. It also provides links to articles on the main Amnesty International website.

PART 5

CONVERGENCE AND DIVERGENCE IN CRIMINAL JUSTICE AND PENAL POLICY

Recent years have seen global criminologists devote increasing attention to attempting to understand patterns of convergence and divergence in the criminal justice and penal policies of selected countries. In earlier parts of the present book, you have already been exposed, at least in an introductory manner, to some of this research, for example in the chapters by Michael J. Gilbert and Steve Russell (Chapter 5) on different national responses to the problem of transnational corporate crime, by Hartmut Aden (Chapter 8) on the convergence of policing policies in Europe, and by Yue Ma (Chapter 12) on signs of growing similarity in the use of prosecutorial discretion and plea bargaining in the United States, France, Germany, and Italy. The following chapters in Part 5 highlight the research findings of criminologists who have given more explicit attention to the challenge of identifying and explaining patterns of convergence (emergent similarities) and divergence (emergent differences) in the criminal justice and penal policies of various countries. Collectively, these chapters contribute further to developing a more nuanced understanding of significant current cross-national developments and issues in criminal justice and penal policy.

In Chapter 17, Trevor Jones and Tim Newburn undertake a comparative study of the development of private prisons in the United States and the United Kingdom. In doing so, they draw out the complexities involved in the effort to explain apparent cross-national convergences in criminal justice and penal policy. Jones and Newburn observe that, in recent decades, penal policy discourse in both the US and the UK appear to have become more punitive in nature. At the same time, governments in both countries have adopted a more managerial approach towards criminal justice, which has included—among other policy developments—deliberately expanding the role of the private sector in the criminal justice system. Jones and Newburn address the underlying question: what do evident similarities and differences in the US/UK experience, with regard to the recent growth of private prisons, tell us about how the implementation of new penal policies are affected by the distinctive features of the political system and political culture of the country in which they are adopted? To answer this question, Jones and Newburn compare the process of penal policy change in the US and the UK since the 1980s and analyse the factors that appear to have shaped key policy decisions concerning private prisons in each country. One of the authors' key findings is that, while both the US and the UK have significantly expanded the role of the private sector in corrections since the 1980s, the constellation of factors that contributed to this movement in each country is noticeably different. In essence, they point out that, in the US, a major "problem" that private prisons were designed to solve was the substantial growth of prison populations and the threat of litigation against states with overcrowded prisons. By contrast, in the UK, a major "problem" that was perceived as needing to be solved was the history of poor industrial (labour) relations in UK prisons and the need to reassert managerial control over correctional staff by weakening their union-based collective bargaining power. Jones and Newburn also highlight the influence of differing political systems and political culture on criminal justice and penal policy by showing that, whereas the development of private prisons in the US was initially state and county-based and influenced by practical considerations, in the UK, the privatization of prisons began as a national governmental programme that was also evidently more ideologically than pragmatically inspired. Jones and Newburn conclude with more general observations about the nature of convergence and divergence in the penal policies of different nations. Most significantly, they point to the theoretical importance in any comparative study of simultaneously examining both the "globalizing tendencies" of specific criminal justice policy changes and "the local and particular" influences that affect the direction taken by changes in individual countries.

In Chapter 18, Hanns von Hofer offers another exemplary study of convergence and divergence in criminal justice and penal policies by giving attention to the challenge of explaining different trends in the growth and decline of prison populations in Finland, Holland, and Sweden. Von Hofer shows that, over the past 50 years, Finland, Holland and Sweden witnessed similar economic and social developments and have been affected by similar crime trends. However, over the same period, the daily prison populations in these three Northern European countries have developed very differently. Von Hofer identifies three phases in Dutch sentencing trends since the 1950s. In the 1950s to mid-1960s, the trend was towards shorter sentences due to the growing dominance of a rehabilitative philosophy in corrections. The mid-1960s to mid-1970s saw a continuation of this trend due to constraints on prison capacity; one of the most significant was the limitation on additional cell space due to the "one prisoner per cell" policy that was followed by Dutch correctional authorities. However, since the late-1970s, the trend has been toward longer sentences and increasing prison capacity. Von Hofer also identifies a number of possible factors that have likely contributed to the upward trend in sentence length and prison capacity in Holland since the 1970s, including economic crisis, immigration, the rise in crime levels, the growing perception of the failure of the criminal justice system, and pressure from abroad to abandon liberal policies in relation to drug use. Unlike Holland, Sweden, von Hofer shows, has had a relatively stable prison population for the past 30 years. He observes that, distinctive to Sweden throughout this period, deliberate attempts have been made by criminal justice authorities to bring in new policies to counteract other policies that have started to lead toward higher prison populations. Finally, von Hofer summarizes findings of research on Finland, which show that Finland's prison population has undergone a "stunning decrease" over the last 50 years; specifically, the prison population dropped from nearly 200 per 100,000 of the Finnish population in 1950 to around 70 per 100,000 in 2002. Von Hofer argues that this decrease has been the result of a long-term, conscious, and systematic criminal policy developed and implemented by criminal policy experts in Finland. Among the specific policies put into place to bring about this decrease, were the overall reduction in the length of prison sentences and increase in the use of "conditional sentences"; the "depenalization" of certain offences, such as drunk driving and theft; the increased use of community service; and the implementation of a deliberate policy against the use of imprisonment for young offenders. Von Hofer's analysis leads him to conclude more generally that it is useful to view such diverse cross-national developments in penal policy in light of a perspective that treats prison populations as "political constructs," which is to say that they are ultimately the consequence of political decision making rather than inevitable automatic responses to perceived changing levels of crime.

In Chapter 19, Caroline Chatwin provides an analogous discussion of convergence and divergence in the illegal drug laws and drug-use policies of different countries that are member states of the European Union (EU). In this context, Chatwin devotes particular attention to contrasting the drug laws and policies of the Netherlands, which is known for its liberal approach, and Sweden, which is known for its more repressive approach to drug control. Chatwin highlights the fact that the largely conflicting and incompatible drug policies of the Netherlands and Sweden pose a significant obstacle to the attempt being made by EU member states to develop a common, consensually agreed upon, European-wide approach to illegal drug control. Specifically, Chatwin points to the current division that exists among EU countries over which of the competing drug policy styles, that of the Netherlands or Sweden, should be followed in developing a pan-European approach to illegal drug control. However, rather than concluding that this division will make it impossible to develop such an approach, Chatwin argues, more optimistically, that the battle over the Dutch versus the Swedish drug policy styles may be having a positive effect on the long-term development of a more widely agreed upon European approach. According to Chatwin, one of the positive consequences of this debate is that it has contributed significantly "to the prioritization of the drug problem for the EU." In turn, in the effort to bridge "[t]he division between tolerant Dutch-style policies and prohibitive Swedish-style measures ... the EU has implemented many invaluable research tools and has improved legislation dealing with the control of illegal drugs," and "[a]s a result the nature of the problem and the solutions available are now much more widely understood." Thus, Chatwin concludes, "While the aim of the EU to achieve harmonization of approaches to the drug problem has not been met," EU countries are now collectively "in a much stronger position to manage drug use." The broader lesson that may be learned from Chatwin's research is that, while the goal of harmonizing the criminal justice policies of countries that even agree in principle to such harmonization may be very difficult to achieve, these types of attempts may, nonetheless, have the positive outcome of leading to more coordinated international cooperation along with the development of more deliberately comparative research-based national criminal justice policies in the individual countries that have chosen to adopt a less parochial approach.

Chapter 17

COMPARATIVE CRIMINAL JUSTICE POLICY-MAKING IN THE UNITED STATES AND THE UNITED KINGDOM: THE CASE OF PRIVATE PRISONS

TREVOR JONES AND TIM NEWBURN

Criminologists have become increasingly interested in the ways in which crime-control policies arise and cross national borders and what happens to them when they travel (Newburn and Sparks 2004). The focus of this chapter is upon a specific element within this wider area of interest: the extent to which we have seen the emergence of "United States-style" penal policy developments in the United Kingdom and the processes by which these have come about. A number of authors have commented upon the global spread of a range of penal policies that appeared to originate in the United States (Christie 2000; Jones and Newburn 2002a; Nellis 2000). Discussion of such developments and what might explain them has been focused most recently around the work of David Garland (2000, 2001). Garland has argued that, during the second half of the 20th century, a largely shared "culture of control" arose in both the United Kingdom and the United States. This, he argues, has helped to shape similar developments in popular and political discourse about crime and also penal-policy responses that appear increasingly alike. Against this, another body of work highlights the local and the particular. For example, Tonry (1999, 2001) stresses the striking differences in penal-policy interventions between countries with different historical and cultural traditions. As he argues, "The world increasingly may be a global community, but explanations of penal policy remain curiously local" (2001: 518). In a similar vein, Melossi (2001) has noted the striking differences over time between penal systems in the United States and in Italy, and argued that "(p)unishment is deeply embedded in the national/cultural specificity of the environment which produces it" (2001: 407).

This chapter has two key objectives. The first is to help to address the relative paucity of studies, especially comparative studies, of policy-making in the arena of criminal justice. As we have pointed out elsewhere, criminologists (see Rock 1990, 1995; Rutherford 1996; Ryan 1999; Downes and Morgan 2002, for exceptions) have focused their empirical research upon the content and impact of penal policy rather than its origins (Jones and Newburn 2002a). By contrast, whereas political scientists have undertaken detailed empirical analyses of policy-making in a range of different spheres, from agriculture to telecommunications regulation (Atkinson and Coleman 1992), they have rarely ventured into the field of criminal justice and penal policy. As Michael Tonry (2001) has argued, our knowledge of what shapes criminal-justice policy is still relatively limited.

The second broad aim is to re-emphasize the notion of political agency within considerations of penal-policy formulation. Recent work has focused primarily upon fundamental structural and cultural conditions that provide the broader context for policy formulation. This helps us to identify and understand the broader globalizing tendencies that lie behind a degree of convergence between penal systems (Christie 2000; Garland 2000, 2001). It is, however, also vital that we continue to explore the degree to which important national differences in penal-policy outcomes can be related to historical "path dependencies" (Karstedt 2002) and distinctive national cultural traditions (Melossi 2001). A fuller understanding of penal-policy changes also requires a more detailed understanding of the purposive actions of key agents within the policy process, and the constraints and opportunities provided by the political systems within which they operate. Although some work has begun to address this gap (Rutherford 1996; Nellis 2000; Jones and Newburn 2002a, 2002b), to date, it has not been linked to the broader structural constraints that shape the frameworks, agendas, and decisions of policy-makers. As Richard Sparks has observed, "much criminology and penology only gestures at the political" (2001: 172). The two approaches primarily reflect the "unavoidable tension between broad generalization and the specification of empirical particulars" (Garland 2001: vi). However, it is possible to link the two approaches. Comparative studies that unpick particular "policies" and examine the essentially *political* processes that shape them can help us to explore the ways in which the tensions between globalizing and localizing trends play themselves out in the agendas and decisions of key actors.

The chapter is divided into four main sections. First, we examine what is meant by "policy" in this context and highlight two key dimensions of the concept.[1] These are policy *processes* (the "how") and the substantive *levels* of policy (the "what"). This section also outlines a model of public policy-making (Kingdon 1995) that provides a useful way forward in making sense of the penal-policy process. The second section turns to the experience of prison privatization in the United Kingdom and the United States and provides an overview of the re-emergence of privately managed correctional institutions in both countries in the latter half of the 20th century. Section three explores the similarities and differences in the process and substance of policy change in the United States and the United Kingdom, drawing upon the Kingdon model outlined earlier. The chapter concludes with some observations about what light this case study can shed upon the broader issues outlined by David Garland and others.

EXPLORING "POLICY"

There is a danger in discussions of penal-policy convergence or divergence that we take the term "policy" as a given. Here, we draw a distinction between two dimensions of policy—those concerned with "process" and with "substance," respectively. First, it is important to emphasize that policy-making can be represented as a set of processes involving a number of analytically distinct "stages" or "streams." The structure of these streams and the way in which they interact with one another have an important influence on the second dimension—policy "substance"—

our central concern here. Policy can be considered substantively at a number of different "levels," ranging from the more symbolic elements, such as ideas and rhetoric, on the one hand, to the more concrete manifestations, such as policy instruments and practices, on the other.

Policy process

It is important to recognize that formal "policy" represents the outcome of a set of processes rather than an "event" in itself. There is a large body of work within political science that has analysed policy-making by dividing it up into distinct stages and undertaking detailed examinations of each (Easton 1965). In such approaches, policy is seen as arising from a distinct set of problem-solving processes: problem definition, formulation of alternative solutions, considerations of implications of alternatives, to experimentation with the preferred choice. Whilst recognizing the analytical importance of identifying such stages, a number of authors have pointed out that such an approach runs the risk of implying a rather mechanistic and sequential model of the policy-making process (Hill 1997). Policy-making in practice rarely looks like the textbook discussions of the "policy cycle," and, in particular, it is rarely as rational as many analytical models imply (Nelson 1996). The substantive "content" of policies is clearly shaped, not only by the latter stages of political decision-making, but negotiated continuously in the earlier problem definition, legislation, regulation and court decisions, and again in the subsequent decisions made by practitioners and "street-level" bureaucrats. Nevertheless, breaking the policy-making cycle into distinct stages, whilst not necessarily reflecting the real world, has provided political scientists with a useful analytical tool for empirical exploration of the processes involved.

One model that seeks to "deconstruct" the policy process whilst paying due regard to its apparently somewhat anarchic character is that developed by Kingdon (1995). His general theory of public-policy-making suggests that it consists of a set of processes, including (at a minimum) agenda setting, alternative specification, authoritative choice, and implementation (1995: 2). However, Kingdon emphasizes that policy-making does not proceed in a neat set of sequential stages. Conversely, he argues that there are three distinct "process streams" that can be identified within the system:

- the problem stream (the process of generation of "problems" requiring attention by policy-makers);
- the policy stream (the generation of policy ideas and proposals); and
- the political stream (the outcome of elections, developments in the "public mood," interest group campaigning, etc.).

Kingdon's argument is that these distinct streams operate independently of each other for much of the time. However, the three converge at critical times, whereby "solutions become joined to problems, and both of them are joined to favourable political forces" (1995: 20). From time to time, "policy windows" (i.e., opportunities for promoting certain proposals or conceptions of a problem) are opened by developments in the political stream or the emergence of particularly compelling problems. Such windows provide an opportunity for what Kingdon calls "policy entrepreneurs," whose "defining characteristic, much as in the case of a business entrepreneur, is their willingness to invest their resources—time, energy, reputation, and sometimes money—in the hope of future return" (1995: 122). Policy entrepreneurs not only push their "pet" proposals and problems but are also responsible for linking problems and proposed solutions to the political stream. The success of policy entrepreneurs depends upon their ability to respond quickly to these "windows" of opportunity, before other "solutions" become favoured. Although a good part of this is down to the skill of the policy entrepreneur, crucially, there is also a substantial element of luck involved. In sum, a significant development in policy is most likely when problems, policy proposals and politics are linked together into a clear package. Focusing upon, and detailing the nature of, the relationships between these streams appears to us to be a prerequisite to the development of a realistic understanding of policy.

Policy levels

At any one point, "policy" can be broken down into a number of distinct "levels." Empirical research into policy formulation has tended, for obvious reasons, to focus upon the more "concrete" levels of formal policy statements or legislation. In this vein, authors such as Bernstein and Cashore have argued that empirical studies need to focus upon formal policy decisions, such as statutes, regulations, and statements, because these manifestations of policy capture the "actual choices of government" (2000: 70). However, others have suggested that such definitions present an overly simplified view of policy. Bennett (1991), for example, identifies a number of distinct elements of policy, including policy content (statutes, administrative rules and regulations), policy instruments (institutional tools to achieve goals such as regulatory, administrative, and judicial tools) and policy style (consensual, confrontational, or incremental). Similarly, Dolowitz and Marsh (2000) outline various different elements of policy, including policy goals, content, instruments, programmes, institutions, ideologies, ideas and attitudes. There is not the space to investigate all of these various levels of policy in relation to changes in criminal-justice policy in recent years. However, the important point here is that a distinction may be drawn between *policy styles, symbols, and rhetoric*, and the more concrete and formalized manifestations of policy in terms of *policy content and instruments*. Moreover, the analysis of policy change is enhanced if equal regard is paid to each.

THE REBIRTH OF PRIVATE PRISONS IN THE UNITED STATES AND THE UNITED KINGDOM

United States

Private-sector provision of correctional services has a long history in the United States, dating back to at least the 19th century, when several states leased their state prisons to private contractors (Shichor 1995). However, the recent rebirth of private corrections in the United States began during the 1960s, when the Federal Bureau of Prisons (FBP) contracted with private firms to operate community treatment centres, youth facilities, and "halfway houses" in the shallow end of the criminal-justice system (Ryan and Ward 1989). During the late-1970s, the US Immigration and Naturalisation Service (INS) contracted with private firms to detain illegal immigrants (McDonald 1994).

The first mainstream prison to be run on private lines opened in 1984, in Houston, Texas, run by the newly formed Corrections Corporations of America (CCA). Further establishments were opened in the following year, during which CCA made an unsuccessful bid to run the entire Tennessee state prison system.[2] During the mid- to late 1980s, other private corrections corporations (e.g., the US Corrections Corporation and Wackenhut) also emerged as significant competitors in the growing market at state and local county levels, mainly in the southern states. The issue of private prisons had become sufficiently salient at the national level for the US House of Representatives Judiciary Committee to hold a series of hearings on Private Corrections (United States Congress 1986). Privatization at state and county levels continued, and, by 1988, the private corrections sector was sufficiently large for the National Institute of Justice to organize a conference on the subject (Peterson 1988). However, the federal adult prison sector remained largely impervious to privatization, and the market remained primarily within state and local jurisdictions.

The early- to mid-1990s saw continued growth in the private corrections sector (Mattera and Khan 2001). Once again, the issue attracted the attention of federal bodies when, in 1996, the General Accounting Office (GAO) undertook research that found little evidence that private prisons were significantly less costly than public ones (United States General Accounting Office 1996). By the late-1990s, the private prison sector remained concentrated in 23 western and southern states. High-use states included Texas, Oklahoma, Florida, Louisiana, Tennessee, California, Colorado and Mississippi, and also Washington, DC (McDonald *et al.* 1998). More recent figures show that 19 states in total have no prisoners held in private facilities (United States Department of Justice 2001).

The late-1990s saw a significant slowdown in the US private corrections market. A number of high-profile lawsuits were successfully taken out by inmates of private prisons against the corporations responsible for their institutions. It was argued that these incidents were increasingly typical of the private corrections sector: "Countless instances of escapes, riots, brutality, and other sorts of operational problems came to light in connection with the growing universe of privately-owned correctional facilities" (Mattera and Khan 2001: 6). The confidence of institutional investors in companies like CCA was shaken by such developments, and the late-1990s also saw very substantial falls in the stock-market value of Wackenhut, again following bad publicity regarding alleged mismanagement of its prisons (Green 2001). The early years of the new millennium saw a continued stagnation in the growth of private corrections in the United States. In early 2002, the Sentencing Project (2002: 3) observed that "[s]ince 2000, no states have negotiated new private prison contracts, and several states have curtailed their relationship with the private prison industry." In addition to a slowing down of private contracts, some private corrections facilities have been brought under public-sector control.[3]

Although state governments have been a shrinking source of private corrections contracts, the federal government has, in recent years, provided "a source of salvation for the industry" (Sentencing Project 2002: 3). By 1997, the Federal Bureau of Prisons was the main customer for privately operated custodial facilities, in terms of number of prison places (McDonald *et al.* 1998). The rapid growth in federal prison privatization has been related to the implementation of mandatory minimum sentencing and the "war on drugs" (Sentencing Project 2002). In addition, a further pressure on the federal system has resulted from the 1996 Immigration Reform Act, which meant that even minor offences, when committed by non-US citizens, can be prosecuted under federal law. This has led to further expansion in the federal prison population. In 2001, the Immigration and Naturalization Service and the US Marshall's Service renewed five contracts with CCA, worth over $50 million annually (Mattera and Khan 2001).

United Kingdom

The private provision of prisons in the United Kingdom also has a long history. From the Middle Ages onwards, jails were run as private businesses and, during the 18th and 19th centuries, private entrepreneurs found profit-making opportunity in the policy of transportation to the colonies (McConville 1981; Cavadino and Dignan 2002). As in the United States, the more recent manifestation of private provision of prisons began in the immigration-detention sector. In the early-1970s, the Home Office contracted the private security firm, Securicor, to run detention centres (and associated escort services) for suspected illegal immigrants at the four principal airports in England. However, it was not until 1984 that the contracting-out of mainstream prisons and remand centres to the private sector was advocated by the free-market think tank, the Adam Smith Institute (ASI) (Adam Smith Institute 1984). The ASI continued to canvass support for the idea of privately run prisons and, in 1987, published another report on the subject, describing, in glowing terms, a number of privately managed prisons in the United States (Young 1987).

In 1986, the Home Affairs Select Committee (HAC) of the House of Commons, under the chairmanship of the Conservative MP Sir Edward Gardner, undertook an inquiry into the state of prisons in England and Wales. Members of the Committee visited a number of facilities in the United States, including several institutions operated by CCA. The issue of private prisons dominated subsequent discussion of the Committee's deliberations. Labour members objected to the support of private prisons by some leading Conservatives, and this issue was dealt with in a separate short report (Home Affairs Committee 1987), which recommended that the government conduct an experiment in the private contracting of a remand centre. At around the same time, Lord Windlesham, then a junior Home Office Minister, began to canvass the Prime Minister's support for a separate, privately contracted remand sector and the contracting-out of the court escort service (Windlesham 1993). Though the initial response was not positive, there soon followed a number of events that indicated that prison privatization remained at least on the margins of the agenda. The Home Office minister, Lord Caithness, visited the United States to examine the evidence on prison privatization, and, on his return, he reported positively on what he had seen (Rutherford 1990). At about the same time, UK Detention Services, a consortium comprising CCA and two British construction companies, John Mowlem and Sir Robert McAlpine and Sons Ltd., was formed "specifically to lobby the UK government about the merits of private prisons and to win contracts" (Prison Reform Trust 1994). A Green Paper, *Private Sector Involvement in the Remand System*, was published in July 1988 (Cm. 434), and responses were invited. By this point, commercial lobbying, both inside and outside parliament, was developing apace, with various consortia forming to respond to possible opportunities in the penal sphere. Another new company, Contract Prisons, was formed to exploit new opportunities, with the former HAC chairman, Sir Edward Gardner, as its chief executive. The private security companies, Group 4 Securitas and Securicor, set up subsidiaries specializing in the provision of detention services. By the late-1980s, the remand population was falling quite significantly, and the Home Office remained inclined against including provision for contracting-out in the forthcoming Criminal Justice Bill. However, pressure from the Number 10 Policy Unit resulted in a clause being included that would allow for the contracting-out of new facilities in the remand sector (Windlesham 1993).

The Criminal Justice Bill, introduced in autumn 1990, included a provision to allow for contracting-out, but only of *new* facilities for *remand* prisoners. These restrictions were soon overturned by amendments,[4] introduced at the committee stage and orchestrated by backbenchers and Home Office junior ministers (Windlesham 1993; Cavadino and Dignan 2002). The amendments extended the power to contract-out to facilities for sentenced prisoners and existing prisons and remand centres. During 1991, contract details were announced for two privately contracted penal establishments—the first was the Wolds, won by the security company Group 4, and the first prisoners were received in spring 1992. Despite vociferous criticism from opposition MPs, privatization continued to gather momentum. The contract for a second privately managed prison (Blakenhurst) was signed with UK Detention Services in December 1992. In September 1993, Home Secretary Michael Howard announced that the government planned to privatize about 10 per cent of the prison system in England and Wales. The contract for the third private management-only prison, Doncaster, was signed with Premier Prison Services (jointly owned by the American Wackenhut Corrections Corporation and a British firm, Serco Ltd.) in February 1994.

In August 1994, a shortlist of 20 prisons which were to be "market tested" was announced. However, in October 1994, the Prison Officers' Association (POA) successfully complained to the Central Arbitration Committee that they had not been properly consulted over the proposed market testing. Then, under the European Commission's Acquired Rights Directive, it emerged that private contractors were required to maintain existing jobs and conditions in respect of any new contracts that they won (Cavadino and Dignan 2002: 232). Despite these setbacks, the policy of privatization continued to extend beyond its original scope. The end of 1994 saw the opening of yet another privately run prison, Buckley Hall, to be managed by Group 4.[5] In June 1995, a consortium, including Tarmac and Group 4, won the contract to build and manage a 600-cell category B prison at Fazakerley, Liverpool. Another group, including Costain and Securicor, was contracted to construct and run an 880-place category B prison at Bridgend in South Wales. These were the first of six new penal institutions planned under the Government's Private Finance Initiative (PH). In 1996, the Government published a White Paper proposing to privately finance, design, and build a further 12 prisons, to come on-stream at a rate of one or two a year from 2001–2002 onwards, providing 9,600 new prisoner places (Nathan 1996).

May 1997 saw the election of a Labour government that had been unequivocally opposed to the contracting-out of prisons whilst in opposition. Not long after the election, there were signs that the Labour Party was to reverse its previous position. In June 1997, Home Secretary Jack Straw announced that he had renewed UK Detention Services' management contract for

Blakenhurst and agreed to two new privately financed, designed, built, and run prisons. The following year, Straw confirmed the U-turn in a speech to the POA, when he stated that, henceforth, all new prisons in England and Wales would be privately constructed and run (although, the Prison Service was now also to be allowed to tender for the contracts when current contracts expired). The threat of privatization was also to be used to promote reform in "under-performing" public prisons. In July 1999, the prisons minister, Paul Boateng, announced that Brixton Prison was to be market tested with a view to privatization. In January 2000, he further announced that the Prison Service had won the contracts to manage Blakenhurst and Manchester prisons, beating off competition from the private sector. By early 2004, there were a total of nine privately operated prison service establishments in England and Wales, although that total will shortly rise to 11, with a further two contracts in the pipeline. Though privatization may not have spread as far as some critics initially feared, it is difficult to disagree with Cavadino and Dignan's conclusion that "the policy of encouraging private sector involvement in the design, construction, financing and operation of prisons in England and Wales now appears unassailable, at least for the forseeable future" (2002: 234).

PRISON PRIVATIZATION: POLICY PROCESS

In this section, we draw upon Kingdon's (1995) framework of problems, policies, and politics, to explore how the various streams of influence shaped policy changes in both countries. Our focus here is the processes that led to the policy change in each country, and our argument is that the trajectory followed in the United States differed in several important ways from that in the United Kingdom. Though, on a broad level, the ostensible policy "outcomes" were very similar, the permutations in the streams of problems, policies, and politics were far from identical.

Problems

Kingdon (1995) describes the "problem stream" as being concerned with the ways in which particular issues or problems emerge that command the attention of policy-makers. It is entirely unsurprising that, at a broad level of generality, we can detect similarities between the problem streams visible in the United States and in the United Kingdom at the time that prison privatization emerged. As we have seen, in both countries, the idea first emerged at a time of expanding prison populations and a focus on the related problems caused by overcrowding and prison conditions. However, looking in more detail at the problem stream highlights some interesting and significant differences.

In the United States, the major problem confronting state authorities was the substantial growth of prison populations and the threat of litigation against states with overcrowded prison systems. Other problems experienced during the 1980s included significant funding problems on the part of state and local government with the cutback of federal aid programmes under the Reagan administrations. This exacerbated the problems of state and county governments under pressure to build new prisons, and to do so quickly. Traditional public-sector procurement procedures for major capital projects were protracted and complex. The private sector offered a relatively speedy way of providing new prison capacity without the need for major public capital spending at the outset. More recent developments in privatization within the federal sector can also be related to the emerging problem of growing federal inmate populations, which have expanded enormously in recent years (Sentencing Project 2002). In addition, federal agencies have come under pressure to reduce their numbers of directly employed staff as a result of the "end of the era of big government," announced by President Clinton. This introduced a requirement to reduce the number of federal employees—a pressure that led to an increase in contracting-out across a range of federal government functions. Within the FBP, this has resulted in a general reduction in employment in the public sphere, with a consequent emergence and expansion of the private sector in federal corrections (Gaes and Camp 2002).

There are important contrasts here with the United Kingdom. Like the United States, the United Kingdom, too, faced the problem of an expanding prison population and consequent overcrowding during the 1980s, particularly in the remand sector. However, it is difficult to escape the sheer scale of comparison with the staggering increases in US incarceration (Christie 2000). Furthermore, by the end of the 1980s, this particular problem appeared to be easing in the United Kingdom with the fall in the remand population. However, the particular "problem" of pressure on prison places was, arguably, just part of a broader sense of ongoing "crisis" in the penal system and the need for more radical reform in general. Indeed, it appears that an important area of contrast within the "problem streams" in the United States and the United Kingdom concerns the history of poor industrial relations in the United Kingdom prison systems and the sense that managerial control needed to be reasserted. The POA was viewed as a significant block to effective penal reform, and a protector of inefficient and expensive working practices. The introduction of privately run facilities was, in part at least, seen as a means of reducing the power of the POA by breaking its monopoly (Mellor 2002). This notion of privatization as a tool of more general penal reform is also reflected in the significant early advocacy of private involvement in the prison system by a minority of academic commentators on the left of the political spectrum (McConville and Williams 1985).

Policies

The process of generation of compelling "problems" that require responses from policy-makers and politicians can be analysed quite distinctly from the generation of policy ideas and proposals—the "policy stream." Kingdon (1995) describes how a plethora of policy ideas and proposals float around continuously in what he terms "the policy primeval soup," some of which come to the surface and become attached to particular "problems." The key point is that policy change should not necessarily be seen as a rational response to the emergence of particular problems. Rather, we need to examine how and why certain ideas arise and are promoted, and the circumstances in which they become linked with particular problems. What insight does such an approach provide for the re-emergence of private prisons in the United States and the United Kingdom?

It seems that both prior to and during the emergence of privatization, the "policy stream" in each country included a range of possible alternatives. In the United States, a number of alternatives within the "policy stream" emerged from time to time, although this clearly varied from state to state. Penal-reform groups have continuously advocated the reduction of prison populations via changes in sentencing policy and the development of alternatives to custody. The New York based Vera Institute of Justice established a "State Centered Project" that provided expertise and support to policy-makers in particular states, attempting to develop alternatives to custody and revision of parole (Sarabi 2000). The Washington, DC based Sentencing Project has long been involved in the promotion of policies designed to reduce the use of incarceration, via sentencing reforms and the development of effective alternative sanctions (Mauer 1999). Other penal-reform groups have targeted particular parts of the country, with the Western Prison Project active in the northwestern states, such as Oregon, Washington, and Montana. At times, major public investment in the building of new public-sector prisons has been advocated. During the mid-1990s, the federal government offered grants to state governments to fund prison building, as an incentive to promote the adoption of "truth in sentencing" laws (United States General Accounting Office 1998). During the 1980s and 1990s, a number of states introduced diversion schemes or early-release schemes as part of an attempt to reduce pressures on their prison systems. Private-sector provision of prisons was, therefore, one of a range of possible policies that were floating around. At a broad level of analysis, it is difficult to document how that policy gathered momentum and came to be attached to the "problem" of prison overcrowding. More detailed policy histories of the development of privatization at the state level are required here. For example, Cummins's (2000) analysis of the Texan penal system suggests that certain US states experienced a particularly vigorous marketing of contracting-out as a "solution," [undertaken] by private firms, such as CCA and Wackenhut. The founders of the large corrections corporations were hugely successful "policy" as well as "business" entrepreneurs. They were also well connected in the political sphere. Furthermore, the US story neatly demonstrates how the purveyors of particular policy "solutions" can seek out and develop "problems" to attach them to. Clearly, in its initial stages, the policy of privatization can be seen, in part, as a response to growing prison populations. However, recent studies have indicated that private prison corporations also helped to promote the types of sentencing policies that created, or at least stimulated, the "problem" in the first instance.

The American Legislative Exchange Council (ALEC) has become an increasingly important national player in the United States, promoting both harsher sentencing policies across state legislatures and pro-privatization policies more generally. ALEC is a conservative public policy organization, based in Washington, DC, and it is estimated that 40 per cent of state legislators are members (Sarabi and Bender 2000: 3). One of the main aims of ALEC is to formulate "model legislation" to promote conservative policies, and it has been extremely successful in getting Bills enacted into law across many states. It has not gone unnoticed that corporate donations are an extremely important source of income for ALEC, accounting for almost 70 per cent of the total budget in 1998 (Sarabi and Bender 2000). It is significant that private corrections corporations are prominent supporters of ALEC, including both CCA and Wackenhut. The same research also points out that the Criminal Justice Taskforce (that develops model legislation) in ALEC included high-level representatives from the private corrections sector. For example, the taskforce was co-chaired by senior CCA executives. ALEC has been extremely influential in promoting "truth in sentencing" and "three strikes" legislation during the 1990s. In addition to the work of bodies like the ALEC, private corrections corporations have taken more direct action in the form of increasing amounts of money paid to professional lobbyists, and in terms of making direct donations to political campaigns. Sarabi and Bender (2000) note that, in 1998, contributions to 361 candidates in 25 states were made by private corrections companies or their associates. They argue that "this total represents a significant and growing effort to ensure access to policy-makers at the state level at crucial moments" (2000: 8).

Turning to the United Kingdom, we can also identify a number of distinct alternatives within the "policy stream" during the mid- to late-1980s. In the more centralized and closed world of British penal policy-making, penal-reform groups, such as NACRO, the Howard League and the Prison Reform Trust, had traditionally exerted significant influence (Ryan 1999). Although this influence declined from the 1970s onwards, these groups remained active in promoting sentencing reforms to promote alternatives to imprisonment, improved prison regimes and rehabilitative measures for ex-offenders. During the late-1980s, for a while at least, it appears that some of these "solutions" were in the ascendancy, as indicated by the fact that prison populations did begin to fall (as a result of deliberate policy) during the late-1980s and early-1990s. This is a very important contrast with the policy stream in the United States. Furthermore, the discussion of prison privatization appears to have been very limited, even during the late-1980s. As we noted earlier, even as late as 1988, it appeared that senior ministers (including the Prime Minister) were not inclined to give the idea serious consideration. This was despite the enthusiastic advocacy of supporters of the policy, such as the Adam Smith Institute and Conservative MPs such as Sir Edward Gardner and Sir John Wheeler. There was some commercial lobbying in the United Kingdom, but even this was minimal compared to the activity at the state level in the United States. In order to understand how the "solution" of private prisons came to "rise to the surface" of the policy soup and was eventually implemented, we need to examine the political stream in more detail.

Politics

While there are important contrasts between the streams of "problems" and "policies" that emerged in the United States and the United Kingdom in connection with private prisons, it is in the realm of politics that the differences become most significant. In both nations, but in very different ways, the privatization "solution" became attached to the prison "problem," and both were linked to favourable political developments. Of course, in broad terms, similarities in the political stream are, again, visible. These include the existence of ideological similarities between the ruling administrations (both between Conservative and Republican administrations, and, more recently, between Labour and Democrat administrations). More broadly, both countries were, arguably, in the vanguard of neo-liberal reforms, and governments in both promoted privatization of public services and "new public management" reforms. Furthermore, both countries are two-party systems that have experienced similar developments in the politics of crime. Politicians in both countries have responded to growing public concern about crime by attempting to "out-tough" the other party in terms of penal-policy proposals. However, within the overall picture of similarity, some important differences within the politics of prison privatization are worth emphasizing.

Whilst there were political similarities (in terms of ideology) between the Reagan and Thatcher administrations, privatization as a national governmental programme was far more significant in the United Kingdom than in the United States (Feigenbaum et al. 1999). This relates to fundamental contrasts between the role of federal government in the United States and that of national government in the United Kingdom. Even though the Reagan administration did latterly promote privatization across a range of areas, including corrections (President's Commission on Privatization 1988), in the United States, there was much less opportunity for privatization at the federal level. For much of the 1980s, the radical governments of Margaret Thatcher were ideologically committed to a programme of liberalization and privatization in the economic sphere, and in many areas of social policy. This enthusiasm for the market, however, did not initially extend to the penal system. An important strand within Conservative thinking advocated the strong state in the sphere of law and order, whilst championing the "rolling back" of state influence elsewhere (Windlesham 1993). As outlined earlier, as late as the end of the 1980s, it appeared that prison privatization was seen as politically difficult, even in Conservative circles. There is some evidence that the Prime Minister was, herself, initially sceptical about whether privatization could be extended to the penal system (Windlesham 1993; Wheeler 2001). The eventual U-turn was related not to instrumental concerns about costs and overcrowding, but more to expressive concerns and the need to make a "grand gesture" about the radicalism of the government.

Another important contrast within the "political stream" concerns the stark differences in the political institutions of the two nations. Unsurprisingly, given its size and complexity, the US political system is more fragmented and open than the relatively centralized systems of Western European countries (Chandler 2000). There are more "points of influence" for interest groups to target key decision-makers at federal, state, and local levels. As McDonald has observed, "This nation's federal system of government is a fragmented one, with literally thousands of different governments, and important changes in practice can occur in an incremental fashion almost without being noticed until they become too well-entrenched either to stop or to control effectively" (1990: 3). It is, therefore, not surprising that, in the United States, the political process of privatization was characterized by vigorous lobbying by various supporters of private prisons at the key points of influence (primarily, local state legislatures). We have already referred to the lobbying activities of the private corrections companies, both in indirect form (e.g., funding the activities of bodies like ALEC) and in the more direct form of political contributions. Although, in the United Kingdom, it is clear that there was lobbying of government by private-sector consortia during the late-1980s, it is widely accepted that the nature and degree of this activity simply do not compare with what went on in the United States. Furthermore, in the United States, the lobbying went beyond simply encouraging enabling legislation for private prisons. As we have already suggested, there is clear evidence that private prison corporations have sought to expand their market by actively promoting more punitive sentencing policies. This has not been visible in the United Kingdom.

An additional area of United States-United Kingdom contrast concerns the involvement of local government in the lobbying process. The traditional opposition of local communities to prison construction in their localities began to disappear in deprived rural areas during the 1980s and 1990s (Lapido 2001). Prisons came to be seen as a source of jobs and income in many high-unemployment areas. For example, Cummins (2000) describes the "YIMBY" ("Yes In My Back Yard") element in the lobbying in favour of prison privatization legislation in Texas.

Representatives of county and city governments supported such legislation and actively lobbied for private prisons to be established in their areas. Similar lobbying has been visible in other parts of the United States, and it has been long noted that many new private prisons have been situated in areas suffering from severe economic problems and high unemployment. A number of authors have expressed concern about the growing dependence of these areas upon jobs and income provided by prisons industries (Schlosser 1998). The strategy of deploying prison growth as a tool for economic regeneration of deprived areas has been further confirmed by the importance of economic development subsidies from local, state and federal sources in the development of the private corrections industry (Mattera and Khan 2001).

PRISON PRIVATIZATION: LEVELS OF IMPACT

Even a brief analysis of the development of prison privatization in the United States and the United Kingdom demonstrates, we would argue, some important contrasts in the streams of problems, policies, and politics. This section explores how far these differences have been reflected in the more concrete outputs of the policy process. Here, we explore the two most important dimensions of policy "level," namely the more substantive elements of policy (such as policy content or instruments) and the relatively symbolic or discursive aspects of policy-making (policy style or rhetoric).

Policy content and instruments

By "policy content," we mean the formal manifestations of policy, including statutes, administrative rules, court rulings, etc. The term "policy instruments" refers to the regulatory, administrative or judicial tools used to implement and administer policy.

In terms of policy content and instruments, there is a broad similarity between the US and the UK experience of prison privatization. Taking "policy content" first, in both countries, it appears that legislative action was required to confirm the legality of the contracting-out of prison management. Of course, in the United States, for much of the recent period, the most important legislation has been passed at the state level (see Cummins 2001 for a discussion of the debate in Texas). However, as outlined above, recent years have seen a growth in federal use of private prison facilities. At a broad level of generalization, the policy content appears similar in both the United States and the United Kingdom. This similarity extends to the policy instruments used to implement and administer the policy of privatized prisons. Each country subsequently experienced a growth in the number of contracts between governmental authorities and private-sector companies for the provision of correctional services. Furthermore, some of the key players in the United Kingdom market were part-owned by major US corrections corporations, suggesting the possibility of a broadly similar approach to delivering correctional services.

However, looking in more detail at the actual operation of this policy in both countries, unsurprisingly, we begin to uncover important differences between the two. Many of these relate to the contrasts outlined in the previous section, and, in particular, the huge geographical, institutional, and political differences between the two nations. First, there have been important differences in the approach to contracting in each country. The "market" for prison places is far larger, considerably more open, and more complex in the United States. The sheer magnitude of the difference between the rate and extent of prison population growth in the United States and that in the United Kingdom cannot be overlooked. As Lilly and Knepper (1992) point out, the openings for private-sector involvement are that much greater in a huge continental country, where responsibility for corrections is shared among the federal government, 50 states (plus Washington, DC), over 3000 counties, plus a number of cities: "The absolute number of facilities, inmates, and the size of the US corrections administrative organization make it the most attractive and accessible correctional market" (1992: 179). This has helped to shape a number of further distinctive features in the United States. For example, the practice of "exporting" prisoners between jurisdictions is well established in the United States. This primarily involves states contracting with private prison companies to export some of ... [their] prisoners to out-of-state facilities (McDonald et al. 1998). However, there are other important players in the "market." On the demand side, federal agencies, such as the FBP, INS, and the US Marshalls Service, contract both with private corrections corporations and with state governments to hold prisoners under their jurisdictions. On the supply side, many county and city governments have contracted with states and federal bodies to provide jail places for federal prisoners in what have been termed "public propriety prisons" (Sechrist and Shichor 1993). To add further to the complexity here, many of these local governments contract-out the building and management of these facilities to private companies (Cummins 2000). This tradition of a vibrant "prisoner export" market is simply not a feature of the much smaller and more centralized system in the United Kingdom.

Another contrast concerns "speculative" prison building by some US corrections companies (McDonald 1994). This has not been a feature of the UK experience. The UK system, although clearly experiencing overcrowding and related problems, did not undergo the degree of pressure that existed in the US prison system. Even if private companies had considered speculative prison building in the United Kingdom, this would be constrained by the lack of available cheap land and the relatively stringent planning regulations (Kent 2001). Furthermore, the emphasis on "market testing" of existing public-sector establishments that has been a feature of the more recent British experience has generally been absent in the United States, where privatization has only very recently been applied to existing public-sector institutions (Gaes and Camp 2002). Although further research is required here, it seems that the US experience of private prisons has historically involved a less stringent approach to contracting. The safeguards of tightly specified contracts, and the rigorous monitoring of compliance with contracts, have been a stronger feature of the UK experience (Bronstein 2002). It is important, however, that we be aware of over-generalizing about the US experience. Further, it seems that the late-1990s saw the US private prisons sector operating in an increasingly critical climate. Partly as a result of this, contracts have been tightened, and the state governments have strengthened their approaches to the monitoring and control of private prisons (Cummins 2000). Despite these more recent developments, there remains the strong impression that the tradition within the United Kingdom is of a more closely monitored and controlled private sector. This suggests that the UK private sector has become more integrated within the wider prison system than has been the case in many parts of the United States. Privately run prisons always have an on-site Home Office monitor, both public and private prisons come under the gaze of Her Majesty's Inspectors of Prisons and the Prisons Ombudsman, and the contracting and procurement process has become increasingly rigorous. The procurement process in the United Kingdom involves the independent assessment of three bodies within the Contracts and Competitions Group of the Prison Department. These bodies independently assess the bids according to design, regime quality, and cost. Successful bids have not always necessarily been those with the lowest cost. By contrast, it has been suggested that, in many parts of the United States, the primary driver was cost. Some of the major problems that arose within certain states that enthusiastically embraced private prisons seem to bear this impression out. Cummins (2000) demonstrates the process by which private contractors cut costs by abandoning work and rehabilitative programmes and [by] "warehousing" inmates in their facilities.

A final interesting area of contrast concerns the proportional impact of the policy on the system as a whole. Given the massive increases in the US incarcerated population over the past 30 years or so, despite substantial growth in the private penal sector, it still only accounts for a rather smaller proportion of the total number of prisoners. In the smaller (albeit growing) and more centralized UK system, privatization has had a greater proportional impact on the system as a whole. For example, recent estimates from the United States indicate that about 6 per cent of the total adult imprisoned population were held in private facilities (US Department of Justice 2001). In the United Kingdom, once the latest two private prisons open, it is estimated that about 10 per cent of the total adult imprisoned population will be held in private facilities. Although these differences are not huge, it might be argued that, in the smaller though rapidly expanding UK system, the impact of the existence of a significant private sector in terms of being a lever of reform in public-sector prisons has been more significant.

Policy styles: Ideology and symbolism

In unpicking the more ephemeral aspects of "policy," it appears that there are both important similarities and differences between the policy of contracting-out prisons in the United States and that in the United Kingdom. In terms of similarity, for example, in each country, it appears that both pragmatic and more symbolic/ideological factors were important. The emergence of a private sector in prisons can be broadly related in both societies to a pragmatic response to the twin problems of expanding prison populations and constraints on public expenditure. In both countries, the emergence of the commercial corrections sector led to discussions about legal and moral principles concerning private provision in the arena of state punishment. The US Senate Judiciary Committee hearings questioned whether such a policy would be constitutional, although this was clearly resolved in favour of the pro-privatization lobby (McDonald et al. 1998). Similarly, in some states, the period prior to legislation enabling prison contracting was characterized by debates about the morality of private prisons, as well as the contested issue of effectiveness and cost savings (Cummins 2000). In the United Kingdom, although the HAC did not explore the issue of privatization with any real depth, the debates in parliament (and subsequent political comment) focused upon moral and legal principles.

Despite these similarities, it is possible to detect an ideological element in the initial move to privatization in the United Kingdom that was not as visible in the United States. First, in the United States, the major ideological debates concerning private prisons appeared to develop following the appearance of a private corrections market. In the strongly individualistic political cultures of the southern states, where private prisons first appeared, the ideological principles were, arguably, less contested. By contrast, in the United Kingdom, there was a strong ideological debate surrounding prison privatization that occurred prior to legislation on the issue. The subsequent trajectory of prison privatization in the United Kingdom has seen the ideological sting removed (arguably, along with other areas of public policy), and policy has been developed pragmatically and incrementally (Shaw 2002). Nevertheless, it seems to us to be important that, at one of the key historical "moments" of privatization in the United Kingdom, it was ideology rather than pragmatism that appeared to drive change. Although the prison systems in the United Kingdom were also experiencing problems of overcrowding when the idea of privatization was first touted, that idea came from the avowedly ideological ASI, who promoted the idea on the basis that private provision was *defacto* preferable to public provision, whether or not prison populations and overcrowding were on the increase. By promoting privatization of prisons, the ASI was deliberately "thinking the unthinkable"—a conscious strategy, described to us by senior members of the Institute. For example, Peter Young argued that a key strategy of the ASI was to "push out the boundaries." "The prisons [study] was an attractive one to promote because it seemed to most people to be very radical, and I think initially most people thought it was a joke" (Young 2001).

Furthermore, as noted earlier, the remand and sentenced prison populations were falling significantly by the end of the 1980s, to the extent that the Home Secretary overseeing the introduction of the Criminal Justice Bill was inclined to omit a specific clause enabling private contracting of new remand facilities (Windlesham 1993). It was the specific intervention of the Prime Minister that ensured the inclusion of such a clause.

It is, therefore, possible to argue that, at least at the outset, the policy of prison privatization in the United Kingdom had an avowedly symbolic dimension that was not present to nearly the same degree in the United States. First, prison privatization was both perceived as, and presented as, an "ideological bridgehead" by many of its supporters. Second, the decision to incorporate a clause in the 1991 Criminal Justice Act that would open the way to experiment with a privately managed remand centre, as noted earlier, was primarily driven by the symbolic need to appear radical. Windlesham (1993: 421–22) argues that the decision was taken by the Prime Minister "because of her conviction of the need for radical reform outside the prevailing consensus; not for any reasons of penological principle or administrative practice." The decision "was a symbol as well as an experiment" (1993: 307). For Margaret Thatcher, the decision symbolized her independence, her radicalness, and her belief that her government should be perceived as a "conviction government" (Jenkins 1987: 183).

CONCLUDING REMARKS

In this chapter, we have sought to explore in more detail the development of one apparent example of penal-policy convergence in the United States and the United Kingdom. Viewed in broad terms, the impression is one of similarity between the two countries. Given the time-scale of developments in both countries, it certainly appears that there was at least a degree of "policy transfer" from the United States to the United Kingdom, in terms of both the initial "idea" of privately run penal institutions and, later, in terms of substantive manifestations of policy. Both countries faced similar problems, such as growing prison populations (albeit on very different scales), and [they] faced the difficulty of meeting demand for places within the constraints of traditional public-sector procurement procedures. Developments in privatized prisons occurred first in the United States and followed later in the United Kingdom. It is also possible to identify important links between the policy streams in the United Kingdom and the United States. The key policy entrepreneurs in the genesis of the policy in the United Kingdom all explicitly drew upon US examples as exemplars to promote similar developments on this side of the Atlantic. The first advocate of the policy of private prisons in the United Kingdom, the Adam Smith Institute, had strong links with the US-based Heritage Foundation. The author of the ASI report that later advocated private prisons (Peter Young) was, himself, based in Washington, DC, over a number of years, and based his study entirely on private prisons operating in the United States. Home Office civil servants accompanied ministers on visits to private prisons in the United States during the late-1980s. These links were also visible in the political stream. British politicians made high-profile visits to view private prisons in the United States, including the members of the Home Affairs Committee, and at least two junior Home Office ministers. Many of them later explicitly justified their support for the principle of private-sector involvement with reference to their experiences. Finally, US-based corporations were centrally involved in the lobbying process that preceded legislation on this issue and then in the actual implementation stages of the policy in the United Kingdom (in terms of involvement in consortia that bid and won contracts to run prisons). It is, therefore, unsurprising that we are able to distinguish broad similarities in the "substance" of the policy of prison privatization in the United States and the United Kingdom, in terms of the requirement for legislative change and the administrative instruments of private contracting. It is safe to say, therefore, that there are clearly "globalizing" elements in the story of private prisons, in the way that policy ideas emerge, travel, and are implemented in different jurisdictions when the political conditions are right.

However, it is also clear that the story is not so simple as this. By attempting to break down what we mean by "policy" in particular instances and by analysing the processes of its formulation, we have also highlighted a range of significant distinctions between the experiences of the two nations. These differences apply to the "substance" of policy, in terms of the specific ways in which it was implemented and took shape. They also apply to the processes that led to the adoption and development of this policy. Many of these differences can be sensibly related to the distinctive features of the political systems (and, perhaps, political cultures) of the United States and the United Kingdom. However, some of these differences cannot easily be explained by such factors. An important finding of any study of policy-making is to highlight the haphazard nature of the processes that led to change. It is possible to focus upon seemingly intractable global or cultural forces, but, in studying the activities of key agents in the process, it is impossible to overlook the importance of contingency and happenstance. As Kingdon (1995: 206) has noted, "we still encounter considerable doses of messiness, accident, fortuitous coupling and dumb luck" in the policy process. However, this way of approaching the analysis of policy-making does allow us to begin to make links between the broader structures within which agents operate and the particular patterns of actions that they take. Thus, Kingdon argues, "Individuals do not control events or structures, but can anticipate them and bend them to their purposes to some degree" (1995: 225).

At key moments in the trajectories of the policies in each country, agents took decisions that were essentially unpredictable yet crucial. To take some key examples, in the United Kingdom, the Prime Minister intervened at a crucial moment to establish the legal principle of contracting-out. Various parliamentarians worked behind the scenes to amend the legislation in order to extend the remit of privatization. Senior POA officials decided against taking industrial action against prison privatization (a decision that they came to regret). Senior Labour Party politicians executed their own U-turn on private prisons and became enthusiastic advocates. At each stage, it is quite conceivable that these key players could have chosen to act differently—indeed, in precisely the opposite way.

Given the size and complexity of the United States, it is more difficult to provide examples of key moments, because privatization developed to different extents and at different paces in the different state jurisdictions and in the federal sector. However, detailed case studies of the development of the policy in particular states display a similar range of key moments. For example, Cummins (2000) has shown how the expansion of private prisons in Texas proceeded in an unpredictable and haphazard way. Furthermore, it is important to note that a significant number of states in the United States still have no private prisons. This almost certainly reflects a combination of "structural" factors, including the political traditions and cultures of the states concerned, the differing legal systems, the degree of penal expansion, etc. But it also reflects the importance of political *agency* in terms of the various strategies adopted by key actors responding to these broader constraints and opportunities. Further research is needed here into such questions as why private corrections corporations targeted some states rather than others for expansion, why coalitions of opposition arose in some states and not in others, and under what circumstances each failed or succeeded in its aims.

At the outset, we suggested that it was possible to identify two contrasting approaches to the analysis of penal-policy developments—one that focuses upon globalizing tendencies and the other upon the local and the particular. Each approach has much to offer. The first identifies important commonalities between societies and explains them with reference to global cultural, political, and social changes taking place in advanced democracies or "late modern" societies. The latter reminds us of the abiding importance of national (and, perhaps, sub-national), cultural, and historical traditions in mediating and reworking global trends, and preserving significant degrees of difference. However, in order better to understand the tensions between the global and the local, we argue that there is a need to place the study of human agency and political processes closer to the centre of the account that is offered. This approach focuses more closely on the details of policy development and political influence, and moves from these to the broader issues of emergent social routines and cultural sensibilities. In this paper, we have acknowledged the importance of broad structural changes to an understanding of policy convergence but, within this, have argued that it is useful to "reinsert" a closer study of the role of political actors into the narrative. Doing so, we suggest, is revealing in a number of ways. First, by reinserting agency in this way, a fuller picture of the processes of cultural formation and reproduction is produced. Second, doing so enables a better understanding of the specific nature of "convergence" between the cultures of control in the United States and the United Kingdom. Finally, and linked to this, such an approach illustrates the limits of convergence. That is, it also highlights the continuing existence of dissimilarity and difference. Simultaneously, therefore, it is possible both to acknowledge the existence of elements of cultural convergence in crime control, whilst also drawing attention to important divergences, both within and between particular nation states.

David Garland (1990) has argued that penal policy is the outcome of "a large number of conflicting forces," and it is ultimately impossible to identify and analyse the full range of "swarming circumstances" that work to shape penal developments. Though agreeing with his observation, we would argue that it nonetheless remains the case that more detailed empirical studies of the concrete changes that are occurring, and the processes that lead to change, can significantly add to our knowledge and understanding of the determinants of penal policy. It is only via detailed empirical work that we can begin to map out the reflexive relationships between local, national and global influences that come to shape penal policy.

NOTES

[1] This is not to imply that we think that this is all that there is to policy—merely that we take this distinction to be crucial in developing a more nuanced understanding of policy.

[2] This followed a federal court ruling that the entire state prison system was in violation of the Constitution because of overcrowded conditions of confinement.

[3] For example, two Wackenhut facilities in Arkansas were transferred to public-sector control in 2001.

[4] These amendments would enable the Secretary of State to make an order by statutory instrument, giving effect to the power to contract-out (with none of the previous limitations).

[5] Group 4 lost its contract after re-tendering in 1999. Since June 2000, Buckley Hall has been run by the Prison Service.

REFERENCES

Adam Smith Institute. 1984. *The Omega File*. London: Adam Smith Institute.

Atkinson, M. and W. Coleman. 1992. "Policy Networks, Policy Communities and Problems of Governance." *Governance* 5: 154–80.

Bennett, C. 1991. "What is Policy Convergence and What Causes It?" *British Journal of Political Science* 21: 215–33.

Bernstein, S. and B. Cashore. 2000. "Globalization, Four Paths of Internationalization and Domestic Policy Change: The Case of EcoForestry in British Columbia, Canada." *Canadian Journal of Political Science* 33: 67–99.

Bronstein, A. 2002. [Personal Interview.] National Prison Project, American Civil Liberties Union.

Cavadino, M. and J. Dignan. 2002. *The Penal System: An Introduction.* 3rd ed. London: Sage.

Chandler, J. (Ed.). 2000. *Comparative Public Administration.* London: Routledge.

Christie, N. 2000. *Crime Control as Industry.* 3rd ed. London: Routledge.

Cummins, C.E. 2000. *Private Prisons in Texas, 1987–2000: The Legal, Economic and Political Influences on Policy Implementation.* Unpublished doctoral thesis. Washington, DC: The American University.

Downes, D. 2001. "The Macho Penal Economy: Mass Incarceration in the US, a European Perspective." *Punishment and Society* 3: 61–80.

Downes, D. and R. Moran. 2002. "The Skeletons in the Cupboard: The Politics of Law and Order at the Turn of the Millennium." Pp. 286–321 in *The Oxford Handbook of Criminology.* 3rd ed., edited by M. Maguire, R. Morgan, and R. Reiner. Oxford: Oxford University Press.

Drakeford, M. 2000. *Privatization and Social Policy.* Harlow: Longman.

Easton, D. 1965. *A Systems Analysis of Political Life.* Chicago: University of Chicago Press.

Faulkner, D. 2001. *Crime, State and Citizen: A Field Full of Folk.* Winchester: Waterside Press.

Feigeniiaum, H., J. Henig, and C. Hamnett. 1999. *Shrinking the State: The Political Underpinnings of Privatization.* Cambridge: Cambridge University Press.

Gars, G. and S. Camp. 2002. [Personal Interview.] Office of Research, Federal Bureau of Prisons.

Garland, D. 1990. *Punishment and Modern Society.* Oxford: Oxford University Press.

Garland, D. 2000. "The Culture of High Crime Societies: Some Preconditions of Recent 'Law and Order' Policies." *British Journal of Criminology* 40: 347–75.

Garland, D. 2001. *The Culture of Control: Crime and Social Order in Contemporary Society.* Oxford: Oxford University Press.

Greene, J. 2001. "Bailing Out Private Jails." *The American Prospect* 12 (16): 23–27.

Fiaroing, R.W. 1997. *Private Prisons and Public Accountability.* New Brunswick: Transaction Books.

Hill, M. 1997. *The Policy Process in the Modern State.* 3rd ed. London: Prentice Hall/ Harvester Wheatsheaf.

Home Affairs Committee. 1987. *Contract Provision of Prisons.* Fourth Report, Session 1986–1987. London: HMSO.

Home Affairs Committee. 1996. *The Management of the Prison Service (Public and Private).* Volume 1, Second Report, Session 1996–1997. London: HMSO.

Hued, D. 1987. "Statement to the House of Commons." *Hansard,* 16 July 1987, Col. 1303.

James, A.L., A.K. Bottomley, A. Liebling, and E. Clare. 1997. *Privatizing Prisons: Rhetoric and Reality.* London: Sage.

Jenkins, P. 1987. *Mrs Thatcher's Revolution: The Ending of the Socialist Era.* London: Pan Books.

Jones, T., T. Newburn, and D.J. Smith. 1994. *Democracy and Policing.* London: Policy Studies Institute.

Jones, T. and T. Newburn. 2002a. "Learning from Uncle Sam? Understanding US Influences over UK Crime Control Policy." *Governance* 15: 97–199.

Jones, T. and T. Newburn. 2002b. "Policy Convergence and Crime Control in the USA and UK: Streams of Influence and Levels of Impact." *Criminal Justice* 2: 173–203.

Jones, T. and T. Newburn. 2002c. "The Transformation of Policing? Understanding Current Trends in Policing Systems." *British Journal of Criminology* 42: 129–46.

Karstedt, S. 2002. "Durkheim, Tarde and Beyond: The Global Travel of Crime Policies." *Criminal Justice* 2: 111–24.

Kent, D. 2001. "A New Prison for Peterborough." *Public Service Review* (Winter): 190–91.

Kiekbusch, R.G. 2001. "Jail Privatization: The Next Frontier." Pp. 133–68 in *Privatization in Criminal Justice: Past, Present and Future*, edited by D. Schichor and M.J. Gilbert. Cincinnati: Anderson Publishing.

Kingdon, J. 1995. *Agendas, Alternatives and Public Policies*. 2nd ed. New York: Harper Collins.

Lapidvo, D. 2001. "The Rise of America's Prison-Industrial Complex." *New Left Review* 7 (January/February): 109–23.

Lilly, J.R. and P. Knepper. 1992. "An International Perspective on the Privatization of Corrections." *Howard Journal* 31: 174–91.

McConville, S. 1981. *A History of English Prison Administration: Volume 1, 1760–1877*. London: Routledge and Kegan Paul.

McConville, S. and J. Williams. 1985. *Crime and Punishment: A Radical Rethink*. London: Tawney Society.

McDonald, D. (Ed.). 1990. *Private Prisons and the Public Interest*. New Brunswick, NJ: Rutgers University Press.

McDonald, D. 1994. "Public Imprisonment by Private Means." *British Journal of Criminology* 34 (Special Issue): 29–48.

McDonald, D., R. Fournier, M. Russell-Einhourn, and S. Crawford. 1998. *Private Prisons in the United States: An Assessment of Current Practice*. Cambridge, MA: Abt Associates Inc.

Mattera, P. and M. Khan. 2001. *Jail Breaks: Economic Development Subsidies Given to Private Prisons*. Washington, DC: Good Jobs First.

Mauer, M. 1999. *Race to Incarcerate*. New York: The New Press.

Mellor, D. 2002. [Personal Interview.]

Melossi, D. 2004. "The Cultural Embeddedness of Social Control: Reflections on the Comparison of Italian and North-American Cultures Concerning Punishment." Pp. 80–103 in *Criminal Justice and Political Cultures*, edited by T. Newbam and R. Sparks. Cullompton: Willan.

Nathan, S. 1996. *Prison Privatization Report International, No. 1*. London: Prison Reform Trust.

Nellis, M. 2000. "Law and Order: The Electronic Monitoring of Offenders." Pp. 98–117 in *Policy Transfer and British Social Policy*, edited by D. Dolowitz. Buckingham: Open University Press.

Newburn, T. and R. Sparks. (Eds.). 2004. *Criminal Justice and Political Cultures: National and International Dimensions of Crime Control*. Cullompton: Willan.

Newburn, T. and R. Sparks. 2004. "Criminal Justice and Political Cultures." Pp. 1–15 in *Criminal Justice and Political Cultures*, edited by T. Newburn and R. Sparks. Cullompton: Willan.

Peterson, J. 1988. *Corrections and the Private Sector: A National Forum*. Washington, DC: National Institute of Justice.

Presidents Commission on Privatization. 1988. *Privatization: Toward More Effective Government*. Washington, DC: The White House.

Prison Reform Trust. 1994. *Privatization and Market Testing in the Prison Service*. London: Prison Reform Trust.

Rock, P. 1990. *Helping Victims of Crime: The Home Office and the Rise of Victim Support in England and Wales.* Oxford: Clarendon Press.

Rock, P. 1995. "The Opening Stages of Criminal Justice Policy-Making." *British Journal of Criminology* 35: 1–16.

Rutherford, A. 1990. "British Penal Policy and the Idea of Prison Privatization." Pp. 42–65 in *Private Prisons and the Public Interest*, edited by D. C. McDonald. New Brunswick: Rutgers University Press.

Rutherford, A. 2000. "An Elephant on the Doorstep: Criminal Policy without Crime in New Labour's Britain." Pp. 33–61 *Criminal Policy in Transition*, edited by P. Green and A. Rutherford. Oxford: Hart.

Ryan, M. 1996. "Private Prisons: Contexts, Performance and Issues." *European Journal on Criminal Policy and Research* 4: 92–107.

Ryan, M. 1999. "Penal Policy-Making Towards the Millennium: Elites and Populists; New Labour and the New Criminology." *International Journal of the Sociology of Law* 27: 1–22.

Ryan, M. and T. Waju. 1989. *Privatization and the Penal System: The American Experience and the Debate in Britain.* Milton Keynes: Open University Press.

Sarabi, B. 2000. *ALEC in the House: Corporate Bias in Criminal Justice Legislation.* Portland, OR: Western Prison Project.

Sarabi, B. and E. Bender. 2000. *The Prison Payoff: The Role of Politics and Private Prisons in the Incarceration Boom.* Portland, OR: Western Prison Project.

Schlosser, E. 1998. "The Prison-Industrial Complex." *Atlantic Monthly* (December): 51–77.

Sechrist, D. and D. Shichor. 1993. "Corrections Goes Public and Private in California." *Federal Probation* 57: 3–8.

Sentencing Project. 2002. *Prison Privatization and the Use of Incarceration.* Washington, DC: The Sentencing Project.

Shichor, D. 1995. *Punishment for Profit.* Thousand Oaks, CA: Sage.

Sparks, R. 2001. "Degrees of Estrangement: The Cultural Theory of Risk and Comparative Penology." *Theoretical Criminology* 5: 159–76.

Tonry, M. 1999. "Parochialism in US Sentencing Policy." *Crime and Delinquency* 45: 48–65.

Tonry, M. 2001. "Symbol, Substance and Severity in Western Penal Policies." *Punishment and Society* 3: 517–36.

United States Congress. House Committee of the Judiciary. 1986. *Privatization of Corrections: Hearings before the Subcommittee on Courts, Civil Liberties and the Administration of Justice of the Committee of the Judiciary.* 99th Cong., 1st sess., November 13, 1985 and March 18, 1986. Washington, DC: US Government Printing Office.

United States Department Of Justice. Bureau Of Justice Statistics. 2001. *Prisoners in 2000.* Washington, DC: US Department of Justice.

United States General Accounting Office. 1996. *Private and Public Prisons: Studies Comparing Operational Costs and/or Quality of Service.* Washington, DC: US General Accounting Office.

United States General Accounting Office. 1998. *Truth in Sentencing: Availability of Federal Grants Influenced Laws in Some States.* Washington, DC: US General Accounting Office.

Walker, D. 1984. "Prisons: Must Britain be a Slave to Tradition?" *The Times*, 24 (April 11): 12.

Wacquant, L. 1999. "How Penal Common Sense Comes to Europeans: Notes on the Transatlantic Diffusion of the Neoliberal Doxa." *European Societies* 1: 319–52.

Weiss, R. 1989. "Private Prisons and the State." Pp. 24–51 in *Privatizing Criminal Justice*, edited by P. Matthews. London: Sage.

Wheeler, J. 2001. [Personal Interview.] Former Chair of the Home Affairs Committee.

Windlesham, Lord. 1993. *Responses to Crime*. Vol. 2. Oxford: Oxford University Press.

Windlesham, Lord. 1998. *Politics, Punishment and Populism*. New York: Oxford University Press.

Wolman, H. 1992. "Understanding Cross-National Policy Transfers: The Case of Britain and the United States." *Governance* 5: 27–45.

Young, P. 1987. *The Prison Cell: The Start of a Better Approach to Prison Management* London: Adam Smith Institute.

Young, P. 2001. [Personal Interview.]

CHAPTER STUDY QUESTIONS

- Recent years have seen a growing focus upon perceived similarities in criminal justice and penal policies in the United States and the United Kingdom. Discuss the privatization of prisons as one example of penal-policy convergence between the United States and the United Kingdom that has occurred in recent decades.

- How can the implementation of a new criminal justice policy, through an attempt made at policy transfer from one country to another, be affected by the distinctive features of the political system and political culture of the country in which the new criminal justice policy is being implemented? Address this question in light of the findings of Jones's and Newburn's comparative study of policy transfer between the United States and United Kingdom regarding private prisons.

- According to Jones and Newburn, "there are clearly 'globalizing' elements in the story of private prisons." In light of your reading of the Jones and Newburn chapter, would you consider this to be a valid statement? Explain your answer.

- Imagine that you have been hired by the government of your country to examine the feasibility of introducing a new criminal justice policy that is modelled on a criminal justice policy already in effect in another country. In light of your reading of Jones and Newburn, what kinds of advice would you give your country's government concerning the problems and issues involved in attempting to transfer criminal justice policies from one country to another?

RELATED WEB LINKS

Corrections Corporation of America – "Prison Privatization at its Best"
http://www.correctionscorp.com/
> The official corporate website of the Corrections Corporation of America (CCA), described as a private corporation that "designs, builds and manages prisons, jails and detention facilities and provides inmate residential and prisoner transportation services in partnership with government."

The Geo Group Inc.
http://www.thegeogroupinc.com/
> The official corporate website of Geo Group Inc., described as a "world leader in privatized correctional and detention management," with operations in North America, Australia, South Africa, and the United Kingdom.

HM Prison Service – Contracted Out Prisons
http://www.hmprisonservice.gov.uk/prisoninformation/privateprison/
> This website provides information on privately-managed prisons currently operating in the United Kingdom.

Prison Policy Initiative
http://www.prisonpolicy.org/index.html
> An anti-prison advocacy organization concerned with documenting "the disastrous impact of mass incarceration on individuals, communities, and the national welfare" and with providing "accessible and innovative research to empower the public to participate in creating better criminal justice policy."

Chapter 18

PRISON POPULATIONS AS POLITICAL CONSTRUCTS: THE CASE OF FINLAND, HOLLAND, AND SWEDEN

HANNS VON HOFER

During the past 50 years, prison populations in Finland, Holland, and Sweden have followed different trends. The Finnish prison population has shown a marked decrease, in Sweden it has remained more or less stable, whilst the prison population in Holland has followed a U-shaped trend.

Keeping people in prison is costly—not only in financial but also in humanitarian terms. For these reasons, it is of great political and scientific interest to try to understand the driving forces that underlie both the size of prison populations and trends in this size over time. How is it possible that three Northern European countries such as Finland, Sweden, and Holland can have witnessed three principally different trends in prison population size?

Caveats

When reading this chapter, ... [keep] in mind that it stresses a dynamic and developmental perspective. On the basis of such a perspective, it is easy to discern important differences between the three countries. At the same time, it is interesting to note that the level of differences at the end of the period examined are rather small. In fact, in 1995, the prison population rates were very similar across the three countries—indicating that there might be some kind of an adaptation process at work (the mysterious "regression to the mean"?) somehow pulling prison populations towards some kind of "standard" (see Figure 1).

The time horizon is also significant for potential explanations. One reasonably sound hypothesis is that the longer the time perspective, the more clearly will structural factors, common to the three countries, appear to constitute a crucial driving force behind the changes in prison populations. The shorter the period, the greater will be the emphasis on systemic factors such as crime rates, sentencing practices, and so forth. Thus, prison data dating back to the early 19th century show very high prison rates in all three countries during the first half of the 19th century (Christie 1968; Junger-Tas 2001: 181 citing van Ruller and Beijers 1995). Since then, prison populations have decreased considerably.

The main focus of this paper is directed at a middle-range time frame covering approximately 30–40 years.

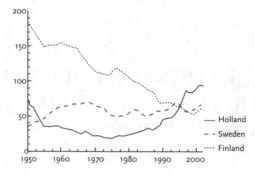

Figure 1. Daily prison populations in Finland, Holland, and Sweden, 1950–2002. Per 100,000 population.

Previous research and hypotheses

In line with the main body of existing research in this area (cf. Kuhn 2003), trends[1] in the daily prison populations of Finland, Holland, and Sweden do not mirror the trends followed by registered criminality in these countries. In all three countries, officially registered offences (e.g., violence, theft, drug, and traffic offences) have increased significantly over the past 50 years (von Hofer 1997; Westfelt 2001, Huls et al. n.d.) (see Table 1). According to data from victim surveys (both national and international, dating back to the 1980s), this increase had slowed down or may even have levelled off completely in all three countries by the end of the period examined (van Kesteren et al. 2000; National Research Institute of Legal Policy 2002; Westfelt 2001; Wittebrood and Junger 2002). Nor do factors such as economic development, unemployment or social marginalisation appear to provide particularly good uniform explanations for the long-term decrease in Finland, the stability in Sweden and the U-shaped trend witnessed in Holland.

Table 1. Reported offences in Finland, Holland and Sweden, 1950–2000. Per 100,000 of the population.

	1950	1960	1970	1980	1990	2000
Homicide (completed)						
Finland	3	2	..	2	3	3
Holland	..	..	1	1	1	1
Sweden	1	1	1	2	1	1
Assault						
Finland	148	126	246	292	414	537
Holland	81	76	67	97	151	278
Sweden	105	116	229	297	475	663
Robbery						
Finland	5	7	21	39	53	50
Holland	..	..	..	30	80	117
Sweden	3	6	19	41	70	101
Theft						
Finland	507	700	1,359	2,280	3,648	4,217
Holland	459	650	1,368	3,427	5,552	5,403
Sweden	1,575	2,723	4,855	6,187	8,581	7,832

Sources: von Hofer (1997); Westfelt (2001); Council of Europe (1999).

This chapter therefore examines a third set of hypotheses.[2] Daily prison rates may be understood as a political construct, i.e., given a certain framework,[3] "prisoner rates are to a great degree a function of criminal justice and social policies that either encourage or discourage the use of incarceration" (Aebi and Kuhn 2000: 66 with explicit references to Young and Brown 1993, Killias 1991, Morris 1991, and Tonry 1999).[4]At the superficial level, the mechanism behind this "construction" process is quite simple. Since prisons are financed through state budgets, governments and parliaments have to monitor[5]developments in prison rates in order to allocate what are deemed to be adequate resources. In theory, this monitoring process provides a continuous opportunity for the regulation of prison populations. Whether or not such regulation takes place in practice, however, is an open question, and one that is very difficult to answer because it is always up to politicians whether they choose to act or to react or whether they choose to do nothing and simply allow things to ride.

In the following section, a short account is provided of *criminal justice* policies in Holland, Sweden, and Finland in order to illustrate that it is indeed feasible to treat daily prison populations as political constructs. The analyses are, first and foremost, restricted to criminal policy decisions at the surface level, for the most part leaving aside the deeper structures involved.

HOLLAND

The decrease in the Dutch prison population during the 1950s and the 1960s has been described in detail by von Hofer (1975) and analysed by Downes (1982, 1988, 1998; see also Franke 1990; Downes 1990). Downes concluded his analysis by stating that,

> In sum, three phases in post-war sentencing trends in the Netherlands can be discerned. In the first, ranging from the early 1950s to the mid-1960s, the impact of a rehabilitative anti-penal philosophy seems crucial in explaining the trend towards shorter sentences. In the second, from roughly the mid-1960s until the mid-1970s, constraints of the capacity of the criminal justice system as a whole [...], assume an increasing importance in enabling the judiciary to effect a continuation of these trends. In the third period, from the late 1970s to date, the period of shortening sentences has ended, and pressure to expand the capacity of the system is working through the political processes. (Downes 1982: 355)

Indeed, in 1972, prison capacity had been decreased as part of a general restructuring of the Dutch system. This drop in capacity coincided with a growing need for more inmate places, however. The 1972 decision resulted in a serious shortage of prison cells, and persons sentenced to short terms in prison were at times collectively reprieved at the same time as it took longer and longer to put short prison sentences into effect (Haen Marshall 1988; Baerveldt and Bunkers 1996).

It was not until February 1981 that a working group was appointed (Capacity Problems in the Prison Service), which one year later proposed introducing permanent increases to prison capacity (SCP 1983). In 1983, a large majority in the second chamber of the Dutch parliament demanded that the coalition government—comprised of Christian Democrats and Liberals—produce a plan for the maintenance of law and order. The resolution motivated this demand by reference to 1) increasing levels of concern about rising crime within the population at large, 2) the risk that the public might lose confidence in the government and its role as guarantor of private and public interests, and 3) fears of an ongoing undermining of citizens' perceptions of norms and social control (Ministerie van Justitie 1985). The so-called "Roethof-Committee" was appointed (cf. Tak 2001), and the decisive step towards an increase in prison numbers was then taken in 1985 in the Justice Ministry's policy statement entitled *Society and Crime. A Policy Plan for The Netherlands*, which was in turn based on preliminary proposals put forward by the Roethof-Committee (see Fogure 2).

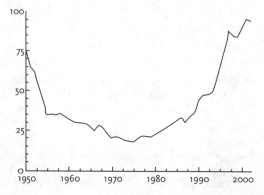

Figure 2. Daily prison population in Holland, 1950–2002. Yearly average. Per 100,000 population. (Preliminary data for 2001–2002)

The policy statement reported that crime in Holland had increased very substantially, and particularly organised crime that was deemed to lie behind much of the drug-related offending in the form of property crime and violent offences. The rise in crime and reduced levels of resources within the justice system were perceived as having led to a dramatic decline in efficiency within the justice system, which had in turn undermined the general credibility and preventive function of the penal system. Profound changes would therefore be required. A bi-level strategy was proposed. The control of petty crime would be transferred to the management of the local community, whilst the combat of serious crime would be pursued through intensified criminal justice measures by means of increasing the risk of discovery, more prosecutions and harsher sanctions. As a consequence, proposals were also put forward for a far-reaching program to extend existing prisons and to construct new ones.

The Minister of Justice was

> forced to conclude that the criminal justice system is no longer able, with its present resources, to maintain a minimum standard of law-enforcement which is essential in a state based on the rule of law. The gap between the number of infringements of standards embodied in the criminal law and the number of real responses to them by the criminal justice authorities had become unacceptably wide.
>
> In the present situation, not only was it impossible to secure the objectives of deterrence and standard-reinforcement to an adequate degree, it was even

feared that the ever-present tendency of citizens to take the law into their own hands can no longer be satisfactorily kept in check. [...] Order must be restored in the affairs of criminal justice [...]. (Ministerie van Justitie 1985: 20)

The plans for expansion and to increase prison service resources were put into effect and reliance on this strategy was re-confirmed in a renewed policy plan in 1990. The plan stated dryly that "Despite the efforts made by the authorities to tackle the causes of the increase in the prison population [...], it will be necessary to make further increases in capacity [...]" (Netherlands Ministry of Justice 1990: 70–71). In all, between 1985 and 2000, the penitentiary capacity increased from 5,900 places to 15,700 (Tak 2003: 123) and the expenditures rose at an even faster pace (CBS 1996: 13; DJI 2001:11, 13). Dutch commentators have reasonably drawn the conclusion that the expansion in prison places led to a *structural* increase in the prison population in Holland, which is very likely to endure for some considerable time to come (van Kalmthout and Tak 2001). Not even a further increase seems to be out of the question (Justitie 2002a).

The underlying reasons

What, then, might be the underlying reasons for this shift in strategy in an apparently liberal country, such as Holland, with a record of hostility toward the use of prisons? Within the space of approximately ten years—between around 1975 to 1985—Holland witnessed a fundamental shift in crime policy strategy, from decarceration to incarceration. What factors might have served to condition such a shift? The following possible scenario of how politicians understood the situation and reacted to it may be inferred from the available Dutch literature.

The 1985 policy document was published towards the end of a period, at the beginning of the 1980s, during which Holland had experienced a deep economic crisis (after the second oil shock in 1979). Even prior to this point, however, the traditional foundations of Dutch society were perceived to have become subject to a severe stress, something which had been further intensified during the mid-1970s as a result of immigration (Junger-Tas 1997; de Haan 1997) and the establishment of the drug problem (Leuw 1991; Korf 1995). The steep rise in crime levels (according to official police statistics) that was also witnessed during this period came then to be associated with an all-encompassing process of secularisation and with the crumbling of the so-called "pillars,"[6] together with a growing material surplus and the shift from tolerance to permissiveness witnessed during the 1960s and 1970s (de Haan 1997).

The justice system was considered unable to meet the growing demands for increased control as a result of its poorly dimensioned resources and the diffuse nature of the objectives that criminal justice interventions were intended to achieve. The likelihood of sanctioning was perceived to be dropping rapidly in line with the falling risk of discovery, as was the likelihood that those penalties that *were* imposed would actually be put into effect. This last factor in particular created public indignation and "ill will" in relation to the justice system. "It hardly needs to be said that failing to place remand prisoners in custody constitutes a disturbing breach of a fundamental judicial principle, namely that rulings issued by judges must also be put into effect" (Ministerie van Justitie 1985: 16).[7]

As distinct from the 1960s and 1970s, at which time crime policy issues were not a major focus for the interest of the press and politicians (Johnson and Jeijder 1983) and "tolerance from above" could be practiced more or less unhindered by the functionaries of the justice system (Christie 2000: 55), law and order had now become a "hot" political question (Beki et al. 1999: 403). Both politicians and the mass media[8] came to place an increasingly strong emphasis on effective crime control. Here the perception that the handling of narcotics was of central importance to the crime situation played a key role (Haen Marshall et al. 1990; cf. Martineau and Gomart 2001): drug use, which was visible everywhere, had given rise to petty crime and public order disturbances that the general public experienced as both irritating and disturbing. Junger-Tas (2001: 188) summarises:

> Others have observed that the Dutch criminal justice system and the Ministry of Justice have long been operated by a liberal and tolerant elite of experts, legislators, and high-ranking civil servants. [...] However, this situation has changed dramatically as the numbers of victims of petty offences increased. Moreover, crime became a highly topical and marketable subject in the media. [...] Pressures on the government, Parliament, and the judiciary for tougher laws and harsher penalties increased.

It is also worth noting that, as Frank (1990: 90) has pointed out, there has been no previous organised political opposition to the plans for expansion. An alliance of prison staff, inmates, inmate organisations, and pressure groups *against* the introduction of *multi-inmate cells* (as a means of creating space in prisons) in fact helped to pave the way for the next building program. "Partly due to this unanimous resistance, the Minister of Justice had to abandon his plan for group cells, although a large majority in Parliament would have supported him. Criticism of the building of new prisons was thus regarded as antisocial and accordingly died down."

In addition to these domestic trends there was also pressure from abroad (primarily from France, Sweden, the USA, and the then West Germany) to abandon liberal policies in relation to the drug issue (Downes 1988; Fiselier 1992; Baerveldt and Bunkers 1996). Up until the early 1980s, Dutch drug policy appeared to be moving even further from the control strategies of other Western countries. Holland promoted her own isolation by exaggerating her liberal view in the international arena (Haen Marshall et al. 1990).

In summary, the formally appropriate description of Dutch crime policy (Downes 1982) as not being the result of systematic political planning (but rather the consequence of a host of different circumstances) needs now to be replaced by the opposite description (cf. van Swaaningen and de Jonge 1995; Rutherford 1996; Downes 1998): crime policy is today to a large extent characterised by what the literature refers to as "planned justice" or "managerialism," i.e., "a bureaucratic quest for greater cost-effective forms of social regulation" (Cavadino and Dignan 1997: 222)—in relation to which an expanding body of criminologists, specializing in both planning and evaluation,[9] appears to play an important role. According to Rutherford (1996), the Netherlands experienced a loss of popularity of the socio-liberal model, with increases in the moralistic law-and-order rhetoric and actual policy reflecting planned justice. The role of the joint moral community in shaping criminal justice policy during the 1990s had become more precarious. The populist agenda, combined with the pressure of managerialism, served to dilute and perhaps even eliminate the limits that protected society from seeking more simplistic and authoritarian solutions to crime (Rutherford 1996).

SWEDEN

Against the backdrop of a rising prison population, the Swedish Prison Administration fore-casted in the early 1960s that Swedish inmate numbers would increase to 6,200 in 1967 (Sveriges Officiella Statistik 1964: 15), and a program of building new prisons was initiated in the mean-time. However, the forecast turned out to be an overestimate, the prison building program was checked, and prison population size did not reach the forecast figure until 30 years later in 1993/94. But why did the forecast increase fail to materialise?

During the 1960s and early 1970s, grass roots movements such as KRUM (cf. Mathiesen 1974) introduced a view of imprisonment as being an expensive, ineffective, and detrimental form of punishment, the use of which should be limited to as great an extent as possible. This view also came to be accepted by the political establishment (both social democratic and cen-tre-right governments and parliament), by those responsible for the administration of justice (the judiciary and the prison administration) and by the media. This becomes very clear when trends in inmate numbers are examined over the last 30 years. Figure 3 shows that, since the mid-1970s, there has been an underlying pressure towards an increase in inmate numbers. This increase has been capped on several occasions, however, by means of focused legislative changes that have decreased the size of the prison population.

The fall in inmate numbers at the end of the 1960s and the beginning of the 1970s coincided with the widespread criticism of the prison sanction that characterised this period (Tham 2001a). The introduction of the rules for discounting time served on remand[10] further reduced the prison population at the beginning of 1974. The upward pressure on inmate numbers continued to increase however—particularly in connection with major police operations directed against the street-level drug trade during the years 1980 to 1982—and the next measure to regulate the size of the prison population came in the summer of 1983 with the introduction of release on parole after serving half the sentence for those sentenced to a prison term of between four months and two years.

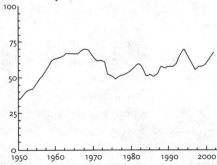

Figure 3. Sweden: Daily prison population, 1950–2002. Yearly average. Per 100,000 population.

The introduction of new remand regulations—as a result of a court ruling against Sweden in the European Court—increased the number of remand inmates and thus also the size of the prison population. At the end of the 1980s, however, contractual treatment was introduced partly as an alternative to a short prison sentence. The use of the prison sanction for drunk-driving offences became restricted in 1990. It was not until the short period of centre-right government (1991–1994) that certain more expansionist decisions were taken (such as the return to release on parole after two-thirds of the sentence had been served), and the inmate population was allowed to grow past the 5,000 mark. New steps were taken to regulate inmate numbers at the end of the period however, *inter alia*, through the introduction of supervision by means of electronic monitoring in 1994 and the extended use of community service in 1999.

At the general level, Swedish prison policy over the past 30 years may be characterised as having constituted a relatively successful attempt at keeping increases in the prison population under control in line with crime policy ambitions of the time to restrict the negative effects of prison sentencing.

Since the end of the 1990s, however, the trend has been such as to indicate that the inmate population will be settling permanently above the 6,000 mark. The principal reason for this prognosis is that, in 2002, the Prison Administration pronounced plans to expand prison capacity (with approximately 1,000 places) for the first time in a very long time. The plan had not been preceded by a public political debate of any kind but should rather be regarded as an administrative measure aimed at reducing the level of crowding in prisons. In exactly the same way as in Holland, the temporary doubling of the inmates-to-cell ratio has led to protests from both prison service staff and from inmates. The lack of any public political discussion on the dimensioning of the prison system is in turn a result of the fact that—unlike the situation at the end of the 1960s—the use of prison sanctions *per se* is no longer in question as a crime policy measure. On the contrary, the demand for more and longer prison sentences has once again become a common feature of the crime policy debate, and, during the period between 1991 and 2001, the sentencing scale has been tightened in relation to a number of different offences (Andersson et al. 2001). In addition, the government appointed a commission of inquiry in 2002 with the task of producing a proposal for new prison and probation service legislation, prioritising "the work of preventing re-offending" and "the requirement of the secure and credible execution of sentences" (Dir 2002: 90; 96). The direction of this focus is very reminiscent of what had already happened in Holland. There, a new Prisons Act had been in force since 1999, which toned down the importance of rehabilitation as a goal connected to the execution of sentences, focusing instead on the importance of security and sobriety (Pakes 2000; Tak 2001; Tak 2003).

The renewed popularity of the prison sanction in both Holland[11] and Sweden[12] has also manifested itself in various survey studies.[13] The well-known *International Crime Victims Survey* (ICVS) (van Kesteren et al. 2000) asked respondents to choose which of a variety of sanctions they felt to be most suitable for a 21-year-old male being found guilty of his second burglary, this time stealing a colour television set in the process. Given the choice between fines, a prison sentence, community service, a suspended sentence, or any other sentence, the answers were distributed in the following way (see Table 2).

Whilst the number reporting a preference for a prison term is generally high in the English speaking countries (cf. Kuhn 1993), Sweden and Holland differ significantly at the end of the period from the rest of the non-English speaking countries, and Sweden also differs significantly from both Denmark and Finland.

FINLAND

The stunning decrease in the Finnish prison population has been analysed in detail by Törnudd (1993) and Lappi-Seppälä (1998, 2000). Only a short summary of the trend is therefore required here. This summary focuses on the different techniques employed to bring about the decrease.

Technically, the decrease was brought about by two groups of measures. On the one hand, admissions were reduced through the depenalisation of certain offence types (such as drunken driving and theft), the increased use of suspended prison sentences, and the introduction of community service as an alternative to unconditional imprisonment (1991). On the other hand, the size of the inmate population was reduced through the use of shorter prison sentences and the expanded use of the parole system. The combined effect of all these measures has been the continuous decrease of the size of the inmate population, whilst the average length of stay in prison seems to have varied very little since the middle of the 1950s (see Figure 4).

Table 2. Sentencing preferences for a young recidivist burglar, percentage in favour of a prison sentence.

	1989	1992	1996	2000
Austria	..	..	10	..
Belgium	26	19	..	21
Denmark	..	..	..	20
England & Wales	38	37	49	51
Finland	15	14	18	19
France	13	..	11	12
Germany (West)	13	..	..	..
Italy	..	22	..	..
Netherlands	26	26	31	37
Northern Ireland	45	..	49	54
Norway	14	..	..	..
Poland	..	31	17	21
Portugal	..	..	..	26
Scotland	39	..	48	52
Spain	27	..	..	..
Catalonia	..	..	..	7
Sweden	9	..	9	..
All countries	24	25	26	29

Source: van Kesteren et al., 2000: Table 27.

Equally important is Lappi-Seppälä's assertion that "the decrease in the Finnish prison population has been the result of a conscious, long-term and systematic criminal policy." This has been due to 1) the fact that Finnish criminal policy has been exceptionally expert-oriented; 2) the existence of an "attitudinal readiness" among the judiciary—particularly within the courts of first instance; 3) an absence of political opposition to reform proposals prepared by the Ministry of Justice; and 4) the fact that, until the early 1990s, at least, the Finnish media retained a "fairly sober and reasonable attitude towards issues of criminal policy" (Lappi-Seppälä 2000: 37–38).

Kekkonen (2003; see also Christie 1968: 171) goes a step further by claiming that the decrease in the Finnish prison population should be understood in the light of the Finnish civil war, which broke out in late January 1918 and is counted among the bloodiest internal conflicts to have taken place in Europe during the 20th century. In its aftermath, Finnish control policy became harsher and, by comparison with the other Nordic countries, it contained fewer alternatives of either an ideological or legislative character. This situation did not begin to change until the 1960s when Finnish society became subject to major structural changes which would in turn pave the way for the experts' reform endeavours.

In light of the Dutch and the Swedish case histories described above, one might point to two additional circumstances that may have facilitated the reduction in the large numbers of Finnish prison inmates: the one relates to the question of immigrants and the other to the question of narcotics.[14] Due to its geopolitical location, Finland has been insulated from these two major sources of political concern. In both Holland and Sweden, the way the issues of immigrants and drugs have been dealt with politically has played an important role and has been among the driving forces behind increases in prison admissions and changes in the daily routines within the prison system. In both countries, immigration has served as a catalyst for real or constructed popular fears, and foreigners constitute a substantial proportion of the prison populations in both Sweden and Holland. By contrast, Finland experienced a net emigration during the 1960s and 1970s;[15] and "drugs have been overpowered by the extremely strong position of alcohol in Finnish culture. Due to this, drug issues have long remained a strange element for Finns" (Hakkarainen et al. 1996: 16).

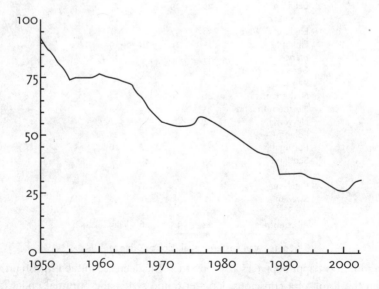

Figure 4. Finland: Daily Prison Population, 1950–2002. Yearly average. Per 100,000 population.

CONCLUSION

Much of the research on prison populations and crime policies in general is of an *ad hoc* and rather speculative nature because we lack good theories or at least good empirical generalisations (Tonry 2001: 531). Even the explanations put forward here suffer from this weakness. This is easily understood when looking at the prison populations in the neighbouring countries of Denmark and Norway. Both countries define drug use and immigration as major political problems and, in addition, prominent extreme right-wing populist parties (Rydgren 2002)—taking law-and-order to market—have had representatives in parliament for many years. Nevertheless, prison populations show different paths over the past 50 years, with a decrease in Denmark and an increase in Norway (see Figure 5).[16]

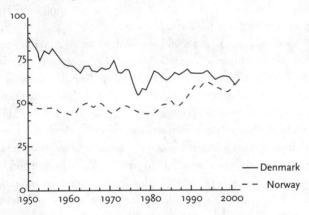

Figure 5. Daily prison population in Denmark (1950–2002) and Norway (1950–2001). Yearly average. Per 100,000 population.

In summary, the case histories presented in this paper show very different patterns. One common trait appears to be discernible, though. The increase in Holland, the decrease in Finland, and the long stability in Sweden were made possible because no strong political opposition challenged the course of events. Thus, political power and counter-power and the absence of counter-power seem to play an important role in relation to the size of prison populations. For this reason, it will be most interesting to follow what does or does not happen in these countries over the coming years. For Holland, the question is whether the prison population is allowed to continue its increase. In October 2002, the Minister of Justice announced that the Dutch prison population could increase by another 5,000 places as a consequence of a newly adopted Security Plan (Justitie 2002a, 2002b). For Finland, the question arises whether prison figures will be kept low despite the prospects of increasing drug use and increasing immigration due to Finland's ongoing integration into the European Union. For Sweden, finally, the question is whether some form of political opposition will emerge and gain sufficient strength to pull the country's prison population back to the "standard" Nordic level.

NOTES

[1] It should be noted that this ...[chapter] focuses on a trend-based perspective and not on annual fluctuations. Research into annual and short-term fluctuations has produced results that differ in some respects from those presented here (see, e.g., Sutton 2003).

[2] This perspective has, nevertheless, been contested by eminent writers such as Bauman (1998: 115–116).

[3] For example, macroeconomic conditions (Rusche and Kirchheimer 1968); degree of inequality (Wilkens and Pease 1987); public sensibilities (Garland 1990); market state versus welfare state (Weiss 1998); the nation-specific institutionalisation of knowledge production and decision making (Savelsberg 1999); national and cultural idiosyncrasies (Tonry 2001).

[4] One should also mention Christie (1993: 13) who wrote: "The size of the prison population is a result of decisions. We are free to choose. It is only when we are not aware of this freedom that the economic material conditions are given free rein."

[5] See, for instance, Moolenaar et al. (2002) and Direktoratet for Kriminalforsorgen (2002).

[6] This concept attempts to summarise a number of essential characteristics of the Dutch social structure. The following description is to be found in the *Encyclopaedia Suecia*: "Political life in the Netherlands, like social life in general, has for a long time been characterised by the *Verzuiling*-system. The designation is based on the Dutch *zuil* or 'pillar' and proceeds from the way in which society has been strictly divided on the basis of religious and socio-political affiliation, which has affected people's social and political lives and determined for example the clubs and societies to which people have belonged and the way they have voted. These divisions have become institutionalised, and have given rise to very powerful interest groups. These have been regarded as the 'pillars' on which Dutch society rests, and the interaction and compromises taking place between them have determined the political life of the Netherlands. [...] the *Verzuiling*-system has been broken down over recent decades [...]" (Johansson 1994: 87 [my translation]; see also Therborn 1989).

[7] This problem does not seem to have been resolved, however. The number of remand detainees released as a result of lack of prison space is reported to have varied between 1,200 and 5,300 during the period 1987–1995 (CBS 1996, Table 3.10) and the criticisms remain (for details, see Tak and van Kalmtouth 2001: 162).

[8] On the media's importance for prison growth, see Mathiesen (1996).

[9] See, for example, van Tulder's (2000) paper on "Crimes and the need for sanction capacity in the Netherlands."

[10] Namely, time served on remand prior to a court hearing is automatically deducted from the prison term to which the court then sentences the individual.

[11] See also SCP (1995: 424–427) and Downes (1998).

[12] See, e.g., Jareborg (1995) and Tham (1995, 2001a).

[13] Correlational analyses used to indicate that there is a positive relationship between national incarceration rates and the proportion of the population that chose prison (Kuhn 1993: Besserer 2002). It remains, however, an open question whether these changes should be regarded as having been triggered from "above" and/or from "below" (cf. Beckett 1997, Tham 2001b).

[14] The importance of narcotics and immigrant policies for prison populations has been shown, for example, by Christie (2000: 69–74) and Wacquant (2001). See also Weiss (1998).

[15] Lenke (1983) has maintained that a group of Finnish emigrants who came to Sweden in the 1970s included persons with serious social problems. These people came to Sweden because the opportunities to "make it" were greater in Sweden than in Finland, even for people with serious problems. In this connection, Lenke refers to "social political refugees."

[16] The increase in Norway between 1987 and 1994 (from 48 to 62 prisoners per 100,000 of the population) is largely due to intensified drug controls (Christie 2000: 71–72).

REFERENCES

Aebi, M.F. and A. Kuhn. 2000. "Influences on the Prisoner Rate: Number of Entries into Prison, Length of Sentences and Crime Rate." *European Journal on Criminal Policy and Research* 8: 65–75.

Andersson, U., H. Örnemark, S. Jönsson, and P.O. Träskman. 2001. "Svensk krönika." [Swedish chronicle] *Nordisk Tidsskrift for Kriminalvidenskab* 88: 51–65.

Baervelt, C. and H. Bunkers. 1996. "Limits To Growth: The Case of Dutch Prison Capacity." *Crime, Law, and Social Change* 25: 153–72.

Bauman, Z. 1998. *Globalization: The Human Consequences*. Cambridge: Polity Press.

Beckett, K. 1997. *Making Crime Pay: Law and Order in Contemporary America*. Oxford: Oxford University Press.

Beki, C., K. Zeelenberg, and K. van Montfort. 1999. "An Analysis of the Crime Rate in The Netherlands 1950–1993." *British Journal of Criminology* 39: 401–15.

Besserer, S. 2002. "Attitudes Toward Sentencing in Nine Industrialized Countries." Pp. 391–409 in *Crime Victimization in Comparative Perspective: Results from the International Crime Victims Survey, 1989–2000*, edited by P. Nieuwbeerta. Den Haag: Boom Juridische uitgevers.

Cavadino, M. and J. Dignan. 1997. *The Penal System*. 2nd ed. London: Sage.

CBS. 1996. *Gevangenisstatistiek 1995*. [Prison Statistics 1995] Voorburg/Heerlen: Centraal Bureau voor de Statistiek.

Christie, N. 1968. "Changes in Penal Values." *Scandinavian Studies in Criminology* 2: 161–72.

Christie, N. 1993. *Crime Control as Industry: Towards Gulags, Western Style*. London: Routledge.

Christie, N. 2000. *Crime Control as Industry: Towards Gulags, Western Style*. 3rd ed. London: Routledge.

Council of Europe. 1999. *European Sourcebook of Crime and Criminal Justice Statistics*. Strasbourg: Council of Europe.

National Research Institute of Legal Policy. 2002. *Crime in Finland 2001: Summary*. Publication number 190. Helsinki: The National Research Institute of Legal Policy. http://www.op-tula.om.fi/15540.htm

Dir. 2002. *En ny kriminalvårdslag*. [A new prison and probation service legislation.] Stockholm: Justitiedepartementet.

Direktoratet for Kriminalforsorgen. 2002. Kriminalforsorgens belægsprognose for 2003. [Projections of the prison population in 2003.] October 2002. http://www.kriminalforsorgen.dk/

DJI. 2001. *Jaarverslag 2000: Samenverken aan en visie.* [Co-operation for a vision.] Den Haag: Dienst Justitiële Inrichtingen.

Downes, D. 1982. "The Origins and Consequences of Dutch Penal Policy Since 1945." *British Journal of Criminology* 22: 325–62.

Downes, D. 1988. *Contrasts in Tolerance: Post-war Penal Policy in The Netherlands and England and Wales.* Oxford: Clarendon Press.

Downes, D. 1990. "Response to Herman Franke." *British Journal of Criminology* 30: 94–96.

Downes, D. 1998. "The Buckling of the Shields: Dutch Penal Policy 1985–1995." Pp. 143–74 in *Comparing Prison Systems. Toward a Comparative and International Penology,* edited by R.P. Weis and N. South. Amsterdam: Gordon and Breach Publishers.

Fiselier, J.P.S. 1992. "A Test of the Stability of Punishment Hypothesis: The Dutch Case." *Journal of Quantitative Criminology* 8: 133–51.

Franke, H. 1990. "Dutch Tolerance: Facts and Fables." *British Journal of Criminology* 30: 81–93.

Garland, D. 1990. *Punishment and Modern Society: A Study in Social Theory.* Oxford: Oxford University Press.

de Haan, W. 1997. "Minorities, Crime and Criminal Justice in the Netherlands." Pp. 198–223 in *Minorities, Migrants, and Crime: Diversity and Similarity across Europe and the United States,* edited by I. Haen Marshall. Thousand Oaks: Sage.

Haen Marshall, I. 1988. "Trends in Crime Rates, Certainty of Punishment and Severity of Punishment in the Netherlands." *Criminal Justice Review* 1: 21–52.

Haen Marshall, I., O. Anjewierden, and H. van Attevald. 1990. "Toward an 'Americanization' of Dutch Drug Policy?" *Justice Quarterly* 7: 391–420.

Hakkarainen P., L. Laursen, and C. Tigerstedt. (Eds.). 1997. *Discussing Drugs and Control Policy: Comparative Studies on Four Nordic Countries.* NAD Publication No. 31. Helsinki: Nordic Council for Alcohol and Drug Research.

von Hofer, H. 1975. "Dutch Prison Population." Pp. 104–50 in *Rapport fra 17:e Nordiska Forskarseminariet, Norefjell Norge, 1975.* Stockholm: Nordiska Samarbetsrådet för Kriminologi. [Scandinavian Research Council for Criminology.]

von Hofer, H. (Ed.). 1997. *Nordic Criminal Statistics 1950–1995.* Report 1997: 2. Stockholm: Stockholm University Department of Criminology.

Huls F.W.M., M.M. Schreuders, M.H. Ter Horst-van Breukelen, and F.P. van Tulder. (Eds.). 2001. *Criminaliteit en rechtshandhaving 2000: Ontwikkelingen en samenhangen.* [Criminality and Criminal Justice 2000: Trends and Contexts.] Onderzoek en beleid 189. Den Haag: Wetenschappelijk Onderzoek- en Documentatiecentrum (WODC).

Jareborg, N. 1995. "What Kind of Criminal Law Do We Want? On Defensive and Offensive Criminal Law Policy." Pp. 17–36 in *Beware of Punishment: On the Utility and Futility of Criminal Law,* edited by A. Snare. Scandinavian Studies in Criminology 14. Norway: Pax Forlag.

Johansson, R. 1994. "Nederländerna, Staatsskick och politik." [The Netherlands, Constitution and politics.] P. 87 in the *Nationalencyklopedin, Vol. 14.* Höganäs: Bokförlaget Bra Böcker.

Johnson, E.H. and A. Heider. 1983. "The Dutch De-emphasize Imprisonment: Sociocultural and Structural Explanations." *International Journal of Comparative and Applied Criminal Justice* 7: 3–19.

Junger-Tas, J. 1997. "Ethnic Minorities and Criminal Justice in the Netherlands." Pp. 257–310 in *Ethnicity, Crime and Immigration. Comparative and Cross-National Perspectives*. Vol. 21 *Crime and Justice*, edited by M. Tonry. Chicago: Chicago University Press.

Junger-Tas, J. 2001. "Dutch Penal Policies Changing Direction." Pp. 179–89 in *Penal Reform in Overcrowded Times*, edited by M. Tonry. Oxford: Oxford University Press.

Justitie. 2002a. "Donner: Increase of Detention Capacity by Maximum of 5000 Places is Possible." *Press Releases* (October 17). http://english.justitie.nl/

Justitie. 2002b. "Cabinet: Netherlands Safer in Coming Years." *Press Releases* (October 17). http://english.justitie.nl/

van Kalmthout, A.M. and P.J.P. Tak. 2001. "Prison Population Growing Faster in the Netherlands than in the United States." Pp. 161–168 in *Penal Reform in Overcrowded Times*, edited by M. Tonry. Oxford: Oxford University Press.

Kekkonen, J. 2003. "From Rule of Law to Law and Order: A Century of Violence, Control, and Discipline." Unpublished paper. University of Helsinki.

van Kesteren, J., P. Mayhew, and P. Nieuwbeerta. 2000. *Criminal Victimization in Seventeen Industrialized Countries: Key Findings from the 2000 International Crime Victims Survey*. Onderzoek en beleid 187. The Hague: WODC/ NSCR.

Killias, M. 1991. *Précis de criminologie*. Bern: Staempfli.

Korf, D.J. 1995. Dutch Treat: Formal Control and Illicit Drug Use in The Netherlands. Amsterdam: Thesis Publishers.

Kuhn, A. 1993. "Attitudes Towards Punishment." Pp. 271–288 in *Understanding Crime Experiences of Crime and Crime Control*, edited by A. Alvazzi del Frate, U. Zvekic, and J.J.M. van Dijk. Publication No. 49. Rome: UNICRI.

Kuhn, A. 2003. "Prison Population Trends in Western Europe." *Criminology in Europe* 2: 12–16.

Lappi-Seppälä, T. 1998. *Regulating the Prison Population: Experiences from a Long-Term Policy in Finland*. Research Communications 38. Helsinki: National Research Institute of Legal Policy.

Lappi-Seppälä, T. 2000. "The Fall of the Finnish Prison Population." *Journal of Scandinavian Studies in Criminology and Crime Prevention* 1: 27–40.

Lenke, L. 1983. De *"socialpolitiska flyktingarna"—Ett fall av selektiv migration.*[The "socio-political refugees"—A case of selective migration.] Pp. 215–24 in *Utlänningarna och brottsligheten*. Brottsförebyggande rådet, Rapport 1983: 4, edited by U. Eiksson and H. Tham. Stockholm: Liber.

Leuw, E. 1991. "Drugs and Drug Policy in the Netherlands." Pp. 229–76 in *Crime and Justice, Volume 14: An Annual Review of Research*, edited by M. Tonry. Chicago: University of Chicago Press.

Martineau, H and E. Gomart. 2001. "Drug-Related Nuisances: How the Dutch Handle the Problem." *Penal Issues* 14 (1). http://www.cesdip.org/Questions-Penales-Archives-de-sa.html

Mathiesen, T. 1974. *The Politics of Abolition: Essays in Political Action Theory.* Scandinavian Studies in Criminology 4. Oslo: Universitetsforlaget.

Mathiesen, T. 1996. "Driving Forces Behind Prison Growth: The Mass Media." *Nordisk Tidsskrift for Kriminalvidenskab* 83: 133–43.

Ministerie van Justitie. 1985. *Society and Crime. A Policy Plan for The Netherlands.* Schiedam: van Rossum.

Moolenaar, D.E.G., F.P. van Tulder, G.L.A.M. Huijbregts, and W. van der Heide. 2002. *Prognose van de sanctiecapaciteit tot en met 2006.* [Prognosis of the volume of sanctions up to 2006.] Onderzoek en beleid, nr. 196. Den Haag: Ministerie van Justitie, WODC.

Morris, N. 1991. "Deinstitutionalization of Correctional Measures." Pp. 339–350 in *Crime and Crime Control: Past, Present, and Future.* Seoul: Korean Institute of Criminology.

Netherlands Ministry of Justice. 1990. *Law in Motion: A Policy Plan for Justice in the Years Ahead.* The Hague: Information Department.

Pakes, F.J. 2000. "League Champion in the Mid Table: On the Major Changes in Dutch Prison Policy." *The Howard Journal* 39: 30–39.

Rusche, G. and O. Kirchheimer. 1968. *Punishment and Social Structure.* Reissued ed. New York: Russel and Russel.

Rutherford, A. 1996. *Transforming Criminal Policy.* Winchester: Waterside Press.

Rydgren, J. 2002. *Political Protest and Ethno-Nationalist Mobilization: The Case of the French Front National.* Stockholm Studies on Social Mechanism. Stockholm: Stockholm University Department of Sociology.

Savelsberg, J.J. 1999. "Knowledge, Domination and Criminal Punishment Revisited: Incorporating State Socialism." *Punishment and Society* 1: 45–70.

Sociaal en Cultureel Planbureau (SCP). 1983. *Social and Cultural Report 1982.* Rijswijk, Den Haag: SCP.

Sociaal en Cultureel Planbureau (SCP). 1995. *Social and Cultural Report 1994.* Rijswijk, Den Haag: SCP.

Sveriges Officiella Statistik. (1964). *Kriminalvården 1963.* [The Correctional System 1963.] Stockholm: Fångvårdsstyrelsen.

van Swaaningen, R. and G. de Jonge. 1995. "The Dutch Prison System and Penal Policy in the 1990s: From Humanitarian Paternalism to Penal Business Management." Pp. 24–45 in *Western European Penal Systems,* edited by V. Ruggiero, M. Ryan, and J. Sim. London: Sage.

Sutton, J.R. 2003. "The Political Economy of Imprisonment Among Affluent Western Democracies, 1960–1990." Unpublished paper. Santa Barbara: University of California.

Tak, P.J.P. 2001. "Sentencing and Punishment in the Netherlands." Pp. 156–161 in *Penal Reform in Overcrowded Times,* edited by M. Tonry. Oxford: Oxford University Press.

Tak, P.J.P. 2003. *The Dutch Criminal Justice System: Organization and Operation.* 2nd ed. Onderzoek en beleid 205. Den Haag: WODC/Justitie/Boom Juridische uitgevers. http://www.wodc.nl/Onderzoeken/Onderzoek_W00205.asp

Tham, H. 1995. "From Treatment to Just Deserts in a Changing Welfare State." Pp. 89–122 in *Beware of Punishment: On the Utility and Futility of Criminal Law.* Scandinavian Studies in Criminology 14, edited by A. Snare. Norway: Pax Forlag.

Tham, H. 2001a. "Law and Order as a Leftist Project? The Case of Sweden." *Punishment and Society* 3: 409–26.

Tham, H. 2001b. "Law and order—from below or from above?" Paper presented at the 1st Conference of the European Society of Criminology, Lausanne, September.

Therborn, G. 1989. " 'Pillarization' and 'Popular Movements': Two Variants of Welfare State Capitalism: the Netherlands and Sweden." Pp. 192–241 in *The Comparative History of Public Policy,* edited by F.G. Castles. Cambridge: Polity Press.

Tonry, M. 1999. "Why are U.S. Incarceration Rates so High?" *Overcrowded Times* 10: 8–16.

Tonry, M. 2001. "Symbol, Substance, and Severity in Western Penal Policies." *Punishment and Society* 3: 517–36.

Törnudd, P. 1993. *Fifteen Years of Decreasing Prisoner Rates in Finland.* Research Communication 8. Helsinki: National Research Institute of Legal Policy.

van Tulder, F. 2000. "Crime and the Need for Sanction Capacity in The Netherlands: Trends and Backgrounds." *European Journal on Criminal Policy and Research* 8: 91–106.

Wacquant, L. 1999. "'Suitable Enemies': Foreigners and Immigrants in the Prisons of Europe." *Punishment and Society* 1: 215–22.

Weiss, R.P. 1998. "Conclusion: Imprisonment at the Millennium 2000—Its Variety and Patterns Throughout the World." Pp. 427–81 in *Comparing Prison Systems: Toward a Comparative and International Penology,* edited by R.P. Weis and N. South. Amsterdam: Gordon and Breach Publishers.

Westfelt, L. 2001. *Brott och straff i Sverige och Europa: En studie i komparativ kriminologi.* [Crime and punishment in Sweden and Europe: A study in comparative criminology.] Avhandlingsserie Nr 5. Stockholm: Stockholms universitet, Kriminologiska institutionen.

Wilkens, L.T. and K. Pease. 1987. "Public Demand for Punishment." *International Journal of Sociology and Social Policy* 7: 16–29.

Wittebrood, K. and M. Junger. 2002. "Trends in Violent Crime: A Comparison Between Police Statistics and Victimization Surveys." *Social Indicators Research* 59: 153–73.

Young, W. and M. Brown. 1993. "Cross-National Comparisons of Imprisonment." *Crime and Justice* 17: 1–49.

CHAPTER STUDY QUESTIONS

- What does von Hofer mean by the statement that prison populations are "political constructs"?

- How specifically can the prison populations of Finland, Holland, and Sweden be shown to be the product of political choices made about the use of incarceration as a form of criminal punishment?

- Over the past 50 years, the prison population of Finland has decreased substantially. What are the reasons for the relatively dramatic decline in the prison population of Finland? In your view, can Finland's success in reducing prison populations be reproduced by other countries? Explain your answer.

- Why has the prison population of Holland increased substantially over the past 20 years while, over the same period, the prison population of Sweden has remained relatively stable? What is the likely direction of future prison population trends in these countries? Why?

RELATED WEB LINKS

International Centre for Prison Studies
http://www.kcl.ac.uk/depsta/rel/icps/about.html
> This is the homepage of an independent research centre concerned with undertaking projects and disseminating the findings of international research on prisons.

European Institute for Crime Prevention and Control, affiliated with the United Nations (HEUNI)
http://www.heuni.fi/
> The homepage of this research institute, which is concerned with promoting the international exchange of information on crime prevention and control among European countries, contains links to projects and publications on the prison systems of numerous European and other countries.

Scandinavian Research Council for Criminology
http://www.nsfk.org/
> This is the homepage of a research council dedicated to furthering criminological research in Scandinavian countries and advising Scandinavian governments on issues related to criminology. It provides links to numerous publications, reports, and databases relevant to crime and corrections in Scandinavian countries.

Prison and Probation Services in Finland
http://www.rikosseuraamus.fi/16019.htm
> This is the official English-language homepage of the government of Finland's "Criminal Sanctions Agency." It contains links to information on prison and probation services in Finland.

Chapter 19

DRUG POLICY DEVELOPMENTS WITHIN THE EUROPEAN UNION: THE DESTABILIZING EFFECTS OF DUTCH AND SWEDISH DRUG POLICIES

CAROLINE CHATWIN

Since the formalization of the EU, with the signing of the Maastricht Treaty in 1991, the problem of drug control has presented significant difficulties for policy makers. This problem of drug control can be said to be relatively similar in all member states of the EU. Regardless of actual official statistics and recorded numbers, it is a fact that, in all EU member states, certain drugs are illegal and yet are used and possessed by a number of people within each country. Each member state therefore has to deal with those who use and possess drugs as well as those who supply, cultivate, and/or traffic drugs. Issues such as dealing with drug-related deaths, curbing drug-related street level crime and organized crime networks, finding appropriate treatment for those addicted to drugs and, suppressing public nuisance and open drug scenes connected with drug taking face each EU member state to a greater or lesser extent. With regard to this problem, individual member states have developed their own, often significantly differing, national policies in which "prevalence of both cannabis and hard drug use bears little relationship to the type of policy in operation in any particular country" (Reuband 1995). More recently, the harmonization of drug-control policies has become increasingly important with a developing emphasis on international cooperation in the fight against drugs and particularly in an effort to curb large-scale drug trafficking crime organizations. However, in acknowledgement of the entrenched nature of many member states' national policies, the emphasis has remained on countries working together rather than having identical drug-control policies. Before 1995, the national drug policy of the Netherlands, with its tendencies towards liberalization and tolerance, was distinctive when compared with the drug policies of other member states. Originally highly criticized, policy measures adopted in the Netherlands were beginning to make an impression elsewhere within the EU, and a general shift towards a more pragmatic solution to the problems of drug control could be identified elsewhere. However, in 1995, Sweden entered the EU and brought a strictly repressive policy approach to drug control. Their national policy is severely prohibitive and has caused a backlash within the EU leading to a generally more punitive attitude towards the problem of drug control. There now exists a serious divide within the EU between the tolerant policies favoured by the Netherlands and the repressive policies followed in Sweden. In the face of this divide, the EU must find a middle road between prohibition and legalization if its centralized aims of cooperation and harmonization are to be met.

DUTCH DRUG POLICY

Dutch drug policy is based on normalization: drugs are seen as a normal problem affecting society in general rather than a problem facing the abnormal and therefore isolated individual user (Van Vliet 1990). In turn, drug addicts have always been regarded as patients in need of help rather than as criminals requiring punishment. These underlying conceptions have led to a national drug policy for the Netherlands generally regarded as being liberal and tolerant. The foundations for such a pragmatic policy can, to some extent, be traced to the early involvement of the Netherlands in the legal trade of coca and opium and their financial dependence on this trade (De Kort and Korf 1992). The first Opium Act in 1919, adopted largely due to pressure from abroad, made transporting and dealing in drugs illegal, but it was not until the 1960s that drug addiction was viewed as a social problem, and not until 1976 that the Opium Act was revised in order to make provisions for drug addicts. The main aim of this revised Opium Act was to "protect [the] health of individual users, people around them and society as a whole. Priority must be given to vulnerable groups" (Netherlands Ministry of Foreign Affairs 1997: 1).

In order to achieve this aim, the Dutch, as a nation, have consistently practiced a policy of harm reduction with regard to the drug problems they have faced. The principle of harm reduction is encapsulated by an understanding that a drug addict suffers primary harm from the effects of the drugs that they are taking, and [the policy] also aims to reduce any secondary harms the addict may be in danger of suffering as a result of his addiction. Excessive repression and the American "war against drugs" are seen, in the Netherlands, as being counterproductive in that they cause more pain to the drug user without successfully making headway against drug problems. Dutch government officials have decided that it is an unrealistic aim to completely eradicate drugs from any society—it is far more realistic to contain the damage caused by them (Korfet et al. 1999). It is this principle which has led to Dutch initiatives such as needle exchanges, the free testing of ecstasy pills for purity, reception rooms where users can take drugs without making a nuisance of themselves on the streets, and methadone programmes in which those addicted to heroin receive free methadone in an attempt to control their addiction. The Netherlands, along with Britain, are also one of the first countries to get involved with running trials of marijuana treatment in patients with multiple sclerosis (Sheldon 2002). These practices have resulted in a situation in which Dutch drug addicts are relatively visible to the authorities and far more of them come into contact with care and treatment than in countries with more repressive regimes.

The second major strand of Dutch drug policy is the principle of the separation of markets. In the Netherlands, as in many other countries, a distinction is drawn between "hard" and "soft" drugs. "Hard" drugs are those such as heroin, cocaine, crack cocaine, and amphetamines, which are judged to present an unacceptable risk to society. In comparison, cannabis and marijuana products are categorized as "soft" drugs and are thus assigned a far lower risk status. It has been suggested often, and in many contexts, that becoming involved with soft drugs leads to an introduction to harder drugs, and thus that cannabis is a "gateway" drug leading to cocaine and heroin addiction. By permitting the establishment of coffee shops which sell cannabis and marijuana in a controlled, semi-legal environment, the Dutch have effected a separation of the markets for soft and hard drugs. This is a major difference in drug policy between the Netherlands and other countries. The sale of drugs in coffee shops is tolerated in parts of the Netherlands so long as the shops themselves adhere to a set of carefully laid down rules. No hard drugs may be sold in coffee shops; there can be no advertising, no sales to minors, and no nuisance caused to neighbours. Trade stock cannot exceed 500 grams and each customer can buy up to only 5 grams per day (Van Dijk 1998). Therefore, in the Netherlands, there now exists a situation in which it is possible to obtain cannabis products without coming into contact with any more potentially dangerous drugs. Cannabis itself remains illegal but such a situation can be justified by employing the expediency principle: while it would be possible to prosecute people for the possession or consumption of small amounts of cannabis, it would not be in the interest of society in general to implement such repressive action. Although [the] coffee shops themselves are legal, they are dependent on an illegal market to supply them and this creates a paradoxical situation in the Netherlands (De Kort and Cramer 1999). Coffee shops are officially approved to sell small amounts of cannabis but not to grow it in large amounts or import it. Nevertheless, the Dutch generally regard their separation of markets policy as being successful, and it is so deeply entrenched in their society that it would be difficult to make any significant changes at this stage.

The one area in which repressive measures are strongly enforced is that concerning trafficking in drugs. The Netherlands have declared that they will cooperate in and actively support any action against trafficking in drugs and, indeed, have a relatively strict policy in this area themselves. Other than this, their liberalized twin policies of harm reduction and the separation of markets has led to a situation in which drug addicts in the Netherlands are highly visible, have easy access to treatment, and thus can be extensively monitored by the authorities. Needle exchange programmes and other harm reduction initiatives are successful in that they have led to a lower drug-related death rate without causing an increase in the overall number of users (Netherlands Ministry of Foreign Affairs 1997, "Prevention and Care": 1–2). Dutch drug policy, in the past, has taken severe criticism from other countries, but it is increasingly true that schemes initially seen as too radical are now being adopted by other countries. Two examples are the decriminalization of cannabis possession in Germany, Belgium, and Portugal and the provision of methadone programmes in Switzerland (Lemmens and Garretsen 1998). In the eyes of the Dutch, a drug-free society is not a realistic outcome. They recognize their drug problem as being dynamic and have implemented a dynamic, innovative, and flexible drug policy as a result (De Kort and Cramer 1999).

To some extent, a drug policy such as that employed in the Netherlands relies on the tolerance of its national neighbours. Dutch drug policy can be viewed as an anti-prohibitionist style of controlling drugs, which does not enjoy support everywhere. Criminal law is employed only against large-scale drug traffickers while users and small-scale dealers are tolerated and/or treated. The United States has a diametrically opposite prohibitionist policy in which users, dealers, and traffickers are all treated punitively, and it has become routine for senators, such as General McCaffrey, to publicly castigate the Dutch approach (van Solinge 1999: 517). Although the United States is an undeniably powerful foe to have, the legitimacy of their criticism can be brought into question by the fact that they have arguably the worst drug problem in the world with laws that have "served mainly to create enormous profits for drug dealers and traffickers, overcrowded jails, police and other government corruption ... predatory street crime ... and urban areas ... terrorized by violent drug gangs" (Inciardi 1991). With the current state of the American drug situation and its unfavourable comparison with that of the Netherlands, this criticism loses a lot of its influence. The US-fuelled "war against drugs" provides a vehement criticism of Dutch drug policy, but, in terms of the EU, there are many critics much closer to home.

In the 1980s, German authorities expressed criticism against Dutch drug policy as large numbers of Germans were crossing the border to purchase drugs in the Netherlands. However, it was felt by Dutch commentators that Germany's repressive drug policy was pushing German drug users into the Netherlands more strongly than the liberal Dutch policy was actually pulling them there (van Solinge 1999). More recently Germany's drug policy has become less repressive and has focused more strongly on the treatment and understanding of addicts resulting in far fewer Germans going to the Netherlands for drugs. In 1995, President Chirac of France accused the Netherlands of being the chief supplier of drugs to the French market and became vocally very critical of Dutch drug policy. Chirac spoke out at several European summits and won the support of German Chancellor Kohl and British Prime Minister Major (van Solinge 1999: 518). Chirac even went as far as threatening to close the border with the Netherlands—impressive fervour even if, in the real world, the two countries do not share a border. Concerns of countries actually bordering the Netherlands have been aggravated by the 1985 Schengen Agreement, which largely removed border controls between Belgium, the Netherlands, Luxembourg, Germany, and France. In order to deal with these concerns, the Netherlands have undertaken to ensure that any effects their domestic drug policy may have on other countries will be anticipated and dealt with by themselves. The police and customs officials of the relevant countries are now working together to control large-scale drug trafficking organizations operating across these borders.

Through signing the Maastricht Treaty, all countries in the EU have committed themselves to the fight against drugs, and they continue to commit themselves by supporting various UN drug conventions. Although each individual member state has been given free reign to develop its own policy, no country has managed to develop a policy which has succeeded in curbing drug use. Perhaps because of this, the pragmatic Dutch approach has recently enjoyed increasing popularity. Austria, Denmark, Italy, and Portugal are now becoming more liberal, in line with Dutch-style policy, and are placing increasing emphasis on social needs (Blom and van Mastrigt 1994).

SWEDISH DRUG POLICY

Unlike many other European countries which reject the total abolition of drugs as an unrealistic objective, the main aim of current Swedish drug policy can be identified as a bid to entirely free society of illegal drugs and the problems they cause. During the 1960s and 1970s, the Swedes operated a relatively liberal drug policy not dissimilar to practices in the Netherlands today. However, during the late 1970s, a far more repressive policy began to be implemented (Johansson 1998). Previously, it had been judged not to be in the interest of the public to prosecute in the majority of cases of possession of narcotics, but, by 1980, the law was changed to ensure that every incidence of possession of illegal drugs was to be taken to court. Throughout the 1980s, campaigners fought to introduce laws against even the consumption of illegal drugs, and, in 1988, this was passed into the legal framework. By 1993 the police were allowed to do blood and urine tests in order to determine whether illegal drugs had been consumed, and, in the event that such tests apparently demonstrated that they had been, to prosecute from this evidence alone. Three basic laws regulate Swedish drug control: The Smuggling of Goods Act (1960), The Narcotic Drugs Ordinance (1962), and the Narcotic Drugs Act (1968). Revised versions of these laws have drastically increased the original maximum sentence of two years for drug offences in Sweden. Serious drug offences now carry penalties of between two and ten years in prison, and possession of any amount can now be punished by up to six months' imprisonment. Only sentences for murder, aggravated robbery, and aggravated arson are harsher than those for serious drug offences (Solarz 1989). These repressive changes have taken place in the space of no more than 20 years. When Sweden entered the EU in 1995, ... [the country] paralyzed the general trend towards liberalism that had been developing. Unlike the policy in the Netherlands that had been gaining in popularity elsewhere, ...[Swedish policy] does not distinguish between measures to limit supply and measures to reduce demand. While other countries have focused their drug-control policy on large-scale drug traffickers (leaving small scale users and dealers in relative peace) Sweden believes that every user and dealer should be targeted in an attempt to create a totally drug-free society. Neither does Sweden differentiate between soft and hard drugs; in Sweden, even cannabis is regarded as causing psychological damage, making people irresponsible, being addictive, and [it] is [viewed] as [being] a gateway leading to other, potentially more damaging, drugs (Westerberg 1994). The Swedes thus view Dutch drug policy as a direct threat to their aims for a drug-free society, and have condemned their liberalized approach as "giving up."

Sweden has always been a country with a strong temperance culture. For example, the consumption of alcohol has long been strictly controlled and regarded as extremely dangerous (Gould 1988). In addition to this, conformity is important and liberalism is viewed very negatively (Daun 1989). Within such a national paradigm, it is hardly surprising that drug policy has become, in recent years, so repressive. Tham (1995) describes how the drug problem in Sweden has become entwined with forming a national identity and fighting against outsiders. Citizenship is very important in Sweden and the life of the drug abuser is held up as the antithesis of the life of a good citizen. Drugs are seen as being part of a hippie, decadent culture that "normal" people would wish to eradicate from society. In this way it is claimed that a strict drug policy has widespread support from the general population of Sweden. This is emphasized by the many pressure groups that show support for a repressive drug policy. These groups are not all government controlled. Others are run by parents, Parents Against Drugs (FMN), or by groups of volunteers, the Workers Temperance Association (Verdandi) and the National Association to Help Addicts (RFHL) (Gould 1988). As policy has become more repressive drugs have become a problem that supersedes political party interests. Instead they are seen as a problem that has come from outside Sweden and, as such, constitute a threat to the Swedish lifestyle. In the words of an eminent Swedish drug researcher: "drugs have no place in Sweden and have been brought in from the outside—they are an attack on the kingdom of Sweden both culturally and territorially" (Tham 1995: 120). This is an opinion that is often expounded in the national press, which reinforces many elements of the restrictive policy and gives little consideration to liberal alternatives— often linking articles on narcotics with foreign countries (Gould 1996).

Like the Netherlands, although not on the same scale or for the same reasons, the Swedish method of dealing with the drug problem has attracted criticism from the outside. Liberal drug policy makers have criticized repressive policies for breeding large-scale rings of organized crime, drug traffickers, isolating individual drug users, and being counterproductive to aims of reducing drug-related deaths. Swedish drug campaigners, such as Olsson (1998), refute these lines of thought as ideological theories paying no attention to the practicalities of the situation. Continuing this debate in an article for the *Scandinavian Journal of Social Welfare*, Gould (1994) criticizes Swedish policy for reducing its welfare and treatment options while at the same time increasing control measures. He condemns the aim of a drug-free society and denounces the Swedes for placing a higher emphasis on a drug-free environment than [on] the rights of individual integrity. New and increasingly repressive policies are described as "dangerous and extreme." Westerberg (1994) replied to these claims in the same journal issue. He cites the fact that most Swedes agree with the repressive aims and the fact that drug policy is not political but part of general social policy, as defence against Gould's criticisms. He charges Gould with inhumanity for his refusal to believe in the ideal of a drug-free society and further defends Swedish policy by claiming that ... [Sweden is] committed to international cooperation but also recognizes the European-wide right to pursue its own national policy within international aims. Up-to-date statistics on the drug problem within Sweden have also been cited as criticism of the repressive policy. Yates (1998) reports an increase in serious drug addicts from 12,000 in 1980 to 22,000 in 1998. A government report (CAN 2000) supports Yates's findings by claiming that, although drug seizures are up by 50 per cent and prosecutions are up by 66 per cent since 1990, the level of drug abuse among young people is the same as in the 1970s. Further, drug-related deaths have increased from 50 per year in the 1970s to 250 per year in 2000 and are said to be the highest in Europe (Yates 2001), and availability of illegal drugs is at an all time high.

As the situation stands, the respective drug-control polices of Sweden and the Netherlands are so opposed it is difficult to imagine a situation in which the two countries could work together to combat the drug problem that faces them individually and the EU as a whole. The policies of each country are so entrenched in their differing national values and so supported by their differing societal structures that the possibility of them embracing each other's ideas in an effort to achieve harmonization is extremely unlikely. The situation is further complicated by the fact that Sweden used to be a relatively liberal country in terms of drug policy but has written this period off as a disaster in terms of drug control. It is ironic that both Sweden and the Netherlands have declared a reduction in the number of young cannabis users in recent years, and each country has claimed the reason for this trend is due to the success of their respective, and very different, drug policies.

It would be possible to compare the extent of the drug problem in Sweden and the Netherlands on the basis of available statistics relating to matters such as the number of problem drug users recorded in each country or the number of young people who report recent cannabis use. However it is highly debatable as to whether such comparisons constitute any useful information. The European Monitoring Centre for Drugs and Drug Addiction (EMCDDA) states in its

2000 report that "there are differences across countries in methods of data collection, sampling sizes, and frames, which could influence the precision and validity of estimates. Until these issues are solved, direct comparisons between levels of use in Member States should be made with caution." In addition, whereas Sweden's drug users are largely a hidden population, due to policy which drives them into isolation, in the Netherlands, numbers of drug users seem relatively high since they can be readily identified through their use of benefits and services and because they need not fear government recrimination.

THE PROBLEM OF DRUG CONTROL WITHIN THE EUROPEAN UNION

In order to assess fully the impact of these two such different drug policies on the EU as a whole, it is important to look in detail at the existing position of the EU itself on matters of drug control. As issues of drug control have become increasingly important over recent years, several organizations have been set up in order to facilitate international cooperation, amass data, and compare new ideas and experiences. The first working group to be set up was the European Committee to Combat Drugs (CELAD) in 1989, which brought together the national coordinators in this field from different Member States. It also provides legal bases for EU action in internal and external affairs. During the first half of 1995, the European Monitoring Centre for Drugs and Drug Addiction (EMCDDA) was established. The Centre's main objective is to collect and analyse information relating to drugs and to make this information available to a wide audience including academics, policy makers, journalists, and the general public. Surveys, studies, and pilot projects are carried out by the Centre, and the exchange of information between specialists is facilitated (EMCDDA 1998b). The priorities of the EMCDDA have been identified as the reduction of the demand for drugs, international cooperation, the control of trade, and an examination of the implications of the drug phenomenon for producer, consumer, and transit countries (EMCDDA 2001).

One of the most consistently raised themes by the new groups formed to combat the drug problem is the necessity of international cooperation. A state of cooperation is expected to flow from the work of the EMCDDA, and an important tool in the pursuit of this aim is the European Information Network on Drugs and Drug Addiction (REITOX), created in 1993. REITOX is a computer network at the heart of the collection and exchange of drug information and documentation in Europe, which stores national statistics on drugs from each member state of the EU. Finally, a further tool in the fight against drugs was envisioned in July 1995 by the establishment of a European Police Office (Europol), which was actualized on 1 October 1998. This new body was designed to provide a structure for "developing police cooperation between Member States in preventing and combating serious forms of international crime, including terrorism and drug trafficking" (SCADplus 1998a: 2). Before it became fully operational in July 1999, a temporary Europol Drugs Unit (EDU) was established to combat drug trafficking and associated money laundering, with powers to take effect immediately. Europol took over the duties of the EDU with effect from January 1999, and is particularly helpful in organized crime investigations.

This emergence of drug-control problems as a priority for the EU is also evidenced in new legislation. The Amsterdam Treaty, signed in October 1997, has as a main aim to "enable the EU to deal with the globalization and evolution of the international situation" (SCADplus 1998b: 1–2). Within its broad objective to ensure freedom, security, and justice, the fight against drugs is given special attention. Prior to the signing of the Amsterdam Treaty, the main piece of legislation stipulating guidelines for the control of the drug problem had been the Maastricht Treaty signed in November 1991. Regarding the regulation of drug control, this treaty was largely unsatisfactory as it failed to lay down sufficient provisions for international cooperation and for effective methods for fighting the drug problem in Europe. Individual member states were left to fight international crime relatively informally—much as they had been doing for the previous 20 years. The implementation of the Amsterdam Treaty reshaped international cooperation and introduced effective methods of reaching this cooperation in the fight against international crime and control of the drug problem within Europe.

Since the Maastricht Treaty, the EU has been organized on the basis of three "pillars" as described by van Solinge (1999), each of which has relevance to the problem of drug control. The first pillar deals mainly with the traditional economic policy of the EU. However, Article 129 of this pillar stipulates a responsibility of the EU to deal with the "prevention of diseases, in particular the major health scourges, including drug dependence," although it is left up to the individual member states to coordinate their own policies and programmes to achieve this objective. The second pillar covers cooperation in external relations and deals with drugs in terms of supply reduction and the fight against drug trafficking. The third pillar regulates cooperation in justice and home affairs and therefore deals with many of the important decisions that are now being made on drug issues. Drug issues can therefore be said to come under all three pillars, which has made regulation somewhat difficult. In order to combat this problem, a horizontal drug group was set up to coordinate drug issues across the three pillars. The Amsterdam Treaty has, however, gone some way towards reorganizing drug issues within the EU. Title IV of the Amsterdam Treaty now deals with checks at external borders and judicial cooperation in criminal matters. It aims to make freedom of movement easier while at the same time building up effective international cooperation. Title VI also deals with drugs in terms of trafficking and building up an international network of cooperation between police, customs, and judicial authorities. This new organization has focused more on international cooperation and may allow more effective methods of drug control to be developed. A closer examination of the statistics gathered by agencies such as the EMCDDA and REITOX allows an insight into the extent of the drug problem in Europe, and into the solutions developed to overcome it.

CURRENT TRENDS IN DRUG USE WITHIN THE EUROPEAN UNION

The EMCDDA report on *Trends in Drug Use* (1999) creates a clear picture of the current situation regarding the use of illicit drugs within the EU. Cannabis is identified as the most widely used illicit drug having been used by 40 million people across the EU. It is the main drug to be involved in arrests for drug offences, although most of these arrests relate to use of the drug rather than trafficking. It is not associated with any particular social or recreational context or with any particular situation, suggesting that its use is prevalent across all sections of society. Amphetamines are the second most widely used drug and show particular association with young people. Levels of cocaine and ecstasy use are moderately but steadily rising, heroin use remains relatively constant, and crack cocaine use is still a relatively limited phenomenon. Solvents are consistently popular but only among adolescents, and, conversely, misuse of medicines such as benzodiazepines is rising among adults. In health terms, the levels of reported AIDS cases are levelling out but hepatitis cases are rising at a serious rate. Drug-related deaths are stable or decreasing in most countries. Law enforcement measures show that police arrest mostly for drug use, and the proportion of arrests for trafficking is not generally increasing. Rather worryingly, a fairly high proportion of the prison population in every country are drug users, even though they are not necessarily imprisoned for drug offences. In many countries within the EU, community work is being considered increasingly important in the prevention of drug use. Problematic drug use has been consistently linked to social exclusion, and therefore prevention and treatment options are becoming more comprehensive. It has also been noted that the borders between licit and illicit drugs are blurring in terms of treatment and development.

As well as these fairly specific statistics relating to current trends in drug use, the EMCDDA also collects data on methods of drug prevention and control within the EU, and these are presented in the *EMCDDA General Report* (EMCDDA 1998a). The *EMCDDA General Report* evaluates the extent of cooperation to date and identifies where it is most needed. The findings show that, across Europe, cooperation between agencies within member states appears to be increasing. Cooperation between the criminal justice system and health and social sectors is also developing, resulting in increased use of schemes for drug using offenders and projects for imprisoned drug users. The report also looks in detail at the preventative position adopted by the majority of member states and current trends in repression or liberalization in terms of drug-control policy.

The principle of therapy instead of punishment has been adopted in the general guidelines of drug policies in a growing number of countries. Some member states have consolidated social and medical support towards drug-addicted offenders, and increasingly, the first contact with law enforcement authorities is being used as a door to treatment or counselling activities. The EMCDDA interpret this as a sign that the EU is gradually moving away from repressive responses to the drug problem and focusing more on prevention and treatment in an effort to reduce the risks caused by drug use. Further evidence of this is provided by new projects aiming to give legal, professional, and political recognition to a range of activities such as needle exchange, injecting rooms, or substitution treatment, which have been implemented in many countries. This can be interpreted as an attempt to reduce the health and social damage often caused by drug addiction. However, it is still most definitely the case that prohibition of possession and use of drugs is the basic precept followed by all EU countries. Legalization is not currently considered an option in any member state, although there is consistent evidence of awareness that prosecution and imprisonment of individuals with drug problems can cause escalations of their problems. Drug consumption in general seems not to be prosecuted in most European countries. However, debate continues on how to deal with consumers in possession of small quantities of drugs for personal use or who commit petty crimes because of their drug dependence. To sum up, it can be said that developments in European drug polices and new legal approaches towards illicit drugs show a shift towards decriminalizing some behaviour linked to consuming and possessing drugs for personal use. However, most member states reject extreme solutions, such as full legalization or harsh repression, but continue to prohibit drug consumption while modifying the penalties and measures applied to it.

THE *EUROPEAN UNION ACTION PLAN TO COMBAT DRUGS (2000–2004)*

The most recent document outlining the position of the EU on drug control is the current *European Union Action Plan to Combat Drugs (2000–2004)*, which outlines the methods and policies to be put into practice regarding dealing with the problem of drug control. This is a document which must attempt to reconcile the positions of Dutch liberalism with Swedish repression if it is to have any success in implementing the objective stated in almost every piece of EU legislation: to encourage international cooperation and harmonization in the fight against drugs. It builds upon the 1995–1999 drug plan which aimed to work on demand reduction, supply reduction, and the fight against illicit trafficking, as well as on international cooperation and coordination at national and EU levels. The 2000–2004 action plan develops further aims in the fight against drugs and defines more carefully the role of international cooperation. Each member state is expected to develop its own individual policy but also to participate in interaction with the policies of other member states. "Not everyone has to fight on the same fronts at the same time but coordination and interaction of players and approaches must be ensured to reach maximum efficiency" (European Union 1999: 2). The EU is publicly declaring its support for both the Swedish and the Dutch models of drug control, but it remains to be seen how interaction between these two opposed styles of drug control will be effectively implemented.

The action plan emphasizes the importance of collecting, analysing, and disseminating data on the drug phenomenon in the EU. In the area of demand reduction, two specific aims over the next five years have been defined: to reduce significantly the prevalence of illicit drug use among young people under 18 and to reduce substantially the number of drug-related deaths. In addition, several new challenges have been determined. One of these new challenges deals with the area of amphetamines and ecstasy and the other with urban delinquency. The plan focuses on fighting the production and abuse of increasingly popular drugs like ecstasy and amphetamine, especially among young people. Efforts will be made to curb the increasing number of juveniles involved in criminal groups and in the sale of illicit drugs in general. Other new areas of concern that are outlined are poly drug use, drug use in prisons, and alternatives to punishment for drug users. Finally the new action plan to combat drugs makes preparations for the enlargement of the fight against drugs.

A DIVIDED EUROPEAN UNION

Despite the official prolific cooperative measures implemented by the EU, the current position held on matters of drug control remains, in reality, very much divided. Several countries are embracing the pragmatic approaches of the Netherlands and are gradually introducing some of them to their own national drug policies. However, other countries are joining Sweden and the United States in their strict adherence to repressive measures. Complicating the situation further is the fact that this division in methods of drug control is not just an international phenomenon: some countries are also internally divided. For example, in Germany, where drug control is a federal matter but implementation of policy is left up to individual states (Länder), Northern states have increasingly adopted a liberal position matching that of the Dutch, while Southern states are still very much pursuing repressive policies (Albrecht and van Kalmthout 1989). Even the European Parliament, which should be sending out a consistent message regarding drug control, reflects the divisions seen elsewhere.

The European Parliament has organized and headed two drug reports: one headed by Stewart-Clark and known as the Stewart-Clark report (1986) and one headed by Cooney and known as the Cooney report (1991). Both reports are discussed in an article by Blom and van Mastrigt (1994) and demonstrate divided opinions and relatively inconclusive findings. Stewart-Clark, a British conservative, headed the 1986 report, which ended in a majority/minority divide of positions within the group. Overall, the group members agreed that large-scale dealing should be treated with a strict enforcement policy but agreement ended here. The majority position held that a repressive approach should be maintained in drug-control problems while the minority position linked large-scale, organized drug trafficking to repressive policies and allowed for the possibility that legalization could be an effective tool in controlling trafficking. The majority group cited brief periods of legalization in Spain and Sweden as a failure resulting in an increased number of drug addicts. It also criticized the contradictory policy currently operating in the Netherlands whereby trade and supply in cannabis is illegal but sale and small-scale possession is legal. Conversely, the minority position found that Dutch policies made sense and favoured the decriminalization of use, possession, and small-scale dealing. They found it incomprehensible that some drugs, such as alcohol and nicotine, are legal but others are not. The European Parliament judged the findings to be inconclusive and, ignoring the main debate surrounding prohibition versus legalization, recommended the implementation of educational programmes, the establishment of research centres and the improvement of national and international coordination.

In 1991, the Cooney report was published and focused particularly on the problems associated with illegal drug trafficking. Again opinions were divided, but this time the majority group was more in favour of liberal methods and it was the minority group that remained dedicated to repressive measures. Dutch policies had been more closely researched and this time were judged in a much more favourable light. The distinction between soft and hard drugs, the high priority placed on prevention projects, the general assistance of addicts and, in particular, programmes implementing free treatment, needles, and substitute drugs were upheld by the majority group. They were also impressed by the growing view that drug problems should be seen as a public health problem and possession of drugs for personal use should not be regarded as a criminal offence. However, they did maintain that legalization should be rejected as the EU must follow the United Nations in the aim to minimize the use of drugs. Meanwhile, the minority group protested that possession should stay illegal and the illogical policy adopted by the Netherlands (legalizing sale and small-scale possession of drugs in an overall system where trade and supply is still illegal) should be eradicated. It is a measure of the success and spreading implementation of Dutch drug-control policies that such a turn around in opinion can be observed in the five years separating these reports. However, when the second report was presented to the European Parliament, the majority view was rejected and the minority one upheld—possibly due to the condemnation of the report by the United States (Blom and van Mastrigt 1994). Obviously, opinion within the European Parliament is incredibly divided between support for Dutch style liberalism and Swedish style repression, but a predominantly prohibitionist front has been presented, which is not encouraging to those opting for the spread of the Dutch model.

Another area in which the diverse ethics of the Swedish and Dutch drug policies can be seen emphatically is in the establishment of two diametrically opposed European city networks, as described by Kaplan and Leuw (1996). In November 1990, the Frankfurt resolution was signed, forming a network of European cities devoted to the problem of drug control, known as European Cities on Drug Policy (ECDP). Originally, this agreement was signed by Amsterdam, Frankfurt am Main, Hamburg, and Zurich, who all agreed to work towards the principles of "legalization, liberalization and harm reduction." These cities subscribe to a Dutch-style drug policy committed to reintegrating addicts into society and treating rather than punishing them. Drugs are a problem to be shared equally by the police and welfare groups, and the legalization of cannabis is a goal that is being worked towards.

In response to this experimentalist network, the Stockholm resolution was signed in April 1994, forming the network of European Cities Against Drugs (ECAD). The founder members (Berlin, Dublin, London, Paris, Madrid, and Stockholm) were later joined by 19 major European cities in signing this resolution and thereby dedicating themselves to "prohibition, zero tolerance and a war on drugs." ECAD adopted the Swedish style aim of freeing Europe from all kinds of drugs. Both networks aim to unite European cities in an attempt to control the drug problem, but they have conflicting aims and strategies, both of which have attracted considerable support. The development of these networks has shattered hopes for a united European front against drugs. It is a considerable challenge for the EU to develop these networks in such a way that they can interact and cooperate with each other.

BRIDGING THE DIVIDE: UP TO DATE STRATEGIES FOR DEALING WITH THE PROBLEM OF DRUG CONTROL WITHIN THE EUROPEAN UNION

As can be seen from the reports presented to the European Parliament and the city networks developing within the EU, it is proving difficult to find a middle road between the contrasting policies of prohibition and legalization. Most recently, the European Parliament can be described as focusing on individual policy measures judged to be successful in controlling drugs rather than dwelling overly on the fruitless debate of liberal against repressive measures (Diez-Ripolles 1989). The European Parliament has pledged to continue to intervene in all stages of the drug problem, from production to consumption, and will continue to underline the illegality of drugs in general. However, ... [members] will hold regular conferences to evaluate all the implications and effects of new projects designed to tackle the trafficking, dealing, possession, and consumption of drugs whether they are prohibitive or repressive. This rather vague, general objective allows the Parliament to side step the issue of which policy style is inherently better, instead introducing the idea of embracing any policy measure which proves successful. More specific individual aims are also professed by the Parliament. It will continue to fight against criminal organizations and put pressure on drug-producing countries with regard to their crop cultivation programmes. Effective measures with regard to controlling money laundering will be adopted, and extradition agreements and the freezing and confiscation of the assets of large-scale traffickers will be facilitated. Finally, preventive education will be improved throughout member states, as will rehabilitation and treatment programmes. Essentially, the Parliament is backing all the ventures it has previously supported in an environment which proclaims to be repressive but also makes provision for the more successful of the liberal approaches. Within the generally repressive parameters there is thus a definite emphasis on using education, information, and rehabilitation to reduce the demand for illegal drugs.

Albrecht and van Kalmthout (1989) describe the various models that have been suggested in recent years for the liberalization of the drug-control problem. The first model would be total legalization in which all kinds of drugs are totally decriminalized and it would not be considered an offence to buy, sell, possess, consume, or traffic in drugs of any sort. The second and third models suggest partial decriminalization. This could be partial in the sense of drugs being categorized due to their high or low risk value and then implementing the removal of prohibition with respect to the lowest risk drugs. Alternatively, partial decriminalization could refer to the decriminalization of the possession and consumption of very small amounts of any drug. Finally, a fourth model suggests keeping drugs predominantly illegal but to identify seriously addicted users and allow them a controlled amount of illegal drugs through the medium of a legal prescription. None of these models has been, or indeed is likely to be, implemented across Europe in the near future. However, it is indicative of the new, more open environment which surrounds the drug debate that such models can even be discussed. The entire topic of legalization with reference to illegal drugs used to be one of total taboo. It is now the case, as conflicting ideas about the best way to deal with the drug-control problem abound, that there is much more scope for debate.

CONCLUDING REMARKS

It is fairly obvious that Dutch drug policy has had a significant effect on the drug policies in other European member states. Principles of harm reduction and differentiating between hard and soft drugs as well as specific measures such as needle exchange programmes and shooting galleries, have spread to an increasing number of countries, e.g., as shown earlier, Germany and Switzerland. A general regime of tolerance and liberalization regarding drugs seems to be hitting many European countries with new policy initiatives that are influenced by developments in Dutch drug policy. For example, the European Legal Database on Drugs (ELDD) (2001) reports that, in April 2001, a law passed in Luxembourg [that] decriminalized cannabis consumption, as well as its transportation, possession, and acquisition for personal use, and, in Portugal, the decriminalization of possession and use of all drugs has been effective since 1 July 2001. In other countries, specific laws have not yet been passed but regimes can nevertheless be described as becoming more liberal. For example, in January 2001, Belgium expressed the intention to modify its main drug law in order to make non-problematic use of cannabis non-punishable, and, in Britain, since October 2001, moving cannabis from a class B drug to a class C drug, has been extensively and seriously debated. Sweden's influence is more subtle and perhaps less impressive. However, since ...[Sweden] joined the EU in 1995, ... [it has] provided a powerful opponent to Dutch-style policy and does not allow this regime of tolerance to reign unchecked. The success and popularity of European Cities Against Drugs (ECAD), initiated by Sweden, is a direct setback for the Dutch-born European Cities on Drug Policy (ECDP). Any radical, liberal initiatives attempted to be implemented by the ECDP now face a direct challenger, and members of the ECDP must now realize they have rivals in the ECAD who will fight them all the way on new policy initiatives. While Sweden does not have as many drug policy "converts" as the Netherlands, it does have allies, and there is evidence that some countries are moving closer to a Swedish-style policy. Finland and Norway, which together with Sweden make up part of the Nordic Council, are also strongly repressive towards drug users, dealers, and traffickers, with no policy of separation between hard and soft drugs and little differentiation in penalties between drug users and dealers. Denmark, which is also part of the Nordic Council, has, in the past, displayed a relatively liberal policy towards drugs allowing the free city of Christiania in Copenhagen to flourish despite openly selling and smoking cannabis in hash markets. This situation was tolerated as a social experiment but the Danish government has been cracking down recently on drug users and the current policy in Christiania, as a response to considerable criticism for ... [its] policies from the rest of the Nordic Council. An article published in the *Copenhagen Post* (10 March 2002) reports the government's intention to close down Christiania unless all drugs and drug dealers are got rid of.

The opposed styles of drug control seen in Sweden and the Netherlands have made it nearly impossible for a harmonized approach to be adopted throughout the EU. This may be viewed negatively by EU policy makers who are hoping for an immediate Europe-wide united front on dealing with drugs or positively by those who are not convinced that either Swedish-style total repression or Dutch-style liberalism are the order of the day and think that a drug policy considering the positive aspects of both sides of the argument is the way forward. What they have done is significantly contribute to the prioritization of the drug problem for the EU. The division between tolerant Dutch-style policies and prohibitive Swedish-style measures has ensured an increasing focus on the drug problem. In an effort to bridge the division, the EU has implemented many invaluable research tools and has improved legislation dealing with the control of illegal drugs. As a result, the nature of the problem and the solutions available are now much more widely understood. While the aim of the EU to achieve harmonization of approaches to the drug problem has not been met, ... [member countries] are now in a much stronger position to manage drug use. No one style of control has been singled out as being morally better or inherently more successful, but the split has allowed a more diverse range of methods to be developed as each member state devises its own national policy within the parameters of legalization and prohibition (Boekhout van Solinge 2002). No single policy is likely to be universally adopted, but the battle centred on Sweden and the Netherlands has ensured that drug-control policy will remain a priority for the EU and increasing numbers of possible solutions to the problem will become available in the near future.

REFERENCES

Albrecht, H. and A. van Kalmthout. 1989. "European Perspectives on Drug Policies." Pp. 425–73 in *Drug Policies in Western Europe*, edited by H. Albrecht and A. Van Kalmthout. Criminological Research Reports 41. Freiburg: Max Planck Institute for Foreign and International Penal Law.

Blom, I. and H. van Mastrigt. 1994. "The Future of the Dutch Model in the Context of the War on Drugs." Pp. 255–81 in *Between Prohibition and Legalization: The Dutch Experiment*, edited by E. Leuw and I. Haen Marshall. Amsterdam: Kugler Publications.

Boekhout van Solinge, T. 2002. *Drugs and Decision Making in the European Union*. Amsterdam: CEDRO/Mets en Schilt. http://www.cedro-uva.org/lib/boekhout.eu.html

CAN. 2000. *Drug Developments in Sweden, Report (2000)*. Stockholm: Swedish Council for Information on Alcohol and Other Drugs.

Cooney, P. 1992. *Report Drawn Up by the Committee of Enquiry into the Spread of Organized Crime Linked to Drug Trafficking in the Member States of the European Union*. European Parliament Document A3-0358/91, 23 April.

Daun, A. 1989. *Swedish Mentality*. University Park, PA: Pennsylvania State University Press.

De Kort, M. and T. Cramer. 1999. "Pragmatism Versus Ideology: Dutch Drug Policy Continued." *Journal of Drug Issues* 29: 473–92.

De Kort, M. and D.J. Korf. 1992. "The Development of Drug Trade and Drug Control in the Netherlands: A Historical Perspective." *Crime, Law and Social Change* 17: 123–44.

Diez-Ripolles, J.L. 1989. "Current Trends on the Works of the European Parliament with Regard to Narcotic Drugs." Pp. 21–28 in *Drug Policies in Western Europe*, edited by H. Albrecht and A. Van Kalmthout. Criminological Research Reports 41. Freiburg: Max Planck Institute for Foreign and International Penal Law.

ELDD. 2001. *Decriminalization in Europe? Recent Developments in Legal Approaches to Drug Use*. ELDD Comparative Analysis, November. Lisbon: European Monitoring Centre for Drugs and Drug Addiction (EMCDDA).

EMCDDA. 1998a. *EMCDDA General Report (1998)*. Lisbon: EMCDDA. http://www.emcdda. europa.eu/

EMCDDA. 1998b. *EMCDDA in Brief*. Lisbon: EMCDDA. http://www.emcdda.europa.eu/

EMCDDA. 1999. *Trends in Drug Use: Problems and Answers (1999)*. Lisbon: EMCDDA. http://www.cmcdda.europa.eu/

EMCDDA. 2001. *Annual Report on the State of the Drug Problem in the European Union*. Lisbon: EMCDDA. http://www.emcdda.europa.eu/

European Parliament. 1986. "Report Drawn Up on Behalf of the Committee of Enquiry into the Drug Problem in the Member States of the Community by the Chair, Sir Jack

Stewart-Clark." *European Parliament Working Documents.* Document A 2-114/86/Corr. October 2. Strasbourg: European Communities.

European Union. 1999. *The European Union Action Plan to Combat Drugs (2000–2004).* Brussels: European Union. http://ec.europa.eu/external_relations/drugs/ap00_04.pdf.

Gould, A. 1988. *Conflict and Control in Welfare Policy: The Swedish Experience.* London: Longman.

Gould, A. 1994. "Pollution Rituals in Sweden: The Pursuit of a Drug-Free Society." *Scandinavian Journal of Social Welfare* 3: 85–93.

Gould, A. 1996. "Drug Issues and the Swedish Press." *The International Journal of Drug Policy* 7: 91–104.

Inciardi, J.A. 1991. "American Drug Policy and the Legalization Debate." Pp. 7–15 in *The Drug Legalization Debate,* edited by J.A. Inciardi. Newbury Park, CA: Sage.

Johansson, P. 1998. "Address at a Meeting in Stockholm July 12 (1998) with General Barry McCaffrey, Director of the Office of National Drug Control Policy, Held by Per Johansson, Secretary General of RNS. *Riksforbundet Narkotikafritt Samhalle.* http://www.rns.se/

Kaplan, C.D. and E. Leuw. 1996. "A Tale of Two Cities: Drug Policy Instruments and City Networks in the European Union." *European Journal on Criminal Policy and Research* 4: 74–89.

Kaplan, C.D., D.J. Haanraadts, H.J. Van Vliet, and J.P. Grund. 1994. "Is Dutch Drug Policy an Example to the World?" Pp. 311–35 in *Between Prohibition and Legalization: The Dutch Experiment,* edited by E. Leuw and I. Haen Marshall. Amsterdam: Kugler Publications.

Knowles, H.R. 2002. "Denmark: Cannabis Showdown in Christiania." *The Copenhagen Post* (March 8). http://www.cphpost.dk/get/63463.html

Korf, D.J., H. Riper and B. Bullington. 1999. "Windmills in Their Minds? Drug Policy and Drug Research in the Netherlands." *Journal of Drug Issues* 29: 451–72.

Lemmens, P. and H. Garretsen. 1998. "Unstable Pragmatism: Dutch Drug Policy under National and International Pressure." *Addiction* 93: 157–62.

Netherlands Ministry of Foreign Affairs. 1997. *Dutch Drug Policy, January (1997).* Utrecht, Netherlands: Ministry of Foreign Affairs.

Olsson, P. 1998. *Arguments Against the Legalization of Narcotic Drugs.* Stockholm: Riksforbundet Narkotikafritt Samhalle. http://www.rns.se/

Reuband, K.H. 1995. "Drug Use and Drug Policy in Western Europe." *European Addiction Research* 1: 32–41.

SCADplus. 1998a. *Europol (European Police Office).* European Union. http://europa.eu/scadplus/leg/en/lvb/l14005b.htm

SCADplus. 1998b. *The Amsterdam Treaty: A Comprehensive Guide.* European Union. http://europa.eu/scadplus/leg/en/s50000.htm

Sheldon, T. 2002. "Netherlands to Run Trials of Marijuana in Patients with Multiple Sclerosis." *British Medical Journal* 324: 504.

Solarz, A. 1989. "Drug Policy in Sweden." Pp. 343–360 in *Drug Policies in Western Europe,* edited by H. Albrecht and A. Van Kalmthout. Criminological Research Reports 41. Freiburg: Max Planck Institute for Foreign and International Penal Law.

Tham, H. 1995. "Drug Control as a National Project: The Case of Sweden." *The Journal of Drug Issues* 25: 113–28.

Van Dijk, J.M. 1998. "The Narrow Margins of the Dutch Drug Policy: A Cost Benefit Analysis." *European Journal on Criminal Policy and Research* 6: 369–94.

Van Solinge, T. 1999. "Dutch Drug Policy in a European Context." *Journal of Drug Issues* 29: 511–28.

Van Vliet, H.J. 1990. "Separation of Drug Markets and the Normalization of Drug Problems in the Netherlands: An Example for Other Nations?" *Journal of Drug Issues* 20: 463–71.

Westerberg, B. 1994. "Reply to Arthur Gould: 'Pollution Rituals in Sweden: The Pursuit of a Drug Free Society.'" *Scandinavian Journal of Social Welfare* 3: 94–96.

Yates, J. 2001. "Swedish Drug Deaths Highest in Europe." *Expressen*, http://www.expressen.se/article.asp?id=86453.

Yates, J. 1998. "Sweden: A Totalitarian Threat to Europe." *International Journal of Drug Policy* 9: 233-37.

CHAPTER STUDY QUESTIONS

- Compare and contrast the legal policies controlling illegal drugs in the Netherlands and Sweden. How can the differences in Dutch and Swedish drug-law policies be explained?

- What have European Union (EU) countries done to try to come up with a common action plan to combat the trafficking and use of illegal drugs? How successful have the EU countries been at implementing a common approach to controlling the use of illegal drugs? Why?

- What effect have the different Dutch and Swedish drug laws had on the attempt made by European Union (EU) countries to develop a common action plan to combat the trafficking and use of illegal drugs?

- Imagine that you were asked by the government of your country to draft a set of recommendations for reforming the laws and policies controlling illegal drugs for your country. Would having knowledge of the European Union experience be helpful to you in drafting your recommendations? Would you recommend either the Dutch or Swedish policy approach? Why?

RELATED WEB LINKS

Justitie – Dutch Ministry of Justice
http://english.justitie.nl/
    This is the official English-language homepage of the Dutch Ministry of Justice, with links to information on crime and criminal justice policy in the Netherlands.

United Nations – Office on Drugs and Crime
http://www.unodc.org/unodc/index.html

> This UN organization provides current information on national and global trends in drug legislation, trafficking, consumption, and international law enforcement.

DrugScope
http://www.drugscope.org.uk/home.asp

> This is the homepage of the leading independent centre of expertise on drugs in the United Kingdom. The centre is concerned with informing policy development and reducing drug-related risk. Links to numerous reports, publications, and current news items on drug-use policy, education, and prevention are provided.

Drug Policy Alliance
http://www.drugpolicy.org/homepage.cfm

> This is the website of the leading organization in the United States concerned with promoting alternatives to the war on drugs. It contains extensive links to information on drug laws and policies around the world.

PART 6

CHALLENGES FOR A GLOBAL CRIMINOLOGY: HUMAN RIGHTS CRIMES AND INTERNATIONAL CRIMINAL JUSTICE

Human rights abuses and war crimes represent two of the thorniest issues facing global policy-makers in an increasingly conflict-ridden world. Violations of basic human rights have become routine during most contemporary world conflicts, and there is increasing evidence that atrocities constituting war crimes are also common in many conflicts. It is now clear that war crimes occurred on a massive scale during the conflicts in the former Yugoslavia, Rwanda, East Timor, and Iraq, among many others. Although such events typically engender outrage and condemnation when they are reported in the media, this outrage is often short-lived, as public attention quickly shifts to other issues. Unfortunately, however, the short-term media sensationalism frequently precipitates further atrocities as each side tries to even the score, and the different parties respond by trying to manipulate domestic and international public opinion to favour their side. Because the fluid and chaotic nature of many conflicts makes it difficult to identify the perpetrators and implement immediate control policies, officials frequently concentrate on ending the major conflict before attempting remedial action against the abuses. However, once the main conflict is contained, it is not always an easy matter to develop effective policies for dealing with past atrocities, or for preventing new ones.

Several factors contribute to the difficulties inherent in developing appropriate solutions to human rights abuses and war crimes in the aftermath of serious conflict. First, the fact that all sides in a conflict frequently commit human rights abuses and war crimes makes it difficult to gain the political will necessary to actively pursue the perpetrators. This problem is exacerbated by the fact that many serious offenders frequently remain very popular with their own people and may even retain considerable power and influence. These two factors make it difficult to move decisively to detain and punish offenders even when the evidence is clear and an established mechanism is in place to deal with the situation. This was certainly the case during the recent Balkan conflict, during which Slobodan Milošević remained President of the Federal

Republic of Yugoslavia (comprised of Serbia and Montenegro) while he was under indictment by the international tribunal established to deal with war crimes committed in the former Yugoslavia. Indeed, many Serbians considered him a hero right up until his death, and his arrest and trial caused considerable unrest in Serbia. This latter situation is common to many conflicts and leads to the very real possibility that adopting a strict criminal justice approach to the problem may actually harm attempts to prevent future conflict. All of these problems underscore the fact that the most appropriate course of action in the face of human rights abuses and war crimes is not always clear. The three articles contained in this part discuss these issues in more detail.

In "Dealing with the Legacy of Past War Crimes and Human Rights Abuses," Ivan Šimonović discusses several different ways in which transitional societies that are either recovering from conflict or moving from oppression to democracy deal with past war crimes and human rights abuses. He commences his discussion by noting that transitional societies must resolve two main dilemmas before they can deal adequately with the issue. First, a society must decide the degree to which it will either forget about past abuses or seek to uncover the truth about them. Following this, citizens must also decide the degree to which offenders should be forgiven or punished for their roles in committing the abuses. Within this context, Šimonović centres much of his discussion on the advantages and disadvantages of amnesties and truth commissions and on the enforcement of individual criminal responsibility. He notes that, while amnesties can be very useful in facilitating post-conflict peace building, they should not be granted for the most serious abuses and war crimes. Not only would this contravene international law, he argues, but also any resulting peace would likely be unstable. He further argues that amnesties are particularly effective when used in conjunction with truth commissions, as was the case in South Africa during the post-apartheid era. Using the South African Truth and Reconciliation Commission as an example, Šimonović argues that truth commissions help establish an accurate and reliable historical record and also precipitate institutional reforms that help prevent the abuses from occurring in the future.

Šimonović argues that proceedings based on individual criminal responsibility constitute the fastest growing approach to dealing with war crimes and human rights abuses. Individual criminal responsibility, he notes, can be established though three main avenues: national proceedings, proceedings based on universal jurisdiction, and proceedings before *ad hoc* tribunals or hybrid tribunals. (He also touches on the International Criminal Court, but this avenue is much less commonly used.) He notes that holding national proceedings in the immediate aftermath of a major conflict is difficult because there is a lack of political will and the rule of law has broken down. However, national court proceeding have the most impact on a society's values, and they frequently force a society to face problems to a much greater degree than occurs with *ad hoc* tribunals or with proceedings based on universal jurisdiction, which are often held in third countries (ones not involved in the initial conflict or abuse). Although the latter remind war criminals that they are never completely safe from prosecution, they are also subject to misuse by politically motivated foreign judges and prosecutors. *Ad hoc* tribunals, on the other hand, are usually far removed from the society in which the atrocities occurred, and thus their impact on the local population is much more limited than national proceedings.

Šimonović argues that hybrid tribunals, composed of a combination of local and international judges, represent a promising compromise between national and *ad hoc* tribunals, and he suggests that they will become more common as international reactions to war crimes become "embedded in … the globalization of human rights."

The second chapter in Part 6 discusses the major theoretical and empirical questions addressed in the literature on international tribunals and transitional justice. In "Advocacy and Scholarship in the Study of International War Crimes Tribunals and Transitional Justice," Vinjamuri and Snyder argue that two main perspectives have dominated the literature on war crimes tribunals and transitional justice. The most dominant of these perspectives is the legalist approach, which is based on a "logic of appropriateness." This approach stresses the importance of universal standards of justice and believes that actors in the international political arena are guided by the norms that they consider appropriate in a particular context. Thus, the legalists argue, there is a compelling need to persuade people to adhere to internationally accepted humanitarian norms as a strategy for reducing atrocities. They further argue that accountability is crucial to this process and should never be sacrificed in response to the needs of political expediency through amnesties and other mechanisms that shield the perpetrators of atrocities from responsibility for their actions. Ultimately, according to Vinjamuri and Snyder, legalists favour trials over mechanisms such as truth commissions because the latter are subject to political manipulation and fail to safeguard the rights of either victims or perpetrators. Public trials, on the other hand, serve a deterrent function that stresses individual rather than group responsibility. This factor may help to reduce further atrocities based on inter-group conflict because it shifts responsibility away from a religious or ethnic group. In addition, trials may well serve an educational function that helps socialize transitional societies into more democratic patterns of behaviour based on the rule of law.

In contrast to the strict accountability endorsed by legalist scholars, many international legal scholars argue that legal approaches to accountability should be analysed in terms of their pragmatic consequences, according to Vinjamuri and Snyder. The pragmatist approach to transitional justice focuses on explaining who is tried and punished for abuses, what the resulting consequences are of such a process, and whether any ethical rules can be deduced from the entire process. Pragmatists argue that political considerations are very important and that the long-term goal of achieving peace and democracy overrides the legalist prescription of strict legal accountability. In many cases, they argue, the creation of stable, functioning democratic institutions may be better served if societies emphasize reconciliation rather than accountability and punishment. This emphasis is particularly useful when perpetrators remain strong because the political costs of prosecution would be too great in such cases. Vinjamuri and Snyder conclude their discussion by arguing that much of the literature on transitional justice fails to explicitly incorporate the "logic of emotions" into their accounts. This latter approach rests on the assertion that achieving long-term peace and stability depends on eliminating the conditions that give rise to atrocities, which in turn depends on the achievement of emotional catharsis by victims and the acceptance of blame by the perpetrators. This process of reconciliation is frequently operationalized through the mechanism of truth commissions, which also promote reform by fostering public debate over human rights abuses in addition to reducing tensions between groups. However, Vinjamuri and Snyder argue that truth commissions focus primarily on tensions at the mass level and that strategies to counter the role of elites will also need to be implemented in many cases.

In "War, Aggression, and State Crime," Kramer and Michalowski conduct an *integrated* analysis of the invasion of Iraq by British and American forces. They commence their discussion by arguing that the invasion constitutes a form of state crime that is prohibited by both the Nuremburg Convention and the UN Charter. They further argue that many activities carried out during the occupation that followed the invasion violated the principles of the Geneva Convention as well as widely accepted principles of international humanitarian law (IHL). After reviewing several different definitions of "state crime," Kramer and Michalowski ultimately conclude that it is any state organizational deviance that precipitates human rights violations and that would be subject to widespread censure or condemnation if known. They argue that the invasion of Iraq clearly fits this definition on empirical grounds alone, with 10,000 civilian deaths, rampant use of torture, and other human rights abuses too numerous to count. They note that the US initially tried to justify the invasion on the grounds that Iraq constituted a *potential* threat to US interests because it possessed weapons of mass destruction (WMD). When it became clear that Iraq did not possess WMD, the US subsequently argued that the invasion was justified by the humanitarian goal of protecting Iraqis from human rights abuses carried out by Saddam Hussein's forces. The US and the UK also argued that the invasion was justified because Iraq was in violation of previous UN resolutions. Kramer and Michalowski dismiss all of these claims as factually unfounded, conceptually specious, or irrelevant under international law because the UN Security Council had already rejected them when refusing to authorize the invasion.

The second part of Kramer and Michalowski's article consists of an integrated analysis of the Iraq invasion that merges structural-level political and economic pressures with internal organizational factors and individual-level differential association. This tri-level analysis is further linked with three catalysts for action that include motivation, opportunity, and social control. Kramer and Michalowski argue that the invasion of Iraq must be analysed within the context of the long-standing US policy of "open door" imperialism, which focuses on control of access to markets rather than on the control of territory that characterizes traditional imperialism. At the end of the Second World War, the United States emerged as a military and economic superpower with virtual hegemony over key aspects of the global economy. However, two factors threatened US dominance of the global political economy. First, the rise of the Soviet Union presented the US with a clear ideological challenge to its policy of open door imperialism, and this challenge ultimately led to the "Cold War," with its attendant military build up. In addition, attempts by radical regimes and nationalists in the Third World to improve the living standards of the masses were seen as threats to US interests because they impeded the free flow of capital and the access to markets and cheap labour that capitalism generally requires. These threats were dealt with by working with capitalist elites in the affected countries and, in some cases, by direct military intervention.

The end of the Cold War presented the US with a different set of opportunities and challenges related to its goal of global military and economic hegemony. While the US now had the unchallenged ability to use its military power to curb the activities of nationalist regimes such as Panama and Grenada, it also had to find a new justification for continuing the military build up that had characterized the Cold War. One possible solution, proposed by the neo-conservative faction within the Republican Party, centred on the consolidation of US power in the Middle East. This proposal was not taken seriously for many years because the neocon-servatives had very little influence over US foreign policy, even when the Republicans were in power. However, the fact that the Supreme Court awarded a contested Presidency to George W. Bush provided the neoconservatives with an ideological ally in the White House for the first time. (Ronald Reagan and George H. W. Bush, although staunch conservatives, had little in common with the neoconservatives.) This set of events was followed by the 9/11 attacks, which focused American attention on the threat from the Middle East and provided the neoconserva-tives with the political clout they needed to influence US foreign policy in favour of a general war on terrorism. Kramer and Michalowski conclude their analysis by arguing that the war on terrorism was subsequently used to obscure the real economic and political goals behind the invasion of Iraq. They further conclude that there is no effective social control mechanism capable of controlling unilateral US action, even when that action constitutes a state crime. In the case of Iraq, not only was the UN ineffective, they argue, but also the US media, which abdicated their responsibility to provide the American public with a balanced perspective. This abdication was a crucial factor in fostering public support for the invasion of Iraq.

Chapter 20

DEALING WITH THE LEGACY OF PAST WAR CRIMES AND HUMAN RIGHTS ABUSES: EXPERIENCES AND TRENDS

IVAN ŠIMONOVIĆ

Transitional societies, recovering from conflict or moving from oppression towards democracy, have developed a range of ways of dealing with past war crimes and human rights abuses.[1] To various degrees, they have combined the short-term and long-term goals of ending the conflict and preventing its recurrence ... [with] achieving social stability and reconciliation.[2] In this comment, I will try to systematize the most important experiences and identify the relevant trends.

The framework for the systematization of experiences arises from the institutional answers to two dilemmas. First, to what extent should we *forget or establish the truth* about past war crimes and human rights abuses? Secondly, to what extent should we *pardon or punish* the perpetrators?[3]

EXPERIENCES WITH TRANSITIONAL JUSTICE

Amnesties and truth commissions

Amnesties seem to be very useful tools in peace negotiations and post-conflict peace building and reconciliation, but they should not cover the gravest abuses and war crimes. International humanitarian law and human rights law have established certain limits on the use of amnesties to obtain peace: it is the international legal obligation of a state to prosecute certain crimes, and no political or pragmatic argumentation can help to avoid it.[4] The International Committee of the Red Cross (ICRC) interprets the Geneva Convention accordingly (Martin 2002),[5] and it is very important that the United Nations has finally taken a firm stand on this matter.[6] It might be easier to negotiate a peace agreement with an unlimited amnesty, but it is unlikely that such a peace would be sustainable.[7] Conditional and individual amnesty, which retains the possibility to prosecute the gravest crimes (such as those in South Africa and, even more so, in East Timor) is fully compatible, not only with international law, but also with other institutions such as truth commissions and proceedings based on individual or collective responsibility.

Truth commissions have proved to be a powerful instrument not only for establishing truth and a reliable record of past human rights abuses but also for initiating the institutional change necessary to prevent abuses from reoccurring.[8] Truth commissions have benefited greatly from the process of transnational learning and burden sharing: reports and experiences, methodologies, computer software, and even veteran staff from previous commissions have facilitated considerably the establishment and work of each new commission. Truth commissions have had different prerogatives, roles, compositions, and features. Granting an amnesty for confession (as practiced by the South African Truth and Reconciliation Commission) appears to be an effective tool for the establishment of a reliable historical record. Truth commissions' findings can also represent an important source of information on crimes that are not covered by the amnesty. The Commission for Reception, Truth, and Reconciliation, established in 2002 in East Timor, relies on South Africa's experiences but does not allow immunity for serious crimes such as murder or rape. It allows immunity for lesser crimes such as looting, burning, and minor assault only when the confessor undertakes community service or makes a symbolic payment in addition to a confession (Orentlicher 2004). Truth commissions can more easily absorb many cases, hear more victims, and involve civil society because their methods of work are less formal than those of the courts. In this way, they can help to establish patterns of abuse, analyse their root causes, and suggest institutional reforms to prevent their recurring (van Zyl and Freeman 2002). Even in cases where they did not have a direct mandate, truth commissions tended to issue broad and future-oriented recommendations.[9] The inclusion of foreigners in truth commissions has proved to be a mixed blessing. In situations of strong social and political divisions, such as that in El Salvador, appointing foreigners to the truth commission was the only way to ensure objectivity. However, the inherent problem is that the historical record established by foreigners has a reduced impact on the local population.[10] A hybrid commission, composed of foreigners and nationals, such as the Guatemalan *Comisión de Esclarecimiento Histórico* (CEH or Truth Commission), is a compromise solution.

Lustration processes and substitute criminal proceedings

These are fast and pragmatic solutions to remove war criminals and abusers from public life without raising controversial issues from the past. In this context, pragmatism is regarded as more important than justice. It is considered important to eliminate perpetrators of abuse from political life by reducing their opportunities to participate in it through administrative measures or through criminal proceedings (these criminal proceedings do not directly address war crimes and abuses and tend not to be politically divisive). During the Communist regime, many people in Eastern Europe, in one way or another, were involved in human rights abuses. After the political changes, it was considered destabilizing to launch criminal proceedings against all of them. As a result, transitions from the Communist rule of the late 1980s and early 1990s were not accompanied by a large number of prosecutions.[11] Unlike criminal proceedings, some administrative measures were often taken to limit the participation of alleged former abusers in political life. Through the process of *lustration*, they were excluded from active political life and were prohibited from participating in public administration (especially in military and police forces). The process was based on a review of secret police records and the elimination of former collaborators.[12] Even in rare cases of criminal proceedings, they tended to be limited to non-controversial issues. The essence of these *substitute criminal proceedings* was that war criminals and abusers were treated as common criminals (which, quite often, they also were). For example, in the Federal Republic of Yugoslavia (now Serbia and Montenegro), its former president, Slobodan Milošević, was charged with corruption and arranging the murder of his political opponent, but not with genocide and war crimes against Croats, Muslims, and Albanians.[13]

The advantages of lustration are its quick application and its capacity to easily deal with many cases. The disadvantage is that there are no reliable procedural guarantees for the due process of law. Nobody goes to jail, but people can easily get hurt because of mistakes or political or personal revenge. As with amnesties and truth commissions, lustration is most useful when combined with compensation to the victims and the criminal prosecution of those most responsible, when conditions permit adequate processes. Substitute criminal proceedings can have practical value if there is a need to ease public opinion towards accepting that former high officials were not nice people. Their potential shortcoming is the possibility that war crimes and abuses will happen again because they were never really confronted and condemned. For the sake of establishing the truth and bringing justice to the victims, substitute criminal proceedings should be followed by proceedings for war crimes and abuses as soon as the conditions permit. Once the fact that a former leader is a corrupt murderer is established, it might be easier to accept that he or she is a war criminal as well.

Proceedings based on collective responsibility

Such proceedings are growing in number and importance and therefore require our special attention. *Proceedings based on collective responsibility* are targeted against a collective body considered responsible for the abuse of victims, who are entitled to compensation. Recent forced *labour reparations*, awarded by some companies for forced labour during the Second World War, are, in this respect, similar to war *reparations*, ... [as are] the claims of Bosnia and Herzegovina or Croatia against the Federal Republic of Yugoslavia (later named Serbia and Montenegro) before the International Court of Justice (ICJ) for the alleged genocide [committed by the Serbs against Croats and Bosnians].[14] Proceedings based on collective responsibility can enable victims to obtain financial compensation that alleviates their often very difficult economic situation. It is much faster to establish the status of the victim than to identify and prosecute the abuser. However, the utility of these measures is limited because post-conflict and transition societies are usually poor and scarce resources have to be used strategically to enable recovery; fair compensation to the victims is simply not realistic (Martin 2002; Kritz 2002).[15] Proceedings based on collective responsibility can also be used for the symbolic satisfaction of the victims and the establishment of truth, even many years after the abuses have taken place.[16]

Proceedings based on individual criminal responsibility

This is the fastest developing category of institutional answers to war crimes and human rights abuses under the strong influence of non-governmental organizations (NGOs), the media, international organizations, and legal scholars. Individual criminal responsibility can be established through *national proceedings*, proceedings in third countries based on *universal jurisdiction*, or by proceedings before *ad hoc tribunals*, such as those for the former Yugoslavia and Rwanda, *hybrid tribunals* involving national and international judges and prosecutors (such as those in Cambodia, East Timor, Kosovo, and Sierra Leone), or before the *International Criminal Court* (ICC).

In post-conflict and transition societies, it is often very difficult to (re)establish the rule of law, and particularly hard to commence *national proceedings* for past war crimes and human rights abuses. In some cases, there is not enough political will, the justice system has previously been involved in oppression, infrastructure has been destroyed, or qualified personnel have been killed or left the country (Šimonović 2003: 260–262).[17] Whether there is a problem of political will, capacity, or both, international assistance or even more direct involvement is sometimes a precondition for successfully dealing with the past.[18] International staff can contribute much, through their skills, experience and objectivity, towards achieving stability in the country. International involvement, however, also has its costs: international staff use resources that could have been used locally, and there is a danger of developing a "culture of dependency," threatening the sustainability of the rule of law when foreign experts are gone.

Proceedings in third countries based on *universal jurisdiction* represent powerful tools against impunity?[19] War criminals and abusers cannot feel safe anymore, even if their national justice system protects them or if they have managed to escape from its reach. In recent years, a growing number of national courts have acted on the basis of universal jurisdiction over such crimes as genocide, crimes against humanity, war crimes, and torture, to permit the prosecution of foreign perpetrators.[20] However, these proceedings can also represent a serious problem with potentially far-reaching political consequences if ambitious prosecutors and judges interfere in affairs that they do not fully understand (van Zyl and Freeman 2002). Hypothetically, universal jurisdiction can also be deliberately misused to hurt political opponents and to, at least temporarily, prevent their travelling abroad.

The establishment of *ad hoc international tribunals* for the former Yugoslavia (ITY) and Rwanda (ITR) expressed the commitment of the international community to help to establish truth and punish the perpetrators of war crimes and abuses.[21] They were relatively successful in helping to establish a reliable historical record through their proceedings, but sometimes they had serious difficulties with ensuring the cooperation of states in fulfilling their mandate in areas like documentation delivery, and, especially, in bringing high-profile perpetrators to justice. Their work was also quite slow, violating the principle of expeditious dispensation of justice, and extremely expensive, raising doubts about their cost-effectiveness.[22] Providing translation services, using foreign judges, undertaking complicated logistics, and complying with highly demanding procedural rules (sometimes much above the standard of the countries in their mandate) are objective problems which require time and resources. They represent a warning regarding the constraints on the future work of the ICC. However, perhaps, the greatest concern is the insufficient impact of the Tribunals on the population of the countries in their mandate.

The removal of proceedings from the country where the crimes have been committed and the use of foreign languages and unfamiliar legal rules seem to have contributed to the psychological distance and diminished local media coverage.[23] It is shocking that, in spite of all the international efforts, some high-profile indicted war criminals, such as Milošević and Šešelj, were still locally regarded as heroes and remained party leaders, heading the party lists and winning the elections in spite of being in the ICTY's custody.[24] In general, national courts have a greater impact on the society and its values and beliefs than international tribunals. Through national proceedings, societies more directly face their own problems and mistakes, and learn from them.[25] For example, in the Republic of Croatia, national proceedings against the young and popular general, Mirko Norac (nationally regarded as a hero for his military merits during the liberation war) for previously publicly unknown war crimes that he had committed have had a much more sobering effect and have done more for the re-establishment of the rule of law in Croatia than any of the ICTY's proceedings against its citizens.[26] When General Norac was accused of war crimes, there was a public outcry and his supporters were on the streets, wearing T-shirts with the slogan: "We are all Mirko Norac." After the trial, when the conviction and sentence had been handed down, there was silence.[27] Intensive media coverage of the trial, exhibited evidence, and the General's own remorse have made the difference. This experience suggests that to address the practical problems of transitional societies in a sustainable manner, one should not introduce expensive and sophisticated, but distant, international tribunals that can process very few cases and keep them completely separate from domestic courts, which remain underfinanced, understaffed, and, very often, in a mess.[28] It is national courts that will have to deal with all other cases and other legal problems of the societies in transition, and they should be assisted and strengthened.

Hybrid tribunals, involving both national and international judges and prosecutors acting upon an amalgam of national and international law, with locally held trials (such as in Cambodia, East Timor, Kosovo, and Sierra Leone) are an attempt at compromise.[29] The inclusion of local judges makes the work of the court faster (because they do not have a language barrier and possess a better understanding of local laws and customs), but it also brings into the proceedings the values, including the political values, of the local judges. The "mutiny" of local Albanian judges (and its eventual success) in choosing which laws to implement is a striking example.[30] When courts are hybrid, it might be decisive on which judges represent the majority, local or international ones.[31] A convincing argument in favour of hybrid courts (and the financial and educational strengthening of national courts) is the impact of courts established immediately following the conflict on the sustainability of the justice system in the country in question.[32] Sooner or later, internationals have to leave and locals have to take over. Therefore, investment in the strengthening of the national justice system seems to be most effective when long-term sustainability is taken into account. Hybrid courts, first established within the framework of UN transitional administrations (in Kosovo and East Timor), are now also being established by agreement between the United Nations and national governments (Sierra Leone is the first case, with Cambodia to follow).

The experiences of ad hoc tribunals are helpful in preparing for the challenges of the ICC. The ICC is also composed of international judges and prosecutors, its proceedings will be conducted in foreign languages, and they will usually take place far away from the site of the crimes and abuses. However, its global character will attract public attention and ensure media coverage of its proceedings. The fact that it has global jurisdiction, that it has been established for future crimes, that its rules have been adopted consensually and in advance, and that it will assume jurisdiction only when [a] national justice system is either unable or unwilling to do so, will certainly contribute to its legitimacy. This might facilitate the ICC's cooperation with national justice systems, but there are also serious causes for concern. Unlike the ad hoc tribunals for the former Yugoslavia and Rwanda, the ICC was not established [by the UN Security Council] and is not backed up by the power of the UN Security Council, and some countries are reluctant to accept its jurisdiction. In the long run, the future of the ICC will be determined by the attitude of the United States. Although the United States, after initial general support, withdrew its signature from the ICC Treaty, the ICC's potential in the fight against terrorism might make the United States reconsider its position.[33] If the United States accepts the jurisdiction of the ICC, it is likely that it would lobby for the Court as hard as it is now lobbying against it, making it very difficult for all other states to deny the ICC's jurisdiction.

TRENDS IN TRANSITIONAL JUSTICE

On the basis of the practical experiences that we have examined, we can identify two trends. First, social reactions to past war crimes and human rights abuses are becoming more oriented towards establishing truth and punishing perpetrators. Secondly, social reactions are becoming internationalized.

As a result, new institutional mechanisms to establish collective or individual responsibility are being created and are being used more often. This especially concerns international or internationalized criminal courts. Hybrid tribunals seem to be a particularly promising new institution in this regard, and their proliferation is to be expected. They benefit from international expert knowledge and impartiality, while, compared with fully international tribunals, they have advantages related to financial costs, efficiency, legitimacy, psychological impact, and the capacity-building necessary for sustaining legal standards and the rule of law.

The legal view prevails that, at the very least, the gravest crimes must be met with criminal proceedings. Amnesties are more and more often used to cover only minor crimes and are sometimes conditioned on cooperation with truth commissions. Although, for long-term stability and reconciliation, the establishment of legal responsibility seems to be unavoidable, in the short run, amnesties are a useful tool to help end the conflict and attain social stability and reintegration. Truth commissions (unlike criminal proceedings, during which victims are subjected to hostile cross-examination) are victim-centred, and can involve large numbers of people. No other criminal proceedings can be as fast at putting away people who could endanger democratic transition as are lustration processes.

The trends toward establishing the truth and punishing the perpetrators of war crimes and human rights abuses, and the internationalization of the reaction to such crimes, will probably remain quite stable. They are embedded in a broader process of the globalization of human rights and the development of international mechanisms for their protection.[34]

NOTES

[1] For a comprehensive overview and analysis of transitional societies, emphasizing the legal aspect, see Teitel (2000).

[2] It is not only societies that have taken different paths. Different international actors, observing problems from different perspectives, have suggested various approaches. There is a tendency on the part of human rights advocates to regard norms and institutions of justice as an omnipotent cure against war crimes and human rights abuses, while diplomats and other peace-makers are far more sceptical, sometimes regarding justice as mere window dressing, or, even worse, as a straightforward impediment to peace (Williams and Scharf 2002).

[3] For how to identify social attitudes toward past war crimes and human rights abuses from social choices in these dilemmas, and which social reaction corresponds to each attitude, see Šimonović (2004).

[4] In cases where amnesty is granted against the rules of international law that prohibit amnesty for certain crimes, perpetrators could still be prosecuted in a third country on the basis of universal jurisdiction. The *Cour de cassation* of France, in a 2002 decision, upheld the decision that had rejected the application of a 1993 Mauritanian amnesty in the *Ely Ould Dah* case. The explanation was that recognizing the applicability of the amnesty would be tantamount to a violation of international obligations and would deprive the principle of universal jurisdiction of its purpose.

[5] The ICRC encourages amnesties at the end of hostilities "for those detained or punished for the mere fact of having participated in hostilities" (Martin 2002). However, a firm stand about the necessity of prosecuting war crimes can become a problem in messy situations such as prisoner exchange during the war. The ICRC, represented at the meeting by its president, Corneio Sommaruga, refused to become a co-signatory of the "All for all" exchange of prisoners agreement between Croatia and the Federal Republic of Yugoslavia because war-crimes proceedings had started and some sentences had been handed down (including a couple of death sentences) against some of the Croatians included in the exchange. The ICRC was aware that those were, by and large, mock trials, but, nevertheless, did not want to get involved in potentially sensitive legal issues.

[6] Even in the early 1990s, the UN was involved in encouraging and even drafting very broad amnesty agreements, covering war crimes of military leaders (Martin 1999, 2002). The turning point was probably the peace agreement for Sierra Leone, signed in Lomé. Foday Sankoh's Revolutionary United Front conditioned signing on having the broadest possible amnesty which provided "absolute and free pardon to all combatants and collaborators in respect of anything done by them in pursuit of their objectives" (Kriis 1999). At the last moment, the UN Secretary General's special envoy appended to his signature a disclaimer to the effect that the amnesty provisions should not apply to international crimes of genocide, crimes against humanity, war crimes, and other serious violations of international humanitarian law (Martin 1999). In practice, such decisions are often not easy. The head of the UN Transitional Administration for Eastern Slavonia (part of Croatia occupied during the war and slowly reintegrated back into it with UN support), Jacques Klein, demanded that

Croatian authorities numerically limit the number of proceedings for war crimes against Serbs from that region in order to prevent their fleeing.

7 The aforementioned Lomé Peace Agreement and the impunity that it allowed did not ultimately provide for a lasting peace in Sierra Leone. Hopefully, the Truth and Reconciliation Commission and the Special Court will provide a more sustainable solution.

8 For an overview of the truth commissions, their achievements, shortcomings, and potential, see Hayner (2001).

9 Guatemala's Truth Commission, in spite of complaints that it went beyond its mandate, included, in its final report, issues such as the social and political participation of indigenous peoples. Similarly, South Africa's Truth and Reconciliation Commission recommended measures to address accountability, prevent future human rights violations, provide reparations and rehabilitation for victims, and reform the security forces (Kritz 2002).

10 "Outsider quality" was cause for some rejection of the work of [the El Salvador] Commission, even though its report was regarded as generally accurate (Kritz 2002).

11 The trials of border guards in Eastern Germany and some others were exceptions (Kritz 2002).

12 Lustration processes were not limited to ex-Communist countries: in El Salvador, on the basis of the review by the "Ad hoc Commission," the retirement of 100 senior military officers was recommended (Kritz 2002).

13 However, Milošević was indicted and was being prosecuted for the aforementioned crimes by the ICTY before his death in March 2006 (Scharf and Schabas 2002).

14 It is only possible to start a proceeding before the ICJ against a state. In the case of the success of the aforementioned processes, Serbia and Montenegro would be (among others) obliged to pay compensation related to the genocide. The author of this article is the Agent of the Republic of Croatia in proceedings against the Federal Republic of Yugoslavia (Serbia and Montenegro) for genocide before the ICJ.

15 Success with compensation paid to the victims of abuses in Chile can be attributed to a relatively small class of eligible victims and a good economic situation, and is therefore difficult to repeat.

16 Only recently have the German government and industry agreed to pay compensation for slave and forced labor during the Second World War to 900,000 surviving victims (van Zyl and Freeman 2002).

17 For the rule of law to become a reality, the complete spectrum of components must be developed, including laws, judiciary, police, and the penal system (United States Institute for Peace 2002: 12–13).

18 Levels of foreign involvement may vary "from the light footprint in Afghanistan through the ambiguous sovereignty in Kosovo to benevolent despotism in East Timor" (Chesterman 2002).

19 On the present state of the discussion on universal jurisdiction, see Summers (2003) and Van der Vyver (2001).

20 For a list of countries where criminal cases have been opened on the basis of universal jurisdiction, see Kritz (2002).

21 ICTY has been established by the UN Security Council Resolution 827, 25 May 1993, UN SCOR, 48th Sess., UN doc. S/RES/827, 1993. About a year and a half later, the Security

Council, by its Res. 955, established ICTR (UN SCOR, 49th Sess., 3543 mtg, Annex, UN doc. S/RES/955, 1994).

[22] It can be estimated that, until now, over $1 billion each has been spent on the ICTY and the ICTR. Taking into account the foreseeable duration of the work of the Tribunals (investigations to be finished by 2004, first instance trials by 2008 and appeals by 2010), the overall expenses of the Tribunals will be substantial. It is interesting to note that a number of states clearly consider the costs of these Tribunals as being too high. The issue was informally raised on a number of occasions (The Stanley Foundation 2002: 16). It has been noted that the UN and the international community continue to pour hundreds of millions of dollars into ad hoc tribunals, while failing to meaningfully invest in rebuilding domestic judicial systems. According to a budgetary report, less than 30% of Member States have paid in full their 2002 Tribunal Assessments. This is particularly striking when compared to regular budget payments, covered in full by 56% of Member States. The fact that a substantial number of states has given priority to the regular budget over the Tribunals is a strong indicator of their position on the best use of their resources.

[23] The decision of the Rwanda Tribunal to conduct some of its proceedings in Kigali (Rwanda) instead of Anisha (Tanzania), where it has its seat, should therefore be welcomed, in spite of numerous logistical difficulties.

[24] Slobodan Milošević was the former president of Serbia (1989–1997) and the Federal Republic of Yugoslavia (1997–2000). Vojislav Šešelj was former Deputy Prime Minister of Serbia, a warlord, and leader of the extremist Radical Party. In spite of the fact that both were indicted and in the ICTY's custody, they headed their parties' lists for the Serbian elections, held in 2003. Šešelj's party won the most seats in the Parliament.

[25] It has been argued that, for example, national proceedings had a much stronger psychological and moral impact on population and contributed more to the denazification of Germany than Nuremberg and other international trials.

[26] General Mirko Norac has been prosecuted and sentenced for his personal involvement in war crimes. Indictments based exclusively on command responsibility, as the ICTY's indictments often are, cannot have such psychological impact as evidence on direct involvement in war crimes. On legal difficulties regarding command responsibility, see Damaška (2001: 455–496).

[27] Almost silence: only a smaller group around his home town was protesting.

[28] A drastic example of the absurdity of such a sharp division is Rwanda. Overall costs of the Rwanda Tribunal, until the expiration of its mandate, can be estimated at about $2 billion, and the expected number of processed persons at about 100, so the costs of the process can be assessed at about $20 million per person. If the same amount per person was spent on all 130,000 people detained for crimes related to the 1994 genocide, then it would require $2.6 trillion, which corresponds to about 300 years of Rwanda's total GDP. It would cost every citizen of Rwanda about $370,000, while, in Rwanda, GDP per capita is about $1,200. It is not only that Rwanda could not afford such expensive trials but that it could not manage any regular trials. Trials (shortened and made less expensive by introducing plea-bargaining) were preserved only for the gravest crimes, while, for others, a new

mechanism, relying on traditional community-level dispensation of justice, called *garaca*, has been introduced. *Garaca* lies somewhere between tribunals and truth commissions: participation is massive and almost a quarter of a million people are envisaged to take part in the process as judges; besides revealing the truth (as envisaged by the Truth and Reconciliation Commission in South Africa), those subjected to the procedure are expected to apologize, express remorse, and ask for forgiveness.

[29] This compromise may be based on various institutional arrangements: the aforementioned hybrid tribunals differ from each other substantially.

[30] In line with the UN SC Res. 1244, 1999 and under strong Russian pressure, the first UNMIK regulation provided that the applicable law would be the law in force on 24 March 1999, when NATO's air campaign started. The predominantly Albanian judiciary put in place by UNMIK insisted, however, on applying the Kosovo Criminal Code and other provincial laws that had been in effect in March 1989, before being illegally revoked by Belgrade. Under strong pressure, UNMIK finally reversed its decision and passed a regulation along the lines of the Albanian demands (Chesterman 2002).

[31] For this very reason, after some experimenting, the UN Administrator in Kosovo decided that, in proceedings for more serious crimes, there should be a majority of international judges. According to a *Financial Times* report, when international judges sat on a Bench with a majority of Kosovar colleagues, they were always outvoted because Serbs were automatically regarded as guilty, while Albanians were rarely condemned. That has led to a push for a majority of "internationals" (Lloyd 2002: 3).

[32] Sometimes, there will simply have to be trade-offs in terms of the higher formal qualifications of foreigners and the higher level of sustainability generated by the early inclusion of locals. For example, none of the East Timorese have ever served as a judge or a prosecutor before UNTAET. If they were not given a chance within a hybrid tribunal, how could East Timor proceed on its own?

[33] On the ICC's potential in the fight against terrorism, see Scheffer (2002: 47).

[34] On such a trend, see Šimonović (2000). For the development of international criminal adjudication, see McCormack (1997) and Šimonović (1999).

REFERENCES

Chesterman, S. 2002. *Justice Under International Administration*. New York: International Peace Academy. http://www.ipacademy.org/pdfs/JUSTICE_UNDER_INTL.pdf

Commission for Reception, Truth and Reconciliation in East Timor. 2004. *Homepage*: http://www.easttimor-reconciliation.org/

Damaška, M. 2001. "The Shadow Side of Command Responsibility." *The American Journal of Comparative Law* 49: 455–96.

Hayner, P. 2001. *Unspeakable Truths: Confronting State Terror and Atrocity*. New York: Routlege.

Kriis, N.J. 2002. "Where We Are and How We Got Here: An Overview of Developments in the Search for Justice and Reconciliation." Pp. 21–46 in *The Legacy of Abuse—Confronting the*

Past, Facing the Future, edited by A.H. Henkin. New York: The Aspen Institute and New York University School of Law.

Lloyd, J. 2002. "We come here to build." *Financial Times* (December 31): 3.

Martin, I. 1999. "Haiti: International Force or National Compromise?" *Journal of Latin American Studies* 31: 711–34.

Martin, I. 2002. "Justice and Reconciliation: Responsibilities and Dilemmas of Peace-makers and Peace-builders." Pp. 81–90 in *The Legacy of Abuse—Confronting the Past, Facing the Future*, edited by A.H. Henkin. New York: The Aspen Institute and New York University School of Law.

McCormack, T.L.H. 1997. "Selective Reaction to Atrocity: War Crimes and the Development of International Criminal Law." *Albany Law Review* 60: 681–732.

Orentlicher, D. 2004. *Independent Study on Best Practices, Including Recommendations, to Assist States in Strengthening Their Domestic Capacity to Combat All Aspects of Impunity.* Submitted to the Commission on Human Rights, E/CN.412004J88, 27 February 2004.

Scharf, M.P. and W.A. Schabas. 2002. *Slobodan Milošević's Trial: A Companion*. New York: Continuum Publishing Group.

Scheffer, D.J. 2002. "Staying the Course with the International Criminal Court." *Cornell International Law Journal* 35: 47–100.

Šimonović, I. 1999. "The Role of the ICTY in the Development of International Criminal Adjudication." *Fordham International Law Journal* 23: 1401–421.

Šimonović, I. 2000. "State Sovereignty and Globalization: Are Some States More Equal?" *Georgia Journal of International and Comparative Law* 3 (28): 381–404.

Šimonović, I. 2003. "Post-Conflict Peace Building: The New Trends." *International Journal of Legal Information* 2 (31): 251–63.

Šimonović, I. 2004. "Attitudes and Types of Reaction Towards Past War Crimes and Human Rights Abuses." *The Yale Journal of International Law* 29: 343–62.

Summers, M.A. 2003. "The International Court of Justice's Decision in *Congo v Belgium*: How Has It Affected the Development of a Principle of Universal Jurisdiction That Would Obligate All States to Prosecute War Criminals?" *Boston University International Law Journal* 21: 64–100.

Teitel, R.G. 2000. *Transitional Justice*. New York: Oxford University Press.

The Stanley Foundation. 2002. *Laying a Durable Foundation for Post-Conflict Societies.* Proceedings of the 37th Conference on the United Nations of the Next Decade. Carmel, CA: The Stanley Foundation.

United States Institute for Peace. 2002. *Lawless Role vs. Rule of Law in the Balkans*. Special Report No. 97. Washington, DC: United States Institute for Peace.

Van der Vyver, J.D. 2001. "International Human Rights: Human Rights, International Criminal Justice and National Self-righteousness." *Emory Law Journal* 50: 775.

van Zyl, P. and M. Freeman. 2002. "The Legacy of Abuse—Conference Report." Pp. 3–20 in *The Legacy of Abuse—Confronting the Past, Facing the Future*, edited by A.H. Henkin. New York: The Aspen Institute and New York University School of Law.

Williams, P.R. and M.P. Scharf. 2002. *Peace with Justice? War Crimes and Accountability in the Former Yugoslavia*. Lanham, MD: Rowman and Littlefield.

CHAPTER STUDY QUESTIONS

- Provide an overview of the range of ways in which post-conflict and transitional societies have attempted to deal with past war crimes and human rights abuses, and highlight what they reflect about recent trends in transitional justice.

- Šimonović argues that amnesties should never cover war crimes and other grave abuses. Why does he make this statement? What are the ramifications of such a policy for the negotiation of lasting peace treaties?

- Why is it often difficult to commence national criminal proceedings based on individual criminal responsibility? How do international tribunals based on universal jurisdiction help remedy the limitations of national criminal proceedings? Outline several advantages and disadvantages of international tribunals for bringing war criminals to justice.

- How does the International Criminal Court (ICC) differ from the ad hoc tribunals established to deal with war crimes in Rwanda and the former Yugoslavia? Does it offer any advantages or disadvantages over them? Why is the US so opposed to its jurisdiction?

RELATED WEB LINKS

Global Policy Forum
http://www.globalpolicy.org/intljustice/tribindx.htm
>This website provides access to a series of links to other sites that cover the war crimes tribunals for Rwanda and Yugoslavia as well as special courts established to deal with genocide and war crimes in Sierra Leone, Cambodia, and East Timor. General articles on war crimes are also provided.

Beyond Intractability
http://www.beyondintractability.org/essay/int_war_crime_tribunals/
>This website provides a discussion of the advantages and limitations of international war crimes tribunals. Links are also provided to other organizations and to articles dealing with war crimes, international tribunals, and the International Criminal Court.

Wikipedia Free Dictionary
http://en.wikipedia.org/wiki/Nuremberg_Trials
>This website provides an overview of the Nuremberg Trials (arguably the first international war crimes tribunal) of Nazi war criminals at the end of World War II. A brief discussion is also provided of the influence of the Nuremberg Trials on subsequent international criminal law. Numerous links are provided to other sites covering many related events and issues related to the Nuremberg Trials.

International Criminal Court
http://www.icc-cpi.int/
This is the home website of the International Criminal Court, which provides details on the structure and operation of the ICC.

Chapter 21

ADVOCACY AND SCHOLARSHIP IN THE STUDY OF INTERNATIONAL WAR CRIME TRIBUNALS AND TRANSITIONAL JUSTICE

LESLIE VINJAMURI AND JACK SNYDER

INTRODUCTION

In the wake of widespread atrocities in the former Yugoslavia and Rwanda, questions of justice and the accountability of perpetrators have energized the worlds of scholarship, advocacy, and policy making. It has become virtually impossible to read the daily news without encountering some reference to international or domestic war crime tribunals, truth commissions, or amnesty for perpetrators of atrocities.

In the years after the Nuremberg Trials, war crimes were a scholarly preoccupation mainly for international lawyers and historians. More recently, however, scholarship on atrocities and transitional justice has also come to occupy an important place within the political science subfields of comparative politics, international relations, and political theory, as well as in philosophy and sociology. International lawyers and human rights advocates have also made significant contributions to the literature on war crime trials and truth commissions. More than in most areas of political science, the linkages between scholars, practitioners, and advocates on questions of justice have had a lasting influence on the evolution of both theory and practice.

In this chapter, we survey the literature on international criminal tribunals and transitional justice. Our primary concern is with scholarship in political science, although we also consider work from the disciplines of law, history, and sociology and from practitioners and advocates. We find that the normative positions of scholars have heavily influenced the development of literature in this field, in which scholarship, practice, and advocacy are deeply intertwined. Advocates and individuals who have played key roles in the development of international criminal justice institutions, domestic tribunals, and truth commissions have been prominent in setting the agenda for scholars. Nonetheless, there is also a growing body of rigorous social science research that attempts to assess empirically—and sometimes critically—the claims of advocates and practitioners and to explain changing strategies of justice.

We consider the major theoretical and empirical questions addressed by the literature on international criminal tribunals and transitional justice. Broadly speaking, we argue that the

471

literature has been dominated by two general orientations, a legalism that is premised on a logic of appropriateness and a pragmatism premised on a logic of consequences. After discussing each of these, we consider a third orientation, guided by a logic of emotions, that recognizes the significance of transitional justice but emphasizes strategies that diverge from the model of legalism. In our survey of each of these orientations, we consider the nexus between scholarship and practice. In our conclusion, we consider how work in international relations and comparative politics can contribute to the study of transitional justice and international war crimes tribunals.

THE LEGALIST APPROACH

The dominant perspective from which scholarship on international war crime tribunals has drawn is legalism. Shklar's landmark book, *Legalism*, defined this as "the ethical attitude that holds that moral conduct is to be a matter of rule following, and moral relationships to consist of duties and rights determined by rules" (Shklar 1964: 1; Teitel 1999). The glue that binds scholars working within this tradition is a shared belief in the importance of promoting universal standards of justice. Underpinning much of the scholarship in this tradition is the assumption that the behavior of actors in international politics is guided by norms that they believe to be appropriate. This "logic of appropriateness" dictates that reducing atrocities is in part a matter of persuading elites and masses to comply with international humanitarian norms. More specifically, advocates and scholars who write from a legalist perspective stress the need to create tribunals that can enforce international law and, especially, international humanitarian and human rights law. Legalists recognize a complicated relationship between peace and justice but submit that accountability is critical to a lasting peace and that "accountability should never be bartered in a *realpolitik* fashion in order to arrive at political expediency" (Bassiouni 2002a: 41). Unlike pragmatists, legalists oppose the granting of amnesty for international crimes.

Legalist scholars and advocates offer several arguments in favor of trials for war crimes, crimes against humanity, genocide, and torture (Bassiouni 2002a: 25). First, they argue that war crime trials that adhere to international standards are the appropriate method for dealing with the perpetrators of mass atrocities and should replace alternatives ranging from vengeance to assassinations or executions. Neier argues that punishment fulfills society's duty "to honor and redeem the suffering of the individual victim" (Orentlicher 1991). Some legalists also argue against alternative strategies of accountability currently in fashion, notably truth commissions; they stress that these strategies represent a compromise of justice because they fail to guarantee the legitimate rights of either victims or perpetrators. Truth commissions, legalists argue, are not a substitute for justice (Seils 2002: 775–95). More worrisome from this perspective, the legal void inherent in truth commissions makes them strong candidates for political manipulation.

Second, legalist scholarship has stressed the potential significance of war crime tribunals in both preventing and deterring future conflicts (Malamud-Goti 1990; Roth 1998, 1999; Seils 2002: 40). According to Diane Orentlicher, a prominent legal scholar, "The fulcrum of the case for criminal punishment is that it is the most effective insurance against future repression"

(Orentlicher 1991: 2540). War crime tribunals deter by placing guilt for crimes such as ethnic cleansing, genocide, and crimes against humanity on the shoulders of individuals deemed responsible for the actions of larger groups. Kenneth Roth, Executive Director of Human Rights Watch, argued that the U.S. government's failure to support the International Criminal Court (ICC) was "shortsighted" because "an effective ICC could help avoid" the risk that U.S. troops faced abroad when conducting humanitarian missions by "deterring the atrocities in the first place" (Roth 1998: 47). Others who have stressed the significance of prosecutions in preventing future atrocities underscore the need for trials to complement a broader commitment to using the tools of military, political, and economic resources if they are to be effective in achieving this goal (Akhavan 2001: 7–31). International courts also aid efforts to prevent future crimes by breaking future cycles of violence. Public trials demonstrate to people that justice will be done publicly and not privately (Rosenberg 1995). Although legalists particularly stress the accountability of war criminals at the top of the chain of command, they rule out lower-level officials' perennial excuse that they were just following orders. This strategy strengthens the deterrent capacity of trials, they suggest, by sending a signal to both those who issue orders and those who obey them.

The link between individual accountability and deterrence stressed by legalists to justify war crime trials became especially important in the 1990s when ethnic conflict broke out in the Balkans, Rwanda, and parts of the former Soviet Union. Legalists believed that individual war crime trials would defuse intergroup conflict and deter future cycles of violence by removing blame from ethnic groups and placing it on individual leaders who could be removed from positions of power. As Meron (1998: 282) has argued, "The great hope of tribunal advocates was that the individualization and decollectivization of guilt ... would help bring about peace and reconciliation."

Finally, legalists argue that war crime trials serve as an education in the rule of law to the peoples of new democracies, authoritarian regimes, and failed states. Trials show the appropriate means of holding perpetrators responsible and help to socialize people into patterns of behavior that conform to liberal and democratic norms. Orentlicher (1991: 2540) suggests that "trials may, as well, inspire societies that are reexamining their basic values to affirm the fundamental principles of respect for the rule of law and for the inherent dignity of individuals." One variant of this argument suggests that the ICC is especially well equipped "through its symbolism and its interaction with domestic legal systems ... to transform political culture (Mayerfeld 2001: 107). Another variant suggests that the mixed tribunal model, best represented by the Special Court for Sierra Leone, is in theory best designed to help bolster domestic judicial institutions and thereby transmit norms of accountability (Sieff and Vinjamuri 2002).

Legalists who stress these justifications for war crime tribunals have permeated human rights-based nongovernmental organizations (NGOs), international organizations, and universities. More than any other professional class, lawyers have moved freely among these institutions and taken leadership roles in the international tribunals whose creation they have advocated. Theodor Meron of New York University's Law School, who has written extensively on international criminal tribunals and was a strong advocate of an international tribunal for the former Yugoslavia, later became President of the International Criminal Tribunal for the former Yugoslavia (Meron 1993, 1997, 1998). Similarly, Ruth Wedgwood, a prominent legal scholar from Yale University, has played an important role in advising the Bush Administration's Defense Department on military tribunals following September 11, and, in 2002, she was elected to the Human Rights Committee, the implementation body for the International Covenant on Civil and Political Rights (Wedgwood 1999). Cherif Bassiouni, Professor of Law at De Paul University and a preeminent scholar of international criminal law and human rights, was from 1992 to 1994, the Chairman of the Commission of Experts that led the war crime investigations in the former Yugoslavia.

The transfer of knowledge, expertise, and values has also moved in the reverse direction; individuals directly employed by tribunals or truth commissions have later created NGOs or written extensive works on the subject. After serving as Deputy Chair of the South African Truth and Reconciliation Commission, Alex Borraine has joined Priscilla Hayner, a scholar practitioner of truth commissions, to create a New York based NGO, the International Center for Transitional Justice, dedicated to the study and advocacy of transitional justice (Borraine 2000; Hayner 2001).

If a shared belief in international criminal justice is what unites legalists, the core concerns that shape legalist scholarship have centered on (a) the appropriate forum for prosecuting war criminals and (b) the implications of war crime tribunals for the further development of international humanitarian law and, more generally, of the international criminal justice system. According to Bassiouni, the legalist position suggests that the choice of the appropriate forum for accountability should depend on four factors: the gravity of the violation, the extent and severity of the victimization, the number of individuals accused, and the degree of command responsibility of those accused. International trials may be more appropriate where the violator regime is still in power, where conflict has not yet been concluded, where the domestic community lacks the will to prosecute, or where one side is significantly less committed to complying with standards for international criminal justice than another. International trials are, however, to be reserved for the prosecution of leaders, policy makers, and other senior officials responsible for mass crimes. Practical criteria also enter the equation and often lead legalists to press for an international trial or significant international participation in local trials, as has been the case in discussions concerning a trial of Saddam Hussein. Domestic trials are deemed appropriate only if the domestic judiciary is independent and if the state's judicial infrastructure is functioning well (Bassiouni 2002a: 26–42).

Legalists see the ICC as "the most appropriate international mechanism through which the proscriptive norms against genocide, crimes against humanity and war crimes can become more effective instrumental norms .... An instrumental norm ... is characterized by repeated and consistent application." Bassiouni argues that "the public processes of the ICC will reinforce social values and expectations concerning international conduct, and that will in turn contribute to the individual internalization of these values." Through a combination of proscriptive norms and its sanctions capabilities, the ICC will "enhance individual and collective compliance, and thus reduce harmful results" (Bassiouni 2002c: 820–21).

Some international lawyers, however, criticize the design of the ICC as being heavily influenced by power politics. For example, some legalists sought to create a court that could examine past perpetrators of mass atrocities, such as Ethiopia's Haile Mariam Mengistu and Chile's Augusto Pinochet, on the grounds that genocide, war crimes, and crimes against humanity were established in customary international law long before the 1998 Rome Statute that created the ICC. Moreover, precedents for retroactive trials had been established earlier by the trials of Adolf Eichmann and Klaus Barbie. Thus, activist legalists felt that politics, not legal considerations, had restricted the ICC to a strictly forward-looking jurisdiction. In the words of one legal scholar, the NGOs "got their court all right, but it ended up being a court of a curious sort, where superpowers pull the strings (through the Security Council) yet at the same time (in the case of the US and China) refuse to support it" (Robertson 1999: 364–67).

Scholars working within the legalist framework have also advocated the prosecution of suspected perpetrators of serious crimes under international law in national courts of any state under the theory that certain crimes carry a universal jurisdiction and can therefore be tried in any court. Bassiouni has argued that crimes against humanity, genocide, and war crimes all carry a universal jurisdiction. In 2001, a group of scholars and NGOs gathered at Princeton University's Woodrow Wilson School to issue the Princeton Principles on Universal Jurisdiction. According to this document, piracy, slavery, war crimes, crimes against peace, crimes against humanity, genocide, and torture are all "serious crimes under international law" that can and should be tried by a "competent and ordinary judicial body of any state." Courts may prosecute these crimes under a universal jurisdiction, the Princeton Principles claim, "even if their national legislation does not specifically provide for it" (Bassiouni 2002b: 1003–005). According to Bassiouni, legal scholars who advocate universal jurisdiction consider it the "most effective method to deter and prevent international crimes" because enabling courts anywhere to prosecute these crimes increases the chances that perpetrators will be held accountable (Bassiouni 2002d: 998; Joyner 1996: 153; Kritz 1996; Meron 1998: 260; Morris 1996; Orentlicher 1991: 2537).

Apart from debates about appropriate legal forums, legalists have continued to discuss the longer-term effects of trials. They contend that trials, despite short-term failures of justice, may still make a significant contribution to the development of international humanitarian law (Boed 2002: 487–98; Meron 1998). Legalists view norms as cumulative and evolving toward ever more standardized and universalized enforcement. Falk (1999: 440), for example, sees the "beginnings of an ethos of criminal accountability that contains no exemptions for political leaders and is being implemented at the global level."

Orentlicher (1991: 2593) suggests that this began with the Nuremberg Tribunal, which contributed to the evolution of the law that now requires states to punish crimes against humanity committed in their own territories. Minow (1998: 50) claims that trials contribute to the project of international criminal justice by helping to "articulate both norms and a commitment to work to realize them ... Even when sharply limited in their numbers, their reach, or their results, indictments, prosecutions, and convictions can build up the materials of international human rights and the notions of individual responsibility, conscience, and human dignity that imbue them." Even politically marred trials, she argues, can "produce some sense of accountability. Then claims for the power of the rule of law can grow, even in the face of demonstrable failures in its implementation" (Minow 1998: 50).

Some suggest that the most useful aspect of the ad hoc tribunals has been the propagation of norms of accountability. Indeed, many legalists argue that these courts have "mainstreamed accountability in international relations" (Akhavan 2001: 95). Meron (1998: 304) says the tribunals of the 1990s spurred "the elevation of many principles of international humanitarian law from the rhetorical to the normative, and from the merely normative to the effectively criminalized." Meron argues that the International Criminal Tribunal for the former Yugoslavia's failure to deter, highlighted by the massacre at Srebrenica, is largely a product of the international community's inability to enforce indictments. However, he argues that the tribunal has been more successful in strengthening international law (Meron 1998: 282–283). In particular, he suggests that the statutes for the two ad hoc tribunals were critical in extending international humanitarian law to the domain of civil wars (Meron 1998: 229).

Michael Scharf, a legal scholar who worked in the State Department's Office of the Legal Advisor when it was involved in creating the Yugoslav Tribunal, has described the creation of a permanent ICC as the product of the momentum generated by the ad hoc tribunals for Yugoslavia and Rwanda, which demonstrated a need for more routinized justice (Scharf 1999: 621–646). Legalists suggest the ICC has had a similar effect. According to Schabas (2001: 19), who has written extensively on the ICC, "The influence of the Rome Statute will extend deep into domestic criminal law, enriching the jurisprudence of national courts and challenging prosecutors and judges to greater zeal in the repression of serious violations of human rights."

A few prominent international legal scholars have criticized prevailing legalistic approaches and urge that legal remedies be scrutinized in terms of their pragmatic consequences. Meron cautions that "the enforcement of international humanitarian law cannot depend on international tribunals alone. There will never be a substitute for national courts." However, his assessment of the record of national prosecutions for violators of international humanitarian laws is gloomy. "A lack of resources, evidence and, above all, political will has stood in the way" (Meron 1998: 230).

Another international legal expert who is critical of the prevailing legalism, José Alvarez, argues that the international tribunal following the 1994 Rwanda genocide "provides a cautionary tale against a 'one size fits all' approach to international criminal justice" (Alvarez 1999: 365–483). Most survivors preferred local trials, for reasons that are both practical and psychological. Local criminal processes, if done properly, can have a greater impact on the preservation of collective memory, victim mollification, and the national rule of law, Alvarez writes. In contrast, the international tribunal's vision of justice has been scarcely visible within Rwanda and has made no contribution to national reconciliation.

Others have addressed the relationship between legal principles and political consequences in a different way. Legal scholar Ruti Teitel has written extensively on the functions that justice plays in securing transitions from authoritarianism to a new regime. Instances of transitional justice "reflect a balancing and accommodation of ideal theories of law and the political circumstances of the transition" (Teitel 2000: 224). Teitel's work suggests that empirical evaluations of the capacity of trials to deter atrocities fail to capture their real purpose. Transitional justice, Teitel argues, serves to construct a liberal political identity for the new state: "transitional justice offers a way to reconstitute the collective—across potentially divisive racial, ethnic, and religious lines" (Teitel 2000: 225).

Empirical social scientists have also begun to evaluate the claims of legalist proponents of war crime tribunals. Political scientist Gary Bass tries to both explain and evaluate the emergence of war crime tribunals as a prominent tool of public policy. Based on detailed case histories of international justice after the Napoleonic wars, World War I, the Armenian genocide, World War II, the Yugoslav breakup, and the Rwanda genocide, Bass (2000: 7) argues that leaders turn to legalistic approaches when they are seized "in the grip of a principled *idea*." Only liberal democracies pursue war crime tribunals, he says, because this form of justice meshes with their basic ideal of due process. He adds, however, that legalist ideas do not always hold sway in liberal democracies. "Nonrhetorical calls for justice are fitful," he observes, because pragmatic considerations also come into play (Bass 2000: 8). Even liberal states are selfish. They are almost never willing to risk their own soldiers simply to bring war criminals to justice and are rarely willing to pursue criminals who victimize only foreigners. To overcome this indifference, legalism is not enough, he concludes—"one also needs outrage," which has recently been effectively promoted by NGOs such as Human Rights Watch (Bass 2000: 31, 33).

Bass (2000: 282) seeks common ground between the legalist and pragmatic concerns, arguing that there is a "self-serving case for a more legalist world" in which aggression and violent bigotry would be effectively punished. However, Bass finds that we do not yet live in a world in which the legalists' empirical claims are borne out. It is not true, he says, that the threat of trials has a strong deterrent effect on potential war criminals. Nor do trials unambiguously help to rehabilitate former enemy countries or to place blame for atrocities on individuals rather than on whole ethnic groups.

Despite his acknowledgment of the limitations of trials, Bass (2000: 304) concludes with a positive net evaluation of their impact because he sees the alternative to trials as "uncontrolled vengeance," not "a painless kind of forgetting." The "great advantage of legalism is that it institutionalizes and moderates desires for revenge." Here Bass's argument resembles the more general position of many legalists that tribunals socialize states into patterns of behavior that draw on legal traditions. These positive effects of trials may, he argues, be deferred to successive generations, as was the case in Germany, where trials were held by the post-Nazi generation (Bass 2003: 95). He also notes that trials are indeed helpful in setting the historical record straight (Bass 2000: 286–304).

However, these findings are debatable. Pragmatists dispute Bass's claim that the international tribunal for the former Yugoslavia has socialized the younger generations of Serbs into supporting war crime trials (Snyder and Vinjamuri 2003: 39). Legal processes may also create a narrow view of the past. The Rwanda tribunal looked exclusively at a small segment of the events of 1994 and thus failed to produce a historically deep, comprehensive picture of the causes and meaning of the genocide. Pragmatists' research also suggests that revenge is unlikely to be a highly disruptive, enduring feature of the political landscape. Their critiques of legalism are more fundamental than those of Bass.

THE PRAGMATIST APPROACH

A second approach to issues of transitional justice is pragmatic. Pragmatists are interested in, first, explaining who gets tried for abuses and with what consequences and, second, deriving consequentialist ethical prescriptions from that explanatory account. The power and self-interest of political actors loom large in such accounts. Proponents of legalistic justice who underrate the centrality of these political considerations cause more abuses than they prevent, in this view. In the evaluation of outcomes, the consequences of trials for the consolidation of peace and democracy trump the goal of justice per se, since the future prospects for justice depend on the establishment of social peace and unshakeable democratic institutions.

Some, though not all, pragmatists are political realists. Pragmatists incorporate ethical and legal goals in their objectives and analyses, but they take a firmly consequentialist view of how to achieve them. Empirical studies of the actual consequences of justice strategies—or at any rate, testable assertions about those consequences—are central to the pragmatists' case.

Henry Kissinger is not only a public figure but also a card-carrying political scientist who has written about the doctrine of universal jurisdiction for war crimes and crimes against humanity from a classical realist perspective. He also came under the scrutiny of a Belgian court for alleged war crimes himself under the theory of universal jurisdiction. Notwithstanding his personal interest in the topic, his philosophical stance toward the legalism of the courts is what might be expected of a scholar with longstanding realist credentials. Writing in *Foreign Affairs* in 2001, Kissinger complains that "distrusting national governments, many of the advocates of universal jurisdiction seek to place politicians under the supervision of magistrates and the judicial system" (Kissinger 2001: 94). These advocates, he claims, "argue that the state is the basic cause of war and cannot be trusted to deliver justice. But even a cursory examination of history shows that there is no evidence to support such a theory." Prudent, flexible political judgment yields better outcomes than rigid, apolitical legalism: "The role of the statesman is to choose the best option when seeking to advance peace and justice, realizing that there is frequently a tension between the two and that any reconciliation is likely to be partial" (Kissinger 2001: 95).

• Prescriptively, Kissinger argues that political authorities should be in charge of the judicial process. The UN Security Council, where the United States has a veto, should set up a Human Rights Commission to report on abuses that may warrant judicial actions. When the legal system of the state where the alleged crime occurred, is undemocratic or incapable of judging the crime, the Security Council should set up an ad hoc tribunal on the model of the ones for Yugoslavia and Rwanda with a precisely defined scope (Kissinger 2001: 95–96).

Among the more empirical contributions to the pragmatist literature, Huntington's (1991) discussion of post-transitional justice in *The Third Wave* offers several of the most basic and enduring hypotheses about the causes and consequences of justice strategies. Huntington asks whether it is more appropriate, by which he means more prudent, to punish past atrocities in newly democratizing states or to forget them. He begins with lists of contradictory legal and moral assertions that underpin each view: "democracy depends on demonstrating the rule of law through trials" versus "democracy has to be based on reconciliation in which all groups set aside divisions of the past," "prosecution deters future crimes" versus "amnesty is needed to reconcile perpetrators to the new order," and so forth. But "in actual practice," says Huntington, "what happened was little affected by moral and legal considerations. It was shaped almost exclusively by politics, by the nature of the democratization process, and by the distribution of political power during and after the transition" (Huntington 1991: 213–15).

In about half of the pre-1990 transitional countries, Huntington finds, leaders of the existing authoritarian regimes initiated the democratization. They were hardly going to allow their crimes to be prosecuted. They gave themselves amnesties. In countries where the dictatorship simply collapsed, however, some top leaders were often put on trial, because they no longer had the power to prevent it. Finally, in transitions that were negotiated between state leaders and powerful opposition forces, the terms of an amnesty were often part of the bargain (Huntington 1991: 211–25). In short, "officials of strong authoritarian regimes that voluntarily ended themselves were not prosecuted; officials of weak authoritarian regimes that collapsed were punished, if they were promptly prosecuted" before the public lost interest (Huntington 1991: 228). In international wars, similar analyses suggest that external conquest provides the best conditions for trials (Zalaquett 1995).

Huntington then derives prescriptive "guidelines for democratizers" from these empirical findings. These prescriptions accord with those earlier elaborated by scholars who studied transitions from authoritarian rule (e.g., Stepan 1986: 64). Thus, if the perpetrators remain strong, "do not attempt to prosecute" because "the political costs will outweigh any moral gains." If they are weak, and "if you feel it is morally and politically desirable, prosecute the leaders of the authoritarian regime promptly (within one year of your coming to power) while making it clear that you will not prosecute middle- and lower-ranking officials," who otherwise might form a powerful constituency opposing democracy. When facing tradeoffs, "do not prosecute, do not punish, do not forgive, and, above all, do not forget" (Huntington 1991: 231).

Other scholars working within this tradition have built on Huntington's basic ideas but diverged in significant ways. In a study of transitions in three countries (South Korea, Greece, and Argentina), Roehrig also suggests that a more cautious approach toward prosecuting the military may be more conducive to a smooth transition to democracy. Roehrig suggests several criteria for holding trials. First, efforts to reassert civilian control over the military are critical and should take place before trials of the military begin. Second, trials of the military should be designed such that they do not threaten the military as an institution. Trials should be of a limited scope, and, if they go deeper than a few top officers, careful thought should be given before pursuing radical cuts to the military budget. Retaining an important mission for the military is also an effective way of achieving this goal. In Greece and South Korea, the military was reined in before trials took place, and trials were limited in their scope (Roehrig 2002: 198–99).

Some pragmatists have argued that the feasibility of trials depends in part on the stage of the conflict. They agree that justice should be deferred until peace is secured but differ as to the timing of successive attempts to prosecute. Some argue that an attempt to uncover the truth should follow successful efforts to secure peace, and only after a democratic culture has taken root should trials be considered (Roehrig 2002: 186–88). Others argue that, even after peace is secured, the pursuit of justice should be contingent on underlying balances of power between the major ethnic groups in society or on the effective containment of potential spoilers (Snyder and Vinjamuri 2003; Vinjamuri 2003).

Many pragmatist scholars contend that state behavior typically follows the dictates of pragmatic behavior. States may pay lip service to the norm of prosecuting war criminals, but they seldom support such efforts where spoilers present a great risk to stability (Snyder and Vinjamuri 2003). One scholar of Nuremberg labels this tendency to manipulate the law to fit with political objectives "strategic legalism." He claims that this has characterized American policy makers both before and since Nuremberg (Maguire 2000).

Another effort to build on Huntington-style pragmatism argues that trials can be tools that enable societies to alter underlying power structures. Nino's *Radical Evil on Trial* accepts Huntington's pragmatic criteria and agrees with much of his political analysis. However, he parts company with Huntington in his assessment of Argentina, the central case study of his book. Nino points out that Huntington's strongest objection to trials is that they may destroy the basis for democracy, on which justice depends. But this, says Nino, hinges on a narrow view of "what makes democracy self-sustainable. If one believes that self-interested motivations are enough, then the balance works heavily against retroactive justice. On the other hand, if one believes that impartial value judgments contribute to the consolidation of democracy, there is a compelling political case for retroactive justice" (Nino 1996: 134). "Authoritarianism," he contends, "is the product of certain social trends that cannot be overcome merely because the interests of some powerful people happen to favor democratic resolution of conflicts." In Argentina, those underlying trends led to the entrenchment of unlawfulness, military privilege and concentrated social power. Trials are "great occasions for social deliberation and for collective examination of the moral values underlying public institutions," which can help break that power structure and invent a new, democratic society (Nino 1996: 131).

In short, Nino is just as consequentialist and pragmatic as Huntington, and he accepts much of Huntington's political analysis of self-interested motives. He is highly critical of Argentine human rights groups, whom he says "held a Kantian view of punishment; even if society were on the verge of dissolution, it had the duty to punish the last offender" (Nino 1996: 112). However, he extends consequentialist reasoning past the myopically self-interested motives of actors to assess the effect of normative deliberation on political outcomes.

Elster (1998: 7–48) likewise tries to integrate self-interested and normative (or impartial) factors in developing hypotheses about the causes of transitional justice outcomes, lightly illustrating them with examples. He groups these causes under the headings of actors, constraints on their decisions, their motives, their beliefs, and the mechanisms for aggregating their preferences into binding decisions. The strength of the piece lies mainly in its careful disentangling of different kinds of causes and reasons, which advocates' arguments often jumble together.

Regarding motives, Elster begins with impartial reason, distinguishing between backward-looking motives such as retribution and forward-looking motives such as deterrence. He complains that "backward-looking considerations are often conflated with consequentialist arguments," for example, by confusing the rights of victims with their psychological needs, which is "shaky on moral as well as factual grounds." Morally, it is not clear that the needs of victims can justify a particular treatment of wrongdoers. Many would find repugnant the implication that wrongdoers whose victims happened to have died should, other things being equal, be let off more lightly. Factually, it is not clear that truthfinding not followed by punishment will produce catharsis" (Elster 1998: 35).

After discussing self-interest, which dominates Huntington's analysis, Elster moves on to passion. Although he sees anger as a powerful motive for justice, he also argues that passion "spends itself" quickly. Citing the prosecution of Nazi collaborators after World War II, he notes that convictions and sentences became much more lax after an initial period of outrage (Elster 1998: 40–41). If true more generally, this calls into question the common assertion that failures to deliver justice will fester and threaten the social peace.

Overall, Elster's analysis shows that pragmatic, consequentialist, and utilitarian approaches to transitional justice need not be as narrowly focused on political power and bargaining as Huntington's seminal argument. Impartial normative persuasion, moral judgments, and passions may all affect assessments of what is prudent and possible.

Finally, Goldsmith and Krasner (2003) apply a sophisticated consequentialist, modified realist yardstick to measure the prudence of the ICC and other modalities of justice favored by activists. These authors argue that they come up short. They criticize legalists and idealists both for ignoring power and for overestimating the normative consensus on which law must be based if it is to be legitimate and effective. Like Elster's and Nino's, their stance is engaged with the consequentialist dimensions of normative arguments and is in no way narrowly realist.

A few international lawyers and empirical social scientists influenced by the scholarship of those working within this tradition have also begun to evaluate the consequences of war crime trials. Wedgwood (1998: 24), for example, argues that the United States should take the ICC seriously, not for legalistic reasons but to enhance the "power and prestige" of the United States. In a study of war crime trials, truth commissions, and amnesties pursued in civil wars that have ended since 1989, Snyder and Vinjamuri (2003) find that states have tended to follow the dictates of pragmatism while paying lip service to legalist arguments for justice. They also find that throughout the post Cold War era, powerful states have been effective at pushing the development of the norm in directions that reinforce the authority of states and especially of liberal states. The Bush Administration's emphasis on "mixed" tribunals that emphasize local participation and the complementarity principle of the ICC both underscore this trend (Snyder and Vinjamuri 2003).

THE EMOTIONAL PSYCHOLOGY APPROACH

A third approach to issues of transitional justice emphasizes the social psychology of emotions. Scholars and advocates who explore the "logic of emotions" seek, first, to develop an explanatory account of the establishment of social peace in the wake of widespread atrocities and, second, to derive policy prescriptions from that explanatory account. Typically, they argue that eliminating the conditions that breed atrocities depends on achieving an emotional catharsis in the community of victims and an acceptance of blame by the perpetrators. Without an effort to establish a consensus on the truth about past abuses, national reconciliation will be impossible, as resentful groups will continue to use violence to voice their emotions. A successful process of truth telling, they argue, can "promote and protect a culture of human rights" in part by recognizing and vindicating the experiences of victims (van Zyl 2002: 745–60). Truth commissions could serve the goal of "healing for individuals and reconciliation across social divisions" even better, scholars have argued, if they diverged "even more than they usually do from prosecutions" and offered "more extensive therapeutic assistance and relief from threats of prosecution" (Minow 1998: 88). For these reasons, proponents of truth commissions stress the importance of encouraging perpetrators to admit responsibility for their crimes, sometimes in exchange for amnesty (Kiss 2000: 216–30; Minow 2000: 235–60).

Advocates of this approach propound a conception of justice that is centered on the survivors and victims, not on retribution against the perpetrator. They argue, moreover, that cathartic truth telling has the benefits of strengthening civil society, compensating victims psychologically and materially, and telling a more coherent narrative than do trials focused narrowly on the guilt of individuals (Borraine 2000; Minow 2000). Some advocates also argue that truth commissions can play a pivotal role in moving the process of institutional reform forward. Van Zyl (2002: 745–60) argues that, in South Africa, the truth commission did this by generating widespread public debate about human rights abuse and official culpability, thereby strengthening the hand of those working to promote change and working against bureaucratic inertia that might impede reform.

Some proponents of cathartic truth telling speak in the language of psychotherapy. Scholars have criticized this view, which is popular with some advocates, on empirical grounds (Pupavac 2001: 358–72). A more rationalistic interpretation, examined in a comparative study of the reconciliation processes pursued in international and civil wars, emphasizes the role of justice in signaling a state's commitment to reconcile with its adversary in the aftermath of conflict (Long and Brecke 2003: 31). Long and Brecke hypothesize that reconciliation initiatives work when they constitute costly, risky, novel, voluntary, noncontingent, and/or irrevocable signals of intentions toward the aggrieved party. They find some support for this signaling model, especially in settlements of international conflicts.

For the settlement of civil wars, however, Long and Brecke find more empirical support for an argument grounded in evolutionary biology, which claims that social cohesion hinges on the emotions of reconciliation and the practice of forgiveness. They find that successful civil war settlements tend to go through a trajectory that starts with truth telling and limited justice, culminates in an emotionally salient call for a new relationship between former enemies, and sometimes accomplishes a redefinition of social identities. One problem with their research design, however, is the difficulty of knowing whether the emotional theater of reconciliation is causally central to establishing peace or whether it is mainly window dressing that makes political bargaining and amnesties more palatable to the public. Their brief, descriptive case studies establish the minimal plausibility of the explanation based on emotion and forgiveness, but they do not probe hard for alternative interpretations.

An alternative conceptual basis for strategies based on the psychology of emotions might be found in the burgeoning literature on the role of emotion, resentment, and status reversal in sparking ethnic violence (Horowitz 2001; Petersen 2002). Arguably, institutionally structured truth telling or punishment might serve as a release valve for resentments that might otherwise be expressed as riots, pogroms, or exclusionary ethnonational political movements. Such arguments might be located more broadly in recent theoretical developments that demonstrate the intimate connection between cognition and emotion in appraising political situations and deciding how to act (Elster 1999; Goodwin 2001: 1–57).

All of these approaches based on the psychology of emotions locate the solution to human rights abuses at the popular level. Reconciliation, in this view, resolves conflict because it reduces tensions between peoples, not between elites. However, elites, not masses, have instigated many recent ethnic conflicts with high levels of civilian atrocities. Solutions that mitigate tensions at the mass level need to be combined with strategies that effectively neutralize elite spoilers and manipulators (Kaufman 2001).

Political scientist James Gibson has tried to assess the impact of truth telling on social reconciliation based on his surveys of attitudes toward the South African Truth and Reconciliation Commission (TRC). His initial studies noted that the TRC provoked the anger of some victims' relatives, who watched revealed perpetrators walk free (Gibson and Gouws 1999: 501–18). His subsequent research shows that South Africans consider amnesty to be necessary but unfair. This perceived unfairness could be mitigated, according to the survey's findings, if victims' families had a voice in truth commission proceedings, if perpetrators' apologies were perceived to be sincere, and if victims were financially compensated (Gibson 2002: 540–56).

Overall, Gibson finds that white South Africans who accept the truth as told at the TRC forum are more likely to be reconciled to positive race relations (Gibson 2003). This finding does not hold for black South Africans, however—perhaps because the TRC's stories were not news to them, Gibson speculates. Even for the whites, Gibson admits that it is difficult to prove that those who became more conciliatory did so because they were persuaded by the TRC's version of the truth. It is possible that many decided to reconcile for other reasons and came to accept the TRC's truth later. Lacking data to measure change over time, Gibson relies on the two-stage least squares statistical method to aid his speculation about causal direction (Gibson 2003).

A final limitation of Gibson's study is that it addresses reconciliation only from the viewpoint of individual attitudes. He acknowledges that "not all questions of reconciliation can be understood in terms of the attributes of citizens. Groups are important, institutions are important, and some individuals (elites) are more important than others" (Gibson 2003). Indeed, South Africa's truth telling and reconciliation, such as it was, could happen only because of the favorable political context created by political deals and coalition politics of the kind that pragmatists study.

CONCLUSIONS

The literature on international war crime tribunals and transitional justice has been heavily influenced by the normative views of human rights advocates and international lawyers. In particular, the nexus between advocacy, practice, and scholarship has shaped the scholarship that has come out of the legalist tradition. Individuals working in this mode have moved between roles as scholars, advocates, and practitioners.

In principle, there should be no objection to scholars doing policy-relevant work in this or any other field. Indeed, the relevance of the legalists' ideas to compelling moral and political concerns explains why they have attracted so much attention. Sometimes, however, the commitment to advocacy has come at the expense of progress in empirical research. Some of the writings of these advocate-scholars have treated the benefits of war crime trials as an assumption rather than an empirical proposition to be tested rigorously.

Increasingly, however, scholars taking all three approaches—legalist, pragmatist, and emotional psychology—have begun to undertake systematic empirical studies of the factors that have driven states' choices of different strategies of justice and the effectiveness of these strategies in achieving the goals that their proponents claim for them. This presents a new opportunity for mainstreaming the study of war crime tribunals and transitional justice in political science. Because of their broader understanding of processes of democracy building and democratic consolidation, liberalization, and transitions from authoritarianism during which decisions are made about justice, students of comparative politics are well placed to analyze the implications of these strategies of justice for broader social and political trends. Similarly, international relations scholars have a wealth of knowledge about the factors that shape the successes or failures of postwar reconstruction efforts and nation building. Strategies of justice are one component of these frameworks for reconstituting political order in the aftermath of war. This knowledge will allow political scientists to design more careful studies to assess the influence of justice on political order and on democracy.

Already, a number of political scientists have begun to develop hypotheses grounded in careful empirical investigation, rather than simply more conviction, concerning the effects of war crime trials and truth commissions on peace and on the consolidation of democracy. Some have even begun to develop criteria for pursuing justice based on empirical analysis that move beyond the divisions between legalists and pragmatists. Ultimately, these studies are likely to be the most fruitful, both for the practitioners and for scholarship.

REFERENCES

Akhavan, P. 2001. "Beyond Impunity: Can International Criminal Justice Prevent Future Atrocities?" *American Journal of International Law* 95: 7–31.

Alvarez, J. 1999. "Crimes of States/Crimes of Hate: Lessons from Rwanda." *Yale Journal of International Law* 24: 365–483.

Bass, G. 2000. *Staying the Hand of Vengeance.* Princeton: Princeton University Press.

Bass, G. 2003. "Milošević in The Hague." *Foreign Affairs* 82: 82–96.

Bassiouni, M.C. (Ed.). 2002. *Post-Conflict Justice.* Ardsley, NY: Transnational.

Bassiouni, M.C. 2002a. "Accountability for Violations of International Humanitarian Law and Other Serious Violations of Human Rights." Pp. 3–54 in *Post-Conflict Justice,* edited by M. C. Bassiouni. Ardsley, NY: Transnational.

Bassiouni, M.C. 2002b. "The Princeton Principles on Universal Jurisdiction." Pp. 1003–05 in *Post-Conflict Justice*, edited by M.C. Bassiouni. Ardsley, NY: Transnational.

Bassiouni, M.C. 2002c. "The Universal Model: The International Criminal Court." Pp. 813–28 in *Post-Conflict Justice*, edited by M.C. Bassiouni. Ardsley, NY: Transnational.

Bassiouni, M.C. 2002d. "Universal Jurisdiction for International Crimes: Historical Perspectives and Contemporary Practice. Pp. 945–1002 in *Post-Conflict Justice*, edited by M.C. Bassiouni. Ardsley, NY: Transnational.

Boed, R. 2002. "The International Criminal Tribunal for Rwanda." Pp. 487–498 in *Post-Conflict Justice*, edited by M.C. Bassiouni. Ardsley, NY: Transnational.

Borraine, A. 2000. *A Country Unmasked*. Oxford: Oxford University Press.

Elster, J. 1998. "Coming to Terms with the Past: A Framework for the Study of Justice in the Transition to Democracy." *Archives of European Sociology* 39: 7– 48.

Elster, J. 1999. *Alchemies of the Mind: Rationality and the Emotions*. Cambridge: Cambridge University Press.

Falk, R. 1999. "The Pursuit of International Justice: Present Dilemmas and an Imagined Future." *Journal of International Affairs* 52: 409–444.

Gibson, J.L. 2002. "Truth, Justice, and Reconciliation: Judging the Fairness of Amnesty in South Africa." *American Journal of Political Science* 46: 540–56.

Gibson, J.L. 2003. *Overcoming Intolerance in South Africa: Experiments in Democratic Persuasion*. Cambridge: Cambridge University Press.

Gibson, J.L. and A. Gouws. 1999. "Truth and Reconciliation in South Africa: Attributions of Blame and the Struggle over Apartheid." *American Political Science Review* 93: 501–518.

Goldsmith, J. and S.D. Krasner. 2003. "The Limits of Idealism." *Daedalus* 132: 47–63.

Goodwin, J. 2001. *Passionate Politics: Emotions and Social Movements*. Chicago: University of Chicago Press.

Hayner, P. 2001. *Unspeakable Truths: Confronting State Terror and Atrocity*. New York: Routledge.

Horowitz, D. 2001. *The Deadly Ethnic Riot*. Berkeley: University of California Press.

Huntington, S.R. 1991. *The Third Wave: Democratization in the Late Twentieth Century*. Norman: University of Oklahoma Press.

Joyner, C.C. 1996. "Arresting Impunity: The Case for Universal Jurisdiction in Bringing War Criminals to Accountability." *Law and Contemporary Problems* 59: 153–72.

Kaufman, S.J. 2001. *Modern Hatreds: The Symbolic Politics of Ethnic War*. Ithaca, NY: Cornell University Press.

Kiss, B. 2000. "Moral Ambition Within and Beyond Political Constraints: Reflections on Restorative Justice." Pp. 216–30 in *Truth vs. Justice: The Morality of Truth Commissions*, edited by R.I. Rotberg and D. Thompson. Princeton: Princeton University Press.

Kissinger, H. 2001. "The Pitfalls of Universal Jurisdiction." *Foreign Affairs* 80: 94–95.

Kritz, N.J. 1996. "Coming to Terms with Atrocities: A Review of Accountability Mechanisms for Mass Violations of Human Rights." *Law and Contemporary Problems* 59: 127–52.

Long, W.J. and P. Brecke. 2003. *War and Reconciliation: Reason and Emotion in Conflict Resolution*. Cambridge, MA: MIT Press.

Maguire, R. 2000. *Law and War: An American Story*. New York: Columbia University Press.

Malamud-Goti, J. 1990. "Transitional Governments in the Breach: Why Punish State Criminals?" *Human Rights Quarterly* 12: 1–16.

Mayerfeld, J. 2001. "The Mutual Dependence of External and Internal Justice: The Democratic Achievement of the International Criminal Court." *Finnish Yearbook of International Law* 12: 71–107.

Meron, T. 1993. "The Case for War Crime Trials in Yugoslavia." *Foreign Affairs* 72: 122–35.

Meron, T. 1997. "Answering for War Crimes: Lessons from the Balkans." *Foreign Affairs* 76: 2–8.

Meron, T. 1998. *War Crimes Law Comes of Age: Essays.* Oxford: Oxford University Press.

Minow, M. 1998. *Between Vengeance and Forgiveness: Facing History after Genocide and Mass Violence.* Boston: Beacon.

Minow, M. 2000. "The Hope for Healing: What Can Truth Commissions Do?" Pp. 216–30 in *Truth vs. Justice: The Morality of Truth Commissions,* edited by R.I. Rotberg and D. Thompson. Princeton: Princeton University Press.

Morris, M.R. 1996. "International Guidelines Against Impunity: Facilitating Accountability." *Law and Contemporary Problems* 59: 29–40.

Nino, C. 1996. *Radical Evil on Trial.* New Raven: Yale University Press.

Orentlicher, D.R. 1991. "Settling Accounts: The Duty to Prosecute Human Rights Violations of a Prior Regime." *Yale Law Journal* 100: 2537– 615.

Petersen, R. 2002. *Understanding Ethnic Violence: Fear, Hatred, and Resentment in Twentieth Century Eastern Europe.* Cambridge: Cambridge University Press.

Pupavac, V. 2001. "Therapeutic Governance: Psycho-Social Intervention and Trauma Risk Management." *Disasters* 25: 358–72.

Robertson, G. 1999. *Crimes Against Humanity: The Struggle for Global Justice.* New York: New Press.

Roehrig, T. 2002. *The Prosecution of Former Military Leaders in Newly Democratic Nations: The Cases of Argentina, Greece, and South Korea.* Jefferson, NC: McFarland.

Rosenberg, T. 1995. "Tipping the Scales of Justice." *World Political Journal* 12 (3): 55–64.

Rotberg, R.I. and D. Thompson. (Eds.). 2000. *Truth vs. Justice: The Morality of Truth Commissions.* Princeton: Princeton University Press.

Roth, K. 1998. "The Court the US Doesn't Want." *New York Review of Books* 45 (18): 45–47.

Roth, K. 1999. "Speech One: Endorse the International Criminal Court." Pp. 19–36 in *Toward an International Criminal Court?* edited by A.M. Slaughter, K. Roth, J. Bolton, and R. Wedgwood. New York: Council on Foreign Relations.

Schabas, W.A. 2001. *An Introduction to the International Criminal Court.* Cambridge, UK: Cambridge University Press.

Scharf, M.R. 1999. "Responding to Rwanda: Accountability Mechanisms in the Aftermath of Genocide." *Journal of International Affairs* 52: 621–646.

Seils, P. 2002. "The Limits of Truth Commissions in the Search for Justice: An Analysis of the Truth Commissions of El Salvador and Guatemala and Their Effect in Achieving Post-Conflict Justice." Pp. 775–95 in *Post-Conflict Justice,* edited by M. C. Bassiouni. Ardsley, NY: Transnational.

Shklar, J. 1964. *Legalism.* Cambridge, MA: Harvard University Press.

Sieff, M. and L. Vinjamuri. 2002. "Prosecuting War Criminals: An Argument for Decentralization." *Conflict, Security, Development* 2: 103–113.

Snyder, J. and L. Vinjamuri. 2003/2004. "Trials and Errors: Principle and Pragmatism in Strategies of International Justice." *International Security* 28: 5–44.

Stepan, A. 1986. "Paths Toward Redemocratization: Theoretical and Comparative Considerations." Pp. 64–84 in *Transitions from Authoritarian Rule: Comparative Perspectives*, edited by G. O'Donnell, P. Schmitter, and L. Whitehead. Baltimore, MD: Johns Hopkins University Press.

Teitel, R.G. 1999. "Bringing the Messiah Through the Law." Pp. 177–93 in *Human Rights in Political Transitions: Gettysburg to Bosnia*, edited by C. Hesse and R. Post. New York: Zone Books.

Teitel, R.G. 2000. *Transitional Justice.* Oxford: Oxford University Press.

van Zyl, P. 2002. "Unfinished Business: The Truth and Reconciliation Commission's Contribution to Justice in Post-Apartheid South Africa." Pp. 745–60 in *Post-Conflict Justice*, edited by M. C. Bassiouni. Ardsley, NY: Transnational.

Vinjamuri, L. 2003. "Order and Justice in Iraq." *Survival* 45: 135–52.

Wedgwood, R. 1998. "Fiddling in Rome: America and the International Criminal Court." *Foreign Affairs* 77: 20–24.

Zalaquett, J. 1995. "Confronting Human Rights Violations Committed by Former Governments: Applicable Principles and Political Constraints." *Transitional Justice* 1: 3–31.

CHAPTER STUDY QUESTIONS

- Provide an overview of the three different approaches reflected in recent advocacy and scholarship literature on international war crime tribunals and transitional justice. What are the recognized strengths and weaknesses of these approaches?

- The legalist approach to war crimes argues that legal accountability should never be sacrificed in the name of political expediency. Why do its advocates make this argument? Do you agree with their arguments? Why? Why not?

- According to Huntington (*The Third Wave*), one of the major contradictions between the legalist and pragmatist approaches lies in the distinction between "democracy depends on demonstrating the rule of law through trials" and "democracy has to be based on reconciliation in which all groups set aside divisions of the past." Discuss the practical and moral implications of both positions. Do you think it is possible to satisfy both goals in a given situation?

- Discuss the major principles incorporated in the emotional psychology approach to handling war crimes and human rights abuses. Outline at least two major purported advantages that this approach offers over the legalist and pragmatist approaches. In practice, how successful have "truth commissions" (a major mechanism associated with this approach) been?

RELATED WEB LINKS

International Center for Transitional Justice
http://www.ictj.org/en/index.html
> This website provides information on a wide range of issues related to transitional justice.
> Links are provided to full-text articles as well as to other organizations.

African Transitional Justice Research Network
http://www.transitionaljustice.org.za/
> This website provides access to many full-text articles and research reports on transitional
> justice in Africa. Links are also provided to other organizations.

Minnesota Advocates for Human Rights
http://www.mnadvocates.org/Transitional_Justice_Mechanisms.html
> This website provides access to information on a wide range of human rights issues, in-
> cluding human rights abuses arising from civil wars and other conflicts. Links are provided
> to information on truth commissions in South Africa, Sierra Leone, Chile, Argentina,
> Peru, Guatemala, and El Salvador.

United Nations Office for the Coordination of Humanitarian Affairs
http://www.irinnews.org/webspecials/RightsAndReconciliation/54270.asp
> This website provides access to information on a range of transitional justice issues, includ-
> ing peace building, political and economic reform, and security. Links are also provided
> to news reports, country profiles, and feature articles on many different topics. Available
> offerings change periodically, so it's wise to check more than once.

Chapter 22

WAR, AGGRESSION, AND STATE CRIME: A CRIMINOLOGICAL ANALYSIS OF THE INVASION AND OCCUPATION OF IRAQ

RONALD C. KRAMER AND RAYMOND J. MICHALOWSKI

INTRODUCTION

Wars of aggression are, by far, the most destructive and destabilizing of all state crimes. In the words of the Nuremberg Charter, they are "the supreme international crime"—a term, we argue, that appropriately characterizes the invasion and occupation of Iraq by the United States and its main ally, the United Kingdom. A strong case can and has been made that the invasion of Iraq was not a legitimate defensive move by the United States, but rather an aggressive war that, as UN Secretary General Kofi Annan reiterated in September 2004, violated the UN Charter and the international rule of law (Lynch 2004a, 2004b).[1] In the following pages, we provide a brief overview of the case for labelling the Iraq War as a state crime, followed by a narrative analysis of the historical and contemporary origins of this crime. We do so through the lens of an integrated model for the study of organizational deviance that has proved useful in the analysis of a number of other upper-world crimes (Kramer and Michalowski 1990; Kramer 1992; Aulette and Michalowski 1993; Kauzlarich and Kramer 1998; Matthews and Kauzlarich 2000; Wonders and Danner 2002; Whyte 2003). In this analysis, we locate the invasion of Iraq first in the general context of America's long history of "open door" imperialism and then within the specific framework of the neoconservative revolution under George W. Bush, which brought a new climate of unilateralism and militarism to the long-standing American project of making the world safe for international capitalism under the aegis of an American hegemony.

DEFINING STATE CRIME

In his 1988 Presidential Address to the American Society of Criminology, William Chambliss (1989: 184) described state crimes as "acts defined by law as criminal and committed by state officials in the pursuit of their job as representatives of the state." Despite its utility, this definition limited the study of state crime to harms that political states *had chosen* to criminalize.

The historical record, however, suggests that states rarely criminalize the social harms they commit. A few years later, Chambliss (1995: 9) addressed the limitation in his earlier definition by suggesting that criminological analyses of state crime should include "behavior that violates international agreements and principles established in the courts and treaties of international bodies." This approach is consistent with our contention that the study of state crime must include governmental acts that violate international law, even when they do not violate domestic law (Kauzlarich et al. 1992; Kauzlarich and Kramer 1998; Michalowski 1985). Thus, we begin from the premise that violations of international law *are* state crimes.

Some have argued that international law is an inadequate framework for evaluating state behaviour. Post-colonial and feminist theorists have argued that UN-sponsored international law frequently encodes the political hegemony of white, Western liberalism rather than representing universally valid conceptions of human nature (Lambert et al. 2003; Otto 1997; Sihna et al. 1999). In this vein, Eric Hobswam (1996) has criticized the present order as "human rights imperialism." Others have suggested that the notion of state sovereignty—the touchstone of international law since the 17th century—has lost much of its viability in the contemporary world (Falk 1993; Hardt and Negri 2000). Defenders of a global human rights agenda counter with the claim that governing documents such as the UN Charter and the Universal Declaration of Human Rights were forged through open international debate and, as such, represent the best available global standard for distinguishing between legal and illegal state actions (Schultz 2003; Steiner and Aiston 2000).

We cannot here resolve the question of whether current international law enshrines genuinely universal human rights or narrow sectoral interests. Our argument rests instead on the proposition that, although debates may exist over its universality, existing international law has been accepted *as law* by most nations of the world—including the United States—and, thus, violations of these laws are criminal wrongs under the existing international legal order.

WAR AS CRIME

The horrors of the Second World War provoked a significant expansion and codification of public international law, particularly rules concerning war. The central elements of this expansion were the adoption of the UN Charter, the creation of the United Nations, and the promulgation of the Nuremberg Charter that not only authorized the prosecution of Nazi leaders for war crimes but also declared waging aggressive war to be a state crime under both treaty and customary law (Henkin 1995: 111). These developments created a relatively new branch of public international law known as "international criminal law" that codified a number of specific international crimes and created obligations and precedents for their prosecution and punishment. This evolution of international criminal law has recognized that states as well as individuals can be held liable for the commission of political crimes (Jorgensen 2000). Based on these precedents, we define state crime as follows:

> State crime is any action that violates public international law, international criminal law, or domestic law when these actions are committed by individuals acting in official or covert capacity as agents of the state pursu-

ant to expressed or implied orders of the state, or resulting from state failure
to exercise due diligence over the actions of its agents.

Green and Ward (2000) have argued that definitions of state crime that rely primarily on a
legalistic framework are too narrow in scope.[2] As an alternative, they define state crime as the
area of overlap between two distinct phenomena: (1) violations of human rights, and (2) state
organizational deviance that would be subject to widespread censure if it were known. This approach creates an important theoretical opening for criminologists to analyse a variety of social
harms as state crimes, even where these may not be formally recognized as violations by either
national or international law.

The invasion and occupation of Iraq would certainly appear to fit within Green and Ward's
definition of state crime. A death toll that now includes more than 10,000 innocent civilians,
armed attacks on residential neighbourhoods, home invasions, arrests and detentions without
probable cause or due process, and the torture and abuse of prisoners are clear violations of
existing human rights standards (Amnesty International 2004; Gonzales 2002; Schell 2004). In
addition, the Bush and Blair governments have been subject to significant censure from within
their own countries, as well as from the international community, in general, and students of
international law, in particular. We suggest, however, that there is no need to reach beyond the
existing body of international law, in order to bring the Iraq War under the theoretical umbrella
of state crime. Existing international law alone establishes the United States and the United
Kingdom as guilty of state crimes linked to the invasion and occupation of Iraq.

THE IRAQ WAR AS STATE CRIME

With the creation of the United Nations in 1945, the UN Charter became the fundamental law
of international relations, superseding all existing laws and customs (Normand 2003). At the
heart of the Charter is the prohibition of aggressive war found in Article 2 (4): "All members
shall refrain in their international relations from the threat or use of force against the territorial
integrity or political independence of any state, or [behave] in any other manner inconsistent
with the purposes of the United Nations." Article 2 (4) is a peremptory norm having the character of supreme law that cannot be modified by treaty or by ordinary customary law.

In so far as the United States and its allies invaded a sovereign nation without legal authorization from the international community, the invasion of Iraq is a prima facie violation of Article
2 (4). However, US and British state officials have argued that this case is rendered null by the
Charter's exceptions to Article 2 (4), and by the emerging concept of humanitarian intervention.

Article 51 and preventive war

Article 51 of the UN Charter recognizes that states have an "inherent right" to use force in
self-defence in the face of an armed attack (Ratner 2002). Iraq, however, had not attacked the

United States, nor was there ever any claim that such an attack was imminent. Thus, Article 51 would appear to not apply. The Bush administration, however, sought to retain Article 51 justification by linking Iraq to the Al Qaeda attacks of 11 September.

During the public relations campaign to generate political support for an invasion of Iraq, Bush administration officials made continual references to terrorism in general and Al Qaeda, specifically (Prados 2004; Waxman 2004). Not only were the claims of Iraq's links to Al Qaeda questionable, but emerging evidence indicates that the Bush administration knew there were no data to support them (CBS News 2004; Clarke 2004; Corn 2003; Domen 2004; Prados 2004; Rampton and Stauber 2003; Scheer et al. 2003; Suskind 2004). In late 2003, both President Bush and Secretary Powell finally conceded there was no evidence linking Saddam Hussein to 9/11 or other terrorist attacks against the United States (Prados 2004). Recognizing the limitations of Article 51 justifications for aggressive wars, the Bush administration sought to increase its manoeuvring room by promulgating a new National Security Strategy. This new policy claimed the United States had a legal right to attack any nation it perceived as a *potential* threat to US interests (Mahajan 2003). Based on this claim, administration officials repeatedly argued that the United States could legally attack Iraq because Hussein's government possessed weapons of mass destruction (WMD) that might eventually be used against the United States, either directly or through terrorist networks.

The US claim that it possessed the legal right to initiate preventative war was an attempt to unilaterally rewrite international law. International law provides some latitude for pre-emptive strikes in the face of an imminent threat—one that Daniel Webster described as "instant, overwhelming, and leaving no choice of means, and no moment for deliberation" (Webster 2003: 590). It does not, however, authorize the kind of preventive warfare threatened by the Bush National Security Strategy. The reason for this is clear. History is dense with wars initiated by governments that claimed an absolute need to invade enemy territory to prevent some claimed future threat. As international law, the Bush doctrine would provide easy legal cover for any nation with aggressive intentions.

Although it had no status in international law, the administration's claim to a right of preventative war focused much of the pre-war debate around the question of whether or not Iraq possessed WMD—which we now know it did not (Priest and Pincus 2004).[3] What was lost in this debate, however, was the fact that, in the absence of a clearly defined, imminent threat from Iraq, invading that country did not meet the test of legality under international law—i.e., even if Hussein had possessed WMD, absent explicit authorization from the UN Security Council, the invasion would still have been a violation of international law.

UN Security Council authorization

A second exception to Article 2 (4) prohibition against war is found in Chapter Seven of the UN Charter. Article 41 authorizes the UN Security Council to implement various measures, short of war, to respond to a threat to or breach of international peace and security, as determined by Article 39. If the non-military measures allowed under Article 41 are judged to have failed, then, and only then, can the Security Council authorize the use of force to restore or maintain international peace and security under the auspices of Article 42.

There was no such authorization for the use of force against Iraq in March of 2003. In early 2003, the United States, along with the United Kingdom and Spain, sought Security Council support for a draft resolution that would declare Iraq to be in violation of an earlier disarmament resolution (Resolution 1441) and that [would state that] this non-compliance posed a threat to international peace and security. Although the draft resolution did not explicitly authorize war, it was clear to Security Council members that the drafters intended to use it as a warrant to invade Iraq. Faced with strong resistance from Security Council members: France, Russia and Germany; the pro-invasion forces withdrew their resolution. As weapons inspector Hans Blix (2004: 218) concluded, "By withholding an authorization desired, if not formally requested, the Council dissociated the UN from an armed action that most member: states thought was not justified."

Lacking Security Council authorization, American and British officials argued that previous Security Council resolutions already provided sufficient legal justification for the invasion of Iraq. Indeed, this is the only argument that Lord Goldsmith, the UK Attorney General, utilized in his 17 March 2003 presentation to Parliament seeking support for the invasion of Iraq (Singh and Kilroy 2003). At the start of the invasion, US Ambassador to the United Nations John Negroponte made similar claims to the Security Council, as did legal advisors for the US Department of State (Ritter 2003; Taft and Buchwald 2003). These claims, however, have proven to be little more than "selective," "misleading," "creative," "problematic," and ultimately "unsustainable" interpretations of the resolutions in question (Franck 2003; Charlesworth 2003; Normand 2003; Ratner 2002). Simply put, if the members of the UN Security Council had believed that an invasion of Iraq was legally justified, they would have endorsed the draft resolution authorizing invasion instead of forcing its withdrawal.

The legality of humanitarian intervention

The third possible exception to Article 2 (4) can be found in what Normand (2003: 8) calls "the legally dubious doctrine of humanitarian intervention." The United States and the United Kingdom argued that they had a right and a duty to use military force for the humanitarian purpose of saving Iraqis from human rights violations by the Hussein government. In pre-war arguments for invading Iraq, however, Bush and Blair rarely discussed liberation of the Iraqi people, and, when they did, it was most often a distant third to the threat of WMD and Iraq's ties to terrorism (Prados 2004; Waxman 2004). It was only in the aftermath of the invasion, once the WMD argument proved to be hollow, that humanitarian concerns were reframed as the primary justification for the invasion of Iraq.[4]

Even if the Bush and Blair administrations were motivated primarily by humanitarian concerns, the legality of humanitarian invasion remains in question. Many international lawyers question this legality because unilateral humanitarian invasions circumvent established procedures and principles within the UN Charter and international law for addressing humanitarian crises (Normand 2003: 8).[5] Beyond the question of legality, there is also little evidence that

Hussein's government was engaged in large-scale political atrocities at the time of the invasion (Charlesworth 2003; Roth 2004). The worst offences of Hussein's Baathist regime occurred in the 1980s and early 1990s. By the 1990s, the government in Baghdad had made important home-rule concessions to Iraq's northern Kurds and, in the aftermath of the Gulf War, UN weapons inspections, Security Council sanctions, and no-fly zones reduced the likelihood of major human rights crimes. Human Rights Watch concluded that, at the time of the US/UK invasion, political killings in Iraq were "not of the exceptional nature that would justify such intervention," nor was invasion "the last reasonable option to stop Iraqi atrocities" (Roth 2004: 9).

Invasion and international humanitarian law

International humanitarian law (IHL), also known as the "law of armed conflict," rests on the 1907 Hague Convention, the four Geneva Conventions of 1949, and the First Additional Protocol of 1977 to the 1949 Geneva Conventions (Protocol I). This body of international law requires that parties to armed conflict protect civilians and noncombatants, limit the means or methods that are permissible during warfare, and conform to rules governing the behaviour of occupying forces. Violations of IHL are considered war crimes. The US Congress incorporated the 1949 Geneva Conventions into federal law with the ratification of the Geneva treaties and the passage of the War Crimes Act of 1996 (Slomanson 2003).

IHL specifically forbids direct assaults on civilians and civilian objects, and it prohibits indiscriminate attacks that, in the language of Protocol I, are "expected to cause incidental loss of civilian life, injury to civilians [or] damage to civilian objectives ... which would be excessive in relation to the concrete and direct military advantage anticipated" from that attack (Human Rights Watch 2003: 9). Yet, Amnesty International (2004) estimates that over 10,000 civilians were killed during the invasion and first year of occupation. According to Human Rights Watch (2003), the widespread use of cluster bombs and numerous attempted "decapitation" strikes targeting senior Iraqi officials— often based on scanty or questionable intelligence—were responsible for the deaths of hundreds of Iraqi civilians during the early days of the invasion. Coalition forces exposed Iraqi civilians to significant "collateral damage" through the deployment of napalm-like Mark 77 firebombs (Buncombe 2003; Ridha 2004) and through widespread use of depleted uranium munitions that release dangerous radioactive debris in the short term (Miller 2003) and pose long-term environmental hazards to people exposed to uranium-contaminated soil or water (Michalowski and Bitten 2004).

Occupation and IHL crimes

Under IHL, at least four types of war crimes were committed by coalition forces during the ongoing (as of October 2004) occupation of Iraq: (1) the failure to secure public safety and protect civilian rights; (2) the illegal transformation of the Iraqi economy; (3) indiscriminate responses to Iraqi resistance actions, resulting in further civilian casualties; and (4) the torture and abuse of Iraqi prisoners (see Normand 2004).

Although the invasion of Iraq itself was not authorized by the UN Security Council, faced with the reality of an occupied Iraq, the UN Security Council passed Resolution 1483 recognizing the US and UK as the occupying powers in Iraq. This Resolution required the Coalition Provisional Authority (CPA) to comply fully with their obligations under international law, including the Geneva Conventions of 1949 and The Hague Regulations of 1907. Specifically, under the Fourth Geneva Convention, the occupying power must ensure public safety and order and guarantee the civilian population's fundamental rights to food, health care, education, work, and freedom of movement. The lives and property of civilians must be respected at all times.

Contrary to these requirements, death, looting, fear, and insecurity have characterized the reality of occupied Iraq. In the early weeks following the overthrow of the Hussein government, US and UK troops did nothing to stop the looting of Iraq's most important public buildings. The immediate outlawing of the Iraqi Army and criminalization of all government leaders meant that, at the moment of defeat, there was no recognized Iraqi authority that could surrender to invading forces while providing a continuity of government services, including security services. As of this writing, 18 months after the occupation of Iraq began, the security situation for Iraqi civilians continues to deteriorate (Krane 2004).

The Fourth Geneva Convention of 1949 specifically prohibits conquering powers from restructuring the economy of a conquered nation in accordance with the ideology and economics of the conqueror (Greider 2003: 5). In direct contravention of this requirement, the occupying powers sought to transform Iraq's state-dominated economic system into a market economy committed to free trade, supply-side tax policy, privatization of key economic sectors, and widespread foreign ownership in those sectors (Bacon 2004; Juhasz 2004; Krugman 2004a). These strategies contributed significantly to creating a 70 per cent rate of unemployment in a country that now lacked a social welfare system to ameliorate the worst consequences of "shock" capitalism (Bacon 2004: 1; Klein 2003).

Fighting insurgency

The third category of occupation crimes involves the US/UK response to Iraqi insurgents. The occupation provoked fierce armed resistance by militant Sunni and Shiite sectors of the Iraqi populace. Faced with a rising tide of opposition, the occupying powers engaged in numerous violations of IHL in their attempts to quell the insurgency, contributing to a cycle of resistance and repression that deepened the daily security crisis for average Iraqi citizens (Andersen 2004). American and British forces have shot and killed demonstrators, bombed civilian areas, invaded homes in the search for insurgents, demolished homes and destroyed property as collective punishment, abused prisoners, and violated deep cultural rules of gender and social respect (Amnesty International 2004; Packer 2003; Schell 2004). Coalition forces have used hostage taking in order to root out suspected insurgents, made arbitrary arrests, and held detainees indefinitely without charges or access to lawyers. Nearly 90 per cent of all prisoners held by US authorities in its now infamous Abu Ghraib prison were arrested "in error," without probable cause that they were guilty of violations of law or aggression against the occupying authorities (ICRC 2004).

In April 2004, the known scope of US violations of IHL in Iraq expanded significantly with revelations of the abuse of Iraqi prisoners in the Abu Ghraib prison. Documents analysed by reporter Seymour Hersh (2004) and photos released by CBS's 60 *Minutes II* in 2004 revealed physical and psycho-sexual abuse being inflicted on Iraqi detainees by US military personnel at the prison. As Marjorie Cohn (2004: 1), executive vice-president of the US National Lawyers Guild, noted, "These actions are not only offensive to human dignity; they violate the Geneva Convention, and the Convention Against Torture and Other Cruel, Inhuman or Degrading Treatment or Punishment."

ANALYSING STATE CRIME: AN INTEGRATED APPROACH

There are three major theoretical approaches to the study of organizational wrongdoing, each corresponding to a different level of social inquiry. The broadest level is characterized by political–economic analyses, particularly those examining how structural demands and internal contradictions can create criminogenic pressures in economic and political organizations (Barnett 1981; Michalowski 1985; Quinney 1977; Young 1981). At the intermediary level, organizational approaches examine how defective standard operating procedures and/or maladaptive emphases on performance goals within organizations increase the likelihood of deviant outcomes (Finney and Lesieur 1982; Gross 1978; Hopkins 1978; Kramer 1982). When merged with anomie theory, this perspective has generated valuable narratives of both corporate and state crime (Braithwaite 1989; Passas 1990; Vaughan 1982, 1983, 1996). At the level of individual behaviour, Sutherland's (1940, 1949) theory of differential association established the importance of understanding the role of grounded human interaction in the process toward deviant organizational activities.

Despite their different foci, the theoretical and lived intersections suggested by these different approaches provide a sensitizing, integrated framework for analysing organizational deviance (Kramer et al. 2002). The historical contours of the political–economic arrangements and dominant ideologies of the capitalist world system are reflected differentially, but reflected nonetheless, in the positions, procedures, goals, means and constraints that define concrete organizations of governance, production, and redistribution in contemporary nation states. At the same time, direct and indirect communications among people within and across specific political, economic, and social organizations, i.e., differential association, translate the formal elements of organizations into the work-related thoughts and actions of the people in them. At every moment in time, each of these levels is manifest in the others, with organizations serving as the site in which large-scale political–economic arrangements and small-scale human actions intersect in ways that generate either conformity or deviance.

Our approach links these three levels of analysis with three catalysts for action: motivation, opportunity, and social control. Our goal is to highlight the key factors that contribute to or restrain organizational deviance at each intersection of a catalyst for action and a level of analysis. According to this approach, organizational deviance is most likely to occur when pressures for goal attainment and/or faulty operating procedures intersect with attractive and available illegitimate means in the absence or neutralization of effective social control.

MOTIVATION AND OPPORTUNITY

When applied to the US decision to invade Iraq, our approach reveals how a presidential administration, embedded in the history and ideology of US imperial designs, faced with opportunities and constraints presented by the end of the Cold War, the attacks of 11 September 2001, and a bizarre electoral outcome, deployed a messianic vision of America's global role in a way that led to the commission of state crime against the people of Iraq.

America as imperial project

America has been an imperial project from its earliest years (Ferguson 2004, Garrison 2004). Throughout the 19th century, American growth relied on expansion through force, including enslavement of Africans, expropriation of Native lands in the name of "manifest destiny," claiming North and South America as an exclusive American sphere of influence (the Monroe Doctrine), expansionist war with Mexico, and using American warships to ensure Asian trading partners (Beard and Beard 1930; Kolko 1984; Sewall 1995; Williams 1959; Williams 1969).

As the 19th century drew to a close, structural contradictions in American capitalism provoked an intensification of America's imperial reach. With the frontier expansion stalled at the Pacific Ocean and the economic infrastructure fully capitalized, surplus productive capacity in the United States began to generate significant pressures for new markets and cheaper sources of material and labour (Sklar 1987). In 1898, increased pressures for new economic frontiers motivated an imperialist war against Spain. Although it was publicly justified as bringing "freedom" to Spain's remaining colonies, instead of liberation, the people of the Philippines, Hawaii, and Puerto Rico were annexed and colonized by the United States, while those in Cuba were subject to a virtual colonization that did not end until the Cuban revolution of 1959 (Thomas 1971). In a foreshadowing of future American imperialism, the acquisition of these territories was construed not as expansionism but rather as a moral duty to uplift and civilize other races by spreading the American system of business and government—what Ferguson (2004: 54) calls "the paradox of dictating democracy, of enforcing freedom, of exporting emancipation."

The United States would soon abandon its brief experiment with formal colonization as too economically and politically costly. Moreover, America's political and ideological roots were more purely commercial than [those of] European mercantile nations whose feudal history was rooted in the control of land. As a result, US leaders were quicker to recognize that, in the emerging commercial era, "what mattered was not ownership or even administrative control but commercial access" (Bacevich 2002: 25).

Hints of this change are found in the 1899 *Open Door Notes* of Secretary of State John Hay. Hay promoted what Williams (1959) termed "Open Door" imperialism based on diplomacy among the major capitalist powers to keep foreign markets open to trade, rather than dividing the world into the closed trading blocs typical of mercantile capitalism since the British and Dutch East India trading companies of the 18th century. Although it was based on considerable military might (by 1905, the US Navy was second only to that of Great Britain), the strategy of controlling without owning became the basic design of American foreign policy in the 20th century (Williams 1959).

Consolidating imperialism in the 20th century

Despite this early imperial history, the United States has always been, in Ferguson's (2004) apt phrase, "an empire in denial." Through a rhetorical move that equated capitalist markets with "freedom," two centuries of American leaders have established a political habit of mind that comprehends any war or invasion as noble sacrifice rather than self-interest. By conveniently limiting the conception of imperialism to the direct colonization of physical territory, for more than a century, the Open Door ideology has enabled Americans to avoid recognizing that market imperialism is imperialism nonetheless.

As it rose to ever greater power after the First World War and then the Second World War, the United States clung to its self-image as a "reluctant superpower"—a master narrative claiming the United States involved itself in world affairs only under duress, and then always for selfless reasons (Bacevich 2002). President Woodrow Wilson's famous claim that the United States must enter the First World War "to make the world safe for democracy" exemplifies this narrative in action. The need to ensure the United States could play a significant role in creating a new political and economic order out of the collapse of the Ottoman and Austro-Hungarian empires was carefully crafted as selflessness rather than self-interest (Johnson 2004: 48).

In the years between the First and Second World Wars, America's strategy of securing the benefits of imperialism by dominating an open trade system was threatened by the Great Depression and the economic expansionism of Nazi Germany and imperial Japan (Kolko 1968; Zinn 1980). The Second World War, however, lifted the United States out of economic depression and established it as both the world's dominant military power and the economic hegemon in charge of the key institutions of global capitalism, such as the International Monetary Fund (IMF), the World Bank, and the General Agreement on Trade and Tariffs (Derber 2002; Friedrichs 2004).

There were two challenges to the US imperial project in the post-Second World War era: the threat of independent nationalism and the Soviet Union. Nations on the periphery and semi-periphery of the world system, many of them former colonies of the world's wealthy capitalist nations, were limited to service roles in the global capitalist economy, providing resources, cheap labour, and retail markets for consumer products and finance capital (Frank 1969; Wallerstein 1989). US planners were concerned that "radical and nationalistic regimes," more responsive to popular pressures for immediate improvement in the living standards of the masses than advancing the interests of foreign capital, could become a "virus" infecting other countries and threatening the "overall framework of order" that Washington had constructed (Chomsky 2003).

The Soviet Union, with its rival ideology, its own imperialistic goals, and its own atomic weapons, also threatened American domination. Neither the United States nor the Soviet Union seriously challenged the overall framework of power sharing established at Yalta near the end of the Second World War. Instead, the two "superpowers" pursued their global interests through client states in the less developed world, with the Soviet Union frequently courting the favour of independent nationalist movements and the United States working with local elites to limit the expansion of such movements. In this struggle, the Soviet Union and the United States also were able to periodically stalemate one another's interests by exercising their veto powers in the UN Security Council.

While it represented constraints, the Cold War was *consciously* recognized by growth-oriented government and corporate leaders in the United States as an opportunity to justify expanding military budgets, establish a "permanent war economy," and strengthen the military–industrial complex (Elliot 1955). America's post-Second World War imperial project began with a far-flung empire of military bases justified as necessary tools in the fight against communism, thereby linking America's imperial project to a rhetoric of liberation rather than one of geo-political expansion (Johnson 2004). Or, in Ferguson's words (2004: 78):

> For an empire in denial, there is really only one way to act imperially with a clear conscience, and that is to combat someone else's imperialism. In the doctrine of containment, born in 1947, the United States hit on the perfect ideology for its own peculiar kind of empire: the imperialism of anti-imperialism.

Opportunities and motivations in the "unipolar moment"

The fall of the Berlin Wall in 1989 and the collapse of the Soviet Union in 1991 brought the Cold War to an end, presenting the United States with a new set of opportunities and challenges. With the Soviet Union out of the way and American military supremacy unrivalled, the "unipolar moment" had arrived (Krauthammer 1989, 1991). The goals of Open Door imperialism never seemed more realizable. American military power—a primary tool at Washington's disposal to achieve global hegemony—could now be used with relative impunity, whether it was invading small neighbours such as Panama and Grenada or using Iraq's incursion into Kuwait to establish a more permanent US military presence in the oil-rich Persian Gulf region.

The unipolar moment was not without its challenges, however. The fall of the Soviet Union removed the primary ideological justification for the suppression of independent nationalism, and it weakened domestic political support for expanding military budgets and a permanent war economy. Many Americans expected the end of the Cold War to produce a "peace dividend" (Zinn 1980).

Economic and political elites linked to the military–industrial complex, however, did not acquiesce to the reduction in their power that would have resulted from such a realignment of American goals. Instead, they were soon searching for new "enemies" and, with them, new justifications for continued imperial expansion. A sharp struggle soon emerged between rival factions over how to capitalize on the opportunities offered by the fall of the Soviet Union while deflecting threats presented by the possibility of a new isolationism. One group supported a globalist and internationalist approach typical of the administrations of George H.W. Bush and Bill Clinton. The other, often referred to as "neoconservatives," argued for a more nationalist, unilateralist, and militarist revision of America's Open Door imperialism. It was this latter group that would, surprisingly, find itself in a position to shape America's imperial project for the 21st century.

Neoconservatives and the new Pax Americana

The term "neoconservative" (often abridged as "neocon") was first used by the American democratic socialist leader Michael Harrington in the early 1970s to describe a group of political figures and intellectuals who had been his comrades in the US Socialist Party but were now moving politically to the right. Many of this original neoconservative group, such as Irving Kristol and Norman Podhoretz, had been associated with the Henry "Scoop" Jackson wing of the Democratic Party, but, in reaction to the cultural liberalism and anti-Vietnam war stance associated with the 1972 Democratic presidential candidate George McGovern, they moved to the right, eventually joining the Republican Party (Dorrien 2004: 9–10).

A number of neoconservatives were affiliated with the Reagan administration, often providing intellectual justification for that administration's policies of military growth and the rollback of détente rather than encourageing coexistence with the Soviet Union. While the first generation of neoconservatives also addressed economic and cultural issues, their primary foreign policy goal was confronting what they claimed to be the globe-girdling threat of the Soviet Union's "evil empire." As the Soviet Union began to weaken, neocons in the administration of George H.W. Bush began forcefully promoting an aggressive post-Soviet neo-imperialism. Their first concern, shared by many within the military–industrial complex, was to stave off cuts in the military budget in response to the weakened Soviet threat and popular expectations for a peace dividend. In order to justify continued high levels of military spending, General Colin Powell, Chairman of the Joint Chiefs of Staff, and Secretary of Defense Dick Cheney both prepared plans to fill in the "threat blank" vacated by the Soviet Union (Armstrong 2001). Although the first Gulf War temporarily reduced the pressure to cut the defence budget, the swift victory in Kuwait and the complete disintegration of the Soviet Union in 1991 reinvigorated calls for a peace dividend and, with them, the threat of cuts to critical military–industrial budgets.

In 1992, aides to Secretary Cheney, supervised by neocons Paul Wolfowitz and I. Lewis (Scooter) Libby, prepared a draft document entitled *Defense Planning Guidance* (DPG)—a classified, internal Pentagon policy statement used to guide military officials in the planning process. The draft 1992 DPG provides a first look at the emerging neoconservative imperialist agenda. As Armstrong (2002: 78) notes, the DPG "depicted a world dominated by the United States, which would maintain its superpower status through a combination of positive guidance and overwhelming military might. The image was one of a heavily armed City on a Hill."

The draft DPG stated that the first objective of US defence policy should be to prevent the re-emergence of a new rival. It also endorsed the use of pre-emptive military force to achieve its goal. The document called for the United States to maintain a substantial arsenal of nuclear weapons and to develop a missile defence shield. The DPG was a clear statement of the neo-conservative vision of unilateral use of military supremacy to defend US interests anywhere in the world, including protecting US access to vital raw materials such as Persian Gulf oil

(Armstrong 2002; Halper and Clarke 2004; Mann 2004). The aggressive tone of the DPG generated a firestorm of criticism when a draft was leaked to the press. President George H.W. Bush and Secretary Cheney quickly distanced themselves from the DPG, and ordered a less obviously imperialist version prepared.

The surprisingly rapid collapse of the Soviet Union ultimately revealed that the "neocons" had been wrong on almost every issue concerning the Soviet threat. As a consequence, neoconservatism lost much of its legitimacy as a mainstream political ideology, and these early neocons would eventually find themselves in political exile as part of a far-right wing of the Republican Party.

The election of President Bill Clinton removed the neocons from positions within the US government, but not from policy debates. From the sidelines, they generated a steady stream of books, articles, reports, and op-ed pieces in an effort to influence the direction of US foreign policy. In 1995, second-generation neoconservative William Kristol (son of Irving Kristol) founded the right-wing magazine *The Weekly Standard*, which quickly became a major outlet for neocon thinking. Many of the neoconservatives also joined well-funded conservative think-tanks to advocate for their agenda.

Throughout the Clinton years, the neocons opined about new threats to American security, continually calling for greater use of US military power to address them (Mann 2004). One persistent theme in their writings was the need to eliminate Saddam Hussein's government from Iraq, consolidate American power in the Middle East, and change the political culture of the region (Dorrien 2004).

In many ways, the Clinton administration's foreign policy was consistent with that of the previous administration. Clinton shared the elder Bush's views of America as a global leader that should use its economic and military power to ensure openness and integration in the world economic system (Bacevich 2002). In this sense, Clinton-era foreign policy remained consistent with the Open Door system of informal imperialism practiced by the United States since the beginning of the 20th century, stressing global economic integration through free trade and democracy (Dorrien 2004: 225).

Where Iraq was concerned, the Clinton administration developed a policy of "containment plus regime change" (Rai 2003). Despite their devastating human costs, Clinton continued the comprehensive economic sanctions that had been imposed on Iraq following the 1991 war, pursued low-level warfare against Iraq in the form of unauthorized "no-fly zones," and used UN weapons inspections (UNSCOM) as a way of spying on the Iraqi military (Rai 2003; Ritter 2003; Simons 2002). Although the Clinton administration hoped to provoke regime change in Iraq, it did not, however, consider doing so without UN authorization.

Neoconservatives subjected the Clinton administration to a barrage of foreign-policy criticism, particularly with respect to Clinton's handling of the Middle East and Iraq. In early 1998, the Project for the New American Century, a key neoconservative think-tank, released an open letter to President Clinton, urging him to forcefully remove Hussein from power (Halper and Clarke 2004; Mann 2004). In September of 2000, the Project for the New American Century issued a report entitled *Rebuilding America's Defenses: Strategy, Forces and Resources for a New Century*. This report resurrected core ideas in the controversial draft *Defense Planning Guidance* of 1992. The report called for massive increases in military spending, the expansion of US military bases, and the establishment of client states supportive of American economic and political interests. The imperial goals of the neocons were clear. What they lacked was the opportunity to implement these goals. Two unanticipated events gave them the opportunity to do so.

Motive, happenstance, and opportunity

In December 2000, after a botched election put the question in their lap, the Supreme Court of the United States awarded the US Presidency to George W. Bush, despite his having lost the popular vote by over half-a-million ballots. This odd political turnabout would soon restore the neocons to power, with more than 20 neoconservatives and hard-line nationalists being awarded high-ranking positions in the new administration (Dorrien 2004). In a classic demonstration of the creation of shared understandings through differential association, the Pentagon and the Vice-President's office became unipolarist strongholds, reflecting the longstanding working relationship between neoconservatives and Vice-President Dick Cheney and the new Secretary of Defense, Donald Rumsfeld (Moore 2001).

Even though a stroke of good luck had placed them near the centre of power, neoconservative unipolarists found that the new President remained more persuaded by "pragmatic realists" in his administration, such as Secretary of State Colin Powell, than by their aggressive foreign policy agenda (Dorrien 2004). This was to be expected. The PNAC report *Rebuilding American Defenses* had predicted that "the process of transformation is likely to be a long one, absent some catastrophic or catalyzing event—like a new Pearl Harbor." The neoconservatives needed another stroke of good luck.

The 9/11 attacks presented the neocons with the "catalyzing event" they needed to transform their agenda into actual policy. The terror attacks were a "political godsend" that created a climate of fear and anxiety, which the unipolarists mobilized to promote their geopolitical strategy to a President who lacked a coherent foreign policy, as well as to the nation as a whole (Hartung 2004). As former Treasury Secretary Paul O'Neill revealed, the goal of the unipolarists in the Bush administration had always been to attack Iraq and oust Saddam Hussein (Susskind 2004). This, they believed, would allow the United States to consolidate its power in the strategically significant Middle East and to change the political culture of the region.

On the evening of 11 September 2001 and in the days following, unipolarists in the Bush administration advocated attacking Iraq immediately, even though there was no evidence linking Iraq to the events of the day (Clarke 2004; Woodward 2004). After an internal struggle between the "pragmatic realists" led by Secretary of State Powell and the unipolarists led by Vice President Cheney and Secretary of Defense Rumsfeld, the decision was eventually made to launch a general "war on terrorism" and to begin it by attacking Al Qaeda's home-base in Afghanistan and removing that country's Taliban government (Mann 2004). The unipolarists were only temporarily delayed in so far as they had achieved agreement that as soon as the Afghanistan war was under way, the United States would begin planning an invasion of Iraq (Clarke 2004; Fallows 2004). By November, barely one month after the invasion of Afghanistan, Bush and Rumsfeld ordered the Department of Defense to formulate a war plan for Iraq (Woodward 2004). Throughout 2002, as plans for the war on Iraq were being formulated, the Bush administration made a number of formal pronouncements that demonstrated that the goals of the unipolarists were now the official goals of the US government. In the 29 January State of the Union address, Bush honed the focus of the "war on terrorism" by associating terrorism with specific rogue states, such as Iran, Iraq, and North Korea (the "axis of evil"), who were presented as legitimate targets for military action (Callinicos 2003). In a speech to the graduating cadets at West Point on 1 June, the President unveiled a doctrine of preventative war—a policy that many judged as "the most open statement yet made of imperial globalization" (Falk 2004: 189), soon to be followed by the new *National Security Strategy*. This document not only claimed the right to wage preventative war as previously discussed, it also claimed that the United States would use its military power to spread "democracy" and American-style laissez-faire capitalism around the world as the "single sustainable model for national success" (Callinicos 2003: 29). As Roy (2004: 56) notes, "Democracy has become Empire's euphemism for neo-liberal capitalism."

In the campaign to build public support for the invasion of Iraq, the Bush administration skillfully exploited the political opportunities provided by the fear and anger over the 9/11 attacks. By linking Saddam Hussein and Iraq to the wider war on terrorism, the government was able to establish the idea that security required the ability to attack any nation believed to be supporting terror, no mater how weak the evidence. This strategy obscured the more specific geopolitical and economic goals of creating a neoconservative Pax Americana behind the smokescreen of fighting terrorism. In Falk's (2004: 195) words, "the Iraq debate was colored by the dogs that didn't bark: oil, geopolitical goals in the region and beyond, and the security of Israel."

Messianic militarism

The final factor to consider in understanding the Bush administration's war on Iraq is the fusion of a neoconservative imperial agenda with the fundamentalist Christian religious convictions of George W. Bush—a convergence that has been variously referred to as "messianic militarism" (*The Progressive* 2003), "political fundamentalism" (Domke 2004), or "fundamentalist geopolitics" (Falk 2004). Bush's evangelical moralism creates a Manichean vision which views the world as a struggle between good and evil—a struggle that requires him to act on behalf of the good. In his West Point speech, for instance, Bush (2002) insisted that "we are in a conflict between good and evil, and America will call evil by its name. By confronting evil and lawless regimes, we do not create a problem, we reveal a problem. And we will lead the world in opposing it."

George W. Bush is not the first US president to justify his foreign policy on ideological or moral grounds. As we noted above in our historical overview of the American imperial project, many presidents have rationalized the pursuit of empire on the basis of ideological claims such as "white man's burden" or "making the world safe for democracy." But George W. Bush presents himself as more explicitly motivated by a specific religious doctrine than past presidents, as well as apparently more willing to act on those convictions. As Domke (2004; 116) observes, "The Bush administration offered a dangerous combination: the president claimed to know God's wishes and presided over a global landscape in which the United States could act upon such beliefs without compunction." Thus, at this moment, the leader of the global hegemony claims to be "divinely inspired to reshape the world through violent means"—a "messiah complex" that conveniently fuses with the unipolarist dream of American global imperial domination (*The Progressive* 2003: 8).

The failure of effective social control

Motivations and opportunities alone are not sufficient to generate organizational deviance. Although policy planners who supported aggressive American unilateralism as a route to global dominance enjoyed insider positions in a presidential administration willing to embrace just such a strategy, this alone is not a sufficient explanation of how the United States found itself on the pathway to committing state crime against Iraq and the Iraqi people.

Despite the desire of Bush administration unipolarists to invade Iraq, the military power of the United States and the political opportunities provided by the 9/11 attacks, strong social control mechanisms could have blocked the march to war. No such mechanisms emerged, however. Our integrated approach requires that we also consider the social control context of the Iraq War and explain why these mechanisms failed to prevent the state crime of aggressive war against Iraq. Specifically, the model directs us to examine potential controls at the intersections of the structural, organizational, and international levels of analysis.

At the level of the international system, the United Nations failed to provide an effective deterrent to a US invasion of Iraq largely because it has little ability to *compel* powerful nations to comply with international law if they choose to do otherwise. There are two reasons for this. First, the use of sanctions or force to compel compliance requires a Security Council vote, and the world's most powerful nations, as permanent members of the Security Council, can and do veto any action against their own interests, just as the United States would have in this situation. It could be said that the UN Security Council "served the purpose of its founding by its refusal to endorse recourse to a war that could not be persuasively reconciled with the UN Charter and international law" (Falk 2004: 201). While this may be true, it is also true that the assembled nations of the world, most of whom opposed the invasion of Iraq, had no structural power to prevent the US from violating the UN Charter. Falk (2004) goes so far as to suggest that the United Nation's inability to deter the war on Iraq calls into question the very future of the Charter system.

Second, much of the power of the United Nations rests with its ability to extract a price in terms of negative world opinion against those who would violate international law. When a nation enjoys a hegemonic economic and military position, as did the United States in 2003, it can easily believe it need not be overly concerned with world opinion. This is precisely the understanding that informed the neoconservative vision underlying the move to invade Iraq. Whether the United States is, in fact, free to do just what it wants with no cost in the world community remains to be seen. At this point, however, potential world opinion appears to exert little social control over the neoconservatives shaping US foreign policy.

Like the United Nations, world public opinion, including massive antiwar protests, had little impact on the Bush administration's desire to invade Iraq. As the unipolarists pushed for the invasion of Iraq, a global antiwar movement came to life. On 15 February 2003, as US military forces were poised for the invasion, over 10 million people across the globe participated in antiwar demonstrations. These protests "were the single largest public political demonstration in history" (Jensen 2004: xvii). The next day, the *New York Times* editorialized that there were now two superpowers in the world: the United States and world public opinion. The "superpower" of world public opinion, however, proved to be powerless, exerting no deterrent effect on US plans to invade Iraq. As Jensen (2004: xviii) notes, "the antiwar movement had channeled the people's voices" but it had not "made pursuing the war politically costly enough to elites to stop it." Indeed, it is unlikely, given US economic and military power, that world public opinion is capable of altering US government policies, unless this opinion is translated into consequential actions such as a global boycott on US products.

While world public opinion was overwhelmingly against the Bush administration's war plans, within the US, public opinion shifted from initial opposition to a preventative attack without UN sanction to majority support for the war, despite a substantial US antiwar movement. Two interrelated factors appear to explain the US public's support for the invasion of Iraq. First, the Bush administration engaged in an effective public relations campaign that persuaded many Americans of the necessity of a war in Iraq (Rutherford 2004). As we previously noted, this propaganda campaign rested mainly on false claims about Iraqi WMD, ties to Al Qaeda, and complicity in the 9/11 tragedy (Corn 2003; Rampton and Stauber 2003; Scheer et al. 2003). It was also undertaken at a time when many Americans were in a wounded, vengeful and hyper-patriotic mood as a result of the 9/11 terrorist attacks. Public opinion polls taken on the eve of the war show that the government's public relations blitz had successfully convinced a majority of the American polity that Saddam Hussein was threatening the United States with WMD and had also convinced an astounding 70 per cent of its American audience that Iraq was directly involved with the 9/11 attacks (Berman 2003; Corn 2003). As Rutherford (2004: 193) concludes in his study of the marketing of the war against Iraq, "democracy was overwhelmed by a torrent of lies, half-truths, infotainment, and marketing." This was not the first time in American history that a "big lie" repeated frequently enough from a high enough platform would create public support for war. What is significant, however, is that it could do so even in the face of large-scale counter-efforts, and in the face of mounting evidence that many of its claims were, in fact, false.

An important factor explaining public support for the invasion of Iraq was the failure of the media in the United States to perform their critical role as "watchdogs" over government power (Schell 2004). It is one thing to have evidence that government claims are weak. It is another to be able to insert those claims into the same high-profile media where the government is promoting its PR message. A number of studies document that the media failed to provide the American public with an accurate assessment of Bush administration claims about Iraq; nor did they provide any useful historical or political context within which the public could assess those claims (Alterman 2003; Massing 2004; Moeller 2004; Miller 2004; Solomon and Erlich 2003). Most news reports promoted the administration's official line and marginalized dissenters (Rendall and Broughel 2003). As Moeller (2004: 3) concluded, most "stories stenographically reported the incumbent administration's perspective on WMD, giving too little critical examination of the way officials framed the events, issues, threats, and policy options." Both the *New*

York Times and the *Washington Post* would later acknowledge that they should have challenged the administration's claims and assumptions more thoroughly (*New York Times* 2004; Kurtz 2004). As Orville Schell (2004: iv) points out, an independent press in a "free" country allowed itself "to become so paralyzed that it not only failed to investigate thoroughly the rationales for war, but also took so little account of the myriad other cautionary voices in the on-line, alternative, and world press." The performance of the media in the period leading up to the invasion is a near-perfect illustration of Herman and Chomsky's (1988) "propaganda model."

In addition to the institutional failure of the media, the US Congress also failed to provide an effective constraint on the Bush administration's war plans. This represented a significant institutional failure of the formal system of checks and balances among the three branches of government built into the US Constitution. Article I, Section 8, Clause 11 of the US Constitution grants the power to declare war to Congress and Congress alone. The framers of the Constitution explicitly stated their desire that the power to take the country to war not rest on the shoulders of the President, but should be reserved to the people through their representatives in Congress.

On 16 October 2002, immediately before the mid-term elections, Congress abdicated its responsibility to determine when the country would go to war by passing a resolution that authorized the President "to use the Armed Forces of the United States as he determines to be necessary and appropriate in order to 1) defend the national security of the United States against the continuing threat posed by Iraq; and 2) enforce all relevant United Nations Security Council resolutions regarding Iraq" (Bonifaz 2003: 11). As Congressman John Conyers (2003: xi) pointed out, by taking this action, "Congress had unconstitutionally delegated to the President its exclusive power to declare war." Thus, in the aftermath of the 9/11 tragedy, Congress (including many members of the Democratic Party) voluntarily removed itself as a significant player in the unfolding events leading to the invasion and occupation of Iraq.

Sources of organizational and interactional control within the Bush administration were also ineffective. The pragmatic realists within the administration, led by Secretary of State Colin Powell, were not in full support of the unipolarist agenda. But, in a struggle for control of the administration's foreign policy, Powell and the pragmatists lost out to neoconservatives pushing for war against Iraq (Dorrien 2004; Halper and Clarke 2004; Mann 2004).

Among the unipolarists, there is a strong "subculture of resistance" to international law and institutions (Schell 2004). According to Braithwaite (1989: 346), such organizational subcultures "neutralize the moral bond of the law and communicate knowledge about how to create and seize illegitimate opportunities and how to cover up offending."

The group dynamics involved in the decision making of the unipolarists also demonstrate classic characteristics of "groupthink," as described by Janis (1982). The unipolarists were a highly cohesive group with a strong commitment to their assumptions and beliefs about America's role in the world. They valued loyalty, believed in the inherent morality of their position, had an illusion of invulnerability, and shared stereotypes of outgroups. But, most importantly for this analysis, the unipolarists within the Bush administration were highly selective in gathering information, ignored, discounted, or ridiculed contrary views, engaged in self-censorship, and protected the group from examining alternatives to their war plans.

Finally, the administration used a variety of "techniques of neutralization" (Sykes and Matza 1957) in an effort to rationalize its criminal acts in Iraq. They denied responsibility (the war was Saddam's fault), denied the victims (most were terrorists), denied injury (there was only limited "collateral damage"), condemned the condemners (protesters were unpatriotic and the French were ungrateful and cowardly), and appealed to higher loyalties (God directed Bush to liberate the Iraqi people).

CONCLUSION

The invasion and occupation of Iraq by the United States and its allies is a violation of international law and, as such, constitutes a state crime. It is a state crime, however, over which there is no effective social control, and for which there is no likelihood of formal sanction. As the most militarily and economically powerful nation in the world system, it appears that the United States and its leaders can, if they choose, violate international law with relative impunity. Unpunishability, however, does not render illegal acts legal; nor should it place them beyond criminological scrutiny.

From a criminological standpoint, the invasion and occupation of Iraq by the United States and its allies reveal a complex interaction among historical and contemporary political and economic forces, as well a need to recognize how the "butterfly effect," as both chaos theorists and moviemakers term it, can impact the production of state crime. In the case of Iraq, we suggest that the interaction of less than 600 votes in the 2000 presidential election with the external events of 9/11 made the difference between no invasion and one of the most important acts of illegal aggression in recent decades. At the same time, neither 9/11 nor the selection of George W. Bush as US President is adequate in itself to explain the state crimes encompassed by the invasion and occupation of Iraq. The fuller explanation resides in the dynamics of America's long-standing will to empire, with its success in achieving global political–economic dominance, and with the construction and dissemination of an ideology which enables many Americans to embrace the fantasy that the US pursuit of global dominance is a noble sacrifice in the name of worldwide human liberation.

NOTES

[1] For expanded legal arguments regarding the illegality of the war on Iraq, see Boyle (2004), Falk (2004), and Weeramantry (2003).

[2] See also Ward and Green (2000).

[3] For details regarding the absence of weapons of mass destruction in Iraq, see Pitt (2002), Rai (2002), Corn (2003), Ratner, Green, and Olshansky (2003), Rampton and Stauber (2003), Scheer, Scheer, and Chaudhry (2003), Solomon and Erlich (2003), Rai (2003), Allman (2004), Blix (2004), Eisendrath and Goodman (2004), Everest (2004), Gellman (2004), Hiro (2004), Prados (2004). In early October 2004, the Bush administration's own Iraq

Survey Group, under the direction of Charles Duelfer, concluded that the first Gulf War and UN inspections destroyed Iraq's illicit weapons and Saddam Hussein did not try to rebuild them (Priest and Pincus 2004).

[4] Contrary to its humanitarian rhetoric, the US government had a history of supporting human rights violations by Saddam Hussein. The Reagan and first Bush administrations provided Iraq with loans and satellite intelligence during the Iran-Iraq war despite Iraq's use of chemical weapons against Iran. They continued doing so even after Iraqi helicopters gassed villagers in northern Kurdistan—the case of Hussein "gassing his own people," so frequently used by George W. Bush to explain why the United States must bring about "regime change" in Iraq (Chomsky 2003; Mahajan 2003: 124; Zunes 2003). In addition, nearly a million Iraqis died as a result of U.S. sanctions and bombing campaigns between the two wars further calling into question the Bush administration's claim that concern for the Iraqi people was the primary reason for invasion (Simons 2002).

[5] We do not mean to suggest that these laws and procedures are not without their problems and limitations. The failure of effective UN action in cases [such] as genocide in Rwanda and the Darfur region of the Sudan speak to the weaknesses of the existing system. We are suggesting that unilateral "humanitarian" intervention in countries where the intervening nations have high political and economic stakes are questionable morally, as well as legally.

REFERENCES

Anderson, J. 2004. *The Fall of Baghdad*. New York: Penguin Books.

Allman T.D. 2004. *Rogue State: America at War with the World*. New York: Nation Books.

Alterman, E. 2003. *What Liberal Media? The Truth about Bias and the News*. Paperback ed. New York: Basic Books.

Amnesty International. 2004. *Iraq: One Year on the Human Rights Situation Remains Dire*, March 18, http://web.amnesty.org/library/index/engmde140062004.

Armstrong, D. 2002. "Dick Cheney's Song of America: Drafting a Plan for Global Dominance." *Harper's Magazine* (October): 76–83.

Aulette, J. and R. Michalowski. 1998. "Fire in Hamlet: A Case Study of State-Corporate Crime." Pp. 171–206 in *Political Crime in Contemporary America: A Critical Approach*, edited by K. Tunnell. New York: Garland Press.

Bacevich, A. 2002. *American Empire: The Realities and Consequences of U.S. Diplomacy*. Cambridge, MA: Harvard University Press.

Bacon, D. 2004. "Whose Human Rights is the Occupation Defending." *ZNet: Activism* April 17, http://www.zmag.org/content/showarticle.cfm?ItemID=5349.

Barnett H. 1981. "Corporate Capitalism, Corporate Crime." *Crime and Delinquency* 27: 4–23.

Beard, C. and M. Beard. 1930. *The Rise of American Civilization*. New York: Macmillan.

Berman, A. 2003. "Polls Suggest Media Failure in Pre-War Coverage." *Editor and Publisher* March 26, http://www.mediainfo.com/eandp/news/article_display.jsp?vnu_content_id=1848576

Blix, H. 2004. *Disarming Iraq*. New York: Pantheon Books.

Bonifaz, J. 2003. *Warrior-King: The Case for Impeaching George W. Bush.* New York: Nation Books.

Boyle, F. 2004. *Destroying World Order: U.S. Imperialism in the Middle East Before and After September 11.* Atlanta: Clarity Press.

Braithwaite, J. 1989. "Criminological Theory and Organizational Crime." *Justice Quarterly* 6: 333–58.

Buncombe A. 2003. "U.S. Admits It Used Napalm Bombs in Iraq." *The Independent* August 10, http://news.independent.co.uk/world/americas/article99716.ece.

Bush, G.W. 2002. "Remarks by the President at 2002 Graduation Exercise of the United States Military Academy, West Point, New York." June 1, www.whitehouse.gov.

Callinicos, A. 2003. *The New Mandarins of American Power.* Cambridge, UK: Polity Press.

CBS News 2002. "Plans For Iraq Attack Began On 9/11." *CBS News Online* (September 4), http://www.cbsnews.com/stories/2002/09/04/september11/main520830.shtml.

Conyers, J. 2003. "Foreword." Pp. ix–xii in *Warrior-King: The Case for Impeaching George W. Bush,* edited by K. Tunnell. New York: Nation Books.

Chambliss, W. 1989. "State-Organized Crime." *Criminology* 27: 183–208.

Chambliss, W. 1995. "Commentary." *Society for the Study of Social Problems (SSSP) Newsletter* 26: 9.

Charlesworth, H. 2003. "Is International Law Relevant to the War in Iraq and Its Aftermath?" Telstra Address, National Press Club, Canberra, Australia, October 29.

Chomsky, N. 2003. *Hegemony or Survival: America's Quest for Global Dominance.* New York: Metropolitan Books.

Clarke, R. 2004. *Against All Enemies: Inside America's War on Terror.* New York: Free Press.

Cohn, M. 2004. "Torturing Hearts and Minds." *Truthout* May 4, http://www.truthout.org/cgi-bin/artman/exec/view.cgi/4/4361.

Corn, D. 2003. *The Lies of George W. Bush: Mastering the Politics of Deception.* New York: Crown Publishers.

Derber, C. 2002. *People Before Profit: The New Globalization in An Age of Terror, Big Money, and Economic Crisis.* New York: St Martin's Press.

Domke, D. 2004. *God Willing? Political Fundamentalism in the White House, the "War On Terror," and the Echoing Press.* London: Pluto Press.

Dorrien, G. 2004. *Imperial Designs: Neo-conservatism and the New Pax Americana.* New York: Routledge.

Eisendrath, C. and M. Goodman. 2004. *Bush League Diplomacy: How the Neoconservatives Are Putting the World at Risk.* Amherst, NY: Prometheus Books.

Elliot, W. (Ed.). 1955. *The Political Economy of American Foreign Policy: Its Concepts, Strategy and Limits.* New York: Henry Holt and Co.

Everrest, L. 2004. *Oil, Power, and Empire: Iraq and the US Global Agenda.* Monroe, ME: Common Courage Press.

Falk, R. 1993. "Rethinking the Agenda of International Law." Pp. 418–431 in *National Sovereignty: International Communication in the 1990s,* edited by K. Nordenstreng and H. Schiller. Norwood, NJ: Ablex.

Falk, R. 2004. *The Declining World Order: America's Imperial Geopolitics.* New York: Routledge.

Fallows, J. 2004. "Bush's Lost Year." *The Atlantic Monthly* 294 (October): 68–84.

Ferguson, N. 2004. *Colossus: The Price of America's Empire*. New York: The Penguin Press.

Finney, H. and H. Lesier. 1982. "A Contingency Theory of Organizational Crime." Pp. 255–299 in *Research in the Sociology of Organizations*, edited by S. Bacharach. NewYork: Random House.

Franck, T. 2003. "What Happens Now? The United Nations after Iraq." *American Journal of International Law* 97: 607–20.

Frank, A.G. 1969. *Capitalism and the Underdevelopment of Latin America*. New York: Monthly Review Press.

Friedrichs, D. 2004. *Trusted Criminals: White Collar Crime in Contemporary Society*. Belmont, CA: Wadsworth.

Gardner, R. 2003. "Neither Bush nor the Jurisprudes." *American Journal of International Law* 97: 585–90.

Garrison, J. 2004. *America as Empire: Global Leader or Rogue Power?* San Francisco: Berrett Koehier.

Gellman, B. 2004. "Iraq's Arsenal Was Only on Paper." *Washington Post* January 7: AOl.

Gonzales, A. 2002. "Memorandum for the President: Decision Re Application of the Geneva Convention on Prisoners of War to the Conflict with Al Qaeda and the Taliban." http://msnbc.msn.com/id/4999148/site/newsweek/

Green, P. and Ward, T. 2000. "State Crime, Human Rights, and the Limits of Criminology." *Social Justice* 27: 101–15.

Greider, W. 2003. "Occupiers and the Law." *The Nation* November 17: 5–6.

Gross, E. 1978. "Organizational Crime: A Theoretical Perspective." Pp. 55–85 in *Studies in Symbolic Interaction*, edited by N. Denzin. Greenwich, CN: JAI Press.

Halper, S. and J. Clarke. 2004. *America Alone: The Neoconservatives and the Global Order*. Cambridge: Cambridge University Press.

Hardt, M. and A. Negri. 2000. *Empire*. Cambridge, MA: Harvard University Press.

Hartung, W. 2004. *How Much Are You Making on the War Daddy? A Quick and Dirty Guide to War Profiteering in the Bush Administration*. New York: Nation Books.

Henkin, L. 1995. *International Law: Politics and Values*. Dordrecht, The Netherlands: Martinus Nijhoff.

Herman, E. and N. Chomsky. 1988. *Manufacturing Consent: The Political Economy of the Mass Media*. New York: Pantheon Books.

Hersh, S. 2004. *Chain of Command: The Road from 9–11 to Abu Ghraib*. New York: HarperCollins.

Hero, D. 2004. *Secrets and Lies: Operation "Iraqi Freedom" and After*. New York: Nation Books.

Hobswam, E. 1996. *Age of Extremes*. New York: Vintage Books.

Hopkins, A. 1978. "The Anatomy of Corporate Crime." Pp. 79–91 in *Two Faces of Deviance: Crimes of the Powerless and Powerful*, edited by P. Wilson and J. Braithwaite. Brisbane: University of Queensland Press.

Human Rights Watch. 2003. *Off Target: The Conduct of the War and Civilian Casualties in Iraq*. New York: Human Rights Watch.

International Committee of the Red Cross. 2004. *Report of the International Committee of the Red Cross (ICRC) on the Treatment by the Coalition Forces of Prisoners of War and Other Persons Protected by the Geneva Conventions in Iraq During Arrest, Internment and Interrogation*. Geneva: ICRC.

Janis, I. 1982. *Groupthink*. Boston: Houghton Muffin.

Jensen, R. 2004. *Citizens of the Empire: The Struggle to Claim Our Humanity*. San Francisco: City Lights Books.

Johnson, C. 2004. *The Sorrows of Empire: Militarism, Secrecy, and the End of the Republic*. New York: Metropolitan/Holt.

Jorgensen, N. 2000. *The Responsibility of States for International Crimes*. Oxford: Oxford University Press.

Juhasz, A. 2004. "Ambitions of Empire: The Bush Administration Economic Plan for Iraq (and Beyond)." *Left Turn Magazine* 12 (February/March). http://www.ifg.org/analysis/globalization/ambition.htm

Klein, N. 2003. "Bring Halliburton Home." *The Nation* November 24: 10.

Kauzlarich, D. and R. Kramer. 1998. *Crimes of the American Nuclear State: At Home and Abroad*. Boston: Northeastern University Press.

Kauzlarich, D., R. Kramer, and B. Smith. 1992. "Toward the Study of Governmental Crime: Nuclear Weapons, Foreign Intervention, and International Law." *Humanity and Society* 16: 543–63.

Kolko, G. 1968. *The Politics of War: The World and United States Foreign Policy, 1943–1945*. New York: Random House.

Kolko, G. 1984. *Main Currents in Modern American History*. New York: Pantheon Books.

Kramer, R. 1982. "Corporate Crime: An Organizational Perspective." Pp. 75–94 in *White-Collar and Economic Crime*, edited by P. Wickman and T. Dailey. Lexington, MA: Lexington Books.

Kramer, R. 1992. "The Space Shuttle Challenger Explosion: A Case Study of State-Corporate Crime." Pp. 214–43 in *White-Collar Crime Reconsidered*, edited by K. Schlegel and D. Weisburd. Boston: Northeastern University Press.

Kramer R. and R. Michalowski. 1990. "Toward an Integrated Theory of State-Corporate Crime." Paper presented at the annual meeting of the American Society of Criminology, November, Baltimore.

Kramer, R., R. Mickalowski, and D. Kauzlarich. 2002. "The Origins and Development of the Concept and Theory of State-Corporate Crime." *Crime and Delinquency* 48: 263–82.

Krane, J. 2004. "Bush, Allawi Say Most of Iraq is Stable: Map, However, Is Dotted with Violence." *Associated Press*. http://www.kurd.org/newsletters/20040924171722.html#1

Krauthammer, C. 1989. "Universal Domination: Toward a Unipolar World." *National Interest* 18 (Winter): 48–49.

Krauthammer, C. 1991. "The Unipolar Moment." *Foreign Affairs* 70: 23–33.

Krugman, P. 2004. "Battlefield of Dreams." *New York Times* May 4.

Kurtz, H. 2004. "The Post on WMDs: An Inside Story; Prewar Articles Questioning Threat Often Didn't Make Front Page." *Washington Post* August 12: A0l.

Lambert, C., S. Pickering, and C. Alder. 2003. *Critical Chatter: Women and Human Rights in South East Asia*. Durham, NC: Carolina Academic Press.

Lynch, C. 2004a. "U.S. Allies Dispute Annan on Iraq War." *Washington Post* September 17: 18.

Lynch, C. 2004b. "Annan Faults Both Sides of Terror War for Eroding Rule of Law." *Washington Post* September 21: A02.

Mahajan, R. 2003. *Full Spectrum Dominance: US Power in Iraq and Beyond.* New York: Seven Stories Press.

Mann, J. 2004. *Rise of the Vulcans: The History of Bush's War Cabinet.* New York: Viking.

Massing, M. 2004. *Now They Tell Us: The American Press and Iraq.* New York: New York Review of Books.

Matthews, R. and D. Kauzlarich. 2000. "The Crash of ValuJet 592: A Case Study in State–Corporate Crime." *Sociological Focus* 3: 281–98.

Michalowski, R. 1985. *Order, Law, and Crime.* New York: Random House.

Michalowski, R. and K. Bitten. 2004. "Transnational Environmental Crime." Pp. 139–159 in *Handbook of Transnational Crime and Justice,* edited by P. Reichel. Beverly Hills: Sage.

Miller, D. (Ed.). 2004. *Tell Me Lies: Propaganda and Media Distortion in the Attack on Iraq.* London: Pluto Press.

Miller, R. S. 2003. *Collateral Damage from US. Depleted Uranium Munitions in Iraq.* Winter Springs, FL: ZOR Foundation Inc.

Moeller, S. 2004. *Media Coverage of Weapons of Mass Destruction.* College Park, MD: Center for International Studies at Maryland, University of Maryland.

Moore, M. 2001. *Stupid White Men.* New York: Harper Collins.

New York Times. 2004. "From the Editors: *The Times* and Iraq." *New York Times* May 26: A10.

Normand, R. 2003. *Tearing Up the Rules: The Illegality of Invading Iraq.* Brooklyn, New York: The Center for Economic and Social Rights.

Normand, R. 2004. "Presentation on Crimes Committed During the Ongoing Occupation." *World Tribunal On Iraq,* New York, May 8, http://www.worldtribunal.org/main.htm.

Otto, D. 1997. "Rethinking the Universality of "Human Rights" Law." *Columbia Human Rights Law Review* 29: 1–46.

Packer. G. 2004. "Letter from Baghdad: War After War, What Washington Doesn't See." *The New Yorker* November 24: 58–85.

Passas, N. 1990. "Anomie and Corporate Deviance." *Contemporary Crises* 14: 157–78.

Pitt, W.R. 2002. *War on Iraq.* New York: Context Books.

Prados, J. 2004. *Hoodwinked: The Documents that Reveal How Bush Sold Us a War.* New York: The New Press.

Priest, D. and W. Pincus. 2004. "U.S. 'Almost All Wrong' on Weapons: Report on Iraq Contradicts Bush Administration Claims." *Washington Post* October 7: A01.

Project for the New American Century. 2000. *Rebuilding America's Defenses: Strategy, Forces and Resources for a New Century.* Washington, DC: Project for The New American Century.

Progressive Magazine 2003. "Comment: Bush's Messiah Complex." *The Progressive* (February): 8–10.

Quinney, R. 1977. *Class, State and Crime: On the Theory and Practice of Criminal Justice.* New York: David McKay Company.

Rai, M. 2002. *War Plan Iraq: Ten Reasons Against War on Iraq.* London: Verso.

Rai, M. 2003. *Regime Unchanged: Why the War on Iraq Changed Nothing.* London: Pluto Press.

Rampton, S. and J. Srauber. 2003. *Weapons of Mass Deception: The Uses of Propaganda in Bush's War on Iraq.* New York: Jeremy P. Tarcher/Penguin.

Ratner, M. 2002. "The United Nations Charter and the Use of Force Against Iraq." *Lawyers Against the War (LAW)*, http://www.lawyersagainstthewar.org/legalarticles/ratner.html.

Ratner, M., J. Green, and B. Olshansky. 2003. *Against War with Iraq.* New York: Seven Stories Press.

Rendall, S. and T. Broufhel. 2003. "Amplifying Officials, Squelching Dissent." *Extra* 16 (May–June): 12–14.

Ridha, J. 2004. "Presentation on the Use of Incendiary Weapons." *World Tribunal on Iraq*, New York, May 8, http://www.worldtribunal.org/main.htm.

Ritter, S. 2003. *Frontier Justice: Weapons of Mass Destruction and the Bushwhacking of America.* New York: Context Books.

Roth, K 2004. *War in Iraq: Not a Humanitarian Intervention.* New York: Human Rights Watch.

Roy, A. 2004. *An Ordinary Person's Guide to Empire.* Cambridge, MA: South End Press.

Rutherford, P. 2004. *Weapons of Mass Persuasion: Marketing the War Against Iraq.* Toronto: University of Toronto Press.

Scheer, C., R. Scheer, and L. Chaudrey. 2003. *The Five Biggest Lies Bush Told Us About Iraq.* New York: Seven Stories Press and Akashic Books.

Schell, J. 2004. *A Hole in the World: An Unfolding Story of War, Protest and the New American Order.* New York: Nation Books.

Schell, J. 2004. "Preface." Pp. ii–xviii in *Now They Tell Us: The American Press and Iraq*, edited by M. Massing. New York: New York Review of Books.

Schultz, W, 2003. *Tainted Legacy: 9/11 and the Ruin of Human Rights.* New York: Nation Books.

Sellin, T. 1938. *Culture Conflict and Crime.* New York: Social Science Research Council.

Sewell, J. [1905] 1995. *The Log Book of the Captain's Clerk.* Chicago: R.R. Donnelly and Sons.

Sklar, M. 1988. *The Corporate Reconstruction of American Capitalism.* New York: Cambridge University Press.

Sinch, R. and C. Kilroy. 2003. "In the Matter of the Legality of the Use of Force Against Iraq and the Alleged Existence of Weapons of Mass Destruction." *Campaign for Nuclear Disarmament*, June 6, http://www.cnduk.org/pages/campaign/opn3.html.

Sinha, M., D. Guy, and A. Wollacorr. 1999. *Feminisms and Internationalisms.* London: Blackwell Publishers.

Simons, G. 2002. *Targeting Iraq: Sanctions & Bombing in U.S. Policy.* London: Saqi Books.

Slomanson, W. 2003. *Fundamental Perspectives on International Law.* 4th ed. Belmont, CA: Thomson/West.

Solomon, N. and R. Erlich. 2003. *Target Iraq: What the News Media Didn't Tell You.* New York: Context Books.

Steiner, H. and P. Alston. 2000. *International Human Rights in Context: Law, Politics, Morals.* New York: Oxford University Press.

Suskind, R. 2004. *The Price of Loyalty: George W. Bush, the White House, and the Education of Paul O'Neill.* New York: Simon and Schuster.

Sutherland, E. 1940. "White Collar Criminality." *American Sociological Review* 5: 1–12.

Sutherland, E. 1949. *White Collar Crime.* New York: Holt, Rinehart and Winston.

Sykes, G. and D. Matza. 1957. "Techniques of Neutralization: A Theory of Delinquency." *American Sociological Review* 22: 664–70.

Taft, W.H. and T. Buchwald. 2003. "Preemption, Iraq, and International Law." *American Journal of International Law* 97: 557–63.

Thomas, H. 1971. *Cuba: The Pursuit of Freedom.* New York: Harper and Row.

Vaughn, D. 1982. "Toward Understanding Unlawful Organizational Behavior." *Michigan Law Review* 80: 377–402.

Vaughn, D. 1983. *Controlling Unlawful Organizational Behavior: Social Structure and Corporate Misconduct.* Chicago: University of Chicago Press.

Vaughn, D. 1996. *The Challenger Launch Decision: Risky Technology, Culture, and Deviance at NASA.* Chicago: University of Chicago Press.

Wallerstein, I. 1989. *The Modern World System.* New York: Academic Press.

Ward, T. and P. Green. 2000. "Legitimacy, Civil Society, and State Crime." *Social Justice* 27: 76–93.

Waxman, H. 2004. *Iraq on the Record: The Bush Administration's Public Statements on Iraq.* Committee on Government Reform, Minority Staff, Special Investigative Division, Washington, DC: US House of Representatives.

Whyte, D. 2003. "Lethal Regulation: State-Corporate Crime and the United Kingdom Government's New Mercenaries." *Journal of Law and Society* 30: 575–600.

Williams, W.A. [1959] 1988. *The Tragedy of American Diplomacy.* Paperback ed. New York: Norton.

Williams, W.A. 1969. *The Roots of the Modern American Empire: A Study of the Growth and Shaping of Social Consciousness in a Marketplace Society.* New York: Random House.

Wonders, N. and M. Danner. 2002. "Globalization, State-Corporate Crime, and Women: The Strategic Role of Women's NGO's in the New World Order." Pp. 165–82 in *Controversies in White Collar Crime,* edited by G. Potter. Cincinnati: Anderson.

Woodward, B. 2004. *Plan of Attack.* New York: Simon and Schuster.

Weeramantry, C.G. 2003. *Armageddon or Brave New World? Reflections on the Hostilities in Iraq.* Ratmalana, Sri Lanka: Sarvodaya Vishva Lekha.

Young, T.R. 1981. "Corporate Crime: A Critique of the Clinard Report." *Contemporary Crises* 5: 323–336.

Zinn, H. 1980. *A People's History of the United States: 1492–Present.* New York: Harper Collins.

Zunes, S. 2003. *Tinderbox: US Middle East Policy and the Roots of Terrorism.* Monroe, ME: Common Courage Press.

CHAPTER STUDY QUESTIONS

- Kramer and Michalowski argue that the 2003 United States/United Kingdom invasion and occupation of Iraq was a form of state crime. What evidence do Kramer and Michalowski provide to support this argument? Do you agree with their argument? Explain your answer.

- Do you believe that the invasion of Iraq was justified under the "preventative war" provisions of Article 51 of the UN Charter? What factors would support such a course of action? What factors would militate against using Article 51 to justify the invasion?

- Kramer and Michalowski argue that the invasion of Iraq represents an ongoing step in the evolution of American "imperialist" ambitions that can be traced to US involvement in WWI and up through to the present day. Do you agree with this assessment? How do the policies of the George W. Bush presidency support this argument? How are they different from the policies of the Clinton and George H.W. Bush administrations?

- Discuss several factors that Kramer and Michalowski argue were central to the decision to invade Iraq. Based on a consideration of these factors, do you feel that it is likely that future administrations will make the same mistakes elsewhere in the world? Why? Why not?

RELATED WEB LINKS

Wikipedia Free Dictionary
http://en.wikipedia.org/wiki/Iraq_War
> This website presents a general overview of the events leading up to the invasion as well as an analysis of US motivations and rationales for the invasion. It also presents statistics on the situation in Iraq.

El Ahram
http://weekly.ahram.org.eg/2003/invasion.htm
> This website is maintained by a major Arab English language newspaper. It contains analyses of the invasion of Iraq from an Arab point of view.

Foreign Policy in Focus
http://www.fpif.org/fpiftxt/3011
> This website analyses the invasion of Iraq in terms of whether Israel influenced or benefited from the invasion.

Centre for Research on Globalization
http://www.globalresearch.ca/
> This website is the official website of the Canadian-based Centre for Research on Globalization. It provides many links to research and commentary on worldwide issues related to globalization, including many on the Middle East and Iraq.

Sources

Aden, Hartmut. "Convergence of Policing Policies and Transnational Policing in Europe." *European Journal of Crime, Criminal Law, and Criminal Justice* 9.2 (2001): 99-122. Reprinted by permission of Brill Academic Publishers.

Chatwin, Caroline. "Drug Policy Developments with the European Union: The Destabilizing Effects of Dutch and Swedish Drug Policies." *British Journal of Criminology* 43.3 (2003): 567-82. Reprinted by permission of Oxford University Press.

Chen, Xiaoming. "Social and Legal Control in China: A Comparative Perspective." *International Journal of Offender Therapy and Comparative Criminology* 48.5 (2004): 523-36. Copyright 2004 by Sage Publications. Reprinted by permission of Sage Publications.

Friedrichs, David O. and Jessica Friedrichs. "The World Bank and Crimes of Globalization: A Case Study." *Social Justice: A Journal of Crime, Conflict and World Order* 29.1-2 (2002): 13-36. Reprinted by permission of Social Justice.

Gilbert, Michael J. and Steve Russell. "Globalization of Criminal Justice in the Corporate Context." *Law, Crime and Social Change* 38.3 (2002): 211-38. Reprinted by permission of Springer Science + Business Media.

Gros, Jean-Germain. "Trouble in Paradise: Crime and Collapsed States in the Age of Globalization." *British Journal of Criminology* 43.1 (2003): 63-80. Reprinted by permission of Oxford University Press.

Haen Marshall, Ineke. "The Criminology Enterprise in Europe and the United States: A Contextual Exploration." *European Journal on Criminal Policy and Research* 9.3 (2001): 235-37. Reprinted by permission of Springer Science + Business Media.

Hodgson, Jacqueline. "The Police, The Prosecutor and The Juge D'instruction: Judicial Supervision in France, Theory and Practice." *British Journal of Criminology* 41.2 (2001): 342-61. Reprinted by permission of Oxford University Press.

Jones, Trevor and Tim Newburn. "Comparative Criminal Justice Policy-Making in the United State and the United Kingdom: The Case of Private Prisons." *British Journal of Criminology* 45.1 (2005): 58-80; "The Transformation of Policing? Understanding Current Policing Systems." *British Journal of Criminology* 42.1 (2002): 129-49. Reprinted by permission of Oxford University Press.

Karstedt, Susanne. "Comparing Cultures, Comparing Crime: Challenges, Prospects and Problems for a Criminology." *Law, Crime and Social Change* 36.3 (2001): 285-308. Reprinted by permission of Springer Science + Business Media.

Kramer, Ronald and Raymond Michalowski. "War, Aggression and State Crime: A Criminological Analysis of the Invasion and Occupation of Iraq." *British Journal of Criminology* 45.4 (2005): 446-69. Reprinted by permission of Oxford University Press.

Ma, Yue. "Prosecutorial Discretion and Plea Bargaining in the United States, France, Germany, and Italy: A Comparative Perspective." *International Criminal Justice Review* 12.1 (2002): 22-52. Copyright 2002 Georgia State University, College of Health and Human Sciences. Reprinted by permission of Sage Publications.

Mameli, Peter A. "Stopping the Illegal Trafficking of Human Beings: How Transnational Police Work Can Stem the Flow of Forced Prostituion." *Law, Crime and Social Change* 38.1 (2002): 67-80. Reprinted by permission of Springer Science + Business Media.

O'Malley, Pat. "Globalizing Risk? Distinguishing Styles of 'Neo-Liberal' Criminal Justice in Australia and the USA." *Criminal Justice* 2.2 (2002): 205-22. Copyright 2002 by Sage Publications. Reprinted by permission of Sage Publications.

Rezaei, Hassan. "Iranian Criminal Justice under the Islamization Project." *European Journal of Crime, Criminal Law, and Criminal Justice* 10.1 (2002): 54-69. Reprinted by permission of Brill Academic Publishers.

Sheptycki, James. "The Accountability of Transnational Policing Institutions: The Strange Case of Interpol" *Canadian Journal of Law and Society* 19.1 (2004): 107-34. Reprinted by permission of the Canadian Journal of Law and Society.

Šimonović, Ivan. "Dealing with the Legacy of Past War Crimes and Human Rights Abuses: Experiences and Trends." *Journal of International Criminal Justice* 2.3 (2004): 701-10. Reprinted by permission of Oxford University Press.

Vinjamuri, Leslie and Jack Snyder. "Advocacy and Scholarship in the Study of International War Crime Tribunals and Transitional Justice." *Annual Review of Political Science* 7.1 (2004): 345-62. Copyright 2004 by Annual Reviews. Reprinted by permission of the Annual Review of Political Science. www.annualreviews.org

von Hofer, Hanns. "Prison Populations as Political Constructs: The Case of Finland, Holland and Sweden." *Journal of Scandinavian Studies in Criminology and Crime Prevention* 4 (2003): 21-38. Reprinted by permission of Taylor & Francis Ltd.

Wardak, Ali. "Building a Post-War Justice System in Afghanistan." *Law, Crime and Social Change* 41.4 (2004): 319-41. Reprinted by permission of Springer Science + Business Media.

Weber, Leanne and Benjamin Bowling. "Policing Migration: A Framework for Investigating the Regulation of Global Mobility." *Policing and Society* 14.3 (2004): 195-212. Reprinted by permission of Taylor and Francis Ltd.

Wonders, Nancy and Raymond Michalowski. "Bodies, Borders, and Sex Tourism in a Globalized World. A Tale of Two Cities—Amsterdam and Havana." *Social Problems* 48.4 (2001): 545-71. Reprinted by permission of The University of California Press.

The publisher has endeavored to contact rights holders of all copyright material and would appreciate receiving any information as to errors or omissions.